ELIZABETHAN AND
JACOBEAN COMEDIES

THE NEW MERMAIDS

General Editor
BRIAN GIBBONS
Professor of English Literature,
University of Zurich

Previous General Editors
PHILIP BROCKBANK
BRIAN MORRIS
ROMA GILL

Elizabethan and Jacobean Comedies

Introduced by
BRIAN GIBBONS

THE OLD WIFE'S TALE
THE SHOEMAKERS' HOLIDAY
EASTWARD HO!
BARTHOLMEW FAIR
THE MALCONTENT
A TRICK TO CATCH THE OLD ONE

ERNEST BENN LIMITED

First published in this form 1984
by Ernest Benn Limited
Sovereign Way, Tonbridge, Kent, TN9 1RW
© *Ernest Benn Limited 1984*

Printed in Great Britain by
Richard Clay (The Chaucer Press) Ltd,
Bungay, Suffolk

ISBN 0-510-00165-3

NOTE

NEW MERMAIDS are modern-spelling, fully annotated editions of important English plays. Each play in this anthology is also available individually, with a critical introduction, biography of the author, discussions of dates and sources, textual details, and a bibliography. The reader is recommended to consult these editions for fuller information.

CONTENTS

ABBREVIATIONS

ed.	editor
O.E.D.	*The Oxford English Dictionary*
om.	omit
s.d.	stage direction
s.p.	speech prefix
Tilley	M. P. Tilley, *A Dictionary of the Proverbs in England in the Sixteenth and Seventeenth Centuries,* Ann Arbor, 1950

Names of periodicals abbreviated:

E.L.H.	*English Literary History*
E.S.	*English Studies*
E & S	*Essays and Studies*
J.E.G.P.	*Journal of English and Germanic Philology*
M.L.N.	*Modern Language Notes*
M.L.R.	*Modern Language Review*
N & Q	*Notes & Queries*
P.M.L.A.	*Publications of the Modern Language Association of America*
P.Q.	*Philological Quarterly*
R.E.S.	*Review of English Studies*
S.P.	*Studies in Philology*
T.L.S.	*The Times Literary Supplement*

INTRODUCTION

THIS ANTHOLOGY SELECTS six intrinsically interesting and varied plays out of the large corpus of surviving comedies from the heyday of Elizabethan and Jacobean drama. The six plays were written between about 1590, when Shakespeare was beginning to become famous, and 1614, the year in which the new Hope Theatre, as well as the second Globe, opened.

These plays may be read in the order they are here printed, that is to say chronologically, but there are many other equally valuable and enjoyable patterns in which they may be arranged. To read these plays chronologically may perhaps encourage a search for quasi-Darwinian evolution in style and form, but although processes of modification can certainly be seen, given the changing rigours and opportunities of the times, nevertheless a comedy has roots that are too profound, and a surface that is too brilliantly opalescent, for us to pluck out the heart of its mystery with any one line of approach. In the discussion of the plays which follows below, a number of possible lines of enquiry are indicated, and some interesting features sketched, but the reader is encouraged to discover for himself the rich variety of issues touched on in these plays and the remarkable diversity of comic experiences created by the playwrights.

This volume may be read for itself alone, or it may be combined with its companion New Mermaid Anthology of Elizabethan and Jacobean Tragedies. It is also designed to accompany a selection of Shakespeare's comedies. A choice of five or six, perhaps two from the early period, *The Taming of the Shrew*, *A Midsummer Night's Dream*, two from the middle period, *The Merry Wives* or *I Henry IV*, *Much Ado*, and two Jacobean plays, *Measure for Measure*, *The Winter's Tale* or *The Tempest*, would provide an exciting and complex sense of the relationship of Shakespeare to his contemporaries in the art of comedy at large; but some direct connections can be made between comedies in the present anthology and certain specific plays of Shakespeare: one might recognise the memory of plays like *The Old Wife's Tale* in *The Winter's Tale* (1611), or *King Henry IV* and *King Henry V* in *The Shoemakers' Holiday*, or consider the very pointed likenesses and differences between *The Malcontent* and *Measure for Measure* (both 1604).

The two earliest plays in the present anthology, Peele's *The Old Wife's Tale* (about 1590) and Dekker's *The Shoemakers' Holiday* (1599) illustrate many attractive features of Elizabethan popular comedy, as performed by adult companies in public theatres. Dance,

song and colourful spectacle augment dramatic narratives rooted in
the traditions of an old-established, predominantly rural, culture:
such as folk-tale, popular romances and jest books. The final years of
Elizabeth's reign, her death, and the accession of King James I in
1603, saw the rise of a literary and dramatic fashion for satire, which
rivalled, without obliterating, more genial kinds of comedy.
Marston's *The Malcontent* (1604) a satiric tragi-comedy offering a
fashionably Italianate depiction of Court life, is representative of this
movement, while the collaborative comedy of 1605, *Eastward Ho!*,
takes up some of the stock conventions of citizen comedy and makes
of them an hilarious satiric burlesque. Finally there are two contrasting representations of immediately contemporary London
scenes, designed to interest audiences for whom the comic mirror
was not always flattering in its reflection. Middleton's *A Trick to
Catch the Old One* is set among London merchants, and given that
the ostensible subject is community and good cheer, Middleton's
seemingly neutral gaze has a disconcerting effect — it sees rather too
much for comfort. Jonson's *Bartholmew Fair* brings into the theatre
the great annual event in Smithfield, which most spectators at the
time would themselves have visited.

In Jonson's version contemporary characters are assembled from
all over the kingdom, provincial dialects and rural attitudes collide
with London wits, fools and rogues, and an intricately plotted design
rapidly produces the effect of inspired surrealist carnival.

The years from 1590 to 1614 saw the rise of the professional
playwright and of professional acting companies in playhouses, some
purpose-built, in London. The successes of the players were achiev-
ed with the support of aristocratic patrons and despite the opposition
of city authorities and the interruptions caused by some severe out-
breaks of plague. Elizabethan London was rapidly expanding and
over-crowded. The dense city within the walls had begun to
overflow, though it was still some distance separated from the Court
at Whitehall. Open countryside was still close at hand; one of Jonson's poems speaks of "all the grass in Chelsea fields", and we can
see from Norden's map of 1600 the nearby green hills of Hampstead
and Highgate forming a pleasant rural backdrop. The Thames
waterfront on the Southwark side of old London Bridge was however
already a busy and built-up area. Five theatres were built there, the
last being the Hope, which opened in 1614, and in which *Bartholmew Fair* was first performed in the same year.

In the Induction to that play Jonson seems to acknowledge, in his
spacious (if curmudgeonly) survey of drama in the preceding two
decades, that an era is on the point of ending. Characteristically, Jonson has no thought of regret, let alone defeatism, in looking back to
the past. He obliquely includes his own youthful self in the mockery

of those early plays, *"Jeronimo or Andronicus"*, and he is not in-dulgent towards Shakespeare's last phase, "to make Nature afraid . . . like those that beget Tales, Tempests, and suchlike drolleries". So much then, we note, for such a kind of comedy as Peele's *Old Wife's Tale*. There, disregard for probability is virtually a structural principle, and fantastic or marvellous episodes are the very stuff of the narrative. Jonson shows himself critical of other comedy; soft-hearted representations of city life (as made on Dekker's broad last) earn mockery in *Eastward Ho!*; plays featuring disguised rulers, like Marston's *The Malcontent*, are incidentally burlesqued in *Bar-tholmew Fair*. All this may remind us that Jonson had been, for his time, a serious, persistent and vocal theorist of comedy and that his early comedies were themselves designed to embody and advocate certain strict principles of integrity in style and form in a deliberately limited kind of critical comedy. Jonson in those plays had in mind some of the recommendations of Sir Philip Sidney, whose strictures on earlier stage comedy can be found in the lively pages of his *Apology for Poetry*. There Sidney certainly can be found to complain of play-makers and stage-keepers who have made the Comic merely something odious (to the discriminating): partly by ignoring the disintegrating effects of gratuitous comic business, partly by offen-ding good taste, in the quality of performance and the subjects chosen for comic treatment. Sidney objects to mere doltishness, to the stirring of laughter in sinful things, "for what is it to make folks gape at a wretched beggar, or a beggarly clown; or against the law of hospitality, to jest at strangers because they speak not English so well as we do? What do we learn . . . ?"

Sidney's essay is only partly concerned with comedy, but given his pioneering enterprise in this first sustained attempt in English to develop a philosophic literary theory, it is remarkable that Sidney touches on some profound and subtle problems connected with com-edy. He notices that laughter very often implies scornful superiority — "we laugh at deformed creatures" — but sometimes a recognition of our own or another's discomfiture, so then we are "rather pained than delighted with laugher". He points out that delight is a proper emotion in comedy and "hath a joy in it whether permanent or pre-sent". We delight in good chances, or to hear the happiness of our friends or of our country; in such cases, Sidney observes, delight and laughter may go together; even so, though laughter "may come with delight it cometh not of delight". Sidney is reluctant to grant laughter more than a low status, as is implied by his referring to it as "a scornful tickling", but he does grant it a place as part of the valuable, enriching experience of comedy at its best, "that delightful teaching that is the end of Poesy".

Sidney wrote his essay before any of the great triumphs of

Elizabethan theatre; his imaginative and subtle mind would clearly have been eager to extend and modify theories and judgements inevitably restricted, as well as coloured by polemical intent. Jonson, with *Epicoene* and *The Alchemist* behind him by 1614, was triumphantly the master of his own distinctive comic art and imaginative world; in *Bartholmew Fair* he seems determined to acknowledge how much he has changed, how the whole issue of comedy and laughter now in 1614 is to be reconciled to the educative and corrective impulses commended by Sidney before Jonson began to write.

In representing the Jacobean professional theatre in terms of a puppet-play in a fairground, with a play-script in which Hero and Leander are up-dated and presented as Cockneys (on the predictable grounds that market-forces and audience taste require Marlowe's poem to be made "a little easy, and modern for the times"), Jonson makes forthright criticism; and certainly there was much to criticise in that history of disordered and shabby acting companies, with their precarious fortunes and muddy provincial tours, hack-work plays made up of odd old ends stolen from true poets, of coarse showmanship winning mindless applause, of prejudice and stupidity, fraud and incompetence. Still in Jonson's memory would be the audience rejection of his *Sejanus* (1603) and *Catiline* (1611), and Jonson in certain moods certainly loathed the stage. Yet in *Bartholmew Fair* the spirit of comedy seems to be granted a licence to express itself with unbounded energy and what we may properly call delight, even though the variety of forms include some which are rough-hewn, deformed, and invite the scornful laughter described by Sidney. Jonson seems to acknowledge that the theatre is self-contradictory, at once art and business, calculating and generous, rehearsed yet dependent on spontaneity; his play will strive to be inclusive, then, it will revel in self-contradiction, depose the author from control so as to welcome the vulgarity, the warm spirit of holiday, tolerance and popular custom, which he fears as enemies of art's integrity and "teaching delightfulness". Yet if in one sense this is a work with a displaced author (even *before* the actors, the director, and the stage hands get their chance to mangle, bungle, misread and distort) yet in another sense Jonson never lets the unconfined joy, the very different kinds of laughter released in this play, turn the whole affair into shapelessness. *Bartholmew Fair* is plotted with a precision and intricacy that would deserve the admiration of such an admired classical predecessor as the Roman comic dramatist Terence himself.

The final act of *Bartholmew Fair* not only presents a highly derogatory image of the Jacobean professional theatre, it also presents a mocking image of the audience (throughout the play there has been persistent attention to crowds, as spectators or customers, watching the fair people perform their sales-talk). By insisting on the whole question of audience response, Jonson seeks to heighten audience self-consciousness about the different ways in which to react to those events which are traditional in stage comedy though not of necessity amusing in themselves — such as theft, vomiting, scalding, abuse, regional dialects, being locked in the stocks, and the spectacle of persons with various types of mental derangement and physical defects. The comic incidents *are* irresistibly hilarious, and laughter arises from an audience which senses that the conventions of stage comedy licence it to enjoy breaking taboos, to recognise the power of anarchy which it is the business of responsible men to try to mitigate and to keep at bay in ordinary life. Instinctual energies are necessary and threatening at one and the same time. Jonson presents grotesque episodes in the play and makes us laugh at them; he also makes us aware that we ought not to laugh at them: we express our common humanity in responding to the liberation of riot and comic anarchy, but we are also made conscious of this and so feel guilty. In this way *Bartholmew Fair* generates the many kinds of laughter possible in a comedy, and it teaches an audience something about itself, for better and for worse. The view seems double though not equivocal: the theatre is seen for itself as it is, in all the common sordid circumstances that obtained during Jonson's working life; but it is also seen as the product of humanity, requiring an attitude which takes self-contradiction to be of the essence.

It is worth insisting for a little longer on the realities of those commercial pressures in the theatre of Jonson's time which the puppet-master so disarmingly discusses. The King's Men, Shakespeare's company and by far the most successful players of the time, accepted in their repertory along with the new *Othello* and *Measure for Measure* such plain fare as *The Fair Maid of Bristow* and *The London Prodigal*. Evidently the audience was not expected to become educated by seeing Shakespeare's profound new masterpieces, and in any case the audience was evidently felt to have an appetite for novelty and variety so that considerations of artistic quality could not be allowed to overrule everything else; as the circus-master Mr Sleary says in Dickens's novel *Hard Times*, "well thquire, people muth be amuthed". Shakespeare's whole idea of comedy, as well as his dramatic artistry, may have undergone the profoundest change and evolution between, say, his early comedy *Love's Labour's Lost* (early 1590s) and his *Measure for Measure* of 1604, but it does not follow necessarily that, for his public at the time, the new work made the old redundant. Thus, as a matter of fact, we can note that *Love's Labour's Lost* was revived at Court only a month after the first performance of *Measure for Measure* in 1604.

The impresarios of the time in the public theatres did their best to get the dramatists organised to turn out new scripts as if on an assembly line, and (to judge by the prompt imitations of any new play that promised to spark off a new fashion) the writers were trying to serve an audience greedy for variety and novelty. This is often supposed to be a characteristic of the lowest classes — though wrongly. Certainly in the early period of the reign of James I, after 1603, Ben Jonson virtually invented a new form of theatre to respond to the Court's craze for medieval chivalric romance (a revival of an Elizabethan Court fashion). Jonson developed the Jacobean Court Masque rapidly to extravagant lengths. His masque *Oberon, the Fairy Prince,* performed in 1611, for example, opened with a wonderfully shaggy panorama of mountain scenery. The rocky pile then opened to discover, within, a complete Renaissance palace, its windows ablaze with light, then (in Jonson's own stage directions)

the whole palace opened, and the nation of Fays were discovered, some with instruments, some bearing lights, others singing; and within, afar off in perspective, the Knights Masquers sitting in their several sieges. At the further end of all, Oberon in a chariot, which to a loud triumphant music began to move forward, drawn by two white bears and on either side guarded by three Sylvans, with one going in front.

It is relevant and amusing to note that this appeared in the same year as Shakespeare's *The Winter's Tale,* with its memorable episode involving old Antigonus making a hasty exit pursued by a bear. Jonson, in the specialised decorum of his exotic form, gives himself licence for a considerably more fantastic happening, with this entrance in a chariot drawn by two bears! We recall that there had been in 1610 a revival by the King's Men of the popular old play *Mucedorus* in which a character *enters* pursued by a bear! (If the dancing bear was a popular entertainment, it appears that bear-baiting drew better crowds in the London of this period; the spectacle of bears being harried to death by dogs regularly filled an adjacent arena known as the Bear Garden, and near the Globe on Bankside.)

The professional theatre brings the poet into the marketplace, and in the Elizabethan and Jacobean period the public taste for comedy seems not to evolve simply in tune with the personal artistic evolution of the great playwrights Shakespeare, Jonson and Middleton. The choice of plays in the present anthology is not therefore to be taken too simply as representing an evolution in audience taste away from folk tale and rural settings to sex-and-money intrigue in the city. In fact relatively simple kinds of popular comedy continued right through the period, though at the less successful playhouses on the whole. There were some distinctive new styles, especially the satiric wave from the children's companies at the · indoor playhouses Blackfriars and Paul's; but there were many revivals to complicate the view we derive from a list of new plays alone.

Revivals of old plays need not imply audiences athirst with nostalgia — as we can see from complaints about repeats on television today — but the fact that in 1610, in the same year that the King's Men performed their dazzling new Jonson play (the precision-engineered, fast, and up-to-date comedy *The Alchemist*) they should have also presented a revival of the old comedy *Mucedorus*, is probably an important testimony to the audience's undiminished enthusiasm for the more primitive comedy of the past. The revival seems moreover to have directly influenced the very next plays that Shakespeare wrote, in 1611. Certainly, if we take a different perspective, we can see that marvels, monsters and the fantastic have an honoured place in English drama from Marlowe to Milton, as witness *Dr Faustus*, *The Tempest* and *Comus*. It may then be appropriate to turn to a short consideration of Peele's comedy *The Old Wife's Tale*, exactly the kind of improbable play that aroused Sidney's critical hostility in *The Apology*, and Jonson's as late as 1632 in his comedy *The Magnetic Lady*.

To start with, the title of Peele's comedy is significant: it signals an entertainment along entirely familiar and traditional lines, with sources buried deep in the anonymous past. The title has a proverbial ring to it, as if Peele would disclaim any authorial responsibility for the work; no more would any old wife claim to have invented the traditional story, learned by ear, which she in turn passes on in the oral tradition. This emphasis on tradition reassures an audience that familiar pleasures are to be gratified, pleasures enjoyed by custom since childhood. Listening to such tales returns a spectator to his childhood, to some extent; he can recover something of the child's spontaneous and complete pleasure in a story as story, the delight in using one's imagination with little enough anxiety about probability, so long as the fantasy and nonsense comprise a good game. The child takes pleasure in the idea of a game, and mysterious and savage games are one staple element in folk tale narratives. The child accepts narrative rules as part of the artifice: it is a sign of the special precociousness of the young Pages in the Induction to Peele's comedy, then, that they ask inappropriate questions as the tale begins:

MADGE

Now this bargain, my masters, must I make with you, that you will say 'hum' and 'ha' to my tale; so shall I know you are awake.

BOTH

Content, gammer; that will we do.

MADGE

Once upon a time, there was a king or a lord or a duke that had a fair daughter, the fairest that ever was, as white as snow, and as red as blood; and once upon a time, his daughter was stolen away, and he sent all his men to seek out his daughter, and he sent so long that he sent all his men out of his land.

FROLIC
Who dressed his dinner then?

MADGE
Nay, either hear my tale or kiss my tail!

FANTASTIC
Well said! On with your tale, gammer.

MADGE
O Lord, I quite forgot! There was a conjurer, and this conjurer could do anything, and he turned himself into a great dragon and carried the king's daughter away in his mouth to a castle that he made of stone, and there he kept her I know not how long, till at last all the king's men went out so long that her own brothers went to seek her. O, I forget: she—he, I would say—turned a proper young man to a bear in the night and a man in the day, and keeps by a cross that parts three several ways, and he made his lady run mad. God's me bones! Who comes here?

Enter the two brothers

FROLIC
Soft, gammer, here some come to tell your tale for you.

Peele expects a sophisticated spectator to remain self-conscious, a little condescending, as he stoops to play such childish games, and so he entertains him with this highly absurd (because extreme) narrative confusion. The Old Wife's bad memory and lack of art serve to emphasise only the incredibility, not the marvellousness: the more she struggles to give causal and sequential justification (which nobody seriously would expect) the more Sidney's famous objections to dramatisations of such material seem thoroughly well-founded. It is hard not to think that Peele combines parody (and witty allusion to Sidney) with a straightforward piece of popular naive comedy here. The particular folk tales that Peele chooses are wittily adapted to his overall theme of metamorphosis, but we are also half-reminded of numerous other similar but not identical tales and motifs, with the effect of dream.

Each action has its own uninfringed integrity, based on long-established pattern; "the Grateful Dead", "The Three Heads of the Well" are fully presented, and motifs are taken from "Childe Roland", "Red Ettin" and "Jack the Giantkiller"; at the same time the spectator is made conscious of his separateness by the intervening on-stage audience of Madge and the Pages, who interrupt occasionally, and in another sense our experience of sudden and abrupt transitions from one level of the action to another induces the half-detached stance of the dreamer in relation to his dream: at times absorbed, then abruptly withdrawn, a passive spectator even when most deeply engaged. The key to Peele's art in this play would seem to be his careful control of the material that needs to be protected from questioning and mockery, so that wonder can be created. Here the physical fact of performance — the immediacy of action and spectacle, the impact of three-dimensional representation — is especially important. Audiences can be aroused to simple wonder by the tale of the three heads of the well, but the play's spectator senses the richness of the implicit symbolism when he not only hears but *sees*. As Celanta the foul wench dips her pitcher into the well a second time, a pure lyric renders the moment perfect and profoundly strange. The daemons of very ancient rites are glimpsed as the charm is sung:

> *A head comes up full of gold; she combs it into her lap*
> Gently dip, but not too deep,
> For fear thou make the golden bird to weep.
> Fair maiden, white and red,
> Comb me smooth, and stroke my head;
> And every hair a sheaf shall be,
> And every sheaf a golden tree.

The play's lightness of touch seems right: the imaginative power of such material can be trusted to exert its fascination when carefully prepared for; Peele seems to want his play to retain something of the sheer inexplicability of folk tale, with its gaps and opacities that are the result of many generations of oral transmission.

The abrupt and unexplained juxtaposition of vividly contrasting material also has a high aesthetic interrest. In the Romantic period we see a comparable interest in serious pastiche: there is Coleridge's *Ancient Mariner*, and *Ossian*, and Hogg's *Private Memoirs and Confessions*. Peele's achievement in *The Old Wife's Tale* may perhaps be understood best, when seen in the context of the intricately sophisticated phase of English culture around 1590 (the heyday of the sonnet, *The Arcadia*, and the music of Dowland, Weelkes and Morley), as an attempt to revive the simple power of the native culture's heritage of oral and performance art, in origin primitive yet also delicate and humorous. This hidden power is represented as something that needs patience and sympathy to unearth, like the light under the hill which, in the play, Jack explains:

> Master, without this the conjuror could do nothing; and so long as this light lasts, so long doth his art edure.

This can stand as a fitting epigraph of the importance of native tradition, which no major dramatist of the times neglects in practice.

The concept of a literary form deliberately intended to be filled with different things was available to the Elizabethans, for this is the meaning of the classical Roman term *satura*, but instead the Elizabethans supposed the form of satire derived from the Greek satyr plays, in which creatures from the woods, half-man and half-goat, were represented attacking the vices of society in crude, elliptic and harsh language, and in the low style. Puttenham in his *Art of English Poetry* for example says "the auncient Poets . . . made wise as if the gods of the woods, whom they called *Satyres* or *Siluanes*

should appear and recite those verses of rebuke, whereas indeede
they were but disguised persons under the shape of *Satyres*".

Satyrs appear in Spenser's *Faery Queene*, where they are
uninhibited in their animality and untamed natural state.

> All day they daunced with great lustihed,
> And with their horned feet the greene grasse wore,
> The whiles their gotes vpon the brouzes fed. (III, x 45)

The style and attitude of Elizabethan satiric writing has the rough
abruptness of manner, the barbarous diction and vocabulary, and the
low and ugly subject-matter, appropriate to the goat-footed creature,
and because reprisals are supposedly to be feared (so powerful does
the poet imagine his indictment to be) there is much obscurity and
obliqueness. It is the prime aim of satire to lash abuses and vice, so in
this sense it is normative, corrective and conservative. The wild and
shaggy creature is more truly in touch with what is good than the
metropolitan city-dweller (*civis*, hence "civilised"). This paradox
produces a profound destabilising force in all satiric writing — it is
much more than a witty paradox. The satyr himself is grotesque, and
in rebuking the ugliness he sees in the city, he explores the special
consciousness of the exiled, the scorned yet feared iconoclast. The
satirist's violent energy is ostensibly corrective but it often becomes
fantastic, absurd, nihilistic. In standing out against the crowd the
satirist can find self-delighting freedom; he can release suppressed
feelings and thoughts, for good and ill; he can subvert evil and op-
pression and he can be swept up himself by anarchic impulses that
arise within himself but become too strong for him to control. It is
the discovery of such things which is the most important feature in
the rise of satire in the Elizabethan and Jacobean period, explored
and expressed with consummate power as it is in *Hamlet*; not the
least interesting feature of Marston's *The Malcontent* is its treatment
of similar material from a different angle and in the mode of comedy
rather than tragedy.

The relation of satire to play, to the licence of reckless irrespon-
sibility, to the release of inhibitions either in the spirit of carnival or
nightmare, is very clear in Marston's Duke Altofront as he performs
the role of Malevole. With the licence given by his disguise,
Altofront as Malevole can create and transmit turbulent excitement
as he intuitively divines the hidden anxieties of the jealous Bilioso;
yet as he does so Malevole reaches the border of his own self-
conscious control, is and is not himself a participant in the feeling he
finds repulsive:

MALEVOLE

   Elder of Israel, thou honest defect of wicked nature and obstinate ignorance, when did thy wife let thee lie with her?

BILIOSO

   I am going ambassador to Florence.

MALEVOLE

Ambassador? Now, for thy country's honour, prithee do not put up mutton and porridge in thy cloak-bag. Thy young lady wife goes to Florence with thee too, does she not?

BILIOSO

No, I leave her at the palace.

MALEVOLE

At the palace? Now discretion shield man! For God's love, let's ha' no more cuckolds. Hymen begins to put off his saffron robe. Keep thy wife i' the state of grace. Heart o' truth, I would sooner leave my lady singled in a bordello than in the Genoa palace.

Sin there appearing in her sluttish shape,
Would soon grow loathsome, even to blushes' sense;
Surfeit would choke intemperate appetite,
Make the soul scent the rotten breath of lust.
When in an Italian lascivious palace,
A lady guardianless,
Left to the push of all allurement,
The strongest incitements to immodesty,
To have her bound, incensed with wanton sweets,
Her veins filled high with heating delicates,
Soft rest, sweet music, amorous masquerers,
Lascivious banquets, sin itself gilt o'er,
Strong fantasy tricking up strange delights, (III.ii, 16-40)

The ambivalence of caricature which can shade off into uncontrolled nightmare is not the province of comedy; in Marston's own tragedies, and especially in the tragedies of Webster, it is deeply explored; but nevertheless it is important to see how strong is the current of satire which produces this turbulence of language and state of mind.

For satire in a more firmly comic key, we may turn to another play in which Marston had a hand, the collaborative *Eastward Ho!*, written perhaps a year after *The Malcontent*. The act of collaboration seems to have brought out the sunniest aspect of all three writers, and the play is marked by some excellent parody of dramatic conventions and verbal styles in preceding popular comedies about the city. The title refers to the major episode in the play, in which a shipload of adventurers set off to make their fortunes in Virginia, drawn by the lure of gold: as the ship's captain Seagull assures the company gathered for the farewell in the Anchor Tavern, Billingsgate, in Virginia

I tell thee, gold is more plentiful there than copper is with us; and for as much red copper as I can bring, I'll have thrice the weight in gold. Why, man, all their dripping-pans and their chamber-pots are pure gold; and all the chains with which they chain up their streets are massy gold; all the prisoners they take are fettered in gold; and for rubies and diamonds, they go forth on holidays and gather 'em by the seashore to hang on their children's coats, and stick in their caps. (III. iii, 23-30)

Sir Petronell Flash the destitute knight, Security the usurer, Master Bramble the lawyer, Security's wife disguised as a sailor for adulterous purposes, and the captain's mates Spendall and Scapethrift, together with the idle apprentice Quicksilver, drink deep; the men "Compass in Winifred, dance the drunken round, and drink carouses", and the gallant company of voyagers departs.

This is an entertaining if sardonic view of the quality, motives and manners of the early colonisers of America, and aptly reverses cheerful patriotic sentiments towards the city and its worthies as found in *The Shoemakers' Holiday*, for instance. But the playwrights in *Eastward Ho!* have yet to complete the climactic episode. What they choose to do is to make an actor enter with a cumbrous great pair of ox-horns; these he must carry while shinning up a tall post and delivering a choric soliloquy. He is Slitgut, a butcher's apprentice, sent to perform the annual London ritual at Cuckoldshaven. Slitgut complains as he climbs the pole that there is a full gale blowing — comically ominous in view of the voyage that has just begun. Slitgut hangs on at the top of his pole (resembling at once a lookout in a ship's crowsnest and an ornament on a carnival maypole) while the storm breaks below: — the usurer discovering his cuckoldry, the ship wrecked and the mariners staggering in wet and addressing Cockneys in fractured French on the beach of the Isle of Dogs. Slitgut, aloft, with the ox-horns, is a lord of misrule (against his will) and a chorus to the mock-heroic absurdities below. We may detect the combined forces of Chapman the translator of Homer, and Jonson the critic of Shakespeare's *Henry V*, in this superb, good-natured parody of the Chorus describing the English fleet's voyage to France; and we may also think of Falstaff ludicrously garbed as Herne the Hunter at the end of *The Merry Wives*. Yet the achievement in *Eastward Ho!* is successful in its own right, and does not *depend* on such allusiveness; this scene offers a satiric rival to the official London Lord Mayor's Show; it has a true Dionysiac comic spirit, and wryly celebrates the instinctual needs which the city's guilds and ceremonies strive to dignify with their companies of Vintners, Fishmongers, and what not, all in solemn robes. Slitgut presides over a very different feast and carnival; in the spirit of Dionysiac comedy, appetite, unbridled licence, is the true heart of the city:

SLITGUT

Now will I descend my honourable prospect, the farthest seeing seamark of the world; no marvel, then, if I could see two miles about me. I hope the red tempest's anger be now overblown, which sure I think heaven sent as a punishment for profaning holy Saint Luke's memory with so ridiculous a custom. Thou dishonest satyr, farewell to honest married men; farewell to all sorts and degrees of thee! Farewell, thou horn of hunger, that call'st th'Inns o' Court to their manger! Farewell, thou horn of abundance, that adornest the headsmen of the commonwealth! Farewell, thou horn of direction, that is the city lanthorn! Farewell, thou horn of pleasure, the ensign of the huntsman! Farewell, thou horn of destiny, th'ensign of the married man! Farewell, thou horn tree, that bearest nothing but stone-fruit! *Exit*

It is with such insights that Middleton begins his comedy of London life, at once signalling its heritage of Roman New Comedy and its sharp modernity in the slickly urban catch-phrase, *A Trick to Catch the Old One*. The reader is invited to now make his own way into Middleton's comedy: this introduction hopes only to whet the appetite.

BRIAN GIBBONS

FURTHER READING

General
1 Eric Bentley, *The Life of the Drama* (1964)
2 M. C. Bradbrook, *The Growth and Structure of Elizabethan Comedy* (1955)
3 T. S. Eliot, *Elizabethan Dramatists* (1963)
4 Una Ellis-Fermor, *The Jacobean Drama* (1936)
5 Brian Gibbons, *Jacobean City Comedy* (rev. ed. 1980)
6 Michael Hattaway, *Elizabethan Popular Theatre* (1982)
7 G. K. Hunter, *Dramatic Identities and Cultural Tradition* (1978)
8 L. C. Knights, *Drama and Society in the Age of Jonson* (1936)
9 Alexander Leggatt, *Citizen Comedy in the Age of Shakespeare* (1973)
10 Richard Levin, *The Multiple Plot in English Renaissance Drama* (1971)

Playhouses and Companies
11 C. Walter Hodges, *The Globe Restored* (1968)
12 C. J. Sisson, *The Boar's Head Theatre* (1972)
13 Richard Hosley, The Blackfriars Theatre, in *The Revels History of Drama in English* vol. III, pt 3, ch. 4.
14 M. C. Bradbrook, Shakespeare and the Multiple Theatres of Jacobean London, in *The Elizabethan Theatre*, ed. G. R. Hibbard, vol. VI (1978)
15 Peter Thomson, *Shakespeare's Theatre* (1983)

Individual Dramatists
Peele
16 *The Life and Works of George Peele*, gen. ed. C. T. Prouty (Yale, 1952-70)

Dekker
17 M. T. Jones-Davies, *Thomas Dekker* (1958)
18 G. R. Price, *Thomas Dekker* (1969)
19 Joel Kaplan, Virtue's Holiday: Thomas Dekker and Simon Eyre, *Ren. D.* II (1969)
20 H. E. Toliver, *The Shoemakers' Holiday:* Theme and Image, Boston Univ. Studies in English, V (1961)
& Essays in 2 and 9 above

Marston

21 Philip Finkelpearl, *John Marston of the Inner Temple* (1969)
22 G. K. Hunter, Introduction to *The Malcontent* (Revels Plays 1975)
& Essays in 3, 4, 5, 7, 10 above
23 Arthur Kirsh, *Jacobean Dramatic Perspectives* (1972)

Middleton

24 Margot Heinemann, *Puritanism and Theatre* (1980)
25 R. B. Parker, Middleton's Experiments with Comedy and Judgment, in J. R. Brown and Bernard Harris, ed., Stratford-upon-Avon Studies, vol. I (1960)
& Essays in 2, 4, 5, 8, 9, 10 above.

Jonson

26 Jonas Barish, ed., *Ben Jonson: Twentieth Century Views* (1963)
27 Ian Donaldson, *The World Upside Down* (1970)
28 Douglas Duncan, *Ben Jonson and the Lucianic Tradition* (1979)
29 William Blissett, Your Majesty is welcome to a Fair, in G. R. Hibbard ed., *The Elizabethan Theatre IV* (1974)
30 G. R. Hibbard, Three Times *Ho* and a Brace of Widows, in *The Elizabethan Theatre III* (1973)
& Discussions in 2, 3, 4, 5, 8, 10 above.

More extensive reading lists can be found in the annual *Year's Work in English Studies* and in the Renaissance Drama issue of *Studies in English Literature*, also annual. The annual volumes of *Renaissance Drama* (new series ed. L. Barkan, Northwestern Univ. Press) and of *The Elizabethan Theatre* (ed. Galloway, Hibbard, Waterloo Ont. & London), contain many good articles on the plays in the present anthology, and may be expected to continue to do so.

The Old Wife's Tale

GEORGE PEELE

Edited by
CHARLES W. WHITWORTH, JR.

ABBREVIATIONS

Q	The quarto of 1595.
OWT	*The Old Wife's Tale*
RD	*Roister Doister*
Binnie	Patricia Binnie, ed., *The Old Wives Tale*, The Revels Plays (Manchester and Baltimore, 1980)
Brooke and Paradise	C. F. Tucker Brooke and N. B. Paradise, eds., *English Drama 1580–1642* (Boston, 1933)
Bullen	A. H. Bullen, ed., *The Works of George Peele*, 2 vols (1888), I
Dyce	Alexander Dyce, ed., *The Dramatic and Poetical Works of Robert Greene and George Peele* (1861)
Gayley	Charles Mills Gayley, ed., *Representative English Comedies* (1903)
Greg	W. W. Greg. ed., *The Old Wives Tale*, MSR (Oxford, 1909)
Gummere	F. B. Gummere, ed., *The Old Wives' Tale*, in Gayley
Hook	Frank S. Hook, ed., *The Old Wives Tale*, in *The Life and Works of George Peele*, 3 vols, gen. ed. C. T. Prouty, III (New Haven, 1970)
McIlwraith	A. K. McIlwraith, ed., *Five Elizabethan Comedies* (1934, etc.)

THE
Old Wiues Tale.

A pleasant conceited Comedie, played by the Queenes Maiesties players.

Written by G. Peele.

Printed at London by *Iohn Danter*, and are to
be sold by *Raph Hancocke*, and *Iohn
Hardie*, 1 5 9 5.

[Dramatis Personae

ANTIC
FROLIC } *pages*
FANTASTIC
CLUNCH, *a smith*
MADGE, *an old woman, the smith's wife*   5

FIRST BROTHER (Calypha) } *brothers to Delia*
SECOND BROTHER (Thelea)
OLD MAN *at the cross* (Erestus)
VENELIA, *his betrothed*
LAMPRISCUS   10
HUANEBANGO, *a braggart knight*
BOOBY, *the Clown, his companion and rival*
SACRAPANT, *the Conjurer*
DELIA, *daughter to the King of Thessaly, abducted by Sacrapant*
EUMENIDES, *the Wandering Knight, in love with Delia*   15

1–3 *pages* Based on the reference by Fantastic in ll. 11–12 to 'our young master'.

4 CLUNCH Named at 32, and called 'Smith' in Q speech prefixes. The word means 'a lumpish fellow, clodhopper or boor', but Peele's use of it as a name suggests no more than a rustic or a country fellow. It must have been current by the time the play was written, though the earliest recorded occurrence of the noun in *OED* is 1602 (see C. W. Whitworth, 'Some Words in Two Thomas Lodge Romances (1591–2)', *N&Q*, N.S.24 (1977), 516).

5 MADGE Named by the Smith at 53. Called 'Old Woman' in Q speech prefixes.

6 FIRST BROTHER Named 'Calypha' at 388. This edition retains Q's titles for the two brothers in speech prefixes; their names occur late and almost incidentally, and it is their status as Delia's brothers which identifies them in the play.

7 SECOND BROTHER Not named as 'Thelea' until 853.

8 OLD MAN Called 'Erestus' only at the end of the play (852). His function as a kind of benevolent presiding figure, a counterpart to the evil Sacrapant, is suggested by his namelessness, and this edition retains Q's speech prefixes.

11 HUANEBANGO M.C. Bradbrook thinks 'Juan y Bango' is meant, suggesting a Spanish braggart (*ES*, 43, p. 325). The braggart soldier, or captain, was a familiar character in all European comedy, and was a principal figure in *commedia dell'arte* where he often bore a Spanish name, e.g. 'Sangre y Fuego'.

12 BOOBY So called in Q throughout his first scene (248–325); thereafter called 'Corebus'. This change of name is the source of a major confusion in the play, as one of Jack's friends who try to get the Churchwarden to bury him is also called Corebus. This edition retains the name 'Booby' for Huanebango's companion throughout. He is designated as 'the Clown' at his entrances both as 'Booby' at 248 and as 'Corebus' at 537.

13 SACRAPANT Peele may have taken the name from Ariosto's epic *Orlando Furioso* (Sacrapante) or from Robert Greene's play of the same name, where it is spelled 'Sacripant'.

15 EUMENIDES Possibly from the romantic hero of John Lyly's play *Endymion* (1588).

7

WIGGEN ⎱ *friends of Jack*
COREBUS ⎰

CHURCHWARDEN (Steven Loach)

SEXTON

ZANTIPPA, *the Curst Daughter* ⎱
                          ⎰ *daughters to Lampriscus*   20
CELANTA, *the Foul Wench* ⎰

A VOICE *in the well*

A HEAD *in the well*

JACK, *a ghost*

HOSTESS   25

Friar, Echo, Two Furies, Harvest-men and women, Fiddlers]

---

20 *Curst* shrewish

---

18 CHURCHWARDEN So called in stage directions and speech prefixes, except at 447, where the s.p. is 'Simon'; this may refer to the name of an actor, John Symons (see Chambers, II, 111). He refers to himself as 'Stephen Loach' at 483.

20 ZANTIPPA From 'Xanthippe', name of the shrewish wife of the Greek philosopher Socrates.

22–3 A VOICE . . . A HEAD This edition distinguishes between the VOICE, which speaks from the well, and the HEAD, which is mute, rising and descending from the well with gifts. Q conflates them, using the speech prefix 'Head' at 621, and 'Voice' at 756.

The Old Wife's Tale

Enter ANTIC, FROLIC *and* FANTASTIC

ANTIC
How now, fellow Frolic! What, all amort? Doth this
sadness become thy madness? What though we have lost
our way in the woods? Yet never hang the head as though
thou hadst no hope to live till tomorrow. For Fantastic
and I will warrant thy life tonight for twenty in   5
the hundred.

FROLIC
Antic and Fantastic, as I am frolic franion, never in all my
life was I so dead slain. What, to lose our way in the wood,
without either fire or candle, so uncomfortable? *O coelum!*
O terra! O maria! O Neptune!   10

FANTASTIC
Why makes thou it so strange, seeing Cupid hath led our
young master to the fair lady, and she is the only saint he
hath sworn to serve?

FROLIC
What resteth then, but we commit him to his wench, and
each of us take his stand up in a tree and sing out our ill   15
fortune to the tune of 'O man in desperation'?

ANTIC
Desperately spoken, fellow Frolic, in the dark; but seeing
it falls out thus, let us rehearse the old proverb:

1 *Frolic* eds. (Franticke Q)
  all amort (Fr., *à la mort;* literally 'mortally sick') dejected, dispirited
5 *warrant . . . hundred* lay five-to-one odds against your being killed
7 *franion* gay, reckless fellow
8 *dead slain* exhausted *or* frightened to death
11 *makes . . . strange* do you carry on so

9–10 *O coelum . . . Neptune* O heaven! O earth! O sea (and/or 'Mary')! O Neptune!
The classical source is Terence's *Adelphoe (The Brothers),* 1. 790: *'o caelum, o terra, o
maria Neptuni'.* Hook (p. 422n.) notes that it is similarly misquoted in Kyd's
Soliman and Perseda, IV.ii, 67.
12–13 *she . . . serve* A parallel is suggested between the action of the play-within where
Eumenides has sworn his love to Delia with whom he is united at last, and that of
the frame, or 'outer' world. This has led some critics to consider *OWT* as an
afterpiece, others to conclude that it was written and played for a marriage feast.
16 *'O . . . desperation'* A popular tune, to which many songs were set.

9

Three merry men, and three merry men,
And three merry men be we;   20
I in the wood, and thou on the ground,
And Jack sleeps in the tree.

[*A dog barks*]

FANTASTIC
Hush! A dog in the wood, or a wooden dog! O
comfortable hearing! I had even as lief the chamberlain of
the White Horse had called me up to bed.   25

FROLIC
Either hath this trotting cur gone out of his circuit, or else
are we near some village,

Enter a smith with a lantern and candle

which should not be far off, for I perceive the glimmering
of a glow-worm, a candle, or a cat's eye, my life for a
halfpenny.—In the name of my own father, be thou ox or   30
ass that appearest, tell us what thou art!

CLUNCH
What am I? Why, I am Clunch the smith. What are you?
What make you in my territories at this time of the night?

23 *wooden* (wood) mad
24 *even as lief* just as soon
29–30 *my . . . halfpenny* (oath)
32 *(and passim)* s.p. CLUNCH eds. (Smith Q)
33 *make you* are you doing

19–22 *Three merry men . . . in the tree* Another popular song, recorded elsewhere with
the same words sung here. It had its own tune, so was not 'to the tune of "O man in
desperation" '; the pages sing something 'merry' rather than 'desperate', although
in some versions the 'tree' in question is a gallows, as in *Rollo, Duke of Normandy*,
by John Fletcher *et al.* (ed. J.D. Jump, 1948), III.ii. The story is quoted in several
plays of the period and Sir Toby Belch sings the first line in *Twelfth Night* (II.iii,
74); the new Arden and New Penguin editions of that play print the tunes. See also
W. Chappell, *Popular Music of the Olden Time* (1859; repr. 1965), I, 216–18, and
P.J. Seng, *The Vocal Songs in the Plays of Shakespeare* (1967), pp. 101–3.

25 *White Horse* Many London taverns have this name. The reference is probably to
the one in Friday Street, near St. Paul's, frequented by Peele himself, according to
an anecdote in *The Merry Conceited Jests of George Peele* (1607) (ed. Bullen, *The
Works of George Peele* (1888), II, 386).

26 *trotting . . . circuit* Perhaps an allusion to the use of dogs to work treadmills, or
tread-wheels, to pump water, turn spits, etc. Dromio of Syracuse, in *The Comedy of
Errors*, fears being 'transformed . . . to a curtal dog, and made [to] turn i' the wheel'
(III.ii, 144).

ANTIC

What do we make, dost thou ask? Why, we make faces for
fear; such as if thy mortal eye could behold, would make   35
thee water the long seams of thy side slops, smith.

FROLIC

And, in faith, sir, unless your hospitality do relieve us, we
are like to wander with a sorrowful 'heigh-ho' among the
owlets and hobgoblins of the forest. Good Vulcan, for
Cupid's sake that hath cozened us all, befriend us as thou   40
mayest, and command us howsoever, wheresoever, when-
soever, in whatsoever, for ever and ever.

CLUNCH

Well, masters, it seems to me you have lost your way in
the wood. In consideration whereof, if you will go with
Clunch to his cottage, you shall have house-room and a   45
good fire to sit by, although we have no bedding to put
you in.

ALL

O blessed smith, O bountiful Clunch!

CLUNCH

For your further entertainment, it shall be as it may be, so
and so.   50

Hear a dog bark

Hark! This is Ball, my dog, that bids you welcome in his
own language. Come, take heed for stumbling on the
threshold. Open door, Madge; take in guests.

Enter old woman

36 *side slops* wide, baggy breeches
40 *cozened* tricked

39 *Vulcan* Vulcanus, the Roman name for the Greek god of fire, Hephaestus. He built
palaces for the other Olympian gods and fashioned armour and jewellery from
metal, hence his traditional role as patron of smiths.
49 *it . . . be* Proverbial (Tilley T202): 'Things must be as they may'.
50 s.d. *Hear . . . bark* An example of the authorial stage direction, telling us that the
characters hear something, rather than providing an instruction for the sound to be
made at this point. Some editors emend to 'Here a dog barks'.
52–3 *stumbling . . . threshold* A bad omen.

MADGE

    Welcome, Clunch, and good fellows all, that come with
    my good man. For my good man's sake, come on, sit   55
    down. Here is a piece of cheese and a pudding of my own
    making.

ANTIC

    Thanks, gammer. A good example for the wives of our
    town.

FROLIC

    Gammer, thou and thy good man sit lovingly together.   60
    We come to chat and not to eat.

CLUNCH

    Well, masters, if you will eat nothing, take away. Come,
    what do we to pass away the time? Lay a crab in the fire to
    roast for lamb's-wool. What, shall we have a game at
    trump or ruff to drive away the time? How say you?   65

FANTASTIC

    This smith leads a life as merry as a king with Madge his
    wife. Sirrah Frolic, I am sure thou art not without some
    round or other; no doubt but Clunch can bear his part.

FROLIC

    Else think you me ill brought up! So set to it when you
    will.   70

They sing

Song

    Whenas the rye reach to the chin,
    And chopcherry, chopcherry ripe within,
    Strawberries swimming in the cream,
    And schoolboys playing in the stream.
    Then 'O', then 'O', then 'O' my true love said,   75

54 *(and passim)* s.p. MADGE eds. *(variously,* Ol., Old woman, Old wom., etc. Q)
55 *good man. For* ed. (good man for Q)
63 *crab* crabapple

---

64 *lamb's-wool* A drink consisting of hot ale mixed with the pulp of roasted apples or
    crabapples and sugared and spiced.
65 *trump or ruff* Card games similar to but less complicated than whist and bridge, and
    popular in the sixteenth century.
71 *Song* No early tune seems to have survived. Benjamin Britten set it to music in his
    Spring Symphony (1949).
72 *chopcherry* 'A game in which one tries to catch a suspended cherry with the teeth;
    bob-cherry' *(OED).*

Till that time come again,
She could not live a maid.

ANTIC
This sport does well. But methinks, gammer, a merry
winter's tale would drive away the time trimly. Come, I
am sure you are not without a score.   80

FANTASTIC
I' faith, gammer, a tale of an hour long were as good as an
hour's sleep.

FROLIC
Look you, gammer, of the giant and the king's daughter,
and I know not what. I have seen the day, when I was a
little one, you might have drawn me a mile after you with   85
such a discourse.

MADGE
Well, since you be so importunate, my good man shall fill
the pot and get him to bed. They that ply their work must
keep good hours. One of you go lie with him; he is a
clean-skinned man, I tell you, without either spavin or   90
windgall. So I am content to drive away the time with an
old wife's winter's tale.

FANTASTIC
No better hay in Devonshire. A' my word, gammer, I'll be
one of your audience.

FROLIC
And I another, that's flat.   95

ANTIC
Then must I to bed with the good man. *Bona nox*,
gammer. Good night, Frolic.

92 *wife's* ed. (wives Q)
93 *A'* at, upon
95 *flat* definite
96 *Bona nox* good night
97 *Good* eds. (God Q)

---

90 *spavin* A hard, bony tumour resulting from inflammation of cartilage joining bones
in a horse's leg.
91 *windgall* A soft tumour on either side of a horse's leg just above the fetlock.
93 *No ... Devonshire* Proverbial? (unrecorded). There's no better way to spend our
time.

CLUNCH
Come on, my lad. Thou shalt take thy unnatural rest with
me.

Exeunt ANTIC *and the Smith*

FROLIC
Yet this vantage shall we have of them in the morning, to   100
be ready at the sight thereof extempore.

MADGE
Now this bargain, my masters, must I make with you, that
you will say 'hum' and 'ha' to my tale; so shall I know you
are awake.

BOTH
Content, gammer; that will we do.   105

MADGE
Once upon a time, there was a king or a lord or a duke
that had a fair daughter, the fairest that ever was, as white
as snow, and as red as blood; and once upon a time, his
daughter was stolen away, and he sent all his men to seek
out his daughter, and he sent so long that he sent all his   110
men out of his land.

*c. P.
Winter
Tale*

FROLIC
Who dressed his dinner then?

MADGE
Nay, either hear my tale or kiss my tail!

FANTASTIC
Well said! On with your tale, gammer.

MADGE
O Lord, I quite forgot! There was a conjurer, and this   115
conjurer could do anything, and he turned himself into a
great dragon and carried the king's daughter away in his
mouth to a castle that he made of stone, and there he kept

112 *dressed* served

---

98 *unnatural* Because a man and a boy are sharing a bed.
99 s.d. *Exeunt . . . Smith* The actors playing these two parts are presumably needed to
   play other roles in the inner play; Madge, Frolic and Fantastic remain onstage as
   audience for the inner play.
100-1 *Yet . . . extempore* But we shall see the dawn as soon as it appears, unlike those
   who will be asleep.

O, I forget: she—he, I would say—turned a proper young
man to a bear in the night and a man in the day, and
keeps by a cross that parts three several ways, and he
made his lady run mad. God's me bones! Who comes
here?   125

Enter the two brothers

FROLIC
Soft, gammer, here some come to tell your tale for you.

FANTASTIC
Let them alone; let us hear what they will say.

FIRST BROTHER
Upon these chalky cliffs of Albion
We are arrived now with tedious toil,
And compassing the wide world round about   130
To seek our sister, to seek fair Delia forth,
Yet cannot we so much as hear of her.

SECOND BROTHER
O fortune cruel, cruel and unkind,
Unkind in that we cannot find our sister,
Our hapless sister in her cruel chance—   135
Soft! Who have we here?

Enter the OLD MAN *at the cross, stooping to gather*

124 *God's* ed. (gods Q)
136 s.d *the* OLD MAN ed. (Senex Q)

---

123 *keeps . . . cross* This formulation may lend weight to the suggestion that the Old
   Man (Erestus) remains onstage (though perhaps not always visible) at his station,
   the cross, throughout the inner play (see below, 234 s.d. and note), and indicates a
   feature of the setting ('three several ways'). Madge is not to be relied upon for
   consistency or preciseness, however. This passage (115–25) and her previous one
   (106–11) set the fairy-tale, 'Once upon a time' atmosphere of her tale, and her
   forgetfulness as regards certain details (115, 121) and the imprecise use of
   pronouns—'she', 'he' (121, 123), omission of 'he' (123)—enhance the effect. We
   do not see Sacrapant's stone castle (118), only a cell or study (326 s.d.), and Madge
   neglects to say that Erestus is turned into an *old* man (122).
136 s.d. *Enter . . . gather* The Old Man cannot both 'enter' and be 'at the cross'
   simultaneously, of course (see above, 123n.), and 'at the cross' here may be
   intended as identification rather than as indicating location. He must, however, get
   onstage for the first time, as the inner play begins. A director might want to have
   him in place as the brothers enter, especially if he is to be seen as a sort of presiding
   figure; 'who comes here' (124–5) and 'here some come' (126) might include him as
   well as the brothers. They then become aware of him at 136; compare 294 and see
   234n., below.

FIRST BROTHER
  Now father, God be your speed. What do you gather
  there?

OLD MAN
  Hips and haws, and sticks and straws, and things that I
  gather on the ground, my son.   140

FIRST BROTHER
  Hips and haws, and sticks and straws! Why, is that all
  your food, father?

OLD MAN
  Yea, son.

SECOND BROTHER
  Father, here is an alms-penny for me, and if I speed in
  that I go for, I will give thee as good a gown of grey as   145
  ever thou didst wear.

FIRST BROTHER
  And father, here is another alms-penny for me, and if I
  speed in my journey, I will give thee a palmer's staff of
  ivory and a scallop shell of beaten gold.

OLD MAN
  Was she fair?   150

SECOND BROTHER
  Ay, the fairest for white and the purest for red, as the
  blood of the deer or the driven snow.

139 *Hips* fruit of the wild rose
    haws fruit of the hawthorn
144 *alms-penny* penny given for charity
    speed am successful
148 *palmer's* pilgrim's

---

145 *gown of grey* Traditional garb of a pilgrim.
148 *palmer's . . . gold* A pilgrim to the Holy Land brought a palm branch back with him;
    hence the name 'palmer'. The staff would be simply a walking stick. The scallop
    shell was a badge or sign, like the palm: pilgrims to the shrine of St. James of
    Compostella in Spain wore or carried one back with them (whence the French
    name for scallops, *coquilles Saint Jacques*). Hook (p. 425) quotes Sir Walter
    Raleigh's poem 'The Passionate Man's Pilgrimage', which mentions staff and shell.
150 *Was she fair?* It is not necessary to assume, as some editors have, that something is
    omitted in the text just before the Old Man asks this question. He has perhaps
    overheard the two brothers talking about their sister, or reads their minds, or
    simply divines the object of their quest.

SECOND BROTHER
    Ay, the fairest for white and the purest for red, as the
    blood of the deer or the driven snow.

OLD MAN
    Then hark well and mark well my old spell:
        Be not afraid of every stranger,
        Start not aside at every danger;   155
        Things that seem are not the same.
        Blow a blast at every flame;
        For when one flame of fire goes out,
        Then comes your wishes well about.
        If any ask who told you this good,   160
        Say the White Bear of England's wood.

FIRST BROTHER
    Brother, heard you not what the old man said?
        'Be not afraid of every stranger,
        Start not aside for every danger;
        Things that seem are not the same.   165
        Blow a blast at every flame;
        [For when one flame of fire goes out,
        Then comes your wishes well about.]
        If any ask who told you this good,
        Say the White Bear of England's wood.'   170

SECOND BROTHER
    Well, if this do us any good,
    Well fare the White Bear of England's wood!

                  Exeunt [*the two brothers*]

---

161 (also 170, 172) *White Bear* eds. (white Beare Q)
167–8 *For... about* eds. (not in Q)
172 s.d. *Exeunt... brothers* eds. (*ex.* Q)

---

159 *comes* The third person singular verb with a plural noun is common in Elizabethan
    English; other examples in this play occur at 412, 505 and 660.
161 *White... wood* No heraldic significance has been discovered which would make
    this a reference to a particular person or family. Gummere (p. 345) observes that
    Merlin appears in the form of a bear in the old ballad 'Childe Rowland'.
167–8 Most editors have followed Dyce in supplying these two lines from the Old
    Man's preceding speech (158–9). There is no good reason for the brother to omit
    them when repeating the instructions, and the exact repetition of such charms,
    incantations and the like heightens their portent and serves to fix them in the
    memory, both the characters' and the audience's.

The hard mishap of thy most wretched state.
In Thessaly I lived in sweet content,
Until that Fortune wrought my overthrow;
For there I wedded was unto a dame
That lived in honour, virtue, love and fame.   180
But Sacrapant, that cursed sorcerer,
Being besotted with my beauteous love,
My dearest love, my true betrothed wife,
Did seek the means to rid me of my life.
But worse than this, he with his chanting spells   185
Did turn me straight into an ugly bear;
And when the sun doth settle in the west,
Then I begin to don my ugly hide.
And all the day I sit as now you see,
And speak in riddles, all inspired with rage,   190
Seeming an old and miserable man;
And yet I am in April of my age.

Enter VENELIA *his lady, mad; and goes in again*

See where Venelia, my betrothed love,
Runs madding all enraged about the woods,
All by his cursed and enchanting spells.   195

Enter LAMPRISCUS *with a pot of honey*

But here comes Lampriscus, my discontented neighbour.——
How now, neighbour? You look toward the ground as well as I.
You muse on something.

---

190 *rage* prophetic inspiration

---

177 *Thessaly* A division of ancient Greece, on the eastern (Aegean) side, now part of
Macedonia. Hook cites Apuleius, *The Golden Ass* (second century A.D.), whose
narrator says: 'I was very desirous to know and see some marvellous and strange
things, remembering with myself that I was in the midst parts of all Thessaly,
where, by the common report of all the world, is the birthplace of sorceries and
enchantments' (Loeb edition, p. 49).

179 *wedded* There is no need to worry unduly about the apparent impreciseness in the
Old Man's account of his relationship with Venelia: *wedded . . . betrothed wife*
(183) . . . *betrothed love* (193). Her status is similar to that of Juliet and, later,
Mariana in *Measure for Measure,* where the latter is referred to by the Duke as
'neither maid, widow nor wife' (V.i, 178). Venelia is 'neither wife, widow nor maid'
(417), and is thus the one who will break Sacrapant's glass, destroying his power.

192 *April . . . age* The cliché is repeated at 654 and 675. Youth and old age, actual and
apparent, are a major motif in the play, one of several aspects of the central truth-
and-illusion theme.

But here comes Lampriscus, my discontented neighbour.—How now, neighbour? You look toward the
ground as well as I. You muse on something.

LAMPRISCUS
Neighbour, on nothing but on the matter I so often
moved to you. If you do anything for charity, help me; if   200
for neighbourhood or brotherhood, help me. Never was
one so cumbered as is poor Lampriscus. And to begin, I
pray, receive this pot of honey to mend your fare.

OLD MAN
Thanks, neighbour, set it down. [*Aside*] Honey is always
welcome to the bear.—And now, neighbour, let me hear   205
the cause of your coming.

LAMPRISCUS
I am, as you know, neighbour, a man unmarried, and
lived so unquietly with my two wives that I keep every
year holy the day wherein I buried them both. The first
was on Saint Andrew's Day, the other on Saint Luke's.   210

OLD MAN
And now, neighbour, you of this country say, your
custom is out. But on with your tale, neighbour.

LAMPRISCUS
By my first wife, whose tongue wearied me alive, and

200 *moved* spoke about
202 *cumbered* encumbered, burdened
203 *mend your fare* improve your diet
204 s.d. *Aside* Binnie
211 *this country* (i.e., England)
212 *custom* obligatory service, as to a feudal master
    out over, done
213 *alive* when she was alive

204–5 *Honey ... bear* This looks as if it may be a line of verse in Q; Binnie prints it as
   one in view of its 'gnomic flavour'. But Q's arrangement may be meant to indicate
   only that the line is spoken aside. Bears' taste for honey is recognized in proverbs,
   e.g. Tilley B130 and H551.
210 *Saint Andrew's ... Saint Luke's* November 30th and October 18th, respectively.
   Both days were traditionally believed to be propitious for choosing a husband
   and/or discovering the identity of a future spouse. In *Measure for Measure*, the
   'dejected Mariana', who is to be reunited with her betrothed who had abandoned
   her, resides at Saint Luke's. Hook notes (p. 426) that St. Luke was patron of
   horned creatures (from his symbol, a winged ox), including cuckolds, an ironic
   association in view of his feast day's supposed propitiousness where lovers and their
   desires were concerned. Lampriscus's good luck was to have buried his two
   insupportable wives on these favourable days.

sounded in my ears like the clapper of a great bell, whose
talk was a continual torment to all that dwelt by her or 215
lived nigh her, you have heard me say I had a handsome
daughter.

OLD MAN
True, neighbour.

LAMPRISCUS
She it is that afflicts me with her continual clamours and
hangs on me like a bur. Poor she is, and proud she is; as 220
poor as a sheep new-shorn, and as proud of her hopes as a
peacock of her tail well-grown.

OLD MAN
Well said, Lampriscus! You speak it like an Englishman.

LAMPRISCUS
As curst as a wasp, and as froward as a child new-taken
from the mother's teat. She is to my age as smoke to the 225
eyes, or as vinegar to the teeth.

OLD MAN
Holily praised, neighbour. As much for the next.

LAMPRISCUS
By my other wife I had a daughter, so hard-favoured, so
foul and ill-faced, that I think a grove full of golden trees,
and the leaves of rubies and diamonds, would not be a 230
dowry answerable to her deformity.

OLD MAN
Well, neighbour, now you have spoke, hear me speak.

---

224 *curst* shrewish, ill-tempered
   froward refractory

---

220 *hangs... bur* Proverbial (Tilley B723).
   Poor... proud Proverbial (Tilley, P474, P475): 'Poor and proud...'. Poverty and
   pride are linked in many other proverbs, e.g. Tilley P572, P577, P579, P580; and
   ODEP: 'A proud beggar that makes his own alms'.
220-1 *as poor... new-shorn* Proverbial (Tilley S295): 'As rich as a new-shorn sheep'
   (used ironically); *ODEP* cites this line from *OWT*, but Tilley does not.
221-2 *as proud... tail* Proverbial (Tilley P157). 'Her' is the wrong pronoun for the
   pea*cock*, the male, but the pea*hen* does not have a fine tail.
224 *As... wasp* Proverbial (Tilley W76): 'As angry as a wasp'.
225-6 *as smoke... teeth* Scriptural: 'As vinegar to the teeth, and as smoke to the eyes, so
   is the sluggard to them that send him' (Proverbs 10:26). This explains the Old
   Man's comment 'Holily praised' in the next line.

Send them to the well for the water of life; there shall they
find their fortunes unlooked for. Neighbour, farewell.

[*Withdraws*]

LAMPRISCUS
Farewell and a thousand! And now goeth poor Lampris- 235
cus to put in execution this excellent counsel.

Exit

FROLIC
Why, this goes round without a fiddling stick. But do you
hear, gammer, was this the man that was a bear in the
night and a man in the day?

MADGE
Ay, this is he; and this man that came to him was a beggar 240
and dwelt upon a green. But soft, who comes here? O,
these are the harvest-men. Ten to one, they sing a song of
mowing.

Enter the Harvest-men a-singing, with this song double repeated

All ye that lovely lovers be, pray you for me.
Lo, here we come a-sowing, a-sowing, 245

---

234 s.d. *Withdraws* Binnie (Exit Q)
235 *Farewell... thousand* a thousand times farewell
236 s.d. *Exit* eds. (Exeunt Q)
243 s.d. *double repeated* (a pleonasm) repeated

---

233 *well... water of life* Possibly an echo of the story of Jesus and the Samaritan woman
at Jacob's Well (John 4:5–26), in which he speaks to her of 'living water' (v. 10)
and 'a well of water springing up into everlasting life' (v. 14).
234 s.d. I follow Binnie's suggestion that the Old Man does not actually leave the stage.
At 294–5, Booby says 'Soft, here is an old man at the cross', and no entrance is
marked, implying that he has been there at the cross and is only then noticed by
Booby, or perhaps emerges from his hut by the cross. See 123 n. and 136 n., above.
237 *this... stick* This tale is moving along rapidly, even without the help of a musical
accompaniment. The expression may be proverbial; Hook cites 'The devil rides on
a fiddlestick' (Tilley D263).
242–3 *Ten... mowing* Madge would lose her bet, logical though it is: the Harvest-men's
song is of sowing. Although a misprint is possible, the juxtaposition of spring and
autumn activities in rural festivals was common (Hook, pp. 427–8). The sudden,
unrelated appearance of the Harvest-men with their song is simply part of the
dream-like fantasy quality of the play; Madge has no control over who or what may
intrude into her 'tale'.

And sow sweet fruits of love:
In your sweethearts well may it prove.

Exeunt [*Harvest-men*]

Enter HUANEBANGO *with his two-hand sword, and* BOOBY *the Clown*

FANTASTIC
Gammer, what is he?

MADGE
O, this is one that is going to the conjurer. Let him alone;
hear what he says.   250

HUANEBANGO
Now by Mars and Mercury, Jupiter and Janus, Sol and
Saturnus, Venus and Vesta, Pallas and Proserpina, and by
the honour of my house Polimackeroeplacidus, it is a
wonder to see what this love will make silly fellows
adventure, even in the wane of their wits and and infancy   255
of their discretion. Alas, my friend, what fortune calls
thee forth to seek thy fortune among brazen gates,
enchanted towers, fire and brimstone, thunder and
lightning? Beauty, I tell thee, is peerless, and she precious
whom thou affectest. Do off these desires, good country-   260
man; good friend, run away from thyself, and so soon as
thou canst, forget her whom none must inherit but he
that can monsters tame, labours achieve, riddles absolve,
loose enchantments, murder magic, and kill conjuring
—and that is the great and mighty Huanebango!   265

BOOBY
Hark you, sir, hark you. First, know I have here the

256 *my friend* i.e., Booby (?)
260 *affectest* love; seek to obtain
263 *absolve* solve
266 *here* i.e., in his hat

247 s.d. *two-hand sword* A two-hand sword, long, heavy and obsolete in the sixteenth
century, was the standard weapon for braggarts and bullies and for giants and other
performers in mummings and pageants. References in the accounts for Midsummer
and Lord Mayor's shows to this essential property are frequent (see MSC, III
(1954), e.g. pp. 17, 23, 24, 29, 65). Because of its obsoleteness, it was also the
weapon ascribed, humorously or insultingly, to old men, as in *2 Henry VI*, II.i, 46
and *Romeo and Juliet*, I.i, 73–4.
253 *Polimackeroeplacidus* The name is borrowed from Plautus's *Pseudolus;* the person so
named (Polymachaeroplagides) does not appear, but is mentioned. He is the
master of Harpax, whose name Udall borrowed in *RD*.

flirting feather, and have given the parish the start for the
long stock. Now, sir, if it be no more but running through
a little lightning and thunder, and 'Riddle me, riddle me,
what's this?', I'll have the wench from the conjurer if he 270
were ten conjurers.

HUANEBANGO

I have abandoned the court and honourable company, to
do my devoir against this sore sorcerer and mighty
magician. If this lady be so fair as she is said to be, she is
mine, she is mine! *Meus, mea, meum, in contemptum* 275
omnium grammaticorum.

BOOBY

O falsum Latinum! The fair maid is *minum, cum apurti-
nantibus gibletes* and all.

HUANEBANGO

If she be mine, as I assure myself the heavens will do
somewhat to reward my worthiness, she shall be allied to 280
none of the meanest gods, but be invested in the most
famous stock of Huanebango Polimackeroeplacidus, my
grandfather; my father, Pergopolineo; my mother, Dionora de Sardinia, famously descended—

---

267 *flirting* ed. (flurting Q) tossing, waving jauntily
273 *devoir* duty (Fr.)

267–8 *have... stock* Have startled the whole parish (or, perhaps, got ahead of them
where fashion is concerned) with my long stockings. Booby is showing off his
clothes, which may be not quite of the latest fashion, despite his boast. As the
clown, he is identified by his outlandish dress, as Huanebango is identified by his
outlandish speech and manners. For a resumé of various interpretations of *stock*, see
Hook, p. 428. *OED* gives no example of *start* (a (the) start to' as 'startle' before the
nineteenth century. Compare 'got the start of you' at 615–16.
275–6 *Meus... grammaticorum* 'Mine, mine, mine, in disregard of all grammars'.
Huanebango uses all three Latin genders (masculine, feminine, neuter) to refer to
his lady, to whom, of course, only the feminine is appropriate.
277 *O... minum* Booby's Latin is also false; *minum* is nonsense. Dyce arranged these
lines as verse and was followed by other editors. But internal rhymes occur in other
prose passages in Q (e.g. 139, 153).
277–8 *cum... gibletes* More nonsense. *Cum appertinentibus* (or *pertinentiis*) was a legal
phrase, meaning 'with its appurtenances'; *gibletes* (presumably 'giblets') was
'corrected' by Dyce to *gibletis*, and some other editors have followed him.
283 *Pergopolineo* Another Plautine name. Pyrgopolynices is the braggart soldier of
Miles Gloriosus.
283–4 *Dionora de Sardinia* Untraced. Perhaps just another exotic-sounding name,
invented by Peele.

BOOBY
Do you hear, sir? Had not you a cousin that was called 285
Gusteceridis?

HUANEBANGO
Indeed I had a cousin that sometime followed the court
infortunately, and his name, Bustegusteceridis.

BOOBY
O Lord, I know him well! He is the Knight of the Neat's
Feet. 290

HUANEBANGO
O, he loved no capon better. He hath oftentimes deceived
his boy of his dinner. That was his fault, good Bustegusteceridis.

BOOBY
Come, shall we go along? Soft, here is an old man at the
cross. Let us ask him the way thither.—Ho you, gaffer! I 295
pray you tell where the wise man, the conjurer, dwells.

HUANEBANGO
Where that earthly goddess keepeth her abode, the
commander of my thoughts, and fair mistress of my heart.

OLD MAN
Fair enough, and far enough from thy fingering, son.

HUANEBANGO
I will follow my fortune after mine own fancy, and do 300
according to mine own discretion.

OLD MAN
Yet give something to an old man before you go.

---

288 *infortunately* without success
292 *boy* page, servant
295 *you, gaffer* ed. (you gaffer Q, eds.)

---

286 *Gusteceridis* This and the longer name at 288 are Peele's versions of such Plautine
   monstrosities as 'Bumbomachides Clutomistaridysarchides', mentioned by Pyrgopolynices near the beginning of *Miles Gloriosus* (I,14).
289–90 *Knight . . . Feet* Neat's, or ox's, feet were scraps, used to make brawn. Binnie
   suggests something like 'Knight of the Leftovers' as conveying the meaning of the
   epithet. In the light of Huanebango's next speech, Hook's comment that the cousin
   was 'a noble trencherman' is obviously accurate.
294–5 *Soft . . . cross* See note on 234, above. Editors who retain Q's exit for the Old Man
   at 234 are obliged to provide an entrance here.

HUANEBANGO
Father, methinks a piece of this cake might serve your
turn.

OLD MAN
Yea, son.   305

HUANEBANGO
Huanebango giveth no cakes for alms; ask of them that
give gifts for poor beggars.—Fair lady, if thou wert once
shrined in this bosom, I would buckler thee! Haratantara!

Exit

BOOBY
Father, do you see this man? You little think he'll run a
mile or two for such a cake, or pass for a pudding. I tell 310
you, father, he has kept such a begging of me for a piece
of this cake! Whoo! He comes upon me with a 'superfantial substance and the foison of the earth', that I know not
what he means. If he came to me thus, and said 'My
friend Booby' or so, why I could spare him a piece, with 315
all my heart. But when he tells me how God hath
enriched me above other fellows with a cake, why, he
makes me blind and deaf at once! Yet, father, here is a
piece of cake for you, as hard as the world goes.

308 *buckler* shield, protect
   thee! Haratantara! Binnie (thee haratantara Q)
310 *pass for* care for
312–13 a 'superfantial... earth' McIlwraith (*quotation marks*)
313 *foison* plentiful harvest
319 *as ... goes* even though times are hard

312–13 *superfantial ... earth* Booby is imitating Huanebango's bombast. As McIlwraith
   notes, *OED*, like Booby, is ignorant of 'superfantial'. As it stands it is sheer
   nonsense, and that is sufficient in the context, whether Booby is correctly quoting
   or misquoting Huanebango. It is just possible, however, that Peele wrote
   'superstantial'; a compositor might have misread a manuscript 'st' as 'f' (especially
   with so many other 's's', 'st's' and 'f's' in the immediate vicinity). Two medieval
   Latin philosophical terms, *superstantia* and *supersubstantia*, meant, respectively,
   'formally (but not physically) existent' and 'transcending substance'. Thus
   'superstantial substance' would be *clever* nonsense: it would be literally self-contradictory. It would thus also continue the Latin wordplay of 275–8, and it *sounds* as if
   it means 'super-abundance', i.e. 'foison'.
318 *blind... once* Booby, speaking figuratively of the effect upon him of Huanebango's
   verbal barrage, anticipates the fate pronounced by the Old Man a few lines later.

OLD MAN
>Thanks, son, but list to me: 320
>He shall be deaf when thou shalt not see.
>Farewell, my son; things may so hit,
>Thou mayst have wealth to mend thy wit.

BOOBY
>Farewell, father, farewell, for I must make haste after my
>two-hand sword that is gone before.   325

[*Exit* BOOBY. OLD MAN *withdraws*]

Enter SACRAPANT *in his study*

SACRAPANT
>The day is clear, the welkin bright and gray,
>The lark is merry and records her notes;
>Each thing rejoiceth underneath the sky,
>But only I whom heaven hath in hate,
>Wretched and miserable Sacrapant.   330
>In Thessaly was I born and brought up;
>My mother Meroe hight, a famous witch,
>And by her cunning I of her did learn
>To change and alter shapes of mortal men.
>There did I turn myself into a dragon,   335

325 s.d. *Exit . . . withdraws* ed. (Exeunt omnes Q)
326 *welkin* sky
329 *But only* except
332 *hight* is called

---

325 s.d. *withdraws* Again, the decision whether to leave the Old Man onstage or not is
one that a director must make. His 'exit' might, in any case, be into a hut or hovel,
his 'station' near the cross, and thus not really 'off'. This edition repeats 'withdraws'
here for consistency's sake. See notes on 136, 234 and 294–5 above, and 419 below.
s.d. *Enter . . . study* This probably means that a curtain is drawn, revealing
Sacrapant already 'in his study'. Compare, for example, Marlowe's *Doctor Faustus*,
I.i ('Enter Faustus in his study' (A-text, 1604, only)) and *The Jew of Malta*, I.i
('Enter Barabas in his counting-house'). The study is also referred to as a 'cell'
(614 s.d.). This may be the so-called 'discovery-space', of the Elizabethan public
theatre, a recessed area at the rear of the stage which could be curtained off, or a
portable curtained booth, set up for productions in which it was needed. A curtain
is drawn later to reveal the sleeping Delia (822 s.d.), and the two brothers propose
to 'enter' (402). See the discussion of staging in the Introduction, p. 1vi.
326 *gray* Q's spelling; some eds. emend to *grey*, though *OED* states that both forms have
equal weight. It seems to mean here 'blue', or 'bluish', and not 'overcast' or 'dull'.
332 *Meroe* According to *The Golden Ass* (Loeb edn., pp. 13–35), a Thessalonian witch
who specialized in changing men into beasts. Hook (p. 337) notes that only
Apuleius and Peele ascribe the name to a woman; elsewhere, Meroe is an island in
the Nile in Ethiopia.

And stole away the daughter to the king,
Fair Delia, the mistress of my heart,
And brought her hither to revive the man
That seemeth young and pleasant to behold,
And yet is aged, crooked, weak and numb.   340
Thus by enchanting spells I do deceive
Those that behold and look upon my face;
But well may I bid youthful years adieu.

Enter DELIA *with a pot in her hand*

See where she comes from whence my sorrows grow.—
How now, fair Delia, where have you been?   345

DELIA
At the foot of the rock for running water, and gathering
roots for your dinner, sir.

SACRAPANT
Ah, Delia, fairer art thou than the running water, yet
harder far than steel or adamant.

DELIA
Will it please you to sit down, sir?   350

SACRAPANT
Ay, Delia, sit and ask me what thou wilt. Thou shalt have
it brought into thy lap.

DELIA
Then I pray you, sir, let me have the best meat from the
king of England's table, and the best wine in all France,
brought in by the veriest knave in all Spain.   355

SACRAPANT
Delia, I am glad to see you so pleasant. Well, sit thee
down.
Spread, table, spread; meat, drink and bread.
Ever may I have what I ever crave,
When I am spread, for meat for my black cock,   360
And meat for my red.

Enter a Friar with a chine of beef and a pot of wine

355 *veriest* most extreme, worst
361 s.d. *chine of beef* part of the backbone

338–43 *the man . . . adieu* Sacrapant is thus in the opposite case to that to which he has
condemned Erestus, who is young but appears old (189–92). Jack explains at the
end (846–50).
344 *sorrows* Because his love for her is unrequited.

SACRAPANT
  Here, Delia; will ye fall to?

DELIA
  Is this the best meat in England?

SACRAPANT
  Yea.

DELIA
  What is it?   365

SACRAPANT
  A chine of English beef, meat for a king and a king's
  followers.

DELIA
  Is this the best wine in France?

SACRAPANT
  Yea.

DELIA
  What wine is it?   370

SACRAPANT
  A cup of neat wine of Orleans, that never came near the
  brewers in England.

DELIA
  Is this the veriest knave in all Spain?

SACRAPANT
  Yea.

DELIA
  What is he? A friar?   375

SACRAPANT
  Yea, a friar indefinite and a knave infinite.

---

362 *fall to* begin eating
371 *neat* undiluted

---

371 *Orleans* On the Loire River, whose valley is one of the major wine-producing
   regions in France.
372 *brewers* Dealers who bought wine and diluted or mixed it before selling it.
376 *friar indefinite* Perhaps a friar of no particular order (Dominican, Franciscan,
   Carmelite, etc.), or, as Hook suggests (p. 431), the opposite of a 'limiter' like
   Chaucer's friar in *The Canterbury Tales* (I, 209), who had a license to beg in a
   particular area only. Or merely a play on words.

DELIA
Then I pray ye, sir friar, tell me before you go: which is
the most greediest Englishman?

FRIAR
The miserable and most covetous usurer.

SACRAPANT
Hold thee there, friar! 380

Exit FRIAR

But soft, who have we here? Delia, away, begone!

Enter the two brothers

Delia, away, for beset are we!
But heaven or hell shall rescue her for me!

[*Exeunt* SACRAPANT *and* DELIA]

FIRST BROTHER
Brother, was not that Delia did appear?
Or was it but her shadow that was here? 385

SECOND BROTHER
Sister, where art thou? Delia, come again!
He calls, that of thy absence doth complain.
Call out, Calypha, that she may hear,
And cry aloud, for Delia is near.

ECHO
Near. 390

380 *Hold thee there* stick to that opinion
383 *But . . . me* neither heaven nor hell shall rescue her if I can prevent it
s.d. *Exeunt . . .* DELIA eds.

---

378 *most greediest* The double superlative is a common Elizabethan form. Compare, e.g.,
'the most unkindest cut of all' (*Julius Caesar*, III.ii, 183).
383 s.d. Sacrapant and Delia clearly go out here, since the former re-enters at 403 and
Delia is not seen again until 560. They would doubtless retreat into the study or
cell, wherever it is located and whatever form it has; see 325 s.d., note.
388 *Calypha* The first time the First Brother is named. See Dramatis Personae, 6n.
390–6 The echo device was popular in Elizabethan drama. Earlier examples than this
are in Thomas Lodge's *The Wounds of Civil War* (c. 1587) and Robert Wilson's *The
Cobbler's Prophecy* (c. 1590), a play that may have influenced Peele (see
Bradbrook, *ES*, 43 (1962), pp. 325–6). In Wilson's play, the echo is 'artificial' and
leads the person who hears it astray (ed. W. W. Greg, MSR (1914), 11.502–22).
Likewise, this echo which seems to be helpful, is not; it leads the brothers into
danger. The lines would be most effective if seen to be spoken by Sacrapant, from
hiding; the brothers would think it an echo, the audience would know better. It
indicates 'this' way, i.e., toward Sacrapant's cell.

FIRST BROTHER
Near! Oh, where? Hast thou any tidings?

ECHO
Tidings.

SECOND BROTHER
Which way is Delia then? Or that, or this?

ECHO
This.

FIRST BROTHER
And may we safely come where Delia is?   395

ECHO
Yes.

SECOND BROTHER
Brother, remember you the White Bear of England's
wood:
'Start not aside for every danger,
Be not afeard of every stranger;
Things that seem are not the same.'   400

FIRST BROTHER
Brother, why do we not then courageously enter?

SECOND BROTHER
Then, brother, draw thy sword and follow me.

Enter the Conjurer; it lightens and thunders. The SECOND BROTHER
falls down

FIRST BROTHER
What, brother, dost thou fall?

SACRAPANT
Ay, and thou too, Calypha.   405

Fall FIRST BROTHER. *Enter two Furies*

399–401 *'Start...same'* The Second Brother misremembers slightly; see 154–6.
403 s.d. *Enter...Conjurer* Peele reverts to Sacrapant's function here; it is as conjurer
that he will now act.
405 *Calypha* Sacrapant has presumably overheard the brothers' conversation from his
hiding place; the Second Brother called Calypha by name at 388.

Adeste Daemones! Away with them!
Go carry them straight to Sacrapanto's cell,
There in despair and torture for to dwell.
                    [*Exeunt Furies with the two brothers*]

These are Thenore's sons of Thessaly,
That come to seek Delia their sister forth.   410
But with a potion I to her have given,
My arts hath made her to forget herself.

          He removes a turf, and shows a light in a glass

See here the thing which doth prolong my life.
With this enchantment I do anything.
And till this fade, my skill shall still endure;   415
And never none shall break this little glass,
But she that's neither wife, widow nor maid.
Then cheer thyself; this is thy destiny,
Never to die but by a dead man's hand.

                                        Exit

          Enter EUMENIDES, *the Wandering Knight, and the*
                    OLD MAN *at the cross*

EUMENIDES
Tell me, Time, tell me, just Time,   420
When shall I Delia see?
When shall I see the lodestar of my life?
When shall my wandering course end with her sight,
Or I but view my hope, my heart's delight?—
[*Sees* OLD MAN] Father, God speed! If you tell fortunes, I   425
pray, good father, tell me mine.

406 Adeste eds. (Adestes Q) come forth, attend
     Daemones spirits
408 s.d. *Exeunt... brothers* eds. (no s.d. in Q)
412 *arts hath* (see 159 n.)
419 s.d. *Exit* eds. (Exeunt Q)
422 *lodestar* guiding light

_____

419 s.d. *Exit* Q's *Exeunt* includes the Furies and the brothers. But editors since Dyce
     have sent them off after 408, as Sacrapant's speech (409–19) seems to be addressed
     to the audience, and the Furies have been sent away at 406–7.
     s.d. *Enter... cross* If the Old Man has withdrawn to the cross or into a hut at 325
     (see note), he enters, or comes forward, from there. Eumenides then sees him at
     425 (compare 294–5).

OLD MAN
 Son, I do see in thy face
 Thy blessed fortune work apace.
 I do perceive that thou hast wit;
 Beg of thy fate to govern it,   430
 For wisdom governed by advice
 Makes many fortunate and wise.
 Bestow thy alms, give more than all,
 Till dead men's bones come at thy call.
 Farewell, my son; dream of no rest,   435
 Till thou repent that thou didst best.

                                        [*Withdraws*]

EUMENIDES
 This man hath left me in a labyrinth:
 He biddeth me give more than all,
 'Till dead men's bones come at thy call'.
 He biddeth me dream of no rest,   440
 Till I repent that I do best.   [*Lies down and sleeps*]

     Enter WIGGEN, COREBUS, CHURCHWARDEN *and* SEXTON

WIGGEN
 You may be ashamed, you whoreson scald sexton and
 churchwarden, if you had any shame in those shameless
 faces of yours, to let a poor man lie so long above ground
 unburied! A rot on you all, that have no more compassion 445
 of a good fellow when he is gone!

CHURCHWARDEN
 What, would you have us to bury him, and to answer it
 ourselves to the parish?

431 *advice* ed. (advise Q)
436 s.d. *Withdraws* ed. (Exit Old m. Q)
439 '*Till ... call*' (quotation marks) Bullen
441 s.d. *Lies ... sleeps* eds.
     s.d. COREBUS eds. (Corobus Q)
442 *scald* scurvy, contemptible
447 s.p. CHURCHWARDEN eds. (Simon Q; see Dramatis Personae, 18n.)
447-8 *answer ... parish* pay the fee (for burial) to the parish treasury out of our own
     pockets

441 s.d. *Lies ... sleeps* Despite the fact that it contradicts the Old Man's injunction to
     'dream of no rest', repeated by Eumenides, this seems to be required by Q's
     direction at 466: '*Eumenides awakes ...* '.

SEXTON
> Parish me no parishes! Pay me my fees and let the rest run
> on in the quarter's accounts, and put it down for one of 450
> your good deeds, a' God's name, for I am not one that
> curiously stands upon merits.

COREBUS
> You whoreson sodden-headed sheep's face! Shall a good
> fellow do less service and more honesty to the parish, and
> will you not when he is dead let him have Christmas 455
> burial?

WIGGEN
> Peace, Corebus! As sure as Jack was Jack, the frolic'st
> franion amongst you, and I, Wiggen, his sweet sworn
> brother, Jack shall have his funerals, or some of them
> shall lie on God's dear earth for it, that's once! 460

CHURCHWARDEN
> Wiggen, I hope thou wilt do no more than thou darest
> answer.

WIGGEN [*Beats* CHURCHWARDEN]
> Sir, sir, dare or dare not, more or less, answer or not
> answer, do this, or have this!

SEXTON
> Help, help, help! Wiggen sets upon the parish with a 465
> pikestaff!

452 *curiously* fastidiously
453 s.p. COREBUS eds. (Corobus Q)
455 *Christmas* Christian (a malapropism)
460 *once* final, certain

449–52 *Pay ... merits* The sexton is saying that as long as he receives his own fee for
   burying Jack, he doesn't mind if the other costs are borne by the parish ('one of
   your good deeds') out of existing funds; he isn't 'particular' about anything—
   except his fee.
454 *less ... honesty* Corebus means *more* service. Such confusions and malapropisms as
   well as vivid epithets are characteristics of his speech.
463–4 The rhythm of the speech suggests the action of the beating that Wiggen is
   administering. The sexton's next speech confirms that this action has been going on
   during Wiggen's speech.
465–6 *Wiggen ... pikestaff* Some editors (but not Gummere, McIlwraith, Hook,
   Binnie) have followed Dyce in making this a stage direction.
465 *parish* From the context, the churchwarden would seem to be meant; he is the
   representative of the parish. *OED* records no such usage of the word. The sexton is
   unlikely to be referring to himself in the third person. Brooke and Paradise assume
   that *both* officers are being referred to, but Wiggen's 'Sir, sir' and Corebus's 'this
   shake-rotten parish' (468–9) sound like the singular. Elsewhere, *parish* is given its
   common meaning.

EUMENIDES *awakes and comes to them*

EUMENIDES [*To* WIGGEN]
Hold thy hands, good fellow.

COREBUS
Can you blame him, sir, if he take Jack's part against this
shake-rotten parish that will not bury Jack?

EUMENIDES
Why, what was that Jack?   470

COREBUS
Who, Jack, sir? Who, our Jack, sir? As good a fellow as
ever trod upon neat's leather.

WIGGEN
Look you, sir: he gave fourscore and nineteen mourning
gowns to the parish when he died, and because he would
not make them up a full hundred they would not bury 475
him. Was this not good dealing?

CHURCHWARDEN
O Lord, sir, how he lies! He was not worth a halfpenny,
and drunk out every penny; and now his fellows, his
drunken companions, would have us to bury him at the
charge of the parish. And we make many such matches, 480
we may pull down the steeple, sell the bells, and thatch
the chancel. He shall lie above ground till he dance a
galliard about the churchyard, for Steven Loach!

469 *shake-rotten* (term of abuse; *OED*'s only example)
472 *neat* cow, ox
   neat's leather shoes
480 *And* if
483 *galliard* quick, lively dance
   for . . . Loach as far as I'm concerned

473-4 *mourning gowns* In which to dress poor members of the parish who would walk in
   the funeral procession as official mourners.
481-2 *thatch the chancel* To replace the lead or slate roof sold, with the bell, to raise
   money.
483 *Steven Loach* The Churchwarden's own name; confirmed by Wiggen's address to
   him in the next line. See Dramatis Personae, 18n. A loach is a small, barbelled
   freshwater fish; the Churchwarden's name may connote his appearance. The word
   is used figuratively (e.g., in *The Merry Conceited Jests of George Peele*) for
   'simpleton'.

WIGGEN
Sic argumentaris, domine Loach: 'And we make many such
matches, we may pull down the steeple, sell the bells, and   485
thatch the chancel.' In good time, sir, and hang yourselves
in the bell-ropes when you have done! *Domine, opponens
praepono tibi hanc questionem:* whether will you have the
ground broken or your pates broken first? For one of
them shall be done presently, and to begin mine, I'll seal   490
it upon your coxcomb!

EUMENIDES
Hold thy hands! I pray thee, good fellow, be not too hasty.

COREBUS [*To* CHURCHWARDEN]
You capon's face! We shall have you turned out of the
parish one of these days with never a tatter to your arse.
Then you are in worse taking than Jack.   495

EUMENIDES
Faith, and he is bad enough. [*To* CHURCHWARDEN *and*
SEXTON] This fellow does but the part of a friend, to seek
to bury his friend. How much will bury him?

WIGGEN
Faith, about some fifteen or sixteen shillings will bestow
him honestly.   500

SEXTON
Ay, even thereabouts, sir.

EUMENIDES
Here, hold it then. [*Aside*] And I have left me but one
poor three half-pence. Now do I remember the words the
old man spake at the cross: 'Bestow all thou hast'—and

---

484 *Sic . . . Loach* Thus you argue, Master Loach
487–8 *Domine . . . questionem* Sir, in opposition, I propose to you this question
489 *broken first? For* eds. (broken: first, for Q)
490 *presently* immediately
     to begin mine to implement my preference
491 *coxcomb* head
495 *taking* condition
499 *bestow* dispose of, provide for
502 *hold it* take it
504–6 *'Bestow . . . call'* (*prose* Q) (*verse* Hook, Binnie) (*quotation marks* eds.)

---

484 *Sic . . . Loach; Domine . . . questionem* Formulae from formal disputation, still an
     obligatory part of university education in Peele's day.
503 *three half-pence* An Elizabethan silver coin worth one-and-a-half pence.

this is all—'till dead men's bones comes at thy 505
call'.—Here, hold it, and so farewell.

[*Exit*]

WIGGEN

God and all good be with you, sir.—Nay, you cormorants,
I'll bestow one peal of Jack at mine own proper costs and
charges.

COREBUS

You may thank God the long staff and the bilbo-blade 510
crossed not your coxcomb. Well, we'll to the church stile
and have a pot and so, trill-lill.

BOTH

Come, let's go.   *Exeunt*

FANTASTIC

But, hark you, gammer, methinks this Jack bore a great
sway in the parish.   515

MADGE

O, this Jack was a marvellous fellow! He was but a poor
man, but very well beloved. You shall see anon what this
Jack will come to.

Enter the Harvest-men singing, with women in their hands

---

505 *bones comes* (see 159 n.)
506 s.d. *Exit* ed. (no s.d. in Q)
507 *cormorants* large, voracious sea birds; hence, greedy persons
508 *bestow . . . Jack* pay for a peal of bells to be rung in Jack's memory
510 *bilbo-blade* eds. (bilbowe blade Q)
512 *trill-lill* (sound of drink flowing down the throat)
513 s.p. BOTH (i.e., Wiggen and Corebus)
518 s.d. *in . . . hands* hand in hand

---

510 *bilbo-blade* A sword from Bilbao in northern Spain, highly prized for its temper;
   generally any sword.
511–12 *church stile . . . pot* The church and the alehouse, focal points of social life, were
   often in close proximity, as Sir Thomas Overbury observed in his sketch of 'A
   Sexton' in *Characters* (1616): 'He could willingly all his life time be confinde to the
   church-yard; at least within five foot on't: for at every church stile, commonly ther's
   an ale-house' (*Works*, ed. E. F. Rimbault (1856; repr. 1890), p.145).
513 s.d. *Exeunt* Wiggen and Corebus would go out together, and the Churchwarden
   and the Sexton would follow, or go out a different way, perhaps 'counting the
   money that has come in so unexpectedly' (Hook, p. 435).

FROLIC
Soft, who have we here? Our amorous harvesters.

FANTASTIC
Ay, ay; let us sit still and let them alone.   520

       Here they begin to sing, the song doubled

Lo, here we come a-reaping, a-reaping,
To reap our harvest fruit;
And thus we pass the year so long,
And never be we mute.

       Exeunt the Harvest-men [and women]

       Enter HUANEBANGO

FROLIC
Soft, who have we here?   525

MADGE
O, this is a choleric gentleman! All you that love your
lives, keep out of the smell of his two-hand sword. Now
goes he to the conjurer.

FANTASTIC
Methinks the conjurer should put the fool into a juggling
box.   530

HUANEBANGO
Fee, fa, fum!
Here is the Englishman—
Conquer him that can—

519 *harvesters* eds. (harvest starres Q)
524 s.d. *Exeunt* eds. (Exit Q)
527 *smell* reach, vicinity
531–2 *Fee ... fum!/Here ... Englishman* eds. (one line in Q)
533–4 *Conquer ... can—/Came ... bright* eds. (one line in Q)

---

520 s.d. *Here ... doubled* If they 'begin to sing' here, what were they singing when they
    entered (518 s.d.)? These are more authorial stage directions, indicating that they
    sing, but not concerned with the specifics of stage business. 'Doubled' means
    simply 'repeated' (Compare 243 s.d.) in which case it would presumably be
    repeated several times.
526–8 Madge introduces Huanebango, although we already know who and what he is.
    She (or Peele) is forgetful.
529–30 *juggling box* If any specific apparatus is meant, it is unknown. 'Juggling' meant
    the practice of magic or legerdemain, or deception generally.
531–2 *Fee ... Englishman* A version of the familiar folk tale giant's roar, as in 'Jack the
    Giant-Killer', 'Jack and the Beanstalk' and 'Childe Rowland'.

Came for his lady bright,
To prove himself a knight,   535
And win her love in fight.

[*Enter* BOOBY *the Clown*]

BOOBY
Hoo-haw, Master Bango, are you here? Hear you, you
had best sit down here and beg an alms with me.

HUANEBANGO
Hence, base cullion! Here is he that commandeth ingress
and egress with his weapon, and will enter at his   540
voluntary, whosoever saith no.

A voice and flame of fire. HUANEBANGO *falleth down*

VOICE
No.

MADGE
So with that they kissed, and spoiled the edge of as good a
two-hand sword as ever God put life in. Now goes Booby
in, spite of the conjurer.   545

536 s.d. *Enter . . . Clown* Dyce, Bullen (part of 524 s.d. in Q)
　　BOOBY ed. (Corebus Q)
537 s.p. BOOBY ed. (Cor. Q)
　　Hoo-haw ed. (Who hawe Q)
539 *cullion* vile fellow, rascal
539–40 *ingress and egress* entry and exit
541 *voluntary* will
544 *Booby* ed. (Corebus Q)
545 *spite of* in spite of
　　s.d. *Enter . . . Furies* eds. (*Enter the Conjurer, and strike Corebus blind* Q)

---

536 s.d. Dyce and Bullen are right, given Booby's 'are you here?' in 537. Also Madge
refers only to Huanebango in 526–8; Fantastic's 'the fool' would thus refer to him,
and not to the 'clown'.
540 *enter* Like the brothers at 402–3, Huanebango is about to enter Sacrapant's cell to
rescue Delia.
542 s.p. VOICE This is not the voice from the well (see Dramatis Personae), but
Sacrapant's. He intervenes verbally from hiding (compare the Echo at 390–6), then
casts his spell on the inruder. The stage direction indicates that the voice's saying
'No', the appearance of the flame and Huanebango's falling down all occur more or
less simultaneously.
543–4 *they . . . sword* Madge's way of saying that Huanebango and the earth met
('kissed'), and his sword stuck into the ground, which is detrimental to its cutting
efficiency.
545 s.d. The Furies are needed to carry Huanebango away on Sacrapant's command
(546).

Enter the Conjurer [and two Furies]

SACRAPANT
Away with him into the open fields
To be a ravening prey to crows and kites.

[*Exeunt Furies with* HUANEBANGO]

And for this villain, let him wander up and down,
In nought but darkness and eternal night.

[*Strikes* BOOBY *blind*]

BOOBY
Here hast thou slain Huan, a slashing knight,   550
And robbed poor Booby of his sight!

SACRAPANT
Hence, villain, hence!   *Exit* [BOOBY]

Now I have unto Delia
Given a potion of forgetfulness,
That when she comes she shall not know her brothers.
Lo, where they labour like to country slaves,   555

547 s.d. *Exeunt*... HUANEBANGO eds. (no s.d. in Q)
549 s.d. *Strikes*... *blind* eds. (part of 545 s.d. in Q)
    BOOBY ed. (Corebus Q)
550 s.p. BOOBY ed. (Cor Q)
551 *Booby* ed. (Corebus Q)
552 s.d. *Exit* eds. (after 551 Q)
    BOOBY ed.
552-3 *Now... Delia/Given... forgetfulness* eds. (one line in Q)

547 *ravening... kites* An example of the rhetorical and poetical figure *hypallage*. The
    modifier which belongs with *crows and kites* is displaced to give the unexpected and
    hence striking construction, *ravening prey*, which is itself an oxymoron.
    s.d. This seems the appropriate place for the Furies to go out carrying
    Huanebango; no exit is provided in Q. Sacrapant then turns to Booby.
550 *slashing knight* A swashbuckler. A character called 'Bold Slasher' or 'Captain
    Slasher' appears in some mummers' plays.
551 Substitution of 'Booby' for 'Corebus' means the loss of a syllable. As Q stands, 550
    is in trochaic pentameter, lacking the final unstressed syllable (a masculine ending
    on 'knight' is appropriate); and with 'robbed' spoken as two syllables, 551 is in
    iambic pentameter. With the emendation, the trochaic metre is maintained (with,
    perhaps, a spondaic first foot), and the line has the same number of syllables—
    nine—as 550. See Dramatis Personae, 12n.
555-6 No editor has suggested that the brothers should be visible here; their entry is
    announced in the conventional way by Delia at 572. Sacrapant may gesture 'off' as
    he speaks these lines. But a director could have them visible in the 'distance' and
    bring them forward at 572.

With spade and mattock on this enchanted ground.
Now will I call her by another name,
For never shall she know herself again
Until that Sacrapant hath breathed his last.
See where she comes.   560

Enter DELIA

Come hither, Delia; take this goad. Here hard
At hand two slaves do work and dig for gold.
Gore them with this and thou shalt have enough.

He gives her a goad

DELIA
Good sir, I know not what you mean.

SACRAPANT [*Aside*]
She hath forgotten to be Delia,   565
But not forgot the same she should forget.
But I will change her name.—
Fair Berecynthia (so this country calls you),
Go ply these strangers, wench; they dig for gold.

Exit SACRAPANT

DELIA
O heavens! How am I beholding to this fair young man! 570
But I must ply these strangers to their work.
See where they come.

561–2 *Come ... hard/At ... gold* eds. (Come ... goad,/Here ... gold Q)
561 *goad* pointed rod or stick, for driving cattle
565 s.d. *Aside* eds.
569 *ply* drive, keep at work
570 *beholding* beholden, indebted

565–6 She has forgotten her name (575–6), but still remembers too much of her former
    life. Sacrapant gives her a new name to replace the old and orders her, in effect, to
    exorcise the remains of that life, and of reality, by beating her brothers whom he
    describes as 'slaves' and 'strangers'. He also appeals to human greed, harping on
    gold (562–3, 569); this marks him as wicked, in contrast to those in the play who
    give freely.
568 *Berecynthia* A surname of Cybele, ancient Greek earth-goddess, from the mountin
    in Phrygia where she was supposed to reside.
570–2 No amount of rearranging these lines will produce four regular verse lines; Dyce
    tried several different ways. They are here left as they are in Q.

Enter the two brothers in their shirts, with spades, digging

FIRST BROTHER
O brother, see where Delia is!

SECOND BROTHER
O Delia, happy are we to see thee here!

DELIA
What tell you me of Delia, prating swains?   575
I know no Delia, nor know I what you mean.
Ply you your work or else you are like to smart!

FIRST BROTHER
Why, Delia, knowst thou not thy brothers here?
We come from Thessaly to seek thee forth;
And thou deceivest thyself, for thou art Delia.   580

DELIA
Yet more of Delia? Then take this and smart!

[*Pricks them with the goad*]

What, feign you shifts for to defer your labour?
Work, villains, work! It is for gold you dig.

SECOND BROTHER
Peace, brother, peace; this vile enchanter
Hath ravished Delia of her senses clean,   585
And she forgets that she is Delia.

FIRST BROTHER [*To* DELIA]
Leave, cruel thou, to hurt the miserable.—
Dig, brother, dig, for she is hard as steel.

Here they dig and descry the light under a little hill

SECOND BROTHER
Stay, brother, what hast thou descried?

575 *swains* labourers, servants
581 s.d. *Pricks . . . goad* eds.
582 *feign you shifts* are you devising tricks
585 *clean* quite
588 s.d. *descry* perceive, discover

588 s.d. *Here . . . hill* Another authorial direction in which he narrates the action as he
visualizes it rather than simply indicating what occurs on stage. Compare 50 s.d.
and 804 s.d. The repetition of the verb 'descried' in the next line of dialogue is
revealing.

DELIA
Away and touch it not! It is something that my lord hath   590
hidden there.

She covers it again. Enter SACRAPANT

SACRAPANT
Well said! Thou plyest these pioneers well.—Go, get you
in, you labouring slaves!
Come, Berecynthia, let us in likewise,
And hear the nightingale record her notes.   595

Exeunt

Enter ZANTIPPA, *the Curst Daughter, to the well, with a pot in her
hand*

ZANTIPPA
Now for a husband, house and home! God send a good
one or none, I pray God! My father hath sent me to the
well for the water of life, and tells me if I give fair words I
shall have a husband.

Enter [CELANTA], *the Foul Wench, to the well for water, with a pot
in her hand*

But here comes Celanta, my sweet sister. I'll stand by and   600
hear what she says.

[Withdraws]

590-1 *Away... there* (*prose* Q) (that/My eds.; some thing,/That Hook)
592-3 (*prose* Q (well./Go) eds.)
592 *Well said* well done
       pioneers diggers
601 s.d. *Withdraws* Binnie

590-1 Why Delia should shift to prose here is unclear, but attempts to sort the
      seventeen syllables into two lines of verse are not very satisfactory; Hook's is the
      best. It would be irregular, like much other verse in the play. But Peele may be
      using prose for contrast (see 592-3).
592-3 These lines divide more easily into verse than the preceding ones, though they
      would be tetrameters, while 594-5 are pentameters. But Peele may have wanted
      prose, to contrast the harshness of Delia's and Sacrapant's words to the brothers
      with both their preceding sorrowful exchange in verse (584-8) and Sacrapant's
      romantic invitation to Delia (594-5).

CELANTA
My father hath sent me to the well for water, and he tells
me if I speak fair, I shall have a husband and none of the
worst. Well, though I am black I am sure all the world
will not forsake me; and as the old proverb is, 'Though I   605
am black, I am not the devil'.

ZANTIPPA [*Approaching*]
Marry gup, with a murrain! I know wherefore thou
speakest that, but go thy ways home as wise as thou
camest, or I'll set thee home with a wanion!

*Here she strikes her pitcher against her sister's, and breaks them both
and goes her way*

CELANTA
I think this be the curstest quean in the world! You see   610
what she is—a little fair but as proud as the devil, and the
veriest vixen that lives upon God's earth. Well, I'll let her
alone, and go home and get another pitcher, and for all
this, get me to the well for water.

Exit

Enter two Furies out of the Conjurer's cell and lay HUANEBANGO *by
the well of life,* [*then exeunt*]

Enter ZANTIPPA *with a pitcher to the well*

ZANTIPPA
Once again for a husband, and in faith, Celanta, I have   615

---

604 *black* dark-complexioned
607 s.d *Approaching* Binnie
609 *with a wanion* with a vengence
610 *curstest* cursedest
    quean hussy
614 s.d. *lay* eds. (*laies* Q)
615–16 *have . . . of* have a headstart on

605–6 *Though . . . devil* Proverbial (Tilley D297).
607 *Marry . . . murrain* Interjection expressing indignation or irritation. 'Marry',
originally from 'Mary', thus an oath, had come by the late sixteenth century to
signify no more than an expression of impatience or surprise. 'Gup' *(go up)* is an
exclamation of derision or remonstrance, often coupled with 'Marry' as here. 'With
a murrain', i.e. 'the plague on it', is another common colloquial exclamation of
anger; compare *GGN*, I.iii, 29.
611 *as . . . devil* Proverbial (Tilley L572): 'As proud as Lucifer'.

44

THE OLD WIFE'S TALE

got the start of you! Belike husbands grow by the well-
side. Now my father says I must rule my tongue. Why,
alas, what am I then? A woman without a tongue is as a
soldier without his weapon. But I'll have my water and be
gone.   620

Here she offers to dip her pitcher in, and a [VOICE] *speaks in the well*

VOICE
Gently dip, but not too deep,
For fear you make the golden beard to weep.

[*A* HEAD *comes up with ears of corn*]

Fair maiden, white and red,
Comb me smooth, and stroke my head,
And thou shalt have some cockle-bread.   625

616 *Belike* maybe
620 s.d. VOICE ed. (head Q)
621 s.p. VOICE ed. (Head Q)
622 *beard* eds. (birde Q)
     s.d. *A* HEAD . . . *corn* ed. (no s.d. in Q)
624 *Comb . . . stroke* ed. (Stroke . . . combe Q)

616–17 *Belike . . . well-side* Zantippa has not yet seen Huanebango, so this is wishful
     thinking, which immediately comes true.
618–19 *A woman . . . weapon* Proverbial (Tilley W675): 'A woman's weapon is her
     tongue'.
620 s.d. VOICE See Dramatis Personae, 22–3n.
622 *beard* Although the four extant copies of Q agree on 'birde' here, most editors
     emend to 'beard' because when the voice speaks again at 756–7, the two corrected
     copies read 'beard', which seems right; by metonymy, 'beard' stands for 'head'.
     What does a bird have to do with it? On the other hand, what has logic or
     likelihood to do with this play-world?
     s.d. By analogy with 757 s.d. The Head must appear for Zantippa to break her
     pitcher on it (631 s.d.).
624 Unless we assume that Zantippa misquotes, the line should read 'Comb me smooth
     and stroke my head'. Compare also 759 and 764.
625 *cockle-bread* Cockle is a weed, sometimes called 'corn cockle', which grows in corn-
     and wheatfields. Cockle-bread may have been a kind of cornbread, or perhaps
     inferior bread with cockle mixed, in the harvesting, with the corn; the Head is
     bearing ears of corn. *OED* records no such literal meaning, however. John Aubrey,
     writing in the late seventeenth century, records a 'wanton sport' of 'young wenches'
     called 'moulding of Cocklebread': '*viz.* they get upon a Table-board, and then
     gather-up their knees and their Coates with their hands as high as they can, and
     then they wabble to and fro with their Buttocks as if they were kneading of Dough
     with their Arses', reciting a rhyme meanwhile (*Three Prose Works*, ed. J. Buchanan-
     Brown (1972), p. 254). Another reference associates it with 'playing at
     barleybreak . . . and such like profane exercises' (*OED*). So the Voice may be
     indulging in a bawdy joke. The offer of cockle-bread clearly provokes Zantippa,
     but not her sister (767).

ZANTIPPA
  What is this?
  'Fair maiden, white and red,
  Comb me smooth and stroke my head,
  And thou shalt have some cockle-bread.'
  'Cockle' callest thou it, boy? Faith, I'll give you cockle-   630
  bread!

She breaks her pitcher upon [the] HEAD; *[it descends.] Then it
thunders and lightens, and* HUANEBANGO *rises up.* HUANEBANGO *is
deaf and cannot hear*

HUANEBANGO
  Phylyda phylerydos, Pamphylyda floryda flortos,
  'Dub-dub-a-dub, bounce!' quoth the guns, with a sulphu-
      rous huff-snuff!
  Waked with a wench, pretty peat, pretty love, and my
      sweet pretty pigsnie.
  Just by thy side shall sit surnamed great Huanebango;   635
  Safe in my arms will I keep thee, threat Mars or thunder
      Olympus!

ZANTIPPA [*Aside*]
  Foh! What greasy groom have we here? He looks as
  though he crept out of the backside of the well, and
  speaks like a drum perished at the west end!

HUANEBANGO
  O that I might—but I may not, woe to my destiny
  therefore!—   640

626-7 *this?/'Fair* eds. (one line in Q)
630 s.d. *the* ed. (his Q)
634 *peat* (term of endearment) pet, darling
    pigsnie (= pig's eye; term of endearment)
637 *groom* fellow

632-6 A farrago of bombast and nonsense. Binnie thinks 632 'Spanish-sounding
   nonsense'. 633 is a parody of the style of Richard Stanyhurst, who translated Books
   I–IV of Virgil's *Aeneid* (1582) into just such amazing verses. Samples (which Peele
   may have had in mind): 'Lowd dub a dub tabering with frapping rip rap of Aetna';
   'Of ruff raffe roaring, mens herts with terror agrysing'.
637 s.d. *Aside* It may be thought superfluous to indicate this, as Huanebango 'is deaf
   and cannot hear'. But Zantippa does not know this and would speak the lines to
   herself and for the audience.
639 *a drum . . . end* Exact meaning unknown. Perhaps a drum with one of its heads or
   skins broken, producing a dull thump rather than the normal resonant sound when
   struck on the other, intact head.
640 Dyce pointed out that this line is quoted from Gabriel Harvey's *Encomium Lauri*
   (1580).

Kiss that I clasp, but I cannot! Tell me, my destiny,
   wherefore?

ZANTIPPA [*Aside*]
Whoop! Now I have my dream! Did you never hear so
great a wonder as this?—Three blue beans in a blue
bladder: rattle, bladder, rattle!

HUANEBANGO [*Aside*]
I'll now set my countenance and to her in prose. It may be   645
this 'rim, ram, ruff' is too rude an encounter.—Let me,
fair lady, if you be at leisure, revel with your sweetness,
and rail upon that cowardly conjurer that hath cast me, or
congealed me rather, into an unkind sleep and polluted
my carcass.   650

ZANTIPPA [*Aside*]
Laugh, laugh, Zantippa! Thou hast thy fortune—a fool
and a husband under one!

HUANEBANGO
Truly, sweetheart, as I seem: about some twenty years, the
very April of mine age.

ZANTIPPA [*Aside*]
Why, what a prating ass is this!   655

HUANEBANGO
Her coral lips, her crimson chin,
Her silver teeth so white within,
Her golden locks, her rolling eye,

646 *rim . . . ruff* Q (two copies; rude . . . ruff two copies)
648 *rail upon* utter abusive language against
651 *fortune—a fool* Binnie (fortune, a fool Q)
652 *under one* all in one

643-4 *Three . . . rattle* Proverbial (Tilley B124). Rather a jingle or tongue-twister, used
as a charm, than a true proverb. Learned notes about the prominence of beans in
ritual and folklore are unnecessary. Aubrey recalls that in his boyhood (thus within
a few decades of the date of the play), it was used as a charm against 'an ill tongue'
or evil spirits (*Three Prose Works*, p. 253 n.). Zantippa utters a charm to safeguard
her newfound prize, a husband, or to protect herself against his 'ill tongue'; or else
she is simply trying to converse with Huanebango in language like his own. Jonson
may be alluding to *OWT* when he has Humphrey Wasp speak the words 'Rattle
bladder rattle' and 'O, Madge' in *Bartholmew Fair*, I.iv, 73.
646 *rim, ram, ruff* Huanebango is referring to the verse he has been speaking. In *The
Canterbury Tales*, Chaucer's Parson explains his preference for prose over both
alliterative and rhymed verse: 'But trusteth wel, I am a Southren man,/I kan nat
geeste 'rum, ram, ruf,' by lettre,/Ne, God woot, rym holde I but litel bettre;/And
therfore, if you list— I wil nat glose—/I wol yow telle a myrie tale in prose' ('The
Parsons's Prologue', 42–6). Like the Parson, Huanebango is changing to prose.

Her pretty parts—let them go by—
Heigh-ho, hath wounded me, 660
That I must die this day to see.

ZANTIPPA
By Gog's bones, thou art a flouting knave! 'Her coral lips,
her crimson chin'—ka, wilshaw!

HUANEBANGO
True, my own, and my own because mine, and mine
because mine—ha, ha! Above a thousand pounds in 665
possibility, and things fitting thy desire in possession.

ZANTIPPA [Aside]
The sot thinks I ask of his lands. Lob be your comfort and
cuckold be your destiny!—Hear you, sir: and if you will
have us, you had best say so betime.

HUANEBANGO
True, sweetheart, and will royalize thy progeny with my 670
pedigree.

Exeunt

Enter EUMENIDES, *the Wandering Knight*

EUMENIDES
Wretched Eumenides, still unfortunate,
Envied by Fortune, and forlorn by Fate;
Here pine and die, wretched Eumenides.
Die in the spring, the April of my age? 675
Here sit thee down; repent what thou hast done.
I would to God that it were ne'er begun!

---

660 *hath* (see 159n.)
662 *Gog's* God's
   flouting jeering, scoffing
663 *ka* (=quotha) said he
   wilshaw (meaning unknown; ? will ich ha(ve) (Gayley))
667 *Lob* clown, lout
669 *betime* in good time

664–5 *True... because mine* Recalls the Latin word-play at 274–8.
667 *Lob... comfort* May your simple-mindedness prevent you from knowing the truth
   about your destiny. But Bullen quotes *The Bachelor's Banquet* (1603), formerly
   attributed to Dekker, where the proverbial expression 'Lob's Pound' (Tilley
   L403), originally simply 'prison', is used to connote the married man's state of
   entanglement and thraldom. See also Eric Partridge, ed., *A Classical Dictionary of
   the Vulgar Tongue* (1931; repr. 1963), p. 221.

Enter JACK

JACK
You are well overtaken, sir.

EUMENDIES
Who's that?

JACK
You are heartily well met, sir.   680

EUMENIDES
Forbear, I say! Who is that which pincheth me?

JACK
Trusting in God, good Master Eumenides, that you are in
so good health as all your friends were at the making
hereof, God give you good morrow, sir. Lack you not a
neat, handsome and cleanly young lad, about the age of   685
fifteen or sixteen years, that can run by your horse, and
for a need, make your mastership's shoes as black as ink?
How say you, sir?

EUMENIDES
Alas, pretty lad, I know not how to keep myself, and
much less a servant, my pretty boy, my state is so bad.   690

JACK
Content yourself, you shall not be so ill a master but I'll
be as bad a servant. Tut, sir, I know you though you know
not me. Are not you the man, sir—deny it if you can,

---

684 *good* eds. (God Q)

---

681 *Who ... me* Pinching is a common way for invisible spirits to manifest their
presence. Here it is not malicious, but see *The Tempest*, II.ii, 4 and V.i., 276.
Eumenides obviously does not see Jack when he speaks at 679 and 681, but does see
him by 689. Peele may have imagined Jack to 'materialize' after 681, but that is
scarcely within an actor's capability. He might come up behind Eumenides,
dodging out of sight until he introduces himself at, say 684. Compare 788 s.d. and
note.

682–4 *Trusting ... hereof* A formulaic epistolary greeting, puzzling here since no letter is
involved. Perhaps Jack refers humorously to himself ('hereof') in his ghostly form,
released ('made') by Wiggen and Corebus ('your friends') who, thanks to
Eumenides's gift, were able to pay for Jack's funeral. Compare *Arden of Faversham*,
ed. Martin White (1982), sc.iii, ll. 3–4: '... hoping in God you be in good health,
as I, Michael, was at the making hereof'; a letter is being read. See E. Legouis, 'The
Epistolary Past in English', *N&Q*, 198 (1953),111–12.

sir—that came from a strange place in the land of Catita, where Jackanapes flies with his tail in his mouth, to seek 695 out a lady as white as snow and as red as blood? Ha, ha! Have I touched you now?

EUMENIDES [*Aside*]
I think this boy be a spirit!—How knowst thou all this?

JACK
Tut, are not you the man, sir—deny it if you can, sir—that gave all the money you had to the burying of a 700 poor man, and but one three half-pence left in your purse? Content you, sir, I'll serve you, that is flat.

EUMENIDES
Well, my lad, since thou art so importunate, I am content to entertain thee, not as a servant, but a copartner in my journey. But whither shall we go? For I have not any 705 money more than one bare three half-pence.

JACK
Well, master, content yourself, for if my divination be not out, that shall be spent at the next inn or alehouse we come to, for, master, I know you are passing hungry; therefore I'll go before and provide dinner until that you 710 come. No doubt but you'll come fair and softly after.

EUMENIDES
Ay, go before; I'll follow thee.

JACK
But do you hear, master? Do you know my name?

703 *importunate* eds. (impor-/nate Q) insistent
705 *go? For* eds. (goe for Q)
709 *passing* exceedingly

694–5 *Catita . . . Jackanapes* Catita is obviously a far-away land, apparently the creation of Peele's imagination, since no trace of it has been found, although the possibility of a misprint (of 'Caria', 'Catina', 'Cataea', 'Carcina', etc.—all real places in the ancient world) cannot be ruled out. There, as in Thessaly, strange things are commonplace. We are not to question how Eumenides knew of Delia if he did not come from Thessaly, nor how, later, he seems to know everyone's name (852–3). 'Jackanapes' too is of uncertain origin (see *OED*). Here an animal, an ape or monkey or some fabulous creature, is meant, with perhaps a glance at Jack's own name, a veiled hint to the baffled Eumenides. See a similar use of both words, probably borrowed from Peele, in Marston's *The Malcontent*, ed. B. Harris (1967), I.iii, 54–5.
711 *fair* and *softly* Proverbial (Tilley S601): 'Fair and softly goes far'. Here it means leisurely, easily.

EUMENIDES
No, I promise thee, not yet.

JACK
Why, I am Jack.   *Exit* 715

EUMENIDES
Jack. Why, be it so then.

Enter the HOSTESS *and* JACK, *setting meat on the table, and Fiddlers
come to play.* EUMENIDES *walketh up and down, and will eat no meat*

HOSTESS
How say you, sir? Do you please to sit down?

EUMENIDES
Hostess, I thank you, I have no great stomach.

HOSTESS [*To* JACK]
Pray, sir, what is the reason your master is so strange?
Doth not this meat please him?   720

JACK
Yes, hostess, but it is my master's fashion to pay before he
eats; therefore, a reckoning, good hostess.

HOSTESS
Marry, shall you, sir, presently.   *Exit*

EUMENIDES
Why, Jack what dost thou mean? Thou knowest I have
not any money. Therefore, sweet Jack, tell me, what shall 725
I do?

---

715 s.d. *Exit* eds. (Exeunt Jack Q)
718 *stomach* appetite
719 s.d. *To* JACK Binnie
723 *shall you* you shall have it

---

716 *Jack . . . then* Eumenides still has not made the connection between the Old Man's
    prophecy about 'dead men's bones' (439), the lad named Jack for whose burial he
    gave money, and this mysterious visitor who has pressed his service upon him.
    s.d. This authorial direction represents a sort of silent interlude, since the actions of
    bringing on the table, and setting it, and of the fiddlers coming in take place before
    the Hostess speaks. Where the 'inn or alehouse' was to be located on the stage did
    not worry Peele. A table (perhaps the one from Sacrapant's magic banquet),
    carried on and set down, and a few chairs would have sufficed. An indefinite lapse
    of time is assumed, for Eumenides to 'arrive', though an impression of the inn's
    coming to him, magically, would be in keeping with the spirit of the play. See
    Hook's discussion of the scene (p. 376), and Chambers, *ES*, III, 48.

JACK
Well, master, look in your purse.

EUMENIDES
Why, faith, it is a folly, for I have no money.

JACK
Why, look you, master, do so much for me.

EUMENIDES
Alas, Jack, my purse is full of money! 730

JACK
'Alas', master? Does that word belong to this accident?
Why, methinks I should have seen you cast away your
cloak and in a bravado dance a galliard round about the
chamber. Why, master, your man can teach you more wit
than this.—Come, hostess, cheer up my master. 735

[Enter HOSTESS]

HOSTESS
You are heartily welcome. And if it please you to eat of a
fat capon, a fairer bird, a finer bird, a sweeter bird, a
crisper bird, a neater bird your worship never eat of.

EUMENIDES
Thanks, my fine, eloquent hostess.

731 'Alas', master? Does ed. (Alas, maister, does Q)
733 bravado gay mood
    dance eds. (daunced Q)
735 s.d. Enter HOSTESS eds.
738 eat ate

734 chamber This suggests that Peele had in mind an indoor setting for this scene. But
    given the non-representational staging of plays in public theatres, no more than the
    table and its accoutrements and the presence of the Hostess were needed to signify
    'inn' (see preceding note).
737-8 a fairer... eat of Some eds. quote lines spoken by Dandaline, a hostess, in the
    anonymous Liberality and Prodigality:
       A better bird, a fairer bird, a finer bird,
       A sweeter bird, a yonger bird, a tenderer bird
       A daintier bird, a crisper bird, a more delicate bird,
       Was there never set upon any Gentlemans board.
                              (ed. W. W. Greg, MSR (1913), ll. 519–22)
    This play was acted in 1601 and published in 1602, but may have been written
    much earlier, so indebtedness in either direction cannot be affirmed.

JACK
But, hear you, master, one word by the way. Are you   740
content I shall be halves in all you get in your journey?

EUMENIDES
I am, Jack; here is my hand.

JACK
Enough, master. I ask no more.

EUMENIDES
Come, hostess, receive your money, and I thank you for
my good entertainment.   745

HOSTESS
You are heartily welcome, sir.

EUMENIDES
Come, Jack, whither go we now?

JACK
Marry, master, to the conjurer's presently.

EUMENIDES
Content, Jack. Hostess, farewell.   *Exeunt*

Enter BOOBY *and* CELANTA, *the Foul Wench, to the well for water*

BOOBY
Come, my duck, come.—I have now got a wife.—Thou   750
art fair, art thou not?

CELANTA
My Booby, the fairest alive, make no doubt of that.

BOOBY
Come, wench, are we almost at the well?

CELANTA
Ay, Booby, we are almost at the well now. I'll go fetch
some water; sit down while I dip my pitcher in.   755

---

741 *be halves* share equally
749 s.d. BOOBY ed. (Corebus Q)
       CELANTA eds. (Zelanto Q)
750 s.p. BOOBY ed. (Coreb. Q; *passim* to 773)
752 s.p. CELANTA eds. (Zelan. Q; *passim* to 772)
       Booby ed. (Corebus Q; *passim* to 772)

---

749 s.d. CELANTA Q's 'Zelanto' may suggest a recollection by Peele of Zelota, the
    shrewish wife of the cobbler Rafe in Wilson's *The Cobbler's Prophecy* (see 390–6
    n.). She is charmed to sleep by Mercury.

[*She dips her pitcher in the well*]

VOICE [*From the well*]
  Gently dip, but not too deep,
  For fear you make the golden beard to weep.

  A HEAD *comes up with ears of corn*

  Fair maiden, white and red,
  Comb me smooth, and stroke my head,
  And thou shalt have some cockle-bread.   760

  She combs [*the corn*] *into her lap.* [*The* HEAD *descends*]

  Gently dip, but not too deep,
  For fear thou make the golden beard to weep.

  [CELANTA *dips her pitcher again*]

  A HEAD *comes up full of gold*

  Fair maiden, white and red,
  Comb me smooth, and stroke my head,
  And every hair a sheaf shall be,   765
  And every sheaf a golden tree.

  She combs [*the gold*] *into her lap.* [*The* HEAD *descends*]

CELANTA
  O see, Booby, I have combed a great deal of gold into my
  lap and a great deal of corn.

BOOBY
  Well said, wench! Now we shall have toast enough. God

755 s.d. *She... well* ed. (compare 620 s.d.)
760 s.d. *She... lap* ed. (part of 757 s.d. in Q)
    s.d. *The... descends* ed. (Descends Binnie; and at 766 s.d.)
762 s.d. *A* HEAD... *gold* as in Hook (after 766 Q)
763 *maiden* eds. (maide Q)
766 s.d. *she... lap* ed. (part of 762 s.d. in Q)
769 *toast* ed. (tost Q (two copies); just (two copies))

---

760 The offer of cockle-bread does not annoy or offend Celanta as it did Zantippa (625
    and n.). If there is bawdy innuendo, it is lost on or ignored by her.
767 *O see* He cannot, of course.
769 *toast* P. A. Daniel suggested 'toast' to Bullen, who retained his copy's 'just', but
    thought it might be 'grist'. He was on the right track. 'Tost' was one spelling of
    'toast' (see 901 n.); the proofreaders, who improved the BM and Huntington
    copies at 646 and 770, were overzealous here, and the 'uncorrected' Dyce and
    Pforzheimer copies are correct. Celanta's corn would be used to make bread; the
    mundane Booby translates that into toast, as he would translate precious metal into
    spendable coin.

send us coiners to coin our gold. But come, shall we go 770
home, sweetheart?

CELANTA
Nay, come, Booby, I will lead you.

BOOBY
So, Booby, things have well hit;
Thou hast gotten wealth to mend thy wit.

Exeunt

Enter JACK *and the Wandering Knight*

JACK
Come away, master, come. 775

EUMENIDES
Go along, Jack, I'll follow thee. Jack, they say it is good to
go cross-legged and say his prayers backward. How sayest
thou?

JACK
Tut, never fear, master; let me alone. Here sit you still;
speak not a word. And because you shall not be enticed 780
with his enchanting speeches, with this same wool I'll

---

770 *coiners . . . coin* Q (two copies; quoiners . . . quine two copies)
774 s.d. Exeunt eds. (Exit Q)
777 *his* one's
779 *let me alone* leave it to me
780 *because* so that

---

773 *Booby* As at 551, the substitution alters the metre, but the lines scan comfortably as
tetrameters. The stresses would be on 'So', 'Boo-', 'things', 'hit'; 'got-', 'wealth',
'mend', 'wit'. Even with 'Corebus', this line is a tetrameter; the emendation, made
in the interest of the play's clarity, does scant violence to its poetry.
773–4 The lines echo the Old Man's prediction concerning Booby (322–3).
776–7 *they say . . . backward* Going, or sitting, cross-legged seems to have been both an
evil and a good-luck charm (see Hook, pp. 441–2n., and his note to *Edward I*, 1.
2263, in *The Life and Works of George Peele*, II, 199). Gummere and Binnie cite
Milton's *Comus:*

without his rod revers't,
And backward mutters of dissevering power,
We cannot free the Lady.   (815–17)

Saying prayers (as opposed to a conjurer's spell) backward, however, conjures up
the devil (compare Diccon's method in *GGN*, II.i). Eumenides, in his trepidation,
may be recalling the wrong kind of charm, but Jack is in charge.
780–2 *And . . . ears* Peele may have had in mind Homer's *Odyssey*, Book XII, where
Odysseus (Ulysses), on the advice of Circe, puts wax in the ears of all his crew so
that they will not hear the fatally enchanting song of the Sirens.

stop your ears. [*Puts wool into* EUMENIDES' *ears*] And so,
master sit still, for I must to the conjurer.

Exit JACK

Enter the Conjurer to the Wandering Knight

SACRAPANT
How now! What man art thou that sits so sad?
Why dost thou gaze upon these stately trees   785
Without the leave and will of Sacrapant?
What, not a word but mum?
Then, Sacrapant, thou art betrayed!

Enter JACK, *invisible, and taketh off* SACRAPANT'*s wreath from his
head, and his sword out of his hand*

What hand invades the head of Sacrapant?
What hateful fury doth envy my happy state?   790
Then, Sacrapant, these are thy latest days.
Alas, my veins are numbed, my sinews shrink,
My blood is pierced, my breath fleeting away,
And now my timeless date is come to end.
He in whose life his actions hath been so foul,   795
Now in his death to hell descends his soul.

He dieth [*and his body is removed*]

782 s.d. *Puts . . . ears* eds.
794 *timeless date* (supposedly) eternal life
796 s.d. *and . . . removed* Binnie

---

782 s.d. *Puts . . . ears* Called for by 801 s.d.
787 *not . . . mum* Proverbial (Tilley W767).
788 Sacrapant said nothing about a threat from a silent man at 413–19, but he may
believe that the silent, unhearing Eumenides is the dead man who is destined to kill
him.
  s.d. *Enter* JACK, *invisible* A delightfully offhand direction. How was it done?
Compare 679, where Jack is invisible to Eumenides at first, then becomes visible.
Here he presumably remains invisible to Sacrapant, but is visible to Eumenides. Or
does Eumenides neither see nor hear him until 802? This too seems to betray the
author drafting his plot, not yet giving thought to the playing of it.
793 *My . . . pierced* The sense is clear, even if, literally speaking, it would be his veins or
his body that was pierced, letting out his blood. Hook notes (p. 442) that Peele
liked the word 'pierced' and used it frequently in other works.
796 s.d. The body must be removed, since Jack enters with the head at 842. It would be
appropriate for the Furies to carry off Sacrapant's body, as they have carried off his
victims previously.

JACK

O sir, are you gone? Now I hope we shall have some other
coil. Now, master, how like you this? The conjurer, he is
dead, and vows never to trouble us more. Now get you to
your fair lady, and see what you can do with her.—Alas, 800
he heareth me not all this while. But I will help that.

He pulls the wool out of his ears

EUMENIDES

How now, Jack! What news?

JACK

Here, master, take this sword and dig with it at the foot of
this hill.

He digs and spies a light

EUMENIDES

How now, Jack! What is this?   805

JACK

Master, without this the conjurer could do nothing, and
so long as this light lasts, so long doth his art endure, and
this being out, then doth his art decay.

EUMENIDES

Why then, Jack, I will soon put out this light.

JACK

Ay, master, how?   810

EUMENIDES

Why, with a stone I'll break the glass, and then blow it
out.

JACK

No, master, you may as soon break the smith's anvil as
this little vial, nor the biggest blast that ever Boreas blew
cannot blow out this little light; but she that is neither   815

---

798 *coil* ado, business
814 *Boreas* the north wind
815–16 *but ... widow* only she that is . . can do it

---

804 s.d. *He ... light* Compare 588 s.d. and note.

maid, wife nor widow. Master, wind this horn, and see
what will happen.

He winds the horn

Here enters VENELIA *and breaks the glass, and blows out the light, and
goeth in again*

JACK
So master, how like you this? This is she that ran madding
in the woods, his betrothed love that keeps the cross; and
now this light being out, all are restored to their former   820
liberty. And now, master, to the lady that you have so
long looked for.

He draweth a curtain, and there DELIA *sitteth asleep*

EUMENIDES
God speed, fair maid, sitting alone: there is once.
God speed, fair maid, [sitting alone]: there is twice.
God speed, fair maid, [sitting alone]: there is thrice.   825

DELIA
Not so, good sir, for you are by.

JACK
Enough, master; she hath spoke. Now I will leave her
with you.   [*Exit*]

EUMENIDES
Thou fairest flower of these western parts,
Whose beauty so reflecteth in my sight   830
As doth a crystal mirror in the sun,
For thy sweet sake I have crossed the frozen Rhine;

816 *wind* blow
828 s.d. *Exit* eds. (no s.d. in Q)

---

817 s.d. *Hear . . . again* This two-line direction describes an action that might consume
  several minutes. Such moments of silent action are a notable feature of the play.
  Compare, e.g., the narrative directions at 192, 403, 518, 541, 588, 631, 716. Venelia,
  who speaks no lines, must rely on behaviour to convey the differences in her state
  of mind at 192, here, and at 851.
823–5 *God speed . . . thrice* I incorporate a suggestion by G. R. Proudfoot (recorded by
  Binnie) that 'sitting alone' should be repeated in each line. It is, after all, a charm,
  and 'there is twice' and 'there is thrice' make good sense only if Eumenides is
  enumerating repetitions of the magic greeting which will waken the sleeping
  princess.
826 *Not . . . by* Delia means that she is not alone now, for Eumenides is there.

Leaving fair Po, I sailed up Danuby
As far as Saba, whose enhancing streams
Cuts 'twixt the Tartars and the Russians.   835
These have I crossed for thee, fair Delia:
Then grant me that which I have sued for long.

DELIA
Thou gentle knight, whose fortune is so good
To find me out, and set my brothers free,
My faith, my heart, my hand I give to thee.   840

EUMENIDES
Thanks, gentle madam. But here comes Jack. Thank him,
for he is the best friend that we have.

Enter JACK *with a head in his hand*

How now, Jack! What hast thou there?

JACK
Marry, master, the head of the conjurer.

EUMENIDES
Why, Jack, that is impossible—he was a young man!   845

JACK
Ah, master, so he deceived them that beheld him. But he
was a miserable, old and crooked man, though to each
man's eye he seemed young and fresh. For, master, this
conjurer took the shape of the old man that kept the cross, 850

---

835 *Cuts* (see 159 n.)

832-5 Editors quote Greene's *Orlando Furioso*, where Mandricard relates his travels to
   seek the hand of the emperor's daughter:
           I furrowed Neptune's seas
           Northeast as far as is the frozen Rhene;
           Leaving fair Voya, cross'd up Danuby,
           As high as Saba, whose enhancing streams
           Cut 'twixt the Tartars and the Russians.
                            (11. 66–70; Dyce, p. 90)
   Eumenides's preceding lines (829–31) are similar, though less strikingly so, to
   those spoken by the Soldan in Greene's play some fifty lines before those just
   quoted:
           The fairest flower that glories Africa,
           Whose beauty Phoebus dares not dash with showers,
           Over whose climate never hung a cloud,
           But smiling Titan lights the horizon—
                            (11. 17–20)

and that old man was in the likeness of the conjurer. But 850
now, master, wind your horn.

He winds his horn

Enter VENELIA, *the two brothers, and he that was at the cross*

EUMENIDES
Welcome, Erestus! Welcome, fair Venelia!
Welcome, Thelea and Calypha both!
Now have I her that I so long have sought;
So saith fair Delia, if we have your consent. 855

FIRST BROTHER
Valiant Eumenides, thou well deservest
To have our favours; so let us rejoice
That by thy means we are at liberty.
Here may we joy each in other's sight.
And this fair lady have her wandering knight. 860

JACK
So, master, now ye think you have done. But I must have
a saying to you. You know you and I were partners, I to
have half in all you got.

EUMENIDES
Why, so thou shalt, Jack.

JACK
Why then, master, draw your sword, part your lady, let 865
me have half of her presently.

EUMENIDES
Why, I hope, Jack, thou dost but jest! I promised thee half
I got, but not half my lady.

853 *Calypha* eds. (Kalepha Q)
855 *your* (i.e., the brothers')
859 *joy* rejoice

---

851 s.d. *he ... cross* Now, with Sacrapant's spell broken, he would enter in his true
shape, as a young man; his name too is restored to him in the next line.
853 *Thelea* The first mention of the Second Brother's name, though since Calypha has
been named earlier (388, 405), no special significance attaches to this fact. But the
addressing of each person by name may be seen as signalling the breaking of the
evil spell and the restoration of their own identities and true status. Eumenides has
also addressed Delia by name for the first time at 836; before the spell was broken
she was 'fair maid'.
861–82 Eumenides's ultimate trial, the friendship or oath-keeping test. It is not
horrible, because it cannot really happen; it is another of the play's many rituals.
Compare Valentine's offer of his love, Silvia, to his friend Proteus in *The Two
Gentlemen of Verona*, V.iv, 82–3. The episode also recalls the judgement of Solomon
(I Kings 3:16–28).

JACK

But what else, master? Have you not gotten her? Therefore divide her straight, for I will have half. There is 870 no remedy.

EUMENIDES

Well, ere I will falsify my word unto my friend, take her all. Here, Jack, I'll give her thee.

JACK

Nay, neither more nor less, master, but even just half.

EUMENIDES

Before I will falsify my faith unto my friend, I will divide 875 her. Jack, thou shalt have half.

FIRST BROTHER

Be not so cruel unto our sister, gentle knight!

SECOND BROTHER

O, spare fair Delia! She deserves no death!

EUMENIDES

Content yourselves; my word is passed to him. Therefore prepare thyself, Delia, for thou must die.   880

DELIA

Then farewell, world! Adieu, Eumenides!

He offers to strike and JACK *stays him*

JACK

Stay, master! It is sufficient I have tried your constancy. Do you now remember since you paid for the burying of a poor fellow?

EUMENIDES

Ay, very well, Jack.   885

JACK

Then, master, thank that good deed for this good turn. And so, God be with you all!

---

870 *straight* straightaway
879 *my . . . passed* I have sworn

---

886 *this . . . turn* Jack may mean simply his sparing of Delia, but 'this good turn' may also be the whole of his benevolent intervention in the main plot, culminating in liberty and happiness for everyone.

JACK *leaps down in the ground*

EUMENIDES
Jack! What, art thou gone? Then farewell, Jack.
Come, brothers and my beauteous Delia,
Erestus and thy dear Venelia;   890
We will to Thessaly with joyful hearts.

ALL
Agreed! We follow thee and Delia.

Exeunt

FANTASTIC
What, gammer, asleep?

MADGE
By the mass, son, 'tis almost day, and my windows shut at
the cock's crow!   895

FROLIC
Do you hear, gammer? Methinks this Jack bore a great
sway amongst them.

MADGE
O, man, this was the ghost of the poor man that they kept
such a coil to bury, and that makes him to help the
wandering knight so much. But come, let us in. We will 900
have a cup of ale and a toast this morning, and so depart.

FANTASTIC
Then you have made an end of your tale, gammer?

888 *gone? Then* eds. (gone?/Then Q)
894 *shut* eds. (shuts Q)
901 *toast* eds. (tost Q; see 769 n.)

---

887 s.d. JACK . . . *ground* A trap is needed for this. It would probably be used for the well
scenes also, with the well built over the trap for the Head to rise from, and with the
person speaking the Voice's part stationed under it. At some point, the well would
have been removed, perhaps immediately after 774, leaving the trap open for Jack
to leap into here.
894–5 *my . . . crow* My eyes are still closed; they should be open by now. The window
metaphor for the eyes and eyelids is common from the fourteenth century. Madge
is replying in the affirmative to Fantastic's query.
900 *let us in* Madge and the pages were 'in' her cottage already, and have not come out
since the beginning, nor would we expect her to 'depart' from her own home with
the others. But this is being perversely literal-minded. The effect of the words is to
suggest, indirectly, that they—and we—have been somewhere else, in the land of
romance and folktale, watching the events of the inner play unfold. And, at the end
of the play, Madge's invitation to her audience to go 'in' is literally an invitation to
the actors to go 'off'; the play that all of them are in is over. Clunch and Antic are
forgotten.

MADGE

Yes, faith. When this was done I took a piece of bread and cheese, and came my way, and so shall you have too before you go, to your breakfast.   [*Exeunt*]   905

FINIS

905 *to* for
    s.d. *Exeunt* eds. (no s.d. in Q)

903-4 *was done . . . took . . . came* Madge's sudden shift of tense and her reference to 'coming her way', as if she herself had seen or heard the tale somewhere else at some other time, is the final disorientating wrench. Dislocation is now temporal as well as spatial: we shift from the dramatic present, not simply to the narrative past of Madge's 'Once upon a time' (106), but to the implied pluperfect, when she was the auditor/spectator, not the teller. The effect is similar to that of Milton's unexpected shift to a framing, narrative past tense in the final verse-paragraph of *Lycidas*.

The Shoemakers' Holiday

THOMAS DEKKER

Edited by
D. J. PALMER

ABBREVIATIONS

Q1   First Quarto of 1600

THE SHOMAKERS

Holiday.

OR

The Gentle Craft.

With the humorous life of Simon
Eyre, shoomaker, and Lord Maior
of London.

As it was acted before the Queenes most excellent Ma-
iestie on New-yeares day at night last, by the right
honourable the Earle of Notingham, Lord high Ad-
mirall of England, his seruants.

Printed by Valentine Sims dwelling at the foote of Adling
hill, neere Bainards Castle, at the signe of the White
Swanne, and are there to be sold.
1 6 0 0.

THE FIRST THREE-MAN'S SONG

O the month of May, the merry month of May,
So frolic, so gay, and so green, so green, so green;
O and then did I unto my true love say,
Sweet Peg, thou shalt be my Summer's Queen.

Now the Nightingale, the pretty Nightingale,   5
The sweetest singer in all the forest's choir,
Entreats thee, sweet Peggy, to hear thy true love's tale:
Lo, yonder she sitteth, her breast against a brier.

But O I spy the Cuckoo, the Cuckoo, the Cuckoo;
See where she sitteth, come away my joy: 10
Come away I prithee, I do not like the Cuckoo
Should sing where my Peggy and I kiss and toy.

O the month of May, the merry month of May,
So frolic, so gay, and so green, so green, so green;
And then did I unto my true love say,   15
Sweet Peg, thou shalt be my Summer's Queen.

THE FIRST THREE-MAN'S SONG. There is no indication where
this should be sung in the play, but an appropriate point would be in
III. iii, when the shoemakers perform their morris dance, and Rose
recognizes Lacy.
8 *her breast against a brier*. The sweet song of the nightingale was supposed
   to be caused by the pain of a thorn in her side.
9 *the Cuckoo*. The name suggests cuckoldry: cf. *Love's Labour's Lost*,
   V. ii, 897–8, 'Cuckoo, cuckoo—O word of fear, / Unpleasing to a married
   ear'.

THE SECOND THREE-MAN'S SONG

This is to be sung at the latter end
Cold's the wind, and wet's the rain,
   Saint Hugh be our good speed;
Ill is the weather that bringeth no gain,
   Nor helps good hearts in need.

Trowl the bowl, the jolly nut-brown bowl,   5
   And here kind mate to thee;
Let's sing a dirge for Saint Hugh's soul,
   And down it merrily.

Down a down, hey down a down,
   Hey derry derry, down a down; *Close with the tenor boy* 10
Ho well done, to me let come,
   Ring compass gentle joy.

Trowl the bowl, the nut-brown bowl,
   And here kind &c. *as often as there be men to drink*

At last when all have drunk, this verse:
Cold's the wind, and wet's the rain,   15
   Saint Hugh be our good speed;
Ill is the weather that bringeth no gain,
   Nor helps good hearts in need.

---

5 *Trowl* pass round
12 *Ring compass* the full range of harmony, or possibly 'complete the circle'

---

  at the latter end. Either to conclude the play, after the King's final speech,
  or at the beginning of IV. ii, where the shoemakers are singing 'Hey
  down a down, down derry'.
  2 *Saint Hugh.* Patron saint of the shoemakers.

70

THE PROLOGUE AS IT WAS PRONOUNCED
BEFORE THE QUEEN'S MAJESTY

As wretches in a storm, expecting day,
With trembling hands and eyes cast up to heaven,
Make prayers the anchor of their conquered hopes,
So we, dear Goddess, wonder of all eyes,
Your meanest vassals, through mistrust and fear   5
To sink into the bottom of disgrace
By our imperfit pastimes, prostrate thus
On bended knees, our sails of hope do strike,
Dreading the bitter storms of your dislike.
Since then, unhappy men, our hap is such   10
That to ourselves ourselves no help can bring,
But needs must perish, if your saint-like ears,
Locking the temple where all mercy sits,
Refuse the tribute of our begging tongues:
Oh grant, bright mirror of true chastity,   15
From those life-breathing stars your sun-like eyes,
One gracious smile: for your celestial breath
Must send us life, or sentence us to death.

[DRAMATIS PERSONAE

KING OF ENGLAND
EARL OF LINCOLN
EARL OF CORNWALL
SIR ROGER OTLEY, *Lord Mayor of London*
SIMON EYRE, *shoemaker and afterwards Lord Mayor*
ROWLAND LACY, *nephew to Lincoln, afterwards disguised as Hans Meulter*
ASKEW, *cousin to Lacy*
HAMMON, *a city gentleman*
WARNER, *cousin to Hammon*
MASTER SCOTT, *friend to Otley*
HODGE (*also called* ROGER), *foreman to Eyre*
FIRK, *journeyman to Eyre*
RALPH DAMPORT, *journeyman to Eyre*
LOVELL, *servant to the King*
DODGER, *parasite to Lincoln*
Dutch Skipper
Boy, *apprentice to Eyre*
Boy, *servant to Otley*
Servingman *to Hammon*
MARGERY, *wife to Eyre*
ROSE, *daughter to Otley*
JANE, *wife to Ralph Damport*
SYBIL, *maid to Rose*
Noblemen, Soldiers, Huntsmen, Shoemakers, Apprentices, Servants]

A PLEASANT COMEDY OF THE GENTLE CRAFT

[Act I, Scene i]

Enter LORD MAYOR [*and*] LINCOLN

LINCOLN
  My Lord Mayor, you have sundry times
  Feasted myself and many courtiers more;
  Seldom or never can we be so kind
  To make requital of your courtesy.
  But leaving this, I hear my cousin Lacy   5
  Is much affected to your daughter Rose.
LORD MAYOR
  True, my good Lord, and she loves him so well
  That I mislike her boldness in the chase.
LINCOLN
  Why, my Lord Mayor, think you it then a shame
  To join a Lacy with an Otley's name?   10
LORD MAYOR
  Too mean is my poor girl for his high birth;
  Poor citizens must not with courtiers wed,
  Who will in silks and gay apparel spend
  More in one year than I am worth by far.
  Therefore your Honour need not doubt my girl.   15

1 *sundry* several
5 *cousin* kinsman
15 *doubt* fear, mistrust

A PLEASANT COMEDY OF THE GENTLE CRAFT. The
running title of the play in Q1: *The Shoemakers' Holiday* appears only
on the title page.
  LORD MAYOR. So he is named in Q1 stage directions and speech prefixes
throughout, even after Eyre has become Lord Mayor; since confusion is
unlikely, this edition follows suit.

LINCOLN
　Take heed, my Lord, advise you what you do:
　A verier unthrift lives not in the world
　Than is my cousin, for, I'll tell you what,
　'Tis now almost a year since he requested
　To travel countries for experience;　　　　　20
　I furnished him with coin, bills of exchange,
　Letters of credit, men to wait on him,
　Solicited my friends in Italy
　Well to respect him, but see the end:
　Scant had he journeyed through half Germany,　25
　But all his coin was spent, his men cast off,
　His bills embezzled, and my jolly coz,
　Ashamed to show his bankrupt presence here,
　Became a shoemaker in Wittenberg:
　A goodly science for a gentleman　　　　　30
　Of such descent! Now judge the rest by this.
　Suppose your daughter have a thousand pound,
　He did consume me more in one half-year;
　And make him heir to all the wealth you have,
　One twelve-month's rioting will waste it all.　35
　Then seek, my Lord, some honest citizen
　To wed your daughter to.
LORD MAYOR　　　　　　I thank your Lordship.
　[aside] Well, fox, I understand your subtlety.
　As for your nephew, let your Lordship's eyes
　But watch his actions, and you need not fear,　40
　For I have sent my daughter far enough;
　And yet your cousin Rowland might do well
　Now he hath learned an occupation.
　[aside] And yet I scorn to call him son-in-law.
LINCOLN
　Ay, but I have a better trade for him:　　　45
　I thank his Grace he hath appointed him
　Chief colonel of all those companies
　Mustered in London and the shires about

25　Scant scarcely
27　embezzled wasted
35　rioting riotous living, extravagance
41　sent ed. (om. Q1)

To serve his Highness in those wars of France.
See where he comes: Lovell, what news with you?   50
Enter LOVELL, LACY *and* ASKEW

LOVELL
My Lord of Lincoln, 'tis his Highness' will
That presently your cousin ship for France
With all his powers: he would not for a million
But they should land at Deepe within four days.

LINCOLN
Go certify his Grace it shall be done.   55
Exit LOVELL

Now, cousin Lacy, in what forwardness
Are all your companies?

LACY   All well prepared:
The men of Hertfordshire lie at Mile End,
Suffolk and Essex train in Tothill-fields,
The Londoners and those of Middlesex,   60
All gallantly prepared in Finsbury,
With frolic spirits long for their parting hour.

LORD MAYOR
They have their imprest, coats and furniture,
And if it please your cousin Lacy come
To the Guildhall, he shall receive his pay,   65
And twenty pounds beside my brethren
Will freely give him, to approve our loves
We bear unto my Lord your uncle here.

LACY
I thank your Honour.

LINCOLN   Thanks, my good Lord Mayor.

LORD MAYOR
At the Guildhall we will expect your coming.   70
Exit [LORD MAYOR]

---

52 *presently* immediately
53 *powers* forces
54 *Deepe* Dieppe
63 *imprest* recruitment pay
63 *furniture* equipment

58–61 *Mile End . . . Tothill-fields . . . Finsbury.* Three drilling grounds out-
    side the city walls, respectively to the east, west, and north. That in
    Finsbury was used for archery (cf. Firk's reference in II. iii, 60).

LINCOLN

> To approve your loves to me? No, subtlety!
> Nephew, that twenty pound he doth bestow
> For joy to rid you from his daughter Rose.
> But, cousins both, now here are none but friends,
> I would not have you cast an amorous eye 75
> Upon so mean a project as the love
> Of a gay, wanton, painted citizen.
> I know this churl, even in the height of scorn,
> Doth hate the mixture of his blood with thine:
> I pray thee do thou so. Remember, coz, 80
> What honourable fortunes wait on thee:
> Increase the King's love, which so brightly shines
> And gilds thy hopes; I have no heir but thee—
> And yet not thee, if with a wayward spirit
> Thou start from the true bias of my love. 85

LACY

> My Lord, I will for honour, not desire
> Of land or livings, or to be your heir,
> So guide my actions in pursuit of France
> As shall add glory to the Lacys' name.

LINCOLN

> Coz, for those words here's thirty portuguese, 90
> And nephew Askew, there's a few for you.
> Fair Honour in her loftiest eminence
> Stays in France for you till you fetch her thence.
> Then, nephews, clap swift wings on your designs:
> Begone, begone, make haste to the Guildhall. 95
> There presently I'll meet you; do not stay:
> Where Honour beckons, shame attends delay.

Exit [LINCOLN]

ASKEW

> How gladly would your uncle have you gone!

---

97 *beckons* ed. (becomes Q1)

---

85 *true bias.* Proper course: an image from the game of bowls, in which the
    bowl is weighted to roll in a curve.

90 *portuguese.* A gold coin worth about 4 pounds: Lincoln makes a hand-
    some gesture, but twenty of these portuguese are later lent by Lacy to
    Eyre as the down-payment on the Dutch skipper's cargo (II. iii, 24).

LACY

True, coz, but I'll o'erreach his policies.
I have some serious business for three days,   100
Which nothing but my presence can dispatch.
You therefore, cousin, with the companies
Shall haste to Dover; there I'll meet with you,
Or, if I stay past my prefixed time,
Away for France: we'll meet in Normandy.   105
The twenty pounds my Lord Mayor gives to me
You shall receive, and these ten portuguese,
Part of mine uncle's thirty. Gentle coz,
Have care to our great charge: I know your wisdom
Hath tried itself in higher consequence.   110

ASKEW

Coz, all myself am yours; yet have this care,
To lodge in London with all secrecy:
Our uncle Lincoln hath, besides his own,
Many a jealous eye that in your face
Stares only to watch means for your disgrace.   115

LACY

Stay, cousin: who be these?

Enter SIMON EYRE, MARGERY, HODGE, FIRK, JANE, *and* RALPH
with a piece

EYRE

Leave whining, leave whining; away with this whimpering,
this puling, these blubbering tears, and these wet eyes. I'll
get thy husband discharged, I warrant thee, sweet Jane:
go to!   120

HODGE

Master, here be the captains.

EYRE

Peace, Hodge; husht, ye knave, husht!

FIRK

Here be the cavaliers and the coronels, master.

---

  99 *o'erreach his policies* outwit his scheming
 109 *charge* commission
     s.d. *with a piece* a firing-piece, a gun
 118 *puling* snivelling
 123 *cavaliers and . . . coronels* officers, commanders

EYRE

Peace, Firk; peace, my fine Firk! Stand by with your
pishery-pashery, away! I am a man of the best presence: 125
I'll speak to them and they were Popes! Gentlemen, captains, colonels, commanders: brave men, brave leaders,
may it please you to give me audience? I am Simon Eyre,
the mad shoemaker of Tower Street; this wench with the
mealy mouth that will never tire is my wife, I can tell you; 130
here's Hodge, my man and my foreman; here's Firk, my
fine firking journeyman; and this is blubbered Jane. All we
come to be suitors for this honest Ralph: keep him at home,
and as I am a true shoemaker and a gentleman of the Gentle
Craft, buy spurs yourself, and I'll find ye boots these seven 135
years.

MARGERY

Seven years, husband?

EYRE

Peace, midriff, peace! I know what I do: peace!

FIRK

Truly, master cormorant, you shall do God good service to
let Ralph and his wife stay together. She's a young new- 140
married woman; if you take her husband away from her
a-night, you undo her; she may beg in the daytime, for he's
as good a workman at a prick and an awl as any is in our trade.

JANE

O let him stay, else I shall be undone!

FIRK

Ay, truly, she shall be laid at one side like a pair of old shoes 145
else, and be occupied for no use.

124 *Stand by* Out of the way
125 *pishery-pashery* fuss
125 *of the best presence* fit for the noblest company
130 *mealy mouth* genteel way of talking
132 *journeyman* one who has served his apprenticeship

---

132 *firking*. Frisking: Firk's name lends itself to a variety of meanings in
    different contexts throughout the play, all suggesting lively and
    vigorous activity, and many of them bawdy.
138 *midriff*. A reference to Margery's diminutive stature, or possibly to her
    sex as 'Adam's rib'.
139 *cormorant*. Firk's corruption of 'coronel'.
143–6 *prick and an awl ... undone ... occupied*. Bawdy quibbles.

LACY

Truly, my friends, it lies not in my power;
The Londoners are pressed, paid, and set forth
By the Lord Mayor: I cannot change a man.

HODGE

Why, then you were as good be a corporal as a colonel, if   150
you cannot discharge one good fellow; and I tell you true,
I think you do more than you can answer, to press a man
within a year and a day of his marriage.

EYRE

Well said, melancholy Hodge! Gramercy, my fine foreman!

MARGERY

Truly, gentlemen, it were ill done for such as you to stand   155
so stiffly against a poor young wife: considering her case,
she is new-married, but let that pass. I pray, deal not roughly
with her; her husband is a young man and but newly
entered, but let that pass.

EYRE

Away with your pishery-pashery, your polls and your   160
edipolls! Peace, midriff; silence, Cicely Bumtrinket! Let
your head speak.

FIRK

Yea, and the horns too, master.

EYRE

Tawsoone, my fine Firk, tawsoone! Peace, scoundrels!
See you this man, captains? You will not release him? Well,   165
let him go! He's a proper shot: let him vanish! Peace, Jane,
dry up thy tears: they'll make his powder dankish. Take
him, brave men: Hector of Troy was an hackney to him,

148 *pressed* conscripted
148 *set forth* equipped
161 *midriff* ed. (midaffe Q1)
162 *your head* your lord and master
164 *Tawsoone* ed. (Too soone Q1) be quiet
168 *hackney* drudge

---

155 *stand so stiffly . . . newly entered.* Unintentional indecencies.
160 *your polls and your edipolls.* A contracted form of Pollux. Eyre is dis-
     paraging Margery's attempt at genteel remonstration: to swear by
     Pollux is a very mild form of swearing.
163 *and the horns too.* Firk cannot resist the inevitable cuckold joke.

Hercules and Termagant scoundrels; Prince Arthur's
Round Table, by the Lord of Ludgate, ne'er fed such a tall,   170
such a dapper swordman! By the life of Pharaoh, a brave,
resolute swordman! Peace, Jane; I say no more, mad
knaves!

FIRK

See, see, Hodge, how my master raves in commendation of
Ralph!   175

HODGE

Ralph, th'art a gull, by this hand, and thou goest not.

ASKEW

I am glad, good Master Eyre, it is my hap
To meet so resolute a soldier.
Trust me, for your report and love to him,
A common slight regard shall not respect him.   180

LACY

Is thy name Ralph?

RALPH   Yes, sir.

LACY   Give me thy hand;
Thou shalt not want, as I'm a gentleman.
Woman, be patient; God no doubt will send
Thy husband safe again, but he must go:
His country's quarrel says it shall be so.   185

HODGE

Th'art a gull, by my stirrup, if thou dost not go! I will not
have thee strike thy gimlet into these weak vessels: prick
thine enemies, Ralph!

Enter DODGER

170 *tall* brave
171 *dapper* spruce
176 *gull* simpleton
176 *and* if
176 *not* ed. (om. Q1)
180 *A common slight regard shall not respect him* he shall receive particular
     consideration
186 *stirrup* shoemaker's strap for holding the last on his knee
187 *gimlet* boring tool

169 *Termagant.* A fierce heathen god often invoked in the medieval mystery
     plays.
170 *Lord of Ludgate.* Possibly the legendary King Lud, whose statue stood
     in Ludgate, a city thoroughfare.

DODGER
My Lord, your uncle on the Tower Hill
Stays with the Lord Mayor and the Aldermen,   190
And doth request you with all speed you may
To hasten thither.

ASKEW   Cousin, let us go.

LACY
Dodger, run you before; tell them we come.

Exit DODGER

This Dodger is mine uncle's parasite,
The arrant'st varlet that e'er breathed on earth;   195
He sets more discord in a noble house,
By one day's broaching of his pickthank tales,
Than can be salved again in twenty years;
And he, I fear, shall go with us to France,
To pry into our actions.

ASKEW   Therefore, coz,   200
It shall behove you to be circumspect.

LACY
Fear not, good cousin. Ralph, hie to your colours.

[*Exit* LACY *and* ASKEW]

RALPH
I must, because there is no remedy;
But, gentle master and my loving dame,
As you have always been a friend to me,   205
So in my absence think upon my wife.

JANE
Alas, my Ralph.

MARGERY
She cannot speak for weeping.

190 *Stays* waits
192 *let us* ed. (lets Q1)
    s.d. *Exit* DODGER (Q1 places this stage direction at the end of Dodger's
    speech, 192)
195 *arrant'st varlet* most unmitigated rascal
197 *pickthank* currying favour
201 *behove* benefit
202 *colours* regimental standard
203 *there is* ed. (theres Q1)

203 *I must, because there is no remedy.* As a 'serious' character, Ralph speaks
in blank verse.

EYRE

    Peace, you cracked groats, you mustard tokens: disquiet
    not the brave soldier. Go thy ways, Ralph.   210

JANE

    Ay, ay, you bid him go; what shall I do when he is gone?

FIRK

    Why, be doing with me, or my fellow Hodge: be not idle.

EYRE

    Let me see thy hand, Jane: this fine hand, this white hand,
    these pretty fingers must spin, must card, must work!
    Work, you bombast-cotton-candle-quean, work for your   215
    living, with a pox to you! Hold thee, Ralph, here's five
    sixpences for thee: fight for the honour of the Gentle Craft,
    for the gentlemen shoemakers, the courageous cordwainers,
    the flower of Saint Martin's, the mad knaves of Bedlam,
    Fleet Street, Tower Street and Whitechapel! Crack me the   220
    crowns of the French knaves, a pox on them, crack them!
    Fight, by the Lord of Ludgate, fight, my fine boy!

FIRK

    Here, Ralph, here's three twopences: two carry into France,
    the third shall wash our souls at parting, for sorrow is dry.
    For my sake, firk the *Basa mon cues.*   225

HODGE

    Ralph, I am heavy at parting, but here's a shilling for thee.
    God send thee to cram thy slops with French crowns, and
    thy enemies' bellies with bullets!

209 *groats* fourpenny coins, here simply a term of jocular abuse
209 *mustard tokens* yellow plague-spots
214 *card* comb or tease the wool
215 *bombast-cotton-candle-quean* bombast is waste cotton such as might be
    used for candle wicks; a quean is a whore: the expression is merely
    boisterous raillery
218 *cordwainers* leather-workers (from Córdoba, in Spain)
224 *wash our souls* i.e., in drink
225 *Basa mon cues* 'baisez mon cul' (kiss my arse): a derisory term for
    Frenchmen
226 *heavy* sad
227 *slops* breeches
227 *French crowns* money, but also an allusion to venereal disease

219 *Saint Martin's*. The parish of St Martin-le-Grand, in which shoemaking
    flourished.
219 *Bedlam*. Bethlehem hospital, a lunatic asylum, outside Bishopsgate.

RALPH

I thank you, master, and I thank you all.
Now, gentle wife, my loving lovely Jane,   230
Rich men at parting give their wives rich gifts,
Jewels and rings, to grace their lily hands;
Thou know'st our trade makes rings for women's heels:
Here, take this pair of shoes cut out by Hodge,
Stitched by my fellow Firk, seamed by myself,   235
Made up and pinked with letters for thy name.
Wear them, my dear Jane, for thy husband's sake,
And every morning, when thou pull'st them on,
Remember me, and pray for my return.
Make much of them, for I have made them so,   240
That I can know them from a thousand mo.

> *Sound drum: enter* LORD MAYOR, LINCOLN, LACY, ASKEW,
> DODGER, *and soldiers. They pass over the stage,* RALPH *falls
> in amongst them,* FIRK *and the rest cry farewell, &c., and so
> Exeunt*

[Act I, Scene ii]

Enter ROSE *alone, making a garland*

ROSE

Here sit thou down upon this flowery bank,
And make a garland for thy Lacy's head.
These pinks, these roses, and these violets,
These blushing gilliflowers, these marigolds,
The fair embroidery of his coronet,   5
Carry not half such beauty in their cheeks,
As the sweet count'nance of my Lacy doth.
O my most unkind father! O my stars!
Why loured you so at my nativity,
To make me love, yet live robbed of my love?   10
Here as a thief am I imprisoned,
For my dear Lacy's sake, within those walls
Which by my father's cost were builded up
For better purposes; here must I languish

236 *pinked* perforated for eyelets
241 *mo* more

For him that doth as much lament, I know,   15
Mine absence, as for him I pine in woe.

Enter SYBIL

SYBIL

Good morrow, young mistress; I am sure you make that
garland for me, against I shall be Lady of the Harvest.

ROSE

Sybil, what news at London?

SYBIL

None but good: my Lord Mayor your father, and Master   20
Philpot your uncle, and Master Scott your cousin, and
Mistress Frigbottom by Doctors' Commons, do all, by my
troth, send you most hearty commendations.

ROSE

Did Lacy send kind greetings to his love?

SYBIL

O yes, out of cry, by my troth. I scant knew him: here 'a   25
wore a scarf, and here a scarf, here a bunch of feathers, and
here precious stones and jewels, and a pair of garters: O
monstrous! Like one of our yellow silk curtains at home
here in Old Ford House, here in Master Bellymount's
chamber. I stood at our door in Cornhill, looked at him, he   30
at me indeed; spake to him, but he not to me, not a word:
marry gup, thought I, with a wanion! He passed by me as
proud—Marry foh! Are you grown humorous? thought I,
and so shut the door, and in I came.

ROSE

O Sybil, how dost thou my Lacy wrong!   35
My Rowland is as gentle as a lamb,
No dove was ever half so mild as he.

---

18 *against* for the time when
25 *'a wore a scarf* ed. (a wore scarffe Q1)
32 *marry gup* marry go up, get along with you then
32 *with a wanion* the worse for you
33 *humorous* temperamental

---

18 *Lady of the Harvest.* The girl elected to preside over the season's
festivities (cf. May-Queen).
22 *Doctors' Commons.* An area near St Paul's, so called because it was
populated by lawyers.

SYBIL

Mild? Yea, as a bushel of stamped crabs! He looked on me
as sour as verjuice: go thy ways, thought I, thou mayest
be much in my gaskins, but nothing in my netherstocks!   40
This is your fault, mistress, to love him that loves not you;
he thinks scorn to do as he's done to, but if I were as you,
I'd cry: Go by, Jeronimo, go by!
I'd set my old debts against my new driblets,
And the hare's foot against the goose giblets,   45
For if ever I sigh when sleep I should take,
Pray God I may lose my maidenhead when I wake!

ROSE

Will my love leave me then and go to France?

SYBIL

I know not that, but I am sure I see him stalk before the
soldiers. By my troth, he is a proper man, but he is proper   50
that proper doth: let him go snick-up, young mistress!

ROSE

Get thee to London, and learn perfectly
Whether my Lacy go to France or no:
Do this, and I will give thee for thy pains
My cambric apron, and my Romish gloves,   55
My purple stockings, and a stomacher.
Say, wilt thou do this, Sybil, for my sake?

SYBIL

Will I, quoth a? At whose suit? By my troth, yes, I'll go:
a cambric apron, gloves, a pair of purple stockings, and a

38 *stamped crabs* crab apples crushed to make cider
39 *verjuice* sour juice of unripe fruit
49 *stalk* march
51 *go snick-up* go hang himself
55 *cambric* fine white linen (from Cambray, in Flanders)
56 *stomacher* ornamental chest-covering, often studded with jewels

---

40 *much in my gaskins, but nothing in my netherstocks.* Probably proverbial.
Gaskins were wide breeches, and netherstocks stockings worn underneath; hence, 'don't mistake my friendly greeting for anything more
personal'.
43 *Go by, Jeronimo, go by!* A catch-phrase deriving from Kyd's *Spanish
Tragedy*, III. xii, 31, meaning 'have nothing to do with that'.
44 *driblets.* Petty cash. The couplet is proverbial, meaning 'set the good
against the bad and take things as they are'.

stomacher! I'll sweat in purple, mistress, for you; I'll take   60
anything that comes, a God's name! O rich, a cambric
apron! Faith then, have at Up Tails All: I'll go jiggy-joggy
to London and be here in a trice, young mistress.

Exit [SYBIL]

ROSE

Do so, good Sybil; meantime wretched I
Will sit and sigh for his lost company.   65

Exit [ROSE]

[Act I, Scene iii]

Enter ROWLAND LACY *like a Dutch shoemaker*

LACY

How many shapes have gods and kings devised,
Thereby to compass their desired loves!
It is no shame for Rowland Lacy then
To clothe his cunning with the Gentle Craft,
That thus disguised I may unknown possess   5
The only happy presence of my Rose.
For her have I forsook my charge in France,
Incurred the King's displeasure, and stirred up
Rough hatred in mine uncle Lincoln's breast.
O Love, how powerful art thou, that canst change   10
High birth to bareness, and a noble mind
To the mean semblance of a shoemaker!
But thus it must be: for her cruel father,
Hating the single union of our souls,
Hath secretly conveyed my Rose from London   15
To bar me of her presence; but I trust
Fortune and this disguise will further me
Once more to view her beauty, gain her sight.
Here in Tower Street, with Eyre the shoemaker,
Mean I a while to work: I know the trade,   20
I learned it when I was in Wittenberg.

62 *Up Tails All*. A catch-phrase from a popular song, meaning 'let's get
  cracking'.
1 *How many shapes have gods and kings devised*. Lacy justifies his disguise
  by reference to Ovid's tales of metamorphosis.

Then cheer thy hoping spirits, be not dismayed;
Thou canst not want, do Fortune what she can:
The Gentle Craft is living for a man.

Exit [LACY]

[Act I, Scene iv]

Enter EYRE *making himself ready*

EYRE

Where be these boys, these girls, these drabs, these scoundrels? They wallow in the fat brewis of my bounty, and
lick up the crumbs of my table, yet will not rise to see my
walks cleansed. Come out, you powder-beef-queans!
What, Nan! What, Madge Mumblecrust! Come out, you   5
fat midriff-swag-belly whores, and sweep me these kennels,
that the noisome stench offend not the nose of my neighbours. What, Firk, I say! What, Hodge! Open my shop
windows! What, Firk, I say!

Enter FIRK

FIRK

O master, is't you that speak bandog and bedlam this   10
morning? I was in a dream, and mused what madman was
got into the street so early. Have you drunk this morning
that your throat is so clear?

EYRE

Ah, well said, Firk; well said, Firk. To work, my fine
knave, to work! Wash thy face, and thou'lt be more blest.   15

FIRK

Let them wash my face that will eat it; good master, send
for a souse-wife, if you'll have my face cleaner.

Enter HODGE

s.d. *making himself ready* putting on his dress
2 *brewis* thick broth
4 *powder-beef*, salted beef, i.e., cheap meat
6 *kennels* channels, gutters
7 *noisome* unpleasant
10 *bandog and bedlam* roaring like a ferocious watchdog and a lunatic
17 *souse-wife* woman who pickled pigs' trotters

---

5 *Madge Mumblecrust.* The rustic crone in Udall's *Ralph Roister Doister.*

EYRE

Away, sloven! Avaunt, scoundrel! Good morrow, Hodge:
good morrow, my fine foreman!

HODGE

O master, good morrow; y'are an early stirrer. Here's a   20
fair morning! Good morrow, Firk. I could have slept this
hour. Here's a brave day toward!

EYRE

O haste to work, my fine foreman, haste to work!

FIRK

Master, I am as dry as dust to hear my fellow Roger talk
of fair weather: let us pray for good leather, and let clowns   25
and ploughboys, and those that work in the fields, pray for
brave days. We work in a dry shop; what care I if it rain?

Enter MARGERY

EYRE

How now, Dame Margery, can you see to rise? Trip and go,
call up the drabs your maids.

MARGERY

See to rise? I hope 'tis time enough: 'tis early enough for   30
any woman to be seen abroad. I marvel how many wives in
Tower Street are up so soon? Gods me, 'tis not noon!
Here's a yawling!

EYRE

Peace, Margery, peace. Where's Cicely Bumtrinket your
maid? She has a privy fault: she farts in her sleep. Call   35
the quean up: if my men want shoethread, I'll swing her
in a stirrup!

FIRK

Yet that's but a dry beating: here's still a sign of drought.

Enter LACY *singing*

LACY

Der was een bore van Gelderland,

25 *clowns* rustics
37 *stirrup* strap (see note on I. i, 186)
39-44 *Der was een bore* . . . 'There was a farmer from Gelderland, /
   Merry they are, / He was so drunk he could not stand, / Drunken they
   are. / Clink once the cannikin, / Drink pretty mannikin'.

35 *privy.* A pun on 'secret' and 'lavatory'.

    Frolick si byen,   40
He was als dronck he cold nyet stand,
    Upsolce se byen.
Tap eens de canneken,
    Drincke schone mannekin.

FIRK

Master, for my life, yonder's a brother of the Gentle Craft.   45
If he bear not Saint Hugh's bones, I'll forfeit my bones.
He's some uplandish workman; hire him, good master, that
I may learn some gibble-gabble: 'twill make us work the
faster.

EYRE

Peace, Firk. A hard world: let him pass, let him vanish!   50
We have a journeyman enow: peace, my fine Firk.

MARGERY

Nay, nay, y'are best follow your man's counsel; you shall
see what will come on't. We have not men enow, but we must
entertain every butter-box: but let that pass.

HODGE

Dame, 'fore God, if my master follow your counsel, he'll   55
consume little beef. He shall be glad of men and he can
catch them.

FIRK

Ay, that he shall!

HODGE

'Fore God, a proper man, and I warrant a fine workman!
Master, farewell; dame, adieu: if such a man as he cannot   60
find work, Hodge is not for you!   *Offer to go*

EYRE

Stay, my fine Hodge.

FIRK

Faith, and your foreman go, dame, you must take a journey
to seek a new journeyman! If Roger remove, Firk follows;
if Saint Hugh's bones shall not be set a-work, I may prick   65

44 *schone* ed. (shoue Q1)
47 *uplandish* outlandish, foreign
51 *enow* enough

---

46 *Saint Hugh's bones*. The shoemaker's tools: see Introduction, p. ix.
54 *butter-box* Dutchmen were thought to be prone to gluttony (cf. II. iii,
    141 and IV. iv, 42).

mine awl in the walls and go play! Fare ye well, master;
God buy, dame.

EYRE

Tarry, my fine Hodge, my brisk foreman! Stay, Firk!
Peace, pudding-broth! By the Lord of Ludgate, I love my
men as my life. Peace, you gallimaufry! Hodge, if he want   70
work I'll hire him. One of you to him; stay, he comes to us.

LACY

Goeden dach, meester, ende u vro oak.

FIRK

Nails, if I should speak after him without drinking, I should
choke! And you, friend Oak, are you of the Gentle Craft?

LACY

Yaw, yaw, ik bin den skomawker.   75

FIRK

Den skomaker, quoth a! And hark you, skomaker, have you
all your tools? A good rubbing-pin, a good stopper, a good
dresser, your four sorts of awls and your two balls of wax,
your paring-knife, your hand- and thumb-leathers, and good
Saint Hugh's bones to smooth up your work?   80

LACY

Yaw, yaw; be niet vorveard, ik hab all de dingen voour
mack skoes groot and cleane.

FIRK

Ha, ha! Good master, hire him: he'll make me laugh so
that I shall work more in mirth than I can in earnest.

EYRE

Hear ye, friend: have ye any skill in the mystery of   85
cordwainers?

---

67 *God buy* good-bye (i.e., *God-be-with-you*)
70 *gallimaufry* hotch-potch
72 *Goeden dach, meester, ende u vro oak* 'Good day, master, and to you
   mistress also'
73 *Nails* the nails of the Cross, an oath used by Firk again at II. iii, 115
75 *Yaw, yaw, ik bin den skomawker* 'Yes, yes, I am a shoemaker'
75 *bin* ed. (vin Q1)
81 *Yaw, yaw; be niet vorveard . . .* 'Yes, yes; be not afraid, I have all the
   things for making shoes large and small'

---

86 *cordwainers* see note on I. i, 218.

LACY

Ik weet niet wat yow seg; ich verstaw you niet.

FIRK

Why, thus, man. [*Mimes a shoemaker at work*] Ich verste
u niet, quoth a!

LACY

Yaw, yaw, yaw, ick can dat well doen.   90

FIRK

Yaw, yaw: he speaks yawing like a jackdaw that gapes to
be fed with cheese-curds! O, he'll give a villainous pull at
a can of double-beer! But Hodge and I have the vantage:
we must drink first, because we are the eldest journeymen.

EYRE

What is thy name?   95

LACY

Hans: Hans Meulter.

EYRE

Give me thy hand, th'art welcome! Hodge, entertain him;
Firk, bid him welcome. Come, Hans; run, wife, bid your
maids, your trullibubs, make ready my fine men's breakfasts.
To him, Hodge!   100

HODGE

Hans, th'art welcome. Use thyself friendly, for we are good
fellows; if not, thou shalt be fought with, wert thou bigger
than a giant.

FIRK

Yea, and drunk with, wert thou Gargantua! My master keeps
no cowards, I tell thee! Ho, boy, bring him an heel-block: 105
here's a new journeyman.

Enter Boy

LACY

O ich wersto you: ich moet een halve dossen cans betaelen.

87 *Ik weet niet wat yow seg* . . . 'I know not what you say; I understand you
      not'
87 *verstaw* ed. (vestaw Q1)
90 *Yaw, yaw, yaw, ick can dat wel doen* 'Yes, yes, yes, I can do that well'
99 *trullibubs* trollops
107 *O ich wersto you* . . . 'Oh, I understand you: I must pay for a half dozen
      cans. Here, boy, take this shilling, tap once [i.e., draw a round?] freely'

104 *Gargantua.* The voracious giant in Rabelais's *Gargantua and Pantagruel.*

Here, boy, nempt dis skilling, tap eens freelicke.

Exit Boy

EYRE

Quick, snipper-snapper, away! Firk, scour thy throat, thou
shalt wash it with Castilian liquor. Come, my last of the   110
fives!

Enter Boy

Give me a can: have to thee, Hans; here, Hodge; here, Firk.
Drink, you mad Greeks, and work like true Trojans, and
pray for Simon Eyre the shoemaker! Here, Hans, and
th'art welcome.   115

FIRK

Lo, dame, you would have lost a good fellow that will teach
us to laugh. This beer came hopping in well!

MARGERY

Simon, it is almost seven.

EYRE

Is't so, Dame Clapper-dudgeon? Is't seven o'clock, and my
men's breakfasts not ready? Trip and go, you soused conger,   120
away! Come, you mad Hyperboreans! Follow me, Hodge;
follow me, Hans; come after, my fine Firk: to work, to work
a while, and then to breakfast!   *Exit* [EYRE]

FIRK

Soft! Yaw, yaw, good Hans: though my master have no
more wit but to call you afore me, I am not so foolish to go   125

---

110 *last of the fives* a last for small shoes, i.e., little one

s.d. *Exit Boy ... Enter Boy*. The brevity of the interval for fetching
these drinks suggests that Dekker was more concerned to maintain un-
broken the rhythm and pace of the action than with off-stage probability.
Cf. II. iii, 76 and III. iii, 59.
119 *Clapper-dudgeon*. 'A clapperdudgeon is, in English, a beggar born'
(Dekker's *Villainies Discovered*). Steane suggests that Margery's unwelcome interruption of the drinking is being compared to the noise
of the clap-dish by which a beggar attracted attention.
121 *Hyperboreans*. The legendary race of happy folk who were supposed to
live beyond the north wind, out of reach of its blast. Eyre is fond of this
kind of jocular appellation for his workmen, cf. 'mad Greeks' and 'true
Trojans' at 113 above, and 'mad Mesopotamians', II. iii, 78, and 'mad
Cappadocians', V. i, 45.

behind you, I being the elder journeyman. *Exeunt*

[Act II, Scene i]

Hallooing within. Enter WARNER *and* HAMMON *like hunters*

HAMMON
Cousin, beat every brake, the game's not far:
This way with winged feet he fled from death,
Whilst the pursuing hounds, scenting his steps,
Find out his highway to destruction;
Besides, the miller's boy told me even now   5
He saw him take soil, and he hallooed him,
Affirming him so embossed
That long he could not hold.
WARNER   If it be so,
'Tis best we trace these meadows by Old Ford.
A noise of hunters within. Enter a Boy

HAMMON
How now, boy, where's the deer? Speak, saw'st thou him?   10
BOY
O yea, I saw him leap through a hedge, and then over a
ditch, then at my Lord Mayor's pale: over he skipped me,
and in he went me, and halloo the hunters cried, and there
boy, there boy! But there he is, 'a mine honesty.
HAMMON
Boy, God amercy; cousin, let's away: 15
I hope we shall find better sport today.
                              Exeunt

6 *take soil* ed. (take saile Q1) take to watery ground
7 *embossed* foaming at the mouth from exhaustion
12 *pale* fence

126 *the elder journeyman.* Firk has developed a concern for the niceties of
precedence, now he is no longer the bottom dog. Cf. 'But Hodge and I
have the vantage: we must drink first' at 93 above, and the processional
exit at the end of II. iii.

[Act II, Scene ii]

Hunting within. Enter ROSE *and* SYBIL

ROSE

Why, Sybil, wilt thou prove a forester?

SYBIL

Upon some, no! Forester, go by! No, faith, mistress!
The deer came running into the barn, through the orchard,
and over the pale: I wot well, I looked as pale as a new
cheese to see him, but whip! says goodman Pin-close, up   5
with his flail, and our Nick with a prong, and down he
fell, and they upon him, and I upon them. By my troth,
we had such sport! And in the end we ended him, his throat
we cut, flayed him, unhorned him, and my Lord Mayor shall
eat of him anon when he comes.   10

Horns sound within

ROSE

Hark, hark the hunters come: y'are best take heed,
They'll have a saying to you for this deed.

Enter HAMMON, WARNER, *Huntsmen and Boy*

HAMMON

God save you, fair ladies.

SYBIL   Ladies! O gross!

WARNER

Came not a buck this way?

ROSE   No, but two does.

HAMMON

And which way went they? Faith, we'll hunt at those.   15

SYBIL

At those? Upon some, no! When, can you tell?

WARNER

Upon some, ay!

SYBIL   Good Lord!

WARNER   Wounds! Then farewell.

2 *Upon some* goodness me, upon my soul (also at 16 and 17)
4 *wot* know
10 *anon* presently
17 *Wounds* God's wounds, an oath

---

13 *Ladies! O gross!* Davies cites *A Dictionary of the Canting Crew* (*c.* 1700),
which glosses 'lady' as 'a very crooked, deformed and ill shapen woman'.
Sybil deliberately misconstrues Hammon's courtly greeting.

HAMMON
  Boy, which way went he?
BOY   This way, sir, he ran.
HAMMON
  This way he ran indeed; fair Mistress Rose,
  Our game was lately in your orchard seen.   20
WARNER
  Can you advise which way he took his flight?
SYBIL
  Follow your nose: his horns will guide you right.
WARNER
  Th'art a mad wench.
SYBIL   O rich!
ROSE   Trust me, not I.
  It is not like the wild forest deer
  Would come so near to places of resort: 25
  You are deceived, he fled some other way.
WARNER
  Which way, my sugar-candy, can you show?
SYBIL
  Come up, good honeysops; upon some, no.
ROSE
  Why do you stay, and not pursue your game?
SYBIL
  I'll hold my life their hunting nags be lame.   30
HAMMON
  A deer more dear is found within this place.
ROSE
  But not the deer, sir, which you had in chase.
HAMMON
  I chased the deer, but this dear chaseth me.
ROSE
  The strangest hunting that ever I see:
  But where's your park?   *She offers to go away*
HAMMON   'Tis here: O stay!   35

25 *places of resort* frequented places
35 *park* deer-enclosure

---

31 *A deer more dear.* The rhyming stychomythia of this scene turns upon
   some well-worn Elizabethan puns relating courtship to hunting.

ROSE

Impale me, and then I will not stray.

WARNER

They wrangle, wench; we are more kind than they.

SYBIL

What kind of hart is that, dear heart, you seek?

WARNER

A hart, dear heart.

SYBIL   Who ever saw the like?

ROSE

To lose your heart, is't possible you can?   40

HAMMON

My heart is lost.

ROSE   Alack, good gentleman!

HAMMON

This poor lost heart would I wish you might find.

ROSE

You by such luck might prove your hart a hind.

HAMMON

Why, Luck had horns, so have I heard some say.

ROSE

Now, God, and't be his will, send luck into your way!   45

Enter LORD MAYOR *and Servants*

LORD MAYOR

What, Master Hammon! Welcome to Old Ford.

SYBIL

God's pittikins, hands off, sir! Here's my Lord!

LORD MAYOR

I hear you had ill luck, and lost your game.

HAMMON

'Tis true, my Lord.

LORD MAYOR   I am sorry for the same.

What gentleman is this?

HAMMON   My brother-in-law.   50

LORD MAYOR

Y'are welcome both; sith Fortune offers you

36 *Impale me* fence me in   51 *sith* since

---

39 *A hart, dear heart.* Another quibble overworked by Elizabethan love
poets. The conventional nature of this verbal game prevents us from
taking Hammon's avowals of love too seriously.

Into my hands, you shall not part from hence
Until you have refreshed your wearied limbs.
Go, Sybil, cover the board; you shall be guest
To no good cheer, but even a hunter's feast.   55

HAMMON

I thank your Lordship. [*Aside*] Cousin, on my life,
For our lost venison I shall find a wife!

Exeunt [*all except* LORD MAYOR]

LORD MAYOR

In, gentlemen: I'll not be absent long.
This Hammon is a proper gentleman:
A citizen by birth, fairly allied.   60
How fit an husband were he for my girl!
Well, I will in, and do the best I can,
To match my daughter to this gentleman.

Exit [LORD MAYOR]

[Act II, Scene iii]

Enter LACY, *Skipper,* HODGE *and* FIRK

SKIPPER

Ick sal yow wat seggen, Hans: dis skip dat comen from
Candy is al wol, by Got's sacrament, van sugar, civet,
almonds, cambric, end alle dingen, towsand towsand ding.
Nempt it, Hans, nempt it vor u meester; daer be de bils
van laden. Your meester Simon Eyre sal hae good copen: 5
wat seggen yow, Hans?

FIRK

Wat seggen de reggen de copen, slopen? Laugh, Hodge,
laugh!

LACY

Mine liever broder Firk, bringt Meester Eyre tot den signe

1 *Ick sal yow wat seggen* . . . 'I shall tell you what, Hans: this ship that
comes from Candia [i.e., Crete] is all full, by God's sacrament, of sugar,
civet, almonds, cambric, and all things, a thousand thousand things.
Take it, Hans, take it for your master; there be the bills of lading. Your
master Simon Eyre will have a good bargain: what say you, Hans?'
2 *civet* perfume
9 *Mine liever broder Firk* . . . 'My dear brother Firk, bring Master Eyre to
the sign of the Swan: there shall you find this skipper and me. What say
you, brother Firk? Do it, Hodge. Come, skipper'

un Swannekin: daer sal yow finde dis skipper end me. Wat   10
seggen yow, broder Firk? Doot it, Hodge. Come, skipper.

Exeunt [LACY *and Skipper*]

FIRK

Bring him, quoth you? Here's no knavery, to bring my
master to buy a ship worth the lading of two or three
hundred thousand pounds! Alas, that's nothing, a trifle, a
bauble, Hodge!   15

HODGE

The truth is, Firk, that the merchant owner of the ship
dares not show his head, and therefore this skipper that
deals for him, for the love he bears to Hans, offers my
master Eyre a bargain in the commodities. He shall have a
reasonable day of payment; he may sell the wares by that   20
time, and be an huge gainer himself.

FIRK

Yea, but can my fellow Hans lend my master twenty
porpentines as an earnest penny?

HODGE

Portuguese, thou would'st say; here they be, Firk: hark,
they jingle in my pocket like Saint Mary Overy's bells.   25

Enter EYRE, MARGERY [*and a Boy*]

FIRK

Mum: here comes my dame and my master. She'll scold,
on my life, for loitering this Monday; but all's one, let them
all say what they can, Monday's our holiday.

---

15 *bauble* toy, trifle
23 *porpentines* porcupines
23 *earnest penny* down-payment
24 *Portuguese* see note on I. i, 90
25 *Overy's* ed. (Queries Q1)

---

20 *a reasonable day of payment.* Fair time in which to raise the money. As
Davies suggests, Eyre is being given the opportunity to benefit from
what is either a shady business or an Elizabethan trade policy that
discriminated against foreigners. See Introduction, pp. xv–xvi.
24 *Portuguese.* The twenty portuguese which Lacy lends to Eyre are
presumably those he was given by his uncle Lincoln at I. i, 90. Lacy
gave the other ten to Askew at I. i, 107.
25 *Saint Mary Overy.* The church, now the Cathedral of St Saviour, in
Southwark.

MARGERY

You sing, Sir Sauce, but I beshrew your heart;
I fear for this your singing we shall smart.   30

FIRK

Smart for me, dame? Why, dame, why?

HODGE

Master, I hope you'll not suffer my dame to take down
your journeymen.

FIRK

If she take me down, I'll take her up! Yea, and take her
down too, a button-hole lower!   35

EYRE

Peace, Firk! Not I, Hodge! By the life of Pharaoh, by the
Lord of Ludgate, by this beard, every hair whereof I value
at a king's ransom, she shall not meddle with you. Peace,
you bombast-cotton-candle-quean! Away, Queen of Clubs!
Quarrel not with me and my men, with me and my fine Firk: 40
I'll firk you if you do.

MARGERY

Yea, yea, man, you may use me as you please; but let that
pass.

EYRE

Let it pass? Let it vanish away! Peace: am I not Simon
Eyre? Are not these my brave men? Brave shocmakers, all   45
gentleman of the Gentle Craft? Prince am I none, yet am I
nobly born, as being the sole son of a shoemaker. Away,
rubbish! Vanish, melt like kitchen-stuff!

MARGERY

Yea, yea, 'tis well: I must be called rubbish, kitchen-stuff,
for a sort of knaves.   50

---

29 *beshrew* curse
32 *take down* humiliate
47 *sole* (a pun)

---

39 *Queen of Clubs.* Troublemaker (with a pun on the playing card, cf.
V. ii, 30).
46 *Prince am I none, yet am I nobly born.* One of the stories in Deloney's
The Gentle Craft tells 'how the proverb first grew: "A Shoemaker's son
is a prince born"'. W. F. McNeir suggested that Dekker's wording of
Eyre's catch-phrase derives from a line in Greene's *Orlando Furioso*, 'I
am no king, yet am I princely born'.

FIRK

Nay, dame, you shall not weep and wail in woe for me.
Master, I'll stay no longer: here's a venentory of my shop-
tools. Adieu, master; Hodge, farewell.

HODGE

Nay, stay, Firk, thou shalt not go alone.

MARGERY

I pray, let them go; there be mo maids than Mawkin, more   55
men than Hodge, and more fools than Firk.

FIRK

Fools? Nails, if I tarry now, I would my guts might be
turned to shoethread!

HODGE

And if I stay, I pray God I may be turned to a Turk, and
set in Finsbury for boys to shoot at! Come, Firk.   60

EYRE

Stay, my fine knaves, you arms of my trade, you pillars of
my profession. What, shall a tittle-tattle's words make you
forsake Simon Eyre? Avaunt, kitchen-stuff! Rip, you brown-
bread tannikin! Out of my sight, move me not! Have not I
ta'en you from selling tripes in Eastcheap, and set you in   65
my shop, and made you hail-fellow with Simon Eyre the
shoemaker? And now do you deal thus with my journeymen?
Look, you powder-beef-quean, on the face of Hodge:
here's a face for a lord!

FIRK

And here's a face for any lady in Christendom.   70

EYRE

[to Boy] Rip, you chitterling; avaunt, boy: bid the tapster
of the Boar's Head fill me a dozen cans of beer for my
journeymen.

FIRK

A dozen cans? O brave! Hodge, now I'll stay.

52 *venentory* Firk's corruption of 'inventory'
55 *mo* more *Mawkin* a slattern (the phrase is proverbial)
64 *tannikin* diminutive form of Anna; cf. 'plain Jane'
71 *chitterling* the edible small-guts of a pig, i.e., 'small fry'

72 *Boar's Head.* There were several taverns of this name in Elizabethan
London, including that in Eastcheap celebrated in Shakespeare's
Henry IV.

EYRE

[*Aside to Boy*] And the knave fills any more than two, he   75
pays for them. [*Exit Boy*] A dozen cans of beer for my
journeymen!

      [*Enter Boy with two cans; puts them down and exit*]

Hear you, mad Mesopotamians! Wash your livers with this
liquor. Where be the odd ten? No more, Madge, no more.
Well said: drink and to work! What work dost thou, Hodge,   80
what work?

HODGE

I am making a pair of shoes for my Lord Mayor's daughter,
Mistress Rose.

FIRK

And I a pair of shoes for Sybil, my Lord's maid: I deal
with her.   85

EYRE

Sybil? Fie, defile not thy fine workmanly fingers with the
feet of kitchen-stuff and basting-ladles! Ladies of the court,
fine ladies, my lads, commit their feet to our apparelling:
put gross work to Hans. Yark and seam, yark and seam!

FIRK

For yarking and seaming let me alone, and I come to't.   90

HODGE

Well, master, all this is from the bias: do you remember
the ship my fellow Hans told you of? The skipper and he
are both drinking at the Swan. Here be the portuguese to
give earnest: if you go through with it, you cannot choose
but be a lord at least.   95

FIRK

Nay, dame, if my master prove not a lord, and you a lady,
hang me.

89 *Yark* pull the stitches tight
91 *from the bias* off the point (cf. note to I. i, 85)
93 *earnest* down-payment (cf. note to II. iii, 24)

---

s.d. [*Exit Boy*] . . . [*Enter Boy*]. Q1 gives no stage directions, but the
Boy cannot leave before Eyre's aside to him that only two cans will be
paid for, and he must return before Eyre slily asks after 'the odd ten'.
See note to I. iv, 108.
78 *Mesopotamians.* See note to I. iv, 121. Presumably a quibble on 'mess'
and 'pot' is involved.

MARGERY

Yea, like enough, if you may loiter and tipple thus.

FIRK

Tipple, dame? No, we have been bargaining with Skellum-
Skanderbag-can-you-Dutch-spreaken for a ship of silk   100
Cyprus, lady with sugar-candy.

Enter the Boy with a velvet coat and an alderman's gown.
EYRE *puts it on*

EYRE

Peace, Firk; silence, tittle-tattle. Hodge, I'll go through
with it. Here's a seal-ring, and I have sent for a guarded
gown and a damask cassock—see where it comes! Look
here, Maggy: help me, Firk; apparel me, Hodge. Silk and   105
satin, you mad Philistines, silk and satin!

FIRK

Ha, ha! My master will be as proud as a dog in a doublet,
all in beaten damask and velvet.

EYRE

Softly, Firk, for rearing of the nap, and wearing threadbare
my garments. How dost like me, Firk? How do I look, my   110
fine Hodge?

HODGE

Why, now you look like yourself, master! I warrant you,
there's few in the city, but will give you the wall, and come
upon you with the right-worshipful!

FIRK

Nails, my master looks like a threadbare cloak new turned   115
and dressed. Lord, Lord, to see what good raiment doth!
Dame, dame, are you not enamoured?

---

103 *guarded* embroidered round the edges
113 *give you the wall* allow you to pass on the inside

---

99 *Skellum-Skanderbag*. As Davies notes, 'Skellum' is probably from the
  German 'schelm' ('scoundrel'), while 'Skanderbag' is a corruption of
  'Iskander Bey', the Turkish name for a fifteenth-century Albanian
  patriot, George Castriot. Here Firk's xenophobic humour equates
  'foreigner' and 'rogue' by alliterative association: 'Skanderbag' presumably suggests 'scandal', to echo the word for 'scoundrel'.
100 *silk Cyprus . . . sugar-candy*. Either a confusion or an expansion of the
  merchandise as described by the Skipper at II. iii, 1. 'Silk Cyprus' is
  black lawn.

EYRE

How sayest thou, Maggy? Am I not brisk? Am I not fine?

MARGERY

Fine? By my troth, sweetheart, very fine! By my troth, I
never liked thee so well in my life, sweetheart! But let that   120
pass: I warrant there be many women in the city have not
such handsome husbands, but only for their apparel: but let
that pass too.

Enter LACY *and Skipper*

LACY

Godden day, mester, dis be de skipper dat heb de skip van
marchandice. De commodity ben good: nempt it, master,   125
nempt it.

EYRE

God amercy, Hans; welcome, skipper. Where lies this ship
of merchandise?

SKIPPER

De skip ben in revere; dor be van sugar, civet, almonds,
cambric, and a towsand towsand tings! Gotz sacrament,   130
nempt it, master: yo sal heb good copen.

FIRK

To him, master, O sweet master! O sweet wares: prunes,
almonds, sugar-candy, carrot-roots, turnips! O brave
fatting meat! Let not a man buy a nutmeg but yourself!

EYRE

Peace, Firk. Come, skipper, I'll go aboard with you. Hans,   135
have you made him drink?

SKIPPER

Yaw, yaw, ic heb veale ge drunck.

---

118 *brisk* smart
   s.d. LACY ed. (Hans Q1 and for the remainder of the play in stage directions and speech prefixes)
124 *Godden day, mester* . . . 'Good day, master, this is the skipper that has
   the ship of merchandise. The commodity is good: take it, master, take it'
129 *De skip ben in revere* . . . ed. (rovere Q1): 'The ship is in the river; there
   is sugar, civet, almonds, cambric, and a thousand thousand things!
   God's sacrament, take it, master: you shall have a good bargain'
135 *aboard* ed. (abroade Q1)
137 *Yaw, yaw, ic heb veale ge drunck* 'Yes, yes, I have drunk much'

C

EYRE

Come, Hans, follow me. Skipper, thou shalt have my
countenance in the city.

Exeunt [EYRE, LACY *and Skipper*]

FIRK

Yaw heb veale ge drunck, quoth a. They may well be called   140
butter-boxes, when they drink fat veal and thick beer too!
But come, dame, I hope you'll chide us no more.

MARGERY

No, faith, Firk; no, perdy, Hodge. I do feel honour creep
upon me, and which is more, a certain rising in my flesh:
but let that pass.   145

FIRK

Rising in your flesh do you feel, say you? Ay, you may be
with child, but why should not my master feel a rising in
his flesh, having a gown and a gold ring on? But you are
such a shrew, you'll soon pull him down.

MARGERY

Ha, ha! Prithee, peace: thou mak'st my worship laugh, but   150
that pass. Come, I'll go in. Hodge, prithee go before me,
Firk follow me.

FIRK

Firk doth follow; Hodge, pass out in state.

Exeunt

[Act II, Scene iv]

Enter LINCOLN *and* DODGER

LINCOLN

How now, good Dodger, what's the news in France?

DODGER

My Lord, upon the eighteenth day of May,
The French and English were prepared to fight;
Each side with eager fury gave the sign

139 *countenance* support, protection
141 *butter-boxes* see note to I. iv, 54
141 *veal* Firk mistakes the skipper's 'veale'

147 *rising in his flesh.* The gown and the gold ring befit a bridegroom as well
as an alderman.

Of a most hot encounter; five long hours   5
Both armies fought together; at the length,
The lot of victory fell on our sides.
Twelve thousand of the Frenchmen that day died,
Four thousand English, and no man of name
But Captain Hyam and young Ardington.   10

LINCOLN
Two gallant gentlemen: I knew them well.
But, Dodger, prithee tell me, in this fight
How did my cousin Lacy bear himself?

DODGER
My Lord, your cousin Lacy was not there.

LINCOLN
Not there?

DODGER   No, my good Lord.

LINCOLN   Sure thou mistakest!   15
I saw him shipped, and a thousand eyes beside
Were witnesses of the farewells which he gave,
When I with weeping eyes bid him adieu.
Dodger, take heed!

DODGER   My Lord, I am advised
That what I spake is true; to prove it so,   20
His cousin Askew that supplied his place
Sent me for him from France, that secretly
He might convey himself hither.

LINCOLN   Is't even so?
Dares he so carelessly venture his life
Upon the indignation of a King?   25
Hath he despised my love, and spurned those favours
Which I with prodigal hand poured on his head?
He shall repent his rashness with his soul;
Since of my love he makes no estimate,
I'll make him wish he had not known my hate!   30
Thou hast no other news?

DODGER   None else, my Lord.

LINCOLN
None worse I know thou hast. Procure the King
To crown his giddy brows with ample honours,

---

11 *Two gallant gentlemen: I knew them well* Q1 gives this as the last line of
Dodger's speech

Send him chief colonel, and all my hope
Thus to be dashed? But 'tis in vain to grieve: 35
One evil cannot a worse relieve.
Upon my life, I have found out his plot!
That old dog Love that fawned upon him so,
Love to that puling girl, his fair-cheeked Rose,
The Lord Mayor's daughter, hath distracted him;   40
And in the fire of that love's lunacy
Hath he burnt up himself, consumed his credit,
Lost the King's love, yea and I fear, his life,
Only to get a wanton to his wife!
Dodger, it is so.

DODGER   I fear so, my good Lord.   45

LINCOLN
It is so—nay, sure, it cannot be!
I am at my wits' end. Dodger!

DODGER   Yea, my Lord?

LINCOLN
Thou art acquainted with my nephew's haunts:
Spend this gold for thy pains, go seek him out.
Watch at my Lord Mayor's: there, if he live,   50
Dodger, thou shalt be sure to meet with him:
Prithee, be diligent. Lacy, thy name
Lived once in honour, now dead in shame!
Be circumspect.

                                        Exit [LINCOLN]

DODGER   I warrant you, my Lord.

                                        Exit [DODGER]

[Act III, Scene i]

Enter LORD MAYOR *and* MASTER SCOTT

LORD MAYOR
Good Master Scott, I have been bold with you,
To be a witness to a wedding-knot
Betwixt young Master Hammon and my daughter—
O stand aside, see where the lovers come.

Enter HAMMON *and* ROSE

ROSE

    Can it be possible you love me so?   5
    No, no, within those eyeballs I espy
    Apparent likelihoods of flattery.
    Pray now, let go my hand.

HAMMON   Sweet Mistress Rose,

    Misconstrue not my words, nor misconceive
    Of my affection, whose devoted soul   10
    Swears that I love thee dearer than my heart.

ROSE

    As dear as your own heart? I judge it right:
    Men love their hearts best when th'are out of sight.

HAMMON

    I love you, by this hand.

ROSE   Yet hands off now:

    If flesh be frail, how weak and frail's your vow!   15

HAMMON

    Then by my life I swear.

ROSE   Then do not brawl:

    One quarrel loseth wife and life and all.
    Is not your meaning thus?

HAMMON   In faith, you jest.

ROSE

    Love loves to sport: therefore leave love y'are best.

LORD MAYOR

    [*Aside*] What, square they, Master Scott?

SCOTT   [*Aside*] Sir, never doubt.   20

    Lovers are quickly in, and quickly out.

HAMMON

    Sweet Rose, be not so strange in fancying me;
    Nay, never turn aside, shun not my sight.
    I am not grown so fond, to found my love
    On any that shall quit it with disdain: 25
    If you will love me, so; if not, farewell.

LORD MAYOR

    Why, how now, lovers, are you both agreed?

20 *square* quarrel
22 *strange* distant, aloof
24 *fond* foolish
25 *quit* requite

HAMMON
　　Yes, faith, my Lord.
LORD MAYOR　　　　　'Tis well, give me your hand;
　　Give me yours, daughter. How now, both pull back?
　　What means this, girl?
ROSE　　　　　　　　I mean to live a maid.　　　　　　30
HAMMON
　　[*Aside*] But not to die one: pause ere that be said!
LORD MAYOR
　　Will you still cross me? Still be obstinate?
HAMMON
　　Nay, chide her not, my Lord, for doing well!
　　If she can live an happy virgin's life,
　　'Tis far more blessed than to be a wife.　　　　　　35
ROSE
　　Say, sir, I cannot: I have made a vow,
　　Whoever be my husband, 'tis not you.
LORD MAYOR
　　Your tongue is quick; but, Master Hammon, know
　　I bade you welcome to another end.
HAMMON
　　What, would you have me pule, and pine, and pray,　　40
　　With lovely lady, mistress of my heart,
　　Pardon your servant, and the rhymer play,
　　Railing on Cupid and his tyrant's dart?
　　Or shall I undertake some martial spoil,
　　Wearing your glove at tourney and at tilt,　　　　　45
　　And tell how many gallants I unhorsed?
　　Sweet, will this pleasure you?
ROSE　　　　　　　　Yea, when wilt thou begin?
　　What, love-rhymes, man? Fie on that deadly sin!
LORD MAYOR
　　If you will have her, I'll make her agree.
HAMMON
　　Enforced love is worse than hate to me.　　　　　　50

39 *end* purpose, outcome
40 *pule* whine　　　　　　　　　44 *spoil* conquest

---

40 *What, would you have me pule, and pine, and pray.* Hammon retrieves
　　some dignity in defeat by refusing to adopt the poses of the con-
　　ventional courtly lover.

There is a wench keeps shop in the Old 'Change:
To her will I; it is not wealth I seek;
I have enough, and will prefer her love
Before the world. My good Lord Mayor, adieu:
Old love for me, I have no luck with new.   55

                              Exit [HAMMON]

LORD MAYOR
Now, mammet, you have well behaved yourself!
But you shall curse your coyness, if I live.
Who's within, there! See you convey your mistress
Straight to th'Old Ford. I'll keep you straight enough!
'Fore God, I would have sworn the puling girl   60
Would willingly accepted Hammon's love;
But banish him my thoughts: go, minion, in!   *Exit* ROSE
Now tell me, Master Scott, would you have thought
That Master Simon Eyre the shoemaker
Had been of wealth to buy such merchandise?   65
SCOTT
'Twas well, my Lord, your Honour and myself
Grew partners with him, for your bills of lading
Show that Eyre's gains in one commodity
Rise at the least to full three thousand pound,
Beside like gain in other merchandise.   70
LORD MAYOR
Well, he shall spend some of his thousands now,
For I have sent for him to the Guildhall.

                         Enter EYRE

See where he comes. Good morrow, Master Eyre.
EYRE
Poor Simon Eyre, my Lord, your shoemaker.
LORD MAYOR
Well, well, it likes yourself to term you so.   75

                        Enter DODGER

56 *mammet* doll, little miss

---

51 *the Old 'Change.* The Old Exchange, at the west end of St Paul's.
59 *Old Ford.* A village 3½ miles north-east of St Paul's where the road from
   Essex to London formerly forded the River Lea.
63 *Now tell me, Master Scott* ... A very abrupt and awkward shift of
   subject. Eyre's brief appearance hardly seems dramatically justified.

Now, Master Dodger, what's the news with you?

DODGER
I'd gladly speak in private to your Honour.

LORD MAYOR
You shall, you shall. Master Eyre and Master Scott,
I have some business with this gentleman:
I pray, let me entreat you to walk before   80
To the Guildhall; I'll follow presently.
Master Eyre, I hope ere noon to call you Sheriff.

EYRE
I would not care, my Lord, if you might call me King of
Spain. Come, Master Scott.

Exeunt [EYRE *and* SCOTT]

LORD MAYOR
Now, Master Dodger, what's the news you bring?   85

DODGER
The Earl of Lincoln by me greets your Lordship,
And earnestly requests you, if you can,
Inform him where his nephew Lacy keeps.

LORD MAYOR
Is not his nephew Lacy now in France?

DODGER
No, I assure your Lordship, but disguised   90
Lurks here in London.

LORD MAYOR   London? Is't even so?
It may be, but upon my faith and soul,
I know not where he lives, or whether he lives.
So tell my Lord of Lincoln. Lurk in London?
Well, Master Dodger, you perhaps may start him;   95
Be but the means to rid him into France,
I'll give you a dozen angels for your pains:
So much I love his Honour, hate his nephew,
And prithee so inform thy lord from me.

DODGER
I take my leave.

LORD MAYOR   Farewell, Master Dodger.   100

Exit DODGER

Lacy in London! I dare pawn my life,

95 *start him* flush him out
97 *angels* a gold coin worth about 50p

My daughter knows thereof, and for that cause
Denied young Master Hammon in his love.
Well, I am glad I sent her to Old Ford.
God's Lord, 'tis late! To Guildhall I must hie: 105
I know my brethren stay my company.

Exit

[Act III, Scene ii]

Enter FIRK, MARGERY, LACY, *and* HODGE

MARGERY
Thou goest too fast for me, Roger. O Firk!
FIRK
Ay, forsooth.
MARGERY
I pray thee run—do you hear?—run to Guildhall and learn
if my husband Master Eyre will take that worshipful voca-
tion of Master Sheriff upon him. Hie thee, good Firk!   5
FIRK
Take it? Well, I go. And he should not take it, Firk swears
to forswear him. Yes, forsooth, I go to Guildhall.
MARGERY
Nay, when? Thou art too compendious and tedious.
FIRK
O rare! Your Excellence is full of eloquence! [*Aside*] How
like a new cart-wheel my dame speaks, and she looks like an   10
old musty ale-bottle going to scalding.
MARGERY
Nay, when? Thou wilt make me melancholy.
FIRK
God forbid your Worship should fall into that humour.
I run!

Exit [FIRK]

MARGERY
Let me see now, Roger and Hans.   15

---

1 *O Firk* ed. (om. Q1)
7 *forswear him* leave him
8 *compendious* succinct, brief (Margery means the opposite)

HODGE

Ay, forsooth, dame—mistress, I should say, but the old
term so sticks to the roof of my mouth, I can hardly lick
it off.

MARGERY

Even what thou wilt, good Roger: dame is a fair name for
any honest Christian, but let that pass. How dost thou, Hans?   20

LACY

Mee tanck you, vro.

MARGERY

Well, Hans and Roger, you see God hath blest your master,
and, perdy, if ever he comes to be Master Sheriff of London,
as we are all mortal, you shall see I will have some odd
thing or other in a corner for you: I will not be your back-   25
friend, but let that pass. Hans, pray thee tie my shoe.

LACY

Yaw, ic sal, vro.

MARGERY

Roger, thou knowest the length of my foot: as it is none of
the biggest, so I thank God it is handsome enough. Prithee,
let me have a pair of shoes made, cork, good Roger, wooden   30
heel too.

HODGE

You shall.

MARGERY

Art thou acquainted with never a farthingale-maker, nor
a French-hood maker? I must enlarge my bum, ha, ha!
How shall I look in a hood, I wonder? Perdy, oddly, I think.   35

HODGE

[*Aside*] As a cat out of a pillory—very well, I warrant you,
mistress.

21 *Mee tanck you, vro* 'I thank you, mistress'
25 *I will not be your back-friend* I will not let you down (with another, un-
    intentional, bawdy sense)
27 *Yaw, ic sal, vro* 'Yes, I will, mistress'
35 *Perdy* bless my soul (from 'par dieu')
36 s.p. HODGE ed. (Roger Q1 from here to the end of the scene)

---

33 *farthingale-maker*. A farthingale was a hooped underskirt to make the
    lower part of the dress project out from the waist down.
34 *French-hood*. A hood with flaps on either side of the head (hence
    Hodge's reference to the pillory).

MARGERY

Indeed, all flesh is grass; and Roger, canst thou tell where
I may buy a good hair?

HODGE

Yes, forsooth, at the poulterers in Gracious Street.   40

MARGERY

Thou art an ungracious wag, perdy! I mean a false hair
for my periwig.

HODGE

Why, mistress, the next time I cut my beard you shall have
the shavings of it, but they are all true hairs.

MARGERY

It is very hot: I must get me a fan, or else a mask.   45

HODGE

[*Aside*] So you had need, to hide your wicked face!

MARGERY

Fie upon it, how costly this world's calling is, perdy! But
that it is one of the wonderful works of God, I would not
deal with it. Is not Firk come yet? Hans, be not so sad:
let it pass and vanish, as my husband's Worship says.   50

LACY

Ick bin vrolicke, lot see yow soo.

HODGE

Mistress, will you drink a pipe of tobacco?

MARGERY

O fie upon it, Roger, perdy! These filthy tobacco-pipes are
the most idle slavering baubles that ever I felt. Out upon
it, God bless us, men look not like men that use them!   55

Enter RALPH *being lame*

HODGE

What, fellow Ralph? Mistress, look here: Jane's husband!
Why, how now, lame? Hans, make much of him: he's a
brother of our trade, a good workman, and a tall soldier.

46 *wicked* ugly
51 *Ick bin vrolicke, lot see yow soo* 'I am merry, let me see you so'
58 *tall* brave

40 *Gracious Street.* Alternatively Gracechurch Street, leading northwards
from London Bridge.
52 *drink a pipe of tobacco.* The usual Elizabethan expression.

LACY
You be welcome, broder.

MARGERY
Perdy, I knew him not. How dost thou, good Ralph? I am   60
glad to see thee well.

RALPH
I would God you saw me, dame, as well
As when I went from London into France.

MARGERY
Trust me, I am sorry, Ralph, to see thee impotent. Lord,
how the wars have made him sunburnt! The left leg is not   65
well: 'twas a fair gift of God the infirmity took not hold a
little higher, considering thou camest from France, but let
that pass.

RALPH
I am glad to see you well, and I rejoice
To hear that God hath blest my master so   70
Since my departure.

MARGERY
Yea, truly, Ralph, but let that pass.

HODGE
And, sirrah Ralph, what news, what news in France?

RALPH
Tell me, good Roger, first, what news in England?
How does my Jane? When didst thou see my wife?   75
Where lives my poor heart? She'll be poor indeed,
Now I want limbs to get whereon to feed.

HODGE
Limbs? Hast thou not hands, man? Thou shalt never see
a shoemaker want bread, though he have but three fingers
on a hand.   80

RALPH
Yet all this while I hear not of my Jane!

---

64 *impotent* maimed

---

62. *I would God you saw me, dame, as well.* Ralph speaks in blank verse, as
before.
66 *a little higher.* An allusion to venereal disease, known as 'the French
disease'. Not in the best of taste, but typical of Margery's tactlessness
(assuming it to be intentional).

MARGERY

O Ralph, your wife! Perdy, we know not what's become of
her. She was here a while, and because she was married
grew more stately than became her: I checked her, and so
forth: away she flung, never returned, nor said bye nor   85
bah—and Ralph, you know: ka me, ka thee. And so as I
tell ye. Roger, is not Firk come yet?

HODGE

No, forsooth.

MARGERY

And so indeed we heard not of her; but I hear she lives in
London, but let that pass. If she had wanted, she might   90
have opened her case to me or my husband, or to any of
my men. I am sure there's not any of them, perdy, but
would have done her good to his power. Hans, look if Firk
be come.

LACY

Yaw, ic sal, vro.   95

Exit LACY

MARGERY

And so, as I said: but Ralph, why dost thou weep? Thou
knowest that naked we came out of our mother's womb, and
naked we must return, and therefore thank God for all
things.

HODGE

No, faith, Jane is a stranger here. But Ralph, pull up a   100
good heart: I know thou hast one. Thy wife, man, is in
London: one told me he saw her a while ago, very brave
and neat. We'll ferret her out, and London hold her.

MARGERY

Alas, poor, soul, he's overcome with sorrow. He does but
as I do, weep for the loss of any good thing. But Ralph,   105
get thee in: call for some meat and drink. Thou shalt find
me worshipful towards thee.

84 *stately* ladylike
86 *ka me, ka thee* proverbial expression of mutual help
95 *Yaw, ic sal, vro* 'Yes, I shall, mistress'
95 *ic* ed. (it Q1)   102 *brave* well-dressed   103 *and* if

107 *worshipful.* As bountiful as becomes his Worship the Sheriff's lady.
Margery has not yet learned to use the new title properly.

RALPH

   I thank you, dame; since I want limbs and lands,
   I'll to God, my good friends, and to these my hands.

                        Exit [RALPH]

        Enter LACY *and* FIRK, *running*

FIRK

   Run, good Hans! O Hodge! O mistress! Hodge, heave up   110
thine ears; mistress, smug up your looks, on with your
best apparel! My master is chosen, my master is called—
nay, condemned—by the cry of the country to be Sheriff
of the city, for this famous year now to come, and time
now being. A great many men in black gowns were asked   115
for their voices and their hands, and my master had all their
fists about his ears presently, and they cried Ay, Ay, Ay, Ay,
and so I came away.
   Wherefore, without all other grieve,
   I do salute you, Mistress Shrieve.   120

LACY

   Yaw, my mester is de groot man, de shrieve.

HODGE

   Did not I tell you, mistress? Now I may boldly say good
morrow to your Worship.

MARGERY

   Good morrow, good Roger; I thank you, my good people
all. Firk, hold up thy hand, here's a threepenny-piece for   125
thy tidings.

FIRK

   'Tis but three halfpence, I think. Yes, 'tis threepence, I
smell the rose.

HODGE

   But, mistress, be ruled by me and do not speak so pulingly.

111 *smug up* smarten up
112 *condemned* Firk's version of 'confirmed', perhaps
120 *Shrieve* Sheriff
121 *Yaw, my mester is de groot man, de shrieve* 'Yes, my master is the great man, the Sheriff'
129 *pulingly* mincingly (cf. 'mealy mouth', I. i, 130)

---

128 *I smell the rose.* The threepenny-piece bore a profile of Elizabeth wearing a rose behind her ear. Since this was the coin distributed as maundy-money, Margery's largesse here is truly regal, befitting her new sense of status.

FIRK

'Tis her Worship speaks so, and not she. No, faith, mistress,   130
speak me in the old key: to it, Firk; there, good Firk; ply
your business, Hodge; Hodge—with a full mouth—I'll fill
your bellies with good cheer 'till they cry twang.

Enter SIMON EYRE *wearing a gold chain*

LACY

See, myn liever broder, heer compt my meester.

MARGERY

Welcome home, Master Shrieve, I pray God continue you   135
in health and wealth.

EYRE

See here, my Maggy, a chain, a gold chain for Simon Eyre!
I shall make thee a lady: here's a French hood for thee.
On with it, on with it, dress thy brows with this flap of a
shoulder of mutton to make thee look lovely. Where be my   140
fine men? Roger, I'll make over my shop and tools to thee;
Firk, thou shalt be the foreman; Hans, thou shalt have an
hundred for twenty. Be as mad knaves as your master
Simon Eyre hath been, and you shall live to be Sheriffs of
London! How dost thou like me, Margery? Prince am I   145
none, yet am I princely born. Firk, Hodge, and Hans!

ALL THREE

Ay, forsooth, what says your Worship, Mistress Sheriff?

EYRE

Worship and honour, you Babylonian knaves, for the Gentle
Craft! But I forget myself: I am bidden by my Lord
Mayor to dinner to Old Ford. He's gone before; I must   150
after. Come, Madge, on with your trinkets! Now, my true
Trojans, my fine Firk, my dapper Hodge, my honest Hans:
some device, some odd crotchets, some morris or suchlike,
for the honour of the gentle shoemakers. Meet me at Old
Ford: you know my mind.   155

---

134 *See, myn liever broder, heer compt my meester* 'See, my dear brothers, here
comes my master'
149 *forget* ed. (forgot Q1)   153 *crotchets* pranks

---

139 *flap of a shoulder of mutton.* The flap of the French hood (see note to 34
above), perhaps from a resemblance in shape.
143 *an hundred for twenty.* For the twenty portuguese lent to Eyre by Hans.
153 *morris.* A festive dance in costume.

Come, Madge, away;
Shut up the shop, knaves, and make holiday.

Exeunt [EYRE *and* MARGERY]

FIRK

O rare! O brave! Come, Hodge; follow me, Hans;
We'll be with them for a morris-dance!

Exeunt [FIRK, HODGE, *and* LACY]

[Act III, Scene iii]

Enter LORD MAYOR, EYRE, MARGERY *in a French hood,*
[ROSE,] SYBIL *and other Servants*

LORD MAYOR

Trust me, you are as welcome to Old Ford
As I myself.

MARGERY

Truly, I thank your Lordship.

LORD MAYOR

Would our bad cheer were worth the thanks you give.

EYRE

Good cheer, my Lord Mayor, fine cheer; a fine house, fine   5
walls, all fine and neat.

LORD MAYOR

Now, by my troth, I'll tell thee, Master Eyre,
It does me good, and all my brethren,
That such a madcap fellow as thyself
Is entered into our society.   10

MARGERY

Ay, but, my Lord, he must learn now to put on gravity.

EYRE

Peace, Maggy, a fig for gravity! When I go to Guildhall in
my scarlet gown, I'll look as demurely as a saint, and speak
as gravely as a justice of peace; but now I am here at Old
Ford, at my good Lord Mayor's house, let it go by, vanish,   15
Maggy. I'll be merry: away with flip-flap, these fooleries,
these gulleries! What, honey? Prince am I none, yet am I
princely born. What says my Lord Mayor?

s.d. MARGERY *in a French hood*, [ROSE,] SYBIL . . . ed. (wife, Sibill in a
French hood Q1)

LORD MAYOR

Ha, ha, ha! I had rather than a thousand pound
I had an heart but half so light as yours.   20

EYRE

Why, what should I do, my Lord? A pound of care pays
not a dram of debt. Hum, let's be merry whiles we are
young: old age, sack and sugar, will steal upon us ere we
be aware.

LORD MAYOR

It's well done. Mistress Eyre, pray give good counsel to my   25
daughter.

MARGERY

I hope Mistress Rose will have the grace to take nothing
that's bad.

LORD MAYOR

Pray God she do, for, i'faith, Mistress Eyre,
I would bestow upon that peevish girl   30
A thousand marks more than I mean to give her,
Upon condition she'd be ruled by me.
The ape still crosseth me: there came of late
A proper gentlemen of fair revenues,
Whom gladly I would call son-in-law,   35
But my fine cockney would have none of him.
You'll prove a coxcomb for it, ere you die:
A courtier, or no man, must please your eye.

EYRE

Be ruled, sweet Rose. Th'art ripe for a man: marry not with
a boy that has no more hair on his face than thou hast on thy   40
cheeks. A courtier? Wash, go by, stand not upon pishery-
pashery! Those silken fellows are but painted images; outsides, outsides, Rose: their inner linings are torn. No, my
fine mouse, marry me with a gentleman grocer, like my
Lord Mayor your father. A grocer is a sweet trade, plums,   45
plums! Had I a son or daughter should marry out of the
generation and blood of the shoemakers, he should pack.

36 *my fine cockney* spoiled child   37 *coxcomb* fool
41 *Wash* no more meaning than an expletive, like 'pshaw'
47 *he should pack* he'd have to go

21 *A pound of care pays not a dram of debt.* Proverbial expression included
in *The Oxford Dictionary of English Proverbs.*

What? The Gentle Trade is a living for a man through
Europe, through the world!

     A noise within of a tabor and a pipe

LORD MAYOR
    What noise is this?   50
EYRE
    O my Lord Mayor, a crew of good fellows that for love to
    your honour are come hither with a morris-dance. Come in,
    my Mesopotamians, cheerily!
       Enter HODGE, LACY, RALPH, FIRK, *and other Shoemakers,*
       in a morris. After a little dancing the LORD MAYOR *speaks*
LORD MAYOR
    Master Eyre, are all these shoemakers?
EYRE
    All cordwainers, my good Lord Mayor.   55
ROSE
    [*Aside*] How like my Lacy looks yond shoemaker!
LACY
    [*Aside*] O that I durst but speak unto my love!
LORD MAYOR
    Sybil, go fetch some wine to make these drink;
    You are all welcome.
                                      [*Exit* SYBIL]
ALL [THE DANCERS]
    We thank your Lordship.   60

    [*Enter* SYBIL *with wine*] ROSE *takes a cup of wine and goes*
                              to LACY

ROSE
    For his sake whose fair shape thou represent'st,
    Good friend, I drink to thee.
LACY
    Ic be dancke, good frister.
MARGERY
    I see, Mistress Rose, you do not want judgment: you have
    drunk to the properest man I keep.   65

    s.d. *tabor* small drum
  63 *Ic be dancke, good frister* 'I thank you, good maid'

---

  53 s.d. The first Three-man's Song would be appropriate here after the
     dance, or possibly immediately before the shoemakers' exit.

FIRK

Here be some have done their parts to be as proper as he.

LORD MAYOR

Well, urgent business calls me back to London:
Good fellows, first go in and taste our cheer,
And, to make merry as you homeward go,
Spend these two angels in beer at Stratford Bow.   70

EYRE

To these two, my mad lads, Sim Eyre adds another. Then
cheerily, Firk, tickle it, Hans, and all for the honour of
shoemakers.

All go dancing out

LORD MAYOR

Come, Master Eyre, let's have your company.
                    Exeunt [LORD MAYOR, EYRE *and* MARGERY]

ROSE

Sybil, what shall I do?   75

SYBIL

Why, what's the matter?

ROSE

That Hans the shoemaker is my love Lacy,
Disguised in that attire to find me out.
How should I find the means to speak with him?

SYBIL

What, mistress, never fear; I dare venture my maidenhead   80
to nothing, and that's great odds, that Hans the Dutchman,
when we come to London, shall not only see and speak with
you, but in spite of all your father's policies, steal you away
and marry you. Will not this please you?

ROSE

Do this, and ever be assured of my love.   85

SYBIL

Away then, and follow your father to London, lest your
absence cause him to suspect something.
Tomorrow, if my counsel be obeyed,
I'll bind you prentice to the Gentle Trade.   [*Exeunt*]

72 *tickle it* put some life into it (cf. IV. ii, 7, V. iv, 19)
83 *policies* scheming

---

70 *Stratford Bow*. Stratford-le-Bow in Dekker's time, as in Chaucer's, was
a small village in the country, some 5 miles from St Paul's.

[Act IV, Scene i]

Enter JANE *in a seamster's shop, working, and* HAMMON
muffled, at another door. He stands aloof

HAMMON

Yonder's the shop, and there my fair love sits:
She's fair and lovely, but she is not mine.
O would she were! Thrice have I courted her,
Thrice hath my hand been moistened with her hand,
Whilst my poor famished eyes do feed on that   5
Which made them famish. I am infortunate:
I still love one, yet nobody loves me.
I muse in other men what women see
That I so want? Fine Mistress Rose was coy,
And this too curious—O no, she is chaste!   10
And for she thinks me wanton, she denies
To cheer my cold heart with her sunny eyes.
How prettily she works! O pretty hand!
O happy work! It doth me good to stand
Unseen to see her; thus I oft have stood,   15
In frosty evenings, a light burning by her,
Enduring biting cold, only to eye her.
One only look hath seemed as rich to me
As a king's crown: such is love's lunacy!
Muffled I'll pass along, and by that try   20
Whether she know me.

JANE   Sir, what is't you buy?
What is't you lack, sir? Callico, or lawn?
Fine cambric shirts, or bands? What will you buy?

HAMMON

[*Aside*] That which thou wilt not sell; faith, yet I'll try:
How do you sell this handkercher?

JANE   Good cheap.   25

HAMMON

And how these ruffs?

---

10 *curious* scrupulous

---

22 *What is't you lack, sir?* The usual Elizabethan form of crying one's
wares, here ironically echoing Hammon's own reflection at 8–9.

JANE   Cheap too.
HAMMON   And how this band?
JANE
  Cheap too.
HAMMON   All cheap? How sell you then this hand?
JANE
  My hands are not to be sold.
HAMMON   To be given, then?
  Nay, faith, I come to buy.
JANE   But none knows when.
HAMMON
  Good sweet, leave work a little while: let's play.   30
JANE
  I cannot live by keeping holiday.
HAMMON
  I'll pay you for the time which shall be lost.
JANE
  With me, you shall not be at so much cost.
HAMMON
  Look, how you wound this cloth, so you wound me.
JANE
  It may be so.
HAMMON   'Tis so.
JANE   What remedy?   35
HAMMON
  Nay, faith, you are too coy.
JANE   Let go my hand.
HAMMON
  I will do any task at your command:
  I would let go this beauty, were I not
  Enjoined to disobey you by a power
  That controls kings: I love you.
JANE   So, now part.   40
HAMMON
  With hands I may, but never with my heart.
  In faith, I love you.
JANE   I believe you do.

34 *wound this cloth* i.e., with her needle
39 *Enjoined* ed. (In mind Q1)

HAMMON
　Shall a true love in me breed hate in you?
JANE
　I hate you not.
HAMMON　　　　Then you must love.
JANE　　　　　　　　　　　I do.
　What, are you better now? I love not you.　　　　　　45
HAMMON
　All this, I hope, is but a woman's fray
　That means, come to me, when she cries, away.
　In earnest, mistress, I do not jest:
　A true chaste love hath entered in my breast.
　I love you dearly as I love my wife:　　　　　　　　50
　I love you as a husband loves a wife.
　That and no other love my love requires;
　Thy wealth I know is little; my desires
　Thirst not for gold; sweet beauteous Jane, what's mine
　Shall, if thou make myself thine, all be thine:　　　55
　Say, judge, what is thy sentence, life or death?
　Mercy or cruelty lies in thy breath.
JANE
　Good sir, I do believe you love me well,
　For 'tis a silly conquest, silly pride,
　For one like you—I mean a gentleman—　　　　　　60
　To boast that by his love-tricks he hath brought
　Such and such women to his amorous lure.
　I think you do not so; yet many do,
　And make it even a very trade to woo.
　I could be coy, as many women be,　　　　　　　　65
　Feed you with sunshine-smiles and wanton looks;
　But I detest witchcraft. Say that I
　Do constantly believe you constant have—
HAMMON
　Why dost thou not believe me?
JANE　　　　　　　　I believe you,
　But yet, good sir, because I will not grieve you　　　70
　With hopes to taste fruit which will never fall,
　In simple truth this is the sum of all:
　My husband lives, at least I hope he lives.

46 *a woman's fray* female wrangling

Pressed was he to these bitter wars in France,
Bitter they are to me by wanting him.   75
I have but one heart, and that heart's his due:
How can I then bestow the same on you?
Whilst he lives, his I live, be it ne'er so poor,
And rather be his wife, than a king's whore.

HAMMON
Chaste and dear woman, I will not abuse thee,   80
Although it cost my life if thou refuse me.
Thy husband pressed for France? What was his name?

JANE
Ralph Damport.

HAMMON   Damport? Here's a letter sent
From France to me, from a dear friend of mine,
A gentleman of place: here he doth write   85
Their names that have been slain in every fight.

JANE
I hope Death's scroll contains not my love's name.

HAMMON
Cannot you read?

JANE   I can.

HAMMON   Peruse the same.
To my remembrance such a name I read
Amongst the rest: see here.

JANE   Ay me, he's dead!   90
He's dead; if this be true, my dear heart's slain.

HAMMON
Have patience, dear love.

JANE   Hence, hence.

HAMMON   Nay, sweet Jane,
Make not poor sorrow proud with these rich tears:
I mourn thy husband's death because thou mourn'st.

JANE
That bill is forged: 'tis signed by forgery.   95

HAMMON
I'll bring thee letters sent besides to many,
Carrying the like report: Jane, 'tis too true.
Come, weep not; mourning, though it rise from love,
Helps not the mourned, yet hurts them that mourn.

74 *Pressed* conscripted

JANE
  For God's sake, leave me.
HAMMON   Whither dost thou turn?   100
  Forget the dead, love them that are alive;
  His love is faded, try how mine will thrive.
JANE
  'Tis now no time for me to think on love.
HAMMON
  'Tis now best time for you to think on love,
  Because your love lives not.
JANE   Though he be dead,   105
  My love to him shall not be buried.
  For God's sake, leave me to myself alone.
HAMMON
  'Twould kill my soul to leave thee drowned in moan.
  Answer to my suit, and I am gone:
  Say to me, yea or no.
JANE   No.
HAMMON   Then farewell—   105
  One farewell will not serve: I come again.
  Come, dry these wet cheeks; tell me, faith, sweet Jane,
  Yea or no, once more.
JANE   Once more I say no;
  Once more begone, I pray, else will I go.
HAMMON
  Nay, then, I will grow rude! By this white hand,   110
  Until you change that cold no, here I'll stand,
  Till by your hard heart—
JANE   Nay, for God's love, peace!
  My sorrows by your presence more increase.
  Not that you thus are present, but all grief
  Desires to be alone; therefore in brief   115
  Thus much I say, and saying bid adieu:
  If ever I wed man it shall be you.
HAMMON
  O blessed voice! Dear Jane, I'll urge no more;
  Thy breath hath made me rich.
JANE   Death makes me poor.
                                        Exeunt

110 *rude* rough, unmannerly

[Act IV, Scene ii]

Enter HODGE *at his shop-board*, RALPH, FIRK, LACY, *and a Boy at work*

ALL
Hey down a down, down derry.

HODGE
Well said, my hearts! Ply your work today; we loitered yesterday. To it, pell-mell, that we may live to be Lord Mayors, or Aldermen at least.

FIRK
Hey down a down derry!   5

HODGE
Well said, i'faith. How sayest thou, Hans, doth not Firk tickle it?

LACY
Yaw, mester.

FIRK
Not so, neither. My organ pipe squeaks this morning, for want of liquoring. Hey down a down derry!   10

LACY
Forware, Firk, tow best un jolly yongster. Hort I, mester, ic bid yo, cut me un pair vampres vor Mester Jeffrey's bootes.

HODGE
Thou shalt, Hans.

FIRK
Master!   15

HODGE
How now, boy?

---

11 *Forware* ed. (Forward Q1)

11 *Forware, Firk, tow best un jolly yongster* ... 'Indeed, Firk, you are a merry youngster. Hear me, master, I pray you, cut me a pair of vamps for Master Jeffrey's boots'

12 *vampres* ed. (văpres Q1): the front end of the upper shoe

1 *Hey down a down, down derry.* The resemblance to the refrain of the second Three-man's Song suggests that it might be sung at the opening of this scene.

FIRK

Pray, now you are in the cutting vein, cut me out a pair of counterfeits, or else my work will not pass current. Hey down a down!

HODGE

Tell me, sirs, are my cousin Mistress Priscilla's shoes done?   20

FIRK

Your cousin? No, master, one of your aunts, hang her! Let them alone.

RALPH

I am in hand with them. She gave charge that none but I should do them for her.

FIRK

Thou do for her? Then 'twill be a lame doing, and that she   25 loves not. Ralph, thou might'st have sent her to me: in faith, I would have yerked and firked your Priscilla. Hey down a down derry! This gear will not hold.

HODGE

How sayest thou, Firk? Were we not merry at Old Ford?

FIRK

How, merry? Why, our buttocks went jiggy-joggy like a   30 quagmire! Well, Sir Roger Oatmeal, if I thought all meal of that nature, I would eat nothing but bagpuddings.

RALPH

Of all good fortunes, my fellow Hans had the best.

FIRK

'Tis true, because Mistress Rose drank to him.

HODGE

Well, well, work apace; they say seven of the Aldermen   35 be dead, or very sick.

FIRK

I care not; I'll be none.

18 *counterfeits* replacements
21 *aunts* whores
27 *yerked and firked* Firk is in his bawdy vein
28 *gear* way of carrying on
31 *Sir Roger Oatmeal* Sir Roger Otley, the Lord Mayor
32 *bagpuddings* stuffed with a mixture of meat and meal

35 *seven of the Aldermen be dead, or very sick.* An artless preparation for the news announced by Lacy in IV. iv, 15.

RALPH

No, nor I; but then my master Eyre will come quickly to
be Lord Mayor.

Enter SYBIL

FIRK

Whoop! Yonder comes Sybil.   40

HODGE

Sybil, welcome, i'faith, and how dost thou, mad wench?

FIRK

Sib-whore, welcome to London.

SYBIL

Godamercy, sweet Firk! Good Lord, Hodge, what a
delicious shop you have got! You tickle it, i'faith.

RALPH

Godamercy, Sybil, for our good cheer at Old Ford.   45

SYBIL

That you shall have, Ralph.

FIRK

Nay, by the mass, we had tickling cheer, Sybil. And how
the plague dost thou and Mistress Rose, and my Lord
Mayor? I put the women in first.

SYBIL

Well, Godamercy. But God's me, I forget myself! Where's   50
Hans the Fleming?

FIRK

Hark, butter-box, now you must yelp out some spreken.

LACY

Vat begaie you, vat vod you, frister?

SYBIL

Marry, you must come to my young mistress, to pull on her
shoes you made last.   55

LACY

Vere ben your edle fro, vare ben your mistress?

SYBIL

Marry, here at our London house in Cornwall.

53 *Vat begaie you* ... 'What do you want, what would you, maid?'
56 *Vere ben your edle fro* ... 'Where is your noble lady, where is your
  mistress?'
57 *Cornwall* Cornhill (cf. I. ii, 30)

FIRK
Will nobody serve her turn but Hans?

SYBIL
No, sir. Come, Hans, I stand upon needles.

HODGE
Why then, Sybil, take heed of pricking!   60

SYBIL
For that let me alone: I have a trick in my budget. Come,
Hans.

LACY
Yaw, yaw, ic sall meete yo gane.

HODGE
Go, Hans; make haste again. Come, who lacks work?

Exit LACY *and* SYBIL

FIRK
I, master, for I lack my breakfast; 'tis munching-time, and   65
past.

HODGE
Is't so? Why then, leave work, Ralph: to breakfast. Boy,
look to the tools; come, Ralph; come, Firk.

Exeunt

[Act IV, Scene iii]

Enter a Servingman

SERVINGMAN
Let me see, now: the sign of the Last in Tower Street.
Mass, yonder's the house! What, haw! Who's within?

Enter RALPH

RALPH
Who calls there? What want you, sir?

SERVINGMAN
Marry, I would have a pair of shoes made for a gentlewoman against tomorrow morning. What, can you do them?   5

61 *a trick in my budget* a gadget in my purse (with a bawdy innuendo)
63 *Yaw, yaw, ic sall meete yo gane* 'Yes, yes, I shall go with you'
64 *make haste again* hurry back
5   *against* by (cf. I. ii, 18)

RALPH

Yes, sir, you shall have them. But what length's her foot?

SERVINGMAN

Why, you must make them in all parts like this shoe, but at any hand fail not to do them, for the gentlewoman is to be married very early in the morning.

RALPH

How? By this shoe must it be made? By this? Are you sure,   10
sir? By this?

SERVINGMAN

How? By this? Am I sure? By this? Art thou in thy wits? I tell thee I must have a pair of shoes, dost thou mark me? A pair of shoes, two shoes, made by this very shoe, this same shoe, against tomorrow morning by four o'clock. Dost   15
understand me? Canst thou do't?

RALPH

Yes, sir, yes; ay, ay, I can do't! By this shoe, you say; I should know this shoe! Yes, sir, yes: by this shoe. I can do't. Four o'clock, well: whither shall I bring them?

SERVINGMAN

To the sign of the Golden Ball in Watling Street. Enquire   20
for one Master Hammon, a gentleman, my master.

RALPH

Yea, sir. By this shoe, you say.

SERVINCMAN

I say Master Hammon at the Golden Ball. He's the bride-groom, and those shoes are for his bride.

RALPH

They shall be done by this shoe. Well, well, Master   25
Hammon at the Golden Shoe—I would say the Golden Ball. Very well, very well; but I pray you, sir, where must Master Hammon be married?

SERVINGMAN

At Saint Faith's Church under Paul's: but what's that to thee? Prithee, dispatch those shoes, and so farewell.   30

Exit [SERVINGMAN]

8 *at any hand* in any case
29 *Saint Faith's Church under Paul's.* A chapel under the choir of the cathedral, used as a parish church by the stationers and others who lived in the precincts.

RALPH

By this shoe, said he. How am I amazed
At this strange accident! Upon my life,
This was the very shoe I gave my wife
When I was pressed for France; since when, alas!
I never could hear of her. It is the same,   35
And Hammon's bride no other but my Jane.

Enter FIRK

FIRK

'Snails, Ralph, thou hast lost thy part of three pots a
countryman of mine gave me to breakfast!

RALPH

I care not: I have found a better thing.

FIRK

A thing? Away! Is it a man's thing, or a woman's thing?   40

RALPH

Firk, dost thou know this shoe?

FIRK

No, by my troth, neither doth that know me! I have no
acquaintance with it, 'tis a mere stranger to me.

RALPH

Why then, I do; this shoe, I durst be sworn,
Once covered the instep of my Jane.   45
This is her size, her breadth; thus trod my love;
These true-love knots I pricked; I hold my life,
By this old shoe I shall find out my wife.

FIRK

Ha, ha! Old shoe, that wert new: how a murrain came this
ague-fit of foolishness upon thee?   50

RALPH

Thus, Firk: even now here came a servingman;
By this shoe would he have a new pair made,
Against tomorrow morning, for his mistress
That's to be married to a gentleman.
And why may not this be my sweet Jane?   55

---

37 *'Snails* God's nails (cf. I. iv, 73)
40 *a man's thing* genital organ (cf. III. ii, 25)
44 *durst* dare
49 *murrain* plague

FIRK

And why mayest not thou be my sweet arse? Ha, ha!

RALPH

Well, laugh, and spare not; but the truth is this:
Against tomorrow morning I'll provide
A lusty crew of honest shoemakers,
To watch the going of the bride to church.   60
If she prove Jane, I'll take her in despite
Of Hammon, and the devil, were he by;
If it be not my Jane, what remedy?
Hereof am I sure: I shall live till I die,
Although I never with a woman lie.   65

Exit [RALPH]

FIRK

Thou lie with a woman, to build nothing but Cripplegates!
Well, God send fools fortune! And it may be he may light
upon his matrimony by such a device, for wedding and
hanging goes by destiny.

Exit [FIRK]

[Act IV, Scene iv]

Enter LACY *and* ROSE, *arm in arm*

LACY

How happy am I by embracing thee!
O I did fear such cross mishaps did reign,
That I should never see my Rose again.

ROSE

Sweet Lacy, since fair Opportunity
Offers herself to further our escape,   5
Let not too over-fond esteem of me
Hinder that happy hour; invent the means,
And Rose will follow thee through all the world.

2 *cross* adverse

---

66 *Cripplegates.* Cripplegate was one of the seven gates in the city walls, so
called because cripples used to beg there. Firk is making rather a heart-
less joke about Ralph's lameness.

68 *wedding and hanging goes by destiny.* Cf. *The Merchant of Venice*,
II. ix, 82–3: 'The ancient saying is no heresy: / Hanging and wiving
goes by destiny'.

LACY

O how I surfeit with excess of joy,
Made happy by thy rich perfection!   10
But since thou payest sweet interest to my hopes,
Redoubling love on love, let me once more,
Like to a bold-faced debtor, crave of thee
This night to steal abroad, and at Eyre's house,
Who now by death of certain Aldermen   15
Is Mayor of London, and my master once,
Meet thou thy Lacy; where, in spite of change,
Your father's anger, and mine uncle's hate,
Our happy nuptials will we consummate.

Enter SYBIL

SYBIL

O God, what will you do, mistress? Shift for yourself, your   20
father is at hand! He's coming, he's coming! Master Lacy,
hide yourself! In, my mistress! For God's sake, shift for
yourselves!

LACY

Your father come! Sweet Rose, what shall I do?
Where shall I hide me? How shall I escape?   25

ROSE

A man, and want wit in extremity?
Come, come, be Hans still: play the shoemaker,
Pull on my shoe.

Enter LORD MAYOR

LACY

          Mass, and that's well remembered!

SYBIL

Here comes your father.   30

LACY

Forware, metresse, tis un good skow; it sal vel dute, or ye

19 *we* ed. (me Q1)
31 *Forware, metresse, tis un good skow* ... 'Indeed, mistress, it is a good
   shoe; it shall do well, or you shall not pay for it'

15 *Who now by death of certain Aldermen | Is Mayor of London.* Not un-
   expected news (cf. IV. ii, 38), but slipped in very casually here.
22 *Master Lacy, hide yourself! In, my mistress!* The punctuation represents
   what Sybil means to say; 'hide your selfe in my mistris' (Q1), however,
   suggests that the line may be played for a bawdy laugh.

sal neit betallen.

ROSE

O God, it pincheth me! What will you do?

LACY

Your father's presence pincheth, not the shoe.

LORD MAYOR

Well done; fit my daughter well, and she shall please thee   35
well.

LACY

Yaw, yaw, ick weit dat well. Forware tis un good skoo, tis
gi mait van neits leither: se ever, mine here.

Enter a Prentice

LORD MAYOR

I do believe it. What's the news with you?

PRENTICE

Please you, the Earl of Lincoln at the gate   40
Is newly lighted, and would speak with you.

LORD MAYOR

The Earl of Lincoln come to speak with me?
Well, well, I know his errand. Daughter Rose,
Send hence your shoemaker: dispatch, have done!
Sib, make things handsome! Sir boy, follow me.   45

Exit [LORD MAYOR, SYBIL *and Prentice*]

LACY

Mine uncle come? O what may this portend?
Sweet Rose, this of our love threatens an end.

ROSE

Be not dismayed at this: whate'er befall,
Rose is thine own. To witness I speak truth,
Where thou appoints the place I'll meet with thee.   50
I will not fix a day to follow thee,
But presently steal hence. Do not reply:

---

37 *Yaw, yaw, ick weit dat well* . . . 'Yes, yes, I know that well. Indeed it is a
good shoe, it is made of neat's leather: just see, my lord'
42 *to* ed. (om. Q1)
52 *presently* immediately

---

35 *fit my daughter well, and she shall please thee well.* Another unintentional
indecency.

Love which gave strength to bear my father's hate,
Shall now add wings to further our escape.

Exeunt

[Act IV, Scene v]

Enter LORD MAYOR *and* LINCOLN

LORD MAYOR
 Believe me, on my credit I speak truth,
 Since first your nephew Lacy went to France
 I have not seen him. It seemed strange to me,
 When Dodger told me that he stayed behind,
 Neglecting the high charge the King imposed.   5

LINCOLN
 Trust me, Sir Roger Otley, I did think
 Your counsel had given head to this attempt,
 Drawn to it by the love he bears your child.
 Here I did hope to find him in your house,
 But now I see mine error, and confess   10
 My judgment wronged you by conceiving so.

LORD MAYOR
 Lodge in my house, say you? Trust me, my Lord,
 I love your nephew Lacy too too dearly
 So much to wrong his honour, and he hath done so,
 That first gave him advice to stay from France.   15
 To witness I speak truth, I let you know
 How careful I have been to keep my daughter
 Free from all conference or speech of him.
 Not that I scorn your nephew, but in love
 I bear your honour, lest your noble blood   20
 Should by my mean worth be dishonoured.

LINCOLN
 [*Aside*] How far the churl's tongue wanders from his heart!
 Well, well, Sir Roger Otley, I believe you,
 With more than many thanks for the kind love
 So much you seem to bear me; but, my Lord,   25
 Let me request your help to seek my nephew,
 Whom, if I find, I'll straight embark for France.

7 *given head* encouraged

So shall your Rose be free, my thoughts at rest,
And much care die which now lies in my breast.

Enter SYBIL

SYBIL
O Lord! Help, for God's sake! My mistress, O my young   30
mistress!

LORD MAYOR
Where is thy mistress? What's become of her?

SYBIL
She's gone, she's fled!

LORD MAYOR
Gone? Whither is she fled?

SYBIL
I know not, forsooth. She's fled out of doors with Hans the   35
shoemaker. I saw them scud, scud, scud, apace, apace!

LORD MAYOR
Which way? What, John! Where be my men? Which way?

SYBIL
I know not, and it please your Worship.

LORD MAYOR
Fled with a shoemaker? Can this be true?

SYBIL
O Lord, sir, as true as God's in heaven!   40

LINCOLN
[*Aside*] Her love turned shoemaker? I am glad of this!

LORD MAYOR
A Fleming butter-box? A shoemaker?
Will she forget her birth? Requite my care
With such ingratitude? Scorned she young Hammon,
To love a honnikin, a needy knave?   45
Well, let her fly, I'll not fly after her.
Let her starve if she will, she's none of mine!

LINCOLN
Be not so cruel, sir.

Enter FIRK *with shoes*

---

28 *your Rose ... my thoughts* ed. (my Rose ... your thoughts Q1)
29 *lies* ed. (dies Q1)
45 *honnikin* contemptuous term for a Dutchman or German ('little Hun'?)

SYBIL

    [*Aside*] I am glad she's 'scaped.

LORD MAYOR

    I'll not account of her as of my child!   50
    Was there no better object for her eyes,
    But a foul, drunken lubber, swill-belly?
    A shoemaker? That's brave!

FIRK

    Yea, forsooth, 'tis a very brave shoe, and as fit as a pudding.

LORD MAYOR

    How now, what knave is this? From whence comest thou?   55

FIRK

    No knave, sir. I am Firk the shoemaker, lusty Roger's chief
    lusty journeyman, and I come hither to take up the pretty
    leg of sweet Mistress Rose, and thus hoping your Worship
    is in good health as I was at the making hereof, I bid you
    farewell, yours, Firk.   60

                                    [*Starts to leave*]

LORD MAYOR

    Stay, stay, sir knave!

LINCOLN

    Come hither, shoemaker.

FIRK

    'Tis happy the knave is put before the shoemaker, or else
    I would not have vouchsafed to come back to you. I am
    moved, for I stir.   65

LORD MAYOR

    My Lord, this villain calls us knaves by craft!

FIRK

    Then 'tis by the Gentle Craft, and to call one knave gently
    is no harm. Sit your Worship merry! [*Aside*] Sib, your
    young mistress! I'll so bob them, now my master, Master
    Eyre, is Lord Mayor of London!   70

---

53 *That's brave* That's wonderful (ironic)
64 *vouchsafed* guaranteed
69 *bob them* ed. (bob then Q1) fool them

---

56 *No knave, sir.* Firk defends the dignity of the Gentle Craft in dealing
    with the Lord Mayor's overbearing manner. His chief purpose in this
    scene, of course, is to cover the retreat of Rose and Lacy, by playing for
    time and then misleading the Lord Mayor and Lincoln.

LORD MAYOR

Tell me, sirrah, whose man are you?

FIRK

I am glad to see your Worship so merry. I have no maw
to this gear, no stomach as yet to a red petticoat.

Pointing to SYBIL

LINCOLN

He means not, sir, to woo you to this maid,
But only doth demand whose man you are.   75

FIRK

I sing now to the tune of Rogero: Roger, my fellow, is now
my master.

LINCOLN

Sirrah, knowest thou one Hans, a shoemaker?

FIRK

Hans, shoemaker? O yes; stay, yes, I have him! I tell you
what, I speak it in secret: Mistress Rose and he are by this   80
time—no, not so, but shortly are to come over one another
with 'Can you dance the shaking of the sheets?' It is that
Hans. [*Aside*] I'll so gull these diggers!

LORD MAYOR

Knowest thou then where he is?

FIRK

Yes, forsooth: yea, marry.   85

LINCOLN

Canst thou, in sadness?

FIRK

No, forsooth: no, marry.

LORD MAYOR

Tell me, good honest fellow, where he is,
And thou shalt see what I'll bestow of thee.

FIRK

Honest fellow? No, sir; not so, sir. My profession is the   90
Gentle Craft: I care not for seeing, I love feeling. Let me

72 *no maw to this gear* no appetite for this kind of game
76 *the tune of Rogero* a popular Elizabethan tune
82 *the shaking of the sheets* the name of an old dance, with an obvious sexual
   allusion (cf. V. v, 29)
83 *gull these diggers* fool them for trying to dig information out of me
86 *sadness* seriousness

feel it here, *aurium tenus*, ten pieces of gold, *genuum tenus*,
ten pieces of silver, and then Firk is your man, in a new pair
of stretchers.

LORD MAYOR

Here is an angel, part of thy reward   95
Which I will give thee: tell me where he is.

FIRK

No point! Shall I betray my brother? No! Shall I prove
Judas to Hans? No! Shall I cry treason to my corporation?
No! I shall be firked and yerked then. But give me your
angel: your angel shall tell you.   100

LINCOLN

Do so, good fellow, 'tis no hurt to thee.

FIRK

Send simpering Sib away.

LORD MAYOR

Huswife, get you in.

Exit SYBIL

FIRK

Pitchers have ears, and maids have wide mouths. But for
Hans-prans, upon my word, tomorrow morning he and   105
young Mistress Rose go to this gear; they shall be married
together, by this rush, or else turn Firk to a firkin of butter
to tan leather withal.

LORD MAYOR

But art thou sure of this?

FIRK

Am I sure that Paul's steeple is a handful higher than 110

---

94 *stretchers* shoe-stretchers, here also truth-stretchers
97 *No point* Absolutely not
98 *corporation* fellow-shoemakers
99 *firked and yerked* worked over (cf. IV. ii, 27)

---

92 *aurium tenus . . . genuum tenus*. 'As far as the ears . . . as far as the knees',
    i.e., gold for the whole truth, silver for part of the truth, with puns on
    'aurium' (gold) and 'tenus' (ten).
107 *by this rush*. Rushes were used as floor-coverings, but a rush-ring was
    said to be used by bridegrooms not intending to keep their vows; so here
    Firk equivocates in swearing that he tells the truth.

London Stone? Or that the pissing-conduit leaks nothing
but pure Mother Bunch? Am I sure I am lusty Firk? God's
nails, do you think I am so base to gull you?

LINCOLN

Where are they married? Dost thou know the church?

FIRK

I never go to church, but I know the name of it. It is a   115
swearing-church: stay a while, 'tis Ay-by-the-mass; no, no,
'tis Ay-by-my-troth; no, nor that, 'tis Ay-by-my-faith.
That, that! 'Tis Ay-by-my-Faith's Church under Paul's
Cross: there they shall be knit, like a pair of stockings, in
matrimony; there they'll be in cony.   120

LINCOLN

Upon my life, my nephew Lacy walks
In the disguise of this Dutch shoemaker!

FIRK

Yes, forsooth.

LINCOLN

Doth he not, honest fellow?

FIRK

No, forsooth. I think Hans is nobody but Hans, no spirit.   125

LORD MAYOR

My mind misgives me now 'tis so indeed!

LINCOLN

My cousin speaks the language, knows the trade.

LORD MAYOR

Let me request your company, my Lord.
Your honourable presence may, no doubt,
Refrain their headstrong rashness, when myself   130
Going alone perchance may be o'erborne.
Shall I request this favour?

LINCOLN   This, or what else.

120 *in cony* set up nicely

---

111 *London Stone.* It marked the converging-point of the old Roman roads.
111 *pissing-conduit.* A water-cistern near the Royal Exchange, probably so
  called because it leaked. Steane cites Jack Cade in *Henry VI*, IV. vi, 3:
  'And here sitting upon London Stone, I charge and command that, of
  the City's cost, the pissing conduit run nothing but claret wine this first
  of my reign'.
112 *Mother Bunch.* An ale-wife notorious for watering her beer.

FIRK

Then you must rise betimes, for they mean to fall to their
hey-pass-and-repass, pindy-pandy, which-hand-will-you-
have very early.   135

LORD MAYOR

My care shall every way equal their haste.
[*To* LINCOLN] This night accept your lodging in my house;
The earlier shall we stir, and at Saint Faith's
Prevent this giddy harebrained nuptial;
This traffic of hot love shall yield cold gains: 140
They ban our loves, and we'll forbid their banns.

                                              [*Exit* LORD MAYOR]

LINCOLN

At Saint Faith's Church, thou sayest?

FIRK

Yes, by their troth.

LINCOLN

Be secret, on thy life!   [*Exit* LINCOLN]

FIRK

Yes, when I kiss your wife! Ha, ha! Here's no craft in the   145
Gentle Craft: I came hither of purpose with shoes to Sir
Roger's Worship, whilst Rose his daughter be conycatched
by Hans. Soft now! These two gulls will be at Saint Faith's
Church tomorrow morning, to take Master Bridegroom
and Mistress Bride napping, and they in the meantime shall   150
chop up the matter at the Savoy! But the best sport is, Sir
Roger Otley will find my fellow lame Ralph's wife going to
marry a gentleman, and then he'll stop her instead of his
daughter! O brave, there will be fine tickling sport! Soft now,
what have I to do? O I know now: a mess of shoemakers   155
meet at the Woolsack in Ivy Lane, to cozen my gentleman

---

134 *hey-pass-and-repass* a conjuring term: 'artful tricks'
134 *pindy-pandy* handy-dandy, i.e., giving of hands in marriage
    s.d. *Exit* [LORD MAYOR] ed. (Exeunt Q1)
    s.d. [*Exit* LINCOLN] ed. (om. Q1)
147 *conycatched* caught by a trick
151 *chop up* swiftly conclude
156 *cozen* cheat

---

151 *the Savoy*. A paupers' hospital the chapel of which was frequently used
    for clandestine marriages.

of lame Ralph's wife, that's true.
Alack, alack!
Girls, hold out tack!
For now smocks for this jumbling   160
Shall go to wrack.

                              Exit [FIRK]

[Act V, Scene i]

Enter EYRE, MARGERY, LACY, *and* ROSE

EYRE

This is the morning then, stay, my bully, my honest Hans,
is it not?

LACY

This is the morning that must make us two
Happy or miserable; therefore, if you—

EYRE

Away with these ifs and ands, Hans, and these etceteras!   5
By mine honour, Rowland Lacy, none but the King shall
wrong thee! Come, fear nothing: am not I Sim Eyre? Is
not Sim Eyre Lord Mayor of London? Fear nothing, Rose,
let them all say what they can. 'Dainty, come thou to me':
laughest thou?   10

MARGERY

Good my Lord, stand her friend in what thing you may.

EYRE

Why, my sweet Lady Madgy, think you Simon Eyre can
forget his fine Dutch journeyman? No, vah! Fie, I scorn
it! It shall never be cast in my teeth that I was unthankful.
Lady Madgy, thou hadst never covered thy saracen's head   15
with this French flap, nor loaden thy bum with this farthing-
gale—'tis trash, trumpery, vanity!—Simon Eyre had never
walked in a red petticoat, nor wore a chain of gold, but for
my fine journeyman's portuguese: and shall I leave him?

159 *hold out tack* be on your guard
160 *smocks* maidenhoods *jumbling* confusion
  1 *stay, my bully* now, my fine fellow
  9 *'Dainty, come thou to me'* the opening of a popular song
 11 *stand her friend in what thing you may.* Another example of Margery's
    habit of unintentional *double-entendre* (cf. V. ii, 159).

No! Prince am I none, yet bear a princely mind.   20

LACY

My Lord, 'tis time for us to part from hence.

EYRE

Lady Madgy, Lady Madgy, take two or three of my
piecrust-eaters, my buff-jerkin varlets, that do walk in black
gowns at Simon Eyre's heels. Take them, good Lady
Madgy. Trip and go, my brown queen of periwigs, with my   25
delicate Rose and my jolly Rowland to the Savoy; see them
linked, countenance the marriage, and when it is done,
cling, cling together, you Hamborow turtle-doves! I'll bear
you out! Come to Simon Eyre, come dwell with me, Hans.
Thou shalt eat minced pies and marchpane. Rose, away,   30
cricket! Trip and go, my Lady Madgy, to the Savoy! Hans,
wed and to bed! Kiss and away, go, vanish!

MARGERY

Farewell, my Lord.

ROSE

Make haste, sweet love.

MARGERY

She'd fain the deed were done.   35

LACY

Come, my sweet Rose, faster than deer we'll run!

They go out

EYRE

Go, vanish, vanish, avaunt, I say! By the Lord of Ludgate,
it's a mad life to be a Lord Mayor, it's a stirring life, a fine
life, a velvet life, a careful life! Well, Simon Eyre, yet set
a good face on it, in the honour of Saint Hugh. Soft! The   40
King this day comes to dine with me, to see my new buildings: His Majesty is welcome, he shall have good cheer,
delicate cheer, princely cheer. This day my fellow prentices
of London come to dine with me too: they shall have fine
cheer, gentlemanlike cheer. I promised the mad Cappadoc-   45

---

27 *countenance* witness   30 *marchpane* marzipan

---

45 *mad Cappadocians.* Another of Eyre's jocular appellations (cf. 'mad
   Greeks', I. iv, 113, 'mad Hyperboreans', I. iv, 121, and 'mad Mesopotamians', II. iii, 78). Here possibly with a pun on 'madcaps' and
   bearing the cant association with imprisonment: N.E.D. cites 'Caper-
   dewsie' and 'Caperdochy' as terms for prison and the stocks.

ians, when we all served at the Conduit together, that if
ever I came to be Mayor of London I would feast them all,
and I'll do't, I'll do't, by the life of Pharoah! By this beard,
Sim Eyre will be no flincher! Besides, I have procured that
upon every Shrove Tuesday, at the sound of the pancake   50
bell, my fine dapper Assyrian lads shall clap up their shop
windows, and away. This is the day, and this day they shall
do't, they shall do't!
Boys, that day are you free: let masters care,
And prentices shall pray for Simon Eyre.   55

                                                    Exit

[Act V, Scene ii]

Enter HODGE, FIRK, RALPH, *and five or six shoemakers, all
with cudgels or such weapons*

HODGE

Come, Ralph; stand to it, Firk. My masters, as we are the
brave bloods of the shoemakers, heirs apparent to Saint
Hugh, and perpetual benefactors to all good fellows, thou
shalt have no wrong. Were Hammon a King of Spades, he
should not delve in thy close without thy sufferance! But   5
tell me, Ralph, art thou sure 'tis thy wife?

RALPH

Am I sure this is Firk? This morning, when I stroked on
her shoes, I looked upon her, and she upon me, and sighed,
asked me if ever I knew one Ralph. Yes, said I; for his
sake, said she, tears standing in her eyes, and for thou art   10
somewhat like him, spend this piece of gold. I took it: my
lame leg, and my travel beyond sea, made me unknown. All
is one for that: I know she's mine.

4 *King of Spades* pun on 'spades': cf. 'Queen of Clubs', II. iii, 39
5 *delve in thy close* dig in your patch
5 *sufferance* permission

---

46 *served at the Conduit.* Alluding to the customary duty of apprentices to
    fetch the water for their masters' houses.
50 *every Shrove Tuesday.* The traditional apprentices' holiday, being the
    day before the beginning of Lent.
50 *the pancake bell.* Originally a summons to confession before Lent, but
    in popular tradition the signal to commence the Shrove Tuesday
    festivities.

FIRK

Did she give thee this gold? O glorious glittering gold!
She's thine own, 'tis thy wife, and she loves thee, for I'll 15
stand to't, there's no woman will give gold to any man but
she thinks better of him than she thinks of them she gives
silver to. And for Hammon, neither Hammon nor hangman
shall wrong thee in London. Is not our old master Eyre
Lord Mayor? Speak, my hearts!　　　　　　　　20

ALL

Yes, and Hammon shall know it to his cost.

　　　　Enter HAMMON, *his Man*, JANE, *and others*

HODGE

Peace, my bullies, yonder they come.

RALPH

Stand to't, my hearts! Firk, let me speak first.

HODGE

No, Ralph, let me. Hammon, whither away so early?

HAMMON

Unmannerly rude slave, what's that to thee?　　　　25

FIRK

To him, sir? Yes, sir, and to me, and others! Good morrow,
Jane, how dost thou? Good Lord, how the world is changed
with you, God be thanked!

HAMMON

Villains, hands off! How dare you touch my love?

ALL

Villains? Down with them! Cry clubs for prentices!　　30

HODGE

Hold, my hearts! Touch her, Hammon? Yea, and more than
that: we'll carry her away with us. My masters and gentlemen, never draw your bird-spits: shoemakers are steel to
the back, men every inch of them, all spirit.

33 *bird-spits* contemptuous term for daggers and swords

---

18 *neither Hammon nor hangman.* A play on the name, with an allusion to the
　　Biblical King Haman (in the Book of Esther) who was hanged on his
　　own gallows.
30 *Cry clubs for prentices.* The rallying cry that brought the apprentices out
　　on the streets for a gang-fight (and possibly with a reference back to
　　Hammon as 'King of Spades' at 4 above?).

ALL OF HAMMON'S SIDE
    Well, and what of all this?   35
HODGE
    I'll show you. Jane, dost thou know this man? 'Tis Ralph,
    I can tell thee. Nay, 'tis he, in faith; though he be lamed
    by the wars, yet look not strange, but run to him, fold him
    about the neck and kiss him!
JANE
    Lives then my husband? O God, let me go!   40
    Let me embrace my Ralph.
HAMMON   What means my Jane?
JANE
    Nay, what meant you, to tell me he was slain?
HAMMON
    Pardon me, dear love, for being misled.
    [*To* RALPH] 'Twas rumoured here in London thou wert dead.
FIRK
    Thou seest he lives. Lass, go pack home with him. Now,   45
    Master Hammon, where's your mistress, your wife?
SERVINGMAN
    'Swounds, master, fight for her! Will you thus lose her?
ALL [OF RALPH'S SIDE]
    Down with that creature! Clubs, down with him!
HODGE
    Hold, hold!
HAMMON
    Hold, fool! Sirs, he shall do no wrong.   50
    Will my Jane leave me thus, and break her faith?
FIRK
    Yea, sir; she must, sir; she shall, sir! What then? Mend it.
HODGE
    Hark, fellow Ralph, follow my counsel. Set the wench in
    the midst, and let her choose her man, and let her be his
    woman.   55
JANE
    Whom should I choose? Whom should my thoughts affect,
    But him whom Heaven hath made to be my love!
    Thou art my husband, and these humble weeds
    Makes thee more beautiful than all his wealth.
    Therefore I will but put off his attire,   60
    Returning it into the owner's hand,

And after ever be thy constant wife.

HODGE

Not a rag, Jane! The law's on our side: he that sows in
another man's ground forfeits his harvest. Get thee home,
Ralph; follow him, Jane. He shall not have so much as a   65
busk-point from thee.

FIRK

Stand to that, Ralph, the appurtenances are thine own.
Hammon, look not at her.

SERVINGMAN

O 'swounds! No!

FIRK

Blue coat, be quiet: we'll give you a new livery else! We'll   70
make Shrove Tuesday Saint George's Day for you! Look
not, Hammon, leer not! I'll firk you! For thy head now:
one glance, one sheep's eye, anything, at her! Touch not a
rag, lest I and my brethren beat you to clouts!

SERVINGMAN

Come, Master Hammon, there's no striving here.   75

HAMMON

Good fellows, hear me speak; and honest Ralph,
Whom I have injured most by loving Jane,
Mark what I offer thee: here in fair gold
Is twenty pound, I'll give it for thy Jane.
If this content thee not, thou shalt have more.   80

HODGE

Sell not thy wife, Ralph, make her not a whore.

HAMMON

Say, wilt thou freely cease thy claim in her,
And let her be my wife?

ALL [OF RALPH'S SIDE]   No, do not, Ralph!

RALPH

Sirrah Hammon, Hammon, dost thou think a shoemaker
is so base, to be a bawd to his own wife for commodity?   85

66 *busk-point* corset-lace
74 *clouts* rags
75 *striving* quarrelling
85 *commodity* profit

71 *Saint George's Day*. When servants might change or renew their terms
of service, i.e., Firk is threatening to beat him black and blue.

Take thy gold, choke with it! Were I not lame, I would
make thee eat thy words!

FIRK

A shoemaker sell his flesh and blood? O indignity!

HODGE

Sirrah, take your pelf and be packing.

HAMMON

I will not touch one penny; but in lieu   90
Of that great wrong I offered thy Jane,
To Jane and thee I give that twenty pound.
Since I have failed of her, during my life
I vow no woman else shall be my wife.
Farewell, good fellows of the Gentle Trade: 95
Your morning's mirth my mourning-day hath made.

                    Exeunt [HAMMON *and those of his side*]

FIRK

[*To Servingman going out*] Touch the gold, creature, if you
dare! Y'are best be trudging! Here, Jane, take thou it.
Now let's home, my hearts!

HODGE

Stay, who comes here? Jane, on again with thy mask.   100

          Enter LINCOLN, LORD MAYOR, *and Servants*

LINCOLN

Yonder's the lying varlet mocked us so!

LORD MAYOR

Come hither, sirrah.

FIRK

Ay, sir, I am sirrah: you mean me, do you not?

LINCOLN

Where is my nephew married?

FIRK

Is he married? God give him joy, I am glad of it. They   105
have a fair day, and the sign is in a good planet: Mars in
Venus.

89 *pelf* money

---

96 *Your morning's mirth my mourning-day hath made.* The unfortunate
Hammon has been extremely persistent, and insensitive to the class-
pride of the shoemakers, but he retires with some dignity and with some
claim on our sympathies.

LORD MAYOR

Villain, thou told'st me that my daughter Rose
This morning should be married at Saint Faith's:
We have watched there these three hours at the least,   110
Yet see we no such thing.

FIRK

Truly, I am sorry for't: a bride's a pretty thing!

HODGE

Come to the purpose: yonder's the bride and bridegroom
you look for, I hope. Though you be lords, you are not to
bar by your authority men from women, are you?   115

LORD MAYOR

See, see, my daughter's masked!

LINCOLN   True, and my nephew,
To hide his guilt, counterfeits him lame.

FIRK

Yea, truly, God help the poor couple! They are lame and
blind.

LORD MAYOR

I'll ease her blindness.

LINCOLN   I'll his lameness cure.   120

FIRK

[Aside] Lie down, sirs, and laugh! My fellow Ralph is
taken for Rowland Lacy, and Jane for Mistress Damask
Rose! This is all my knavery.

LORD MAYOR

What, have I found you, minion?

LINCOLN   O base wretch!
Nay, hide thy face, the horror of thy guilt   125
Can hardly be washed off! Where are thy powers?
What battles have you made? O yes, I see!
Thou fought'st with Shame, and Shame hath conquered
thee.
This lameness will not serve.

LORD MAYOR   Unmask yourself.

LINCOLN

Lead home your daughter.

LORD MAYOR   Take your nephew hence.   130

RALPH

Hence? 'Swounds, what mean you? Are you mad? I hope

you cannot enforce my wife from me. Where's Hammon?

LORD MAYOR
Your wife?

LINCOLN
What Hammon?

RALPH
Yea, my wife: and therefore the proudest of you that lays   135
hands on her first, I'll lay my crutch cross his pate!

FIRK
To him, lame Ralph! Here's brave sport!

RALPH
Rose call you her? Why, her name is Jane! Look here else!
[*Unmasks* JANE] Do you know her now?

LINCOLN
Is this your daughter?

LORD MAYOR   No, nor this your nephew.   140
My Lord of Lincoln, we are both abused
By this base crafty varlet.

FIRK
Yea, forsooth no varlet, forsooth no base, forsooth I am
but mean; no crafty neither, but of the Gentle Craft.

LORD MAYOR
Where is my daughter Rose? Where is my child?   145

LINCOLN
Where is my nephew Lacy married?

FIRK
Why, here is good laced mutton, as I promised you.

LINCOLN
Villain, I'll have thee punished for this wrong!

FIRK
Punish the journeyman villain, but not the journeyman
shoemaker.   150

Enter DODGER

DODGER
My Lord, I come to bring unwelcome news:
Your nephew Lacy, and your daughter Rose
Early this morning wedded at the Savoy,
None being present but the Lady Mayoress.

147 *laced mutton* whore's flesh (with a pun on Lacy)

Besides, I learned among the officers, 155
The Lord Mayor vows to stand in their defence,
'Gainst any that shall seek to cross the match.

LINCOLN

Dares Eyre the shoemaker uphold the deed?

FIRK

Yes, sir: shoemakers dare stand in a woman's quarrel, I
warrant you, as deep as another, and deeper too. 160

DODGER

Besides, His Grace today dines with the Mayor,
Who on his knees humbly intends to fall,
And beg a pardon for your nephew's fault.

LINCOLN

But I'll prevent him. Come, Sir Roger Otley:
The King will do us justice in this cause. 165
Howe'er their hands have made them man and wife,
I will disjoin the match, or lose my life.

Exeunt [LINCOLN *and* LORD MAYOR]

FIRK

Adieu, Monsieur Dodger! Farewell, fools! Ha, ha! O if
they had stayed I would have so lammed them with flouts!
O heart! My codpiece-point is ready to fly in pieces every 170
time I think upon Mistress Rose, but let that pass, as my
Lady Mayoress says.

HODGE

This matter is answered. Come, Ralph, home with thy
wife! Come, my fine shoemakers, let's to our master's the
new Lord Mayor, and there swagger this Shrove Tuesday. 175
I'll promise you wine enough, for Madge keeps the cellar.

ALL

O rare! Madge is a good wench.

FIRK

And I'll promise you meat enough, for simpering Susan
keeps the larder. I'll lead you to victuals, my brave soldiers:
follow your captain! O brave! Hark, hark! 180

Bell rings

159 *stand in a woman's quarrel*. Firk intends another bawdy *double-entendre*.
169 *lammed them with flouts* bombarded them with gibes
175 *swagger* make merry

ALL

The pancake bell rings! The pancake bell, trilill, my hearts!

FIRK

O brave! O sweet bell! O delicate pancakes! Open the
doors, my hearts, and shut up the windows! Keep in the
house, let out the pancakes! O rare, my hearts! Let's march
together for the honour of Saint Hugh to the great new   185
hall in Gracious Street corner, which our master the new
Lord Mayor hath built.

RALPH

O the crew of good fellows that will dine at my Lord
Mayor's cost today!

HODGE

By the Lord, my Lord Mayor is a most brave man! How   190
shall prentices be bound to pray for him and the honour
of the gentlemen shoemakers! Let's feed and be fat with
my Lord's bounty.

FIRK

O musical bell still! O Hodge, O my brethren! There's
cheer for the heavens! Venison pasties walk up and down,   195
piping hot, like sergeants; beef and brewis comes marching
in dry fats; fritters and pancakes comes trowling in in
wheelbarrows; hens and oranges hopping in porters'
baskets; collops and eggs in scuttles; and tarts and custards
comes quavering in in malt-shovels!   200

Enter more Prentices

ALL

Whoop! Look here, look here!

HODGE

How now, mad lads, whither away so fast?

1 PRENTICE

Whither? Why, to the great new hall! Know you not why?
The Lord Mayor hath bidden all the prentices in London
to breakfast this morning.   205

181 *The pancake bell* see note on V. i, 50
195 *pasties* ed. (pastimes Q1)
196 *brewis* thick broth
197 *fats* vats
197 *trowling* rolling
199 *collops* bacon   199 *scuttles* dishes

ALL

O brave shoemaker! O brave lord of incomprehensible good fellowship! Whoo! Hark you, the pancake bell rings!

Cast up caps

FIRK

Nay, more, my hearts! Every Shrove Tuesday is our year of jubilee, and when the pancake bell rings, we are as free as my Lord Mayor. We may shut up our shops, and make 210 holiday. I'll have it called Saint Hugh's Holiday.

ALL

Agreed, agreed! Saint Hugh's Holiday!

HODGE

And this shall continue for ever.

ALL

O brave! Come, come, my hearts, away, away!

FIRK

O eternal credit to us of the Gentle Craft! March fair, my 215 hearts! O rare!

Exeunt

[Act V, Scene iii]

Enter KING *and his train over the stage*

KING

Is our Lord Mayor of London such a gallant?

NOBLEMAN

One of the merriest madcaps in your land.
Your Grace will think, when you behold the man,
He's rather a wild ruffian than a Mayor.
Yet thus much I'll ensure your Majesty: 5
In all his actions that concern his state,
He is as serious, provident, and wise,
As full of gravity amongst the grave,
As any Mayor hath been these many years.

KING

I am with child till I behold this huff-cap, 10

7 *provident* prudent
10 *with child* impatiently expecting   10 *huff-cap* madcap

But all my doubt is, when we come in presence,
His madness will be dashed clean out of countenance.

NOBLEMAN

It may be so, my Liege.

KING   Which to prevent,
Let someone give him notice 'tis our pleasure
That he put on his wonted merriment.   15
Set forward.

ALL

On afore.

Exeunt

[Act V, Scene iv]

Enter EYRE, HODGE, FIRK, RALPH, *and other Shoemakers,
all with napkins on their shoulders*

EYRE

Come, my fine Hodge, my jolly gentlemen shoemakers.
Soft, where be these cannibals, these varlets my officers?
Let them all walk and wait upon my brethren, for my
meaning is that none but shoemakers, none but the livery
of my Company shall in their satin hoods wait upon the   5
trencher of my Sovereign.

FIRK

O my Lord, it will be rare!

EYRE

No more, Firk! Come, lively! Let your fellow prentices
want no cheer; let wine be plentiful as beer, and beer as
water! Hang these penny-pinching fathers, that cram   10
wealth in innocent lambskins! Rip, knaves, avaunt, look to
my guests!

HODGE

My Lord, we are at our wits' end for room; those hundred
tables will not feast the fourth part of them!

---

11 *doubt* fear
15 *wonted* customary
6 *trencher* dinner-plate
11 *innocent lambskins* i.e., purses

EYRE

Then cover me those hundred tables again, and again, till   15
all my jolly prentices be feasted. Avoid, Hodge; run,
Ralph; frisk about, my nimble Firk! Carouse me fathom
healths to the honour of the shoemakers! Do they drink
lively, Hodge? Do they tickle it, Firk?

FIRK

Tickle it? Some of them have taken their liquor standing so   20
long, that they can stand no longer. But for meat, they
would eat it, and they had it.

EYRE

Want they meat? Where's this swag-belly, this greasy
kitchen-stuff cook? Call the varlet to me! Want meat! Firk,
Hodge, lame Ralph, run, my tall men, beleaguer the   25
shambles, beggar all Eastcheap, serve me whole oxen in
chargers, and let sheep whine upon the tables like pigs for
want of good fellows to eat them! Want meat! Vanish,
Firk! Avaunt, Hodge!

HODGE

Your Lordship mistakes my man Firk: he means their   30
bellies want meat, not the boards, for they have drunk so
much they can eat nothing.

Enter LACY, ROSE, *and* MARGERY

MARGERY

Where is my Lord?

EYRE

How now, Lady Madgy?

MARGERY

The King's most excellent Majesty is new come! He sends   35
me for thy Honour: one of his most worshipful peers bade
me tell thou must be merry, and so forth, but let that pass.

EYRE

Is my Sovereign come? Vanish, my tall shoemakers, my
nimble brethren, look to my guests the prentices. Yet stay
a little: how now, Hans? How looks my little Rose?   40

---

19 *tickle it* set to with gusto (cf. III. iii, 72 and IV. ii, 7)
25 *beleaguer the shambles* besiege the meat-market
27 *chargers* large serving-dishes

LACY

Let me request you to remember me:
I know your Honour easily may obtain
Free pardon of the King for me and Rose,
And reconcile me to my uncle's grace.

EYRE

Have done, my good Hans, my honest journeyman. Look   45
cheerily: I'll fall upon both my knees till they be as hard
as horn, but I'll get thy pardon.

MARGERY

Good my Lord, have a care what you speak to his Grace.

EYRE

Away, you Islington whitepot! Hence, you hopperarse,
you barley pudding full of maggots, you broiled carbonado!   50
Avaunt, avaunt, Mephostophilus! Shall Sim Eyre learn to
speak of you, Lady Madgy? Vanish, Mother Miniver-cap,
vanish, go, trip and go, meddle with your partlets and your
pishery-pashery, your flewes and your whirligigs! Go, rub
out of mine alley! Sim Eyre knows how to speak to a Pope,   55
to Sultan Soliman, to Tamburlaine, and he were here: and
shall I melt, shall I droop before my Sovereign? No! Come,
my Lady Madgy; follow me, Hans; about your business, my
frolic free-booters; Firk, frisk about and about and about,
for the honour of mad Simon Eyre, Lord Mayor of London.   60

FIRK

Hey, for the honour of the shoemakers!

Exeunt

44 *grace* favour
49 *whitepot ... hopperarse* rude allusions to the barrel-shape of Margery in
   her farthingale
50 *carbonado* steak
51 *learn* ed. (leaue Q1)
52 *Miniver-cap* headpiece trimmed with ermine
53 *partlets* linen collar with a small ruff
54 *flewes* the flaps of the French hood
54 *whirligigs* fripperies
54 *rub* be off

[Act V, Scene v]

A long flourish or two. Enter KING, *Nobles*, EYRE, MARGERY,
LACY, ROSE. LACY *and* ROSE *kneel*

KING

Well, Lacy, though the fact was very foul
Of your revolting from our kingly love
And your own duty, yet we pardon you.
Rise both, and, Mistress Lacy, thank my Lord Mayor
For your young bridegroom here.   5

EYRE

So, my dear Liege, Sim Eyre and my brethren the gentlemen shoemakers shall set your sweet Majesty's image cheek
by jowl by Saint Hugh, for this honour you have done
poor Simon Eyre. I beseech your Grace, pardon my rude
behaviour; I am a handicraftsman, yet my heart is without   10
craft. I would be sorry at my soul that my boldness should
offend my King.

KING

Nay, I pray thee, good Lord Mayor, be even as merry
As if thou wert among thy shoemakers:
It does me good to see thee in this humour.   15

EYRE

Sayest thou me so, my sweet Diocletian? Then hump!
Prince am I none, yet am I princely born. By the Lord of
Ludgate, I'll be as merry as a pie!

KING

Tell me in faith, mad Eyre, how old thou art.

EYRE

My Liege, a very boy, a stripling, a younker: you see not   20
a white hair on my head, not a grey in this beard. Every
hair, I assure thy Majesty, that sticks in this beard Sim
Eyre values at the King of Babylon's ransom; Tamar

1 *fact* deed
18 *pie* magpie
20 *younker* youth
23 *Tamar* ed. (Tama Q1) another name for Tamburlaine

16 *Diocletian.* A Roman emperor, here simply a term for 'majesty'.
16 *Then hump!* A catch-phrase of Eyre's: cf. 'cry hump' (27).

    Cham's beard was a rubbing-brush to't: yet I'll shave it off
    and stuff tennis balls with it, to please my bully King.   25

KING

    But all this while I do not know your age.

EYRE

    My Liege, I am six and fifty year old, yet I can cry hump
    with a sound heart, for the honour of Saint Hugh. Mark
    this old wench, my King: I danced the shaking of the
    sheets with her six and thirty years ago, and yet I hope to   30
    get two or three young Lord Mayors ere I die! I am lusty
    still, Sim Eyre still: care and cold lodging brings white
    hairs. My sweet Majesty, let care vanish, cast it upon thy
    nobles; it will make thee look always young like Apollo, and
    cry hump! Prince am I none, yet am I princely born.   35

KING

    Ha, ha!
    Say, Cornwall, didst thou ever see his like?

NOBLEMAN

    Not I, my Lord.

        Enter LINCOLN *and* LORD MAYOR

KING   Lincoln, what news with you?

LINCOLN

    My gracious Lord, have care unto yourself,
    For there are traitors here.

ALL   Traitors? Where? Who?   40

EYRE

    Traitors in my house? God forbid! Where be my officers?
    I'll spend my soul ere my King feel harm.

KING

    Where is the traitor, Lincoln?

LINCOLN   Here he stands.

KING

    Cornwall, lay hold on Lacy! Lincoln, speak:
    What canst thou lay unto thy nephew's charge?   45

LINCOLN

    This, my dear Liege: your Grace, to do me honour,
    Heaped on the head of this degenerous boy

29 *shaking of the sheets* see note on IV. v, 82
47 *degenerous* degenerate

Desertless favours; you made choice of him,
To be commander over powers in France,
But he—

KING   Good Lincoln, prithee pause a while: 50
Even in thine eyes I read what thou wouldst speak.
I know how Lacy did neglect our love,
Ran himself deeply, in the highest degree,
Into vile treason.

LINCOLN   Is he not a traitor?

KING

Lincoln, he was; now have we pardoned him.   55
'Twas not a base want of true valour's fire
That held him out of France, but love's desire.

LINCOLN

I will not bear his shame upon my back.

KING

Nor shalt thou, Lincoln: I forgive you both.

LINCOLN

Then good my Leige, forbid the boy to wed   60
One whose mean birth will much disgrace his bed.

KING

Are they not married?

LINCOLN   No, my Liege.

BOTH   We are!

KING

Shall I divorce them then? O be it far
That any hand on earth should dare untie
The sacred knot knit by God's majesty!   65
I would not for my crown disjoin their hands
That are conjoined in holy nuptial bands.
How sayest thou, Lacy? Wouldst thou lose they Rose?

LACY

Not for all India's wealth, my Sovereign.

KING

But Rose, I am sure, her Lacy would forgo.   70

ROSE

If Rose were asked that question, she'd say no.

KING

You hear them, Lincoln?

69 *India's* ed. (Indians Q1)

LINCOLN   Yea, my Liege, I do.

KING
  Yet canst thou find i'th'heart to part these two?
  Who seeks, besides you, to divorce these lovers?

LORD MAYOR
  I do, my gracious Lord: I am her father.   75

KING
  Sir Roger Otley, our last Mayor, I think?

NOBLEMAN
  The same, my Liege.

KING   Would you offend Love's laws?
  Well, you shall have your wills; you sue to me
  To prohibit the match: soft, let me see:
  You both are married, Lacy, art thou not?   80

LACY
  I am, dread Sovereign.

KING   Then, upon thy life,
  I charge thee not to call this woman wife.

LORD MAYOR
  I thank your Grace.

ROSE   O my most gracious Lord! *Kneel*

KING
  Nay, Rose, never woo me; I'll tell you true,
  Although as yet I am a bachelor,   85
  Yet I believe I shall not marry you.

ROSE
  Can you divide the body from the soul,
  Yet make the body live?

KING   Yea, so profound?
  I cannot, Rose; but you I must divide:
  Fair maid, this bridegroom cannot be your bride.   90
  Are you pleased, Lincoln? Otley, are you pleased?

BOTH
  Yes, my Lord.

KING   Then must my heart be eased,
  For, credit me, my conscience lives in pain,

---

90 *this bridegroom cannot be your bride*. As Bowers points out, 'bride' could
   be used of either sex.

Till these whom I divorced be joined again.
Lacy, give me thy hand; Rose, lend me thine: 95
Be what you would be; kiss now; so, that's fine!
At night, lovers, to bed! Now, let me see,
Which of you all mislikes this harmony?

LORD MAYOR
Will you then take from me my child perforce?

KING
Why, tell me, Otley, shines not Lacy's name   100
As bright in the world's eyes as the gay beams
Of any citizen?

LINCOLN   Yea, but, my gracious Lord,
I do mislike the match far more than he:
Her blood is too too base.

KING   Lincoln, no more!
Dost thou not know that love repects no blood,   105
Cares not for difference of birth or state?
The maid is young, well born, fair, virtuous:
A worthy bride for any gentleman!
Beside, your nephew for her sake did stoop
To bare necessity, and, as I hear,   110
Forgetting honours and all courtly pleasures,
To gain her love became a shoemaker.
As for the honour which he lost in France,
Thus I redeem it: Lacy, kneel thee down!
Arise, Sir Rowland Lacy! Tell me now,   115
Tell me in earnest, Otley, canst thou chide,
Seeing thy Rose a lady and a bride?

LORD MAYOR
I am content with what your Grace hath done.

LINCOLN
And I, my Liege, since there's no remedy.

KING
Come on, then, all shake hands: I'll have you friends.   120
Where there is much love, all discord ends.
What says my mad Lord Mayor to all this love?

EYRE
O my Liege, this honour you have done to my fine journeyman here, Rowland Lacy, and all those favours which you
have shown to me this day in my poor house, will make   125

Simon Eyre live longer by one dozen of warm summers
more than he should.

KING

Nay, my mad Lord Mayor—that shall be thy name—
If any grace of mine can length thy life,
One honour more I'll do thee: that new building,   130
Which at thy cost in Cornhill is erected,
Shall take a name from us. We'll have it called
The Leadenhall, because in digging it
You found the lead that covereth the same.

EYRE

I thank your Majesty.   135

MARGERY

God bless your Grace.

KING

Lincoln, a word with you.

Enter HODGE, FIRK, RALPH, *and more Shoemakers*

EYRE

How now, my mad knaves? Peace, speak softly: yonder is
the King.

KING

With the old troop which there we keep in pay,   140
We will incorporate a new supply.
Before one summer more pass o'er my head,
France shall repent England was injured.
What are all those?

LACY   All shoemakers, my Liege,
Sometimes my fellows; in their companies   145
I lived as merry as an emperor.

KING

My mad Lord Mayor, are all these shoemakers?

EYRE

All shoemakers, my Liege, all gentlemen of the Gentle
Craft, true Trojans, courageous cordwainers; they all kneel
to the shrine of holy Saint Hugh.   150

---

130 *that new building.* Leadenhall, in fact an estate belonging to the city, upon
which the historical Eyre erected a public granary in 1419, before his rise to
civic office.

ALL

God save your Majesty! All shoemakers!

KING

Mad Simon, would they anything with us?

EYRE

Mum, mad knaves, not a word! I'll do't, I warrant you.
They are all beggars, my Liege, all for themselves; and I
for them all on both my knees do entreat that for the   155
honour of poor Simon Eyre, and the good of his brethren
these mad knaves, your Grace would vouchsafe some
privilege to my new Leadenhall, that it may be lawful for
us to buy and sell leather there two days a week.

KING

Mad Sim, I grant your suit: you shall have patent   160
To hold two market days in Leadenhall;
Mondays and Fridays, those shall be the times.
Will this content you?

ALL

Jesus bless your Grace!

EYRE

In the name of these my poor brethren shoemakers, I most   165
humbly thank your Grace. But before I rise, seeing you are
in the giving vein, and we in the begging, grant Sim Eyre
one boon more.

KING

What is it, my Lord Mayor?

EYRE

Vouchsafe to taste of a poor banquet that stands sweetly   170
waiting for your sweet presence.

KING

I shall undo thee Eyre, only with feasts.
Already have I been too troublesome:
Say, have I not?

EYRE

O my dear King, Sim Eyre was taken unawares upon a day   175
of shroving which I promised long ago to the prentices of
London, for, and't please your Highness, in time past,

---

151 *All shoemakers* ed. (all shoomaker Q1). Some editors make this a stage
     direction
160 *patent* letters patent, royal licence

I bare the water-tankard, and my coat
Sits not a whit the worse upon my back.
And then, upon a morning, some mad boys   180
—It was Shrove Tuesday even as 'tis now—gave me my
breakfast, and I swore then by the stopple of my tankard,
if ever I came to be Lord Mayor of London, I would feast
all the prentices. This day, my Liege, I did it, and the
slaves had an hundred tables five times covered. They are 185
gone home and vanished:
Yet add more honour to the Gentle Trade:
Taste of Eyre's banquet, Simon's happy made.

KING

Eyre, I will taste of thy banquet, and will say,
I have not met more pleasure on a day.   190
Friends of the Gentle Craft, thanks to you all!
Thanks, my kind Lady Mayoress, for our cheer.
Come, Lords, a while let's revel it at home:
When all our sports and banquetings are done,
Wars must right wrongs which Frenchmen have begun.   195

                                                Exeunt

                    FINIS

---

178 *I bare the water-tankard, and my coat.* The shift from prose to verse
   occurs at the beginning of K4 verso in Q1, although 'for, and't please
   your Highness, in time past', the final words on K4 recto, also form a
   line of blank verse._
187 *Yet add more honour* . . . This couplet is set as prose in Q1.

Eastward Ho!

BEN JONSON
GEORGE CHAPMAN
JOHN MARSTON

Edited by
C. G. PETTER

ABBREVIATIONS

Q	copy text
Qq	all copies of first quarto (1605)
Q2	second quarto, BM 644 d53
Q3	third quarto
Brooke and Paradise	C.F. Brooke and N. Paradise. eds., *English Drama 1580-1642* (1933)
Judges	A.V. Judges, ed., *The Elizabethan Underworld* (reprinted 1965)

EASTWARD
HOE.

As

It was playd in the
Black-friers.

By

The Children of her Maiesties Reuels.

Made by

Geo: Chapman. Ben: Ionson. Ioh: Marston.

23

AT LONDON
Printed for *William Aspley.*
1 6 0 5.

[1–2] *Eastward Hoe.* The cry of Thames boatmen to hail passengers going down-river, i.e. to Greenwich (Court) or Blackwall (harbour).

[5] *Black-friers.* A private (enclosed) theatre within the city precinct which catered to a financial if not social élite. Admission charged was 6*d.*, as compared with 1*d.* in the public amphitheatres (e.g. the Globe), and plays were performed 'once a week' (*Epilogue*) rather than daily. As the opening stage direction indicates, there were three stage doors; the middle one was apparently large enough to have been used as a curtained discovery space. The curtain could be pulled shut for scenes taking place 'outside'. The smaller doorways may have been used as parts of the Counter in Act V.

The space 'above', the balcony referred to by Chapman as the *tarras*, in *May-Day*, is used as the upstairs of a house (II, ii, 186) and as the site of the pole at Cuckold's Haven (IV, i)—*Enter* SLITGUT, *with a pair of ox-horns, discovering Cuckold's Haven, above.* It could also have been conveniently used for the appearance of Mistresses Fond and Gazer (III, ii) to prevent overcrowding on the stage, though the text gives no hint of it.

The 'streets' and 'windows' of the *Epilogue* refer to the floor area and galleries of the Blackfriars.

[7] *her Maiesties Revels.* A boys' company granted a patent by James I in 1604, of which Marston was one of the principal shareholders. The company seems to have been increasingly daring in its contemporary, particularly Scots, satire. There was trouble over Daniel's *Philotas* (1604), *Eastward Ho!*, and finally John Day's *Isle of Gulls* (1606), which lost them the queen's patronage because, according to Sir Thomas Hoby's letter (Chambers, op. cit., III, 286), 'from the highest to the lowest, all men's parts were acted by two divers nations'.

[11] *Aspley.* Seems to have taken an interest in Chapman's work, 1604–07. He apparently bought Thorpe's share of this play, for which he was co-signatory in the Stationers' Register.

[DRAMATIS PERSONAE

WILLIAM TOUCHSTONE, *a goldsmith*
MISTRESS TOUCHSTONE, *his wife*
FRANCIS QUICKSILVER ⎱ *his apprentices*
GOLDING ⎰   5
GERTRUDE ⎱ *his daughters*
MILDRED ⎰
BETTRICE, *Mildred's maid*
POLDAVY, *a tailor*
SIR PETRONEL FLASH, *a new-made knight*   10
SECURITY, *an old usurer*
WINIFRED, *his wife*
SINDEFY, *Quicksilver's mistress*
BRAMBLE, *a lawyer*
SEAGULL, *a sea captain*   15
SCAPETHRIFT ⎱ *adventurers bound for Virginia*
SPENDALL ⎰
HAMLET, *a footman*
POTKIN, *a tankard-bearer*
MISTRESS FOND ⎱ *citizens' wives*   20
MISTRESS GAZER ⎰
SLITGUT, *a butcher's apprentice*
WOLF ⎱ *Officers of the Counter*
HOLDFAST ⎰
A SCRIVENER, A COACHMAN, SIR PETRONEL'S PAGE, A DRAWER *at*   25
the Blue Anchor Tavern, MESSENGER, GENTLEMEN, PRISONERS,
FRIEND]

[1] *Dramatis Personae* following H. & S., IV, 523, absent in Q1, 2, and 3.
The names of the principal characters are derived from alchemy.
These names were not only suitable to the prodigal-son story, but also
provided the authors with a shorthand for character traits, and a
formula for interaction. (For a discussion of Jonson's use of names see
G. B. Jackson, *Vision and Judgement in Ben Jonson's Drama* (New
Haven, Conn., 1968), pp. 57–69, and for an interesting summary of
his alchemical ideas see F. H. Mares, Revels edition of Ben Jonson's
The Alchemist (London, 1967), pp. xxxi–xl.)

173

[2] TOUCHSTONE. A smooth, fine-grained variety of black quartz used for testing gold or silver by the colour produced from rubbing upon it. Fig. to try or test the genuineness of anything. Hence his catchphrase, 'work upon that now', i.e., 'test yourself against that'.

[4] QUICKSILVER. Mercury; also sl. for cheat, thief. Its 'nimble-spirited' antics (especially subduing gold) exasperate the alchemist, but the promise of gold or, still better, *lumen novum*, philosophers' gold, helps him to persist. The process of conversion was variously described but consisted basically of: washing, heating (to drive off sulphur), sublimation, and the addition of gold to the fixed metal. Marriage was often symbolic of conversion.

[5] GOLDING. Good as gold and just as malleable in the goldsmith's hands.

[10] SIR PETRONEL FLASH. (Petronel = carbine), i.e., the sound of a gun's report, suggesting the fustian of a blustering gallant.

[11] SECURITY. A humour figure—melancholy: element, earth; metal, sulphur. Unlike Touchstone, encourages Quicksilver's pretensions which he uses as a tracer for gold.

[13] SINDEFY. Befitting one who is Quicksilver's and later Gertrude's foil. Reveals her background: of Puritan stock corrupted to 'Sin' by the city, and 'sweet Sin' (harlot) by Quicksilver.

[17] SPENDALL. Is twice abbreviated *Spoyl*. (III, i, s.p. 52, 61). H. & S., IX, 647 suggest that the name may have been changed to remove unwanted satire.

[18] HAMLET. Brooke and Paradise, op. cit., p. 412, conjecture that he was named for the actor Robert Hamlett, an adult actor by 1611. This might explain 'Gertrude' who is not named for her humour as is her sister 'Mildred'—i.e., mild.

PROLOGUE

Not out of envy, for there's no effect
Where there's no cause; nor out of imitation,
For we have evermore been imitated;
Nor out of our contention to do better
Than that which is opposed to ours in title,   5
For that was good; and better cannot be:
And for the title, if it seem affected,
We might as well have called it, 'God you good even'.
Only that eastward, westwards still exceeds—
Honour the sun's fair rising, not his setting.   10
Nor is our title utterly enforced,
As by the points we touch at, you shall see.
Bear with our willing pains, if dull or witty;
We only dedicate it to the City.

3 *we have evermore been imitated*. Referring to Dekker and Webster's
   imitation of 'city comedy', *Westward Ho!* and *Northward Ho!* A possible
   reference also to the character of Bellamont (Chapman) of *Northward
   Ho!* (See A. Nicholl, 'The Dramatic Portrait of George Chapman',
   PQ, XLI (1962), 215–28.)
5 *opposed to ours in title*. i.e., *Westward Ho!* (Dekker and Webster) performed by the rival Paul's Children in the late autumn or early winter
   of 1604. See E. E. Stoll, *John Webster* (Boston, Mass., 1905), p. 14 and
   M. L. Hunt, *Thomas Dekker. A Study* (Columbia Studies in English,
   1911), pp. 101–2.
8 *God you good even*. Mocking the use of clichés as titles, as in *What You
   Will*, *As You Like It*, etc.
9 *eastward, westwards still exceeds*. Eastward was the traditional direction
   of good luck; 'still exceeds' may be an ironic reference to the residence
   of the Court at Greenwich from mid-March to mid-June 1605. cf.
   Plutarch's *Morals*, 'More men . . . worship the sun rising than . . .
   setting'. See L. Hotson, *Mr. W. H.* (London, 1964), p. 223.
11 *title utterly enforced*. i.e., the values of those whose ambitions are rising
   with the new king are not unconditionally upheld.
14 *We only dedicate it . . . City*. This polite dedication is probably meant
   in the facetious tone of the rest of the *Prologue*.

EASTWARD HO!

Act I, Scene i

[Goldsmith's Row]

Enter MASTER TOUCHSTONE *and* QUICKSILVER *at several doors;*
QUICKSILVER *with his hat, pumps, short sword and dagger, and a*
racket trussed up under his cloak. At the middle door, enter
GOLDING, *discovering a goldsmith's shop, and walking short turns*
before it

TOUCHSTONE

And whither with you now? What loose action are you bound
for? Come, what comrades are you to meet withal? Where's
the supper? Where's the rendezvous?

QUICKSILVER

Indeed, and in very good sober truth, sir—

TOUCHSTONE

'Indeed, and in very good sober truth, sir'! Behind my back   5
thou wilt swear faster than a French foot-boy, and talk more
bawdily than a common midwife; and now, 'indeed, and in
very good sober truth, sir'! But if a privy search should be
made, with what furniture are you rigged now? Sirrah, I
tell thee, I am thy master, William Touchstone, goldsmith;   10
and thou my prentice, Francis Quicksilver; and I will see
whither you are running. 'Work upon that now'!

QUICKSILVER

Why, sir, I hope a man may use his recreation with his
master's profit.

TOUCHSTONE

Prentices' recreations are seldom with their master's profit.   15
'Work upon that now'! You shall give up your cloak, though

1 s.d. *at several doors* different doors.
9 *furniture* equipage, embellishment, decoration

---

4 *in very good sober truth.* Mocking Touchstone's euphemisms, as he
does in II, i with 'forsooth'.
6 *French foot-boy.* A page, notorious for his swearing.
16–17 *though you be no alderman.* City statutes dictated the manner and
colour of dress worn by citizens. Aldermen wore red robes; artisans,
flat caps; and apprentices, cap and gown.

you be no alderman. Heyday, Ruffians' Hall! Sword, pumps,
here's a racket indeed!

TOUCHSTONE *uncloaks* QUICKSILVER

QUICKSILVER

'Work upon that now'!

TOUCHSTONE

Thou shameless varlet, dost thou jest at thy lawful master   20
contrary to thy indentures?

QUICKSILVER

Why, 'sblood, sir, my mother's a gentlewoman, and my
father a Justice of Peace, and of Quorum. And though I am
a younger brother and a prentice, yet I hope I am my father's
son; and, by God's lid, 'tis for your worship and for your   25
commodity that I keep company. I am entertained among
gallants, true! They call me cousin Frank, right! I lend them
moneys, good! They spend it, well! But when they are
spent, must not they strive to get more? Must not their land
fly? And to whom? Shall not your worship ha' the refusal?   30
Well, I am a good member of the City, if I were well con-
sidered. How would merchants thrive, if gentlemen would
not be unthrifts? How could gentlemen be unthrifts, if their
humours were not fed? How should their humours be fed but
by white-meat and cunning secondings? Well, the City might   35
consider us. I am going to an ordinary now: the gallants fall
to play; I carry light gold with me; the gallants call, 'Cousin
Frank, some gold for silver!'; I change, gain by it; the
gallants lose the gold, and then call, 'Cousin Frank, lend me
some silver!' Why—   40

TOUCHSTONE

Why? I cannot tell. Seven-score pound art thou out in the
cash; but look to it, I will not be gallanted out of my moneys!
And as for my rising by other men's fall; God shield me!

---

17 *Ruffians' Hall* Ed. (Ruffins hall Q)
34 *humours* dispositions, affectations

---

17 *Ruffians' Hall.* A field in West Smithfield: site of brawls.
18 *racket.* Tennis racket; and play on the sense racket, a loud noise.
19 s.d. *uncloaks.* Perhaps part of Touchstone's alchemical role; i.e.,
   calcination, removing the glitter.
23 *Justice . . . of Quorum.* A distinguished Justice who presided over a
   'bench'.
36 *ordinary.* Tavern where gallants met to eat, drink, and gamble.
37 *light gold.* Counterfeit money. Its method of preparation is described by
   Quicksilver (IV, i, 202–24).

Did I gain my wealth by ordinaries? No! By exchanging of
gold? No! By keeping of gallants' company? No! I hired me   45
a little shop, sought low, took small gain, kept no debt-book,
garnished my shop for want of plate, with good wholesome
-thrifty sentences, as, 'Touchstone, keep thy shop, and thy
shop will keep thee'. 'Light gains makes heavy purses'. ' 'Tis
good to be merry and wise'. And when I was wived, having   50
something to stick to, I had the horn of suretyship ever
before my eyes. You all know the device of the horn, where
the young fellow slips in at the butt-end, and comes squeezed
out at the buckle. And I grew up, and, I praise Providence, I
bear my brows now as high as the best of my neighbours: 55

---

46 *sought* ed. (fought Q)
49 *Light gains*, etc. proverbial. Tilley, G7
49-50 *'Tis good*, etc. proverbial. Tilley, G324

51-2 *horn of suretyship . . . device of the horn.* Touchstone alludes to the
notorious method by which London merchants cheated young country
gentlemen of their fortunes and lands. A sixteenth-century panel
(described by J. E. Hodgkin, in *N&Q* (1887), IV, 323-4) illustrates the
moral that 'This horn embleme here doth showe Of suertishipp what
harme doth growe'. The panel shows an enormous horn hanging across
a tree. At the far left stands a wealthy citizen, dressed to suit his
affluence. He supervises a character, dressed like Quicksilver (purple
doublet, profusely slashed; large felt hat and cloak, with a dagger in
his girdle), who is thrusting a victim into the opening of the horn; his
unhappy face and an arm emerging from the narrow end (buckle). The
citizen holds a rope, loosely tied around the victim's legs. To the right
stands another ragged, woebegone, gallant (i.e., the gallant, fleeced). In
William Fennor's seventeenth-century pamphlet, 'The Counter's
Commonwealth', A. V. Judges (ed.), op. cit., pp. 441-8, the emblem is
further elucidated. Citizens would draw in victims by at first refusing
them commodities (the lending of goods by which money could be
raised). This only increased the gallant's determination to get the goods.
The citizen would then send a go-between (probably dressed like
Quicksilver) who would advise the gallant on how to persuade the
merchant to grant him credit. The gallant again approached the merchant who once more stubbornly refused. Finally the merchant agreed,
provided 'an endeared friend' could be found as guarantor. In desperation the gallant would ask the go-between to sign for half the bond.
In order to raise cash quickly the gentleman would then give the goods
to the go-between if the latter would sell them for him. But the gentleman was still totally responsible for the bond, and if he forfeited when
it was due, the citizen would invite him to supper and then have him
arrested. He would only be released on paying back the whole sum,
which usually meant forfeiting his inheritance or ancestral lands.

but thou—well, look to the accounts; your father's bond lies
for you; seven score pound is yet in the rear.

QUICKSILVER

Why, 'slid, sir, I have as good, as proper, gallants' words for
it as any are in London; gentlemen of good phrase, perfect
language, passingly behaved; gallants that wear socks and   60
clean linen, and call me 'kind Cousin Frank', 'good Cousin
Frank'— for they know my father; and, by God's lid, shall
not I trust 'em? Not trust?

Enter a PAGE, *as inquiring for* TOUCHSTONE's *shop*

GOLDING

What do ye lack, sir? What is't you'll buy, sir?

TOUCHSTONE

Ay, marry, sir; there's a youth of another piece. There's thy   65
fellow-prentice, as good a gentleman born as thou art; nay,
and better miened. But does he pump it, or racket it? Well,
if he thrive not, if he outlast not a hundred such crackling
bavins as thou art, God and men neglect industry.

GOLDING

It is his shop, and here my master walks.   70

To the PAGE

TOUCHSTONE

With me, boy?

PAGE

My master, Sir Petronel Flash, recommends his love to you,
and will instantly visit you.

TOUCHSTONE

To make up the match with my eldest daughter, my wife's
dilling, whom she longs to call madam. He shall find me   75
unwillingly ready, boy.   *Exit* PAGE
There's another affliction too. As I have two prentices, the
one of a boundless prodigality, the other of a most hopeful
industry; so have I only two daughters: the eldest, of a

---

67 *miened* ed. (meaned Q)
75 *dilling* darling

---

56 *father's bond.* Obligation to pay a sum of money for an indenture.
62 *by God's lid.* By God's eyelid. Such oaths were banned from the stage
    by an act passed in May 1606, offences being subject to a fine of £10.
    Eastward Ho! may have been the *cause célèbre.*
64 *What do ye lack,* etc. Tradesman's familiar greeting to his customer.
68–9 *crackling bavins.* Twigs used to ignite a fire. cf. *1 Henry IV*, III, ii,
    61–2, 'rash bavin wits, Soon kindled and soon burnt'.

proud ambition and nice wantonness, the other of a modest   80
humility and comely soberness. The one must be ladyfied,
forsooth, and be attired just to the court-cut and long-tail.
So far is she ill-natured to the place and means of my preferment and fortune, that she throws all the contempt and
despite hatred itself can cast upon it. Well, a piece of land   85
she has, 'twas her grandmother's gift: let her, and her Sir
Petronel, flash out that! But as for my substance, she that
scorns me, as I am a citizen and tradesman, shall never
pamper her pride with my industry; shall never use me as
men do foxes: keep themselves warm in the skin, and throw   90
the body that bare it to the dunghill. I must go entertain
this Sir Petronel. Golding, my utmost care's for thee, and
only trust in thee; look to the shop. As for you, Master
Quicksilver, think of husks, for thy course is running
directly to the Prodigals' hogs' trough! Husks, sirrah! 'Work   95
upon that now'!   *Exit* TOUCHSTONE

QUICKSILVER
Marry faugh, goodman flat-cap! 'Sfoot! though I am a
prentice, I can give arms; and my father's a Justice-o'-Peace
by descent; and 'sblood—

GOLDING
Fie, how you swear!   100

QUICKSILVER
'Sfoot man, I am a gentleman, and may swear by my pedigree, God's my life. Sirrah Golding, wilt be ruled by a fool?
Turn good fellow, turn swaggering gallant, and 'Let the
welkin roar, and Erebus also'. Look not westward to the fall
of Don Phoebus, but to the East—Eastward Ho!   105

---

 8 *nice* lascivious, loose
89–90 *as men do foxes*, etc. proverbial. Tilley, M1163
98 *give arms* bear arms, display one's gentlemanly rank
105 *Don Phoebus* the sun

---

82 *court-cut and long-tail.* Alluding to the long flowing gowns worn by
    court ladies; also 'one and all'.
97 *Marry faugh.* Oath of contempt. The name of a bawd in Marston, *The
    Dutch Courtesan* (1605).
97 *flat-cap.* The round cap fashionable in Henry VIII's reign, and later
    characteristic of London merchants and apprentices (see above, note
    I, i, 16–17).
103–4 *Let the welkin roar*, etc. Scraps from Pistol's rant, *2 Henry IV*, II, iv,
    182.

'Where radiant beams of lusty Sol appear,
And bright Eoüs makes the welkin clear'.

We are both gentlemen, and therefore should be no coxcombs; let's be no longer fools to this flat-cap, Touchstone.
Eastward, bully! This satin-belly, and canvas-backed   110
Touchstone—'slife, man, his father was a malt-man, and
his mother sold gingerbread in Christ-church!

GOLDING
What would ye ha' me do?

QUICKSILVER
Why, do nothing, be like a gentleman, be idle; the curse of
man is labour. Wipe thy bum with testons, and make ducks   115
and drakes with shillings. What, Eastward Ho! Wilt thou
cry, 'what is't ye lack?', stand with a bare pate and a dropping
nose under a wooden pent-house, and art a gentleman?
Wilt thou bear tankards, and may'st bear arms? Be ruled,
turn gallant, Eastward Ho! 'Ta ly-re, ly-re ro! Who calls   120
Jeronimo? Speak, here I am!' God's so, how like a sheep
thou look'st! O' my conscience some cowherd begot thee,
thou Golding of Golding Hall, ha, boy?

GOLDING
Go, ye are a prodigal coxcomb; I a cowherd's son, because
I turn not a drunken whore-hunting rake-hell like thyself?   125

107 *Eoüs* the dawn.
107 *welkin* sky
115 *testons* sixpences
125 *rake-hell* scoundrel, wanton, debauchee

106–7 *Where . . . clear.* I have been unable to identify this quotation.
110 *bully.* Term implying friendly admiration: fine fellow, gallant.
110 *satin-belly, and canvas-backed.* Tradesmen's dress consisting of satin-
      fronted canvas. Quicksilver may also intend this as an emblem of the
      tradesman's ethic, i.e., soft(-spoken) before, and tough(-minded) after.
115–16 *ducks and drakes.* A game of making flat stones skip across water.
      Proverbial. Tilley, D632.
118 *wooden pent-house.* Awning projecting over the bench outside the
      goldsmith's shop.
119 *bear tankards.* Apprentices' duties included serving their masters with
      water from the conduits or the Thames.
120–1 *Who calls Jeronimo?* Opening line of one of the most famous speeches
      in Kyd's *Spanish Tragedy*, II, v, 4.

QUICKSILVER

Rake-hell! Rake-hell!

Offers to draw, and GOLDING *trips up his heels and holds him*

GOLDING

Pish, in soft terms ye are a cowardly bragging boy, I'll ha'
you whipped.

QUICKSILVER

Whipped? That's good, i'faith. Untruss me?

GOLDING

No, thou wilt undo thyself. Alas, I behold thee with pity,   130
not with anger, thou common shot-clog, gull of all companies! Methinks I see thee already walking in Moorfields
without a cloak, with half a hat, without a band, a doublet
with three buttons, without a girdle, a hose with one point
and no garter, with a cudgel under thine arm, borrowing   135
and begging threepence.

QUICKSILVER

Nay, 'slife, take this and take all! As I am a gentleman born,
I'll be drunk, grow valiant, and beat thee.   *Exit*

GOLDING

Go, thou most madly vain, whom nothing can recover but
that which reclaims atheists, and makes great persons some-   140
times religious: calamity. As for my place and life, thus I
have read:

'Whate'er some vainer youth may term disgrace,
    The gain of honest pains is never base;
From trades, from arts, from valour, honour springs;   145
These three are founts of gentry, yea of kings'.

[*Retires*]

---

127 s.d. *Offers to draw*, etc. This exchange perfectly illustrates the con-
frontation expected in the attack of gold by mercury.

131 *shot-clog*. A dupe who pays the bill (shot) for the whole company at the
tavern.

132 *Moorfields*. The field lying to the north of the city   (see Appendix for
location), a famous haunt of beggars. W. Peery shows how Field uses a
similar passage in *A Woman is a Weathercock* (sig. G4ʳ) and suggests
that Field might have played Quicksilver's role in the original production. (*MLN*, LXII (1947), 131–2: 'Zoons! methinks I see myself in
Moorfields, upon a wooden leg, begging threepence'.)

143–6 *Whate'er . . . kings*. No source has been found for these lines of
commonplace seventeenth-century morality.

[Act I, Scene ii

A Room in TOUCHSTONE'*s House*]

Enter GERTRUDE, MILDRED, BETTRICE, *and* POLDAVY, *a tailor;*
POLDAVY *with a fair gown, Scotch farthingale, and French fall in
his arms;* GERTRUDE *in a French head-attire and citizen's gown;*
MILDRED *sewing, and* BETTRICE *leading a monkey after her*

GERTRUDE

For the passion of patience, look if Sir Petronel approach;
that sweet, that fine, that delicate, that—for love's sake, tell
me if he come. O sister Mill, though my father be a low-
capped tradesman, yet I must be a lady; and, I praise God,
my mother must call me Madam. (Does he come?) Off with   5
this gown for shame's sake, off with this gown! Let not my

---

1 s.d. GERTRUDE Ed. (*girted* Q)
   Scotch farthingale Ed. (Scotch Varthingall Q)

---

1 s.d. BETTRICE. Makes her only appearance to utter one line (I, ii, 65).
Parrott suggests she is a visual pun reflecting Gertrude's mimicry of
court manners. Earlier (London, 1822) Nares, *A Glossary*, notes that
ape occasionally meant 'a fool'; it probably meant that those coquettes
who made fools of men would have them still to lead against their will.
Beatrice in *Much Ado About Nothing*, II, i, 37, alludes to 'leading apes
into hell' as the proverbial fate of old maids: hence possibly a visual
emblem for Mildred. This scene may have been cut so by far the most
persuasive argument is H. & S.'s, that the passage cut was a s.d. in
which Bettrice makes the monkey perform on the word 'Scot'. cf. Donne,
in his first *Satire*, 79–82: 'He doth move no more/Then . . . thou O
Elephant or Ape wilt doe,/When any names the King of Spaine to you';
or Jonson, in the Induction to *Bartholomew Fair*, who describes an ape
that will 'come over the chaine, for the *King* of *England*, and backe
againe for the *Prince*, and sit still on his arse for the *Pope*, and the *King*
of *Spaine*!' In view of this theory, a s.d. has been inserted by the present
editor at I, ii, 47.
   Scotch farthingale. Hooped petticoat popular in Elizabethan and
Jacobean times. Learning to wear a Scotch farthingale is synonymous
with learning to become a miser in *Westward Ho!*, I, i, 35 (Thomas
Dekker, *Dramatic Works*, ed. Fredson Bowers, 4 vols., Cambridge,
1953–61, II.)
   French fall. Falling band; i.e., type of collar, softer than the stiff-
standing ruff.
   French head-attire. i.e., French hood: headdress worn by women
(*O.E.D.*).

knight take me in the city-cut in any hand. Tear't, pax on't—
does he come?—tear't off! [*Sings*] *Thus whilst she sleeps, I
sorrow for her sake, &c.*

MILDRED

Lord, sister, with what an immodest impatiency and dis-   10
graceful scorn do you put off your city tire; I am sorry to
think you imagine to right yourself in wronging that which
hath made both you and us.

GERTRUDE

I tell you I cannot endure it, I must be a lady: do you wear
your coif with a London licket, your stammel petticoat with   15
two guards, the buffin gown with the tuf-taffety cape, and
the velvet lace. I must be a lady, and I will be a lady. I like
some humours of the city dames well: to eat cherries only
at an angel a pound, good. To dye rich scarlet black, pretty.
To line a grogram gown clean through with velvet, tolerable.   20
Their pure linen, their smocks of three pound a smock, are
to be borne withal. But your mincing niceries, taffeta
pipkins, durance petticoats, and silver bodkins—God's my
life, as I shall be a lady, I cannot endure it! Is he come yet?

7 *in any hand* in any case
21 *smock* woman's undergarment
23 *pipkins* hats
23 *durance* a stout durable cloth (*O.E.D.*)

7 *pax*. Euphemism for pox, i.e., syphilis.
8–9 *Thus whilst she sleeps*, etc. From the song beginning 'Sleep wayward
thoughts' (Dowland, *First Book of Songs* (1597), ed. Fellowes in *The
English School of Lutenist Song Writers*, London, 1921, II, 50–2).
15 *licket*. Lace or ribbon used to tie on coifs.
15 *stammel*. Cheap red woollen cloth worn by the lower classes.
16 *guards*. Ornamental trimming, not lavish enough for Gertrude's
extravagant tastes.
16 *buffin*. Coarse woollen grosgrain; cf. Massinger, *The City Madam*,
IV, iv, 26, where the ruined upstarts appear 'in buffin gowns'.
16 *tuf-taffety*. 'Plain taffeta was not rich enough for Elizabethan taste. It
must be "tufted", i.e. woven with raised stripes or spots' (M. C.
Linthicum, *Costume in the Drama of Shakespeare and His Contemporaries*, Oxford, 1936, p. 124); quoted H. & S., IX, 651.
18 *to eat cherries*, etc. The extravagance of city dames in paying 10
shillings a pound for cherries is satirized also in Dekker's *Batchelor's
Banquet* (1603) (Thomas Dekker, *Non Dramatic Works*, ed. A. B.
Grossart, 5 vols., London, 1884–86, I, 173).
23 *bodkin*. A long pin or pin-shaped ornament used by women to fasten up
the hair.

Lord, what a long knight 'tis! [*Sings*] *And ever she cried,*   25
Shoot home!—and yet I knew one longer—*And ever she cried,*
Shoot home! Fa, la, ly, re, lo, la!

MILDRED
Well, sister, those that scorn their nest, oft fly with a sick
wing.

GERTRUDE
Bow-bell!   30

MILDRED
Where titles presume to thrust before fit means to second
them, wealth and respect often grow sullen and will not
follow. For sure in this, I would for your sake I spoke not
truth: 'Where ambition of place goes before fitness of birth,
contempt and disgrace follow'. I heard a scholar once say   35
that Ulysses, when he counterfeited himself mad, yoked
cats and foxes and dogs together to draw his plough, whilst
he followed and sowed salt; but sure I judge them truly
mad that yoke citizens and courtiers, tradesmen and soldiers,
a goldsmith's daughter and a knight. Well, sister, pray God   40
my father sow not salt too.

GERTRUDE
Alas! Poor Mill, when I am a lady, I'll pray for thee yet,
i'faith: nay, and I'll vouchsafe to call thee Sister Mill still;
for though thou art not like to be a lady as I am, yet sure
thou art a creature of God's making, and mayest peradven-   45
ture to be saved as soon as I—does he come?
        [*Sings, and monkey cartwheels*]
    And ever and anon she doubled in her song.
Now, Lady's my comfort, what a profane ape's here!

26, 27 *Shoot* Ed. (*shout* Q)
28–9 *those that . . . wing* proverbial. Tilley, B377

25–7 *And ever she cried,* etc. An unidentified ballad with markedly sexual
    overtones.
30 *Bow-bell.* Term for a cockney, i.e., one born within the sound of the
    bells of St Mary-le-Bow Church in Cheapside (often pejorative).
    Proverbial. Tilley, S671.
36–8 *Ulysses . . . salt.* Mildred here misinterprets the scholar; to feign
    madness, Ulysses yoked together an ass and an ox, then ploughed sand
    and sowed salt.
47 s.d. H. & S., IV, 496 suggest that here (A4ᵛ) 'nine lines have been
    excised from the text . . .' though 'a vestige of a gibe against the Scotch
    survives'.
47 *doubled.* Repeated a note higher (Brooke and Paradise, op. cit. p. 402.).
48 *Lady's my comfort,* etc. Ref. to Virgin Mary as By'r' Lady.

Tailor, Poldavis, prithee, fit it, fit it! Is this a right Scot?
Does it clip close, and bear up round?   50

POLDAVY

Fine and stiffly, i'faith; 'twill keep your thighs so cool, and
make your waist so small; here was a fault in your body, but
I have supplied the defect with the effect of my steel instrument, which, though it have but one eye, can see to rectify
the imperfection of the proportion.   55

GERTRUDE

Most edifying tailor! I protest you tailors are most sanctified members, and make many crooked things go upright.
How must I bear my hands? Light, light?

POLDAVY

O, ay, now you are in the lady-fashion, you must do all
things light. Tread light, light. Ay, and fall so: that's the   60
court-amble.

She trips about the stage

GERTRUDE

Has the Court ne'er a trot?

POLDAVY

No, but a false gallop, lady.

GERTRUDE

And if she will not go to bed,—

Cantat

BETTRICE

The knight's come, forsooth.   65

Enter SIR PETRONEL, MASTER TOUCHSTONE, *and* MISTRESS
TOUCHSTONE

GERTRUDE

Is my knight come? O the Lord, my band? Sister, do my
cheeks look well? Give me a little box o' the ear that I may
seem to blush; now, now. So, there, there, there! Here he
is! O my dearest delight! Lord, Lord, and how does my
knight?   70

49–50 *Scot . . . round* refers to the Scotch farthingale
57 *things* Ed. (thing Q)
61 *amble* artificial or acquired pace (*N.E.D.*)
65 s.d. *Cantat* she sings
66 *band* husband, and possible pun on falling band

51–5 *Fine . . . proportion*. This *double entendre* in the mouth of the tailor is
    predictable, since tailors were reputedly lecherous.
64 *And . . . bed*. I have been unable to identify this song.

3

TOUCHSTONE
Fie, with more modesty!

GERTRUDE
Modesty! Why, I am no citizen now—modesty! Am I not
to be married? Y'are best to keep me modest, now I am to
be a lady.

SIR PETRONEL
Boldness is good fashion and courtlike.   75

GERTRUDE
Ay, in a country lady I hope it is; as I shall be. And how
chance ye came no sooner, Knight?

SIR PETRONEL
'Faith, I was so entertained in the progress with one Count
Epernoum, a Welsh knight; we had a match at balloon too
with my Lord Whachum, for four crowns.   80

GERTRUDE
At baboon? Jesu! You and I will play at baboon in the
country, Knight?

SIR PETRONEL
O, sweet lady, 'tis a strong play with the arm.

GERTRUDE
With arm or leg or any other member, if it be a court sport.
And when shall's be married, my Knight?   85

SIR PETRONEL
I come now to consummate it, and your father may call a
poor knight son-in-law.

TOUCHSTONE
Sir, ye are come. What is not mine to keep, I must not be
sorry to forgo. A hundred pound land her grandmother left
her, 'tis yours; herself (as her mother's gift) is yours. But if   90
you expect aught from me, know, my hand and mine eyes
open together: I do not give blindly. 'Work upon that now'!

SIR PETRONEL
Sir, you mistrust not my means! I am a knight.

---

79 *Epernoum.* This may be a personal gibe; a Count Peppernoun appears in
    Northward Ho!
79 *balloon.* A game like football, but played entirely in the air with 'bracers',
    flat pieces of wood attached to the arm.
89 *A hundred pound land.* Refers to the yearly income accruing from the
    property. Touchstone's valuation of 'two thousand pounds' worth of
    good land' (IV, ii, 232–3) gives the market value of the estate, including
    'two hundred pounds' worth of wood ready to fell; and a fine sweet
    house . . .' (II, ii, 135–8).

TOUCHSTONE
  Sir, sir, what I know not, you will give me leave to say I am
  ignorant of.   95
MISTRESS TOUCHSTONE
  Yes, that he is a knight; I know where he had money to pay
  the gentlemen-ushers and heralds their fees. Ay, that he is
  a knight; and so might you have been, too, if you had been
  aught else than an ass, as well as some of your neighbours.
  And I thought you would not ha' been knighted (as I am an   100
  honest woman), I would ha' dubbed you myself. I praise
  God I have wherewithal. But as for you, daughter—
GERTRUDE
  Ay, mother, I must be a lady tomorrow; and by your leave,
  mother (I speak it not without my duty, but only in the right
  of my husband), I must take place of you, mother.   105
MISTRESS TOUCHSTONE
  That you shall, Lady-daughter, and have a coach as well as
  I too.
GERTRUDE
  Yes, mother. But by your leave, mother (I speak it not
  without my duty, but only in my husband's right), my
  coach-horses must take the wall of your coach-horses.   110
TOUCHSTONE
  Come, come, the day grows low: 'tis supper-time. Use my
  house; the wedding solemnity is at my wife's cost; thank
  me for nothing but my willing blessing, for (I cannot feign)
  my hopes are faint. And, sir, respect my daughter; she has
  refused for you wealthy and honest matches, known good   115
  men, well-moneyed, better traded, best reputed.
GERTRUDE
  Body o' truth, 'chitizens, chitizens'. Sweet Knight, as soon
  as ever we are married, take me to thy mercy out of this
  miserable 'chity', presently, carry me out of the scent of

118 *to* Ed. (to to Q)

96–7 *I know where he had money*, etc. Refers to the sale of knighthoods. A
  grant of 29 May 1604 fixed the fees paid to the gentlemen-ushers,
  heralds-at-arms, etc.
110 *take the wall.* Have precedence, i.e., the person who walked on the
  outside of the pavement would have to endure the garbage thrown from
  the upstairs windows of the house.
117 *chitizens.* Affected pronunciation of city-dames. (*Eastward Ho!*, ed.
  A. H. Bullen, *The Works of John Marston*, 3 vols., London, 1887,
  III, 1–124.) This speech seems to parody the language of *Westward Ho!*

Newcastle coal, and the hearing of Bow-bell, I beseech thee,   120
down with me, for God's sake!

TOUCHSTONE

Well, daughter, I have read, that old wit sings:
    'The greatest rivers flow from little springs.
    Though thou art full, scorn not thy means at first;
    He that's most drunk may soonest be athirst'.   125
'Work upon that now'!

          All but TOUCHSTONE, MILDRED *and* GOLDING *depart*

No, no! Yond' stand my hopes. Mildred, come hither
daughter. And how approve you your sister's fashion? How
do you fancy her choice? What dost thou think?

MILDRED

I hope, as a sister, well.   130

TOUCHSTONE

Nay but, nay but, how dost thou like her behaviour and
humour? Speak freely.

MILDRED

I am loath to speak ill; and yet, I am sorry of this, I cannot
speak well.

TOUCHSTONE

Well! Very good, as I would wish; a modest answer.   135
Golding, come hither; hither, Golding! How dost thou like
the knight, Sir Flash? Does he not look big? How lik'st thou
the elephant? He says he has a castle in the country.

GOLDING

Pray heaven, the elephant carry not his castle on his back.

TOUCHSTONE

'Fore heaven, very well! But, seriously, how dost repute   140
him?

GOLDING

The best I can say of him is, I know him not.

TOUCHSTONE

Ha, Golding! I commend thee, I approve thee, and will
make it appear my affection is strong to thee. My wife has
her humour, and I will ha' mine. Dost thou see my daughter   145

---

123 *The greatest rivers*, etc. proverbial. Tilley, B681

---

139 *Pray heaven . . . back.* Golding fears that Petronel's only possessions
are his clothes. The elephant in the Middle Ages was frequently represented with a castle on his back. cf. the chess piece, and the district in
South London. To the Elizabethans the elephant and castle was a
well-known pageant. See Robert Whithington, 'A Note on *Eastward
Ho*, I, ii, 178,' *MLN*, XLIII (1928), 28–9.

here? She is not fair, well-favoured or so, indifferent, which
modest measure of beauty shall not make it thy only work
to watch her, nor sufficient mischance, to suspect her. Thou
art towardly, she is modest; thou art provident, she is careful.
She's now mine: give me thy hand, she's now thine. 'Work   150
upon that now'!

GOLDING

Sir, as your son, I honour you; and as your servant, obey
you.

TOUCHSTONE

Sayest thou so? Come hither, Mildred. Do you see yond'
fellow? He is a gentleman, though my prentice, and has   155
somewhat to take to; a youth of good hope, well-friended,
well parted. Are you mine? You are his. 'Work you upon
that now'!

MILDRED

Sir, I am all yours; your body gave me life; your care and
love, happiness of life; let your virtue still direct it, for to   160
your wisdom I wholly dispose myself.

TOUCHSTONE

Sayest thou so? Be you two better acquainted. Lip her, lip
her, knave! So, shut up shop, in! We must make holiday!

                              Exeunt GOLDING *and* MILDRED

'This match shall on, for I intend to prove
Which thrives the best, the mean or lofty love.   165
Whether fit wedlock vowed 'twixt like and like,
Or prouder hopes, which daringly o'erstrike
Their place and means. 'Tis honest time's expense,
When seeming lightness bears a moral sense'.
'Work upon that now'!   170

                                                        Exit

---

157 *well parted.* i.e., furnished with good parts or abilities, talented.
168 *'Tis honest time's expense.* Time is used profitably.

Act II, Scene i

[Goldsmith's Row]

TOUCHSTONE, GOLDING, *and* MILDRED, *sitting on either side of the stall*

TOUCHSTONE

Quicksilver! Master Francis Quicksilver! Master Quicksilver!

Enter QUICKSILVER

QUICKSILVER

Here, sir—ump!

TOUCHSTONE

So, sir; nothing but flat Master Quicksilver (without any familiar addition) will fetch you! Will you truss my points,   5
sir?

QUICKSILVER

Ay, forsooth—ump!

TOUCHSTONE

How now, sir? The drunken hiccup so soon this morning?

QUICKSILVER

'Tis but the coldness of my stomach, forsooth.

TOUCHSTONE

What, have you the cause natural for it? Y'are a very learned   10
drunkard; I believe I shall miss some of my silver spoons with
your learning. The nuptial night will not moisten your
throat sufficiently, but the morning likewise must rain her
dews into your gluttonous weasand.

QUICKSILVER

An't please you, sir, we did but drink—ump!—to the   15
coming off of the knightly bridegroom.

TOUCHSTONE

To the coming off on him?

QUICKSILVER

Ay, forsooth! We drunk to his coming on—ump!—when
we went to bed; and now we are up, we must drink to his

1 s.d. omit QUICKSILVER ed.
14 *weasand* gullet

4–5 *without any familiar addition.* cf. Quicksilver's insolent words of
address, 'now I tell thee, Touchstone' (II, i, 120).
5 *truss my points.* The points or laces fastened the doublet to the hose. It
was one of a valet's duties to 'truss' or tie the points.
18–20 *coming on . . . coming off.* Successful completion of the marriage
ritual.

coming off; for that's the chief honour of a soldier, sir; and   20
therefore we must drink so much the more to it, forsooth—
ump!

TOUCHSTONE

A very capital reason! So that you go to bed late, and rise
early to commit drunkenness; you fulfil the Scripture very
sufficient wickedly, forsooth!   25

QUICKSILVER

The knight's men, forsooth, be still o' their knees at it—
ump!—and because 'tis for your credit, sir, I would be loath
to flinch.

TOUCHSTONE

I pray, sir, e'en to 'em again, then; y'are one of the separated
crew, one of my wife's faction, and my young lady's, with   30
whom, and with their great match, I will have nothing to do.

QUICKSILVER

So, sir; now I will go keep my—ump!—credit with 'em, an't
please you, sir!

TOUCHSTONE

In any case, sir, lay one cup of sack more o' your cold
stomach, I beseech you!   35

QUICKSILVER

Yes, forsooth!

Exit QUICKSILVER

TOUCHSTONE

This is for my credit; servants ever maintain drunkenness
in their master's house, for their master's credit; a good idle
serving-man's reason. I thank Time the night is past! I
ne'er waked to such cost; I think we have stowed more sorts   40
of flesh in our bellies than ever Noah's Ark received; and
for wine, why, my house turns giddy with it, and more noise
in it than at a conduit. Ay me, even beasts condemn our
gluttony! Well, 'tis our City's fault, which, because we
commit seldom, we commit the more sinfully; we lose no   45

---

24 *the Scripture*. Isaiah V, 11—'Woe unto them that rise up early in the
    morning, that they may follow strong drink; that tarry into the night,
    till wine inflame them'.

29–30 *separated crew*. i.e., faction separated from the chosen people.

41 *Noah's Ark*. 'Curious gluttony ransackes, as it were, *Noahs Ark* for food,
    onely to feed the riot of one meale'. (W. J. D. Paylor, ed., *The Over-
    burian Characters*, Oxford, 1936, p. 78.)

43 *conduit*. Here Touchstone alludes to city feasts when the conduits
    (cisterns) were filled with wine.

time in our sensuality, but we make amends for it. O that
we would do so in virtue and religious negligences! But see,
here are all the sober parcels my house can show. I'll eaves-
drop, hear what thoughts they utter this morning.

[He retires]

GOLDING *[and* MILDRED *come forward]*

GOLDING

But is it possible, that you, seeing your sister preferred to   50
the bed of a knight, should contain your affections in the
arms of a prentice?

MILDRED

I had rather make up the garment of my affections in some
of the same piece, than, like a fool, wear gowns of two colours,
or mix sackcloth with satin.   55

GOLDING

And do the costly garments; the title and fame of a lady,
the fashion, observation, and reverence proper to such preferment, no more enflame you, than such convenience as my
poor means and industry can offer to your virtues?

MILDRED

I have observed that the bridle given to those violent flat-   60
teries of fortune is seldom recovered; they bear one headlong
in desire from one novelty to another, and where those
ranging appetites reign, there is ever more passion than
reason; no stay, and so no happiness. These hasty advance-
ments are not natural; Nature hath given us legs to go to our   65
objects, not wings to fly to them.

GOLDING

How dear an object you are to my desires I cannot express;
whose fruition would my master's absolute consent and
yours vouchsafe me, I should be absolutely happy. And
though it were a grace so far beyond my merit, that I should   70
blush with unworthiness to receive it, yet thus far both my
love and my means shall assure your requital: you shall
want nothing fit for your birth and education; what increase
of wealth and advancement the honest and orderly industry
and skill of our trade will afford in any, I doubt not will be   75

50 s.d. GOLDING *[and* MILDRED *come forward]* ed. (*Enter* Golding Q)
60 *bridle* fig. restraint, propriety

46–7 *O that we would do so in virtue and religious negligences.* i.e., Touchstone
wishes that it were as natural for citizens to make up for their 'virtuous
and religious negligences' by indulgence in prayer as it was for them to
compensate for hard work by losing themselves in drink.

aspired by me. I will ever make your contentment the end of
my endeavours; I will love you above all; and only your
grief shall be my misery, and your delight my felicity.

TOUCHSTONE

'Work upon that now'! By my hopes, he woos honestly and
orderly; he shall be anchor of my hopes! Look, see the ill-   80
yoked monster, his fellow!

Enter QUICKSILVER *unlaced, a towel about his neck, in
his flat cap, drunk*

QUICKSILVER

Eastward Ho! 'Holla ye pampered jades of Asia!'

TOUCHSTONE

Drunk now downright, o' my fidelity!

QUICKSILVER

Ump!—Pulldo, pulldo! Showse, quoth the caliver.

GOLDING

Fie, fellow Quicksilver, what a pickle are you in!   85

QUICKSILVER

Pickle? Pickle in thy throat; zounds, pickle! Wa, ha, ho!
Good-morrow, Knight Petronel; 'morrow, lady goldsmith;
come off, Knight, with a counter-buff, for the honour of
knighthood.

GOLDING

Why, how now, sir? Do ye know where you are?   90

QUICKSILVER

Where I am? Why, 'sblood, you jolthead, where I am?

GOLDING

Go to, go to, for shame, go to bed and sleep out this immodesty: thou sham'st both my master and his house!

QUICKSILVER

Shame? What shame? I thought thou wouldst show thy
bringing-up; and thou wert a gentleman as I am, thou   95
wouldst think it no shame to be drunk. Lend me some

80–1 *ill-yoked* ill-matched, or ill-mated
84 *Pulldo . . . caliver* bang went the musket (Schelling)
85 *pickle* a sorry plight; a predicament. Proverbial. Tilley, P 276
88 *counter-buff* returned blow
91 *jolthead* blockhead

---

82 s.d. *unlaced*. Points untied, probably doublet undone.
82 *Holla ye pampered jades of Asia! 2 Tamburlaine*, IV, iii, 1; parodying
    Marlowe's tragic rant. Also in Pistol's speech, *2 Henry IV* (II, iv, 178).
86 *Wa, ha, ho!* Cry of a falconer to the falcon; Cocledemoy's catch-phrase
    in *The Dutch Courtesan*.

money, save my credit; I must dine with the serving-men
and their wives—and their wives, sirrah!

GOLDING

E'en who you will; I'll not lend thee threepence.

QUICKSILVER

'Sfoot, lend me some money! 'Hast thou not Hiren here?'   100

TOUCHSTONE

Why, how now, sirrah, what vein's this, ha?

QUICKSILVER

'Who cries on murther? Lady, was it you?' How does our
master? Pray thee, cry Eastward Ho!

TOUCHSTONE

Sirrah, sirrah, y'are past your hiccup now; I see y'are
drunk—   105

QUICKSILVER

'Tis for your credit, master.

TOUCHSTONE

And hear you keep a whore in town—

QUICKSILVER

'Tis for your credit, master.

TOUCHSTONE

And what you are out in cash, I know.

QUICKSILVER

So do I. My father's a gentleman; 'work upon that now'!   110
Eastward Ho!

TOUCHSTONE

Sir, Eastward Ho will make you go Westward Ho. I will no
longer dishonest my house, nor endanger my stock with
your licence. There, sir, there's your indenture; all your
apparel (that I must know) is on your back; and from this   115
time my door is shut to you: from me be free; but for other
freedom, and the moneys you have wasted, Eastward Ho
shall not serve you.

100 *Hiren* siren, seductive woman
113 *dishonest* dishonour
116–17 *other freedom* i.e., making free

---

100 *Hast thou not Hiren here?* A line from a play also quoted by Pistol in
2 Henry IV (II, iv, 173). Bullen believes it originated in Greene's lost
play *Mahomet and the Fair Greek Hiren.*
102 *Who cries on murther?* Chapman, *Blind Beggar of Alexandria*, IX, 49.
112 *Westward Ho.* i.e., to the gallows at Tyburn.
114 *indenture.* The contract by which an apprentice is bound to a master
for seven years to learn the trade.

QUICKSILVER
Am I free o' my fetters? Rent, fly with a duck in thy mouth!
And now I tell thee, Touchstone—   120
TOUCHSTONE
Good sir—
QUICKSILVER
'When this eternal substance of my soul'—
TOUCHSTONE
Well said; change your gold-ends for your play-ends.
QUICKSILVER
'Did live imprisoned in my wanton flesh'—
TOUCHSTONE
What then, sir?   125
QUICKSILVER
'I was a courtier in the Spanish Court,
And Don Andrea was my name'—
TOUCHSTONE
Good master Don Andrea, will you march?
QUICKSILVER
Sweet Touchstone, will you lend me two shillings?
TOUCHSTONE
Not a penny!   130
QUICKSILVER
Not a penny? I have friends, and I have acquaintance; I will
piss at thy shop posts, and throw rotten eggs at thy sign.
'Work upon that now'!

Exit staggering

TOUCHSTONE
Now, sirrah, you, hear you? You shall serve me no more
neither; not an hour longer!   135

126–7 Prose Q

---

119 *Rent, fly with a duck in thy mouth!* Quicksilver inverts the usual meaning
   of this commercial phrase, i.e., return with a good profit, to mean, as
   H. & S. gloss, 'a good riddance, with a profit to myself'.
122, 124, 126–7 *When . . . soul, Did . . . flesh, I . . . name.* From the opening
   speech of Kyd's *Spanish Tragedy*, I, i, INDUCTION.
                    Enter the Ghost of Andrea, and with him Revenge
   GHOST
      When this eternal substance of my soul
      Did live imprison'd in my wanton flesh,
      Each in their function serving other's need,
      I was a courtier in the Spanish court.
      My name was Don Andrea, . . .
123 *gold-ends.* Basic unit of the goldsmith's trade; also moral tags.

GOLDING
What mean you, sir?

TOUCHSTONE
I mean to give thee thy freedom, and with thy freedom my
daughter, and with my daughter a father's love. And with all
these such a portion as shall make Knight Petronel himself
envy thee! Y'are both agreed, are ye not?   140

BOTH
With all submission, both of thanks and duty.

TOUCHSTONE
Well, then, the great power of heaven bless and confirm you.
And Golding, that my love to thee may not show less than
my wife's love to my eldest daughter, thy marriage-feast
shall equal the knight's and hers.   145

GOLDING
Let me beseech you, no, sir; the superfluity and cold meat
left at their nuptials will with bounty furnish ours. The
grossest prodigality is superfluous cost of the belly; nor would
I wish any invitement of states or friends, only your reverent
presence and witness shall sufficiently grace and confirm us. 150

TOUCHSTONE
Son to mine own bosom, take her and my blessing. The nice
fondling, my lady, sir-reverence, that I must not now
presume to call daughter, is so ravished with desire to hansel
her new coach, and see her knight's eastward castle, that
the next morning will sweat with her busy setting-forth.   155
Away will she and her mother, and while their preparation
is making, ourselves, with some two or three other friends,
will consummate the humble match we have in God's name
concluded.

'"Tis to my wish, for I have often read,   160
Fit birth, fit age, keeps long a quiet bed.
'Tis to my wish: for tradesmen (well 'tis known)
Get with more ease than gentry keeps his own'.

Exeunt

141 s.p. BOTH ed. (*Ambo.* Q)   146 s.p. *Goul* Qq (*Con.* Q)
149 *states* men of rank or dignity (*O.E.D.*)
152 *fondling* a fond or foolish person (*O.E.D.*)
153 *hansel* inaugurate   164 s.d. *Exeunt* Ed. (*Exit* Q)

146 *cold meat*, etc. Parody of *Hamlet* (I, ii, 179–81):
    'Thrift, thrift, Horatio. The funeral baked meats
    Did coldly furnish forth the marriage tables'.
152 *sir-reverence.* 'Save your reverence', with doubtful allusion to sense of
    'excrement'. Brooke and Paradise, op. cit., gloss 'with apologies'.

[Act II, Scene ii

A Room in SECURITY'*s House*]

SECURITY *solus*

SECURITY

My privy guest, lusty Quicksilver, has drunk too deep of
the bride-bowl; but with a little sleep, he is much recovered;
and, I think, is making himself ready to be drunk in a gallanter likeness. My house is, as 'twere, the cave where the
young outlaw hoards the stolen vails of his occupation; and   5
here, when he will revel it in his prodigal similitude, he
retires to his trunks, and (I may say softly) his punks: he
dares trust me with the keeping of both; for I am Security
itself; my name is Security, the famous usurer.

Enter QUICKSILVER *in his prentice's coat and cap, his gallant breeches and stockings, gartering himself;* SECURITY
following

QUICKSILVER

Come, old Security, thou father of destruction! Th' indented   10
sheepskin is burned wherein I was wrapped; and I am now
loose, to get more children of perdition into thy usurous
bonds. Thou feed'st my lechery, and I thy covetousness;
thou art pander to me for my wench, and I to thee for thy
cozenages: 'Ka me, ka thee', runs through court and country.   15

SECURITY

Well said, my subtle Quicksilver! These K's ope the doors

3–4 *gallanter likeness* more finely dressed, more showy in appearance
5 *vails* tips, over and above wages
7 *punks* prostitutes
10–11 *indented sheepskin* indenture
15 *cozenages* cheating, deception, fraud
15 *Ka me, ka thee* Ed. (K. me, K. thee Q)
15 *Ka me, ka thee* proverbial. Tilley, K1. One good turn deserves
   another
16 *K's* pronounced 'keys'

---

7 *trunks.* Short breeches of silk or other material (*O.E.D.*). By city
   regulations, it was illegal for an apprentice to store his apparel outside
   his master's house.
10 s.d. The contrived nature of the above utterance and Security's direction here, when he is already on stage, make it appear probable that
   Security's little set speech was inserted after staging had shown the
   passage following insufficient.

to all this world's felicity; the dullest forehead sees it. Let
not master courtier think he carries all the knavery on his
shoulders: I have known poor Hob in the country, that has
worn hob-nails on's shoes, have as much villainy in's head   20
as he that wears gold buttons in's cap.

QUICKSILVER

Why, man, 'tis the London high-way to thrift; if virtue be
used, 'tis but as a scrap to the net of villainy. They that use it
simply, thrive simply, I warrant. 'Weight and fashion makes
goldsmiths cuckolds'.   25

Enter SINDEFY, *with* QUICKSILVER'*s doublet, cloak, rapier,
and dagger*

SINDEFY

Here, sir, put off the other half of your prenticeship.

QUICKSILVER

Well said, sweet Sin! Bring forth my bravery.
Now let my trunks shoot forth their silks concealed,
I now am free, and now will justify
My trunks and punks. Avaunt, dull flat-cap, then!   30
Via the curtain that shadowed Borgia!
There lie, thou husk of my envassaled state,
I, Samson, now have burst the Philistines' bands,
And in thy lap, my lovely Dalida,
I'll lie, and snore out my enfranchised state.   35

[*Sings*]

19 *Hob* stock term for farm labourer
31 *Via* away

---

23 *'tis but as a scrap in the net of villainy.* Meaning virtue can be a bait with
which the gallant is drawn into the usurer's trap; i.e., Quicksilver pretends
friendship towards gallants, lends them money, and then, by pretending
debt of his own, gets them to sign a bond to Security for a commodity
or an exorbitantly high-interest loan for which they, not he, will be
responsible. See I, i, 51–2 *Suretyship* and A. V. Judges op. cit.,
pp. 448–51.
28 *trunks shoot forth.* Play on the meaning trunks: peashooters.
28 *their silks concealed.* The outer fabric slashed or cut in ribbons to reveal
bright silks beneath.
31 *Via the curtain that shadowed Borgia.* Most eds. ascribe this passage to
Mason's *The Turk*, but as Parrott astutely notes, *The Turk* was not on
the stage until 1607–08. It probably alludes to Cesare Borgia, who at
an early age cast aside the 'curtain' of his clerical state for soldierly
ambition.
34 *Dalida.* From the Greek Bible; Dalila.

'*When Samson was a tall young man,*
His power and strength increased then';
He sold no more nor cup nor can,
But did them all despise.
Old Touchstone, now write to thy friends   40
For one to sell thy base gold-ends;
Quicksilver now no more attends
Thee, Touchstone.
But, Dad, hast thou seen my running gelding dressed today?

SECURITY
That I have, Frank. The ostler o' th' Cock dressed him for   45
a breakfast.

QUICKSILVER
What, did he eat him?

SECURITY
No, but he eat his breakfast for dressing him; and so dressed
him for breakfast.

QUICKSILVER
'O witty age, where age is young in wit,   50
And all youth's words have gray beards full of it'!

SINDEFY
But alas, Frank, how will all this be maintained now? Your
place maintained it before.

QUICKSILVER
Why, and I maintained my place. I'll to the Court, another
manner of place for maintenance, I hope, than the silly City!   55
I heard my father say, I heard my mother sing an old song
and a true: 'Thou art a she fool, and know'st not what
belongs to our male wisdom'. I shall be a merchant, forsooth,
trust my estate in a wooden trough as he does! What are these
ships but tennis-balls for the winds to play withal? Tossed   60
from one wave to another: now under-line, now over the
house; sometimes brick-walled against a rock, so that the

37 *then* Ed. (*than* Q)
45 *Cock* a tavern
50 *young in wit* vigorous
57 *Thou* Ed. (*Tou* Q)
62 *brick-walled* caused to rebound back (*O.E.D.*)

36–7 *When Samson*, etc. An old Roxburghe Ballad (Stationers' Register,
    1563). See W. Chappell, *Popular Music of Olden Time*, 2 vols. (London,
    1885–89) I, 241.
61 *under-line.* Tennis allusion: too low for play.
61–2 *over the house.* Sloping roof of the penthouse at one side and two ends
    of the court, hence too high for play.

guts fly out again; sometimes struck under the wide hazard,
and farewell, master merchant!

SINDEFY

Well, Frank, well; the seas, you say, are uncertain; but he   65
that sails in your court seas shall find 'em ten times fuller of
hazard; wherein to see what is to be seen is torment more
than a free spirit can endure. But when you come to suffer,
how many injuries swallow you! What care and devotion
must you use to humour an imperious lord: proportion your   70
looks to his looks, [your] smiles to his smiles, fit your sails
to the wind of his breath!

QUICKSILVER

Tush, he's no journeyman in his craft that cannot do that!

SINDEFY

But he's worse than a prentice that does it; not only humour-
ing the lord, but every trencher-bearer, every groom that   75
by indulgence and intelligence crept into his favour, and by
panderism into his chamber: he rules the roost; and when
my honourable lord says, 'it shall be thus', my worshipful
rascal, the groom of his close stool, says, 'it shall not be thus',
claps the door after him, and who dares enter? A prentice,   80
quoth you? 'Tis but to learn to live; and does that disgrace
a man? He that rises hardly, stands firmly; but he that rises
with ease, alas, falls as easily!

QUICKSILVER

A pox on you! Who taught you this morality?

SECURITY

'Tis long of this witty age, Master Francis. But indeed,   85
Mistress Sindefy, all trades complain of inconvenience, and

63   *hazard* risk
71   *your* Ed. (not in Q)
85   *long of* owing to, on account of

---

63   *under the wide hazard.* Pun—strike the ball wide, and take a risk.
75   *groom.* From the appearance of C1ᵛ in Q, it is possible that something has
        been struck from this passage by the printer—probably another jest about
        the Scots. It is interesting to note that Sir John Murray, groom of the
        king's bedchamber, was the brother of the Sir James Murray who,
        according to Jonson, reported the offence to the king. It is also suspicious
        that in late 1605 the said John Murray received a large sum of money
        from Salisbury, one of the nobles to whom both Jonson and Chapman
        appealed from prison in 1605.
80–3   *A prentice,* etc. These words fit awkwardly into Sindefy's speech.
        Apart from the innuendo they appear to mean, 'slowly but surely wins'.
        It is possible that this is another of the printer's stop-gaps.

therefore 'tis best to have none. The merchant, he complains
and says, 'traffic is subject to much uncertainty and loss'.
Let 'em keep their goods on dry land, with a vengeance, and
not expose other men's substances to the mercy of the winds,   90
under protection of a wooden wall (as Master Francis says);
and all for greedy desire to enrich themselves with unconscionable gain, two for one, or so; where I, and such other
honest men as live by lending money, are content with
moderate profit—thirty or forty i' th' hundred—so we may   95
have it with quietness, and out of peril of wind and weather,
rather than run those dangerous courses of trading as they
do.

                          [SINDEFY *retires*]

QUICKSILVER

Ay, Dad, thou may'st well be called Security, for thou takest
the safest course.   100

SECURITY

Faith, the quieter and the more contented, and, out of doubt,
the more godly; for merchants, in their courses, are never
pleased, but ever repining against heaven: one prays for a
westerly wind to carry his ship forth; another for an easterly
to bring his ship home; and at every shaking of a leaf he   105
falls into an agony to think what danger his ship is in on
such a coast, and so forth. The farmer, he is ever at odds
with the weather: sometimes the clouds have been too
barren; sometimes the heavens forget themselves, their
harvests answer not their hopes; sometimes the season falls   110
out too fruitful, corn will bear no price, and so forth. Th'
artificer, he's all for a stirring world; if his trade be too dull
and fall short of his expectation, then falls he out of joint.
Where we, that trade nothing but money, are free from all
this; we are pleased with all weathers: let it rain or hold up,   115
be calm or windy, let the season be whatsoever, let trade go
how it will, we take all in good part, e'en what please the
heavens to send us, so the sun stand not still, and the moon
keep her usual returns, and make up days, months, and
years—   120

112 *artificer* deviser, trickster (*O.E.D.*)
112 *dull* Ed. (full Q)
116 *calm* Qq (call me Q)

---

  95 *thirty or forty*. By the 1571 Parliament, the interest rate was fixed at
     10 per cent.
113 *out of joint*. cf. *Hamlet* (I, v, 188): 'The time is out of joint'.

QUICKSILVER
  And you have good security?
SECURITY
  Ay, marry, Frank, that's the special point.
QUICKSILVER
  And yet, forsooth, we must have trades to live withal; for
  we cannot stand without legs, nor fly without wings (and
  a number of such scurvy phrases). No, I say still, he that   125
  has wit, let him live by his wit; he that has none, let him be
  a tradesman.
SECURITY
  Witty Master Francis! 'Tis pity any trade should dull that
  quick brain of yours! Do but bring Knight Petronel into my
  parchment toils once, and you shall never need to toil in any   130
  trade, o' my credit! You know his wife's land?
QUICKSILVER
  Even to a foot, sir; I have been often there; a pretty fine
  seat, good land, all entire within itself.
SECURITY
  Well wooded?
QUICKSILVER
  Two hundred pounds' worth of wood ready to fell; and a   135
  fine sweet house that stands just in the midst on't, like a
  prick in the midst of a circle. Would I were your farmer, for
  a hundred pound a year!
SECURITY
  Excellent Master Francis, how I do long to do thee good!
  'How I do hunger and thirst to have the honour to enrich   140
  thee'! Ay, even to die that thou mightest inherit my living;
  'even hunger and thirst'! For o' my religion, Master Francis—
  and so tell Knight Petronel—I do it to do him a pleasure.
QUICKSILVER
  Marry, Dad, his horses are now coming up to bear down his
  lady; wilt thou lend him thy stable to set 'em in?   145
SECURITY
  Faith, Master Francis, I would be loath to lend my stable

---

124 *we cannot stand without legs, nor fly without wings* proverbial.
   Tilley, F407
125 *scurvy* contemptible
130 *toils* traps

134–7 *Well-wooded? . . . circle.* Bawdy intention is clear.
137 *prick in the midst of a circle.* Bull's eye of a target, or the hole left by the
   compass point after proscribing a circle.

out of doors; in a greater matter I will pleasure him, but not
in this.

QUICKSILVER

A pox of your 'hunger and thirst'! Well, Dad, let him have
money; all he could any way get is bestowed on a ship now   150
bound for Virginia; the frame of which voyage is so closely
conveyed that his new lady nor any of her friends know it.
Notwithstanding, as soon as his lady's hand is gotten to the
sale of her inheritance, and you have furnished him with
money, he will instantly hoist sail and away.   155

SECURITY

Now, a frank gale of wind go with him, Master Frank! We
have too few such knight adventurers. Who would not sell
away competent certainties to purchase, with any danger,
excellent uncertainties? Your true knight venturer ever does
it. Let his wife seal today; he shall have his money today.   160

QUICKSILVER

Tomorrow, she shall, Dad, before she goes into the country.
To work her to which action with the more engines, I purpose presently to prefer my sweet Sin here to the place of
her gentlewoman; whom you (for the more credit) shall
present as your friend's daughter, a gentlewoman of the   165
country new come up with a will for awhile to learn fashions,
forsooth, and be toward some lady; and she shall buzz pretty
devices into her lady's ear, feeding her humours so service-
ably (as the manner of such as she is, you know)—

SECURITY

True, good Master Francis!   170

Enter SINDEFY

QUICKSILVER

That she shall keep her port open to anything she commends
to her.

SECURITY

O' my religion, a most fashionable project; as good she spoil
the lady, as the lady spoil her, for 'tis three to one of one
side. Sweet Mistress Sin, how are you bound to Master   175
Francis! I do not doubt to see you shortly wed one of the
head men of our City.

151 *frame* Ed. (fame Q)
151 *frame* plan
151–2 *closely conveyed* a closely guarded secret
160 *seal* set her seal
162 *engines* plans, plots, devices

SINDEFY
> But, sweet Frank, when shall my father Security present me?

QUICKSILVER
> With all festination; I have broken the ice to it already; and
> will presently to the knight's house, whither, my good old   180
> Dad, let me pray thee with all formality to man her.

SECURITY
> Command me, Master Francis; 'I do hunger and thirst to do
> thee service'. Come, sweet Mistress Sin, take leave of my
> Winifred, and we will instantly meet frank Master Francis at
> your lady's.   185

Enter WINIFRED *above*

WINIFRED
> Where is my Cu there? Cu?

SECURITY
> Ay, Winnie.

WINIFRED
> Wilt thou come in, sweet Cu?

SECURITY
> Ay, Winnie, presently!

Exeunt [all but QUICKSILVER]

QUICKSILVER
> 'Ay, Winnie', quod he! That's all he can do, poor man, he   190
> may well cut off her name at Winnie. O 'tis an egregious
> pander! What will not an usurous knave be, so he may be
> rich? O 'tis a notable Jew's trump! I hope to live to see dog's
> meat made of the old usurer's flesh, dice of his bones, and
> indentures of his skin; and yet his skin is too thick to make   195
> parchment, 'twould make good boots for a peterman to
> catch salmon in. Your only smooth skin to make fine vellum
> is your Puritan's skin; they be the smoothest and slickest
> knaves in a country.

[Exit]

---

179 *festination* haste

---

193 *Jew's trump*. Earlier name for a Jew's harp; cant term for usurers.
196 *peterman*. A fisherman; from Peter boats, early trawlers.

[Act II, Scene iii

Before SIR PETRONEL'*s Lodging*]

Enter SIR PETRONEL *in boots, with a riding wand,*
[*followed by* QUICKSILVER]

PETRONEL

I'll out of this wicked town as fast as my horse can trot.
Here's now no good action for a man to spend his time in.
Taverns grow dead; ordinaries are blown up; plays are at a
stand; houses of hospitality at a fall; not a feather waving,
nor a spur jingling anywhere. I'll away instantly.   5

QUICKSILVER

Y'ad best take some crowns in your purse, Knight, or else
your eastward castle will smoke but miserably.

PETRONEL

O, Frank! My castle? Alas, all the castles I have are built
with air, thou know'st!

QUICKSILVER

I know it, Knight, and therefore wonder whither your lady   10
is going.

PETRONEL

Faith, to seek her fortune, I think. I said I had a castle and
land eastward, and eastward she will, without contradiction.
Her coach and the coach of the sun must meet full butt; and
the sun being outshined with her ladyship's glory, she fears   15
he goes westward to hang himself.

QUICKSILVER

And I fear, when her enchanted castle becomes invisible,
her ladyship will return and follow his example.

PETRONEL

O that she would have the grace, for I shall never be able to
pacify her, when she sees herself deceived so.   20

QUICKSILVER

As easily as can be. Tell her she mistook your directions, and
that shortly yourself will down with her to approve it; then
clothe but her crupper in a new gown, and you may drive

---

1 s.d. *riding wan(d)* a switch
1 *wand* ed. (*wan* Q)
22 *approve* prove
23 *crupper* hindquarters (usually of horse)

---

16 *westward to hang.* Another reference to Tyburn's gallows.

her any way you list. For these women, sir, are like Essex
calves, you must wriggle 'em on by the tail still, or they will   25
never drive orderly.

PETRONEL
But, alas, sweet Frank, thou know'st my hability will not
furnish her blood with those costly humours.

QUICKSILVER
Cast that cost on me, sir. I have spoken to my old pander,
Security, for money or commodity; and commodity (if   30
you will) I know he will procure you.

PETRONEL
Commodity! Alas, what commodity?

QUICKSILVER
Why, sir, what say you to figs and raisins?

PETRONEL
A plague of figs and raisins, and all such frail commodities!
We shall make nothing of 'em.   35

QUICKSILVER
Why, then, sir, what say you to forty pound in roasted beef?

PETRONEL
Out upon't! I have less stomach to that than to the figs and
raisins. I'll out of town, though I sojourn with a friend of
mine; for stay here I must not; my creditors have laid to
arrest me, and I have no friend under heaven but my sword   40
to bail me.

QUICKSILVER
God's me, Knight, put 'em in sufficient sureties, rather than
let your sword bail you! Let 'em take their choice, either the

27 *hability* ability
28 *humours* indulgences
34 *frail* play on the meaning frail: basket
42 *sureties* securities

24–5 *Essex calves.* According to Fuller's *The Worthies of England* (1672),
I, 320, these were proverbially 'the *fattest, fairest* and *finest flesh* in
England'. Proverbial. Tilley, C21.
30 *commodity.* A parcel of goods sold in credit by a usurer to a needy
person, who immediately raised some money by reselling them at a
lower price, generally to the usurer himself (*O.E.D.*).
40–1 *sword to bail me.* Defend himself only with his sword, or perhaps, enlist
in the army.

King's Bench or the Fleet, or which of the two Counters
they like best, for, by the Lord, I like none of 'em.   45

PETRONEL

Well, Frank, there is no jesting with my earnest necessity;
thou know'st if I make not present money to further my
voyage begun, all's lost, and all I have laid out about it.

QUICKSILVER

Why, then, sir, in earnest, if you can get your wise lady to set
her hand to the sale of her inheritance, the bloodhound,   50
Security, will smell out ready money for you instantly.

PETRONEL

There spake an angel! To bring her to which conformity, I
must feign myself extremely amorous; and alleging urgent
excuses for my stay behind, part with her as passionately as
she would from her foisting hound.   55

QUICKSILVER

You have the sow by the right ear, sir. I warrant there was
never child longed more to ride a cock-horse or wear his
new coat, than she longs to ride in her new coach. She would
long for everything when she was a maid; and now she will
run mad for 'em. I lay my life, she will have every year four   60
children; and what charge and change of humour you must
endure while she is with child; and how she will tie you to
your tackling till she be with child, a dog would not endure.

---

55 *foisting* farting
56 *sow by the . . . ear* proverbial. Tilley, S684

---

44 *King's Bench.* A debtors' prison.
44 *the Fleet.* A prison near Fleet ditch.
44 *the two Counters.* The two debtors' prisons of London, under control
of the sheriff, were at Wood Street and at Poultry Street near St
Mildred's Church. 'A man of means could live in comfort in either;
indeed, for some people they served as a favourite retreat . . . An apart-
ment on the Master's Side of the prison was the best accommodation
provided. The Knight's Ward was not so good, but comfortable as
prison usage went. The Twopenny Ward and the Hole were no better
than common jails—in some respects worse, for prisoners could count
on no public assistance of any value in the provision of food, and a
penniless man might actually starve to death in the Hole if he failed to
secure relief or help from one of the citizens' legacies or the Christmas-
treat funds provided for the very poor'. Note 7 to 'The Counter's
Commonwealth', in Judges, ed., op. cit., p. 518.
52 *angel.* Pun on a coin worth 7*s.* 6*d.* cf. *Volpone*, II, iv, 21.

Nay, there is no turnspit dog bound to his wheel more
servilely than you shall be to her wheel; for as that dog can   65
never climb the top of his wheel but when the top comes
under him, so shall you never climb the top of her contentment but when she is under you.

PETRONEL
'Slight, how thou terrifiest me!

QUICKSILVER
Nay, hark you, sir; what nurses, what midwives, what fools,   70
what physicians, what cunning women must be sought for
(fearing sometimes she is bewitched, sometimes in a consumption) to tell her tales, to talk bawdy to her, to make her
laugh, to give her glisters, to let her blood under the tongue,
and betwixt the toes; how she will revile and kiss you, spit   75
in your face, and lick it off again; how she will vaunt you are
her creature; she made you of nothing; how she could have
had thousand-mark jointures; she could have been made a
lady by a Scotch knight, and never ha' married him; she
could have had poynados in her bed every morning; how she   80
set you up, and how she will pull you down: you'll never be
able to stand of your legs to ensure it.

PETRONEL
Out of my fortune! What a death is my life bound face to
face to! The best is, a large time-fitted conscience is bound
to nothing; marriage is but a form in the school of policy,   85
to which scholars sit fastened only with painted chains. Old
Security's young wife is ne'er the further off with me.

---

74 *glisters* clysters, enemas
78 *jointures* dowries
84 *large* liberal, bountiful
85 *policy* politically astute action

64–8 *Nay . . . under you.* Refers to the practice of harnessing dogs within
a kind of treadwheel to turn meat on spits in the kitchens.
69 *'Slight.* Abbreviation for God's light, petty oath.
78 *mark.* English or Scottish coin worth 13*s.* 4*d.*
79 *Scotch knight.* In Scotland marriage was assumed after cohabitation—
sharing a bed and board; consent could be sworn before witnesses
other than magistrates, and providing copulation could be proved by
witnesses or inferred 'by the circumstances ordinarily accompanying
it', the marriage was legal.
80 *poynados.* Daggers (with phallic overtones); also panadas, a kind of
medieval bread-pudding. cf. proverb. Tilley, P633: 'puddings and
paramours would be hotly handled'.

QUICKSILVER

Thereby lies a tale, sir. The old usurer will be here instantly, with my punk Sindefy, whom you know your lady has promised me to entertain for her gentlewoman; and he (with   90
a purpose to feed on you) invites you most solemnly by me to supper.

PETRONEL

It falls out excellently fitly: I see desire of gain makes jealousy venturous.

Enter GERTRUDE

See, Frank, here comes my lady. Lord, how she views thee!   95
She knows thee not, I think, in this bravery.

GERTRUDE

How now? Who be you, I pray?

QUICKSILVER

One Master Francis Quicksilver, an't please your Ladyship.

GERTRUDE

God's my dignity! As I am a lady, if he did not make me blush so that mine eyes stood a-water, would I were un-   100
married again! Where's my woman, I pray?

Enter SECURITY *and* SINDEFY

QUICKSILVER

See, Madam, she now comes to attend you.

SECURITY

God save my honourable Knight and his worshipful Lady!

GERTRUDE

Y'are very welcome; you must not put on your hat yet.

SECURITY

No, Madam; till I know your Ladyship's further pleasure,   105
I will not presume.

GERTRUDE

And is this a gentleman's daughter new come out of the country?

90 *entertain* engage in service
96 *bravery* fine clothes

---

88 *Thereby lies a tale, sir.* cf. *The Merry Wives of Windsor* (I, iv, 159).
90-1 (*with . . . you*). Another echo of *Hamlet* (IV, iii, 19): 'Not where he eats but where he is eaten'.
94 *jealousy.* The first mention of Security's humour (melancholy).
104 *you must not put on your hat yet.* Here Security, who has gallantly removed his hat to observe a lady's entrance, is told hamfistedly to keep if off.

SECURITY
    She is, Madam; and one that her father hath a special care
    to bestow in some honourable lady's service, to put her out   110
    of her honest humours, forsooth; for she had a great desire
    to be a nun, an't please you.

GERTRUDE
    A nun? What nun? A nun substantive, or a nun adjective?

SECURITY
    A nun substantive, Madam, I hope, if a nun be a noun. But
    I mean, Lady, a vowed maid of that order.   115

GERTRUDE
    I'll teach her to be a maid of the order, I warrant you! And
    can you do any work belongs to a lady's chamber?

SINDEFY
    What I cannot do, Madam, I would be glad to learn.

GERTRUDE
    Well said, hold up then; hold up your head, I say! Come
    hither a little.   120

SINDEFY
    I thank your Ladyship.

GERTRUDE
    And hark you—good man, you may put on your hat now;
    I do not look on you—I must have you of my faction now;
    not of my knight's, maid!

SINDEFY
    No, forsooth, Madam, of yours.   125

GERTRUDE
    And draw all my servants in my bow, and keep my counsel,
    and tell me tales, and put me riddles, and read on a book
    sometimes when I am busy, and laugh at country gentle-
    women, and command anything in the house for my retainers,
    and care not what you spend, for it is all mine; and in any   130
    case, be still a maid, whatsoever you do, or whatsoever any
    man can do unto you.

SECURITY
    I warrant your Ladyship for that.

GERTRUDE
    Very well; you shall ride in my coach with me into the
    country tomorrow morning. Come, Knight, pray thee, let's   135
    make a short supper, and to bed presently.

126 *draw . . . in my bow.* Bend to my will, bring under control. Proverbial.
    Tilley, Y35.
131 *maid.* Possible pun on 'maid' = virgin and 'make' = sexual intercourse.

SECURITY

Nay, good Madam, this night I have a short supper at home
waits on his worship's acceptation.

GERTRUDE

By my faith, but he shall not go, sir; I shall swoon and he
sup from me.   140

PETRONEL

Pray thee, forbear; shall he lose his provision?

GERTRUDE

Ay, by'r Lady, sir, rather than I lose my longing. Come in,
I say—as I am a lady, you shall not go!

QUICKSILVER

[*Aside to* SECURITY] I told him what a bur he had gotten.

SECURITY

If you will not sup from your knight, Madam, let me entreat   145
your Ladyship to sup at my house with him.

GERTRUDE

No, by my faith, sir; then we cannot be abed soon enough
after supper.

PETRONEL

What a medicine is this! Well, Master Security, you are new
married as well as I; I hope you are bound as well. We must   150
honour our young wives, you know.

QUICKSILVER

[*Aside to* SECURITY] In policy, Dad, till tomorrow she has
sealed.

SECURITY

I hope in the morning, yet, your Knighthood will breakfast
with me?   155

PETRONEL

As early as you will, sir.

SECURITY

Thank your good worship; 'I do hunger and thirst to do you
good, sir'.

GERTRUDE

Come, sweet Knight, come, 'I do hunger and thirst to be abed
with thee'.   160

Exeunt

142 *by'r Lady* cd. (by lady Q)

Act III, Scene i

[SECURITY's *House*]

Enter PETRONEL, QUICKSILVER, SECURITY, BRAMBLE, *and*
WINIFRED

PETRONEL

Thanks for our feast-like breakfast, good Master Security;
I am sorry (by reason of my instant haste to so long a voyage
as Virginia) I am without means by any kind amends to show
how affectionately I take your kindness, and to confirm by
some worthy ceremony a perpetual league of friendship   5
betwixt us.

SECURITY

Excellent Knight, let this be a token betwixt us of inviolable
friendship: I am new married to this fair gentlewoman, you
know, and by my hope to make her fruitful, though I be
something in years, I vow faithfully unto you to make you   10
godfather (though in your absence) to the first child I am
blessed withal; and henceforth call me Gossip, I beseech
you, if you please to accept it.

PETRONEL

In the highest degree of gratitude, my most worthy Gossip;
for confirmation of which friendly title, let me entreat my   15
fair Gossip, your wife, here, to accept this diamond, and keep
it as my gift to her first child; wheresoever my fortune, in
event of my voyage, shall bestow me.

SECURITY

How now, my coy wedlock! Make you strange of so noble a
favour? Take it, I charge you, with all affection, and, by   20

---

3 *amends* requitals   19 *Make you strange* are you hesitant?

---

12 *Gossip.* Godfather: usually chosen for his spiritual affinity.

8–29 *I am . . . despatch it.* Closely parallels the source, Masuccio's *Il
Novellino*, XL (1476). See Parrott, II, 838: 'Genefra, a rich Catalan,
falls in love with Adriana, the young wife of Cosmo, a silver-smith of
Amalfi. To obtain his end Genefra cultivates Cosmo's friendship and
so far wins over the unsuspecting husband that he is invited to stand
godfather to the first child of the marriage (cf. *Eastward Ho!*, III, i,
8–18). Forced to leave Amalfi, Genefra plots to carry off the wife and
enlists Cosmo as his accomplice by deluding him with a false tale of his
purpose to elope with a boatman's wife (cf. *Eastward Ho!*, III, ii,
204–42). Cosmo gladly promises his aid (cf. *Eastward Ho!*, III, ii, 243–53)
[and] forces his own wife to give a farewell kiss to Genefra (cf. *Eastward
Ho!*, III, i, 19–22) . . .'

way of taking your leave, present boldly your lips to our
honourable gossip.

QUICKSILVER

    [*Aside*] How venturous he is to him, and how jealous to
others!

PETRONEL

    Long may this kind touch of our lips print in our hearts all   25
the forms of affection. And now my good Gossip, if the
writings be ready to which my wife should seal, let them be
brought this morning before she takes coach into the country,
and my kindness shall work her to despatch it.

SECURITY

    The writings are ready, sir. My learned counsel here,   30
Master Bramble the lawyer, hath perused them; and within
this hour, I will bring the scrivener with them to your worshipful lady.

PETRONEL

    Good Master Bramble, I will here take my leave of you,
then. God send you fortunate pleas, sir, and contentious   35
clients!

BRAMBLE

    And you foreright winds, sir, and a fortunate voyage!

                                            Exit

                     Enter a MESSENGER

MESSENGER

    Sir Petronel, here are three or four gentlemen desire to speak
with you.

PETRONEL

    What are they?   40

QUICKSILVER

    They are your followers in this voyage, Knight, Captain
Seagull and his associates; I met them this morning, and
told them you would be here.

PETRONEL

    Let them enter, I pray you; I know they long to be gone,
for their stay is dangerous.   45

      Enter SEAGULL, SCAPETHRIFT, *and* SPENDALL

SEAGULL

    God save my honourable Colonel!

---

37 *foreright* favourable

PETRONEL

Welcome, good Captain Seagull and worthy gentlemen. If
you will meet my friend Frank here, and me, at the Blue
Anchor Tavern by Billingsgate this evening, we will there
drink to our happy voyage, be merry, and take boat to our   50
ship with all expedition.

SPENDALL

Defer it no longer, I beseech you, sir; but as your voyage is
hitherto carried closely, and in another knight's name, so for
your own safety and ours, let it be continued—our meeting
and speedy purpose of departing known to as few as is   55
possible, lest your ship and goods be attached.

QUICKSILVER

Well advised, Captain! Our colonel shall have money this
morning to despatch all our departures. Bring those gentlemen at night to the place appointed, and with our skins full
of vintage we'll take occasion by the 'vantage, and away.   60

SPENDALL

We will not fail but be there, sir.

PETRONEL

Good morrow, good Captain, and my worthy associates.
Health and all sovereignty to my beautiful Gossip. For you,
sir, we shall see you presently with the writings.

SECURITY

With writings and crowns to my honourable Gossip. 'I do   65
hunger and thirst to do you good, sir'!

Exeunt

Act III, Scene ii

[An Inn-yard]

Enter a COACHMAN *in haste, in's frock, feeding*

COACHMAN

Here's a stir when citizens ride out of town, indeed, as if all
the house were afire! 'Slight, they will not give a man leave
to eat's breakfast afore he rises!

Enter HAMLET, *a footman, in haste*

53 *carried closely* kept secret
56 *attached* apprehended by writ, arrested

52, 61 s.p. SPENDALL Ed. (*Spoyl.* Q) See note, *Dramatis Personae*, [17].
  3 s.d. *Enter* HAMLET. See note, *Dramatis Personae*, [18].

HAMLET
   What, coachman! My lady's coach, for shame! Her Ladyship's ready to come down.   5

                Enter POTKIN, *a tankard-bearer*

POTKIN
   'Sfoot, Hamlet, are you mad? Whither run you now? You
   should brush up my old mistress!

                                              [*Exit* HAMLET]

                      Enter SINDEFY

SINDEFY
   What, Potkin? You must put off your tankard, and put on
   your blue coat and wait upon Mistress Touchstone into the
   country.   *Exit*   10
POTKIN
   I will, forsooth, presently.   *Exit*

         Enter MISTRESS FOND *and* MISTRESS GAZER

FOND
   Come, sweet Mistress Gazer, let's watch here, and see my
   Lady Flash take coach.
GAZER
   O' my word, here's a most fine place to stand in. Did you see
   the new ship launched last day, Mistress Fond?   15
FOND
   O God, and we citizens should lose such a sight!
GAZER
   I warrant here will be double as many people to see her take
   coach as there were to see it take water.
FOND
   O, she's married to a most fine castle i' th' country, they
   say.   20
GAZER
   But there are no giants in the castle, are there?
FOND
   O no; they say her knight killed 'em all, and therefore he was
   knighted.

   7 *brush up* brighten up, freshen
   9 *blue coat* footman's livery

   12 s.d. Mistresses Fond and Gazer typify the condescending attitude
      towards city wives in many of the coterie, private theatre, plays.

GAZER
  Would to God her Ladyship would come away!

Enter GERTRUDE, MISTRESS TOUCHSTONE, SINDEFY, HAMLET,
                           POTKIN

FOND
  She comes, she comes, she comes!   25
GAZER ⎫
FOND ⎭
  Pray heaven bless your Ladyship!
GERTRUDE
  Thank you, good people! My coach! For the love of heaven,
  my coach! In good truth I shall swoon else.
HAMLET
  Coach, coach, my lady's coach!   *Exit*
GERTRUDE
  As I am a lady, I think I am with child already, I long for a   30
  coach so. May one be with child afore they are married,
  mother?
MISTRESS TOUCHSTONE
  Ay, by'r Lady, Madam; a little thing does that. I have seen a
  little prick no bigger than a pin's head swell bigger and
  bigger till it has come to an ancome; and e'en so 'tis in these   35
  cases.

                      Enter HAMLET

HAMLET
  Your coach is coming, Madam.
GERTRUDE
  That's well said. Now, heaven! Methinks I am e'en up to the
  knees in preferment!   [*Sings*]
    But a little higher, but a little higher, but a little higher;   40
    There, there, there lies Cupid's fire!
MISTRESS TOUCHSTONE
  But must this young man, an't please you, Madam, run by
  your coach all the way a-foot?
GERTRUDE
  Ay, by my faith, I warrant him! He gives no other milk, as
  I have another servant does.   45

35 *ancome.* Boil or swelling, rising unexpectedly.
40–1 *But a little higher* . . . The refrain of a song in Campion's *Book of Airs*
  (1601), entitled 'Mistress, Since You So Much Desire' (Fellowes ,op. cit.,
  Series I, 13, 59–60). A 1617 version, 'Beauty Since You So Much Desire'
  (Series 2, 11, 40–1), has the innuendo of Gertrude's lines.

MISTRESS TOUCHSTONE

Alas, 'tis e'en pity, methinks! For God's sake, Madam, buy him but a hobby-horse; let the poor youth have something betwixt his legs to ease 'em. Alas, we must do as we would be done to!

GERTRUDE

Go to, hold your peace, dame; you talk like an old fool, I   50
tell you.

Enter PETRONEL *and* QUICKSILVER

PETRONEL

Wilt thou be gone, sweet honeysuckle, before I can go with thee?

GERTRUDE

I pray thee, sweet Knight, let me; I do so long to dress up thy castle afore thou com'st. But I marle how my modest   55
sister occupies herself this morning, that she cannot wait on me to my coach, as well as her mother!

QUICKSILVER

Marry, Madam, she's married by this time to prentice Golding. Your father, and some one more, stole to church with 'em, in all the haste, that the cold meat left at your   60
wedding might serve to furnish their nuptial table.

GERTRUDE

There's no base fellow, my father, now! But he's e'en fit to father such a daughter: he must call me daughter no more now; but 'Madam', and, 'please you Madam', and, 'please your worship, Madam', indeed. Out upon him! Marry his   65
daughter to a base prentice!

MISTRESS TOUCHSTONE

What should one do? Is there no law for one that marries a woman's daughter against her will? How shall we punish him, Madam?

GERTRUDE

As I am a lady, an't would snow, we'd so pebble 'em with   70
snowballs as they come from church! But sirrah, Frank Quicksilver—

QUICKSILVER

Ay, Madam.

55 *marle* marvel

GERTRUDE
Dost remember since thou and I clapped what-d'ye-call'ts
in the garret?   75

QUICKSILVER
I know not what you mean, Madam.

GERTRUDE   [*Sings*]
 His head as white as milk,
 All flaxen was his hair;
 But now he is dead,
 And laid in his bed,   80
 And never will come again.
God be at your labour!

 Enter TOUCHSTONE, GOLDING, MILDRED *with rosemary*

PETRONEL
[*Aside*] Was there ever such a lady?

QUICKSILVER
See, Madam, the bride and bridegroom!

GERTRUDE
God's my precious! God give you joy, Mistress What-lack-   85
you! Now out upon thee, baggage! My sister married in a
taffeta hat! Marry, hang you! Westward with a wanion t' ye!
Nay, I have done wi' ye, minion, then, i'faith; never look to
have my countenance any more, nor anything I can do for
thee. Thou ride in my coach? Or come down to my castle?   90
Fie upon thee! I charge thee in my Ladyship's name, call
me sister no more.

TOUCHSTONE
An't please your worship, this is not your sister; this is my
daughter, and she calls me father, and so does not your
Ladyship, an't please your worship, Madam.   95

MISTRESS TOUCHSTONE
No, nor she must not call thee father by heraldry, because

---

87 *wanion* plague or vengeance (*O.E.D.*)
94 *calls* Q2 (cal Q)

74–5 *clapped . . . garret.* None too subtle reference to sexual matters,
 characteristic of the licentious Gertrude.
77–81 *His head,* etc. Parodies Ophelia's song in *Hamlet,* IV, v, 188–97.
85–6 *Mistress What-lack-you.* Nick-name taken from the greeting of an
 apprentice.

thou mak'st thy prentice thy son as well as she. Ah, thou mis-
proud prentice, dar'st thou presume to marry a lady's
sister?

GOLDING

It pleased my master, forsooth, to embolden me with his   100
favour; and though I confess myself far unworthy so worthy
a wife (being in part her servant, as I am your prentice) yet
(since I may say it without boasting) I am born a gentleman,
and by the trade I have learned of my master (which I trust
taints not my blood) able with mine own industry and   105
portion to maintain your daughter, my hope is, heaven will
so bless our humble beginning, that in the end I shall be no
disgrace to the grace with which my master hath bound me
his double prentice.

TOUCHSTONE

Master me no more, son, if thou think'st me worthy to be   110
thy father.

GERTRUDE

Sun? Now, good Lord, how he shines, and you mark him!
He's a gentleman?

GOLDING

Ay, indeed, Madam, a gentleman born.

PETRONEL

Never stand o' your gentry, Master Bridegroom; if your   115
legs be no better than your arms, you'll be able to stand upon
neither shortly.

TOUCHSTONE

An't please your good worship, sir, there are two sorts of
gentleman.

PETRONEL

What mean you, sir?   120

TOUCHSTONE

Bold to put off my hat to your worship—   [*Doffs his hat*]

PETRONEL

Nay, pray forbear, sir, and then forth with your two sorts
of gentlemen.

TOUCHSTONE

If your worship will have it so: I say there are two sorts of

116 *arms* coat of arms

---

112 *Sun.* The same pun is found in John Donne, 'Ascension', *Divine Poems*,
   ed. H. J. C. Grierson, *The Poems of John Donne* (London, 1939), p. 292.
   'Joy at the uprising of this Sunne, and Sonne'.

gentlemen. There is a gentleman artificial, and a gentleman   125
natural. Now, though your worship be a gentleman natural—
'work upon that now'!

QUICKSILVER
Well said old Touchstone; I am proud to hear thee enter a
set speech, i'faith! Forth, I beseech thee!

TOUCHSTONE
Cry you mercy, sir, your worship's a gentleman I do not   130
know. If you be one of my acquaintance, y'are very much
disguised, sir.

QUICKSILVER
Go to, old quipper! Forth with thy speech, I say!

TOUCHSTONE
What, sir, my speeches were ever in vain to your gracious
worship; and therefore, till I speak to you gallantry indeed,   135
I will save my breath for my broth anon. Come, my poor
son and daughter, let us hide ourselves in our poor humility,
and live safe. Ambition consumes itself with the very show.
'Work upon that now'!

[*Exeunt* TOUCHSTONE, GOLDING *and* MILDRED]

GERTRUDE
Let him go, let him go, for God's sake! Let him make his   140
prentice his son, for God's sake! Give away his daughter,
for God's sake! And when they come a-begging to us, for
God's sake, let's laugh at their good husbandry, for God's
sake! Farewell, sweet Knight, pray thee make haste after.

PETRONEL
What shall I say? I would not have thee go.   145

QUICKSILVER   [*Sings*]
    Now, O now, I must depart;
    Parting though it absence move—
This ditty, Knight, do I see in thy looks in capital letters.
    What a grief 'tis to depart,

130 *Cry you mercy* I beg your pardon
133 *quipper* argumentative person
135 *gallantry* fine language of fops

125–6 *gentleman natural.* Pun meaning a natural gentleman, and idiot.
130–1 *your worship's a gentleman I do not know.* If your worship's a gentle-
    man I cannot tell.
146–52 *Now, O now,* etc. A corruption of a Dowland Song (E. H. Fellowes,
    ed., *Dowland, First Book of Airs* (London, 1920), I, 22–4).
148 *capital letters.* With emphasis, touching on the topic of cuckoldry.

And leave the flower that has my heart!   150
My sweet lady, and alack for woe,
Why should we part so?
Tell truth, Knight, and shame all dissembling lovers; does
not your pain lie on that side?

PETRONEL
If it do, canst thou tell me how I may cure it?   155

QUICKSILVER
Excellent easily! Divide yourself in two halves, just by the
girdlestead; send one half with your lady, and keep the
tother yourself. Or else do as all true lovers do—part with
your heart, and leave your body behind. I have seen't done
a hundred times: 'tis as easy a matter for a lover to part   160
without a heart from his sweetheart, and he ne'er the worse,
as for a mouse to get from a trap and leave his tail behind
him. See, here comes the writings.

Enter SECURITY *with a* SCRIVENER

SECURITY
Good morrow to my worshipful Lady! I present your
Ladyship with this writing, to which if you please to set   165
your hand, with your knight's, a velvet gown shall attend
your journey, o' my credit.

GERTRUDE
What writing is it, Knight?

PETRONEL
The sale, sweetheart, of the poor tenement I told thee of,
only to make a little money to send thee down furniture for   170
my castle, to which my hand shall lead thee.

GERTRUDE
Very well! Now give me your pen, I pray.

QUICKSILVER
[*Aside*] It goes down without chewing, i'faith!

SCRIVENER
Your worships deliver this as your deed?

BOTH
We do.   175

GERTRUDE
So now, Knight, farewell till I see thee!

PETRONEL
All farewell to my sweetheart!

157 *girdlestead* waist
162 *his* ed. (her Q)
175 s.p. BOTH ed. (*Ambo.* Q)

MISTRESS TOUCHSTONE
Good-bye, son Knight!

PETRONEL
Farewell, my good mother!

GERTRUDE
Farewell, Frank; I would fain take thee down if I could.   180

QUICKSILVER
I thank your good Ladyship. Farewell, Mistress Sindefy.

Exeunt [GERTRUDE *and her party*]

PETRONEL
O tedious voyage, whereof there is no end! What will they
think of me?

QUICKSILVER
Think what they list. They longed for a vagary into the
country, and now they are fitted. So a woman marry to ride   185
in a coach, she cares not if she ride to her ruin. 'Tis the great
end of many of their marriages. This is not first time a lady
has rid a false journey in her coach, I hope.

PETRONEL
Nay, 'tis no matter. I care little what they think; he that
weighs men's thoughts has his hands full of nothing. A man,   190
in the course of this world, should be like a surgeon's instrument: work in the wounds of others, and feel nothing himself—the sharper and subtler, the better.

QUICKSILVER
As it falls out now, Knight, you shall not need to devise
excuses, or endure her outcries, when she returns. We shall   195
now be gone before, where they cannot reach us.

PETRONEL
Well, my kind compeer, you have now th'assurance we both
can make you. Let me now entreat you, the money we agreed
on may be brought to the Blue Anchor, near to Billingsgate,

197 *compeer* gossip

---

180 *take thee down.* Travel with, or have sexual intercourse with.
187–8 *This is not first time,* etc. H. & S. note (incorrectly) that this passage
    is paralleled in Field's *A Woman is a Weathercock* (II, iv, D3ᵛ). (It is
    found in Field's *Amends for Ladies*, II, iv, 32.) Nevertheless, this
    confirms Peery's hypothesis that Field played the part of Quicksilver.
    (See note, I, i, 132.)
199 *Blue Anchor.* Tavern mentioned in *The Roxburghe Ballads*, 1607.
199 *Billingsgate.* A river-gate, wharf, and fish-market, on the Thames a
    little below London Bridge. The great market-place of seventeenth-
    century London.

by six o'clock; where I and my chief friends, bound for this   200
voyage, will with feasts attend you.

SECURITY

The money, my most honourable compeer, shall without
fail observe your appointed hour.

PETRONEL

Thanks, my dear Gossip, I must now impart
To your approved love a loving secret,   205
As one on whom my life doth more rely
In friendly trust than any man alive.
Nor shall you be the chosen secretary
Of my affections for affection only:
For if I protest (if God bless my return)   210
To make you partner in my actions' gain
As deeply as if you had ventured with me
Half my expenses. Know then, honest Gossip,
I have enjoyed with such divine contentment
A gentlewoman's bed, whom you well know,   215
That I shall ne'er enjoy this tedious voyage,
Nor live the least part of the time it asketh,
Without her presence; 'so I thirst and hunger'
To taste the dear feast of her company.
And if the hunger and the thirst you vow,   220
(As my sworn gossip) to my wished good
Be (as I know it is) unfeigned and firm,
Do me an easy favour in your power.

SECURITY

Be sure, brave Gossip, all that I can do,
To my best nerve, is wholly at your service: 225
Who is the woman, first, that is your friend?

PETRONEL

The woman is your learned counsel's wife,
The lawyer, Master Bramble; whom would you
Bring out this even', in honest neighbourhood,
To take his leave with you, of me your gossip.   230
I, in the meantime, will send this my friend
Home to his house, to bring his wife disguised,
Before his face, into our company;
For love hath made her look for such a wile
To free her from his tyrannous jealousy.   235
And I would take this course before another,
In stealing her away to make us sport
And gull his circumspection the more grossly.
And I am sure that no man like yourself

Hath credit with him to entice his jealousy   240
To so long stay abroad as may give time
To her enlargement in such safe disguise.

SECURITY
A pretty, pithy, and most pleasant project!
Who would not strain a point of neighbourhood,
For such a point-device, that, as the ship   245
Of famous Draco went about the world,
Will wind about the lawyer, compassing
The world himself; he hath it in his arms,
And that's enough, for him, without his wife.
A lawyer is ambitious, and his head   250
Cannot be praised nor raised too high,
With any fork of highest knavery.
I'll go fetch him straight.

         Exit SECURITY

PETRONEL
So, so. Now, Frank, go thou home to his house,
'Stead of his lawyer's, and bring his wife hither,   255
Who, just like to the lawyer's wife, is prisoned
With his stern usurous jealousy, which could never
Be over-reached thus, but with over-reaching.

      Enter SECURITY

SECURITY
And, Master Francis, watch you th'instant time
To enter with his exit; 'twill be rare,   260
Two fine horned beasts—a camel and a lawyer!   [*Exit*]

QUICKSILVER
How the old villain joys in villainy!

      Enter SECURITY

SECURITY
And hark you, Gossip, when you have her here,

242 *enlargement* freedom of action
253 *him* Ed. (her Q)
257 *his* Qq (eis Q)
261 *Two fine* Qq (To finde Q)

---

245 *point-device.* Pun meaning (1) a point of vice and (2) the best way
 imaginable.
246 *Draco.* Drake's ship at Deptford.
261 *a camel and a lawyer.* Camel; thought to be a horned beast. Frequently
 used by Chapman in the context of cuckoldry. See H. & S., IX, 642.

Have your boat ready; ship her to your ship
With utmost haste, lest Master Bramble stay you.   265
To o'er-reach that head that out-reacheth all heads,
'Tis a trick rampant! 'Tis a very quiblin!
I hope this harvest to pitch cart with lawyers,
Their heads will be so forked. 'This sly touch
Will get apes to invent a number such'.   *Exit* 270

QUICKSILVER
Was ever rascal honeyed so with poison?
'He that delights in slavish avarice,
Is apt to joy in every sort of vice'.
Well, I'll go fetch his wife, whilst he the lawyer.

PETRONEL
But stay, Frank, let's think how we may disguise her   275
Upon this sudden.

QUICKSILVER
God's me, there's the mischief!
But hark you, here's an excellent device;
'Fore God, a rare one! I will carry her
A sailor's gown and cap, and cover her,   280
And a player's beard.

PETRONEL
And what upon her head?

QUICKSILVER
I tell you; a sailor's cap! 'Slight, God forgive me,
What kind of figent memory have you?

PETRONEL
Nay, then, what kind of figent wit hast thou?   285
A sailor's cap? How shall she put it off
When thou present'st her to our company?

QUICKSILVER
Tush, man! For that, make her a saucy sailor.

PETRONEL
Tush, tush, 'tis no fit sauce for such sweet mutton!
I know not what t'advise.   290

267 *rampant* spirited   267 *quiblin* a pun, a trick
270 *apes* imitators, actors
274 *lawyer* Ed. (lawyers Q)
275–84 prose Q
284 *figent* restless, fidgety
289–90 prose Q

289 *mutton*. From the proverb 'sweet meat must have a sour sauce'; Tilley,
    M839. Also mutton: prostitute.

Enter SECURITY, *with his wife's gown*

SECURITY
    Knight, Knight, a rare device!
PETRONEL
    'Swounds, yet again!
QUICKSILVER
    What stratagem have you now?
SECURITY
    The best that ever! You talked of disguising?
PETRONEL
    Ay, marry, Gossip, that's our present care.   295
SECURITY
    Cast care away then; here's the best device
    For plain security (for I am no better),
    I think, that ever lived. Here's my wife's gown,
    Which you may put upon the lawyer's wife,
    And which I brought you, sir, for two great reasons: 300
    One is, that Master Bramble may take hold
    Of some suspicion that it is my wife,
    And gird me so, perhaps, with his law wit;
    The other (which is policy indeed)
    Is, that my wife may now be tied at home,   305
    Having no more but her old gown abroad,
    And not show me a quirk, while I firk others.
    Is not this rare?
BOTH
    The best that ever was!
SECURITY
    Am I not born to furnish gentlemen?   310
PETRONEL
    O my dear Gossip!
SECURITY
    Well, hold, Master Francis!
    Watch when the lawyer's out, and put it in.
    And now I will go fetch him.   *Exit*
QUICKSILVER
    O my Dad!   315

292 *'Swounds* God's wounds
307 *quirk* sudden turn
308 s.p. BOTH ed. (*Ambo.* Q)
312–15 prose Q
_____

307 *firk.* Bedevil. (Security here resembles Vice of the Mystery Play.)

He goes, as 'twere the devil, to fetch the lawyer;
And devil shall he be, if horns will make him.

[*Re-enter* SECURITY]

PETRONEL
Why, how now, Gossip? Why stay you there musing?
SECURITY
A toy, a toy runs in my head, i'faith!
QUICKSILVER
A pox of that head! Is there more toys yet?   320
PETRONEL
What is it, pray thee, Gossip?
SECURITY
Why, sir, what if you
Should slip away now with my wife's best gown,
I have no security for it?
QUICKSILVER
For that, I hope, Dad, you will take our words.   325
SECURITY
Ay, by th'mass, your word! That's a proper staff
For wise Security to lean upon!
But 'tis no matter, once I'll trust my name
On your cracked credits; let it take no shame.
Fetch the wench, Frank!   *Exit* 330
QUICKSILVER
I'll wait upon you, sir,
And fetch you over, you were ne'er so fetched.
Go to the tavern, Knight; your followers
Dare not be drunk, I think, before their captain.   *Exit*
PETRONEL
Would I might lead them to no hotter service,   335
Till our Virginian gold were in our purses!   *Exit*

316 *to fetch* also to trick, gull
316–24 prose Q
319 *toy* prank
335 *them* Qq (then Q)

316 *He goes . . . lawyer*. cf. Chaucer's *Friar's Tale*, where the devil carries
off the lawyer because the villagers mean it literally when they say,
'Devil take you!' Typical of Chapman's habit of matter-of-fact citing
of obscure allusions.

[Act III, Scene iii

Blue Anchor Tavern, Billingsgate]

Enter SEAGULL, SPENDALL, *and* SCAPETHRIFT, *in the tavern,*
with a DRAWER

SEAGULL

Come, drawer, pierce your neatest hogsheads, and let's have
cheer, not fit for your Billingsgate tavern, but for our
Virginian colonel; he will be here instantly.

DRAWER

You shall have all things fit, sir; please you have any more
wine?   5

SPENDALL

More wine, slave! Whether we drink it or no, spill it, and
draw more.

SCAPETHRIFT

Fill all the pots in your house with all sorts of liquor, and
let 'em wait on us here like soldiers in their pewter coats;
and though we do not employ them now, yet we will main-   10
tain 'em till we do.

DRAWER

Said like an honourable captain! You shall have all you can
command, sir!   *Exit* DRAWER

SEAGULL

Come, boys, Virginia longs till we share the rest of her
maidenhead.   15

SPENDALL

Why, is she inhabited already with any English?

SEAGULL

A whole country of English is there, man, bred of those that
were left there in '79. They have married with the Indians,
and make 'em bring forth as beautiful faces as any we have
in England; and therefore the Indians are so in love with 'em,   20
that all the treasure they have they lay at their feet.

SCAPETHRIFT

But is there such treasure there, Captain, as I have heard?

9 *pewter coats* armour

---

18 '79. Grenville's earliest expedition to Virginia was in 1585 (Hakluyt,
Voyages, 1600, VIII, 310). Schelling upholds Edward Channing's
suggestion that the text refers to the 1587 expedition, known as 'the
lost colony', because some of the survivors apparently remained with
the Indians of Pamlico Sound.

SEAGULL

I tell thee, gold is more plentiful there than copper is with
us; and for as much red copper as I can bring, I'll have thrice
the weight in gold. Why, man, all their dripping-pans and   25
their chamber-pots are pure gold; and all the chains with
which they chain up their streets are massy gold; all the
prisoners they take are fettered in gold; and for rubies and
diamonds, they go forth on holidays and gather 'em by the
seashore to hang on their children's coats, and stick in their   30
caps, as commonly as our children wear saffron-gilt brooches,
and groats with holes in 'em.

SCAPETHRIFT

And is it a pleasant country withal?

SEAGULL

As ever the sun shined on; temperate and full of all sorts
of excellent viands; wild boar is as common there as our   35
tamest bacon is here; venison, as mutton. And then you
shall live freely there, without sergeants, or courtiers, or
lawyers, or intelligencers; only a few industrious Scots,
perhaps, who indeed are dispersed over the face of the whole
earth. But as for them, there are no greater friends to   40
Englishmen and England, when they are out on't, in the
world, than they are. And for my part, I would a hundred
thousand of 'em were there; for we are all one countrymen
now, ye know; and we should find ten times more comfort
of them there than we do here. Then for your means to   45
advancement, there it is simple and not preposterously mixed.

---

38 *intelligencers* informers, spies

24–5 *red copper . . . gold.* 'Copper carrieth the price of all, so it be red', . . .
    'Our copper is better than theirs: and the reason is for that it is redder
    and harder . . .' written about the Virginian Indians, and 'copper . . . they
    esteem more than gold, which for the colour they make no account of',
    of the Florida Indians. *Hakluyt's Principal Voyages* (1600), The Hakluyt
    Society Extra Series, 12 vols. (Glasgow, 1904), VIII, 320, 329, 433.
    (Quoted first A. H. Gilbert, *MLN*, XXXIII (1918), 183–4; and H. & S.,
    IX, 663.)
25–32 *Why, man, all their dripping-pans,* etc. Closely parallels Sir Thomas
    More's *Utopia.* Sir Thomas More, *Utopia*, Book II, eds. E. Surtz &
    J. Hexter (New Haven, 1965), 153.
32 *groats.* Coin worth 4*d.* when minted in 1531–32. By 1600 slang for any
    small coin.
38–45 *only . . . here.* The famous gibe which was cancelled in all but two
    existing copies of Q.

You may be an alderman there, and never be scavenger;
you may be a nobleman, and never be a slave; you may
come to preferment enough, and never be a pander; to riches
and fortune enough, and have never the more villainy nor   50
the less wit.

SPENDALL
God's me! And how far is it thither?

SEAGULL
Some six weeks' sail, no more, with any indifferent good
wind. And if I get to any part of the coast of Africa, I'll sail
thither with any wind; or when I come to Cape Finisterre,   55
there's a foreright wind continually wafts us till we come at
Virginia. See, our colonel's come.

Enter SIR PETRONEL *with his followers*

PETRONEL
Well met, good Captain Seagull, and my noble gentlemen!
Now the sweet hour of our freedom is at hand. Come,
drawer, fill us some carouses, and prepare us for the mirth   60
that will be occasioned presently. Here will be a pretty
wench, gentlemen, that will bear us company all our voyage.

SEAGULL
Whatsoever she be, here's to her health, noble Colonel, both
with cap and knee.

PETRONEL
Thanks, kind Captain Seagull! She's one I love dearly, and   65
must not be known till we be free from all that know us.
And so, gentlemen, here's to her health!

BOTH
Let it come, worthy Colonel; 'we do hunger and thirst for it'!

---

53 *indifferent* moderately
58 s.d. PETRONEL *with his followers* Qq (*Petronell* Q)
68 s.p. BOTH ed. (*Ambo.* Q)

---

47 *scavenger*. Officer whose job it was to employ and supervise the poor to
keep the streets clean.
48 Here, 'You may be a nobleman, and never be a slave;' was changed to
the innocuous 'You may be any other officer, . . .'. A passage was
inserted at the end to fill the gap left by the removal of 38–45: 'Besides,
there we shall have no more law than conscience, and not too much of
either; serve God enough, eat and drink enough, and "enough is as
good as a feast"'. Adams believes the last if not all the corrections were
made by the printer and on the basis of the facile proverb thrown in
as a stop-gap, I would tend to agree. See Adams, op. cit., pp. 163-9.
55 *Cape Finisterre*. The most westerly headland of Spain.

PETRONEL

Afore heaven, you have hit the phrase of one that her
presence will touch from the foot to the forehead, if ye knew   70
it.

SPENDALL

Why, then, we will join his forehead with her health, sir;
and, Captain Scapethrift, here's to 'em both!

                         [*All kneel and drink*]

                Enter SECURITY *and* BRAMBLE

SECURITY

See, see, Master Bramble, 'fore heaven, their voyage cannot
but prosper: they are o' their knees for success to it.   75

BRAMBLE

And they pray to god Bacchus.

SECURITY

God save my brave Colonel, with all his tall captains and
corporals! See, sir, my worshipful learned counsel, Master
Bramble, is come to take his leave of you.

PETRONEL

Worshipful Master Bramble, how far do you draw us into   80
the sweet brier of your kindness! Come, Captain Seagull,
another health to this rare Bramble, that hath never a prick
about him.

SEAGULL

I pledge his most smooth disposition, sir. Come, Master
Security, bend your supporters, and pledge this notorious   85
health here.

SECURITY

Bend you yours likewise, Master Bramble; for it is you shall
pledge me.

SEAGULL

Not so, Master Security! He must not pledge his own
health!   90

SECURITY

No, Master Captain?

             Enter QUICKSILVER *with* WINIFRED *disguised*

Why then, here's one is fitly come to do him that honour.

QUICKSILVER

Here's the gentlewoman your cousin, sir, whom, with much

84 s.p. SEAGULL Qq (*Pet.* Q)

74–131 *See, see, . . . lady*. The jesting of the deluded husband at his own
    expense and his misconstruing of his wife's fears derives from
    Masuccio XL.

entreaty, I have brought to take her leave of you in a
tavern; ashamed whereof, you must pardon her if she put   95
not off her mask.

PETRONEL

Pardon me, sweet cousin; my kind desire to see you before
I went, made me so importunate to entreat your presence
here.

SECURITY

How now, Master Francis, have you honoured this presence   100
with a fair gentlewoman?

QUICKSILVER

Pray, sir, take you no notice of her, for she will not be known
to you.

SECURITY

But my learned counsel, Master Bramble here, I hope may
know her.   105

QUICKSILVER

No more than you, sir, at this time; his learning must
pardon her.

SECURITY

Well, God pardon her for my part, and I do, I'll be sworn;
and so, Master Francis, here's to all that are going eastward
tonight, towards Cuckold's Haven; and so, to the health   110
of Master Bramble!

QUICKSILVER

[Kneels] I pledge it, sir. Hath it gone round, Captains?

SEAGULL

It has, sweet Frank; and the round closes with thee.

QUICKSILVER

Well, sir, here's to all eastward and toward cuckolds, and so
to famous Cuckold's Haven, so fatally remembered.   115

Surgit

PETRONEL

[To WINIFRED] Nay, pray thee, coz, weep not. Gossip
Security?

SECURITY

Ay, my brave Gossip.

PETRONEL

A word, I beseech you, sir. Our friend, Mistress Bramble
here, is so dissolved in tears that she drowns the whole   120
mirth of our meeting. Sweet Gossip, take her aside and
comfort her.

116 s.d. *Surgit* stands up

SECURITY

[*Aside to* WINIFRED] Pity of all true love, Mistress Bramble!
What, weep you to enjoy your love? What's the cause, lady?
Is't because your husband is so near, and your heart earns,　　125
to have a little abused him? Alas, alas, the offence is too
common to be respected. So great a grace hath seldom
chanced to so unthankful a woman: to be rid of an old
jealous dotard, to enjoy the arms of a loving young knight,
that, when your prickless Bramble is withered with grief of　　130
your loss, will make you flourish afresh in the bed of a lady.

Enter DRAWER

DRAWER

Sir Petronel, here's one of your watermen come to tell you
it will be flood these three hours; and that 'twill be dangerous
going against the tide, for the sky is overcast, and there was
a porcpisce even now seen at London Bridge, which is　　135
always the messenger of tempests, he says.

PETRONEL

A porcpisce! What's that to th' purpose? Charge him, if he
love his life, to attend us; can we not reach Blackwall (where
my ship lies) against the tide, and in spite of tempests?
Captains and gentlemen, we'll begin a new ceremony at the　　140
beginning of our voyage, which I believe will be followed
of all future adventurers.

SEAGULL

What's that, good Colonel?

PETRONEL

This, Captain Seagull. We'll have our provided supper
brought aboard Sir Francis Drake's ship, that hath com-　　145
passed the world; where, with full cups and banquets, we
will do sacrifice for a prosperous voyage. My mind gives me
that some good spirits of the waters should haunt the desert
ribs of her, and be auspicious to all that honour her memory,
and will with like orgies enter their voyages.　　150

---

125 *earns* feels keen grief

---

137 *porcpisce.* Jonson's spelling (see *Volpone*, II, i, 40). Stow's *Chronicle*
(*Annals*, p. 880, ed. 1615) tells of the appearance of a porpoise on the
Thames. The date recorded for the capture of a porpoise at West Ham
is 19 January 1606, but it must have been seen on the river before this
if *Volpone* was written late in 1605.
138 *Blackwall.* A mooring for merchant-ships, on the Thames below
London.

SEAGULL

Rarely conceited! One health more to this motion, and
aboard to perform it. He that will not this night be drunk,
may he never be sober!

They compass in WINIFRED, *dance the drunken round, and
drink carouses*

BRAMBLE

Sir Petronel and his honourable Captains, in these young
services we old servitors may be spared. We only came to   155
take our leaves, and with one health to you all, I'll be bold
to do so. Here, neighbour Security, to the health of Sir
Petronel and all his captains!

SECURITY

You must bend, then, Master Bramble. [*They kneel*] So, now
I am for you. I have one corner of my brain, I hope, fit to   160
bear one carouse more. Here, lady, to you that are encom-
passed there, and are ashamed of our company! Ha, ha, ha!
By my troth, my learned counsel, Master Bramble, my mind
runs so of Cuckold's Haven tonight, that my head runs over
with admiration.   165

BRAMBLE

[*Aside*] But is not that your wife, neighbour?

SECURITY

[*Aside*] No, by my troth, Master Bramble. Ha, ha, ha! A pox
of all Cuckold's Havens, I say!

BRAMBLE

[*Aside*] O' my faith, her garments are exceeding like your
wife's.   170

SECURITY

[*Aside*] *Cucullus non facit monachum*, my learned counsel;
all are not cuckolds that seem so, nor all seem not that are
so. Give me your hand, my learned counsel; you and I will
sup somewhere else than at Sir Francis Drake's ship tonight.
Adieu, my noble Gossip!   175

BRAMBLE

Good fortune, brave Captains; fair skies God send ye!

ALL

Farewell, my hearts, farewell!

177 s.p. ALL ed. (*Omnes* Q)

171 *Cucullus non facit monachum*. The cowl does not make the monk, with a
play on 'cuckold'. cf. *Twelfth Night*, I, v, 62.

PETRONEL
Gossip, laugh no more at Cuckold's Haven, Gossip.

SECURITY
I have done, I have done, sir. Will you lead, Master Bramble?
Ha, ha, ha!   *Exit* [*with* BRAMBLE]   180

PETRONEL
Captain Seagull, charge a boat!

ALL
A boat, a boat, a boat!   *Exeunt*

DRAWER
Y'are in a proper taking, indeed, to take a boat, especially at
this time of night, and against tide and tempest. They say
yet, 'drunken men never take harm'. This night will try the   185
truth of that proverb.   *Exit*

[Act III, Scene iv

Outside SECURITY's *House*]

Enter SECURITY

SECURITY
What, Winnie? Wife, I say? Out of doors at this time! Where
should I seek the gad-fly? Billingsgate, Billingsgate, Billingsgate! She's gone with the knight, she's gone with the knight!
Woe be to thee, Billingsgate. A boat, a boat, a boat! A full
hundred marks for a boat!   *Exit*   5

180 *Exit* Qq (omitted in Q)
181 *charge* order
182 s.p. ALL ed. (*Omnes* Q)
183 *taking* state
185 *drunken men never take harm* proverbial. Tilley, M94

4–5 *A boat*, etc. Parody on *Richard III*, V, iv, 7, 13. Marston also parodies
    this passage in *The Scourge of Villainy*, Satire VII, i, *Parasiter*, V, i, and
    What you Will, II, i.

Act IV, Scene i

Enter SLITGUT, *with a pair of ox-horns, discovering Cuckold's
Haven, above* [*right*]

SLITGUT
All hail, fair haven of married men only, for there are none
but married men cuckolds! For my part, I presume not to
arrive here, but in my master's behalf (a poor butcher of
Eastcheap), who sends me to set up (in honour of Saint
Luke) these necessary ensigns of his homage. And up I got   5
this morning, thus early, to get up to the top of this famous
tree, that is all fruit and no leaves, to advance this crest of
my master's occupation. Up then; heaven and Saint Luke
bless me, that I be not blown into the Thames as I climb,
with this furious tempest. 'Slight, I think the devil be   10
abroad, in likeness of a storm, to rob me of my horns! Hark
how he roars! Lord, what a coil the Thames keeps! She
bears some unjust burden, I believe, that she kicks and
curvets thus to cast it. Heaven bless all honest passengers
that are upon her back now; for the bit is out of her mouth,   15
I see, and she will run away with 'em! So, so, I think I have
made it look the right way; it runs against London Bridge,
as it were, even full butt. And now, let me discover from this
lofty prospect, what pranks the rude Thames plays in her
desperate lunacy. O me, here's a boat has been cast away   20
hard by! Alas, alas, see one of her passengers, labouring for
his life to land at this haven here! Pray heaven he may
recover it! His next land is even just under me; hold out yet
a little, whatsoever thou art: pray, and take a good heart to
thee. 'Tis a man; take a man's heart to thee; yet a little   25

---

7 *tree* pole
12 *coil* turmoil
23 *recover* regain
23 *next* nearest

---

1 s.d. *Cuckold's Haven.* A point on the Surrey side of the Thames about
a mile below Rotherhithe Church (see Appendix). According to legend
the point had once been the site of a Temple of Fortune which was
later destroyed by fire. It was traditional on St Luke's day, 18 October,
for a butcher of Eastcheap to commemorate King John's cuckolding
of a miller, by erecting a pair of horns on a pole there. The cuckold
symbol is thus ambiguous since it is also the Christian emblem of
St Luke. cf. Breton, *Pasquil's Nightcap* (1612), G1ᵛ–H3ʳ.
4–5 *Saint Luke.* See above, s.d.

further, get up o' thy legs, man; now 'tis shallow enough.
So, so, so! Alas, he's down again! Hold thy wind, father!
'Tis a man in a night-cap. So! Now he's got up again; now
he's past the worst; yet, thanks be to heaven, he comes
toward me pretty and strongly.　　　　　　　　　　　　　　　30

Enter SECURITY *without his hat, in a nightcap, wet band, &c.*
[stage right]

SECURITY
Heaven, I beseech thee, how have I offended thee! Where
am I cast ashore now, that I may go a righter way home by
land? Let me see. O, I am scarce able to look about me!
Where is there any sea-mark that I am acquainted withal?

SLITGUT
Look up, father; are you acquainted with this mark?　　　　35

SECURITY
What! Landed at Cuckold's Haven! Hell and damnation! I
will run back and drown myself.

　　　　　　　　　　　　　　　　　He falls down

SLITGUT
Poor man, how weak he is! The weak water has washed
away his strength.

SECURITY
Landed at Cuckold's Haven! If it had not been to die twenty　40
times alive, I should never have 'scaped death! I will never
arise more; I will grovel here and eat dirt till I be choked. I
will make the gentle earth do that which the cruel water has
denied me!

SLITGUT
Alas, good father, be not so desperate! Rise, man; if you　　45
will, I'll come presently and lead you home.

SECURITY
Home! Shall I make any know my home, that has known me
thus abroad? How low shall I crouch away, that no eye may
see me? I will creep on the earth while I live, and never look
heaven in the face more.　　　　　　　　*Exit creeping*　　50

34 *sea-mark* landmark
50 s.d. *creeping* Ed. (*creep* Q)

---

31 s.d. *band*. The collar which superseded the ruff.
42–50 *I will grovel here . . . face more*. Security is consistently shown to be
　　of a melancholic humour, whose element is earth. His affinity to the
　　earth here is not unnatural; and his exit creeping tallies with earlier
　　hints at his satanic character. cf. the devil of the York Mystery Play
　　who exits crawling.

SLITGUT
What young planet reigns now, trow, that old men are so
foolish? What desperate young swaggerer would have been
abroad such a weather as this upon the water? Ay me, see
another remnant of this unfortunate shipwreck, or some
other! A woman, i'faith, a woman! Though it be almost at   55
Saint Katherine's, I discern it to be a woman, for all her
body is above the water, and her clothes swim about her
most handsomely. O, they bear her up most bravely! Has
not a woman reason to love the taking up of her clothes the
better while she lives, for this? Alas, how busy the rude   60
Thames is about her! A pox o' that wave! It will drown her,
i'faith, 'twill drown her! Cry God mercy, she has 'scaped it,
I thank heaven she has 'scaped it! O, how she swims like a
mermaid! Some vigilant body look out and save her. That's
well said; just where the priest fell in, there's one sets down   65
a ladder, and goes to take her up. God's blessing o' thy heart,
boy! Now, take her up in thy arms and to bed with her.
She's up, she's up! She's a beautiful woman, I warrant her;
the billows durst not devour her.

Enter the DRAWER *in the Tavern before, with* WINIFRED
[stage left]

DRAWER
How fare you now, lady?   70
WINIFRED
Much better, my good friend, than I wish; as one desperate
of her fame, now my life is preserved.
DRAWER
Comfort yourself: that power that preserved you from death

---

51 *trow* pray
65 *well said* well done

---

51 *young planet*. Probably the new star discovered by Kepler on 17 October
  1604. '[It] had burst out in the constellation Serpentarius, and . . . sur-
  passed Jupiter in brightness'. E. B. Knobel, *Shakespeare's England*,
  2 vols. (Oxford, 1916), I, 455. cf. *Volpone*, II, i, 37.
57–8 *her clothes swim* . . . Perhaps another hit at *Hamlet*, IV, vii, 176–7.
  'Her clothes spread wide,/And mermaid-like awhile they bore her up'.
65 *just where the priest fell in*. See John Taylor, the Water Poet, *A Discovery
  by Sea from London to Salisbury*, Spencer Soc., reprint, London, 1869,
  p. 21: 'Down by St. Katherine's where the priest fell in', and Jonson's
  Masque of Augurs, 'We shew th'yron Gate,/The wheele of St. Kate,/And
  the place where the Priest fel in'. (H. & S., VII, 636, l. 201).

can likewise defend you from infamy, howsoever you
deserve it. Were not you one that took boat late this night   75
with a knight and other gentlemen at Billingsgate?

WINIFRED

Unhappy that I am, I was.

DRAWER

I am glad it was my good hap to come down thus far after
you, to a house of my friend's here in St. Katherine's; since
I am now happily made a mean to your rescue from the   80
ruthless tempest, which (when you took boat) was so
extreme, and the gentleman that brought you forth so desperate and unsober, that I feared long ere this I should hear
of your shipwreck, and therefore (with little other reason)
made thus far this way. And this I must tell you, since per-   85
haps you may make use of it: there was left behind you at
our tavern, brought by a porter (hired by the young gentleman that brought you) a gentlewoman's gown, hat, stockings,
and shoes; which, if they be yours, and you please to shift
you, taking a hard bed here in this house of my friend, I will   90
presently go fetch you.

WINIFRED

Thanks, my good friend, for your more than good news.
The gown with all things bound with it are mine; which if
you please to fetch as you have promised, I will boldly
receive the kind favour you have offered till your return;   95
entreating you, by all the good you have done in preserving
me hitherto, to let none take knowledge of what favour you
do me, or where such a one as I am bestowed, lest you incur
me much more damage in my fame than you have done me
pleasure in preserving my life.   100

DRAWER

Come in, lady, and shift yourself; resolve that nothing but
your own pleasure shall be used in your discovery.

WINIFRED

Thank you, good friend. The time may come, I shall requite
you.   *Exeunt*

SLITGUT

See, see, see! I hold my life, there's some other a-taking up   10

89–90 *shift you* change into a new suit of clothes

---

79 *St. Katherine's.* A reformatory for fallen women.

at Wapping now! Look, what a sort of people cluster about
the gallows there! In good troth, it is so. O me, a fine young
gentleman! What, and taken up at the gallows? Heaven
grant he be not one day taken down there! O' my life, it is
ominous! Well, he is delivered for the time. I see the people 110
have all left him; yet will I keep my prospect awhile, to see
if any more have been shipwrecked.

      Enter QUICKSILVER, *bareheaded*

                                   [centre]

QUICKSILVER
  Accursed that ever I was saved or born!
  How fatal is my sad arrival here!
  As if the stars and Providence spake to me,   115
  And said, 'The drift of all unlawful courses
  (Whatever end they dare propose themselves
  In frame of their licentious policies)
  In the firm order of just Destiny,
  They are the ready highways to our ruins'.   120
  I know not what to do; my wicked hopes
  Are, with this tempest, torn up by the roots!
  O, which way shall I bend my desperate steps,
  In which unsufferable shame and misery
  Will not attend them? I will walk this bank   125
  And see if I can meet the other relics
  Of our poor, shipwrecked crew, or hear of them.
  The knight—alas—was so far gone with wine,
  And th'other three, that I refused their boat,
  And took the hapless woman in another,   130
  Who cannot but be sunk, whatever Fortune
  Hath wrought upon the others' desperate lives.   *Exit*

    Enter PETRONEL *and* SEAGULL, *bareheaded*
                        [downstage, right]

PETRONEL
  Zounds, Captain! I tell thee, we are cast up o' the coast of
France! 'Sfoot, I am not drunk still, I hope! Dost remember
where we were last night?   135

---

106 *sort* crowd   112 *bareheaded* ed. (*bareheade* Q)   118 *frame* planning

106–7 *Wapping . . . gallows.* 'The usual place of execution for hanging of
    pirates and sea-rovers, at the low-water mark, and there to remain, till
    three tides had overflowed them'. John Stow, *The Survey of London*,
    ed. H. B. Wheatley (London, 1912; repr. 1965), p. 375. (Wapping
    gallows stood on a bend in the Thames, just below St Katherine's.)
131 *Fortune.* See note, IV, i, 1 s.d. *Cuckold's Haven.*

SEAGULL

No, by my troth, Knight, not I. But methinks we have been
a horrible while upon the water, and in the water.

PETRONEL

Ay me, we are undone for ever! Hast any money about thee?

SEAGULL

Not a penny, by heaven!

PETRONEL

Not a penny betwixt us, and cast ashore in France!   140

SEAGULL

Faith, I cannot tell that; my brains nor mine eyes are not
mine own yet.

Enter TWO GENTLEMEN

PETRONEL

'Sfoot, wilt not believe me? I know't by th'elevation of the
pole, and by the altitude and latitude of the climate. See,
here comes a couple of French gentlemen; I knew we were 145
in France; dost thou think our Englishmen are so Frenchified that a man knows not whether he be in France or in
England when he sees 'em? What shall we do? We must e'en
to 'em, and entreat some relief of 'em. Life is sweet, and we
have no other means to relieve our lives now, but their 150
charities.

SEAGULL

Pray you, do you beg on 'em then; you can speak French.

PETRONEL

*Monsieur, plaist-il d'avoir pitié de nostre grand infortunes. Je
suis un povre chevalier d'Angleterre qui a souffri l'infortune de
naufrage.*   155

1 GENTLEMAN

Un povre chevalier d'Angleterre?

PETRONEL

*Oui, monsieur, il est trop vraye; mais vous scavés bien nous
sommes toutes subject a fortune.*

2 GENTLEMAN

A poor knight of England? A poor knight of Windsor, are

154 *souffri l'infortune* (Qq *souffri'l infortune* Q)

___

143 *by th'elevation.* The latitude; another far-fetched pun.
146–7 *Frenchified.* cf. Fastidious Brisk in Jonson's *Every Man out of His
    Humour*, I, iii, 195; the aping of French manners was a common target
    of the Elizabethan satirist.
159 *A poor knight of Windsor.* A pensioner of the king who was allowed to live
    in the royal chambers at Windsor. By 1604 synonymous with 'pauper'.

you not? Why speak you this broken French when y'are a 160
whole Englishman? On what coast are you, think you?

PETRONEL
On the coast of France, sir.

1 GENTLEMAN
On the coast of Dogs, sir; y'are i'th' Isle o' Dogs, I tell you!
I see y'ave been washed in the Thames here, and I believe
ye were drowned in a tavern before, or else you would never 165
have took boat in such a dawning as this was. Farewell,
farewell; we will not know you for shaming of you.—I ken
the man weel; he's one of my thirty-pound knights.

2 GENTLEMAN
No, no, this is he that stole his knighthood o' the grand day
for four pound, giving to a page all the money in's purse, I 170
wot well.

Exeunt [GENTLEMEN]

SEAGULL
Death, Colonel! I knew you were overshot!

PETRONEL
Sure, I think now, indeed, Captain Seagull, we were something overshot.

Enter QUICKSILVER

What, my sweet Frank Quicksilver! Dost thou survive to 175
rejoice me? But what! Nobody at thy heels, Frank? Ay me,
what is become of poor Mistress Security?

QUICKSILVER
Faith, gone quite from her name, as she is from her fame,
I think; I left her to the mercy of the water.

SEAGULL
Let her go, let her go! Let us go to our ship at Blackwall, and 180
shift us.

---

172 *Death*. i.e., Christ's death   172 *overshot* wide of the mark; drunk

---

163 *Isle o' [of] Dogs.* A low swampy peninsula in the Thames opposite
Greenwich (see Appendix), well-known refuge for debtors and cutpurses. Its proximity to the queen's castle makes it probable that the
play's title is a topical allusion to the royal sojourn there from mid-
March to mid-June 1605. It is also the place where Drake was knighted
and there may be further satirical play with the title of Jonson's
topical satire *Isle of Dogs*, for which he was imprisoned in 1597.

168 *thirty-pound knights.* Referring to James I's lavish creation of knights,
the subject of many a contemporary jest (cf. Appendix). This line was
evidently meant to mimic James's Scots accent.

PETRONEL

Nay, by my troth, let our clothes rot upon us, and let us rot
in them! Twenty to one our ship is attached by this time!
If we set her not under sail this last tide, I never looked for
any other. Woe, woe is me! What shall become of us? The   185
last money we could make, the greedy Thames has devoured,
and if our ship be attached, there is no hope can relieve us.

QUICKSILVER

'Sfoot, Knight, what an unknightly faintness transports thee!
Let our ship sink, and all the world that's without us be
taken from us, I hope I have some tricks in this brain of   190
mine shall not let us perish.

SEAGULL

Well said, Frank, i' faith. O my nimble-spirited Quicksilver!
'Fore God, would thou hadst been our colonel!

PETRONEL

I like his spirit rarely; but I see no means he has to support
that spirit.   195

QUICKSILVER

Go to, Knight! I have more means than thou art aware of.
I have not lived amongst goldsmiths and goldmakers all
this while, but I have learned something worthy of my time
with 'em. And not to let thee stink where thou stand'st,
Knight, I'll let thee know some of my skill presently.   200

SEAGULL

Do, good Frank, I beseech thee!

QUICKSILVER

I will blanch copper so cunningly that it shall endure all
proofs but the test: it shall endure malleation, it shall have
the ponderosity of Luna, and the tenacity of Luna, by no
means friable.   205

PETRONEL

'Slight, where learn'st thou these terms, trow?

QUICKSILVER

Tush, Knight, the terms of this art every ignorant quacksalver is perfect in. But I'll tell you how yourself shall blanch
copper thus cunningly. Take arsenic, otherwise called realgar

---

183 *attached* seized
203 *malleation* hammering
205 *friable* easily reduced to powder
208 *blanch* whiten, turn silvery

---

204 *ponderosity . . . tenacity of Luna*. The weight and toughness of silver.

(which, indeed, is plain ratsbane); sublime 'em three or four 210
times, then take the sublimate of this realgar, and put 'em
into a glass, into *chymia*, and let 'em have a convenient
decoction natural, four-and-twenty hours, and he will
become perfectly fixed; then take this fixed powder, and
project him upon well-purged copper, *et habebis magisterium*. 215

BOTH
Excellent Frank, let us hug thee!

QUICKSILVER
Nay, this I will do besides: I'll take you off twelvepence from
every angel, with a kind of *aqua fortis*, and never deface any
part of the image.

PETRONEL
But then it will want weight? 220

QUICKSILVER
You shall restore that thus: take your *sal achyme*, prepared,
and your distilled urine, and let your angels lie in it but four-
and-twenty hours, and they shall have their perfect weight
again. Come on, now, I hope this is enough to put some
spirit into the livers of you; I'll infuse more another time. 225
We have saluted the proud air long enough with our bare
sconces. Now will I have you to a wench's house of mine
at London; there make shift to shift us, and after, take such
fortunes as the stars shall assign us.

BOTH
Notable Frank, we will ever adore thee!   *Exeunt* 230

Enter DRAWER, *with* WINIFRED, *new-attired*
[*stage left*]

WINIFRED
Now, sweet friend, you have brought me near enough your

210 *sublime* vaporize and solidify
211 *realgar* arsenic disulphide
212 *chymia* kemia, chemical analysis
216 s.p. BOTH ed. (*Ambo.* Q)
218 *aqua fortis* sulphuric acid
221 *sal achyme* salt without chyme
227 *sconces* skulls   230 s.p. BOTH ed. (*Ambo.* Q)

214 *fixed.* Made stable by being deprived of volatility or fluidity.
215 *et habebis magisterium.* Literally 'and you will have the philosopher's
stone'. Ironical since Quicksilver will have only produced false silver.
226 *saluted the proud air* (Ayre Q). A possible pun on the name of the
hero of Dekker's *The Shoemakers' Holiday*, Simon Eyre, who so closely
resembles Touchstone.

tavern, which I desired that I might with some colour be seen near, inquiring for my husband, who, I must tell you, stole thither last night with my wet gown we have left at your friend's—which, to continue your former honest kind- 235 ness, let me pray you to keep close from the knowledge of any; and so, with all vow of your requital, let me now entreat you to leave me to my woman's wit, and fortune.

DRAWER

All shall be done you desire; and so, all the fortune you can wish for attend you! *Exit* DRAWER 240

Enter SECURITY

SECURITY

I will once more to this unhappy tavern before I shift one rag of me more, that I may there know what is left behind, and what news of their passengers. I have bought me a hat and band with the little money I had about me, and made the streets a little leave staring at my night-cap. 245

WINIFRED

O my dear husband! Where have you been tonight? All night abroad at taverns? Rob me of my garments, and fare as one run away from me? Alas, is this seemly for a man of your credit, of your age, and affection to your wife?

SECURITY

What should I say? How miraculously sorts this! Was not 250 I at home, and called thee last night?

WINIFRED

Yes, sir, the harmless sleep you broke, and my answer to you, would have witnessed it, if you had had the patience to have stayed and answered me: but your so sudden retreat made me imagine you were gone to Master Bramble's, and 255 so rested patient and hopeful of your coming again, till this your unbelieved absence brought me abroad with no less than wonder, to seek you where the false knight had carried you.

SECURITY

Villain and monster that I was, how have I abused thee! I 260 was suddenly gone indeed; for my sudden jealousy trans- ferred me. I will say no more but this; dear wife, I suspected thee.

WINIFRED

Did you suspect me?

SECURITY

Talk not of it, I beseech thee; I am ashamed to imagine it. 265

I will home, I will home; and every morning on my knees
ask thee heartily forgiveness.   *Exeunt*

SLITGUT

Now will I descend my honourable prospect, the farthest
seeing sea-mark of the world; no marvel, then, if I could
see two miles about me. I hope the red tempest's anger be   270
now overblown, which sure I think heaven sent as a punishment for profaning holy Saint Luke's memory with so
ridiculous a custom. Thou dishonest satyr, farewell to
honest married men; farewell to all sorts and degrees of
thee! Farewell, thou horn of hunger, that call'st th'Inns o'   275
Court to their manger! Farewell, thou horn of abundance,
that adornest the headsmen of the commonwealth! Farewell,
thou horn of direction, that is the city lanthorn! Farewell,
thou horn of pleasure, the ensign of the huntsman! Farewell, thou horn of destiny, th'ensign of the married man!   280
Farewell, thou horn tree, that bearest nothing but stone-
fruit!   *Exit*

268 s.p. SLITGUT ed. (unassigned Q)
275 *horn of hunger* dinner horn

---

270 *red tempest*. Red may indicate that alchemical change has taken place.
275–6 *Inns o' Court*. The London legal societies: Lincoln's Inn, Inner
   Temple, Middle Temple, and Gray's Inn.
275–82 *Farewell . . . stone-fruit*. The encomium on the horn is similar to
   Valerio's in Chapman, *All Fools* (1605).
276 *horn of abundance*. Cornucopia. Bulls' heads were set up by the Romans
   in honour of the river which brought wealth to the city, cf. Breton, op.
   cit., G1ᵛ.
277 *that adornest the headsmen*. Schelling notes the probable pun 'add-
   hornest', and 'headsmen' as cuckolds as well as dignitaries.
278 *horn of direction*. i.e., pun on lanthorn as 'land-horn', the transparent
   protective case made of 'horn' to shield a lantern from the wind.
281–2 *stone-fruit*. Stone = testicle, hence the tree is recognized as a phallic
   symbol.

Act IV, Scene ii

[*A Room in* TOUCHSTONE's *House*]

Enter TOUCHSTONE

TOUCHSTONE

Ha, sirrah! Thinks my Knight adventurer we can no point
of our compass? Do we not know north-north-east? north-
east-and-by-east? east-and-by-north? nor plain eastward?
Ha! Have we never heard of Virginia? Nor the Cavallaria?
Nor the Colonaria? Can we discover no discoveries? Well,   5
mine errant Sir Flash and my runagate Quicksilver, you
may drink drunk, crack cans, hurl away a brown dozen of
Monmouth caps or so, in sea ceremony to your *bon voyage*;
but for reaching any coast save the coast of Kent or Essex,
with this tide, or with this fleet, I'll be your warrant for a   10
Gravesend toast. There's that gone afore will stay your
admiral and vice-admiral and rear-admiral, were they all (as
they are) but one pinnace and under sail, as well as a remora,
doubt it not, and from this sconce, without either powder or
shot. 'Work upon that now'! Nay, and you'll show tricks,   15
we'll vie with you a little. My daughter, his lady, was sent
eastward by land to a castle of his i' the air (in what region
I know not) and, as I hear, was glad to take up her lodging
in her coach, she and her two waiting-women (her maid and
her mother), like three snails in a shell, and the coachman   20
a-top on 'em, I think. Since they have all found the way

1 *can* know
5 *Nor* Ed. (not Q)
15 *show tricks* pretend, make a fraud

4–5 *Cavallaria . . . Colonaria.* Latin law terms indicating the length of
    tenure for a knight and for an ordinary adventurer. Mocking Petronel's
    Virginian plans.
8 *Monmouth caps.* Flat caps worn by sailors and soldiers.
10 *I'll be your warrant.* I'll be bound. I wouldn't bet more than a Gravesend
    toast.
11 *Gravesend toast.* A phrase of uncertain meaning but denoting something
    worthless.
13 *pinnace.* Small two-masted schooner.
13 *remora.* A sucking fish. Traditionally believed to stay ships by attaching
    itself to the hull.
14 *sconce.* Crown of the head, with play on the sense 'fort'.

back again by Weeping Cross; but I'll not see 'em. And for
two on 'em, madam and her malkin, they are like to bite o'
the bridle for William, as the poor horses have done all this
while that hurried 'em, or else go graze o' the common.   25
So should my Dame Touchstone, too; but she has been my
cross these thirty years, and I'll now keep her, to fright away
sprites, i' faith. I wonder I hear no news of my son Golding.
He was sent for to the Guildhall this morning betimes, and
I marvel at the matter. If I had not laid up comfort and hope   30
in him, I should grow desperate of all.

Enter GOLDING

See, he is come i' my thought! How now, son? What news
at the Court of Aldermen?

GOLDING
Troth, sir, an accident somewhat strange, else it hath little
in it worth the reporting.   35

TOUCHSTONE
What? It is not borrowing of money, then?

GOLDING
No, sir; it hath pleased the worshipful commoners of the
City to take me one i' their number at presentation of the
inquest—

TOUCHSTONE
Ha!   40

GOLDING
And the alderman of the ward wherein I dwell to appoint
me his deputy—

TOUCHSTONE
How!

GOLDING
In which place I have had an oath ministered me, since I
went.   45

---

23 *malkin* slut
32 *i'my* . . . just as I . . . 32 s.d. ed. (34 s.d. Q)

---

22 *Weeping Cross.* Eleanor cross (erected by Edward I in memory of his
    first queen, Eleanor of Castile (d. 1290)), of which there were six in
    England. To return by the Weeping Cross was to return repentant.
    Proverbial. Tilley, W248.
23–4 *bite o' the bridle for William.* Proverbial. Tilley, B670; to fare badly,
    to be cut short, to suffer want.
38–9 *presentation of the inquest.* Report to a committee of inquiry.

TOUCHSTONE

Now, my dear and happy son! Let me kiss thy new worship, and a little boast mine own happiness in thee. What a fortune was it (or rather my judgement, indeed) for me, first to see that in his disposition which a whole city so conspires to second! Ta'en into the livery of his company the first day   50
of his freedom! Now (not a week married) chosen commoner and alderman's deputy in a day! Note but the reward of a thrifty course. The wonder of his time! Well, I will honour Master Alderman for this act (as becomes me) [*doffing his cap*] and shall think the better of the Common Council's   55
wisdom and worship while I live, for thus meeting, or but coming after me, in the opinion of his desert. Forward, my sufficient son, and as this is the first, so esteem it the least step to that high and prime honour that expects thee.

GOLDING

Sir, as I was not ambitious of this, so I covet no higher   60
place; it hath dignity enough, if it will but save me from contempt; and I had rather my bearing in this or any other office should add worth to it, than the place give the least opinion to me.

TOUCHSTONE

Excellently spoken! This modest answer of thine blushes, as   65
if it said, I will wear scarlet shortly. Worshipful son! I cannot contain myself, I must tell thee: I hope to see thee one o' the monuments of our City, and reckoned among her worthies, to be remembered the same day with the Lady Ramsey and grave Gresham, when the famous fable of   70

---

46 *me* Q3 (we Q)
51-2 *commoner* member of the Common Council
56 *worship* repute, good name
58 *sufficient* capable
59 *expects* awaits
64 *opinion* good reputation
66 *wear scarlet* be an alderman and wear red velvet

---

50 *Ta'en . . . livery.* On the same day that Touchstone has declared his apprenticeship complete (making him a freeman able to set up his own business), the select 'livery men' of the Goldsmiths' company have remarkably elevated him to their rank.
69-70 *Lady Ramsey.* Widow of the Lord Mayor, who, in 1577, founded Christ's Hospital.
70 *Gresham.* Sir Thomas Gresham, founder of the Royal Exchange.

Whittington and his puss shall be forgotten, and thou and
thy acts become the posies for hospitals; when thy name
shall be written upon conduits, and thy deeds played i' thy
lifetime by the best companies of actors, and be called their
get-penny. This I divine; this I prophesy.   75

GOLDING

Sir, engage not your expectation farther than my abilities
will answer. I, that know mine own strengths, fear 'em; and
there is so seldom a loss in promising the least, that commonly it brings with it a welcome deceit. I have other news
for you, sir.   80

TOUCHSTONE

None more welcome, I am sure!

GOLDING

They have their degree of welcome, I dare affirm. The
colonel, and all his company, this morning putting forth
drunk from Billingsgate, had like to have been cast away o'
this side Greenwich; and (as I have intelligence, by a false   85
brother) are come dropping to town like so many masterless
men, i' their doublets and hose, without hat, or cloak, or any
other—

TOUCHSTONE

A miracle! The justice of heaven! Where are they? Let's go
presently and lay for 'em.   90

GOLDING

I have done that already, sir, both by constables, and other
officers, who shall take 'em at their old Anchor, and with less
tumult or suspicion than if yourself were seen in't, under

75 *get-penny* box-office success
85–6 *false brother* traitor, informer
90 *lay for 'em* set an ambush or trap

---

71 *Whittington and his puss.* Sir Richard Whittington was a mercer and
three times Lord Mayor of London, remembered for the endowments
he left behind after his death in 1423. The legend of the cat, which has
close similarities with German folk tales, first appeared in English in a
(lost) play performed by the Prince's Servants, 8 February 1605
(Stationers' Register).

72 *posies.* Motto inscribed to the wealthy citizens who donated funds to
build conduits and hospitals.

73–4 *deeds played i'thy lifetime.* This happened to Gresham in a Latin play
by I. Rickets, 1570. Citizen heroes were popular figures, e.g., Heywood's
If You Know Not Me, You Know Nobody, Part II (1605), in which
Whittington, Lady Ramsey, and Gresham are portrayed.

colour of a great press that is now abroad, and they shall
here be brought afore me.   95

TOUCHSTONE

Prudent and politic son! Disgrace 'em all that ever thou
canst; their ship I have already arrested. How to my wish
it falls out, that thou hast the place of a justicer upon 'em!
I am partly glad of the injury done to me, that thou may'st
punish it. Be severe i' thy place, like a new officer o' the first   100
quarter, unreflected. You hear how our lady is come back
with her train from the invisible castle?

GOLDING

No; where is she?

TOUCHSTONE

Within; but I ha' not seen her yet, nor her mother, who now
begins to wish her daughter undubbed, they say, and that   105
she had walked a foot-pace with her sister. Here they come;
stand back.

> [*Enter*] MISTRESS TOUCHSTONE, GERTRUDE, MILDRED,
>   SINDEFY

God save your Ladyship, 'save your good Ladyship! Your
Ladyship is welcome from your enchanted castle, so are
your beauteous retinue. I hear your knight-errant is travelled   110
on strange adventures. Surely, in my mind, your Ladyship
'hath fished fair and caught a frog', as the saying is.

MISTRESS TOUCHSTONE

Speak to your father, Madam, and kneel down.

GERTRUDE

Kneel? I hope I am not brought so low yet! Though my
knight be run away, and has sold my land, I am a lady still!   115

TOUCHSTONE

Your Ladyship says true, Madam; and it is fitter, and a
greater decorum, that I should curtsey to you that are a
knight's wife, and a lady, than you be brought o' your knees
to me, who am a poor cullion, and your father.

---

108 s.d. [*Enter*] MISTRESS TOUCHSTONE, etc. (*Touchstone* and *Goulding*
     included in Q)
112 *fished fair and caught a frog* proverbial. Tilley, F767
119 *cullion* base, despicable, vile fellow

93–4 *under colour . . . press.* Under the pretext of drafting troops or sailors.
101 *unreflected.* A pun: as an officer of the first term, not to be deflected
     from his duty; and as the crescent moon, not reflecting much light.
106 *a foot-pace.* To forego the 'court-amble' for a staid pace.

GERTRUDE

Law! My father knows his duty.   120

MISTRESS TOUCHSTONE

O child!

TOUCHSTONE

And therefore I do desire your Ladyship, my good Lady
Flash, in all humility, to depart my obscure cottage, and
return in quest of your bright and most transparent castle,
'however presently concealed to mortal eyes'. And as for one   125
poor woman of your train here, I will take that order, she
shall no longer be a charge unto you, nor help to spend your
Ladyship; she shall stay at home with me, and not go abroad;
not put you to the pawning of an odd coach-horse or three
wheels, but take part with the Touchstone. If we lack, we   130
will not complain to your Ladyship. And so, good Madam,
with your damsel here, please you to let us see your straight
backs, in equipage; for truly, here is no roost for such
chickens as you are, or birds o' your feather, if it like your
Ladyship.   135

GERTRUDE

Marry, fist o' your kindness! I thought as much. Come
away, Sin. We shall as soon get a fart from a dead man, as a
farthing of courtesy here.

MILDRED

O good sister!

GERTRUDE

Sister, sir-reverence? Come away, I say, hunger drops out   140
at his nose.

GOLDING

O Madam, 'fair words never hurt the tongue'.

GERTRUDE

How say you by that? You   out with your gold-ends
now!

MISTRESS TOUCHSTONE

Stay, Lady-daughter! Good husband!   145

133 *in equipage* at quick march
136 *fist* corruption of foist, i.e., fart
137-8 *get a fart . . . here* proverbial. Tilley, F63
140-1 *hunger . . . nose* proverbial. Tilley, H813
142 *fair words . . . tongue* proverbial. Tilley, W793
143 *gold-ends* moral tags

---

124 *transparent castle*. Easily seen through. cf. 'build castles in the air',
proverbial. Tilley, C126.

TOUCHSTONE

Wife, no man loves his fetters, be they made of gold. I list
not ha' my head fastened under my child's girdle; as she has
brewed, so let her drink, o' God's name! She went witless
to wedding, now she may go wisely a-begging. It's but
honeymoon yet with her ladyship; she has coach-horses,   150
apparel, jewels, yet left; she needs care for no friends, nor
take knowledge of father, mother, brother, sister, or anybody. When those are pawned or spent, perhaps we shall
return into the list of her acquaintance.

GERTRUDE

I scorn it, i'faith! Come, Sin!   155

MISTRESS TOUCHSTONE

O Madam, why do you provoke your father thus?

                           Exit GERTRUDE [*with* SINDEFY]

TOUCHSTONE

Nay, nay; e'en let pride go afore, shame will follow after,
I warrant you. Come, why dost thou weep now? Thou art
not the first good cow hast had an ill calf, I trust.

                    [*Exit* MISTRESS TOUCHSTONE *and*]

                    Enter CONSTABLE

What's the news with that fellow?   160

GOLDING

Sir, the knight and your man Quicksilver are without; will
you ha' 'em brought in?

TOUCHSTONE

O, by any means!

                           [*Exit* CONSTABLE]

And, son, here's a chair; appear terrible unto 'em on the
first interview. Let them behold the melancholy of a   165
magistrate, and taste the fury of a citizen in office.

---

146 *no man . . . gold* proverbial. Tilley, M338
147 *head fastened . . . girdle* proverbial. Tilley, H248
147–8 *as she has brewed,* etc. proverbial. Tilley, B654
157 s.d. ed. (156 s.d. Q)
157 *e'en let pride . . . after* proverbial. Tilley, P576
159 *good cow . . . calf* proverbial. Tilley, C761
160 s.d. *Enter* CONSTABLE ed. (159 s.d. *Enter Const.* Q)
165 *melancholy* (rare sense) irascibility

148–9 *She went . . . a-begging.* Heywood's *Proverbs*, I, chapter 11.

GOLDING

Why, sir, I can do nothing to 'em, except you charge 'em
with somewhat.

TOUCHSTONE

I will charge 'em and recharge 'em, rather than authority
should want foil to set it off.   170

[*Offers* GOLDING *a chair*]

GOLDING

No, good sir, I will not.

TOUCHSTONE

Son, it is your place, by any means!

GOLDING

Believe it, I will not, sir.

Enter KNIGHT PETRONEL, QUICKSILVER, CONSTABLE,
OFFICERS

PETRONEL

How misfortune pursues us still in our misery!

QUICKSILVER

Would it had been my fortune to have been trussed up at   175
Wapping, rather than ever ha' come here!

PETRONEL

Or mine to have famished in the island!

QUICKSILVER

Must Golding sit upon us?

CONSTABLE

You might carry an M. under your girdle to Master Deputy's
worship.   180

GOLDING

What are those, Master Constable?

CONSTABLE

An't please your worship, a couple of masterless men I
pressed for the Low Countries, sir.

170 *foil.* A piece of gold placed under a gem to enhance its lustre.
175 *trussed up.* Hanged on the gallows. See above, note IV, i, 106–7.
177 *in the island.* i.e., the Isle of Dogs. See above, note IV, i, 163.
179 *carry an M. under your girdle.* M. = abbrev. for master, i.e., to use
   respectful language when addressing one's superiors. Tilley, M1.

GOLDING
Why do you not carry 'em to Bridewell, according to your
order, they may be shipped away?   185

CONSTABLE
An't please your worship, one of 'em says he is a knight;
and we thought good to show him to your worship, for our
discharge.

GOLDING
Which is he?

CONSTABLE
This, sir!   190

GOLDING
And what's the other?

CONSTABLE
A knight's fellow, sir, an't please you.

GOLDING
What! A knight and his fellow thus accoutred? Where are
their hats and feathers, their rapiers and their cloaks?

QUICKSILVER
O, they mock us!   195

CONSTABLE
Nay, truly, sir, they had cast both their feathers and hats
too, before we see 'em. Here's all their furniture, an't please
you, that we found. They say knights are now to be known
without feathers, like cockerels by their spurs, sir.

GOLDING
What are their names, say they?   200

TOUCHSTONE
[Aside] Very well, this! He should not take knowledge of
'em in his place, indeed.

CONSTABLE
This is Sir Petronel Flash.

TOUCHSTONE
How!

187–8 *for our discharge* claiming a fee

---

184 *Bridewell.* House of correction since 1553. Originally founded as a
monastery, near St Bride's Church, Fleet Street. Petronel and Quicksilver were to be held there under the Statute against vagabonds and
masterless men (1597), until being conscripted into the army serving
in the Low Countries. (See Stow, *The Survey of London*, ed. Wheatley,
p. 440.)

194 *feathers.* The most conspicuous mark of foppery.

CONSTABLE

And this, Francis Quicksilver.   205

TOUCHSTONE

Is't possible? I thought your worship had been gone for
Virginia, sir. You are welcome home, sir. Your worship has
made a quick return, it seems, and no doubt a good voyage.
Nay, pray you be covered, sir. How did your biscuit hold
out, sir? Methought I had seen this gentleman afore. Good   210
Master Quicksilver, how a degree to the southward has
changed you!

GOLDING

Do you know 'em, father?—forbear your offers a little, you
shall be heard anon.

TOUCHSTONE

Yes, Master Deputy; I had a small venture with them in   215
the voyage—a thing called a son-in-law, or so. Officers, you
may let 'em stand alone, they will not run away; I'll give my
word for them. A couple of very honest gentlemen! One of
'em was my prentice, Master Quicksilver here; and when he
had two year to serve, kept his whore and his hunting nag,   220
would play his hundred pound at gresco, or primero, as
familiarly (and all o' my purse) as any bright piece of
crimson on 'em all; had his changeable trunks of apparel
standing at livery, with his mare, his chest of perfumed
linen, and his bathing-tubs: which when I told him of, why   225
he—he was a gentleman, and I a poor Cheapside groom!
The remedy was, we must part. Since when, he hath had
the gift of gathering up some small parcels of mine, to the
value of five hundred pound, dispersed among my customers,
to furnish this his Virginian venture; wherein this knight was   230
the chief, Sir Flash—one that married a daughter of mine,
ladyfied her, turned two thousand pounds' worth of good
land of hers into cash within the first week, bought her a
new gown and a coach, sent her to seek her fortune by land,

---

221 *gresco, or primero* card games

---

209 *be covered.* Put on your hat, a sarcastic hit at Petronel's having lost
his hat.

209 *biscuit.* Store of ship's biscuits, the staple ration of seamen.

211 *degree to the southward.* Probably mocking Quicksilver's frequenting of
the public theatres in Southwark.

213 *offers.* [*to* CONSTABLE] evidence, or [*to* PRISONERS] petitions.

222-3 *bright piece of crimson.* Scarlet was the colour worn by nobles and
court officials. It is also the colour of 'infected' mercury.

whilst himself prepared for his fortune by sea; took in fresh   235
flesh at Billingsgate, for his own diet, to serve him the whole
voyage—the wife of a certain usurer, called Security, who
hath been the broker for 'em in all this business. Please,
Master Deputy, 'work upon that now'!

GOLDING

If my worshipful father have ended.   240

TOUCHSTONE

I have, it shall please Master Deputy.

GOLDING

Well then, under correction—

TOUCHSTONE

Now, son, come over 'em with some fine gird, as, thus:
'Knight, you shall be encountered', that is, had to the
Counter, or, 'Quicksilver, I will put you in a crucible', or   245
so—

GOLDING

Sir Petronel Flash, I am sorry to see such flashes as these
proceed from a gentleman of your quality and rank; for mine
own part, I could wish I could say I could not see them;
but such is the misery of magistrates and men in place, that 250
they must not wink at offenders. Take him aside: I will hear
you anon, sir.

TOUCHSTONE

I like this well, yet; there's some grace i' the knight left—
he cries!

GOLDING

Francis Quicksilver, would God thou hadst turned quack-   255
salver, rather than run into these dissolute and lewd courses!
It is great pity; thou art a proper young man, of an honest
and clean face, somewhat near a good one (God hath done
his part in thee); but thou hast made too much and been
too proud of that face, with the rest of thy body; for main- 260
tenance of which in neat and garish attire (only to be looked

242 *under correction* confinement and corporal punishment
243 *gird* sharp stroke, blow
255–6 *quacksalver* charlatan, quack

244–5 *encountered . . . the Counter.* This pun is used in *Westward Ho!*, ed.
   Bowers, III, ii, 76. 'I will patiently incounter the Counter'.
245 *Quicksilver, I will put you in a crucible.* Touchstone believes that
   imprisonment and his own wrath will purge the tainted mercury.
250 *men in place.* Ministers of state in the service of the Crown.

upon by some light housewives) thou hast prodigally consumed much of thy master's estate; and being by him gently
admonished, at several times, hast returned thyself haughty
and rebellious in thine answers, thundering out uncivil   265
comparisons, requiting all his kindness with a coarse and
harsh behaviour, never returning thanks for any one benefit,
but receiving all, as if they had been debts to thee and no
courtesies. I must tell thee, Francis, these are manifest signs
of an ill nature; and God doth often punish such pride   270
and *outrecuidance* with scorn and infamy, which is the worst
of misfortune. My worshipful father, what do you please
to charge them withal? From the press I will free 'em,
Master Constable.

CONSTABLE
Then I'll leave your worship, sir.   275

GOLDING
No, you may stay; there will be other matters against 'em.

TOUCHSTONE
Sir, I do charge this gallant, Master Quicksilver, on suspicion of felony; and the knight as being accessory in the
receipt of my goods.

QUICKSILVER
O God, sir!   280

TOUCHSTONE
Hold thy peace, impudent varlet, hold thy peace! With
what forehead or face dost thou offer to chop logic with me,
having run such a race of riot as thou hast done? Does not
the sight of this worshipful man's fortune and temper confound thee, that was thy younger fellow in household, and   285
now come to have the place of a judge upon thee? Dost not
observe this? Which of all thy gallants and gamesters, thy
swearers and thy swaggerers, will come now to moan thy
misfortune, or pity thy penury? They'll look out at a window,
as thou rid'st in triumph to Tyburn, and cry, 'Yonder goes   290
honest Frank, mad Quicksilver'! 'He was a free boon companion, when he had money', says one; 'Hang him, fool'!
says another, 'he could not keep it when he had it'! 'A pox
o' the cullion, his master', says a third, 'he has brought him
to this'; when their pox of pleasure, and their piles of perdi-   295
tion, would have been better bestowed upon thee, that hast

271 *outrecuidance* arrogance, overbearing conceit
282 *chop logic* bicker, exchange disrespectful argument
295–6 *pox of pleasure . . . piles of perdition* infectious malice and
      pointed detraction

ventured for 'em with the best, and by the clew of thy
knavery, brought thyself weeping to the cart of calamity.

QUICKSILVER
Worshipful master!

TOUCHSTONE
Offer not to speak, crocodile; I will not hear a sound come   300
from thee. Thou hast learnt to whine at the play yonder.
Master Deputy, pray you commit 'em both to safe custody,
till I be able farther to charge 'em.

QUICKSILVER
O me, what an infortunate thing am I!

PETRONEL
Will you not take security, sir?   305

TOUCHSTONE
Yes, marry, will I, Sir Flash, if I can find him, and charge
him as deep as the best on you. He has been the plotter of
all this; he is your engineer, I hear. Master Deputy, you'll
dispose of these? In the meantime, I'll to my Lord Mayor,
and get his warrant to seize that serpent Security into my   310
hands, and seal up both house and goods to the King's use
or my satisfaction.

GOLDING
Officers, take 'em to the Counter.

QUICKSILVER⎱
PETRONEL ⎰
O God!

TOUCHSTONE
Nay, on, on! You see the issue of your sloth. Of sloth cometh   315
pleasure, of pleasure cometh riot, of riot comes whoring,
of whoring comes spending, of spending comes want, of
want comes theft, of theft comes hanging; and there is my
Quicksilver fixed.   *Exeunt*

305 *take security* accept bail
308 *engineer* schemer

297 *clew.* Ball of thread; fig. that which guides through intricate courses.
298 *cart of calamity.* The cart which bears criminals to Tyburn.
306 *if I can find him.* Picks up the pun in 305.
310 *serpent.* Security once more associated with the Morality Play Vice.
319 *fixed.* Another example of Touchstone's naïve belief in alchemical cure.

Act V, Scene i

[GERTRUDE's *Lodging*]

GERTRUDE, SINDEFY

GERTRUDE

Ah, Sin! hast thou ever read i'the chronicle of any lady and
her waiting-woman driven to that extremity that we are,
Sin?

SINDEFY

Not I, truly, Madam; and if I had, it were but cold comfort
should come out of books now.   5

GERTRUDE

Why, good faith, Sin, I could dine with a lamentable story
now. *O hone, hone, o no nera,* &c. Canst thou tell ne'er a
one, Sin?

SINDEFY

None but mine own, Madam, which is lamentable enough:
first to be stolen from my friends, which were worshipful   10
and of good accompt, by a prentice in the habit and disguise
of a gentleman, and here brought up to London and promised marriage, and now likely to be forsaken, for he is in
possibility to be hanged!

GERTRUDE

Nay, weep not, good Sin; my Petronel is in as good possi-   15
bility as he. Thy miseries are nothing to mine, Sin; I was
more than promised marriage, Sin; I had it, Sin, and was
made a lady; and by a knight, Sin; which is now as good as
no knight, Sin. And I was born in London, which is more
than brought up, Sin; and already forsaken, which is past   20
likelihood, Sin; and instead of land i' the country, all my
knight's living lies i' the Counter, Sin; there's his castle now!

SINDEFY

Which he cannot be forced out of, Madam.

GERTRUDE

Yes, if he would live hungry a week or two. 'Hunger', they
say, 'breaks stone walls'! But he is e'en well enough served,   25
Sin, that so soon as ever he had got my hand to the sale of
my inheritance, run away from me, and I had been his punk,

4 *cold comfort* proverbial. Tilley, C542
24–5 *Hunger . . . stone walls* proverbial. Tilley, H811

7 '*O hone, hone, o no nera*'. Refrain from an Irish lament.

God bless us! Would the Knight o' the Sun, or Palmerin of
England, have used their ladies so, Sin? or Sir Lancelot? or
Sir Tristram?   30

SINDEFY

I do not know, Madam.

GERTRUDE

Then thou know'st nothing, Sin. Thou art a fool, Sin. The
knighthood nowadays are nothing like the knighthood of old
time. They rid a-horseback; ours go a-foot. They were
attended by their squires; ours by their lackeys. They went   35
buckled in their armour; ours muffled in their cloaks. They
travelled wildernesses and deserts; ours dare scarce walk the
streets. They were still pressed to engage their honour; ours
still ready to pawn their clothes. They would gallop on at
sight of a monster; ours run away at sight of a sergeant.   40
They would help poor ladies; ours make poor ladies.

SINDEFY

Ay, Madam, they were Knights of the Round Table at
Winchester, that sought adventures; but these of the Square
Table at ordinaries, that sit at hazard—

GERTRUDE

True, Sin, let him vanish. And tell me, what shall we pawn   45
next?

SINDEFY

Ay, marry, Madam, a timely consideration; for our hostess
(profane woman!) has sworn by bread and salt, she will not
trust us another meal.

---

44 *hazard* a game of dice

---

28 *Knight o' [of] the Sun.* Hero of the first part of *The Mirror of Princely
Deeds and Knighthood* by Diego Ortuñez, first translated into English
by Margaret Tyler in 1578.

28–9 *Palmerin of England.* By Luis Hurtado, translated into English by
Anthony Munday in 1596. Such Spanish romances were extremely
popular with the London citizenry. cf. *The Knight of the Burning Pestle*,
I, iii, s.d.: '*Enter* RAFE *like a Grocer in's shop, with Two Prentices Reading
Palmerin of England*'.

33–41 *knighthood . . . ladies.* A popular complaint of the time. See
Appendix 1.

40 *sergeant.* Sheriff's officer whose duty it was to arrest debtors.

43 *Winchester.* Thought in the seventeenth century to be the seat of
King Arthur's Court, and where his supposed table, with the figure of
the king painted in the middle, still remains.

GERTRUDE

Let it stink in her hand then! I'll not be beholding to her.   50
Let me see: my jewels be gone, and my gowns, and my red
velvet petticoat that I was married in, and my wedding silk
stockings, and all thy best apparel, poor Sin! Good faith,
rather than thou shouldst pawn a rag more, I'd lay my Ladyship in lavender—if I knew where.   55

SINDEFY

Alas, Madam, your Ladyship?

GERTRUDE

Ay, why? You do not scorn my Ladyship, though it is in a
waistcoat? God's my life, you are a peat indeed! Do I offer to
mortgage my Ladyship, for you and for your avail, and do
you turn the lip and the alas to my Ladyship?   60

SINDEFY

No, Madam; but I make question who will lend anything
upon it?

GERTRUDE

Who? Marry, enow, I warrant you, if you'll seek 'em out.
I'm sure I remember the time when I would ha' given a
thousand pound (if I had had it) to have been a lady; and   65
I hope I was not bred and born with that appetite alone:
some other gentleborn o' the City have the same longing, I
trust. And for my part, I would afford 'em a penny'rth; my
Ladyship is little the worse for the wearing, and yet I would
bate a good deal of the sum. I would lend it (let me see) for   70
forty pound in hand, Sin—that would apparel us—and ten
pound a year. That would keep me and you, Sin (with our
needles)—and we should never need to be beholding to our
scurvy parents! Good Lord, that there are no fairies nowadays, Sin!   75

SINDEFY

Why, Madam?

50 *beholding* obliged
54–5 *lay . . . in lavender* pawn. Proverbial. Tilley, L96
57–8 *in a waistcoat* in shirt-sleeves
58 *peat* term of endearment for a girl or woman
60 *turn the lip* show contempt
63 *enow* enough
68 *penny'rth* pennyworth, i.e., money's worth
69 *worse for the wearing* proverbial. Tilley, W207
70 *bate* bring down the price
72–3 *with our needles* with what we can earn by needlework

GERTRUDE

To do miracles, and bring ladies money. Sure, if we lay in a
cleanly house, they would haunt it, Sin? I'll try. I'll sweep
the chamber soon at night, and set a dish of water o' the
hearth. A fairy may come, and bring a pearl or a diamond.   80
We do not know, Sin? Or, there may be a pot of gold hid o'
the backside, if we had tools to dig for't? Why may not we
two rise early i' the morning, Sin, afore anybody is up, and
find a jewel i' the streets worth a hundred pound? May not
some great court-lady, as she comes from revels at midnight,   85
look out of her coach as 'tis running, and lose such a jewel,
and we find it? Ha?

SINDEFY

They are pretty waking dreams, these.

GERTRUDE

Or may not some old usurer be drunk overnight, with a
bag of money, and leave it behind him on a stall? For God-   90
sake, Sin, let's rise tomorrow by break of day, and see! I
protest, law! if I had as much money as an alderman, I
would scatter some of it i' the streets for poor ladies to find,
when their knights were laid up. And now I remember my
song o' the Golden Shower, why may not I have such a   95
fortune? I'll sing it, and try what luck I shall have after it.
                                                        [Sings]

    Fond fables tell of old
    How Jove in Danaë's lap
    Fell in a shower of gold,
    By which she caught a clap;   100
    O had it been my hap

    (How e'er the blow doth threaten)
    So well I like the play,
    That I could wish all day
    And night to be so beaten.   105

Enter MISTRESS TOUCHSTONE

82 *backside* behind the house   93 *of it* ed. (on 't Q)

95–105 *song o' the Golden Shower*. From the Greek myth. Zeus appears in
    a shower of gold to seduce Danaë in the cell where her father imprisoned
    her. (cf. T. Bateson, Madrigal IX, *The English Madrigal School*, ed.
    Fellowes, XXI, p. xi.)

100 *caught a clap*. i.e., made pregnant. Gertrude wishes to become pregnant
    in this way so that she can have sexual intercourse with a god and also
    have the gold in which he manifests himself.

O here's my mother! Good luck, I hope. Ha' you brought
any money, mother? Pray you, mother, your blessing. Nay,
sweet mother, do not weep.

MISTRESS TOUCHSTONE

God bless you! I would I were in my grave!

GERTRUDE

Nay, dear mother, can you steal no more money from my   110
father? Dry your eyes, and comfort me. Alas, it is my knight's
fault, and not mine, that I am in a waistcoat, and attired thus
simply.

MISTRESS TOUCHSTONE

Simply? 'Tis better than thou deserv'st. Never whimper for
the matter. 'Thou shouldst have looked before thou hadst   115
leaped'. Thou wert afire to be lady, and now your Ladyship
and you may both blow at the coal, for aught I know. 'Self do,
self have'. 'The hasty person never wants woe', they say.

GERTRUDE

Nay, then, mother, you should ha' looked to it. A body
would think you were the older; I did but my kind, I. He   120
was a knight, and I was fit to be a lady. 'Tis not lack of liking,
but lack of living, that severs us. And you talk like yourself
and a cittiner in this, i' faith. You show what husband you
come on, I wis: you smell o'the Touchstone—he that will
do more for his daughter that he has married [to] a scurvy   125
gold-end man, and his prentice, than he will for his tother
daughter, that has wedded a knight, and his customer. By
this light, I think he is not my legitimate father.

SINDEFY

O good Madam, do not take up your mother so!

MISTRESS TOUCHSTONE

Nay, nay, let her e'en alone! Let her Ladyship grieve me   130
still, with her bitter taunts and terms. I have not dole enough
to see her in this miserable case, I, without her velvet gowns,

---

115–16 *shouldst have looked . . . leaped* proverbial. Tilley, L429
117 *blow at the coal* proverbial. Tilley, C460
117–18 *Self do, self have* proverbial. Tilley, S217
118 *hasty . . . woe* proverbial. Tilley, M159
120 *my kind* according to my nature and right of birth
123 *cittiner* colloquial for citizen
124 *I wis* forsooth
124 *o' the* Ed. (the Q)
125 *to* Ed. (omitted in Q)

---

124 *come on.* Pun: come from, and probable sexual connotation.

without ribands, without jewels, without French wires, or
cheat-bread, or quails, or a little dog, or a gentleman-usher,
or anything, indeed, that's fit for a lady—   135

SINDEFY
[*Aside*] Except her tongue.

MISTRESS TOUCHSTONE
And I not able to relieve her, neither, being kept so short
by my husband. Well, God knows my heart. I did little
think that ever she should have had need of her sister
Golding.   140

GERTRUDE
Why, mother, I ha' not yet. Alas, good mother, be not
intoxicate for me; I am well enough. I would not change
husbands with my sister, I. 'The leg of a lark is better than
the body of a kite'.

MISTRESS TOUCHSTONE
I know that, but—   145

GERTRUDE
What, sweet mother, what?

MISTRESS TOUCHSTONE
It's but ill food when nothing's left but the claw.

GERTRUDE
That's true, mother. Ay me!

MISTRESS TOUCHSTONE
Nay, sweet lady-bird, sigh not! Child, Madam, why do you
weep thus? Be of good cheer; I shall die, if you cry and mar   150
your complexion thus.

GERTRUDE
Alas, mother, what should I do?

MISTRESS TOUCHSTONE
Go to thy sister's, child; she'll be proud thy Ladyship will
come under her roof. She'll win thy father to release thy
knight, and redeem thy gowns and thy coach and thy horses,   155
and set thee up again.

GERTRUDE
But will she get him to set my knight up too?

MISTRESS TOUCHSTONE
That she will, or anything else thou'lt ask her.

133 *French wires* supports for the hair and ruff
134 *cheat-bread* inferior bread
142 *intoxicate* intemperate, exasperated
143-4 *leg of a lark . . . kite* proverbial. Tilley, L186

GERTRUDE
I will begin to love her, if I thought she would do this.

MISTRESS TOUCHSTONE
Try her, good chuck, I warrant thee.   160

GERTRUDE
Dost thou think she'll do't?

SINDEFY
Ay, Madam, and be glad you will receive it.

MISTRESS TOUCHSTONE
That's a good maiden; she tells you true. Come, I'll take
order for your debts i' the ale-house.

GERTRUDE
Go, Sin, and pray for thy Frank, as I will for my Pet.   165
                                              [*Exeunt*]

[Act V, Scene ii

Goldsmith's Row]

Enter TOUCHSTONE, GOLDING, WOLF

TOUCHSTONE
I will receive no letters, Master Wolf; you shall pardon me.

GOLDING
Good father, let me entreat you.

TOUCHSTONE
Son Golding, I will not be tempted; I find mine own easy
nature, and I know not what a well-penned subtle letter may
work upon it; there may be tricks, packing, do you see?   5
Return with your packet, sir.

WOLF
Believe it, sir, you need fear no packing here; these are but
letters of submission, all.

TOUCHSTONE
Sir, I do look for no submission. I will bear myself in this
like blind Justice. 'Work upon that now'! When the Sessions 10
come, they shall hear from me.

GOLDING
From whom come your letters, Master Wolf?

WOLF
An't please you, sir, one from Sir Petronel, another from

160 *chuck* term of endearment
  3 *find* perceive
  5 *packing* scheming

Francis Quicksilver, and a third from old Security, who is
almost mad in prison. There are two to your worship; one   15
from Master Francis, sir, another from the knight.

TOUCHSTONE

I do wonder, Master Wolf, why you should travail thus in a
business so contrary to kind or the nature o' your place!
That you, being the keeper of a prison, should labour the
release of your prisoners! Whereas, methinks, it were far   20
more natural and kindly in you to be ranging about for more,
and not let these 'scape you have already under the tooth.
But they say, you wolves, when you ha' sucked the blood
once, that they are dry, you ha' done.

WOLF

Sir, your worship may descant as you please o' my name;   25
but I protest I was never so mortified with any men's discourse or behaviour in prison; yet I have had of all sorts of
men i' the kingdom under my keys, and almost of all
religions i' the land, as: Papist, Protestant, Puritan, Brownist, Anabaptist, Millenary, Family-o'-Love, Jew, Turk,   30
Infidel, Atheist, Good Fellow, &c.

GOLDING

And which of all these, thinks Master Wolf, was the best
religion?

WOLF

Troth, Master Deputy, they that pay fees best: we never
examine their consciences farder.   35

25 *descant* comment, remark
26 *mortified* (rare sense) overcome, depressed
28 *under my keys* under lock and key
31 *Good Fellow* reveller

19–20 *That you ... prisoners.* The gaoler accepted fees from prisoners for
food, lodging, and other favours.
21 *kindly.* Pun: showing favour, and according to your profession.
22 *tooth.* Fig. gaol; play on name Wolf.
29–30 *Brownist.* i.e., follower of Robert Brown (1550–1633); one of the
strictest evangelical Protestant sects.
30 *Millenary.* Believing in the Second Coming of Christ, when He would
reign for a thousand years until the Day of Judgement.
30 *Family-o'-Love.* Dutch sixteenth-century sect whose English advocates
were prosecuted as heretical for practising free love and denying the
immortality of the soul. Mary Faugh and Mulligrub of *The Dutch
Courtesan* (Marston, 1605) belonged to this sect. cf. Middleton's
Family of Love (*c.* 1602–07), in Bullen (ed.), *The Works of Thomas
Middleton* (London, 1885–86), III, 3–5.

GOLDING

I believe you, Master Wolf. Good faith, sir, here's a great
deal of humility i' these letters.

WOLF

Humility, sir? Ay, were your worship an eye-witness of it,
you would say so. The knight will i' the Knight's Ward, do
what we can sir; and Master Quicksilver would be i' the   40
Hole if we would let him. I never knew or saw prisoners
more penitent, or more devout. They will sit you up all
night singing of psalms and edifying the whole prison. Only
Security sings a note too high sometimes, because he lies i'
the two-penny ward, far off, and cannot take his tune. The   45
neighbours cannot rest for him, but come every morning to
ask what godly prisoners we have.

TOUCHSTONE

Which on 'em is't is so devout—the knight, or the tother?

WOLF

Both, sir; but the young man especially! I never heard his
like! He has cut his hair too. He is so well given, and has   50
such good gifts. He can tell you almost all the stories of the
Book of Martyrs, and speak you all the Sick Man's Salve,
without book.

TOUCHSTONE

Ay, if he had had grace—he was brought up where it grew,
I wis. On, Master Wolf!   55

WOLF

And he has converted one Fangs, a sergeant, a fellow could
neither write nor read, he was called the Bandog o' the

---

53 *without book* by heart

39–45 *the Knight's Ward . . . the Hole . . . the two-penny ward.* The
Counter had four types of accommodation, ranging in price from the
Knight's Ward down to the Hole. See 'The Counter's Commonwealth'
in Judges, op. cit., pp. 423–87, and *Westward Ho!* (ed. Bowers), III, ii,
77–9. See above, note II, iii, 44.

50 *cut his hair.* i.e., from the courtier's length.

52 *Book of Martyrs.* John Foxe's famous classic, first published by John
Day in 1561.

52 *Sick Man's Salve.* Thomas Becon's popular devotional prayers, sub-
titled 'wherein all faithful Christians may learn both how to behave
themselves patiently and thankfully in the time of sickness, and also
vertuously to dispose their temporal goods, and finally prepare themselves gladly and godly to die' (1561).

57 *Bandog.* Guard dog which had to be tied up because of its ferocity.

Counter; and he has brought him already to pare his nails,
and say his prayers; and 'tis hoped he will sell his place
shortly, and become an intelligencer.   60

TOUCHSTONE

No more; I am coming already. If I should give any farther
ear, I were taken. Adieu, good Master Wolf! Son, I do feel
mine own weaknesses; do not importune me. Pity is a rheum
that I am subject to; but I will resist it. Master Wolf, 'fish is
cast away that is cast in dry pools'. Tell Hypocrisy it will not   65
do; I have touched and tried too often; I am yet proof, and
I will remain so; when the Sessions come, they shall hear
from me. In the meantime, to all suits, to all entreaties, to
all letters, to all tricks, I will be deaf as an adder, and blind
as a beetle, lay mine ear to the ground, and lock mine eyes   70
i' my hand against all temptations.   *Exit*

GOLDING

You see, Master Wolf, how inexorable he is. There is no
hope to recover him. Pray you commend me to my brother
knight, and to my fellow Francis; present 'em with this small
token of my love [*Giving money*]. Tell 'em, I wish I could   75
do 'em any worthier office; but in this, 'tis desperate; yet
I will not fail to try the uttermost of my power for 'em. And,
sir, as far as I have any credit with you, pray you let 'em want
nothing; though I am not ambitious, they should know so
much.   80

WOLF

Sir, both your actions and words speak you to be a true
gentleman. They shall know only what is fit, and no more.
                                                    Exeunt

60 *intelligencer* informer
61 *coming* yielding
64–5 *fish is cast away*, etc. proverbial. Tilley, F307
66 *proof* impervious, invulnerable
79 *ambitious* eager, keen

66 *I have touched . . . too often.* Alchemical; mercury 'worked upon' the
   touchstone has been found wanting, and Touchstone, as a goldsmith,
   has 'tried' to change Quicksilver's nature.
69 *deaf as an adder*, etc. Refers to a belief that the adder stopped one ear
   with his tail and put the other to the ground, to deafen himself to the
   snakecharmer's music. cf. Psalm 58, 4. Proverbial. Tilley, A32.

[Act V, Scene iii
The Counter]

HOLDFAST, BRAMBLE

HOLDFAST
Who would you speak with, sir?

BRAMBLE
I would speak with one Security, that is prisoner here.

HOLDFAST
You are welcome, sir! Stay there, I'll call him to you. Master
Security!

SECURITY
[*At the grate*] Who calls?   5

HOLDFAST
Here's a gentleman would speak with you.

SECURITY
What is he? Is't one that grafts my forehead now I am in
prison, and comes to see how the horns shoot up and
prosper?

HOLDFAST
You must pardon him, sir; the old man is a little crazed with   10
his imprisonment.

SECURITY
What say you to me, sir? Look you here. My learned counsel,
Master Bramble! Cry you mercy, sir! When saw you my
wife?

BRAMBLE
She is now at my house, sir; and desired me that I would   15
come to visit you, and inquire of you your case, that we might
work some means to get you forth.

SECURITY
My case, Master Bramble, is stone walls and iron grates;
you see it, this is the weakest part on't. And, for getting me
forth, no means but hang myself, and so to be carried forth,   20
from which they have here bound me in intolerable bands.

1 s.d. HOLDFAST, BRAMBLE ed. (*Holdfast, Bramble; Security* Q)
16 *case* both encasement (i.e., prison) and a legal case

---

5 s.d. *At the grate.* Probably a lattice in one of the stage-doors as in
Marston's *Antonio's Revenge*, ed. G. K. Hunter (London, 1966), II, ii,
123. At V, iii, 18 Security complains of the 'iron grates' and at line 29
Quicksilver says 'the light does him harm', implying that the door or
trap could be closed to obscure him from vision. I am not altogether convinced by Irwin Smith's theory that Security appears at a 'window stage'
(*Shakespeare's Blackfriars Playhouse Its History and Its Design*, N.Y.,
1964, pp. 379–80).

BRAMBLE
Why, but what is't you are in for, sir?

SECURITY
For my sins, for my sins, sir, whereof marriage is the
greatest! O, had I never married, I had never known this
purgatory, to which hell is a kind of cool bath in respect.   25
My wife's confederacy, sir, with old Touchstone, that she
might keep her jubilee and the feast of her new moon. Do
you understand me, sir?

Enter QUICKSILVER

QUICKSILVER
Good sir, go in and talk with him. The light does him harm,
and his example will be hurtful to the weak prisoners. Fie,   30
Father Security, that you'll be still so profane! Will nothing
humble you?   [*Exeunt*]

Enter TWO PRISONERS *with a* FRIEND

FRIEND
What's he?

1 PRISONER
O, he is a rare young man! Do you not know him?

FRIEND
Not I! I never saw him, I can remember.   35

2 PRISONER
Why, it is he that was the gallant prentice of London—
Master Touchstone's man.

FRIEND
Who, Quicksilver?

1 PRISONER
Ay, this is he.

FRIEND
Is this he? They say he has been a gallant indeed.   40

1 PRISONER
O' the royalest fellow that ever was bred up i' the city! He
would play you his thousand pound a night at dice; keep
knights and lords company; go with them to bawdy-houses;
and his six men in a livery; kept a stable of hunting-horses,
and his wench in her velvet gown and her cloth of silver.   45
Here's one knight with him here in prison.

25 *in respect* by comparison

---

27 *her jubilee . . . new moon.* Celebration of cuckoldry, the crescent moon
being the symbol of the cuckold's horns.

FRIEND

And how miserably he is changed!

1 PRISONER

O, that's voluntary in him: he gave away all his rich clothes
as soon as ever he came in here among the prisoners; and
will eat o' the basket, for humility. 50

FRIEND

Why will he do so?

1 PRISONER

Alas, he has no hope of life! He mortifies himself. He does
but linger on till the Sessions.

2 PRISONER

O, he has penned the best thing, that he calls his 'Repentance'
or his 'Last Farewell', that ever you heard. He is a pretty 55
poet, and for prose—you would wonder how many prisoners
he has helped out, with penning petitions for 'em, and not
take a penny. Look! This is the knight, in the rug gown.
Stand by!

Enter PETRONEL, BRAMBLE, QUICKSILVER

BRAMBLE

Sir, for Security's case, I have told him. Say he should be 60
condemned to be carted or whipped for a bawd, or so; why,
I'll lay an execution on him o' two hundred pound; let him
acknowledge a judgement, he shall do it in half an hour; they
shall not all fetch him out without paying the execution, o'
my word. 65

PETRONEL

But can we not be bailed, Master Bramble?

BRAMBLE

Hardly; there are none of the judges in town, else you should
remove yourself (in spite of him) with a *habeas corpus*. But
if you have a friend to deliver your tale sensibly to some

---

56 *wonder* be surprised   60 s.d. (*Wolf* omit ed.)

---

50 *the basket.* The alms basket on which poor prisoners depended for their
food, when staying in the Hole.

58 *rug gown.* The equivalent of sackcloth; worn by the penitent (H. & S.,
IX, 676).

62 *lay an execution.* To allay or prevent the execution of sentence by
putting down a bond: i.e., on a bond of £200 made out to Touchstone,
if he agreed to drop the charge.

68 *habeas corpus.* i.e., by invoking this statute they would be moved to a
different court and in the process might escape.

justice o' the town, that he may have feeling of it (do you   70
see) you may be bailed; for as I understand the case, 'tis
only done *in terrorem*; and you shall have an action of false
imprisonment against him when you come out, and perhaps
a thousand pound costs.

Enter MASTER WOLF

QUICKSILVER
How now, Master Wolf? What news? What return?   75
WOLF
Faith, bad all! Yonder will be no letters received. He says
the Sessions shall determine it. Only Master Deputy
Golding commends him to you, and with this token wishes
he could do you other good.

[*Gives money*]

QUICKSILVER
I thank him. Good Master Bramble, trouble our quiet no   80
more; do not molest us in prison thus with your winding
devices. Pray you, depart. For my part, I commit my cause
to him that can succour me; let God work his will. Master
Wolf, I pray you let this be distributed among the prisoners,
and desire 'em to pray for us.   85
WOLF
It shall be done, Master Francis.

[*Exit* QUICKSILVER]

1 PRISONER
An excellent temper!
2 PRISONER
Now God send him good luck!
Exeunt [BRAMBLE, TWO PRISONERS, *and* FRIEND]
PETRONEL
But what said my father-in-law, Master Wolf?

Enter HOLDFAST

HOLDFAST
Here's one would speak with you, sir.   90
WOLF
I'll tell you anon, Sir Petronel. Who is't?
HOLDFAST
A gentleman, sir, that will not be seen.

Enter GOLDING

82 *part* Q2 (pat Q1)

---

72 *in terrorem*. In fear, i.e., that he was blackmailed.

WOLF
  Where is he? Master Deputy! Your worship is welcome—
GOLDING
  Peace!
WOLF
  Away, sirrah!   95

                    [*Exit* HOLDFAST *with* SIR PETRONEL]

GOLDING
  Good faith, Master Wolf, the estate of these gentlemen, for
  whom you were so late and willing a suitor, doth much
  affect me; and because I am desirous to do them some fair
  office, and find there is no means to make my father relent
  so likely as to bring him to be a spectator of their miseries,   100
  I have ventured on a device, which is, to make myself your
  prisoner, entreating you will presently go report it to my
  father, and (feigning an action, at suit of some third person)
  pray him by this token [*Giving a ring*], that he will presently,
  and with all secrecy, come hither for my bail; which train,   105
  if any, I know will bring him abroad; and then, having him
  here, I doubt not but we shall be all fortunate in the event.
WOLF
  Sir, I will put on my best speed to effect it. Please you, come
  in.
GOLDING
  Yes; and let me rest concealed, I pray you.   110
WOLF
  See here a benefit truly done, when it is done timely, freely,
  and to no ambition.   *Exit* [*with* GOLDING]

                    [Act V, Scene iv

               A Room in TOUCHSTONE's *House*]

     Enter TOUCHSTONE, WIFE, DAUGHTERS, SINDEFY, WINIFRED

TOUCHSTONE
  I will sail by you and not hear you, like the wise Ulysses.
MILDRED
  Dear father!
MISTRESS TOUCHSTONE
  Husband!

  ---

  1 *Ulysses.* Ulysses sailed past the islands on which the sirens were singing
    and stuffed his ears with wax until he was out of hearing.

GERTRUDE
Father!

WINIFRED ⎫
SINDEFY ⎬
        Master Touchstone!   5

TOUCHSTONE
Away, sirens, I will immure myself against your cries, and
lock myself up to your lamentations.

MISTRESS TOUCHSTONE
Gentle husband, hear me!

GERTRUDE
Father, it is I, father, my Lady Flash. My sister and I am
friends.   10

MILDRED
Good father!

WINIFRED
Be not hardened, good Master Touchstone!

SINDEFY
I pray you, sir, be merciful!

TOUCHSTONE
I am deaf, I do not hear you. I have stopped mine ears with
shoemakers' wax, and drunk Lethe and mandragora to   15
forget you. All you speak to me I commit to the air.

Enter WOLF

MILDRED
How now, Master Wolf?

WOLF
Where's Master Touchstone? I must speak with him presently—I have lost my breath for haste.

MILDRED
What's the matter, sir? Pray all be well!   20

WOLF
Master Deputy Golding is arrested upon an execution, and
desires him presently to come to him, forthwith.

MILDRED
Ay me! Do you hear, father?

---

15 *shoemakers' wax*. An apt updating of the myth, and perhaps a sly dig at
   Dekker's *The Shoemakers' Holiday* in the pun on air (Ayre Q) in the
   next line, i.e., Simon Eyre.
15 *Lethe*. River of oblivion.
15 *mandragora*. Mandrake, a narcotic used to induce deep sleep.

TOUCHSTONE
Tricks, tricks, confederacy, tricks! I have 'em in my nose—
I scent 'em!   25
WOLF
Who's that? Master Touchstone?
MISTRESS TOUCHSTONE
Why, it is Master Wolf himself, husband.
MILDRED
Father!
TOUCHSTONE
I am deaf still, I say. I will neither yield to the song of the
siren, nor the voice of the hyena, the tears of the crocodile,   30
nor the howling o' the wolf. Avoid my habitation, monsters!
WOLF
Why, you are not mad, sir? I pray you, look forth, and see the
token I have brought you, sir.
TOUCHSTONE
Ha! What token is it?
WOLF
Do you know it, sir?   35
TOUCHSTONE
My son Golding's ring! Are you in earnest, Master Wolf?
WOLF
Ay, by my faith, sir! He is in prison, and required me to use
all speed and secrecy to you.
TOUCHSTONE
My cloak, there! Pray you be patient. I am plagued for my
austerity. My cloak! At whose suit, Master Wolf?   40
WOLF
I'll tell you as we go, sir.   *Exeunt*

[Act V, Scene v

The Counter]

Enter FRIEND, PRISONERS

FRIEND
Why, but is his offence such as he cannot hope of life?
1 PRISONER
Troth, it should seem so; and 'tis great pity, for he is exceeding penitent.

30 *hyena.* Topsell, *The History of the Four Footed Beasts* (1607), p. 437,
describes how the hyena earned his name as a counterfeiter. He could
supposedly mimic a man's cry, and thus lure searchers to their deaths.

FRIEND

They say he is charged but on suspicion of felony, yet.

2 PRISONER

Ay, but his master is a shrewd fellow; he'll prove great   5
matter against him.

FRIEND

I'd as lief as anything I could see his 'Farewell'.

1 PRISONER

O, 'tis rarely written; why, Toby may get him to sing it to
you; he's not curious to anybody.

2 PRISONER

O no! He would that all the world should take knowledge of   10
his 'Repentance', and thinks he merits in't, the more shame
he suffers.

1 PRISONER

Pray thee, try what thou canst do.

2 PRISONER

I warrant you, he will not deny it, if he be not hoarse with
the often repeating of it.   *Exit*   15

1 PRISONER

You never saw a more courteous creature than he is, and the
knight too: the poorest prisoner of the house may command
'em. You shall hear a thing admirably penned.

FRIEND

Is the knight any scholar too?

1 PRISONER

No, but he will speak very well, and discourse admirably of   20
running horses, and Whitefriars, and against bawds, and of
cocks; and talk as loud as a hunter, but is none.

Enter WOLF *and* TOUCHSTONE

WOLF

Please you, stay here, sir: I'll call his worship down to you.
                                                  [*Exit*]

Enter [2ND PRISONER *with*] QUICKSILVER, PETRONEL
[*and* SECURITY; GOLDING *with* WOLF, *who stands aside*]

9 *curious* particular, choosy
10 s.p. 2 PRISONER ed. (1 *Pris.* Q)
24 s.d. moved from line 26, ed. (*Enter Quick. Pet. &c.* Q)

---

21 *Whitefriars.* Sanctuary for debtors, later called Alsatia.

1 PRISONER
See, he has brought him, and the knight too. Salute him, I
pray. Sir, this gentleman, upon our report, is very desirous   25
to hear some piece of your 'Repentance'.

QUICKSILVER
Sir, with all my heart; and, as I told Master Toby, I shall be
glad to have any man a witness of it. And the more openly I
profess it, I hope it will appear the heartier and the more
unfeigned.   30

TOUCHSTONE
[Aside] Who is this? My man Francis, and my son-in-law?

QUICKSILVER
Sir, it is all the testimony I shall leave behind me to the
world, and my master, that I have so offended.

FRIEND
Good sir!

QUICKSILVER
I writ it when my spirits were oppressed.   35

PETRONEL
Ay, I'll be sworn for you, Francis!

QUICKSILVER
It is in imitation of Mannington's: he that was hanged at
Cambridge, that cut off the horse's head at a blow.

FRIEND
So, sir!

QUICKSILVER
To the tune of, 'I wail in woe, I plunge in pain'.   40

---

37 *Mannington's. Mannington's Repentance* is entered in the Stationers'
Register, 7 November 1576, and described as 'a woeful ballad made by
Mr. George Mannington an hour before he suffered [death] at
Cambridge Castle' (for armed robbery). It is included in Clement
Robinson's *A Handful of Pleasant Delights* (1584; ed. Arber, 1880,
pp. 57–9). A different version appears in J. Ritson's *Ancient Songs and
Ballads*, ed. W. C. Hazlitt (London, 1877), pp. 188–91. Hence, there is
no reason to accept Charles Edmonds's suggestion, *Athenaeum*, 13
October 1883, pp. 463–4, that Quicksilver's 'Repentance' is sketched
from Luke Hutton's *The Black Dog of Newgate* (1596), or that Quicksilver is modelled on that figure. Doggerel repentances were, after all,
extremely popular in Jacobean times.
40 *I wail in woe . . . pain*. The first lines of Mannington's *Repentance*.
Quicksilver's song is a parody of the 'neck verses' sung by criminals on
their way to the gallows at Tyburn.

PETRONEL
   An excellent ditty it is, and worthy of a new tune.

QUICKSILVER
In Cheapside, famous for gold and plate,
Quicksilver, I did dwell of late.
I had a master good and kind,
That would have wrought me to his mind.   45
He bade me still, 'Work upon that',
But, alas, I wrought I knew not what!
He was a Touchstone black, but true,
And told me still what would ensue;
Yet, woe is me! I would not learn;   50
I saw, alas, but could not discern!

FRIEND
   Excellent, excellent well!

GOLDING
   [*Aside to* WOLF] O, let him alone; he is taken already.

QUICKSILVER
I cast my coat and cap away,
I went in silks and satins gay;   55
False metal of good manners, I
Did daily coin unlawfully.
I scorned my master, being drunk;
I kept my gelding and my punk;
And with a knight, Sir Flash by name,   60
(Who now is sorry for the same)—

PETRONEL
   I thank you, Francis!

QUICKSILVER
I thought by sea to run away,
But Thames and tempest did me stay.

TOUCHSTONE
   [*Aside*] This cannot be feigned, sure. Heaven pardon my   65
severity! The ragged colt may prove a good horse.

GOLDING
   [*Aside*] How he listens, and is transported! He has forgot me.

53 *is taken* either understood or, more probably, has begun
56 *False metal* i.e., counterfeit
66 *The ragged colt . . . horse* proverbial. Tilley, C522

48 *Touchstone black, but true.* Refers to the property of dark quartz (touch-stone) to reveal the true nature of the metals 'worked' against it.

QUICKSILVER

Still Eastward Ho was all my word;
But westward I had no regard,
Nor never thought what would come after,   70
As did, alas, his youngest daughter!
At last the black ox trod o' my foot,
And I saw then what 'longed unto't.
Now cry I, 'Touchstone, touch me still,
And make me current by thy skill'.   75

TOUCHSTONE

[*Aside*] And I will do it, Francis.

WOLF

[*Aside to* GOLDING] Stay him, Master Deputy; now is [not]
the time; we shall lose the song else.

FRIEND

I protest, it is the best that ever I heard.

QUICKSILVER

How like you it, gentlemen?   80

ALL

O, admirable, sir!

QUICKSILVER

This stanze now following alludes to the story of Mannington, from whence I took my project for my invention.

FRIEND

Pray you, go on, sir.

QUICKSILVER

O Mannington, thy stories show,   85
Thou cut'st a horse-head off at a blow!
But I confess, I have not the force
For to cut off the head of a horse;
Yet I desire this grace to win,

77–8 *now is not the time* ed. (now is the time Q)
83 *project* model

---

71 *his youngest daughter* i.e., Mildred (I, i, 74–81). Not strictly true since
Touchstone (I, i, 95–6) and Golding (I, i, 132–6) predict his downfall.
Probably used because the form 'dafter' rhymes with 'after'.

72 *black ox.* Symbol of adversity. Proverbial. Tilley, O 103.

74 *touch me still.* i.e., continue to test me and reveal my true value.

75 *make me current.* Quicksilver (who has become false metal) wishes
Touchstone to convert him back to current (true) metal; i.e., silver or
gold that is genuine.

That I may cut off the horse-head of Sin,   90
And leave his body in the dust
Of Sin's highway and bogs of Lust,
Whereby I may take Virtue's purse,
And live with her for better, for worse.

FRIEND
Admirable, sir, and excellently conceited!   95

QUICKSILVER
Alas, sir!

TOUCHSTONE
[*Coming to* GOLDING *and* WOLF] Son Golding and Master
Wolf, I thank you: the deceit is welcome, especially from
thee, whose charitable soul in this hath shown a high point
of wisdom and honesty. Listen! I am ravished with his   100
'Repentance', and could stand here a whole prenticeship to
hear him.

FRIEND
Forth, good sir!

QUICKSILVER
This is the last, and the 'Farewell'.

Farewell, Cheapside, farewell, sweet trade   105
Of goldsmiths all, that never shall fade!
Farewell, dear fellow prentices all,
And be you warned by my fall:
Shun usurers, bawds, and dice, and drabs;
Avoid them as you would French scabs.   110
Seek not to go beyond your tether,
But cut your thongs unto your leather;
So shall you thrive by little and little,
'Scape Tyburn, Counters, and the Spital!

103 *Forth* go on
110 *French scabs* syphilis

90–4 *That I may cut off the horse-head of Sin . . . purse.* i.e., like the high-
    wayman he wishes to seize Virtue's purse by slaying the horse on which
    she rides.
101 *whole prenticeship.* i.e., usually seven years.
112 *cut . . . leather.* Proverbial. Tilley, T229. The proverb is: 'It is not
    honest to make large thongs of other men's leather'—i.e., to be lavish
    with that which is another's. Hence Quicksilver is saying: 'live according
    to your means', or, 'cut your coat according to your cloth'.
114 *Spital.* The general term for a charitable institution for the poor,
    specializing in the treatment of venereal diseases.

TOUCHSTONE

And scape them shalt thou, my penitent and dear Francis!   115

QUICKSILVER

Master!

PETRONEL

Father!

TOUCHSTONE

I can no longer forbear to do your humility right. Arise, and
let me honour your 'Repentance' with the hearty and joyful
embraces of a father and friend's love. Quicksilver, thou hast   120
eat into my breast, Quicksilver, with the drops of thy sorrow,
and killed the desperate opinion I had of thy reclaim.

QUICKSILVER

O, sir, I am not worthy to see your worshipful face!

PETRONEL

Forgive me, father!

TOUCHSTONE

Speak no more! All former passages are forgotten, and here   125
my word shall release you. Thank this worthy brother and
kind friend, Francis.—Master Wolf, I am their bail.

A shout in the prison

[SECURITY *appears at the grate*]

SECURITY

Master Touchstone! Master Touchstone!

TOUCHSTONE

Who's that?

WOLF

Security, sir.   130

SECURITY

Pray you, sir, if you'll be won with a song, hear my lamentable tune, too!

SONG

O Master Touchstone,
My heart is full of woe!
Alas, I am a cuckold;   135
And why should it be so?

---

122 *reclaim* i.e., reclamation, conversion
125 *passages* events, happenings

120–1 *Quicksilver, thou hast eat into my breast.* Refers to mercury's characteristic property of dissolving gold; Touchstone's heart of gold is
easily overcome.

Because I was a usurer,
And bawd, as all you know,
For which, again I tell you,
My heart is full of woe.   140

TOUCHSTONE
Bring him forth, Master Wolf, and release his bands. This
day shall be sacred to Mercy and the mirth of this encounter
in the Counter—see, we are encountered with more suitors!

Enter MISTRESS TOUCHSTONE, GERTRUDE, MILDRED,
SINDEFY, WINIFRED, &c.

Save your breath, save your breath! All things have suc-
ceeded to your wishes, and we are heartily satisfied in their   145
events.

GERTRUDE
Ah, runaway, runaway! Have I caught you? And how has
my poor Knight done all this while?

PETRONEL
Dear Lady-wife, forgive me.

GERTRUDE
As heartily as I would be forgiven, Knight. Dear father, give   150
me your blessing, and forgive me too. I ha' been proud and
lascivious, father, and a fool, father; and being raised to the
state of a wanton coy thing, called a lady, father, have
scorned you, father, and my sister, and my sister's velvet
cap, too; and would make a mouth at the City as I rid   155
through it; and stop mine ears at Bow-bell. I have said your
beard was a base one, father; and that you looked like
Twierpipe the taborer; and that my mother was but my
midwife.

MISTRESS TOUCHSTONE
Now God forgi' you, Child Madam!   160

TOUCHSTONE
No more repetitions! What is else wanting to make our
harmony full?

GOLDING
Only this, sir: that my fellow Francis make amends to
Mistress Sindefy with marriage.

158 *Twierpipe the taborer.* Tabor = a small drum, usually played in con-
junction with a pipe and singing. H. & S., IX, 677, note: 'Tweire-pipe
that famous Southern Taberer with the Cowleyan windpipe, who for
whuling hath beene famous through the Globe of the world'. From the
anonymous tract *Old Meg of Herefordshire* (1609), Dedication.

QUICKSILVER
With all my heart!   165

GOLDING
And Security give her a dower, which shall be all the restitu-
tion he shall make of that huge mass he hath so unlawfully
gotten.

TOUCHSTONE
Excellently devised! A good motion! What says Master
Security?   170

SECURITY
I say anything, sir, what you'll ha' me say. Would I were no
cuckold!

WINIFRED
Cuckold, husband? Why, I think this wearing of yellow has
infected you.

TOUCHSTONE
Why, Master Security, that should rather be a comfort to   175
you than a corrosive. If you be a cuckold, it's an argument
you have a beautiful woman to your wife; then, you shall be
much made of; you shall have store of friends; never want
money; you shall be eased of much o' your wedlock pain:
others will take it for you. Besides, you being a usurer, and   180
likely to go to hell, the devils will never torment you; they'll
take you for one o' their own race. Again, if you be a cuckold,
and know it not, you are an innocent; if you know it and
endure it, a true martyr.

SECURITY
I am resolved, sir. Come hither, Winny!   185

TOUCHSTONE
Well, then, all are pleased; or shall be anon. Master Wolf,
you look hungry, methinks; have you no apparel to lend
Francis to shift him?

QUICKSILVER
No, sir, nor I desire none; but here make it my suit, that I

188 *shift him* enable him to change his clothes

173-4 *wearing of yellow*, etc. i.e., the colour of jealousy (cf. Malvolio in
    Twelfth Night).
176-80 *If you . . . for you.* Closely parallels Rabelais, *Gargantua and Panta-
    gruel*, III, chapter xxvii—see trans. T. Urquhart and P. Le Motteux,
    3 vols. (London, 1934), II, 135-6.
176 *corrosive.* Indicates the properties of sulphur, which is precipitated from
    the alchemical solution, just as Security is here cast out of society.
183 *innocent.* With a probable play on the meaning 'idiot' or 'cretin'.

may go home through the streets in these, as a spectacle, or   190
rather an example, to the children of Cheapside.

TOUCHSTONE
Thou hast thy wish. Now, London, look about,
And in this moral see thy glass run out:
Behold the careful father, thrifty son,
The solemn deeds which each of us have done;   195
The usurer punished, and from fall so steep
The prodigal child reclaimed, and the lost sheep.

EPILOGUE

[QUICKSILVER]
Stay, sir, I perceive the multitude are gathered together to
view our coming out at the Counter. See, if the streets and
the fronts of the houses be not stuck with people, and the
windows filled with ladies, as on the solemn day of the
Pageant!   5
O may you find in this our pageant, here,
The same contentment which you came to seek,
And as that show but draws you once a year,
May this attract you hither once a week.   [Exeunt]

FINIS

193 *glass* i.e., hourglass; fig. time

3 *stuck* i.e., stuck full, jammed
9 s.d. moved from line 197, ed.

192–7 *Thou hast . . . sheep.* Reminiscent of the thumping moral verse of
such earlier prodigal son dramas as *Liberality and Prodigality*, presented
at Blackfriars in 1601.
1 s.p. Like Dodsley and other eds., I assign this speech to Quicksilver.
2 *the streets and the fronts of the houses.* Probably referring to the audience:
the streets, i.e., those seated on benches in the pit; *the fronts of the houses*,
i.e., the galleries and boxes. See Gurr, op. cit., p. 105.
9 *once a week.* Plays were usually performed weekly (on Saturday), in the
private theatres.

County of London.

London

Suburbs

County of Westminster

Moor Fields

Temple Bar

Bank Side

Lambeth Marsh

Southwark

St. Georges fields

Lambeth

Part of the County of Su

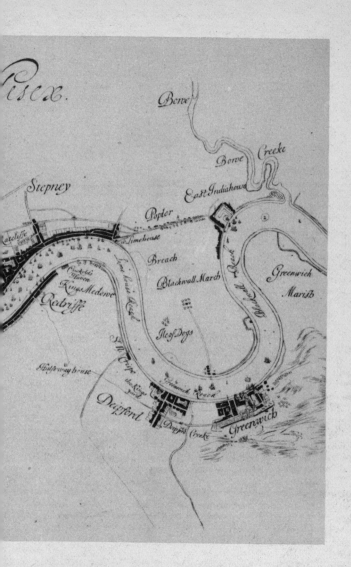

Piscx.

Bowe

Bowe Creeke

East Indiahouse

Stepney

Popler

Ratcliffe

Limehouse

Breach

Blackfold Haven

Kings Medewe

Blackwall Marsh

Greenwich Marish

Ratcliffe

Lime house Reach

Ifeof Dogs

Blackwall Reach

Hatchway house

St. O Crÿse

the Kings yard

Greenwich Reach

Deptford

Deptfort Creeke

Greenwich

APPENDIX B

IMPRISONMENT

One of the most memorable episodes in Jonson's *Conversations with Drummond* is the story surrounding the *Eastward Ho!* imprisonment. He told Drummond:

> He was delated by Sir James Murray to the King for writing something against the Scots in a play Eastward Ho and voluntarily imprisoned himself with Chapman and Marston, who had written it amongst them. The report was that they should then [have] had their ears cut and noses. After their delivery he banqueted all his friends, there was Camden, Selden and others. At the midst of the feast his old mother drank to him and show[ed] him a paper which she had (if the sentence had taken execution) to have mixed in the prison among his drink, which was full of lusty strong poison and that she was no churl she told she minded first to have drunk of it herself.[2]

Besides this account, ten letters, three by Chapman and seven by Jonson, were discovered in a collection of seventeenth-century manuscripts owned by Mr T. A. White of New York. Bertram Dobell published them in the *Athenaeum*, 23, 30 March; 6, 13 April 1901 under the title 'Newly Discovered Elizabethan Documents'. On the basis of their content Dobell conjectured that the letters refer to *Eastward Ho!* and his conclusion is substantiated by Herford and Simpson (*Ben Jonson*, I, 191–3). Dobell thought that Chapman was the probable collector if not the actual scribe. One of the letters (*Jonson* B) is also found in holograph in the Cecil Papers 119, 58. (I have used copies of the letters as found in Schelling and Herford and Simpson, and modernized spelling and punctuation.)

The circumstances of the imprisonment related by Jonson in his conversations concur at several points with the letters. They are in prison because they have aroused 'his Majesty's high displeasure'; they are 'unexamined or unheard'; and the cause is 'not our own'. The letters do not, however, confirm Jonson's story of how he gave himself up nor do they explain the absence of Marston. Jonson's

[2] H. & S., I, 140 (here modernized).

continual plea that *Rumour* is not to be trusted favours the theory that unlicensed production was the actual cause of the offence. (See above, *Date and Sources*, p. xxiii–xxv.)

Whatever the cause, the imprisonment must have been short-lived. Evidently their patrons secured a rapid release. *Chapman* III mentions that D'Aubigny has intervened on behalf of Jonson. We know that Jonson attended a party given by Robert Catesby, a conspirator in the Gunpowder Plot, on 9 October 1605.[3]

I

To His Most Gracious Majesty.

Vouchsafe most excellent Sovereign to take merciful notice of the submissive and amendful sorrows of your two most humble and prostrated subjects for your Highness' displeasure: Geo: Chapman and Ben Jhonson; whose chief offences are but two clauses, and both of them not our own; much less the unnatural issue of our offence-less intents. I hope your Majesty's universal knowledge will deign to remember that all authority in execution of justice especially respects the manners and lives of men commanded before it; and according to their general actions censures anything that hath 'scaped them in particular; which cannot be so disproportionable that one being actually good, the other should be intentionally ill, if not intentionally (howsoever it may lie subject to construction)—where the whole fount of our actions may be justified from being in this kind offensive—I hope the integral parts will taste of the same loyal and dutiful order: which to aspire from your most Caesar-like bounty (who conquered still to spare the conquered, and was glad of offences that he might forgive). In all dejection of never-enough iterated sorrow for your high displeasure, and vow of as much future delight as of your present anger; we cast our best parts at your Highness' feet, and our worst to hell.

GEORGE CHAPMAN.

II

To The Most Worthy and Honourable Protector of Virtue: The Lord Chamberlain.

Most Worthily Honoured:

Of all the oversights for which I suffer none repents me so much as that our unhappy book was presented without your Lordship's

[3] ibid., XI, 578.

allowance. For which we can plead nothing by way of pardon, but your Person so far removed from our required attendance; our play so much importuned; and our clear opinions that nothing it contained could worthily be held offensive. And had your good Lordship vouchsafed this addition of grace to your late free bounties, to have heard our reasons for our well weighed opinions; and the words truly related on which both they and our enemies' complaints were grounded, I make no question but your impartial justice would have stood much further from their clamour than from our acquittal. Which indifferent favour, if yet your no less than princely respect of virtue shall please to bestow on her poor observant and command my appearance; I doubt not but the tempest that hath driven me into this wrackful harbour will clear with my innocence: and withal the most sorrow-inflicting wrath of his excellent Majesty; which to my most humble and zealous affection is so much the more stormy, by how much some of my obscured labours have strived to aspire instead thereof his illustrate favour; and shall not be the least honour to his most Royal virtues.

GEORGE CHAPMAN.

III

[To The Earl of Suffolk:The Lord Chamberlain.]

Notwithstanding your Lordship's infinite free bounty hath pardoned and graced when it might justly have punished; and remembered our poor reputations when our acknowledged duties to your Lordship might worthily seem forgotten; yet since true honour delights to increase with increase of goodness; and that our abilities and healths faint under our irksome burdens; we are with all humility enforced to solicit the propagation of your most noble favours to our present freedom: and the rather since we hear from Lord D'Awbney, that his Highness hath remitted one of us wholly to your Lordship's favour. And that the other had still your Lordship's passing noble remembrance for his joint liberty; which his Highness' self would not be displeased to allow. And thus with all gratitude admiring your no less than sacred respect to the poor estate of virtue, never were our souls more appropriate to the powers of our lives, than our utmost lives are consecrate to your noblest service.

GEORGE CHAPMAN.

A

[To An Unnamed Lord, probably The Earl of Suffolk, 1605.[4]]

Most Honourable Lord:

Although I cannot but know your Lordship to be busied with far greater and higher affairs than to have leisure to descend suddenly on an estate so low and removed as mine; yet since the cause is in us wholly mistaken (at least misconstrued), and that every noble and just man is bound to defend the innocent; I doubt not but to find your Lordship full of that wonted virtue and favour; wherewith you have ever abounded toward the truth. And though the imprisonment itself cannot but grieve me (in respect of his Majesty's high displeasure, from whence it proceeds) yet the manner of it afflicts me more being committed hither, unexamined, nay unheard (a right not commonly denied to the greatest offenders), and I made a guilty man, long before I am one, or ever thought to be. God I call to testimony what my thoughts are and ever have been of his Majesty; and so may I thrive when he comes to be my judge and my King's, as they are most sincere.

And I appeal to posterity that will hereafter read and judge my writings (though now neglected) whether it be possible I should speak of his Majesty as I have done, without the affection of a most zealous and good subject. It hath ever been my destiny to be misreported and condemned on the first tale; but I hope there is an ear left for me, and by your honour I hope it, who have always been friend to justice; a virtue that crowns your nobility. So with my most humble prayer of your pardon, and all advanced wishes for your honour, I begin to know my duty, which is to forbear to trouble your Lordship till my languishing estate may draw free breath from your comfortable word.

BEN: JOHNSON.

B

To The Most Nobly-Virtuous and Thrice-Honoured Earl of Salisbury,[5] 1605.

Most Truly Honourable,/

It hath still been the tyranny of my fortune so to oppress my endeavours that before I can show myself grateful in the least for former benefits, I am enforced to provoke your bounties for more. May it not seem grievous to your Lordship that now my innocence

---

[4] ibid., I, 194.
[5] Created Earl of Salisbury on 5 May 1605.

calls upon you (next the Deity) to her defence—God himself is not averted at just men's cries—and you, that approach that divine goodness and supply it here on earth in your place and honours, cannot employ your aids more worthily than to the commune succour of honesty and virtue, how humbly soever it be placed.

I am here, my most honoured Lord, unexamined or unheard, committed to a vile prison, and with me a gentleman (whose name may perhaps have come to your Lordship), one Mr. *George Chapman*, a learned and honest man. The cause (would I could name some worthier, though I wish we had known none worthy our imprisonment), is (the word irks me that our fortune hath necessitated us to so despised a course), a play, my Lord; whereof we hope there is no man can justly complain that hath the virtue to think but favourably of himself; if our judge bring an equal ear, marry, if with prejudice we be made guilty afore our time, we must embrace the asinine virtue, patience./ My noble Lord, they deal not charitably who are too witty in another man's works, and utter sometimes their own malicious meanings under our words. I protest to your honour, and call God to testimony (since my first error, which yet is punished in me more with my shame than it was then with my bondage),[6] I have so attempered my style, that I have given no cause to any good man of grief, and if to any ill, by touching at any general vice, it hath always been with a regard and sparing of particular persons. I may be otherwise reported; but if all that be accused should be presently guilty, there are few men would stand in the state of innocence./

I beseech your most honourable Lordship, suffer not other men's errors or faults past to be made my crimes; but let me be examined both by all my works past and this present; and not trust to *Rumour* but my books (for she is an unjust deliverer both of great and small actions), whether I have ever (in anything I have written, private, or public) given offence to a nation, to any public order or state, or any person of honour or authority; but have equally laboured to keep their dignity, as mine own person, safe. If others have transgressed, let not me be entitled to their follies. But lest in being too diligent for my excuse, I may incur the suspicion of being guilty, I become a most humble suitor to your Lordship that with the honourable Lord *Chamberlain* (to whom I have in like manner petitioned), you will be pleased to be the grateful means of our coming to answer; or if in your wisdoms it shall be thought unnecessary, that your Lordships will be the most honoured cause of

---

[6] i.e., Jonson's imprisonment for his share in Thomas Nashe's *The Isle of Dogs* (1597), for which he was tried by Salisbury (then Sir Robert Cecil).

our liberty, where freeing us from one prison you shall remove us to another; which is eternally to bind us and our muses, to the thankful honouring of you and yours to posterity; as your own virtues have by many descents of ancestors ennobled you to time./
Your Honour's most devoted in heart as words./
BEN: JONSON.

C

[To an Unnamed Lord, 1605]

Noble Lord,

I have so confirmed opinion of your virtue, and am so fortified in mine own innocence, as I dare (without blushing at anything save your trouble) put my fame into your hands, which I prefer to my life. The cause of my commitment I understand is his Majesty's high displeasure conceived against me; for which I am most inwardly sorry; but how I should deserve it, I have yet, I thank God, so much integrity as to doubt. If I have been misreported to his Majesty, the punishment I now suffer may I hope merit more of his princely favour, when he shall know me truly: every accusation doth not condemn, and there must go much more to the making of a guilty man, than rumour. I therefore crave of your Lordship this noble benefit; rightly to inform his Majesty that I never in thought, word, or act had purpose to offend or grieve him; but with all my powers have studied to show myself most loyal and zealous to his whole designs; that in private and public, by speech and writing, I have ever professed it; and if there be one man or devil to be produced that can affirm the contrary let me suffer under all extremity that justice, nay tyranny, can inflict. I speak not this with any spirit of contumacy, for I know there is no subject hath so safe an innocence but may rejoice to stand justified in sight of his Sovereign's mercy. To which we most humbly submit ourselves, our lives and fortunes.
BEN: JOHNSON.

D

[To An Unnamed Lady, probably The Countess of Bedford. 1605.[7]]

Excellentest of Ladies,

And most honoured of the graces, muses, and me; if it be not a sin to profane your free hand with prison polluted paper, I would entreat some little of your aid to the defence of my innocence, which

[7] H. & S., I, 198. Schelling in his edition of *Eastward Ho!* conjectures that the lady to whom this letter is addressed is the Countess of Rutland.

is as clear as this leaf was (before I stained it) of anything half-
worthy this violent infliction. I am committed and with me a worthy
friend, one Mr. Chapman, a man, I cannot say how known to your
Ladyship, but I am sure known to me to honour you. And our
offence a play, so mistaken, so misconstrued, so misapplied, as I
do wonder whether their ignorance or impudence be most, who are
our adversaries. It is now not disputable for we stand on uneven
bases, and our cause so unequally carried, as we are—without
examining, without hearing, or without any proof but malicious
Rumour—hurried to bondage and fetters. The cause we understand
to be the King's indignation, for which we are heartily sorry, and
the more by how much the less we have deserved it. What our suit is,
the worthy employed solicitor and equal adorer of your virtues, can
best inform you.

BEN: JHONSON.

E

[To Esme, Lord D'Aubigny? 1605.[8]]

The noble favours you have done us, most worthy Lord, cannot
be so concealed or removed but that they have broke in upon us
even where we lie double bound to their comforts. Nor can we
doubt, but he who hath so far and freely adventured to the relief
of our virtue will go on to the utmost release of it. And though I
know your Lordship hath been far from doing anything herein to
your own ambition; yet be pleased to take this protestation, that,
next his Majesty's favour, I shall not covet that thing more in the
world than to express the lasting gratitude I have conceived in soul
towards your Lordship.

BEN: JOHNSON.

F

[To The Earl of] Mon[t]gomerie[9]

Most Worthily Honoured,
    For me not to solicit or call you to succour in a time of such need,
were no less a sin of despair, than a neglect of your honour. Your
power, your place, and readiness to do good invite me, and mine
own cause (which shall never discredit the least of your favours) is
a main encouragement. If I lay here on my desert, I should be the

---

[8] Jonson had been staying with D'Aubigny in 1603.
[9] Patron of the playwright Massinger. According to H. & S. also created earl
on 5 May 1605.

more backward to importune you; but as it is (most worthy Earl) our offence being our misfortune, not our malice; I challenge your aid, as to the common defence of virtue; but more peculiarly to me, who have always in heart so particularly honoured you. I know it is now no time to boast affections, lest, while I sue for favours I should be thought to buy them; but if the future services of a man so removed to you and low in merit may aspire any place in your thoughts; let it lie upon the forfeiture of my humanity, if I omit the least occasion to express them. And so, not doubting of your noble endeavours to reflect his Majesty's most repented on our parts and sorrowed-for displeasure, I commit my fortune, reputation, and innocence into your most happy hands; and reiterated protestation of being ever most grateful.

BEN: JOHNSON.

G

[To The Earl of] Pembroke.

Most Noble Earl:
Neither am I or my cause so much unknown to your Lordship as it should drive me to seek a second means, or despair of this to your favour. You have ever been free and noble to me, and I doubt not the same proportion of your bounties, if I can but answer it with preservation of my virtue and innocence: when I fail of those let me not only be abandoned of you, but of men. 'The anger of the King is death', sayeth the wise man, and in truth it is little less with me and my friend; for it hath buried us quick. And though we know it only the property of men guilty, and worthy of punishment, to invoke *Mercy*; yet now it might relieve us, who have only our fortunes made our fault; and are indeed vexed for other men's licence. Most honoured Earl; be hasty to our succour, and it shall be our care and study not to have you repent the timely benefit you do us; which we will ever gratefully receive and multiply in our acknowledgement.

BEN: JOHNSON.

Bartholmew Fair

BEN JONSON

Edited by
G. R. HIBBARD

ABBREVIATIONS

1. *Texts of* Bartholmew Fair

F   the edition of 1631.

Alden   C. S. Alden, ed., *Bartholomew Fair*, *Yale Studies in English*, 25 (1904).

Spencer   Hazelton Spencer, ed., *Elizabethan Plays*, Boston, 1933.

H & S   C. H. Herford and Percy and Evelyn Simpson, eds., *The Works of Ben Jonson*, 11 vols., 1925–52.

Horsman   E. A. Horsman, ed., *Bartholomew Fair*, The Revels Plays, 1960.

Waith   Eugene M. Waith, ed., *Bartholomew Fair*, The Yale Ben Jonson, 1963.

2. *Other works*

Chambers   E. K. Chambers, *The Elizabethan Stage*, 4 vols., 1923.

Nashe   R. B. McKerrow, ed., *The Works of Thomas Nashe*, 5 vols., 1904–10.

Pepys   R. Garnett, ed., *Diary of Samuel Pepys*, Everyman's Library, 2 vols., 1906.

Shakespeare   Peter Alexander, ed., *The Complete Works of William Shakespeare*, 1951.

Stow   Henry B. Wheatley, ed., John Stow's *The Survey of London* (1598), Everyman's Library, 1912.

BARTHOLMEW FAYRE:

A COMEDIE,

ACTED IN THE
YEARE, 1614.

By the Lady *ELIZABETHS*
Servants.

And then dedicated to King I A M E S, of
most Blessed Memorie;

By the Author, BENIAMIN IOHNSON.

Si foret in terris, rideret Democritus : *nam*
Spectaret populum ludis attentius ipsis,
Vt sibi præbentem, mimo spectacula plura.
Scriptores autem narrare putaret asello
Fabellam surdo.   Hor.lib.2.Epist.1.

LONDON,
Printed by *I. B.* for ROBERT ALLOT, and are
to be sold at the signe of the *Beare*, in *Pauls*
Church-yard. 1631.

BARTHOLMEW FAYRE. The full form of the name *Bartholomew* occurs only once in the play, at 1. i, 3, where, significantly, Littlewit is reading the licence for Cokes's marriage. Everywhere else the preferred form, preserved in this edition, is *Bartholmew* (probably pronounced *Bartlemy*), a spelling which persisted into the nineteenth century.

From 1120 till 1855 a great fair was held annually in Smithfield on 24 August, the feast of St Bartholomew.

the Lady ELIZABETHS SERVANTS. This company of players seems to have come into being in 1611, when a patent was issued to them on 27 April. After various vicissitudes, they established themselves at the newly built theatre called the Hope in the autumn of 1614. See Chambers, ii. 246–58.

Si foret . . . surdo. Quoted from Horace, *Epistles*, II.i. 194–200, with lines 195–6 omitted, *nam* for *seu*, and *asello* misprinted as *assello*. 'If Democritus were still in the land of the living, he would laugh himself silly, for he would pay far more attention to the audience than to the play, since the audience offers the more interesting spectacle. But as for the authors of the plays—he would conclude that they were telling their tales to a deaf donkey'. Characteristically, Jonson is telling his audience what he thinks of them and of the state of the drama.

I.B. The initials of the printer John Beale.

Pauls Church-yard. The churchyard of old St Paul's Cathedral was the centre of the book-trade in London in the sixteenth and early seventeenth centuries.

THE
PROLOGUE
TO
THE KING'S
MAJESTY

Your Majesty is welcome to a Fair;
Such place, such men, such language, and such ware,
You must expect; with these, the zealous noise
Of your land's Faction, scandalized at toys,
As babies, hobby-horses, puppet-plays,   5
And such like rage, whereof the petulant ways
Yourself have known, and have been vexed with long.
These for your sport, without particular wrong,
Or just complaint of any private man
Who of himself or shall think well or can,   10
The Maker doth present; and hopes tonight
To give you, for a fairing, true delight.

 4 *toys* trifles
 5 *babies* dolls
 6 *rage* mad folly
 8 *particular wrong* injurious reference to any individual
11 *Maker* author
12 *fairing* present given at or bought at a fair

PROLOGUE. This prologue took the place of the Induction when the
play was presented before James I at court on 1 November 1614.
 4 *your land's Faction.* Ever since the breakdown of the Hampton Court
Conference in 1604 James I had been embroiled with the Puritans.

THE PERSONS OF THE PLAY

JOHN LITTLEWIT, *a proctor*
[SOLOMON, *his man*]
WIN LITTLEWIT, *his wife*
DAME PURECRAFT, *her mother and a widow*
ZEAL-OF-THE-LAND BUSY, *her suitor, a Banbury man*   5
WINWIFE, *his rival, a gentleman*
QUARLOUS, *his companion, a gamester*
BARTHOLMEW COKES, *an esquire of Harrow*
HUMPHREY WASP, *his man*
ADAM OVERDO, *a Justice of Peace*   10
DAME OVERDO, *his wife*
GRACE WELLBORN, *his ward*
LANTERN LEATHERHEAD, *a hobby-horse-seller*
JOAN TRASH, *a gingerbread-woman*
EZEKIEL EDGWORTH, *a cutpurse*   15
NIGHTINGALE, *a ballad-singer*
URSLA, *a pig-woman*
MOONCALF, *her tapster*
JORDAN KNOCKEM, *a horse-courser, and ranger o' Turnbull*
VAL CUTTING, *a roarer*   20
CAPTAIN WHIT, *a bawd*

---

  1 *proctor* legal agent, attorney
  2 SOLOMON, *his man* Ed. (omitted F)
  7 QUARLOUS combination of 'quarrellous' (= contentious) and
    'parlous' (= dangerously clever)
    gamester (i) gambler (ii) rake (iii) inveterate jeerer
  8 COKES dupe, simpleton
 17 URSLA shortened form of Ursula, Latin for 'little she-bear'
 18 MOONCALF born fool
 19 *horse-courser* horse-dealer, expert in sharp practice
    ranger o' Turnbull gamekeeper of Turnbull Street in London, the
    'game' being the prostitutes for whom the street was notorious
 20 *roarer* noisy bully
 21 WHIT term of abuse of uncertain meaning, also used by Jonson in
    The Alchemist (IV, vii, 45)

---

  5 *a Banbury man.* Banbury, in Oxfordshire, was proverbially famous for
    its cheese, cakes, and ale, and, by the early seventeenth century, it had
    come to be regarded as a centre of Puritanism. Busy, a glutton as well as
    a Puritan, has been a baker (cf. I.iii, 110–20).

304

PUNK ALICE, *mistress o' the game*
TROUBLE-ALL, *a madman*
[HAGGIS,
BRISTLE,] } *watchmen*   25
[POCHER, *a beadle*]
[A] COSTARD-MONGER
[A CORNCUTTER]
[A TINDERBOX-MAN]
[NORTHERN, *a*] *clothier*   30
[PUPPY, *a*] *wrestler*
[FILCHER,
SHARKWELL,] } *doorkeepers* [*at the puppet-shew*]
PUPPETS
[PASSENGERS]   35

The Scene: Smithfield

22 *the game* prostitution
24–6 HAGGIS . . . *beadle* Ed. (WATCHMEN, three. F)
27 A COSTARD-MONGER Ed. (COSTARD-monger. F) costermonger
(originally a vendor of costards, i.e., apples)
28 A CORNCUTTER Ed. (omitted F)
29 A TINDERBOX-MAN Ed. (MOVSETRAP-man. F)
30 NORTHERN, *a* Ed. (CLOTHIER. F)
31 PUPPY, *a* Ed. (WRESTLER. F)
32–3 FILCHER, SHARKWELL, *doorkeepers at the puppet-shew* Ed. (DOORE-
KEEPERS. F)
35 PASSENGERS Ed. (PORTERS F)

THE INDUCTION ON THE STAGE

[Enter] STAGE-KEEPER

STAGE-KEEPER

Gentlemen, have a little patience, they are e'en upon
coming, instantly. He that should begin the play, Master
Littlewit, the Proctor, has a stitch new fallen in his black silk
stocking; 'twill be drawn up ere you can tell twenty. He
plays one o' the Arches, that dwells about the Hospital, and   5
he has a very pretty part. But for the whole play, will you ha'
the truth on't?—I am looking, lest the poet hear me, or his
man, Master Brome, behind the arras—it is like to be a very
conceited scurvy one, in plain English. When't comes to the
Fair once, you were e'en as good go to Virginia for anything   10
there is of Smithfield. He has not hit the humours, he does not
know 'em; he has not conversed with the Bartholmew-birds,
as they say; he has ne'er a sword-and-buckler man in his
Fair, nor a little Davy to take toll o' the bawds there, as in my
time, nor a Kindheart, if anybody's teeth should chance to   15

s.d. STAGE-KEEPER man employed to set and sweep the stage
4 *tell* count
8 *arras* tapestry hanging
9 *conceited* fanciful, unrealistic
11 *hit the humours* hit off the typical oddities of behaviour
12 *Bartholmew-birds* roguish denizens of the Fair (cf. 'jail-birds')
13 *sword-and-buckler man* Ed. (Sword, and Buckler man F) swashbuckler, bragging bully

5 *one o' the Arches.* The Court of Arches, where Littlewit practises, was
held in Bow Church and was the court of appeal from the diocesan
courts.
the Hospital. 'St. Bartlemew, in Smithfield, an hospital of great receipt
and relief for the poor . . . is endowed by the citizens' benevolence'
(Stow, 438).
7–8 *his man, Master Brome.* Richard Brome was for a time Jonson's
'faithful servant', learned from him how to write plays, and eventually
became a dramatist in his own right. Jonson's tribute to him is printed
in H & S, viii. 409.
14 *little Davy.* Referred to in several works of the early seventeenth century, this individual seems to have been a professional bully.
15 *Kindheart.* An itinerant tooth-drawer who gave his name to Henry
Chettle's pamphlet *Kind-Harts Dreame* (1593).

307

ache in his play; nor a juggler with a well-educated ape to
come over the chain for the King of England, and back again
for the Prince, and sit still on his arse for the Pope and the
King of Spain! None o' these fine sights! Nor has he the
canvas cut i' the night for a hobby-horse-man to creep in to   20
his she-neighbour and take his leap there! Nothing! No, an
some writer that I know had had but the penning o' this
matter, he would ha' made you such a jig-a-jog i' the booths,
you should ha' thought an earthquake had been i' the Fair!
But these master-poets, they will ha' their own absurd   25
courses; they will be informed of nothing. He has, sir-
reverence, kicked me three or four times about the tiring-
house, I thank him, for but offering to put in with my
experience. I'll be judged by you, gentlemen, now, but for
one conceit of mine! Would not a fine pump upon the stage   30
ha' done well for a property now? And a punk set under
upon her head, with her stern upward, and ha' been soused
by my witty young masters o' the Inns o' Court? What think
you o' this for a shew, now? He will not hear o' this! I am an
ass! I! And yet I kept the stage in Master Tarlton's time, I   35
thank my stars. Ho! an that man had lived to have played in
Bartholmew Fair, you should ha' seen him ha' come in, and

20 *hobby-horse-man* (i) seller of hobby-horses (ii) frequenter of
   hobby-horses (prostitutes)
21 *take his leap* technical term for the copulation of a stallion with a
   mare
   an if
23 *jig-a-jog* jogging motion (with sexual innuendo)
26–7 *sir-reverence* (originally 'save reverence') I apologize for men-
   tioning it
27–8 *tiring-house* backstage area where the dressing-rooms were
28 *put in* intervene, help him out
30 *conceit* bright idea
31 *punk* whore
32 *soused* soaked to the skin
33 *witty* clever, facetious

33 *young masters o' the Inns o' Court.* The Inns of Court—Lincoln's Inn,
   the Inner Temple, the Middle Temple, and Gray's Inn—where stud-
   ents studied the law, were virtually a third university.
35 *in Master Tarlton's time.* Richard Tarlton, who died in 1588, was the
   most celebrated clown of his time. A member of the Queen's Men from
   the time of that company's foundation in 1583, he became something of
   a legend, and there were numerous stories and anecdotes about him.

ha' been cozened i' the cloth-quarter, so finely! And Adams,
the rogue, ha' leaped and capered upon him, and ha' dealt
his vermin about as though they had cost him nothing. And
then a substantial watch to ha' stolen in upon 'em, and taken
'em away with mistaking words, as the fashion is in the stage
practice.

       [Enter] BOOK-HOLDER, SCRIVENER, *to him*

BOOK-HOLDER

How now? What rare discourse are you fallen upon, ha? Ha'
you found any familiars here, that you are so free? What's the
business?

STAGE-KEEPER

Nothing, but the understanding gentlemen o' the ground
here asked my judgement.

BOOK-HOLDER

Your judgement, rascal? For what? Sweeping the stage? Or
gathering up the broken apples for the bears within? Away,
rogue, it's come to a fine degree in these spectacles when
such a youth as you pretend to a judgement.

                        [Exit STAGE-KEEPER]

And yet he may, i' the most o' this matter i'faith; for the
author hath writ it just to his meridian, and the scale of
the grounded judgements here, his play-fellows in wit.

40
45
50
55

40 *vermin* fleas?
42 *mistaking words* malapropisms (cf. Dogberry and Verges in *Much
    Ado About Nothing*)
43 s.d. BOOK-HOLDER prompter
45 *free* free of speech, forward
52 *pretend* lay claim
54 *just to his meridian* exactly calculated to the limit of his under-
    standing
55 *grounded* (i) well-grounded, proficient (ii) standing on the ground,
    in the pit

---

38 *cozened i' the cloth-quarter*. The cloth-quarter, originally the most
    important part of the Fair, was by the north wall of St Bartholomew's
    Church. An anecdote in the anonymous *Tarltons Jests* (1611) tells how
    the comedian was cheated of his clothes there.
    Adams. John Adams was another member of the Queen's Men at the
    same time as Tarlton (Chambers, ii. 296).
47 *understanding gentlemen o' the ground*. A punning reference to the
    groundlings who stood under, i.e. below, the stage, in the pit.
50 *the bears within*. The Hope Theatre, which opened in 1614, was both a
    playhouse and a bear-garden. The stage was removed on the days when
    bear-baiting was the entertainment offered.

Gentlemen, not for want of a prologue, but by way of a new
one, I am sent out to you here, with a scrivener and certain
articles drawn out in haste between our author and you;
which if you please to hear, and as they appear reasonable, to
approve of, the play will follow presently. Read, scribe; gi’   60
me the counterpane.

SCRIVENER
Articles of Agreement, indented, between the spectators or
hearers at the Hope on the Bankside, in the County of
Surrey, on the one party, and the author of *Bartholmew Fair*,
in the said place and county, on the other party, the one and   65
thirtieth day of October, 1614, and in the twelfth year of the
reign of our Sovereign Lord, James, by the grace of God
King of England, France, and Ireland; Defender of the
Faith; and of Scotland the seven and fortieth.

INPRIMIS, It is covenanted and agreed by and between the   70
parties above-said . . . and the said spectators and hearers, as
well the curious and envious as the favouring and judicious,
as also the grounded judgements and understandings, do
for themselves severally covenant and agree to remain in the
places their money or friends have put them in, with pat-   75
ience, for the space of two hours and an half, and somewhat
more. In which time the author promiseth to present them,
by us, with a new sufficient play called *Bartholmew Fair*,
merry, and as full of noise as sport, made to delight all, and
to offend none—provided they have either the wit or the   80
honesty to think well of themselves.
It is further agreed that every **person here have his or their**

61 *counterpane* other half of the indenture
72 *curious* hypercritical
   envious hostile
78 *sufficient* up to standard, of good quality

63 *the Bankside*. An area on the south side of the river Thames, and therefore not within the jurisdiction of the City of London, which, during the
   decade 1590–1600, became the theatrical centre.
71 *above-said . . . and* ed. (abouesaid, and F). It is very difficult to make
   sense of the long sentence ‘It is . . . more.’ (ll. 70–7) as it stands in the
   Folio. One expects the initial statement ‘It is . . . abovesaid’, to be
   followed by ‘that’, as it is in each of the subsequent articles. The present
   editor assumes that the compositor has omitted a line of Jonson’s manuscript. The difficulty can be got over in the theatre by having the actor
   mumble after ‘above-said’, much as lawyers often do in reading the
   preliminaries of a will or the like.

free-will of censure, to like or dislike at their own charge;
the author having now departed with his right, it shall be
lawful for any man to judge his six penn'orth, his twelve   85
penn'orth, so to his eighteen pence, two shillings, half a
crown, to the value of his place—provided always his place
get not above his wit. And if he pay for half a dozen, he may
censure for all them too, so that he will undertake that they
shall be silent. He shall put in for censures here as they do   90
for lots at the lottery; marry, if he drop but sixpence at the
door, and will censure a crown's worth, it is thought there
is no conscience or justice in that.

It is also agreed that every man here exercise his own
judgement, and not censure by contagion, or upon trust,   95
from another's voice or face that sits by him, be he never so
first in the Commission of Wit; as also that he be fixed and
settled in his censure, that what he approves or not approves
today, he will do the same tomorrow, and if tomorrow, the
next day, and so the next week, if need be; and not to be   100
brought about by any that sits on the bench with him,
though they indict and arraign plays daily. He that will swear
Jeronimo or *Andronicus* are the best plays yet, shall pass
unexcepted at here as a man whose judgement shews it is
constant, and hath stood still these five and twenty or   105

83 *censure* judgement, criticism
    charge; ed. (charge, F)
84 *departed with* surrendered, parted with
    right, ed. (right: F)
89 *so* provided
95 *contagion* infectious influence
101 *brought about* converted, made to change his mind
    bench (i) bench of magistrates (ii) form on the stage occupied by
    the distinguished and fashionable
104 *unexcepted at* unobjected to

85–7 *six penn'orth . . . half a crown.* The list of prices given here is remark-
    ably high for the time, rather more than double what appears to have
    been normal. Chambers suggests (ii. 534) that a possible explanation is
    to be found in the fact that the play was 'not merely a new play, but a
    new play at a new house'.
91 *the lottery.* A lottery, under the patronage of the King, was opened in
    1612 to provide funds for the colonization of Virginia.
97 *the Commission of Wit.* An imaginary body of critics empowered to
    examine and pass judgement on plays, poems, and the like.
103 Jeronimo or Andronicus. Thomas Kyd's *The Spanish Tragedy* (*c.* 1587)
    and Shakespeare's *Titus Andronicus* (1589–90?) had become very old-
    fashioned by 1614.

thirty years. Though it be an ignorance, it is a virtuous and
staid ignorance; and next to truth, a confirmed error does
well. Such a one the author knows where to find him.

It is further covenanted, concluded, and agreed that how
great soever the expectation be, no person here is to expect   110
more than he knows, or better ware than a Fair will afford;
neither to look back to the sword-and-buckler age of Smithfield, but content himself with the present. Instead of a little
Davy to take toll o' the bawds, the author doth promise a
strutting horse-courser, with a leer drunkard, two or three   115
to attend him, in as good equipage as you would wish. And
then for Kindheart, the tooth-drawer, a fine oily pig-woman,
with her tapster to bid you welcome, and a consort of roarers
for music. A wise Justice of Peace *meditant*, instead of a
juggler with an ape. A civil cutpurse *searchant*. A sweet   120
singer of new ballads *allurant*; and as fresh an hypocrite as
ever was broached *rampant*. If there be never a servant-
monster i' the Fair, who can help it? he says; nor a nest of
antics? He is loth to make Nature afraid in his plays, like
those that beget Tales, Tempests, and such like drolleries, to   125
mix his head with other men's heels, let the concupiscence
of jigs and dances reign as strong as it will amongst you; yet
if the puppets will please anybody, they shall be entreated
to come in.

115 *leer* sly
116 *equipage* array
117 *pig-woman*, ed. (*Pig-woman* F)
118 *tapster* ed. (*Tapster*, F)
123–4 *nest of antics* group of clowns
125 *drolleries* comic entertainments of a fantastic kind

112–13 *the sword-and-buckler age of Smithfield*. The 'field commonly called
   West-Smith field, was for many years called *Ruffians hall*, by reason it
   was the usuall place of Frayes and common fighting, during the time that
   Sword-and-Bucklers were in use … This manner of Fight was frequent
   with all men, untill the fight of Rapier and Dagger tooke place,
   and then suddenly the generall quarrell of fighting abated, which began
   about the 20 yeare of Queen *Elizabeth* . . .' (Stow, *Annals*, 1631,
   p. 1024 ab, quoted from Nashe, iv. 111).
119–21 *meditant . . . searchant . . . allurant.* A series of mock heraldic terms
   modelled on such forms as *rampant*.
122–3 *servant-monster.* A patent allusion to Caliban in Shakespeare's *The
   Tempest*, who is repeatedly addressed as 'servant-monster' by Stephano
   and Trinculo at the opening of III.ii.
125 *Tales, Tempests.* An obvious reference to *The Winter's Tale* and *The
   Tempest*.

In consideration of which, it is finally agreed by the   130
foresaid hearers and spectators that they neither in themselves conceal, nor suffer by them to be concealed, any
state-decipherer, or politic picklock of the scene, so solemnly
ridiculous as to search out who was meant by the gingerbread-woman, who by the hobby-horse-man, who by the   135
costard-monger, nay, who by their wares; or that will
pretend to affirm, on his own inspired ignorance, what
Mirror of Magistrates is meant by the Justice, what great
lady by the pig-woman, what concealed statesman by the
seller of mousetraps, and so of the rest. But that such person   140
or persons, so found, be left discovered to the mercy of the
author, as a forfeiture to the stage and your laughter aforesaid; as also, such as shall so desperately or ambitiously
play the fool by his place aforesaid, to challenge the author
of scurrility because the language somewhere savours of   145
Smithfield, the booth, and the pig-broth; or of profaneness
because a madman cries, 'God quit you', or 'bless you'. In
witness whereof, as you have preposterously put to your
seals already, which is your money, you will now add the
other part of suffrage, your hands. The play shall presently   150
begin. And though the Fair be not kept in the same region
that some here, perhaps, would have it, yet think that therein
the author hath observed a special decorum, the place
being as dirty as Smithfield, and as stinking every whit.

133 *state-decipherer* professional informer on the look-out for seditious
     matter
141 *discovered* revealed, exposed
144 *challenge* accuse
148 *preposterously* in reversed order, back to front
     put to affixed
150 *suffrage* approval
     hands (i) signatures (ii) applause
153 *decorum* sense of fitness

---

133 *politic picklock of the scene.* Informers on the look-out for 'lewd,
     seditious, or slanderous matter' were, as Jonson knew to his cost, a
     menace that the playwright had to guard against. He had been im-
     prisoned in 1597 for his share in the lost play *The Isle of Dogs*, and again
     in 1605 for his share in *Eastward Ho!*
138 *Mirror of Magistrates.* The phrase probably has a double meaning:
     (i) paragon of magistrates (ii) in allusion to George Whetstone's *A
     Mirour for Magestrates of Cyties* (1584), in which it is argued that a good
     magistrate should find out the truth for himself by visiting places of
     entertainment in disguise.

Howsoever, he prays you to believe his ware is still the   155
same, else you will make him justly suspect that he that is so
loth to look on a baby or an hobby-horse here, would be
glad to take up a commodity of them, at any laughter or loss,
in another place.   [*Exeunt*]

158-9 *to take up a commodity of them, at any laughter or loss, in another place.*
Jonson refers to a trick, designed to get round the law limiting interest
to 10 per cent, which was commonly practised at the time. The money-
lender, pleading that he was short of ready cash, would persuade his
client to take part or the whole of the loan in the form of goods, such as
'lute-strings and brown paper'. He would then introduce the borrower
to another businessman, with whom he was in collusion, prepared to buy
these goods at a very large discount. Jonson is saying, in effect, that the
spectator who is not willing to pay with laughter for the excellent play
he is being offered will be forced into buying very inferior wares elsewhere and will expose himself to derision as a consequence.

BARTHOLMEW FAIR

Act I, Scene i

[*Enter*] LITTLEWIT

LITTLEWIT
A pretty conceit, and worth the finding! I ha' such luck to
spin out these fine things still, and like a silk-worm, out of
myself. Here's Master Bartholomew Cokes, of Harrow
o'th'Hill, i'th'County of Middlesex, Esquire, takes forth
his licence to marry Mistress Grace Wellborn of the said   5
place and county. And when does he take it forth? Today!
The four-and-twentieth of August! Bartholmew day!
Bartholmew upon Bartholmew! There's the device! Who
would have marked such a leap-frog chance now? A very
less than ames-ace on two dice! Well, go thy ways, John   10
Littlewit, Proctor John Littlewit—one o' the pretty wits o'
Paul's, the Little Wit of London, so thou art called, and

3 *Here's* Ed. (Her's F)
8 *device* clever design
9 *leap-frog chance* chance of two interchangeable things appearing
together
9–10 *very less* truly slighter (with the word 'chance' understood)
10 *ames-ace* ambs-ace, double ace, lowest possible throw with two
dice

---

s.d. *Enter* LITTLEWIT Ed. (LITTLE-WIT {*To him*} WIN. F). Following
classical precedent, Jonson lists all the characters taking part in a scene
at the opening of that scene, irrespective of when they actually enter,
and he does not normally supply stage directions to mark entrances and
exits. The character who is first on the list makes the opening speech,
which has no speech prefix. In this edition that speech prefix is supplied.
A new scene begins when a fresh group of characters appears. It does
not necessarily mark a break in the action, which is usually, though not
invariably, continuous within the act. Act I of *Bartholmew Fair* is set in
Littlewit's house.
3 *Bartholomew.* This is the only occasion on which the full form of this
name occurs in the play. Significantly, Littlewit is reading from an
official legal document, where the full form should be given.
12 *Paul's.* The middle aisle of St Paul's was, in Jonson's day, the great
meeting-place of London. Merchants came there to do business, and the
fashionable to exchange news and gossip.

something beside. When a quirk or a quiblin does scape
thee, and thou dost not watch, and apprehend it, and bring
it afore the constable of conceit—there now, I speak quib   15
too—let 'em carry thee out o' the Archdeacon's court into
his kitchen, and make a Jack of thee, instead of a John.
There I am again, la!

[*Enter*] *to him* WIN

Win, good morrow, Win. Ay, marry, Win! Now you look
finely indeed, Win! This cap does convince! You'd not ha'   20
worn it, Win, nor ha' had it velvet, but a rough country
beaver with a copper band, like the coney-skin woman of
Budge Row? Sweet Win, let me kiss it! And her fine high
shoes, like the Spanish lady! Good Win, go a little; I would
fain see thee pace, pretty Win! By this fine cap, I could   25
never leave kissing on't.

WIN

Come, indeed la, you are such a fool, still!

LITTLEWIT

No, but half a one, Win; you are the tother half: man and
wife make one fool, Win.—Good!—Is there the proctor, or
doctor indeed, i' the diocese, that ever had the fortune to   30
win him such a Win?—There I am again!—I do feel con-

13 *quirk* quip
    quiblin quibble, pun
15 *conceit* wit
17 *Jack* mechanical device for turning the spit when roasting meat
    (*OED*, sb.¹, 7)
20 *does convince* is overwhelming, is a knock-out
22 *beaver* hat made of beaver's fur
    coney-skin woman woman who sells rabbit-skins
23 *kiss it* kiss you (baby language)
24 *go* walk
26 *on't* you (literally 'of it')

---

16 *Archdeacon's court.* The court of Arches, where Littlewit is employed.
23 *Budge Row.* A street where the sellers of budge—a kind of fur, consisting
    of lamb's skin with the wool dressed outwards—had their shops.
24 *the Spanish lady.* The only information we have about this person, who
    evidently caused quite a stir in the fashionable world, is contained in
    Jonson's next play *The Devil is an Ass* (1616). There she is described as
              An *English* widdow, who hath lately trauell'd,
              But shee's call'd the *Spaniard;* 'cause she came
              Latest from thence: and keepes the *Spanish* habit.
              Such a rare woman! (II.viii, 25–39)
    A list of her many accomplishments follows.

ceits coming upon me more than I am able to turn tongue to.
A pox o' these pretenders to wit! your Three Cranes, Mitre,
and Mermaid men! Not a corn of true salt nor a grain of
right mustard amongst them all. They may stand for places   35
or so, again the next witfall, and pay twopence in a quart
more for their canary than other men. But gi' me the man
can start up a Justice of Wit out of six-shillings beer, and
give the law to all the poets and poet-suckers i' town!
Because they are the players' gossips? 'Slid, other men have   40
wives as fine as the players', and as well dressed. Come
hither, Win.   [*Kisses her*]

Act I, Scene ii

[*Enter to them*] WINWIFE

WINWIFE
Why, how now, Master Littlewit? Measuring of lips or
moulding of kisses? Which is it?

LITTLEWIT
Troth, I am a little taken with my Win's dressing here!
Does't not fine, Master Winwife? How do you apprehend,
sir? She would not ha' worn this habit. I challenge all   5

34 *corn* grain
34–5 *salt . . . mustard* sharp pungent wit
35 *stand for* strive for (*OED*, Stand, *v*., 71, † b., quoting *The Devil is
    an Ass*, I.vi, 36)
36 *again* in anticipation of
    witfall the letting-fall of a jest or repartee (Horsman)
37 *canary* light sweet wine from the Canary Islands
38 *six-shillings beer* small beer sold at six shillings a barrel
39 *poet-suckers* sucking poets, fledgling poets
39–40 *town! Because* ed. (Towne, because F)
40 *gossips* familiar acquaintances
    '*Slid* by God's eyelid
  4 *Does't* looks it
    How do you apprehend would you believe it

33–4 *Three Cranes, Mitre, and Mermaid.* London taverns, much frequented
    by playwrights and poets. The Mermaid, Jonson's favourite haunt, was,
    according to Thomas Fuller, the scene of many 'wit-combats' between
    him and Shakespeare (H & S, i. 50. n.3).
40 *Because . . . gossips?* Littlewit's mind suddenly reverts to the 'pretenders
    to wit', who, he thinks, give themselves airs.

Cheapside to shew such another—Moorfields, Pimlico Path,
or the Exchange, in a summer evening—with a lace to boot,
as this has. Dear Win, let Master Winwife kiss you. He
comes a-wooing to our mother, Win, and may be our father
perhaps, Win. There's no harm in him, Win. 10

WINWIFE
None i' the earth, Master Littlewit. [*Kisses her*]

LITTLEWIT
I envy no man my delicates, sir.

WINWIFE
Alas, you ha' the garden where they grow still! A wife here
with a strawberry-breath, cherry-lips, apricot-cheeks, and
a soft velvet head, like a melicotton. 15

LITTLEWIT
Good i'faith!—Now dullness upon me, that I had not that
before him, that I should not light on't as well as he! Velvet
head!

WINWIFE
But my taste, Master Littlewit, tends to fruit of a later kind:
the sober matron, your wife's mother. 20

LITTLEWIT
Ay! We know you are a suitor, sir. Win and I both wish you
well. By this licence here, would you had her, that your two
names were as fast in it as here are a couple. Win would fain
have a fine young father-i'-law with a feather, that her mother
might hood it and chain it with Mistress Overdo. But you 25
do not take the right course, Master Winwife.

WINWIFE
No? Master Littlewit, why?

LITTLEWIT
You are not mad enough.

WINWIFE
How? Is madness a right course?

12 *delicates* delights, delicacies
15 *melicotton* peach grafted on a quince
25 *hood it and chain it* shew an ostentatious pride in her husband's
hood and chain (the marks of his office)

---

6 *Cheapside.* The mercers and haberdashers had their shops in this street.
6–7 *Moorfields, Pimlico Path, or the Exchange.* All places of resort for the
citizens of London. Moorfields, to the north-east of the City walls, had
been laid out as a park in 1606. Pimlico in the village of Hoxton was a
house famous for its cakes and ale; and the New Exchange in the Strand,
built in 1608–09, had milliners' and sempstresses' shops which made it
attractive to women.

LITTLEWIT

    I say nothing, but I wink upon Win. You have a friend, one   30
Master Quarlous, comes here sometimes?

WINWIFE

    Why, he makes no love to her, does he?

LITTLEWIT

    Not a tokenworth that ever I saw, I assure you. But—

WINWIFE

    What?

LITTLEWIT

    He is the more madcap o' the two. You do not apprehend me.   35

WIN

    You have a hot coal i' your mouth now, you cannot hold.

LITTLEWIT

    Let me out with it, dear Win.

WIN

    I'll tell him myself.

LITTLEWIT

    Do, and take all the thanks, and much good do thy pretty
heart, Win.   40

WIN

    Sir, my mother has had her nativity-water cast lately by the
cunning men in Cow-lane, and they ha' told her her fortune,
and do ensure her she shall never have happy hour, unless
she marry within this sennight; and when it is, it must be a
madman, they say.   45

LITTLEWIT

    Ay, but it must be a gentleman madman.

WIN

    Yes, so the tother man of Moorfields says.

WINWIFE

    But does she believe 'em?

---

39 *good do* Ed. (do good F) good may it do
42 *cunning men* fortune-tellers
43 *ensure* assure
44 *sennight* period of seven nights, week

---

33 *tokenworth.* Tokens were pieces of metal issued by tradesmen to overcome the shortage of small change. As they had no general currency, a
'tokenworth' signified 'the least possible amount'.
41 *nativity-water cast.* Win seems to be confusing the casting (calculation)
of a horoscope with the casting (inspection) of urine for the diagnosis of
disease.
42 *Cow-lane.* The modern King Street.

LITTLEWIT

Yes, and has been at Bedlam twice since, every day, to
enquire if any gentleman be there, or to come there, mad!   50

WINWIFE

Why, this is a confederacy, a mere piece of practice upon
her, by these impostors!

LITTLEWIT

I tell her so; or else say I that they mean some young madcap gentleman, for the devil can equivocate as well as a
shopkeeper, and therefore would I advise you to be a little   55
madder than Master Quarlous, hereafter.

WINWIFE

Where is she? Stirring yet?

LITTLEWIT

Stirring! Yes, and studying an old elder, come from Banbury, a suitor that puts in here at meal-tide, to praise the
painful brethren, or pray that the sweet singers may be   60
restored; says a grace as long as his breath lasts him! Sometime the spirit is so strong with him it gets quite out of him,
and then my mother, or Win, are fain to fetch it again with
malmsey, or *aqua coelestis*.

WIN

Yes indeed, we have such a tedious life with him for his diet,   65

51 *confederacy* conspiracy
   mere sheer, downright
   practice trickery or imposture practised (*OED*, Practice, 7., citing
   this passage)
54 *equivocate* deal in ambiguities
60 *painful* diligent
63 *fetch it again* bring it back, i.e., revive him
64 *aqua coelestis* spirit distilled from wine, kind of brandy
65 *tedious* irksome

49 *Bedlam.* The hospital of St Mary of Bethlehem in Bishopsgate was a
   lunatic asylum. Citizens would go to visit it, much as they go to the Zoo
   today.
59 *meal-tide.* Littlewit is jeering at the Puritan habit of replacing 'mass', in
   words such as 'Christmas', with 'tide' meaning 'time'. Cf. *The Alchemist*,
   III.ii, 43, where, when Subtle mentions 'Christ-masse', Ananias inter-
   jects: 'Christ-tide, I pray you'.
60-1 *sweet singers . . . restored.* In the Geneva version of the Bible (1560)
   David is called 'the sweet singer of Israel' (2 Samuel, xxiii. 1). The
   reference here is, however, to the Puritan ministers who had been
   deprived of their livings because they refused to conform to the
   constitution of the Church of England as set out in 1604.

and his clothes too; he breaks his buttons and cracks seams
at every saying he sobs out.

LITTLEWIT

He cannot abide my vocation, he says.

WIN

No, he told my mother a proctor was a claw of the Beast,
and that she had little less than committed abomination in   70
marrying me so as she has done.

LITTLEWIT

Every line, he says, that a proctor writes, when it comes to
be read in the Bishop's court, is a long black hair, kembed
out of the tail of Antichrist.

WINWIFE

When came this proselyte?   75

LITTLEWIT

Some three days since.

Act I, Scene iii

[*Enter to them*] QUARLOUS

QUARLOUS

O sir, ha' you ta'en soil here? It's well a man may reach you
after three hours running, yet! What an unmerciful companion art thou, to quit thy lodging at such ungentlemanly
hours! None but a scattered covey of fiddlers, or one of
these rag-rakers in dunghills, or some marrow-bone man at   5
most, would have been up when thou wert gone abroad, by
all description. I pray thee what ailest thou, thou canst not
sleep? Hast thou thorns i' thy eyelids, or thistles i' thy bed?

WINWIFE

I cannot tell. It seems you had neither i' your feet, that took
this pain to find me.   10

QUARLOUS

No, an I had, all the lime-hounds o' the City should have

---

73 *kembed* combed
 1 *ta'en soil* taken refuge (technical term used in deer-hunting)
 5 *rag-rakers . . . marrow-bone man* equivalents of the modern rag-
   and-bone man
11 *lime-hounds* lyam-hounds, bloodhounds held on a lyam (leash)

---

69 *the Beast*. The Beast of the Apocalypse (Revelation, xiii) was equated by
   the Protestants generally, and especially by the Puritans, with Antichrist, identified as the Pope and the Church of Rome.

drawn after you by the scent rather. Master John Littlewit!
God save you, sir. 'Twas a hot night with some of us, last
night, John. Shall we pluck a hair o' the same wolf today,
Proctor John?   15

LITTLEWIT
Do you remember, Master Quarlous, what we discoursed on
last night?

QUARLOUS
Not I, John: nothing that I either discourse or do at those
times. I forfeit all to forgetfulness.

LITTLEWIT
No? Not concerning Win? Look you, there she is, and   20
dressed as I told you she should be. Hark you, sir, had you
forgot?

QUARLOUS
By this head, I'll beware how I keep you company, John,
when I drink, an you have this dangerous memory! That's
certain.   25

LITTLEWIT
Why, sir?

QUARLOUS
Why? [*To the rest*] We were all a little stained last night,
sprinkled with a cup or two, and I agreed with Proctor John
here to come and do somewhat with Win—I know not what
'twas—today; and he puts me in mind on't now; he says he   30
was coming to fetch me.—Before truth, if you have that fearful quality, John, to remember when you are sober, John,
what you promise drunk, John, I shall take heed of you, John.
For this once, I am content to wink at you. Where's your
wife? Come hither, Win.   *He kisseth her*   35

WIN
Why, John! Do you see this, John? Look you! Help me,
John.

12 *drawn after* tracked
13 *hot* hectic
14 *hair o' the same wolf* cf. 'hair of the dog that bit you'
18 *do* ed. (doe, F)
19 *times*. ed. (times F)
20 *Win*? Ed. (*Win*, F)
24 *drink* Ed. (drunke F)
27 *stained* the worse for drink
34 *wink at you* overlook your indiscretion

27 s.d. *To the rest* ed. (not in F). This direction seems necessary in view of
Quarlous's reference to 'Proctor John here' (ll. 28–9).

LITTLEWIT

O Win, fie, what do you mean, Win? Be womanly, Win.
Make an outcry to your mother, Win? Master Quarlous is an
honest gentleman, and our worshipful good friend, Win; and   40
he is Master Winwife's friend, too. And Master Winwife
comes a suitor to your mother, Win, as I told you before,
Win, and may perhaps be our father, Win. They'll do you no
harm, Win, they are both our worshipful good friends.
Master Quarlous! You must know Master Quarlous, Win;   45
you must not quarrel with Master Quarlous, Win.

QUARLOUS

No, we'll kiss again and fall in.

LITTLEWIT

Yes, do, good Win.

WIN

I'faith you are a fool, John.

LITTLEWIT

A fool-John she calls me, do you mark that, gentlemen?   50
Pretty littlewit of velvet! A fool-John!

QUARLOUS

She may call you an apple-John, if you use this.

WINWIFE

Pray thee forbear, for my respect somewhat.

QUARLOUS

Hoy-day! How respective you are become o' the sudden! I
fear this family will turn you reformed too; pray you come   55
about again. Because she is in possibility to be your daughter-
in-law, and may ask you blessing hereafter, when she courts

41 *friend* Ed. (friends F)
47 *fall in* (i) be reconciled (ii) copulate (cf. *Troilus and Cressida*,
   III.i, 96–7)
52 *use this* behave thus
54 *respective* concerned about good manners
57 *ask you blessing* ask you for your blessing
57–8 *courts it* plays the courtier

50 *fool-John*. As Littlewit seems pleased with this appellation, he is
   probably taking 'fool' as the term of endearment that it could be in the
   early seventeenth century (cf. *King Lear*, V.iii, 305).
52 *apple-John*. A kind of apple that was thought to be at its best when
   shrivelled and withered. It seems to have been regarded as symbolic of
   impotence (cf. *2 Henry IV*, II.iv, 3–10), and this sense fits well with
   Quarlous's jeer.

it to Tottenham to eat cream—well, I will forbear, sir; but
i'faith, would thou wouldst leave thy exercise of widow-
hunting once, this drawing after an old reverend smock by   60
the splay-foot! There cannot be an ancient tripe or trillibub
i' the town, but thou art straight nosing it; and 'tis a fine
occupation thou'lt confine thyself to when thou hast got one
—scrubbing a piece of buff, as if thou hadst the perpetuity of
Pannier-alley to stink in; or perhaps, worse, currying a   65
carcass that thou hast bound thyself to alive. I'll be sworn,
some of them, that thou art or hast been a suitor to, are so old
as no chaste or married pleasure can ever become 'em. The
honest instrument of procreation has, forty years since, left
to belong to 'em. Thou must visit 'em, as thou wouldst do a   70
tomb, with a torch, or three handfuls of link, flaming hot,
and so thou mayst hap to make 'em feel thee, and after, come
to inherit according to thy inches. A sweet course for a man
to waste the brand of life for, to be still raking himself a
fortune in an old woman's embers. We shall ha' thee, after   75
thou hast been but a month married to one of 'em, look like
the quartan ague and the black jaundice met in a face, and
walk as if thou hadst borrowed legs of a spinner and voice of
a cricket. I would endure to hear fifteen sermons a week for
her, and such coarse and loud ones as some of 'em must be;   80

58 *cream—well* Ed. (creame. Well F)
59 *exercise* regular occupation
60 *once* once for all
   drawing after tracking
   smock woman (derogatory)
61 *splay-foot* flat foot that turns outwards
   tripe or trillibub bag of guts (literally 'entrails')
64 *buff* (i) tough leather (ii) bare skin
   perpetuity perpetual tenure
65 *currying* (i) rubbing down (as with a horse) (ii) flattering
69–70 *left to belong* ceased to be of interest (*OED*, Belong, *v.*, 2.)
71 *link* tow and pitch used for torches
73 *inherit* possess your share (of the old woman's fortune)
   inches size, length (of penis)
74 *brand* fire
77 *quartan ague* fever in which the paroxysm occurs every fourth day
78 *spinner* spider
79 *for* instead of

58 *to Tottenham to eat cream.* Tottenham Court was famed for its cream,
   cakes, and ale.
65 *Pannier-alley.* A passage opening out of Pater Noster Row, where tripe
   and skins were sold.

I would e'en desire of Fate I might dwell in a drum, and take
in my sustenance with an old broken tobacco-pipe and a
straw. Dost thou ever think to bring thine ears or stomach to
the patience of a dry grace as long as thy tablecloth, and
droned out by thy son here, that might be thy father, till all   85
the meat o' thy board has forgot it was that day i' the
kitchen? Or to brook the noise made in a question of
predestination, by the good labourers and painful eaters
assembled together, put to 'em by the matron, your spouse,
who moderates with a cup of wine, ever and anon, and a   90
sentence out of Knox between? Or the perpetual spitting
before and after a sober drawn exhortation of six hours,
whose better part was the 'hum-ha-hum'? Or to hear
prayers groaned out over thy iron chests, as if they were
charms to break 'em? And all this, for the hope of two   95
apostle-spoons, to suffer! And a cup to eat a caudle in! For
that will be thy legacy. She'll ha' conveyed her state, safe
enough from thee, an she be a right widow.

WINWIFE
Alas, I am quite off that scent now.

QUARLOUS
How so?   100

WINWIFE
Put off by a brother of Banbury, one that, they say, is come
here, and governs all already.

QUARLOUS
What do you call him? I knew divers of those Banburians
when I was in Oxford.

WINWIFE
Master Littlewit can tell us.   105

LITTLEWIT
Sir!—Good Win, go in, and if Master Bartholmew Cokes

---

84 *patience* enduring, suffering
   dry (i) boring (ii) thirst-inducing (because of its length)
90 *moderates* acts as moderator, arbitrates
91 *sentence* maxim, well-known quotation
96 *caudle* warm concoction given to invalids
97 *conveyed her state* made a legal conveyance of her estate to another

---

91 *Knox*. The works of John Knox (*c*. 1505–1572) the Scottish reformer
   were popular among the Puritans.
96 *apostle-spoons*. It was customary for the sponsors at a baptism to give
   the infant a set of silver spoons with the figure of an apostle on the
   handle of each.

his man come for the licence—the little old fellow—let
him speak with me.   [*Exit* WIN]
What say you, gentlemen?

WINWIFE
What call you the reverend elder you told me of—your   110
Banbury man?

LITTLEWIT
Rabbi Busy, sir. He is more than an elder, he is a prophet,
sir.

QUARLOUS
O, I know him! A baker, is he not?

LITTLEWIT
He was a baker, sir, but he does dream now, and see visions; 115
he has given over his trade.

QUARLOUS
I remember that too—out of a scruple he took that, in spiced
conscience, those cakes he made were served to bridales,
maypoles, morrises, and such profane feasts and meetings.
His Christen name is Zeal-of-the-land.   120

LITTLEWIT
Yes, sir, Zeal-of-the-land Busy.

WINWIFE
How! what a name's there!

LITTLEWIT
O, they have all such names, sir. He was witness for Win here
—they will not be called godfathers—and named her Win-
the-fight. You thought her name had been Winifred, did you   125
not?

WINWIFE
I did indeed.

LITTLEWIT
He would ha' thought himself a stark reprobate, if it had.

QUARLOUS
Ay, for there was a blue-starch-woman o' the name, at the
same time. A notable hypocritical vermin it is; I know him.   130

117 *spiced* tender, scrupulous
118 *bridales* wedding feasts
119 *morrises* morris dances

---

119 *maypoles . . . meetings.* The more rigid Protestants, not merely the
Puritans, were strongly opposed to popular merry-makings such as these,
because they saw them, quite rightly, as survivals of paganism.
129 *blue-starch-woman.* Laundress who used blue starch to whiten and set
ruffs, which were associated with the sin of pride.

One that stands upon his face more than his faith, at all times;
ever in seditious motion, and reproving for vain-glory; of a
most lunatic conscience and spleen, and affects the violence
of singularity in all he does.—He has undone a grocer here,
in Newgate-market, that broked with him, trusted him with   135
currants, as arrant a zeal as he; that's by the way.—By his
profession, he will ever be i' the state of innocence, though,
and childhood; derides all antiquity; defies any other
learning than inspiration; and what discretion soever years
should afford him, it is all prevented in his original   140
ignorance. Ha' not to do with him, for he is a fellow of a most
arrogant and invincible dullness, I assure you. Who is this?

Act I, Scene iv

[*Enter to them*] WASP, [WIN]

WASP

By your leave, gentlemen, with all my heart to you, and God
you good morrow. Master Littlewit, my business is to you.
Is this licence ready?

LITTLEWIT

Here, I ha' it for you in my hand, Master Humphrey.

WASP

That's well. Nay, never open or read it to me; it's labour in   5
vain, you know. I am no clerk, I scorn to be saved by my
book; i'faith I'll hang first. Fold it up o' your word and gi' it
me. What must you ha' for't?

131 *stands upon his face* relies on his effrontery
132 *in seditious motion* causing trouble
136 *zeal* zealot
140 *prevented* balked, precluded
 1–2 *God you* God give you

---

135 *Newgate-market.* Established for the sale of corn and meal, this market
  was, by Jonson's time, dealing in other kinds of foodstuff as well.
  broked ed. (broke F) did business. All other editors retain 'broke', but
  then have difficulty in explaining it. This editor thinks that Jonson wrote
  'brokd', which the compositor turned into 'broke'.
6–7 *to be saved by my book.* Wasp is referring to the 'neck-verse', as it was
  called. Until 1827 anyone who could read a Latin verse (usually the
  beginning of the fifty-first psalm) printed in black-letter was exempted
  from sentence on his first conviction. Also known as 'benefit of clergy',
  since it was originally the privilege of exemption from trial before a
  secular court claimed by clergymen arraigned for felony, the neck-verse
  had saved Jonson's life in October 1598, when he was tried at the Old
  Bailey for killing the actor Gabriel Spencer in a duel.

LITTLEWIT
We'll talk of that anon, Master Humphrey.

WASP
Now, or not at all, good Master Proctor; I am for no anons,   10
I assure you.

LITTLEWIT
Sweet Win, bid Solomon send me the little black box within,
in my study.

WASP
Ay, quickly, good mistress, I pray you, for I have both eggs
o' the spit, and iron i' the fire.   [*Exit* WIN]   15
Say what you must have, good Master Littlewit.

LITTLEWIT
Why, you know the price, Master Numps.

WASP
I know? I know nothing, I. What tell you me of knowing,
now I am in haste? Sir, I do not know, and I will not know,
and I scorn to know; and yet, now I think on't, I will and do   20
know as well as another: you must have a mark for your thing
here, and eightpence for the box. I could ha' saved twopence
i' that, an I had bought it myself, but here's fourteen shillings
for you. Good Lord! How long your little wife stays! Pray
God, Solomon, your clerk, be not looking i' the wrong box,   25
Master Proctor.

LITTLEWIT
Good i'faith! No, I warrant you, Solomon is wiser than so,
sir.

WASP
Fie, fie, fie, by your leave, Master Littlewit, this is scurvy,
idle, foolish, and abominable, with all my heart; I do not like   30
it.

WINWIFE
Do you hear? Jack Littlewit, what business does thy pretty
head think this fellow may have, that he keeps such a coil
with?

18 *nothing, I.* Ed. (nothing. I, F)
18–19 *knowing, now I am in haste? Sir,* Ed. (knowing? (now I am in
     hast) Sir, F)
21 *mark* thirteen shillings and fourpence (two-thirds of a pound
     sterling)
33–4 *keeps such a coil with* makes such a fuss about

14–15 *eggs o'·the spit, and iron i' the fire.* Two proverbial expressions (Tilley,
     E86 and 199) denoting haste.

QUARLOUS

More than buying of gingerbread i' the Cloister here, for   35
that we allow him, or a gilt pouch i' the Fair?

LITTLEWIT

Master Quarlous, do not mistake him. He is his master's
both-hands, I assure you.

QUARLOUS

What? To pull on his boots, a-mornings, or his stockings?
Does he?   40

LITTLEWIT

Sir, if you have a mind to mock him, mock him softly, and
look tother way; for if he apprehend you flout him once, he
will fly at you presently. A terrible testy old fellow, and his
name is Wasp too.

QUARLOUS

Pretty insect! Make much on him.   45

WASP

A plague o' this box, and the pox too, and on him that made
it, and her that went for't, and all that should ha' sought it,
sent it, or brought it! Do you see, sir?

LITTLEWIT

Nay, good Master Wasp.

WASP

Good Master Hornet, turd i' your teeth, hold you your   50
tongue! Do not I know you? Your father was a pothecary, and
sold glisters, more than he gave, I wusse.

[Enter WIN, *with the box]*

And turd i' your little wife's teeth too—here she comes—
'twill make her spit, as fine as she is, for all her velvet-custard
on her head, sir.   55

LITTLEWIT

O! be civil, Master Numps.

WASP

Why, say I have a humour not to be civil; how then? Who
shall compel me? You?

38 *both-hands* factotum
43 *presently* immediately
52 *glisters* clysters, enemas
    I wusse iwis, certainly, truly
54 *velvet-custard* velvet hat in the shape of a pie (custard)
57 *humour* inclination

---

35 *the Cloister.* The Cloisters of Christ Church, near to Smithfield, were
used as a mart for various wares at the time of the Fair.

LITTLEWIT
Here is the box now.

WASP
Why, a pox o' your box, once again! Let your little wife   60
stale in it, an she will. Sir, I would have you to understand,
and these gentlemen too, if they please—

WINWIFE
With all our hearts, sir.

WASP
That I have a charge, gentlemen.

LITTLEWIT
They do apprehend, sir.   65

WASP
Pardon me, sir, neither they nor you can apprehend me
yet.—You are an ass.—I have a young master; he is now
upon his making and marring. The whole care of his well-
doing is now mine. His foolish schoolmasters have done
nothing but run up and down the country with him to beg   70
puddings and cake-bread of his tenants, and almost spoiled
him; he has learned nothing but to sing catches and repeat
Rattle bladder rattle and *O, Madge*. I dare not let him walk
alone, for fear of learning of vile tunes, which he will sing
at supper and in the sermon-times! If he meet but a carman   75
i' the street, and I find him not talk to keep him off on him,
he will whistle him and all his tunes over at night in his
sleep! He has a head full of bees! I am fain now, for this
little time I am absent, to leave him in charge with a gentlewoman. 'Tis true she is a Justice of Peace his wife, and a   80
gentlewoman o' the hood, and his natural sister; but what
may happen under a woman's government, there's the
doubt. Gentlemen, you do not know him; he is another
manner of piece than you think for! But nineteen year old,

61 *stale* piss (usually said of horses and cattle)
71 *puddings* sausages
   cake-bread bread of a fine cake-like quality
75 *carman* carter, carrier
81 *o' the hood* of consequence
83–4 *another manner of piece* a different sort of person

---

73 *Rattle bladder rattle*. Part of a proverbial piece of nonsense which ran:
   'Three blue beans in a blue bladder, rattle, bladder, rattle' (Tilley, B124).
   O, Madge. A ballad about the barn-owl, which was known as Madge or
   Madge-howlet.
78 *He has a head full of bees*. Proverbial (Tilley, H255) for 'he is full of
   crazy notions' (cf. 'He has bees in his bonnet').

and yet he is taller than either of you, by the head, God 85
bless him!

QUARLOUS
Well, methinks this is a fine fellow!

WINWIFE
He has made his master a finer by this description, I should
think.

QUARLOUS
'Faith, much about one; it's cross and pile; whether for a 90
new farthing.

WASP
I'll tell you, gentlemen—

LITTLEWIT
Will't please you drink, Master Wasp?

WASP
Why, I ha' not talked so long to be dry, sir. You see no dust
or cobwebs come out o' my mouth, do you? You'd ha' me 95
gone, would you?

LITTLEWIT
No, but you were in haste e'en now, Master Numps.

WASP
What an I were? So I am still, and yet I will stay too.
Meddle you with your match, your Win there; she has as
little wit as her husband it seems. I have others to talk to. 100

LITTLEWIT
She's my match indeed, and as little wit as I. Good!

WASP
We ha' been but a day and a half in town, gentlemen, 'tis
true. And yesterday i' the afternoon we walked London to
shew the city to the gentlewoman he shall marry, Mistress
Grace. But afore I will endure such another half day with 105
him I'll be drawn with a good gib-cat through the great pond
at home, as his uncle Hodge was! Why, we could not meet
that heathen thing all day but stayed him. He would name

90 *cross and pile* heads and tails. Proverbial (Tilley, C835), French
　　croix et pile (the two sides of a coin)
90-1 *whether for a new farthing* nothing in it, there is not a farthings-
　　worth of difference ('whether' = 'no matter which of the two')
108 *stayed him* stopped him in his tracks

106-7 *drawn . . . home.* The reference is to a rather primitive rustic joke. A
　　bet is made with a foolish person that a gib-cat (tom-cat) will draw him
　　through a pond. A rope is tied round him; the loose end is thrown
　　across the pond; and the cat fastened to it with packthread. Those
　　appointed to guide the cat then haul the victim through the water.

you all the signs over, as he went, aloud; and where he
spied a parrot or a monkey, there he was pitched with all   110
the little long-coats about him, male and female. No getting
him away! I thought he would ha' run mad o' the black
boy in Bucklersbury that takes the scurvy, roguy tobacco
there.

LITTLEWIT
You say true, Master Numps: there's such a one indeed.   115

WASP
It's no matter whether there be or no. What's that to you?

QUARLOUS
He will not allow of John's reading at any hand.

Act I, Scene v

[*Enter to them*] COKES, MISTRESS OVERDO, GRACE

COKES
O Numps! are you here, Numps? Look where I am, Numps!
And Mistress Grace, too! Nay, do not look angerly, Numps.
My sister is here, and all. I do not come without her.

WASP
What the mischief! Do you come with her? Or she with you?

COKES
We came all to seek you, Numps.   5

WASP
To seek me? Why, did you all think I was lost? Or run away
with your fourteen shillingsworth of small ware here? Or
that I had changed it i' the Fair for hobby-horses? 'Sprecious—to seek me!

MISTRESS OVERDO
Nay, good Master Numps, do you shew discretion, though   10
he be exorbitant, as Master Overdo says, an't be but for
conservation of the peace.

110 *pitched* fixed
111 *long-coats* children
117 *reading* comment
     at any hand on any account
  4 *mischief!* ed. (mischiefe, F)
  8 *changed* exchanged
8-9 *'Sprecious* by God's precious blood
 11 *exorbitant* out of hand (like something that has gone out of orbit)

113 *Bucklersbury*. A street in London where herbalists, who also sold
     tobacco, had their shops. Cf. *The Merry Wives of Windsor*, III.iii, 63.

WASP

Marry gip, goody she-Justice, Mistress French-hood!
Turd i' your teeth; and turd i' your French-hood's teeth,
too, to do you service, do you see? Must you quote your   15
Adam to me? You think you are Madam Regent still,
Mistress Overdo, when I am in place? No such matter, I
assure you; your reign is out when I am in, dame.

MISTRESS OVERDO

I am content to be in abeyance, sir, and be governed by
you. So should he too, if he did well. But 'twill be expected   20
you should also govern your passions.

WASP

Will't so forsooth? Good Lord! How sharp you are! With
being at Bedlam yesterday? Whetstone has set an edge
upon you, has he?

MISTRESS OVERDO

Nay, if you know not what belongs to your dignity, I do,   25
yet, to mine.

WASP

Very well, then.

COKES

Is this the licence, Numps? For love's sake, let me see't. I
never saw a licence.

WASP

Did you not so? Why, you shall not see't, then.   30

COKES

An you love me, good Numps.

WASP

Sir, I love you, and yet I do not love you i' these fooleries.
Set your heart at rest; there's nothing in't but hard words.
And what would you see't for?

---

13 *French-hood* kind of hood fashionable among citizens' wives

---

13 *Marry gip.* An exclamatory oath which probably originated from 'By
    Mary Gipcy' ('by St Mary of Egypt'), but then became confused with
    'Gip' meaning (i) gee-up (to a horse) and (ii) 'go along with you' (to a
    person).
23 *Whetstone.* 'A whetstone cannot cut but yet it makes tools cut' was a
    proverbial saying (Tilley, W299), but there is also a reference here to a
    specific person. H & S suggest that Whetstone was probably 'the name
    of a keeper at the Bethlehem Hospital', but, in view of the context, it
    would seem far more likely that it was the name of a well-known inmate.
    Cf. 'the dullness of the fool is the whetstone of the wits' (*As You Like It*,
    I.ii, 49–50).

COKES

I would see the length and the breadth on't, that's all; and 35
I will see't now, so I will.

WASP

You sha' not see it here.

COKES

Then I'll see't at home, and I'll look upo' the case here.

WASP

Why, do so. [*Holds up the box*] A man must give way to him
a little in trifles, gentlemen. These are errors, diseases of 40
youth, which he will mend when he comes to judgement
and knowledge of matters. I pray you conceive so, and
I thank you. And I pray you pardon him, and I thank you
again.

QUARLOUS

Well, this dry nurse, I say still, is a delicate man. 45

WINWIFE

And I am for the cosset, his charge! Did you ever see a
fellow's face more accuse him for an ass?

QUARLOUS

Accuse him? It confesses him one without accusing. What
pity 'tis yonder wench should marry such a cokes!

WINWIFE

'Tis true. 50

QUARLOUS

She seems to be discreet, and as sober as she is handsome.

WINWIFE

Ay, and if you mark her, what a restrained scorn she casts
upon all his behaviour and speeches!

COKES

Well, Numps, I am now for another piece of business more,
the Fair, Numps, and then— 55

WASP

Bless me! deliver me! help! hold me! the Fair!

COKES

Nay, never fidge up and down, Numps, and vex itself. I am
resolute Bartholmew in this. I'll make no suit on't to you.
'Twas all the end of my journey, indeed, to shew Mistress

---

40 *trifles, gentlemen* Ed. (trifles: Gentlemen F)
46 *cosset* spoilt child (literally 'lamb brought up by hand')
49 *cokes* ninny
57 *fidge* move restlessly, fidget
    itself yourself

Grace my Fair. I call't my Fair because of Bartholmew: you   60
know my name is Bartholmew, and Bartholmew Fair.

LITTLEWIT

That was mine afore, gentlemen—this morning. I had that
i'faith, upon his licence; believe me, there he comes after me.

QUARLOUS

Come, John, this ambitious wit of yours, I am afraid, will do
you no good i' the end.   65

LITTLEWIT

No? Why sir?

QUARLOUS

You grow so insolent with it, and overdoing, John, that if you
look not to it, and tie it up, it will bring you to some obscure
place in time, and there 'twill leave you.

WINWIFE

Do not trust it too much, John; be more sparing, and use it   70
but now and then. A wit is a dangerous thing in this age; do
not overbuy it.

LITTLEWIT

Think you so, gentlemen? I'll take heed on't hereafter.

WIN

Yes, do, John.

COKES

A pretty little soul, this same Mistress Littlewit! Would I   75
might marry her.

GRACE

[Aside] So would I, or anybody else, so I might scape you.

COKES

Numps, I will see it, Numps, 'tis decreed. Never be melancholy for the matter.

WASP

Why, see it, sir, see it, do see it! Who hinders you? Why do   80
you not go see it? 'Slid, see it.

COKES

The Fair, Numps, the Fair.

WASP

Would the Fair and all the drums and rattles in't were i' your
belly for me; they are already i' your brain. He that had the
means to travel your head, now, should meet finer sights   85
than any are i' the Fair, and make a finer voyage on't, to see
it all hung with cockle-shells, pebbles, fine wheat-straws,
and here and there a chicken's feather and a cobweb.

67 *insolent* extravagant
72 *overbuy* pay too much for (by allowing it to get you into trouble)

QUARLOUS

Good faith, he looks, methinks, an you mark him, like one
that were made to catch flies, with his Sir Cranion legs.   90

WINWIFE

And his Numps, to flap 'em away.

WASP

God be w'you, sir. There's your bee in a box, and much
good do't you.   [*Gives him the box, and offers to leave*]

COKES

Why, 'your friend and Bartholmew', an you be so con-
tumacious.   95

QUARLOUS

What mean you, Numps?

WASP

I'll not be guilty, I, gentlemen.

MISTRESS OVERDO

You will not let him go, brother, and lose him?

COKES

Who can hold that will away? I had rather lose him than the
Fair, I wusse.   100

WASP

You do not know the inconvenience, gentlemen, you
persuade to; nor what trouble I have with him in these
humours. If he go to the Fair, he will buy of everything to a
baby there; and household-stuff for that too. If a leg or an
arm on him did not grow on, he would lose it i' the press.   105
Pray heaven I bring him off with one stone! And then he is
such a ravener after fruit! You will not believe what a coil I
had t'other day to compound a business between a
Catherine-pear-woman and him about snatching! 'Tis
intolerable, gentlemen.   110

WINWIFE

O! but you must not leave him now to these hazards, Numps.

90 *Sir Cranion* daddy-long-legs
92 *God be w'you* God be with you (original form of 'good-bye')
94 '*your . . . Bartholmew*' ed. (your . . . *Bartholmew* F) farewell.
     Cokes is using a common form of subscribing a letter.
98 *lose* Ed. (loose F)
99 *Who can hold that will away?* Proverbial (Tilley, H515); *that* =
     him who.
     lose Ed. (loose F)
103–4 *buy of everything to a baby there* buy some of everything there,
     down to and including a doll
106 *stone* testicle
107 *coil* trouble, fuss

WASP

Nay, he knows too well I will not leave him, and that makes
him presume. Well, sir, will you go now? If you have such an
itch i' your feet to foot it to the Fair, why do you stop? Am I
your tarriers? Go, will you go! Sir, why do you not go?   115

COKES

O Numps! have I brought you about? Come, Mistress Grace,
and sister, I am resolute Bat, i'faith, still.

GRACE

Truly, I have no such fancy to the Fair, nor ambition to see
it; there's none goes thither of any quality or fashion.

COKES

O Lord, sir! You shall pardon me, Mistress Grace, we are   120
enow of ourselves to make it a fashion; and for qualities, let
Numps alone, he'll find qualities.

       [*Exeunt* COKES, WASP, GRACE, MISTRESS OVERDO]

QUARLOUS

What a rogue in apprehension is this! To understand her
language no better!

WINWIFE

Ay, and offer to marry to her! Well, I will leave the chase of   125
my widow for today, and directly to the Fair. These flies
cannot, this hot season, but engender us excellent creeping
sport.

QUARLOUS

A man that has but a spoonful of brain would think so.
Farewell, John.   [*Exeunt* QUARLOUS, WINWIFE]   130

LITTLEWIT

Win, you see 'tis in fashion to go to the Fair, Win. We must
to the Fair too, you and I, Win. I have an affair i' the Fair,
Win, a puppet-play of mine own making—say nothing—that
I writ for the motion-man, which you must see, Win.

WIN

I would I might, John, but my mother will never consent to   135
such a—'profane motion' she will call it.

115 *tarriers* hinderers
    will you go! ed. (will you goe? F) if you want to go
116 *about* round
119 *quality* social standing
121 *qualities* features of character
121–2 *let Numps alone* leave it to Numps
123 *rogue in apprehension* lack-brain, unintelligent beggar
134 *motion-man* puppet-master
136 *a—'profane motion' she* ed. (a *prophane motion:* she F)

LITTLEWIT

Tut, we'll have a device, a dainty one.—Now, Wit, help at a
pinch; good Wit, come; come, good Wit, an't be thy will.—
I have it, Win, I have it i'faith, and 'tis a fine one. Win, long
to eat of a pig, sweet Win, i' the Fair, do you see? I' the   140
heart o' the Fair; not at Pie-corner. Your mother will do
anything, Win, to satisfy your longing, you know; pray thee
long presently, and be sick o' the sudden, good Win. I'll go
in and tell her. Cut thy lace i' the mean time, and play the
hypocrite, sweet Win.   145

WIN

No, I'll not make me unready for it. I can be hypocrite
enough, though I were never so strait-laced.

LITTLEWIT

You say true. You have been bred i' the family, and brought
up to't. Our mother is a most elect hypocrite, and has maintained us all this seven year with it, like gentlefolks.   150

WIN

Ay, let her alone, John; she is not a wise wilful widow for
nothing, nor a sanctified sister for a song. And let me alone
too; I ha' somewhat o' the mother in me; you shall see.
Fetch her, fetch her! Ah, ah!   [*Exit* LITTLEWIT]

Act I, Scene vi

[*Enter to her*] PURECRAFT, LITTLEWIT

PURECRAFT

Now the blaze of the beauteous discipline fright away this
evil from our house! How now, Win-the-fight, child, how do
you? Sweet child, speak to me.

WIN

Yes, forsooth.

---

146 *make me unready* undress
147 *strait-laced* (i) wearing a tightly laced bodice (ii) rigidly moral
153 *mother* (i) female parent (ii) hysteria
  1 *discipline* religious practice (of the Puritans)

---

141 *Pie-corner*. The site of an old tavern, whose sign was a magpie, this place
   in West Smithfield was given over to cook-shops. It was at Pie-corner
   that Face first met Subtle 'Taking his meale of steeme in, from cookes
   stalls' (*The Alchemist*, I.i, 26).
150 *this seven year*. The statement is endorsed by Purecraft's confession at
   V.ii, 50–60.

PURECRAFT

Look up, sweet Win-the-fight, and suffer not the enemy to   5
enter you at this door; remember that your education has
been with the purest. What polluted one was it that named
first the unclean beast, pig, to you, child?

WIN

Uh, Uh!

LITTLEWIT

Not I, o' my sincerity, mother. She longed above three hours   10
ere she would let me know it. Who was it, Win?

WIN

A profane black thing with a beard, John.

PURECRAFT

O! resist it, Win-the-fight, it is the Tempter, the wicked
Tempter; you may know it by the fleshly motion of pig. Be
strong against it and its foul temptations in these assaults,   15
whereby it broacheth flesh and blood, as it were, on the
weaker side; and pray against its carnal provocations, good
child, sweet child, pray.

LITTLEWIT

Good mother, I pray you that she may eat some pig, and her
belly-ful, too; and do not you cast away your own child, and   20
perhaps one of mine, with your tale of the Tempter. How do
you, Win? Are you not sick?

WIN

Yes, a great deal, John. Uh, uh!

PURECRAFT

What shall we do? Call our zealous brother Busy hither, for
his faithful fortification in this charge of the adversary.   25

[*Exit* LITTLEWIT]

Child, my dear child, you shall eat pig, be comforted, my
sweet child.

WIN

Ay, but i' the Fair, mother.

PURECRAFT

I mean i' the Fair, if it can be any way made or found lawful.

[*Enter* LITTLEWIT]

Where is our brother Busy? Will he not come? Look up, child.   30

LITTLEWIT

Presently, mother, as soon as he has cleansed his beard. I
found him, fast by the teeth i' the cold turkey-pie i' the

14 *motion* prompting

cupboard, with a great white loaf on his left hand, and a glass
of malmsey on his right.

PURECRAFT
Slander not the brethren, wicked one.   35

[*Enter to them*] BUSY

LITTLEWIT
Here he is now, purified, mother.

PURECRAFT
O Brother Busy! your help here to edify and raise us up in a
scruple. My daughter Win-the-fight is visited with a
natural disease of women, called 'A longing to eat pig'.

LITTLEWIT
Ay sir, a Bartholmew pig, and in the Fair.   40

PURECRAFT
And I would be satisfied from you, religiously-wise, whether
a widow of the sanctified assembly, or a widow's daughter,
may commit the act without offence to the weaker sisters.

BUSY
Verily, for the disease of longing, it is a disease, a carnal
disease, or appetite, incident to women; and as it is carnal, 45
and incident, it is natural, very natural. Now pig, it is a meat,
and a meat that is nourishing, and may be longed for, and so
consequently eaten; it may be eaten; very exceeding well
eaten. But in the Fair, and as a Bartholmew-pig, it cannot be
eaten, for the very calling it a Bartholmew-pig, and to eat it   50
so, is a spice of idolatry, and you make the Fair no better than
one of the high places. This, I take it, is the state of the
question. A high place.

LITTLEWIT
Ay, but in state of necessity, place should give place, Master
Busy.—I have a conceit left, yet.   55

PURECRAFT
Good Brother Zeal-of-the-land, think to make it as lawful as
you can.

37–8 *raise us up in a scruple* assist us in a question of conscience
51 *spice* kind, species

---

54 *place should give place*. Littlewit is quibbling, taking Busy's 'high place'
(in the Scriptural sense of a place of idolatrous worship and sacrifice) as
'high rank or position' and saying that a man in high place must yield
precedence to a better man—a version of *noblesse oblige*. Cf. the proverb
(Tilley, M238) 'Man honours the place, not the place the man'.

LITTLEWIT

Yes sir, and as soon as you can; for it must be, sir. You see
the danger my little wife is in, sir.

PURECRAFT

Truly, I do love my child dearly, and I would not have her   60
miscarry, or hazard her first fruits, if it might be otherwise.

BUSY

Surely, it may be otherwise, but it is subject to construction,
subject, and hath a face of offence with the weak, a great face,
a foul face, but that face may have a veil put over it, and be
shadowed, as it were; it may be eaten, and in the Fair, I take   65
it, in a booth, the tents of the wicked. The place is not much,
not very much; we may be religious in midst of the profane,
so it be eaten with a reformed mouth, with sobriety, and
humbleness; not gorged in with gluttony, or greediness;
there's the fear; for, should she go there as taking pride in   70
the place, or delight in the unclean dressing, to feed the
vanity of the eye, or the lust of the palate, it were not well,
it were not fit, it were abominable, and not good.

LITTLEWIT

Nay, I knew that afore, and told her on't. But courage, Win,
we'll be humble enough; we'll seek out the homeliest booth   75
i' the Fair, that's certain; rather than fail, we'll eat it o' the
ground.

PURECRAFT

Ay, and I'll go with you myself, Win-the-fight, and my
brother, Zeal-of-the-land, shall go with us too, for our better
consolation.   80

WIN

Uh, uh!

LITTLEWIT

Ay, and Solomon too, Win; the more the merrier, Win.
[*Aside to* WIN] We'll leave Rabbi Busy in a booth.—
Solomon, my cloak.

[*Enter to them*] SOLOMON

SOLOMON

Here, sir.   85

BUSY

In the way of comfort to the weak, I will go and eat. I will eat
exceedingly, and prophesy. There may be a good use made

63 *face of offence* look of a stumbling-block
70 *fear* thing to be feared

of it, too, now I think on't: by the public eating of swine's
flesh, to profess our hate and loathing of Judaism, whereof
the brethren stand taxed. I will therefore eat, yea, I will eat   90
exceedingly.

LITTLEWIT

Good i'faith, I will eat heartily too, because I will be no Jew;
I could never away with that stiff-necked generation. And
truly, I hope my little one will be like me, that cries for pig
so, i' the mother's belly.   95

BUSY

Very likely, exceeding likely, very exceeding likely.

[Exeunt]

Act II, Scene i

[Enter] JUSTICE OVERDO, [disguised as Mad Arthur of Bradley]

OVERDO

Well, in Justice' name, and the King's, and for the Commonwealth! Defy all the world, Adam Overdo, for a disguise, and
all story; for thou hast fitted thyself, I swear. Fain would I
meet the Lynceus now, that eagle's eye, that piercing
Epidaurian serpent, as my Quintus Horace calls him, that   5

93 *away with* tolerate, put up with
   stiff-necked generation stubborn race (cf. Deuteronomy, ix. 13,
   Acts, vii, 51, etc.)
1-2 *Commonwealth* common weal, general good
3 *fitted* perfectly furnished

89-90 *Judaism, whereof the brethren stand taxed.* The Puritans were accused
   (taxed) of Judaism not only because of the emphasis they placed on the
   Old Testament but also because, very much to their credit, they were,
   first in Holland and then in England, more tolerant in their attitude
   towards the Jews than other Christian sects were. It was Oliver Cromwell
   who allowed the Jews to return to England from which they had been
   expelled by Edward I.
4 *Lynceus.* One of the Argonauts, famous for his extraordinarily keen
   eyesight.
4-5 *piercing Epidaurian serpent . . . him.* Horace writes:
      cur in amicorum vitiis tam cernis acutum
      quam aut aquila aut serpens Epidaurius? (*Satires*, I.iii. 26-7):
   'Why, when you look into the failings of your friends, are you as sharp-
   sighted as an eagle or a serpent of Epidaurus?' Serpents, which were
   supposed to have very keen eyes, were sacred to Aesculapius, the god of
   medicine, who was worshipped in the form of a serpent at Epidaurus in
   Greece.

could discover a Justice of Peace, and lately of the Quorum,
under this covering. They may have seen many a fool in the
habit of a Justice; but never till now a Justice in the habit of
a fool. Thus must we do, though, that wake for the public
good; and thus hath the wise magistrate done in all ages. 10
There is a doing of right out of wrong, if the way be found.
Never shall I enough commend a worthy worshipful man,
sometime a capital member of this city, for his high wisdom in
this point, who would take you, now the habit of a porter,
now of a carman, now of the dog-killer in this month of 15
August, and in the winter of a seller of tinder-boxes. And
what would he do in all these shapes? Marry, go you into
every alehouse, and down into every cellar; measure the
length of puddings, take the gauge of black pots and cans, ay,
and custards, with a stick; and their circumference, with a 20
thread; weigh the loaves of bread on his middle finger. Then
would he send for 'em, home; give the puddings to the poor,
the bread to the hungry, the custards to his children; break
the pots, and burn the cans, himself; he would not trust his
corrupt officers; he would do't himself. Would all men in 25
authority would follow this worthy precedent! For, alas, as
we are public persons, what do we know? Nay, what can we
know? We hear with other men's ears; we see with other
men's eyes; a foolish constable or a sleepy watchman is all our
information. He slanders a gentleman, by the virtue of his 30
place, as he calls it, and we, by the vice of ours, must
believe him; as, a while agone, they made me, yea me, to
mistake an honest zealous pursuivant for a seminary, and a

9 *wake* are vigilant, keep watch and ward
13 *capital* leading
29 *eyes;* Ed. (eyes? F)
33 *pursuivant* state official having power to execute warrants for arrest
seminary Roman Catholic priest trained at one of the seminaries in
Europe

---

6 *Quorum.* Certain justices, selected for their learning and ability, whose
presence was necessary to constitute a bench of magistrates.
12–13 *a worthy . . . city.* C. S. Alden thinks the individual in question was
Sir Thomas Hayes, Lord Mayor of London in 1614, who disguised
himself in order to visit and find out the truth about 'lewd houses' and
the malpractices of those who kept 'victualling houses and ale-houses'
(see H & S, x. 185).
15 *dog-killer.* Acting under the mistaken impression that dogs carried the
infection, the city fathers hired a dog-killer to exterminate all stray dogs
in times of plague, thus freeing the brown rat, whose fleas were the true
source of the infection, from its chief enemy.

proper young Bachelor of Music for a bawd. This we are
subject to, that live in high place: all our intelligence is idle,   35
and most of our intelligencers knaves; and, by your leave,
ourselves thought little better, if not arrant fools, for
believing 'em. I, Adam Overdo, am resolved therefore to
spare spy-money hereafter, and make mine own discoveries.
Many are the yearly enormities of this Fair, in whose courts   40
of Pie-powders I have had the honour, during the three days
sometimes, to sit as judge. But this is the special day for
detection of those foresaid enormities. Here is my black book
for the purpose; this the cloud that hides me; under this
covert I shall see and not be seen. On, Junius Brutus! And   45
as I began, so I'll end: in Justice' name, and the King's, and
for the Commonwealth!   [*Stands aside*]

Act II, Scene ii

[*Enter*] LEATHERHEAD [*and*] TRASH

LEATHERHEAD
The Fair's pestilence dead, methinks. People come not
abroad today, whatever the matter is. Do you hear, Sister
Trash, Lady o' the Basket? Sit farther with your gingerbread-
progeny there, and hinder not the prospect of my shop, or
I'll ha' it proclaimed i' the Fair what stuff they are made on.   5
TRASH
Why, what stuff are they made on, Brother Leatherhead?
Nothing but what's wholesome, I assure you.

35 *intelligence* information
   idle unreliable
36 *intelligencers* spies, informers
40 *enormities* monstrous offences and irregularities
   of Ed. (of of F)
45 *covert* disguise
 1 *pestilence* plaguily

40–1 *courts of Pie-powders*. Summary courts held at fairs and markets to
administer justice among the itinerant dealers and their customers.
'Pie-powders' (French *pied-poudreux*) = 'dustyfoot', 'wayfarer'.
45 *Junius Brutus*. Lucius Junius Brutus, who drove the Tarquins out of
Rome and founded the Roman Republic, is invoked by Overdo for two
reasons: he disguised himself as an idiot in order to escape the vigilance
of Tarquinius Superbus, and he sentenced his own sons to death when
they conspired to restore the Tarquins, thus winning a reputation as an
inflexible judge.

LEATHERHEAD
Yes, stale bread, rotten eggs, musty ginger, and dead honey,
you know.

OVERDO
[*Aside*] Ay! have I met with enormity so soon?   10

LEATHERHEAD
I shall mar your market, old Joan.

TRASH
Mar my market, thou too-proud pedlar? Do thy worst. I
defy thee; ay, and thy stable of hobby-horses. I pay for my
ground as well as thou dost. An thou wrong'st me, for all
thou art parcel-poet and an inginer, I'll find a friend shall   15
right me, and make a ballad of thee and thy cattle all over.
Are you puffed up with the pride of your wares? Your
arsedine?

LEATHERHEAD
Go to, old Joan, I'll talk with you anon; and take you down
too afore Justice Overdo. He is the man must charm you; I'll   20
ha' you i' the Pie-powders.

TRASH
Charm me? I'll meet thee face to face afore his worship when
thou dar'st; and though I be a little crooked o' my body, I'll
be found as upright in my dealing as any woman in
Smithfield, I. Charm me!   25

OVERDO
[*Aside*] I am glad to hear my name is their terror yet; this is
doing of justice.

[*Enter to them*] PASSENGERS

LEATHERHEAD
What do you lack? What is't you buy? What do you lack?
Rattles, drums, halberts, horses, babies o' the best? Fiddles
o'th'finest?   30

Enter COSTARDMONGER [*followed by*] NIGHTINGALE

COSTARDMONGER
Buy any pears, pears, fine, very fine pears!

10 s.p. OVERDO Ed. (IVS. F)
14 *dost. An* Ed. (dost, and F)
15 *parcel-poet* a bit of a poet, part-time poet
   inginer, I'll Ed. (Inginer. I'll F); *inginer* designer, contriver of
   shows
16 *cattle* wares
18 *arsedine* gold-coloured alloy used for ornamenting toys
20 *charm you* subdue your tongue (as though by magic)

TRASH
   Buy any gingerbread, gilt gingerbread!
NIGHTINGALE   [*Sings*]
      Hey, now the Fair's a filling!
      O, for a tune to startle
      The birds o' the booths here billing   35
      Yearly with old Saint Bartle!
      The drunkards they are wading,
      The punks and chapmen trading;
      Who'd see the Fair without his lading?
   Buy any ballads, new ballads?   40

                    [*Enter*] URSLA

URSLA
   Fie upon't! Who would wear out their youth and prime thus
   in roasting of pigs, that had any cooler vocation? Hell's a kind
   of cold cellar to't, a very fine vault, o' my conscience! What,
   Mooncalf!
MOONCALF
   [*Within*] Here, Mistress.   45
NIGHTINGALE
   How now, Ursla? In a heat, in a heat?
URSLA
   [*To* MOONCALF] My chair, you false faucet you; and my
   morning's draught, quickly, a bottle of ale to quench me,
   rascal.—I am all fire and fat, Nightingale, I shall e'en melt
   away to the first woman, a rib, again, I am afraid. I do water   50
   the ground in knots as I go, like a great garden-pot; you may
   follow me by the S's I make.
NIGHTINGALE
   Alas, good Urs! Was Zekiel here this morning?
URSLA
   Zekiel? What Zekiel?
NIGHTINGALE
   Zekiel Edgworth, the civil cutpurse—you know him well   55
   enough—he that talks bawdy to you still. I call him my
   secretary.

   32 *gilt* given a golden appearance (cf. 'to take the gilt off the ginger-
         bread')
   37 *wading* half seas over
   39 *lading* freight (of fairings)
   47 *faucet* tap for a barrel
   51 *knots* intricate figures of criss-cross lines
   57 *secretary* confidant

URSLA
He promised to be here this morning, I remember.

NIGHTINGALE
When he comes, bid him stay. I'll be back again presently.

URSLA
Best take your morning's dew in your belly, Nightingale.   60

MOONCALF brings in the chair

Come, sir, set it here. Did not I bid you should get this chair
let out o' the sides for me, that my hips might play? You'll
never think of anything till your dame be rump-galled. 'Tis
well, changeling; because it can take in your grasshopper's
thighs, you care for no more. Now you look as you had been   65
i' the corner o' the booth, fleaing your breech with a candle's
end, and set fire o' the Fair. Fill, stote, fill.

OVERDO
[*Aside*] This pig-woman do I know, and I will put her in for
my second enormity. She hath been before me, punk,
pinnace, and bawd, any time these two and twenty years,   70
upon record i' the Pie-powders.

URSLA
Fill again, you unlucky vermin.

MOONCALF
'Pray you be not angry, mistress; I'll ha' it widened anon.

URSLA
No, no, I shall e'en dwindle away to't ere the Fair be done,
you think, now you ha' heated me! A poor vexed thing I am.   75
I feel myself dropping already as fast as I can; two stone o'
suet a day is my proportion. I can but hold life and soul
together with this—here's to you, Nightingale—and a whiff
of tobacco at most. Where's my pipe now? Not filled? Thou
arrant incubee!   80

NIGHTINGALE
Nay, Ursla, thou'lt gall between the tongue and the teeth
with fretting now.

URSLA
How can I hope that ever he'll discharge his place of trust—

64 *changeling* stupid or ugly child left by the fairies in place of one
   they have stolen
66 *fleaing* removing fleas from
67 *stote* (i) stoat (ii) stot (clumsy stupid person)
70 *pinnace* go-between
77 *proportion* estimate
80 *incubee* offspring of a woman and an incubus

tapster, a man of reckoning under me—that remembers
nothing I say to him?   [*Exit* NIGHTINGALE]   85
But look to't, sirrah, you were best. Threepence a pipeful I
will ha' made of all my whole half-pound of tobacco, and a
quarter of a pound of coltsfoot mixed with it too, to itch it
out. I that have dealt so long in the fire will not be to seek in
smoke now. Then, six and twenty shillings a barrel I will   90
advance o' my beer, and fifty shillings a hundred o' my bottle-
ale; I ha' told you the ways how to raise it. Froth your cans
well i' the filling at length, rogue, and jog your bottles o' the
buttock, sirrah; then skink out the first glass, ever, and drink
with all companies, though you be sure to be drunk; you'll   95
misreckon the better, and be less ashamed on't. But your
true trick, rascal, must be to be ever busy, and mis-take away
the bottles and cans in haste before they be half drunk off,
and never hear anybody call, if they should chance to mark
you, till you ha' brought fresh, and be able to forswear 'em.   100
Give me a drink of ale.

OVERDO
[*Aside*] This is the very womb and bed of enormity gross as
herself! This must all down for enormity, all, every whit on't.
                                                    One knocks

URSLA
Look who's there, sirrah! Five shillings a pig is my price—
at least. If it be a sow-pig, sixpence more. If she be a great- 105
bellied wife, and long for't, sixpence more for that.

OVERDO
[*Aside*] O tempora! O mores! I would not ha' lost my discovery
of this one grievance for my place and worship o' the bench.
How is the poor subject abused here! Well, I will fall in with
her, and with her Mooncalf, and wind out wonders of   110
enormity.   [*Comes forward*]

88 *itch* eke
89 *to seek in* short of
91 *advance* raise the price
93 *at length* i.e., with the can held as far below the spigot as possible
94 *skink* pour
107 *O tempora! O mores!* (Cicero, *In Catilinam*, I.i. 2) What an age!
    What manners!

110 *wind* ed. (winne F) smell, scent (*OED*, Wind, *v.*², c.). It is difficult to
    find any parallel for 'win out' in the sense it should have here, whereas
    the hunting term 'wind out' fits what Overdo sees himself as doing and
    is consonant with the use of animal imagery in the play. Cf. Barry's *Ram
    Alley* (1607–08): 'No nose to smell, and winde out all your tricks' (II.i).

By thy leave, goodly woman and the fatness of the Fair, oily
as the King's constable's lamp, and shining as his shoeing-
horn! Hath thy ale virtue, or thy beer strength, that the
tongue of man may be tickled, and his palate pleased in the   115
morning? Let thy pretty nephew here go search and see.

URSLA
What new roarer is this?

MOONCALF
O Lord, do you not know him, mistress? 'Tis mad Arthur of
Bradley, that makes the orations.—Brave master, old
Arthur of Bradley, how do you? Welcome to the Fair! When   120
shall we hear you again to handle your matters, with your back
again a booth, ha? I ha' been one o' your little disciples, i' my
days!

OVERDO
Let me drink, boy, with my love, thy aunt here, that I may
be eloquent; but of thy best, lest it be bitter in my mouth,   125
and my words fall foul on the Fair.

URSLA
Why dost thou not fetch him drink? And offer him to sit?

MOONCALF
Is't ale or beer, Master Arthur?

OVERDO
Thy best, pretty stripling, thy best; the same thy dove
drinketh, and thou drawest on holy-days.   130

URSLA
Bring him a sixpenny bottle of ale; they say a fool's handsel
is lucky.

OVERDO
Bring both, child. Ale for Arthur, and beer for Bradley. Ale
for thine aunt, boy.   [*Exit* MOONCALF]
[*Aside*] My disguise takes to the very wish and reach of it. I   135
shall, by the benefit of this, discover enough and more, and

122 *again* against
124 *aunt* gossip
129 *dove* darling
135 *takes* works, succeeds

118–19 *mad Arthur of Bradley*. The hero of an old song, going back at least
    as far as the mid-sixteenth century, called 'The Ballad of the Wedding
    of Arthur of Bradley'. Jonson endows him with a fondness for making
    orations in order to fit him for the role Overdo takes on.
131–2 *a fool's handsel is lucky*. A well-known proverb (Tilley, F517);
    'handsel' is the first money taken in a day.

yet get off with the reputation of what I would be—a
certain middling thing between a fool and a madman.

Act II, Scene iii

[Enter] KNOCKEM *to them*

KNOCKEM

What! my little lean Ursla! my she-bear! art thou alive yet?
With thy litter of pigs to grunt out another Bartholmew Fair,
ha?

URSLA

Yes, and to amble afoot, when the Fair is done, to hear you
groan out of a cart, up the heavy hill.   5

KNOCKEM

Of Holborn, Ursla, meanst thou so? For what? For what,
pretty Urs?

URSLA

For cutting halfpenny purses, or stealing little penny dogs out
o' the Fair.

KNOCKEM

O! good words, good words, Urs.   10

OVERDO

[Aside] Another special enormity. A cutpurse of the sword,
the boot, and the feather! Those are his marks.

[Enter MOONCALF*]*

URSLA

You are one of those horse-leeches that gave out I was dead,
in Turnbull Street, of a surfeit of bottle-ale and tripes?

KNOCKEM

No, 'twas better meat, Urs: cows' udders, cows' udders!   15

URSLA

Well, I shall be meet with your mumbling mouth one day.

KNOCKEM

What? Thou'lt poison me with a neuft in a bottle of ale, wilt

---

11 *sword*, Ed. (sword! F)
13 *horse-leeches* (i) farriers (ii) large blood-sucking leeches (iii)
     rapacious predators
16 *meet with* quits with, revenged on
17 *neuft* newt

---

5 *groan . . . heavy hill.* Criminals sentenced to hanging were conveyed by
   cart from Newgate Gaol, up Holborn Hill, to the gallows at Tyburn;
   'heavy' = 'grievous', 'distressing'.

thou? Or a spider in a tobacco-pipe, Urs? Come, there's no
malice in these fat folks. I never fear thee, an I can scape thy
lean Mooncalf here. Let's drink it out, good Urs, and no   20
vapours!   [*Exit* URSLA]

OVERDO

Dost thou hear, boy?—There's for thy ale, and the remnant
for thee.—Speak in thy faith of a faucet, now. Is this goodly
person before us here, this 'vapours', a knight of the knife?

MOONCALF

What mean you by that, Master Arthur?   25

OVERDO

I mean a child of the horn-thumb, a babe of booty, boy, a
cutpurse.

MOONCALF

O Lord, sir! far from it. This is Master Dan Knockem—
Jordan, the ranger of Turnbull. He is a horse-courser, sir.

OVERDO

Thy dainty dame, though, called him cutpurse.   30

MOONCALF

Like enough, sir. She'll do forty such things in an hour, an
you listen to her, for her recreation, if the toy take her i' the
greasy kerchief. It makes her fat, you see. She battens with
it.

OVERDO

[*Aside*] Here might I ha' been deceived now, and ha' put a   35
fool's blot upon myself, if I had not played an after-game o'
discretion.

> URSLA *comes in again dropping*

29 *Jordan* chamber-pot
32 *toy* whim
33 *kerchief* cloth used as head-cover, but here the head itself
36 *after-game* second game played to reverse the outcome of the first
37 s.d. *dropping* exhausted and dripping with sweat

18–19 *there's no malice in these fat folks.* A version of the proverb 'Fat folks
    are good-natured' (Tilley, F419).
21 *vapours.* This word which is used extensively in the play, is defined by
    Jonson himself in the s.d. at IV.iv, 26 as 'nonsense'. For Knockem, who
    employs it incessantly, it means whatever he wants it to mean—usually
    little or nothing. It seems, however, to have two main connotations:
    (i) fantastic notions (ii) a ridiculous urge to brag and quarrel.
26 *horn-thumb.* Cutpurses protected their thumbs with a piece of horn, so
    that they did not cut themselves in the act of cutting a purse.

KNOCKEM
> Alas, poor Urs, this's an ill season for thee.

URSLA
> Hang yourself, hackney-man.

KNOCKEM
> How, how, Urs? Vapours? Motion breed vapours?   40

URSLA
> Vapours! Never tusk, nor twirl your dibble, good Jordan,
> I know what you'll take to a very drop. Though you be
> captain o' the roarers, and fight well at the case of piss-pots,
> you shall not fright me with your lion-chap, sir, nor your
> tusks. You angry? You are hungry. Come, a pig's head will   45
> stop your mouth and stay your stomach at all times.

KNOCKEM
> Thou art such another mad merry Urs still! Troth, I do make
> conscience of vexing thee now i' the dog-days, this hot
> weather, for fear of foundering thee i' the body, and melting
> down a pillar of the Fair. Pray thee take thy chair again, and   50
> keep state; and let's have a fresh bottle of ale, and a pipe of
> tobacco; and no vapours. I'll ha' this belly o' thine taken up,
> and thy grass scoured, wench. Look! here's Ezekiel
> Edgworth, a fine boy of his inches as any is i' the Fair! Has
> still money in his purse, and will pay all with a kind heart,   55
> and good vapours.

40 *How, how, Urs? Vapours?* Ed. (How? how? *Vrs*, vapours! F)
   Motion breed vapours? Does activity give rise to tantrums?
44 *lion-chap* lion's jaw
49 *foundering* causing a horse to break down by overworking it
51 *keep state* act like a queen
52 *taken up* reduced (farriers' terminology)
53 *scoured* purged out

---

41 *Never tusk, nor twirl your dibble.* An obscure and disputed passage;
   OED suggests that 'tusk' means 'show your teeth', and 'twirl your
   dibble' = 'twist your moustache'. It seems more likely, however, since
   Ursla goes on to refer to Jordan's 'lion-chap' and his 'tusks', that 'tusks'
   are the ends of the moustache and the 'dibble' a little spade beard;
   'tusk' would then mean 'twist up the ends of your moustache', and 'twirl
   your dibble', 'twist your little beard around'.
43 *at the case of piss-pots.* To 'fight at the case of pistols' was to fight with
   a pair of pistols; but Ursla cleverly replaces the expected 'pistols' with
   'piss-pots'.
53–6 *Look! . . . vapours.* While Knockem is saying these words, Edgworth
   makes his way from the rear of the stage to the front, where Knockem
   and Ursla are. He is not regarded as being fully on stage until he joins
   them.

Act II, Scene iv

[*Enter*] *to them* EDGWORTH, NIGHTINGALE, CORNCUTTER, TINDER-
BOX-MAN, PASSENGERS

EDGWORTH
    That I will, indeed, willingly, Master Knockem. [*To*
    MOONCALF] Fetch some ale and tobacco. [*Exit* MOONCALF]
LEATHERHEAD
    What do you lack, gentlemen? Maid, see a fine hobby-horse
    for your young master; cost you but a token a week his
    provender.   5
CORNCUTTER
    Ha' you any corns i' your feet and toes?
TINDERBOX-MAN
    Buy a mousetrap, a mousetrap, or a tormentor for a flea.
TRASH
    Buy some gingerbread.
NIGHTINGALE
    Ballads, ballads! fine new ballads!
        Hear for your love, and buy for your money!   10
        A delicate ballad o' 'The Ferret and the Coney';
        'A Preservative again the Punk's Evil';
        Another of 'Goose-green Starch and the Devil';

---

   1 *Knockem.* Ed. (*Knockhum*, F)
   7 *tormentor* trap
  12 *Punk's Evil* venereal disease
  13 *Goose-green* (more usually 'gooseturd-green') yellowish green

---

    s.d. TINDERBOX-MAN. Here, and in the s.p. of the one speech assigned to
    him (1. 7), the Tinderbox-man takes the place of the Mousetrap-man
    listed among the Persons of the Play, though mousetraps still appear to
    be his main stock in trade.
  10 *Hear . . . money.* Cf. the proverbial 'not to be had for love or money'
    (Tilley, L484).
  11 *The Ferret and the Coney.* The swindler and the dupe (thieves' cant)
  13 *Goose-green Starch and the Devil.* The story on which this 'goodly
    Ballad against Pride' was based is told by Philip Stubbes in his *Anatomie
    of Abuses* (1583). It concerns a proud young woman of Antwerp who,
    dissatisfied with the way in which her ruffs were starched, wished that
    the Devil might take her 'when she weare any of those Neckerchers
    again'. Thereupon, the Devil came to her in the likeness of a young man,
    set her ruffs beautifully, so that she fell in love with him, and then, in
    the act of kissing her, broke her neck (*The Anatomie of Abuses*, ed.
    Furnivall, 1877, i. 71–2).

'*A Dozen of Divine Points*' and '*The Godly Garters*';
'*The Fairing of Good Counsel*', of an ell and three quarters.   15
What is't you buy?
'*The Windmill blown down by the witch's fart!*',
Or '*Saint George, that O! did break the dragon's heart!*'

[*Enter* MOONCALF]

EDGWORTH
Master Nightingale, come hither, leave your mart a little.
NIGHTINGALE
O my secretary! What says my secretary?   20
OVERDO
Child o' the bottles, what's he? What's he?
MOONCALF
A civil young gentleman, Master Arthur, that keeps com-
pany with the roarers, and disburses all still. He has ever
money in his purse. He pays for them, and they roar for
him: one does good offices for another. They call him the   25
secretary, but he serves nobody. A great friend of the ballad-
man's, they are never asunder.
OVERDO
What pity 'tis so civil a young man should haunt this
debauched company! Here's the bane of the youth of our
time apparent. A proper penman, I see't in his countenance; 30
he has a good clerk's look with him, and I warrant him a
quick hand.
MOONCALF
A very quick hand, sir.   [*Exit*]
EDGWORTH
(*This they whisper that* OVERDO *hears it not*)
    All the purses and purchase I give you today by con-
    veyance, bring hither to Ursla's presently. Here we   35

15 *ell* forty-five inches
19 *mart* trade
21 *What's* Ed. (what F)
24 *roar* behave noisily and riotously (to help the cutpurse)
34 *purchase* booty, stolen goods
34–5 *conveyance* sleight of hand

---

14 *A Dozen of Divine Points.* Twelve moral maxims, in the form of a
ballad, 'sent by a gentlewoman to her lover for a new yeares gift'.
The Godly Garters. Probably the ballad which John Charlwood entered
on the Stationers' Register on 20 October 1578 under the title 'A paire
of garters for yonge men to weare that serve the Lord God and Lyve in
his feare'.

will meet at night in her lodge, and share. Look you
choose good places for your standing i' the Fair, when
you sing, Nightingale.

URSLA

Ay, near the fullest passages; and shift 'em often.

EDGWORTH

And i' your singing you must use your hawk's eye   40
nimbly, and fly the purse to a mark still—where 'tis
worn and o' which side—that you may gi' me the sign
with your beak, or hang your head that way i' the tune.

URSLA

Enough, talk no more on't. Your friendship, masters, is not
now to begin. Drink your draught of indenture, your sup   45
of covenant, and away. The Fair fills apace, company begins
to come in, and I ha' ne'er a pig ready yet.

KNOCKEM

Well said! Fill the cups and light the tobacco. Let's give
fire i'th'works, and noble vapours.

EDGWORTH

And shall we ha' smocks, Ursla, and good whimsies, ha?   50

URSLA

Come, you are i' your bawdy vein! The best the Fair will
afford, Zekiel, if bawd Whit keep his word.

[*Enter* MOONCALF]

How do the pigs, Mooncalf?

MOONCALF

Very passionate, mistress; one on 'em has wept out an eye.
Master Arthur o' Bradley is melancholy here; nobody talks   55
to him. Will you any tobacco, Master Arthur?

39 *fullest passages* most crowded thoroughfares
45 *draught of indenture* pledge drunk on the signing of an agreement,
    with a pun on 'draft'
50 *smocks* wenches
54 *passionate* sorrowful, sorry for themselves

41 *fly the purse to a mark.* Indicate precisely where the purse is—an image
    taken from hawking.
44–5 *Your friendship . . . begin.* A significant reminiscence of Chaucer's
    remark about the collusion between the Doctor and the apothecaries:
        For ech of hem made other for to winne;
        Hir frendschipe nas nat newe to beginne. (Prologue to *The Canter-
        bury Tales*, 427–8)
50 *whimsies.* Also occurring in the form 'whimsbies', this is a variant on the
    vulgar 'quims', i.e., 'female genitalia', used as a synonym for 'whores'.

OVERDO

No, boy, let my meditations alone.

MOONCALF

He's studying for an oration now.

OVERDO

[*Aside*] If I can, with this day's travail and all my policy, but
rescue this youth here out of the hands of the lewd man and   60
the strange woman, I will sit down at night and say with my
friend Ovid, *Iamque opus exegi, quod nec Iovis ira, nec ignis,*
etc.

KNOCKEM

Here, Zekiel; here's a health to Ursla, and a kind vapour!
Thou hast money i' thy purse still, and store! How dost thou   65
come by it? Pray thee vapour thy friends some in a courteous vapour.

EDGWORTH

Half I have, Master Dan Knockem, is always at your service.

OVERDO

[*Aside*] Ha, sweet nature! What goshawk would prey upon
such a lamb?   70

KNOCKEM

Let's see what 'tis, Zekiel, count it! [*To* MOONCALF] Come,
fill him to pledge me.

Act II, Scene v

[*Enter*] WINWIFE, QUARLOUS, *to them*

WINWIFE

We are here before 'em, methinks.

QUARLOUS

All the better; we shall see 'em come in now.

LEATHERHEAD

What do you lack, gentlemen, what is't you lack? A fine

---

59 *policy* shrewd contriving
61 *strange woman*, Ed. (strange woman. F) harlot
65 *store* plenty

62–3 *Iamque . . . ignis, etc.* Having completed his *Metamorphoses*, Ovid
expresses, in the last nine lines of that work, his conviction that it will
bring him immortal fame. The passage opens thus:
    Iamque opus exegi, quod nec Iovis ira, nec ignis,
    Nec poterit ferrum, nec edax abolere vetustas (xv. 871–2):
'And now I have finished a work, which neither the anger of Jove, nor
fire, nor sword, nor devouring time will ever destroy'.

horse? A lion? A bull? A bear? A dog or a cat? An excellent
fine Bartholmew-bird? Or an instrument? What is't you   5
lack?

QUARLOUS

'Slid! here's Orpheus among the beasts, with his fiddle and
all!

TRASH

Will you buy any comfortable bread, gentlemen?

QUARLOUS

And Ceres selling her daughter's picture in gingerwork!   10

WINWIFE

That these people should be so ignorant to think us chapmen
for 'em! Do we look as if we would buy gingerbread? Or
hobby-horses?

QUARLOUS

Why, they know no better ware than they have, nor better
customers than come. And our very being here makes us fit   15
to be demanded, as well as others. Would Cokes would
come! There were a true customer for 'em.

KNOCKEM

[*To* EDGWORTH] How much is't? Thirty shillings? Who's
yonder? Ned Winwife? And Tom Quarlous, I think! Yes.—
Gi' me it all, gi' me it all.—Master Winwife! Master Quar-   20
lous! Will you take a pipe of tobacco with us?—Do not
discredit me now, Zekiel.

WINWIFE

Do not see him! He is the roaring horse-courser. Pray thee
let's avoid him; turn down this way.

QUARLOUS

'Slud, I'll see him, and roar with him too, an he roared as   25
loud as Neptune. Pray thee go with me.

---

9 *comfortable bread* bread that does the stomach good
11 *chapmen* customers
25 *'Slud* by God's blood

---

7 *Orpheus among the beasts.* According to Greek myth, Orpheus, the
  greatest poet and musician who ever lived, could charm beasts with the
  sound of his lyre.
10 *Ceres selling . . . gingerwork!* Ceres, goddess of the cornfield, was the
  mother of Proserpina. When her daughter was carried off to Hades by
  Pluto, Ceres wandered about for nine days seeking news of her before
  she discovered what had happened.

WINWIFE

You may draw me to as likely an inconvenience, when you please, as this.

QUARLOUS

Go to then, come along. We ha' nothing to do, man, but to see sights now.   30

KNOCKEM

Welcome, Master Quarlous, and Master Winwife! Will you take any froth and smoke with us?

QUARLOUS

Yes, sir; but you'll pardon us if we knew not of so much familiarity between us afore.

KNOCKEM

As what, sir?   35

QUARLOUS

To be so lightly invited to smoke and froth.

KNOCKEM

A good vapour! Will you sit down, sir? This is old Ursla's mansion; how like you her bower? Here you may ha' your punk and your pig in state, sir, both piping hot.

QUARLOUS

I had rather ha' my punk cold, sir.   40

OVERDO

[*Aside*] There's for me: punk! and pig!

URSLA   *She calls within*

What, Mooncalf, you rogue!

MOONCALF

By and by; the bottle is almost off, mistress. Here, Master Arthur.

URSLA

[*Within*] I'll part you and your play-fellow there i' the   45
guarded coat, an you sunder not the sooner.

KNOCKEM

Master Winwife, you are proud, methinks; you do not talk, nor drink. Are you proud?

WINWIFE

Not of the company I am in, sir, nor the place, I assure you.

KNOCKEM

You do not except at the company, do you? Are you in   50
vapours, sir?

27 *as likely an inconvenience* as promising a piece of mischief (Spencer)
40 *cold* because a 'hot' punk would be one with venereal disease
43 *off* finished
46 *guarded* trimmed (with lace or braid)

MOONCALF

Nay, good Master Dan Knockem, respect my mistress'
bower, as you call it. For the honour of our booth, none o'
your vapours here.

URSLA   *She comes out with a fire-brand*

Why, you thin lean polecat you, an they have a mind to be i'   55
their vapours, must you hinder 'em? What did you know,
vermin, if they would ha' lost a cloak, or such a trifle?
Must you be drawing the air of pacification here, while I am
tormented within, i' the fire, you weasel?

MOONCALF

Good mistress, 'twas in the behalf of your booth's credit   60
that I spoke.

URSLA

Why, would my booth ha' broke if they had fallen out in't,
sir? Or would their heat ha' fired it? In, you rogue, and
wipe the pigs, and mend the fire, that they fall not, or I'll
both baste and roast you till your eyes drop out, like 'em.   65
Leave the bottle behind you, and be curst a while.

                                      [*Exit* MOONCALF]

QUARLOUS

Body o' the Fair! what's this? Mother o' the bawds?

KNOCKEM

No, she's mother o' the pigs, sir, mother o' the pigs!

WINWIFE

Mother o' the Furies, I think, by her fire-brand.

QUARLOUS

Nay, she is too fat to be a Fury, sure; some walking sow of   70
tallow!

WINWIFE

An inspired vessel of kitchen-stuff!   *She drinks this while*

QUARLOUS

She'll make excellent gear for the coach-makers here in
Smithfield to anoint wheels and axle-trees with.

62 *broke* (i) fallen to pieces (ii) gone bankrupt (punning on 'credit')
65 *baste . . . roast* beat (in addition to normal culinary meanings)
70 *sure;* ed. (sure, F)
73 *gear* material, stuff

---

70 *too fat to be a Fury.* Because 'Fat folks are good-natured' (Tilley, F419).
70–1 *walking sow of tallow.* Large oblong mass of tallow endowed with the
   power of movement; cf. 'sow of lead', 'sow of iron' (*OED*, Sow, *sb.*[1] 6.
   a. and b.); a sow of lead weighed about 300 lb.
72 *An inspired vessel of kitchen-stuff.* A container full of dripping that has
   been given the breath of life, with an allusion to Genesis, ii. 7.

URSLA

Ay, ay, gamesters, mock a plain plump soft wench o' the   75
suburbs, do, because she's juicy and wholesome. You
must ha' your thin pinched ware, pent up i' the compass of
a dog-collar—or 'twill not do—that looks like a long laced
conger set upright; and a green feather, like fennel i' the joll
on't.   80

KNOCKEM

Well said, Urs, my good Urs! To 'em, Urs!

QUARLOUS

Is she your quagmire, Dan Knockem? Is this your bog?

NIGHTINGALE

We shall have a quarrel presently.

KNOCKEM

How? Bog? Quagmire? Foul vapours! Hum'h!

QUARLOUS

Yes, he that would venture for't, I assure him, might sink   85
into her, and be drowned a week ere any friend he had
could find where he were.

WINWIFE

And then he would be a fortnight weighing up again.

QUARLOUS

'Twere like falling into a whole shire of butter. They had
need be a team of Dutchmen, should draw him out.   90

KNOCKEM

Answer 'em, Urs. Where's thy Bartholmew-wit now? Urs,
thy Bartholmew-wit?

URSLA

Hang 'em, rotten, roguy cheaters! I hope to see 'em plagued
one day—poxed they are already, I am sure—with lean
playhouse poultry, that has the bony rump sticking out,   95

---

78 *laced* (i) streaked (ii) slashed (ready for cooking)
79 *joll* head (of a fish)
88 *weighing up* raising up (of an anchor or sunken ship)
95 *playhouse poultry* whores (cf. French *poules*) who frequented
   theatres

---

76 *suburbs*. The suburbs of London, especially those on the South Bank,
   were notorious for their brothels; in the City itself prostitution was more
   strictly regulated.
82 *quagmire . . . bog*. Horse-dealers kept a part of their yards in a very soft
   wet condition, so that horses with unsound legs could stand there
   without betraying their deficiencies.
90 *Dutchmen*. Popularly thought of as great consumers of butter.

like the ace of spades or the point of a partizan, that every
rib of 'em is like the tooth of a saw; and will so grate 'em with
their hips and shoulders as, take 'em altogether, they were as
good lie with a hurdle.

QUARLOUS

Out upon her, how she drips! She's able to give a man the   100
sweating sickness with looking on her.

URSLA

Marry look off, with a patch o' your face and a dozen i' your
breech, though they be o' scarlet, sir. I ha' seen as fine outsides as either o' yours bring lousy linings to the broker's,
ere now, twice a week.   105

QUARLOUS

Do you think there may be a fine new cucking-stool i' the
Fair to be purchased? One large enough, I mean. I know
there is a pond of capacity for her.

URSLA

For your mother, you rascal! Out, you rogue, you hedge-
bird, you pimp, you pannier-man's bastard you!   110

QUARLOUS

Ha, ha, ha!

URSLA

Do you sneer, you dog's-head, you trendle-tail? You look
as you were begotten atop of a cart in harvest-time, when
the whelp was hot and eager. Go snuff after your brother's
bitch, Mistress Commodity. That's the livery you wear.   115
'Twill be out at the elbows shortly. It's time you went to't
for the tother remnant.

---

96 *partizan* long-handled spear
101 *sweating sickness* epidemic fever prevalent in the 15th and 16th
    centuries
102–3 *patch . . . breech* symptoms of venereal disease
104 *broker's* ed. (Brokers F)
106 *cucking-stool* chair used for punishing scolds, who were fastened
    in it and then ducked in a pond
109–10 *hedge-bird* foot-pad, vagrant (one born under a hedge)
110 *pannier-man's* hawker's
112 *trendle-tail* cur, mongrel with a curly tail
115 *Commodity* (i) gain (ii) article for sale (whore)

---

104. *bring lousy linings to the broker's.* Either (i) bring lice-infested under-
    clothes to the pawnbroker's, or (ii) bring the diseased contents of your
    breeches, i.e., sexual organs, to the bawd's. (Cf. *OED*, Lining, *vbl. sb.*[1],
    1. b. and 3.)

KNOCKEM
Peace, Urs, peace, Urs!—They'll kill the poor whale and
make oil of her.—Pray thee go in.

URSLA
I'll see 'em poxed first, and piled, and double piled. 120

WINWIFE
Let's away; her language grows greasier than her pigs.

URSLA
Does't so, snotty-nose? Good Lord! are you snivelling?
You were engendered on a she-beggar in a barn when the
bald thrasher, your sire, was scarce warm.

WINWIFE
Pray thee let's go. 125

QUARLOUS
No, faith; I'll stay the end of her now. I know she cannot
last long; I find by her similes she wanes apace.

URSLA
Does she so? I'll set you gone. Gi' me my pig-pan hither a
little. I'll scald you hence, an you will not go. [Exit]

KNOCKEM
Gentlemen, these are very strange vapours! And very idle 130
vapours, I assure you!

QUARLOUS
You are a very serious ass, we assure you.

KNOCKEM
Hum'h! Ass? And serious? Nay, then pardon me my vapour.
I have a foolish vapour, gentlemen: any man that does
vapour me the ass, Master Quarlous— 135

QUARLOUS
What then, Master Jordan?

KNOCKEM
I do vapour him the lie.

QUARLOUS
Faith, and to any man that vapours me the lie, I do vapour
that. [Strikes him]

KNOCKEM
Nay then, vapours upon vapours. 140

EDGWORTH ⎫
NIGHTINGALE ⎭
'Ware the pan, the pan, the pan! She comes with the pan,
gentlemen.

120 *piled* (i) bald (from the pox) (ii) afflicted with piles (iii) threadbare,
reduced to beggary
128 *set you gone* set you going

URSLA *comes in with the scalding-pan. They fight. She falls with it.*
God bless the woman!

URSLA

Oh!   [*Exeunt* QUARLOUS, WINWIFE]

TRASH

What's the matter?   145

OVERDO

Goodly woman!

MOONCALF

Mistress!

URSLA

Curse of hell that ever I saw these fiends! Oh! I ha' scalded
my leg, my leg, my leg, my leg! I ha' lost a limb in the
service! Run for some cream and salad oil, quickly. [*To*   150
MOONCALF] Are you under-peering, you baboon? Rip off my
hose, an you be men, men, men.

MOONCALF

Run you for some cream, good mother Joan. I'll look to
your basket.   [*Exit* TRASH]

LEATHERHEAD

Best sit up i' your chair, Ursla. Help, gentlemen.   155
                                     [*They lift her up*]

KNOCKEM

Be of good cheer, Urs. Thou hast hindered me the currying
of a couple of stallions here, that abused the good race-bawd
o' Smithfield. 'Twas time for 'em to go.

NIGHTINGALE

I'faith, when the pan came. They had made you run else.—
This had been a fine time for purchase, if you had ventured.   160

EDGWORTH

Not a whit, these fellows were too fine to carry money.

KNOCKEM

Nightingale, get some help to carry her leg out o' the air;
take off her shoes. Body o' me, she has the malanders, the
scratches, the crown-scab, and the quitter-bone i' the tother
leg.   165

---

145 s.p. TRASH Ed. (ERA. F)
156 *currying* beating, dressing-down
157 *race-bawd* breeder of bawds, mother-bawd
160 *purchase* theft
161 *fine* smart, clever

163–4 *malanders . . . quitter-bone.* These are all diseases of the leg and hoof
in horses.

URSLA

Oh, the pox! Why do you put me in mind o' my leg thus, to
make it prick and shoot? Would you ha' me i' the Hospital
afore my time?

KNOCKEM

Patience, Urs. Take a good heart; 'tis but a blister as big as
a windgall. I'll take it away with the white of an egg, a little   170
honey, and hog's-grease. Ha' thy pasterns well rolled, and
thou shalt pace again by tomorrow. I'll tend thy booth and
look to thy affairs the while. Thou shalt sit i' thy chair, and
give directions, and shine Ursa major.

[*Exeunt* KNOCKEM *and* MOONCALF *with* URSLA *in her chair*]

Act II, Scene vi

[*Enter*] COKES, WASP, MISTRESS OVERDO, GRACE

OVERDO

These are the fruits of bottle-ale and tobacco! the foam of
the one and the fumes of the other! Stay, young man, and
despise not the wisdom of these few hairs that are grown
grey in care of thee.

EDGWORTH

Nightingale, stay a little. Indeed I'll hear some o' this!   5

COKES

Come, Numps, come, where are you? Welcome into the
Fair, Mistress Grace.

EDGWORTH

[*To* NIGHTINGALE] 'Slight, he will call company, you shall
see, and put us into doings presently.

OVERDO

Thirst not after that frothy liquor, ale; for who knows,   10
when he openeth the stopple, what may be in the bottle?
Hath not a snail, a spider, yea, a neuft been found there?
Thirst not after it, youth; thirst not after it.

COKES

This is a brave fellow, Numps, let's hear him.

170 *windgall* soft tumour on a horse's leg
171 *rolled* bandaged
174 *Ursa major* the constellation of the Great Bear
  8 *'Slight* by God's light
 14 *brave* fine, capital

170–1 *white . . . hog's-grease.* Remedies used by farriers to deal with diseases
in horses.

WASP

'Sblood, how brave is he? In a guarded coat? You were   15
best truck with him; e'en strip, and truck presently; it will
become you. Why will you hear him? Because he is an ass,
and may be akin to the Cokeses?

COKES

O, good Numps!

OVERDO

Neither do thou lust after that tawny weed, tobacco.   20

COKES

Brave words!

OVERDO

Whose complexion is like the Indian's that vents it!

COKES

Are they not brave words, sister?

OVERDO

And who can tell if, before the gathering and making up
thereof, the alligarta hath not pissed thereon?   25

WASP

'Heart, let 'em be brave words, as brave as they will! An
they were all the brave words in a country, how then? Will
you away yet? Ha' you enough on him? Mistress Grace,
come you away, I pray you, be not you accessary. If you do
lose your licence, or somewhat else, sir, with listening to his   30
fables, say Numps is a witch, with all my heart, do, say so.

COKES

Avoid, i' your satin doublet, Numps.

OVERDO

The creeping venom of which subtle serpent, as some late
writers affirm, neither the cutting of the perilous plant, nor
the drying of it, nor the lighting or burning, can any way   35
persway or assuage.

15 *brave* well dressed
16 *truck* make an exchange (of clothes)
17 *him?* Ed. (him, F)
22 *vents* sells (*OED*, Vent, v.³, 1.)
25 *alligarta* alligator
31 *witch* wizard
32 *Avoid* go away, keep off (cf. 'Avoid, Satan')
36 *persway* diminish

33–4 *some late writers.* The most famous of those who wrote to attack the
use of tobacco was James I, whose *Counterblaste to Tobacco* had come
out in 1604.

COKES
> Good, i'faith! is't not, sister?

OVERDO
> Hence it is that the lungs of the tobacconist are rotted, the
> liver spotted, the brain smoked like the backside of the pig-
> woman's booth here, and the whole body within, black as   40
> her pan you saw e'en now without.

COKES
> A fine similitude that, sir! Did you see the pan?

EDGWORTH
> Yes, sir.

OVERDO
> Nay, the hole in the nose here of some tobacco-takers, or the
> third nostril, if I may so call it, which makes that they can   45
> vent the tobacco out like the ace of clubs, or rather the
> flower-de-lys, is caused from the tobacco, the mere tobacco!
> when the poor innocent pox, having nothing to do there, is
> miserably and most unconscionably slandered.

COKES
> Who would ha' missed this, sister?   50

MISTRESS OVERDO
> Not anybody but Numps.

COKES
> He does not understand.

EDGWORTH
> [*Aside*] Nor you feel.   *He picketh his purse*

COKES
> What would you have, sister, of a fellow that knows nothing
> but a basket-hilt and an old fox in't? The best music i' the   55
> Fair will not move a log.

EDGWORTH
> [*Slipping the purse to* NIGHTINGALE] In to Ursla, Night-
> ingale, and carry her comfort. See it told. This fellow was
> sent to us by fortune for our first fairing.
>   [*Exit* NIGHTINGALE]

---

38 *tobacconist* smoker
46 *vent* blow, exhale
55 *basket-hilt* hilt with a basket-like protection for the hand
   fox sword
58 *told* counted

44-5 *hole in the nose . . . third nostril.* An effect of syphilis; but Overdo
prefers to attribute it to smoking.

OVERDO

But what speak I of the diseases of the body, children of   60
the Fair?

COKES

That's to us, sister. Brave i'faith!

OVERDO

Hark, O you sons and daughters of Smithfield! and hear
what malady it doth the mind: it causeth swearing, it causeth
swaggering, it causeth snuffling and snarling, and now and   65
then a hurt.

MISTRESS OVERDO

He hath something of Master Overdo, methinks, brother.

COKES

So methought, sister, very much of my brother Overdo.
And, 'tis when he speaks.

OVERDO

Look into any angle o' the town—the Straits, or the Bermu-   70
das—where the quarrelling lesson is read, and how do
they entertain the time but with bottle-ale and tobacco?
The lecturer is o' one side, and his pupils o' the other;
but the seconds are still bottle-ale and tobacco, for which
the lecturer reads and the novices pay. Thirty pound a   75
week in bottle-ale! forty in tobacco! and ten more in ale
again! Then, for a suit to drink in, so much, and, that being
slavered, so much for another suit, and then a third suit,
and a fourth suit! and still the bottle-ale slavereth, and the
tobacco stinketh!   80

WASP

Heart of a madman! are you rooted here? Will you never

---

65 *snuffling* sniffing with contempt
70 *angle* corner
72 *entertain* occupy, while away
74 *seconds* stand-bys, main supports
78 *slavered* soiled with saliva and sweat
81 *Will* Ed. (well F)

70-1 *the Straits, or the Bermudas.* A disreputable district of narrow lanes
and alleys near Charing Cross, frequented by criminals.

71 *the quarrelling lesson.* The vogue for fencing and duelling with sword and
dagger, which developed in the 1590s, led to the establishment of fencing
academies and to the publication of such works of instruction as
Vincentio Saviola's *Practise of the Rapier and Dagger* (1594–95), which
dealt, among other things, with the right way to go about making a
challenge. See *As You Like It*, V.iv, 45–97, where Touchstone makes
splendid fun of it all.

away? What can any man find out in this bawling fellow, to
grow here for? He is a full handful higher sin' he heard him.
Will you fix here? And set up a booth, sir?

OVERDO

I will conclude briefly—   85

WASP

Hold your peace, you roaring rascal, I'll run my head i' your
chaps else. [*To* COKES] You were best build a booth, and
entertain him; make your will, an you say the word, and
him your heir! Heart, I never knew one taken with a mouth
of a peck afore. By this light, I'll carry you away o' my back,   90
an you will not come.   *He gets him up on pickpack*

COKES

Stay, Numps, stay, set me down. I ha' lost my purse,
Numps. O my purse! One o' my fine purses is gone.

MISTRESS OVERDO

Is't indeed, brother?

COKES

Ay, as I am an honest man; would I were an arrant rogue,   95
else! A plague of all roguy damned cutpurses for me!

WASP

Bless 'em with all my heart, with all my heart, do you see!
Now, as I am no infidel, that I know of, I am glad on't. Ay,
I am; here's my witness! do you see, sir? I did not tell you
of his fables, I? No, no, I am a dull malt-horse, I, I know   100
nothing. Are you not justly served, i' your conscience, now?
Speak i' your conscience. Much good do you with all my
heart, and his good heart that has it, with all my heart again.

EDGWORTH

[*Aside*] This fellow is very charitable; would he had a purse
too! But I must not be too bold all at a time.   105

COKES

Nay, Numps, it is not my best purse.

WASP

Not your best! Death! Why should it be your worst?
Why should it be any, indeed, at all? Answer me to that.
Gi' me a reason from you why it should be any.

83 *him.* Ed. (him, F)
87 *chaps* mouth, chops
88 *entertain* support, maintain
90 *a peck* the capacity of a peck
91 s.d. *pickpack* pick-a-back
98–9 *Ay, I* Ed. (I I F)
100 *malt-horse* heavy horse used to pull brewers' drays

COKES

Nor my gold, Numps; I ha' that yet. Look here else,   110
sister.

[*Shews* MISTRESS OVERDO *his other purse*]

WASP

Why so, there's all the feeling he has!

MISTRESS OVERDO

I pray you have a better care of that, brother.

COKES

Nay, so I will, I warrant you. Let him catch this that catch
can. I would fain see him get this, look you, here.   115

WASP

So, so, so, so, so, so, so, so! Very good.

COKES

I would ha' him come again now, and but offer at it. Sister,
will you take notice of a good jest? I will put it just where
th'other was, and if we ha' good luck, you shall see a delicate
fine trap to catch the cutpurse nibbling.   120

EDGWORTH

[*Aside*] Faith, and he'll try ere you be out o' the Fair.

COKES

Come, Mistress Grace, prithee be not melancholy for my
mischance; sorrow wi' not keep it, sweetheart.

GRACE

I do not think on't, sir.

COKES

'Twas but a little scurvy white money, hang it; it may hang   125
the cutpurse one day. I ha' gold left to gi' thee a fairing yet,
as hard as the world goes. Nothing angers me but that
nobody here looked like a cutpurse, unless 'twere Numps.

WASP

How? I? I look like a cutpurse? Death! your sister's a cutpurse! and your mother and father, and all your kin, were   130
cutpurses! And here is a rogue is the bawd o' the cutpurses,
whom I will beat to begin with.

They speak all together; and WASP *beats the* JUSTICE

OVERDO

Hold thy hand, child of wrath and heir of anger. Make

---

117 *offer at* make an attempt on
125 *white money* silver

---

123 *wi' not keep it*. Will not bring the purse back—a version of the proverb
'Sorrow will pay no debt' (Tilley, S660).

it not Childermas day in thy fury, or the feast of the
French Bartholmew, parent of the Massacre.   135

COKES

Numps, Numps!

MISTRESS OVERDO

Good Master Humphrey!

WASP

You are the Patrico, are you? the patriarch of the
cutpurses? You share, sir, they say; let them share this
with you. Are you i' your hot fit of preaching again? I'll   140
cool you.

OVERDO

Murther, murther, murther!

[*Exeunt*]

Act III, Scene i

[*Enter*] WHIT, HAGGIS, BRISTLE, LEATHERHEAD, TRASH

WHIT

Nay, 'tish all gone now! Dish 'tish phen tou vilt not be
phitin call, Master Offisher! Phat ish a man te better to
lishen out noishes for tee an tou art in anoder 'orld—being
very shuffishient noishes and gallantsh too? One o' their
brabblesh would have fed ush all dish fortnight; but tou   5
art so bushy about beggersh still, tou hast no leishure to
intend shentlemen, an't be.

HAGGIS

Why, I told you, Davy Bristle.

BRISTLE

Come, come, you told me a pudding, Toby Haggis; a matter
of nothing; I am sure it came to nothing! You said, 'Let's go 10

134 *Childermas day* Feast of the Holy Innocents, 28 December
138 *Patrico* hedge-priest of the gypsies and vagabonds
  5 *brabblesh* brabbles, brawls
  7 *intend* pay any attention to
  9 *a pudding* a lot of 'tripe', with a pun on 'Haggis'

---

135 *French Bartholmew.* A reference to the great massacre of Protestants in
    France on 24 August 1572.
  1 *'tish.* 'Tis. The curious and outlandish spellings Jonson resorts to for
    Whit's speeches are intended to represent an Irish brogue, which
    Elizabethan Englishmen, like their modern counterparts, evidently found
    extremely funny. Jonson, understandably, is not consistent in his
    attempts to reproduce it phonetically. Every now and again he forgets
    about it and allows Whit to lapse into standard English forms.

to Ursla's', indeed; but then you met the man with the
monsters, and I could not get you from him. An old fool,
not leave seeing yet?

HAGGIS

Why, who would ha' thought anybody would ha' quarrelled
so early? Or that the ale o' the Fair would ha' been up so   15
soon?

WHIT

Phy, phat o'clock toest tou tink it ish, man?

HAGGIS

I cannot tell.

WHIT

Tou art a vishe vatchman, i' te mean teeme.

HAGGIS

Why, should the watch go by the clock, or the clock by the   20
watch, I pray?

BRISTLE

One should go by another, if they did well.

WHIT

Tou art right now! Phen didst tou ever know or hear of a
shuffishient vatchman but he did tell the clock, phat
bushiness soever he had?   25

BRISTLE

Nay, that's most true, a sufficient watchman knows what
o'clock it is.

WHIT

Shleeping or vaking, ash well as te clock himshelf, or te
Jack dat shtrikes him!

BRISTLE

Let's enquire of Master Leatherhead, or Joan Trash here.   30
Master Leatherhead, do you hear, Master Leatherhead?

WHIT

If it be a Ledderhead, 'tish a very tick Ledderhead, tat sho
mush noish vill not piersh him.

LEATHERHEAD

I have a little business now, good friends, do not trouble me.

WHIT

Phat? Because o' ty wrought neet-cap and ty phelvet   35
sherkin, man? Phy, I have sheen tee in ty ledder sherkin ere
now, Mashter o' de hobby-horses, as bushy and as stately
as tou sheem'st to be.

29 *Jack* mechanical figure which strikes the bell on a public clock
36 *Phy*, ed. (phy? F)

TRASH

Why, what an you have, Captain Whit? He has his choice of
jerkins, you may see by that, and his caps too, I assure you,   40
when he pleases to be either sick or employed.

LEATHERHEAD

God a mercy, Joan, answer for me.

WHIT

Away, be not sheen i' my company; here be shentlemen,
and men of vorship.   [*Exeunt* HAGGIS, BRISTLE]

Act III, Scene ii

[*Enter to them*] QUARLOUS, WINWIFE

QUARLOUS

We had wonderful ill luck to miss this prologue o' the purse,
but the best is we shall have five acts of him ere night. He'll
be spectacle enough! I'll answer for't.

WHIT

O Creesh! Duke Quarlous, how dosht tou? Tou dosht not
know me, I fear? I am te vishesht man, but Justish Overdo,   5
in all Bartholmew Fair now. Gi' me twelvepence from tee,
I vill help tee to a vife vorth forty marks for't, an't be.

QUARLOUS

Away, rogue; pimp, away!

WHIT

And she shall shew tee as fine cut-'ork for't in her shmock,
too, as tou cansht vish i'faith. Vilt tou have her, vorshipful   10
Vinvife? I vill help tee to her here, be an't be, in te pig-
quarter, gi' me ty twel'pence from tee.

WINWIFE

Why, there's twel'pence; pray thee wilt thou be gone?

WHIT

Tou art a vorthy man, and a vorshipful man still.

QUARLOUS

Get you gone, rascal.   15

WHIT

I do mean it, man. Prinsh Quarlous, if tou hasht need on me,

4 *Creesh* Christ
5 *vishesht* wisest
8 *pimp*, Ed. (Pimpe F)
9 *cut-'ork* 'cut work', lace
13 *gone*? Ed. (gone. F)
14 *still* ever

tou shalt find me here at Ursla's. I vill see phat ale and punk
ish i' te pigshty for tee; bless ty good vorship!   [*Exit*]

QUARLOUS

Look who comes here! John Littlewit!

WINWIFE

And his wife, and my widow, her mother: the whole family.   20
          [*Enter*] BUSY, LITTLEWIT, PURECRAFT, WIN

QUARLOUS

'Slight, you must gi' 'em all fairings now!

WINWIFE

Not I, I'll not see 'em.

QUARLOUS

They are going a feasting. What schoolmaster's that is
with 'em?

WINWIFE

That's my rival, I believe, the baker!   25

BUSY

So, walk on in the middle way, fore-right; turn neither to
the right hand nor to the left. Let not your eyes be drawn
aside with vanity, nor your ear with noises.

QUARLOUS

O, I know him by that start!

LEATHERHEAD

What do you lack? What do you buy, pretty Mistress? a   30
fine hobby-horse, to make your son a tilter? a drum, to make
him a soldier? a fiddle, to make him a reveller? What is't you
lack? Little dogs for your daughters? or babies, male or
female?

BUSY

Look not toward them, hearken not. The place is Smith-   35
field, or the field of smiths, the grove of hobby-horses and
trinkets. The wares are the wares of devils; and the whole
Fair is the shop of Satan! They are hooks and baits, very
baits, that are hung out on every side to catch you, and to
hold you, as it were, by the gills, and by the nostrils, as the   40
fisher doth; therefore, you must not look, nor turn toward

---

26 *fore-right* straight ahead
31 *tilter* (i) jouster (ii) lecher, rake

35–6 *Smithfield, or the field of smiths.* The correct etymology is, in fact, as
     the earliest recorded spelling 'Smethefelda' (*c.* 1145) shows, 'Smooth-
     field'.

them—the heathen man could stop his ears with wax
against the harlot o' the sea; do you the like, with your
fingers, against the bells of the Beast.

WINWIFE

What flashes comes from him!   45

QUARLOUS

O, he has those of his oven! A notable hot baker 'twas, when
he plied the peel. He is leading his flock into the Fair now.

WINWIFE

Rather driving 'em to the pens; for he will let 'em look upon
nothing.

[*Enter*] KNOCKEM, WHIT

KNOCKEM

Gentlewomen, the weather's hot! Whither walk you? Have   50
a care o' your fine velvet caps, the Fair is dusty.

LITTLEWIT *is gazing at the sign; which is the Pig's Head with*
a large writing under it

Take a sweet delicate booth, with boughs, here i' the way,
and cool yourselves i' the shade, you and your friends. The
best pig and bottle-ale i' the Fair, sir. Old Ursla is cook,
there you may read: the pig's head speaks it. Poor soul, she   55
has had a stringhalt, the maryhinchco; but she's prettily
amended.

WHIT

A delicate show-pig, little mistress, with shweet sauce, and
crackling like de bay-leaf i' de fire, la! Tou shalt ha' de
clean side o' de table-clot and dy glass vashed with phatersh   60
of Dame Annessh Cleare.

45 *flashes* showy phrases
47 *peel* baker's shovel for putting loaves in the oven and pulling them
   out
52 *delicate* charming, delightful
56 *stringhalt, the maryhinchco* diseases affecting a horse's legs
58 *show-pig* sow-pig (as pronounced by Whit)

42–3 *the heathen man . . . sea.* Busy is somewhat muddled. Ulysses, 'the
   heathen man', had the ears of his crew stopped with wax to prevent them
   from hearing the song of the Sirens, and had himself lashed to the mast
   of his boat, so that he could hear the song but was unable to respond to
   its invitation. (Homer, *The Odyssey*, xii.)
45 *comes.* The third person plural in -s is very common in Elizabethan
   English (see Abbott, 333).
60–1 *phatersh of Dame Annessh Cleare.* Waters from a spring in Hoxton
   called Dame Annis (Agnes) the clear.

LITTLEWIT

This's fine, verily. 'Here be the best pigs, and she does roast 'em as well as ever she did', the pig's head says.

KNOCKEM

Excellent, excellent, mistress, with fire o' juniper and rose-mary branches! The oracle of the pig's head, that, sir.   65

PURECRAFT

Son, were you not warned of the vanity of the eye? Have you forgot the wholesome admonition so soon?

LITTLEWIT

Good mother, how shall we find a pig if we do not look about for't? Will it run off o' the spit into our mouths, think you, as in Lubberland, and cry, 'We, we'?   70

BUSY

No, but your mother, religiously wise, conceiveth it may offer itself by other means to the sense, as by way of steam, which I think it doth, here in this place. Huh, huh!

                    BUSY *scents after it like a hound*

Yes, it doth. And it were a sin of obstinacy, great obstinacy, high and horrible obstinacy, to decline or resist the good   75
titillation of the famelic sense, which is the smell. Therefore be bold (huh, huh, huh), follow the scent. Enter the tents of the unclean, for once, and satisfy your wife's frailty. Let your frail wife be satisfied; your zealous mother, and my suffering self, will also be satisfied.   80

LITTLEWIT

Come, Win, as good winny here as go farther and see nothing.

BUSY

We scape so much of the other vanities by our early entering.

PURECRAFT

It is an edifying consideration.   85

WIN

This is scurvy, that we must come into the Fair and not look on't.

LITTLEWIT

Win, have patience, Win, I'll tell you more anon.

---

76 *famelic* exciting hunger
81 *winny* stay

---

70 *Lubberland.* An imaginary country of plenty and idleness, also known as the Land of Cockaigne and, in German, as 'Schlaraffenland'.

KNOCKEM

Mooncalf, entertain within there; the best pig i' the booth,
a pork-like pig. These are Banbury-bloods, o' the sincere   90
stud, come a pig-hunting. Whit, wait, Whit, look to your
charge.   [*Exit* WHIT]

BUSY

A pig prepare presently, let a pig be prepared to us.
                    [*Exeunt* BUSY, LITTLEWIT, WIN, PURECRAFT]

                    [*Enter*] MOONCALF, URSLA

MOONCALF

'Slight, who be these?

URSLA

Is this the good service, Jordan, you'd do me?   95

KNOCKEM

Why, Urs? Why, Urs? Thou'lt ha' vapours i' thy leg again
presently; pray thee go in; 't may turn to the scratches else.

URSLA

Hang your vapours, they are stale, and stink like you. Are
these the guests o' the game you promised to fill my pit
withal today?   100

KNOCKEM

Ay, what ail they, Urs?

URSLA

Ail they? They are all sippers, sippers o' the City. They look
as they would not drink off two penn'orth of bottle-ale
amongst 'em.

MOONCALF

A body may read that i' their small printed ruffs.   105

KNOCKEM

Away, thou art a fool, Urs, and thy Mooncalf too, i' your
ignorant vapours now! Hence! Good guests, I say, right
hypocrites, good gluttons. In, and set a couple o' pigs o' the
board, and half a dozen of the biggest bottles afore 'em, and
call Whit. I do not love to hear innocents abused: fine   110
ambling hypocrites! and a stone-puritan with a sorrel head

90-1 *sincere stud* true breed
101 *what ail they* what's wrong with them
111 *stone-puritan* lascivious male puritan (by analogy with *stone-
    horse = stallion*)
    sorrel chestnut coloured (of horses)

105 *small printed ruffs.* Puritans wore small ruffs, very carefully set; 'in print'
    was a synonym for 'precise'.

and beard—good-mouthed gluttons, two to a pig. Away!

                                [*Exit* MOONCALF]

URSLA

Are you sure they are such?

KNOCKEM

O' the right breed; thou shalt try 'em by the teeth, Urs.
Where's this Whit?   115

                        [*Enter* WHIT]

WHIT

   Behold, man, and see, what a worthy man am ee!
   With the fury of my sword, and the shaking of my beard,
   I will make ten thousand men afeard.

KNOCKEM

Well said, brave Whit! In, and fear the ale out o' the bottles
into the bellies of the brethren and the sisters; drink to the   120
cause, and pure vapours.   [*Exeunt* KNOCKEM, WHIT, URSLA]

QUARLOUS

My roarer is turned tapster, methinks. Now were a fine time
for thee, Winwife, to lay aboard thy widow; thou'lt never be
master of a better season or place. She that will venture
herself into the Fair, and a pig-box, will admit any assault,   125
be assured of that.

WINWIFE

I love not enterprises of that suddenness, though.

QUARLOUS

I'll warrant thee, then, no wife out o' the widows' hundred.
If I had but as much title to her as to have breathed once on
that strait stomacher of hers, I would now assure myself to   130
carry her yet, ere she went out of Smithfield. Or she should
carry me, which were the fitter sight, I confess. But you are a

---

119 *fear* frighten
120 *brethren and the sisters;* Ed. (brethren, and the sisters F)
123 *lay aboard* make advances to (nautical term for the manoeuvre of
    bringing one ship alongside another in order to board it)
130 *stomacher* ornamental covering for the chest worn by women
    under the lacing of the bodice
131 *carry* win

116–18 *Behold . . . afeard.* Whit's lines smack of the traditional St George
    play, described by Thomas Hardy in *The Return of the Native*, Bk. II,
    Ch. v.
128· *the widow's hundred.* Since a hundred was a sub-division of the English
    shire, the meaning would seem to be 'the widows' section of the
    community', but some topical allusion has probably been lost.

modest undertaker, by circumstances and degrees. Come,
'tis disease in thee, not judgement. I should offer at all
together.—Look, here's the poor fool again that was stung   135
by the wasp erewhile.

Act III, Scene iii

[Enter] OVERDO

OVERDO

I will make no more orations shall draw on these tragical
conclusions. And I begin now to think that, by a spice of
collateral justice, Adam Overdo deserved this beating. For I,
the said Adam, was one cause, a by-cause, why the purse was
lost—and my wife's brother's purse too—which they know   5
not of yet. But I shall make very good mirth with it at
supper—that will be the sport—and put my little friend
Master Humphrey Wasp's choler quite out of countenance,
when, sitting at the upper end o' my table, as I use, and
drinking to my brother Cokes and Mistress Alice Overdo, as   10
I will, my wife, for their good affection to old Bradley, I
deliver to 'em it was I that was cudgelled, and shew 'em the
marks. To see what bad events may peep out o' the tail of
good purposes! The care I had of that civil young man I
took fancy to this morning—and have not left it yet—drew   15
me to that exhortation; which drew the company, indeed;
which drew the cutpurse; which drew the money; which
drew my brother Cokes his loss; which drew on Wasp's
anger; which drew on my beating: a pretty gradation! And
they shall ha' it i' their dish, i'faith, at night for fruit. I love   20
to be merry at my table. I had thought once, at one special
blow he ga' me, to have revealed myself. But then—I thank
thee, fortitude—I remembered that a wise man, and who is
ever so great a part o' the Commonwealth in himself, for no

133 *undertaker* venturer, one who undertakes an enterprise
    circumstances roundabout methods
134–5 *offer at all together* make an all-out attack, risk everything
  1 *shall draw on* which will produce
  3 *collateral* concomitant
  4 *by-cause* secondary or incidental cause
  22 *myself.* Ed. (my selfe? F)

23–4 *and who . . . himself.* Overdo, thinking of himself and petty officers
like him as statesmen, appears to have in mind Cicero's contention (*De
Re Publica*, I.iv and v) that the statesman is at least the equal of the
philosopher (the wise man); 'and who' = 'and anyone who'.

particular disaster ought to abandon a public good design.   25
The husbandman ought not, for one unthankful year, to
forsake the plough; the shepherd ought not, for one
scabbed sheep, to throw by his tar-box; the pilot ought not,
for one leak i' the poop, to quit the helm; nor the alderman
ought not, for one custard more at a meal, to give up his   30
cloak; the constable ought not to break his staff and forswear
the watch, for one roaring night; nor the piper o' the parish—
ut parvis componere magna solebam—to put up his pipes, for
one rainy Sunday. These are certain knocking conclusions;
out of which I am resolved, come what come can—come   35
beating, come imprisonment, come infamy, come banishment, nay, come the rack, come the hurdle, welcome all—
I will not discover who I am till my due time. And yet still
all shall be, as I said ever, in Justice' name, and the King's,
and for the Commonwealth.   40

WINWIFE
What does he talk to himself, and act so seriously? Poor fool!
                                                    [*Exit* OVERDO]

QUARLOUS
No matter what. Here's fresher argument, intend that.

Act III, Scene iv

[*Enter to them*] COKES, MISTRESS OVERDO, GRACE, WASP

COKES
Come, Mistress Grace, come sister, here's more fine sights
yet, i'faith. God's lid, where's Numps?

---

28 *tar-box* box used by shepherds to hold tar employed as a cure for
   skin diseases in sheep
30 *one custard more* i.e., an extra guest
31 *cloak* i.e., office (of which the cloak was the mark)
32 *roaring* tempestuous
   piper o' the parish piper employed by the parish to play at
   church-ales and similar functions
34 *knocking* clinching, decisive
37 *hurdle* a kind of sledge on which traitors were dragged through
   the streets to their execution
41 *What* for what reason, why
42 *fresher argument* more matter for a May morning
   intend pay attention to

---

33 *ut parvis . . . solebam.* Virgil, *Eclogues*, i. 23, with *sic* instead of *ut*: 'thus
it was my habit to compare great things to small ones'.

LEATHERHEAD

What do you lack, gentlemen? What is't you buy? Fine
rattles? Drums? Babies? Little dogs? And birds for ladies?
What do you lack?   5

COKES

Good honest Numps, keep afore, I am so afraid thou'lt lose
somewhat. My heart was at my mouth when I missed thee.

WASP

You were best buy a whip i' your hand to drive me.

COKES

Nay, do not mistake, Numps, thou art so apt to mistake; I
would but watch the goods. Look you now, the treble fiddle   10
was e'en almost like to be lost

WASP

Pray you take heed you lose not yourself. Your best way were
e'en get up and ride for more surety. Buy a token's worth of
great pins to fasten yourself to my shoulder.

LEATHERHEAD

What do you lack, gentlemen? Fine purses, pouches, pin-   15
cases, pipes? What is't you lack? A pair o' smiths to wake you
i' the morning? Or a fine whistling bird?

COKES

Numps, here be finer things than any we ha' bought, by odds!
And more delicate horses, a great deal! Good Numps, stay,
and come hither.   20

WASP

Will you scourse with him? You are in Smithfield; you may
fit yourself with a fine easy-going street-nag for your saddle
again Michaelmas term, do. Has he ne'er a little odd cart for
you to make a caroche on i' the country, with four pied
hobby-horses? Why the measles should you stand here with   25
your train, cheaping of dogs, birds, and babies? You ha' no
children to bestow 'em on, ha' you?

COKES

No, but again I ha' children, Numps, that's all one.

21 *scourse* barter, bargain
23 *again* against, in preparation for
24 *caroche* smart carriage
26 *cheaping of* bargaining for, asking the price of
28 *again* in anticipation of the time when

---

16 *A pair o' smiths*. Presumably a clock of some kind with a pair of 'Jacks'
in the shape of smiths.

WASP

Do, do, do, do! How many shall you have, think you? An I
were as you, I'd buy for all my tenants, too. They are a kind   30
o' civil savages that will part with their children for rattles,
pipes, and knives. You were best buy a hatchet or two, and
truck with 'em.

COKES

Good Numps, hold that little tongue o' thine, and save it a
labour. I am resolute Bat, thou know'st.   35

WASP

A resolute fool you are, I know, and a very sufficient coxcomb. With all my heart—nay, you have it, sir, an you be
angry—turd i' your teeth, twice, if I said it not once afore;
and much good do you.

WINWIFE

Was there ever such a self-affliction? And so impertinent?   40

QUARLOUS

Alas! his care will go near to crack him; let's in and comfort
him.

WASP

Would I had been set i' the ground, all but the head on me,
and had my brains bowled at, or threshed out, when first I
underwent this plague of a charge!   45

QUARLOUS

How now, Numps! Almost tired i' your protectorship?
Overparted? Overparted?

WASP

Why, I cannot tell, sir; it may be I am. Does't grieve you?

QUARLOUS

No, I swear does't not, Numps, to satisfy you.

WASP

Numps? 'Sblood, you are fine and familiar! How long ha' we   50
been acquainted, I pray you?

31 *civil savages* savages of a civilized country
41 *crack him* drive him crazy

43-4 *Would I . . . bowled at.* Cf. *The Merry Wives of Windsor*, III.iv, 85-6,
where Anne Page responds to the suggestion that she marry Dr Caius
by saying:

> Alas, I had rather be set quick i' th' earth,
> And bowl'd to death with turnips.

47 *Overparted.* Given a bigger part than you can play. Cf. *Love's Labour's
Lost*, V.ii, 577-8, where Costard remarks that Sir Nathaniel was 'a little
o'erparted' in taking on the role of Alexander the Great.

QUARLOUS

I think it may be remembered, Numps. That? 'Twas since
morning, sure.

WASP

Why, I hope I know't well enough, sir; I did not ask to be
told.   55

QUARLOUS

No? Why then?

WASP

It's no matter why. You see with your eyes now, what I said
to you today? You'll believe me another time?

QUARLOUS

Are you removing the Fair, Numps?

WASP

A pretty question! and a very civil one! Yes faith, I ha' my   60
lading you see, or shall have anon; you may know whose
beast I am by my burden. If the pannier-man's jack were
ever better known by his loins of mutton, I'll be flayed and
feed dogs for him, when his time comes.

WINWIFE

How melancholy Mistress Grace is yonder! Pray thee let's   65
go enter ourselves in grace with her.

COKES

Those six horses, friend, I'll have—

WASP

How!

COKES

And the three Jew's trumps; and half a dozen o' birds, and
that drum—I have one drum already—and your smiths—   70
I like that device o' your smiths very pretty well—and four
halberts—and, le' me see, that fine painted great lady, and
her three women for state, I'll have.

---

64 *for* in place of
66 *grace* favour
69 *trumps* harps
73 *state* ceremonial shew

---

62 *jack*. Jackass, male ass. Though *OED* cites no instance of 'jackass' prior
to 1727, 'jack' was used in the sixteenth century to denote the male of
some animals and birds. That a jackass is meant here is evident from
the reference to 'beast' and 'burden' (l. 62) and still more from Wasp's
promise to 'be flayed and feed dogs for [in place of] him, when his time
comes', since this is precisely what happened to dead horses and donkeys;
they were flayed and used as dog food.

WASP
   No, the shop; buy the whole shop, it will be best; the shop,
   the shop!   75
LEATHERHEAD
   If his worship please.
WASP
   Yes, and keep it during the Fair, bobchin.
COKES
   Peace, Numps. Friend, do not meddle with him, an you be
   wise and would shew your head above board; he will sting
   thorough your wrought night-cap, believe me. A set of these   80
   violins I would buy too, for a delicate young noise I have i'
   the country, that are every one a size less than another, just
   like your fiddles. I would fain have a fine young masque at my
   marriage, now I think on't. But I do want such a number o'
   things. And Numps will not help me now, and I dare not   85
   speak to him.
TRASH
   Will your worship buy any gingerbread, very good bread,
   comfortable bread?
COKES
   Gingerbread! Yes, let's see.   *He runs to her shop*
WASP
   There's the tother springe!   90
LEATHERHEAD
   Is this well, Goody Joan? To interrupt my market? In the
   midst? And call away my customers? Can you answer this at
   the Pie-powders?
TRASH
   Why, if his mastership have a mind to buy, I hope my
   ware lies as open as another's! I may shew my ware as well   95
   as you yours.
COKES
   Hold your peace; I'll content you both: I'll buy up his shop,
   and thy basket.

79 *above board* in company
80 *thorough* through
81 *delicate* fine   *noise* band of musicians
83 *masque* group of masquers
90 *springe* snare used to catch birds

---

77 *bobchin.* Defined by *OED* as 'one who bobs his chin', an action denoting
   folly, especially in the form of idle chatter.

WASP
Will you i'faith?

LEATHERHEAD
Why should you put him from it, friend? 100

WASP
Cry you mercy! You'd be sold too, would you? What's the
price on you? Jerkin and all, as you stand? Ha' you any
qualities?

TRASH
Yes, goodman angry-man, you shall find he has qualities, if
you cheapen him. 105

WASP
God's so, so you ha' the selling of him! What are they? Will
they be bought for love or money?

TRASH
No indeed, sir.

WASP
For what then? Victuals?

TRASH
He scorns victuals, sir, he has bread and butter at home, 110
thanks be to God! And yet he will do more for a good meal,
if the toy take him i' the belly. Marry, then they must not set
him at lower end. If they do, he'll go away, though he fast.
But put him atop o' the table, where his place is, and he'll do
you forty fine things. He has not been sent for and sought out 115
for nothing at your great city-suppers, to put down Coriat
and Cokeley, and been laughed at for his labour. He'll play
you all the puppets i' the town over, and the players, every
company, and his own company too; he spares nobody!

103 *qualities* accomplishments
106 *God's so* form of *cazzo* (Italian for penis) used as an oath
  so, so you ed. (so, you F)
113 *lower end* (of the table) where inferior guests sat

---

116 *Coriat.* Thomas Coryate (1577?–1617) was a great traveller and,
  according to Jonson, a great bore. His best-known work, *Coryats
  Crudities* (1611), is an account of his 'trauells in France, Sauoy, Italy . . .
  the Grisons . . . Switzerland, some parts of high Germany, and the
  Netherlands'. When it was published, Jonson contributed some mock-
  commendatory verses to it, together with 'The Character' of the author.
  (H & S, viii. 373–8.)
117 *Cokeley.* A jester of the time, who seems to have improvised at entertainments. Jonson also refers to him in *The Devil is an Ass* (I.i, 93) and in
  his poem 'To Mime' (*Epigrams*, cxxix. 16).

COKES

   I'faith?   120

TRASH

   He was the first, sir, that ever baited the fellow i' the bear's
skin, an't like your worship. No dog ever came near him
since. And for fine motions!

COKES

   Is he good at those too? Can he set out a masque, trow?

TRASH

   O Lord, master! sought to, far and near, for his inventions;   125
and he engrosses all, he makes all the puppets i' the Fair.

COKES

   Dost thou, in troth, old velvet jerkin? Give me thy hand.

TRASH

   Nay, sir, you shall see him in his velvet jerkin, and a scarf too,
at night, when you hear him interpret Master Littlewit's
motion.   130

COKES

   Speak no more, but shut up shop presently, friend. I'll buy
both it and thee too, to carry down with me, and her
hamper beside. Thy shop shall furnish out the masque, and
hers the banquet. I cannot go less, to set out anything with
credit. What's the price, at a word, o' thy whole shop, case   135
and all, as it stands?

LEATHERHEAD

   Sir, it stands me in six and twenty shillings sevenpence halfpenny, besides three shillings for my ground.

COKES

   Well, thirty shillings will do all, then! And what comes yours
to?   140

---

123 *motions* puppet-shews
124 *set out* produce (in the theatrical sense), exhibit (*OED*, Set, *v.*,
    149., h.)   *trow* do you think
125 *sought* applied, resorted
126 *engrosses* monopolizes
129 *at night* this evening   *interpret* ventriloquize
134 *banquet* dessert
    I cannot go less it's the least I can do
137 *stands me in* costs me, is worth to me

121–2 *baited . . . bear's skin.* According to Samuel Rowlands, in his *The
    Knave of Harts* (1612), an actor at the Fortune Theatre, playing the
    part of a bear, was 'wel-nye' killed by 'Some Butchers (playing Dogs)'.

TRASH

Four shillings and elevenpence, sir, ground and all, an't like
your worship.

COKES

Yes, it does like my worship very well, poor woman, that's
five shillings more. What a masque shall I furnish out for
forty shillings—twenty pound Scotch! And a banquet of   145
gingerbread! There's a stately thing! Numps! Sister! And
my wedding gloves too! That I never thought on afore. All
my wedding gloves gingerbread! O me! what a device will
there be, to make 'em eat their fingers' ends! And delicate
brooches for the bridemen and all! And then I'll ha' this   150
poesy put to 'em: 'For the best grace', meaning Mistress
Grace, my wedding poesy.

GRACE

I am beholden to you, sir, and to your Bartholmew-wit.

WASP

You do not mean this, do you? Is this your first purchase?

COKES

Yes faith, and I do not think, Numps, but thou'lt say, it was 155
the wisest act that ever I did in my wardship.

WASP

Like enough! I shall say anything, I!

Act III, Scene v

[*Enter to them*] OVERDO, EDGWORTH, NIGHTINGALE

OVERDO

[*Aside*] I cannot beget a project, with all my political brain,
yet; my project is how to fetch off this proper young man
from his debauched company. I have followed him all the
Fair over, and still I find him with this songster; and I begin

150 *bridemen* male attendants on the bridegroom
151 *poesy* posy, motto in metrical form
153 *Bartholmew-wit* foolish attempt to be witty, cheap witticism
  1 *political* shrewd
  2 *fetch off* rescue, save
    proper excellent

---

145 *twenty pound Scotch.* When the Crowns of England and Scotland were
    united on the accession of James I to the throne of England, the Scots
    pound was valued at one-twelfth of a pound sterling, i.e., 1*s*. 8*d*.
147 *wedding gloves.* It was customary to present gloves to the guests at a
    wedding.

shrewdly to suspect their familiarity; and the young man of a   5
terrible taint, poetry! With which idle disease if he be
infected, there's no hope of him in a state-course. *Actum est*
of him for a commonwealth's-man if he go to't in rhyme
once.

EDGWORTH

[*To* NIGHTINGALE] Yonder he is buying o' gingerbread. Set   10
in quickly, before he part with too much on his money.

NIGHTINGALE   [*Sings*]
    My masters and friends, and good people, draw near, etc.

COKES

Ballads! Hark, hark! Pray thee, fellow, stay a little. Good
Numps, look to the goods.   *He runs to the ballad-man*
What ballads hast thou? Let me see, let me see myself.   15

WASP

Why so! He's flown to another lime-bush. There he will
flutter as long more, till he ha' ne'er a feather left. Is there a
vexation like this, gentlemen? Will you believe me now?
Hereafter shall I have credit with you?

QUARLOUS

Yes faith, shalt thou, Numps, and thou art worthy on't, for   20
thou sweatest for't. I never saw a young puny errant and his
squire better matched.

WINWIFE

Faith, the sister comes after 'em well, too.

---

 7 *state-course* career of public service (?)
    Actum est of it's all up with
 8 *commonwealth's man* good citizen
    go to't indulge
10–11 *Set in* begin, go to work
16 *lime-bush* snare (literally, a bush smeared with birdlime)
17 *more* moreover, again
18–19 *now? Hereafter* Ed. (now, hereafter? F)

---

21 *puny* ed. (Pimpe F) ninny, raw novice, French *béjaune*. Cf. Nashe in his
    Christs Teares Over Jerusalem (1593): 'I see others of them [whores]
    sharing halfe with the Baudes their Hostesses, & laughing at the Punies
    they haue lurched [cheated]' (Nashe, ii. 150. 34–36). It is hard to see
    how Cokes, or Wasp who matches him, or Mistress Overdo who
    resembles ('comes after') him, or Overdo who completes the foursome
    ('mess'), can properly be described as a 'pimp' in any recorded sense of
    that word. All four are, however, very emphatically 'punies'; and 'Punye',
    in Jonson's handwriting, might easily have been misread as 'Pimpe',
    especially if a tiny splutter of ink had fallen above the first stroke of the
    'u'.

GRACE

Nay, if you saw the Justice her husband, my guardian, you
were fitted for the mess. He is such a wise one his way—   25

WINWIFE

I wonder we see him not here.

GRACE

O! he is too serious for this place, and yet better sport than
the other three, I assure you, gentlemen, where'er he is,
though't be o' the bench.

COKES

How dost thou call it? *A Caveat against Cutpurses*! A good   30
jest, i'faith. I would fain see that demon, your cutpurse you
talk of, that delicate-handed devil. They say he walks hereabout; I would see him walk now. Look you, sister, here,
here, let him come, sister, and welcome.

He shews his purse boastingly

Ballad-man, does any cutpurses haunt hereabout? Pray thee   35
raise me one or two; begin and shew me one.

NIGHTINGALE

Sir, this is a spell against 'em, spick and span new; and 'tis
made as 'twere in mine own person, and I sing it in mine
own defence. But 'twill cost a penny alone, if you buy it.

COKES

No matter for the price. Thou dost not know me, I see; I am   40
an odd Bartholmew.

MISTRESS OVERDO

Has't a fine picture, brother?

COKES

O sister, do you remember the ballads over the nursery
chimney at home o' my own pasting up? There be brave
pictures! Other manner of pictures than these, friend.   45

WASP

Yet these will serve to pick the pictures out o' your pockets,
you shall see.

COKES

So I heard 'em say. Pray thee mind him not, fellow; he'll
have an oar in everything.

NIGHTINGALE

It was intended, sir, as if a purse should chance to be cut in   50

---

25 *mess* group of four persons who ate together (*OED*, Mess *sb*. II.4);
     cf. *Love's Labour's Lost*, IV.iii, 203: 'you three fools lack'd me
     fool to make up the mess'
27–8 *than the* Ed. (then then the F)
46 *pictures* coins (stamped with the king's head)

my presence, now, I may be blameless though; as by the
sequel will more plainly appear.

COKES

We shall find that i' the matter. Pray thee begin.

NIGHTINGALE

To the tune of *Paggington's Pound*, sir.

COKES	[*Sings*]

Fa, la la la, la la la, fa la la la. Nay, I'll put thee in tune, and	55
all! Mine own country dance! Pray thee begin.

NIGHTINGALE

It is a gentle admonition, you must know, sir, both to the
purse-cutter and the purse-bearer.

COKES

Not a word more out o' the tune, an thou lov'st me. [*Sings*]
Fa, la la la, la la la, fa la la la. Come, when?	60

NIGHTINGALE	[*Sings*]

> *My masters and friends, and good people, draw near,*
> *And look to your purses, for that I do say;*

COKES

Ha, ha, this chimes! Good counsel at first dash.

NIGHTINGALE

> *And though little money in them you do bear,*
> *It cost more to get than to lose in a day.*	65

(COKES

Good!)

> *You oft have been told,*
> *Both the young and the old;*
> *And bidden beware of the cutpurse so bold;*
> *Then if you take heed not, free me from the curse,*
> *Who both give you warning, for and the cutpurse.*	70

(COKES

Well said! He were to blame that would not, i'faith.)

> *Youth, youth, thou hadst better been starved by thy nurse,*
> *Than live to be hangèd for cutting a purse.*

51 *though* nevertheless
59 *out o'* extraneous to, not part of
62 *for that* because of what
63 *chimes* rings true, goes well
    at first dash from the start
70 *for and* and moreover

54 *Paggington's Pound.* Also known as *Packington's Pound*, this old country-
dance tune still survives.

COKES

    Good i'faith, how say you, Numps? Is there any harm i'
this?   75

NIGHTINGALE

       It hath been upbraided to men of my trade,
       That oftentimes we are the cause of this crime.

(COKES

    The more coxcombs they that did it, I wusse.)
       Alack and for pity, why should it be said?
       As if they regarded or places, or time.   80
         Examples have been
         Of some that were seen,
       In Westminster Hall, yea the pleaders between;
       Then why should the judges be free from this curse,
       More than my poor self, for cutting the purse?   85

(COKES

    God a mercy for that! Why should they be more free indeed?)
       Youth, youth, thou hadst better been starved by thy nurse,
       Than live to be hangèd for cutting a purse.

COKES

    That again, good ballad-man, that again!
                  He sings the burden with him
    O rare! I would fain rub mine elbow now, but I dare not pull   90
out my hand. On, I pray thee. He that made this ballad shall
be poet to my masque.

NIGHTINGALE

       At Worcester 'tis known well, and even i' the jail,
       A knight of good worship did there shew his face,
       Against the foul sinners, in zeal for to rail,   95
       And lost (ipso facto) *his purse in the place.*

---

90 *rub mine elbow* (as a sign of glee)

76–7 *It hath . . . crime.* The accusation had been made by Robert Greene in
    his *The Third and Last Part of Cony-Catching* (1592), where one of the
    stories is very similar to the action of this scene. See *Three Elizabethan
    Pamphlets*, ed. G. R. Hibbard (London, 1951), pp. 49–51; or *The
    Elizabethan Underworld*, ed. A. V. Judges (London, 1930) pp. 189–190.
83 *In Westminster Hall.* The courts of Common Pleas, of the King's Bench,
    and of Chancery all sat in the great hall of the Palace of Westminster.
    H & S note that Thomas Dekker, in his *Iests to make you Merie* (1607),
    'has a story of a foreman of the jury, taking pity on a young man who
    had picked a purse, got him acquitted; the man "in recompence
    presently vpon his discharge, paying his fees, came to the place where
    this Juror was, and pickt his pocket" ' (H & S, x. 199).

(COKES
    Is it possible?)
                Nay, once from the seat
                Of judgement so great,
            A judge there did lose a fair pouch of velvet.   100
(COKES
    I'faith?)
                O Lord for thy mercy, how wicked or worse
                Are those that so venture their necks for a purse!
                Youth, youth, etc.
COKES   [Sings the burden with him again]
    Youth, youth, etc.   105
    Pray thee stay a little, friend. Yet o' thy conscience, Numps,
    speak; is there any harm i' this?

WASP
    To tell you true, 'tis too good for you, 'less you had grace to
    follow it.

OVERDO
    [Aside] It doth discover enormity, I'll mark it more; I ha'   110
    not liked a paltry piece of poetry so well a good while.

COKES
    Youth, youth, etc.
    Where's this youth now? A man must call upon him, for his
    own good, and yet he will not appear. Look here, here's for
    him; handy-dandy, which hand will he have?   115
                                        He shews his purse

106 stay pause, break off
     friend. Yet Ed. (friend, yet F)
108 'less unless
115 handy-dandy take your choice (from a children's game of guessing
     in which hand an object is hidden)

98–100 Nay . . . velvet. The allusion is to a story preserved by Cresacre
More in his The Life and Death of Sir Thomas Moore (1631), pp. 115–17.
It tells how More grew tired of hearing one of the Justices at Newgate
upbraid victims of purse-cutting for not keeping their purses more
warily and thus encouraging cutpurses in their activities. Accordingly,
he got in touch with a cutpurse who was about to be tried, and promised
to stand his friend 'if he would cut that Iustice's purse, whilst he sate . . .
on the Benche'. The cutpurse agreed. Coming before the Bench, he
asked to speak privately with the Justice, and, while whispering to him,
cut his purse. This he handed to More, who then restored it to its owner,
telling him not to be so censorious in future. The incident is dramatized,
with some alteration, in Sir Thomas More, the play in which Shakespeare
probably had a hand. See Sir Thomas More, I.ii, in The Shakespeare
Apocrypha, ed. C. F. Tucker Brooke (Oxford, 1918), pp. 387–90.

On, I pray thee, with the rest. I do hear of him, but I cannot
see him, this Master Youth, the cutpurse.

NIGHTINGALE

> *At plays and at sermons, and at the sessions,*
> *'Tis daily their practice such booty to make:*
> *Yea, under the gallows, at executions,*   120
> *They stick not the stare-abouts' purses to take—*
> > *Nay, one without grace,*
> > *At a far better place,*
> *At court, and in Christmas, before the King's face.*

(COKES

That was a fine fellow! I would have him, now.)   125

> *Alack then for pity, must I bear the curse,*
> *That only belongs to the cunning cutpurse?*

COKES

But where's their cunning now, when they should use it?
They are all chained now, I warrant you.

> *Youth, youth, thou hadst better, etc.*   130

The rat-catcher's charm! Are all fools and asses to this? A pox
on 'em, that they will not come! that a man should have such
a desire to a thing and want it.

QUARLOUS

'Fore God, I'd give half the Fair, an 'twere mine, for a cutpurse for him, to save his longing.   135

COKES

Look you, sister, here, here, where is't now? which pocket is't
in, for a wager?   *He shews his purse again*

---

123 *a far better* Ed. (a better F)
133 *to* for
      want be unable to get

122–4 *Nay . . . face.* The cutpurse in question, John Selman, picked a purse
       during a celebration of the sacrament in the King's Chapel at the Palace
       of Whitehall on Christmas Day 1611. He was hanged for it on 7 January
       1612.
131 *The rat-catcher's charm!* Cf. *As You Like It*, III.ii, 163–5, where
       Rosalind says, referring to Orlando's verses: 'I was never so berhym'd
       since Pythagoras' time that I was an Irish rat, which I can hardly
       remember'. The Irish peasantry held the superstitious belief that their
       bards could kill rats or drive them away by the use of magical verses.
       charm! Are . . . this? ed. (charme, are . . . this! F). The Folio punctuation
       does not make sense. Cokes, frustrated by the failure of the cutpurses to
       appear, puts their reluctance down to the effect of the ballad, which has,
       he says, scared them off and made fools and asses of them; 'this' is in
       apposition to 'charm'.

WASP

    I beseech you leave your wagers, and let him end his matter,
    an't may be.

COKES

    O, are you edified, Numps?   140

OVERDO

    [*Aside*] Indeed he does interrupt him too much. There
    Numps spoke to purpose.

COKES

    Sister, I am an ass, I cannot keep my purse?
                            [*He shews his purse*] again
    On, on, I pray thee, friend.
    [*While* COKES *listens to the song*] EDGWORTH *gets up to him, and
    tickles him in the ear with a straw twice, to draw his hand out of
                                                        his pocket*

NIGHTINGALE

        But O, you vile nation of cutpurses all,   145
        Relent and repent, and amend and be sound,
        And know that you ought not, by honest men's fall,
        Advance your own fortunes, to die above ground;

(WINWIFE

    Will you see sport? Look, there's a fellow gathers up to him,
    mark.)   150

        And though you go gay,
        In silks as you may,
        It is not the highway to heaven, as they say.

(QUARLOUS

    Good, i'faith! O, he has lighted on the wrong pocket.)
        Repent then, repent you, for better, for worse;   155
        And kiss not the gallows for cutting a purse.

(WINWIFE

    He has it! 'Fore God, he is a brave fellow; pity he should be
    detected.)
        Youth, youth, thou hadst better been starved by thy nurse,
        Than live to be hangèd for cutting a purse.   160

ALL

    An excellent ballad! an excellent ballad!

EDGWORTH

    Friend, let me ha' the first, let me ha' the first, I pray you.
                            [*He slips the purse to* NIGHTINGALE]

138 *matter* business, performance
143 *purse?* ed. (purse: F)
146 *Relent* abandon your wicked ways
148 *above ground* on the scaffold

COKES

Pardon me, sir. First come, first served; and I'll buy the
whole bundle too.

WINWIFE

That conveyance was better than all, did you see't? He has   165
given the purse to the ballad-singer.

QUARLOUS

Has he?

EDGWORTH

Sir, I cry you mercy; I'll not hinder the poor man's profit;
pray you, mistake me not.

COKES

Sir, I take you for an honest gentleman, if that be mistaking.   170
I met you today afore. Ha! humh! O God! my purse is gone,
my purse, my purse, etc.

WASP

Come, do not make a stir, and cry yourself an ass thorough
the Fair afore your time.

COKES

Why, hast thou it, Numps? Good Numps, how came you by   175
it? I mar'l!

WASP

I pray you seek some other gamester to play the fool with.
You may lose it time enough, for all your Fair-wit.

COKES

By this good hand, glove and all, I ha' lost it already, if thou
hast it not; feel else. And Mistress Grace's handkercher, too,   180
out o' the tother pocket.

WASP

Why, 'tis well; very well, exceeding pretty and well.

EDGWORTH

Are you sure you ha' lost it, sir?

COKES

O God! yes; as I am an honest man, I had it but e'en now, at
'Youth, youth'.   185

NIGHTINGALE

I hope you suspect not me, sir.

EDGWORTH

Thee? that were a jest indeed! Dost thou think the gentleman

---

170 *gentleman, . . . mistaking.* Ed. (Gentleman; . . . mistaking, F)
173 *thorough* throughout, from end to end of
176 *mar'l* marvel
177 *gamester* playmate

is foolish? Where hadst thou hands, I pray thee? Away, ass,
away.

[*Exit* NIGHTINGALE]

OVERDO

[*Aside and beginning to go*] I shall be beaten again if I be   190
spied.

EDGWORTH

Sir, I suspect an odd fellow, yonder, is stealing away.

MISTRESS OVERDO

Brother, it is the preaching fellow! You shall suspect him. He
was at your tother purse, you know!—Nay, stay, sir, and
view the work you ha' done; an you be beneficed at the   195
gallows, and preach there, thank your own handiwork.

COKES

Sir, you shall take no pride in your preferment: you shall be
silenced quickly.

OVERDO

What do you mean, sweet buds of gentility?

COKES

To ha' my pennyworths out on you, bud! No less than two   200
purses a day serve you? I thought you a simple fellow when
my man Numps beat you i' the morning, and pitied you—

MISTRESS OVERDO

So did I, I'll be sworn, brother. But now I see he is a lewd
and pernicious enormity, as Master Overdo calls him.

OVERDO

[*Aside*] Mine own words turned upon me, like swords.   205

COKES

Cannot a man's purse be at quiet for you i' the master's
pocket, but you must entice it forth and debauch it?

WASP

Sir, sir, keep your 'debauch' and your fine Bartholmew-terms
to yourself, and make as much on 'em as you please. But gi'
me this from you i' the mean time. I beseech you see if I can   210
look to this.   [*Tries to take the box*]

COKES

Why, Numps?

193 *shall* ought to, have every reason to
200 *pennyworths* revenge
207 *debauch it* induce it to desert

195–6 *an you . . . there*. If you, who are so given to preaching, suffer a
hanging as your church living—a reference to the speeches of repentance
which were a common feature of executions at the time.

WASP

Why? Because you are an ass, sir. There's a reason the
shortest way, an you will needs ha' it. Now you ha' got the
trick of losing, you'd lose your breech an 'twere loose. I   215
know you, sir. Come, deliver.

                              WASP *takes the licence from him*
You'll go and crack the vermin you breed now, will you?
'Tis very fine! Will you ha' the truth on't? They are such
retchless flies as you are, that blow cutpurses abroad in every
corner; your foolish having of money makes 'em. An there   220
were no wiser than I, sir, the trade should lie open for you,
sir, it should i'faith, sir. I would teach your wit to come to
your head, sir, as well as your land to come into your hand,
I assure you, sir.

WINWIFE

Alack, good Numps.   225

WASP

Nay, gentlemen, never pity me, I am not worth it. Lord send
me at home once, to Harrow o' the Hill again; if I travel any
more, call me Coriat, with all my heart.

        [*Exeunt* WASP, COKES, MISTRESS OVERDO, *with* OVERDO]

QUARLOUS

Stay, sir, I must have a word with you in private. Do you
hear?   230

EDGWORTH

With me, sir? What's your pleasure, good sir?

QUARLOUS

Do not deny it. You are a cutpurse, sir; this gentleman here,
and I, saw you; nor do we mean to detect you, though we can
sufficiently inform ourselves toward the danger of concealing
you; but you must do us a piece of service.   235

EDGWORTH

Good gentlemen, do not undo me; I am a civil young man,
and but a beginner, indeed.

---

216 s.d. WASP *takes the licence from him* (at l. 211 in F)
219 *retchless* heedless
    blow beget (as a fly deposits its eggs and breeds maggots)
220–1 *An there . . . I* if I might have my way without interference
221 *the trade . . . you* you would be apprenticed to some trade
233 *nor do we* and yet we do not
    detect expose, inform on
234 *toward* about
236 *civil* orderly, respectable

QUARLOUS
Sir, your beginning shall bring on your ending, for us. We
are no catchpoles nor constables. That you are to undertake
is this: you saw the old fellow with the black box here?   240

EDGWORTH
The little old governor, sir?

QUARLOUS
That same. I see you have flown him to a mark already. I
would ha' you get away that box from him, and bring it us.

EDGWORTH
Would you ha' the box and all, sir? Or only that that is in't?
I'll get you that, and leave him the box to play with still—   245
which will be the harder o' the two—because I would gain
your worships' good opinion of me.

WINWIFE
He says well, 'tis the greater mastery, and 'twill make the
more sport when 'tis missed.

EDGWORTH
Ay, and 'twill be the longer a-missing, to draw on the sport.   250

QUARLOUS
But look you do it now, sirrah, and keep your word, or—

EDGWORTH
Sir, if ever I break my word with a gentleman, may I never
read word at my need. Where shall I find you?

QUARLOUS
Somewhere i' the Fair, hereabouts. Dispatch it quickly.
                    [*Exit* EDGWORTH]
I would fain see the careful fool deluded! Of all beasts, I   255
love the serious ass: he that takes pains to be one, and plays
the fool with the greatest diligence that can be.

GRACE
Then you would not choose, sir, but love my guardian, Justice Overdo, who is answerable to that description in every
hair of him.   260

QUARLOUS
So I have heard. But how came you, Mistress Wellborn, to
be his ward, or have relation to him, at first?

238 *for us* for all we care
239 *That* that which, what
241 *governor* tutor
242 *flown him to a mark* identified him (cf. II. iv, 41)
248 *mastery* feat, exercise of skill
253 *word* the neck-verse (cf. I, iv, 6–7)
256 *ass: he* Ed. (Asse. He F)

GRACE

Faith, through a common calamity: he bought me, sir. And
now he will marry me to his wife's brother, this wise gentleman that you see, or else I must pay value o' my land.   265

QUARLOUS

'Slid, is there no device of disparagement, or so? Talk with
some crafty fellow, some picklock o' the Law. Would I had
studied a year longer i' the Inns of Court, an't had been but
i' your case!

WINWIFE

[*Aside*] Ay, Master Quarlous, are you proffering?   270

GRACE

You'd bring but little aid, sir.

WINWIFE

[*Aside*] I'll look to you i'faith, gamester.—An unfortunate
foolish tribe you are fallen into, lady; I wonder you can
endure 'em.

GRACE

Sir, they that cannot work their fetters off must wear 'em.   275

WINWIFE

You see what care they have on you, to leave you thus.

GRACE

Faith, the same they have of themselves, sir. I cannot greatly
complain, if this were all the plea I had against 'em.

WINWIFE

'Tis true! But will you please to withdraw with us a little,
and make them think they have lost you? I hope our man-   280
ners ha' been such hitherto, and our language, as will give
you no cause to doubt yourself in our company.

270 *proffering* making an offer, making advances
272 *look to* keep an eye on, beware of
282 *doubt* have fears for

---

263 *he bought me.* Grace is the victim of one of the major abuses of the age.
The Court of Wards, established under Henry VIII, administered the
estates of all wards of the crown, i.e., minors and lunatics inheriting from
tenants of the King. The Court had the power to sell the guardianship,
including control of the ward's marriage, to anyone it pleased for ready
cash. See Joel Hurstfield, *The Queen's Wards* (1958), *passim.*
265 *or else . . . land.* If the ward refused to accept the spouse chosen by the
guardian, the guardian was entitled to recover the value of the marriage
from the ward.
266 *disparagement.* Disparagement was involved, and the match could not go
forward, if the guardian sought to wed his ward to one of inferior rank.

GRACE

Sir, I will give myself no cause; I am so secure of mine own
manners as I suspect not yours.

QUARLOUS

Look where John Littlewit comes.   285

WINWIFE

Away, I'll not be seen by him.

QUARLOUS

No, you were not best, he'd tell his mother, the widow.

WINWIFE

Heart, what do you mean?

QUARLOUS

Cry you mercy, is the wind there? Must not the widow be
named?   290

[*Exeunt* GRACE, WINWIFE, QUARLOUS]

Act III, Scene vi

[*Enter to them*] LITTLEWIT, WIN

LITTLEWIT

Do you hear, Win, Win?

WIN

What say you, John?

LITTLEWIT

While they are paying the reckoning, Win, I'll tell you a
thing, Win: we shall never see any sights i' the Fair, Win,
except you long still, Win. Good Win, sweet Win, long to   5
see some hobby-horses, and some drums, and rattles, and
dogs, and fine devices, Win. The bull with the five legs, Win,
and the great hog. Now you ha' begun with pig, you may
long for anything, Win, and so for my motion, Win.

WIN

But we sha' not eat o' the bull and the hog, John. How shall   10
I long then?

LITTLEWIT

O yes, Win! You may long to see as well as to taste, Win.
How did the pothecary's wife, Win, that longed to see the

---

283 *secure of* confident in
284 *manners* moral code of behaviour
287 *were not best* had best not
289 *is the wind there* is that the case (proverbial, Tilley, W421)

anatomy, Win? Or the lady, Win, that desired to spit i' the
great lawyer's mouth after an eloquent pleading? I assure   15
you they longed, Win. Good Win, go in, and long.

[Exeunt LITTLEWIT, WIN]

TRASH

I think we are rid of our new customer, Brother Leatherhead,
we shall hear no more of him.

They plot to be gone

LEATHERHEAD

All the better. Let's pack up all, and be gone, before he find
us.   20

TRASH

Stay a little, yonder comes a company; it may be we may
take some more money.

[*Enter*] KNOCKEM, BUSY

KNOCKEM

Sir, I will take your counsel, and cut my hair, and leave
vapours. I see that tobacco, and bottle-ale, and pig, and Whit,
and very Ursla herself, is all vanity.   25

BUSY

Only pig was not comprehended in my admonition, the
rest were. For long hair, it is an ensign of pride, a banner,
and the world is full of those banners, very full of banners.
And bottle-ale is a drink of Satan's, a diet-drink of Satan's,
devised to puff us up, and make us swell in this latter age of   30
vanity, as the smoke of tobacco to keep us in mist and error.
But the fleshly woman, which you call Ursla, is above all to
be avoided, having the marks upon her of the three enemies
of man: the World, as being in the Fair; the Devil, as being
in the fire; and the Flesh, as being herself.   35

[*Enter*] PURECRAFT

PURECRAFT

Brother Zeal-of-the-land, what shall we do? My daughter,
Win-the-fight, is fallen into her fit of longing again.

BUSY

For more pig? There is no more, is there?

14 *anatomy* skeleton
14–15 *to spit . . . mouth* (as a form of reward and encouragement—
    proverbial, Tilley, M1255 and M1259)
27 *For* as for
29 *diet-drink* medicine
35 *and the* Ed. (and and the F)

PURECRAFT

To see some sights, i' the Fair.

BUSY

Sister, let her fly the impurity of the place swiftly, lest she   40
partake of the pitch thereof. Thou art the seat of the Beast,
O Smithfield, and I will leave thee. Idolatry peepeth out on
every side of thee.

KNOCKEM

An excellent right hypocrite! Now his belly is full, he falls
a-railing and kicking, the jade. A very good vapour! I'll in,   45
and joy Ursla with telling how her pig works; two and a half
he ate to his share. And he has drunk a pailful. He eats with
his eyes, as well as his teeth.   [*Exit*]

LEATHERHEAD

What do you lack, gentlemen? What is't you buy? Rattles,
drums, babies—   50

BUSY

Peace, with thy apocryphal wares, thou profane publican—
thy bells, thy dragons, and thy Toby's dogs. Thy hobby-
horse is an idol, a very idol, a fierce and rank idol; and thou
the Nebuchadnezzar, the proud Nebuchadnezzar of the
Fair, that sett'st it up, for children to fall down to and   55
worship.

LEATHERHEAD

Cry you mercy, sir, will you buy a fiddle to fill up your
noise?

[*Enter* LITTLEWIT, WIN]

LITTLEWIT

Look, Win; do look o' God's name, and save your longing.
Here be fine sights.   60

PURECRAFT

Ay, child, so you hate 'em, as our brother Zeal does, you
may look on 'em.

LEATHERHEAD

Or what do you say to a drum, sir?

51 *apocryphal* sham, spurious (the Puritans rejected the Apocrypha
    completely)
    publican heathen, excommunicated person
54 *Nebuchadnezzar* King of Babylon who set up a golden idol
    (Daniel, iii)
58 *noise?* Ed. (noise. F)
63 *drum,* Ed. (Drumme. F)

---

52 *thy bells . . . Toby's dogs.* See *Tobit*, v. 16 and *Bel and the Dragon*, in the
    Apocrypha.

BUSY

It is the broken belly of the Beast, and thy bellows there are
his lungs, and these pipes are his throat, those feathers are   65
of his tail, and thy rattles the gnashing of his teeth.

TRASH

And what's my gingerbread, I pray you?

BUSY

The provender that pricks him up. Hence with thy basket of
popery, thy nest of images, and whole legend of ginger-work.

LEATHERHEAD

Sir, if you be not quiet the quicklier, I'll ha' you clapped   70
fairly by the heels, for disturbing the Fair.

BUSY

The sin of the Fair provokes me, I cannot be silent.

PURECRAFT

Good brother Zeal!

LEATHERHEAD

Sir, I'll make you silent, believe it.

LITTLEWIT

I'd give a shilling you could, i' faith, friend.   75

LEATHERHEAD

Sir, give me your shilling; I'll give you my shop if I do not,
and I'll leave it in pawn with you, i' the mean time.

LITTLEWIT

A match i' faith; but do it quickly then.

                              [*Exit* LEATHERHEAD]
BUSY   *He speaks to the widow*

Hinder me not, woman. I was moved in spirit, to be here,
this day, in this Fair, this wicked and foul Fair—and fitter   80
may it be called a foul than a Fair—to protest against the
abuses of it, the foul abuses of it, in regard of the afflicted
saints, that are troubled, very much troubled, exceedingly
troubled, with the opening of the merchandise of Babylon
again, and the peeping of popery upon the stalls here, here in   85

68 *pricks him up* makes him high-spirited (proverbial, Tilley, P615)
75 *shilling you could*, Ed. (shilling, you could F) shilling if you could
81 *be called* Ed. (be a called F)
83 *saints* Puritans

---

69 *images . . . legend of ginger-work*. The Puritans were, of course, strongly
opposed to the use of images in churches—some of Trash's wares are,
presumably, in the shape of St Bartholomew—and they regarded *The
Golden Legend*, the great mediaeval collection of saints' lives, as a pack
of lies.

the high places. See you not Goldylocks, the purple strumpet, there? in her yellow gown, and green sleeves? the profane pipes, the tinkling timbrels? A shop of relics!

LITTLEWIT

Pray you forbear, I am put in trust with 'em.

BUSY

And this idolatrous grove of images, this flasket of idols!   90
which I will pull down—   *Overthrows the gingerbread*

TRASH

O my ware, my ware, God bless it.

BUSY

—in my zeal, and glory to be thus exercised.

LEATHERHEAD *enters with officers*

LEATHERHEAD

Here he is. Pray you lay hold on his zeal; we cannot sell a
whistle, for him, in tune. Stop his noise first!   95

BUSY

Thou canst not; 'tis a sanctified noise. I will make a loud
and most strong noise, till I have daunted the profane
enemy. And for this cause—

LEATHERHEAD

Sir, here's no man afraid of you, or your cause. You shall
swear it, i' the stocks, sir.   100

BUSY

I will thrust myself into the stocks, upon the pikes of the
land.

LEATHERHEAD

Carry him away.

PURECRAFT

What do you mean, wicked men?

BUSY

Let them alone; I fear them not.   105
    [*Exeunt officers with* BUSY, *followed by* PURECRAFT]

LITTLEWIT

Was not this shilling well ventured, Win, for our liberty?
Now we may go play, and see over the Fair, where we list,
ourselves. My mother is gone after him, and let her e'en go,
and loose us.

---

90 *flasket* long shallow basket
95 *for* because of
100 *swear it* do your swearing
101 *thrust myself . . . upon the pikes* rush to destruction (like a martyr)

WIN

Yes, John, but I know not what to do.   110

LITTLEWIT

For what, Win?

WIN

For a thing I am ashamed to tell you, i'faith, and 'tis too far
to go home.

LITTLEWIT

I pray thee be not ashamed, Win. Come, i'faith thou shall
not be ashamed. Is it anything about the hobby-horse-man?   115
An't be, speak freely.

WIN

Hang him, base bobchin, I scorn him. No, I have very great
what-sha-callum, John.

LITTLEWIT

O! Is that all, Win? We'll go back to Captain Jordan, to the
pig-woman's, Win. He'll help us, or she with a dripping   120
pan, or an old kettle, or something. The poor greasy soul
loves you, Win. And after we'll visit the Fair all over, Win,
and see my puppet play, Win. You know it's a fine matter,
Win.

[Exeunt LITTLEWIT, WIN]

LEATHERHEAD

Let's away. I counselled you to pack up afore, Joan.   125

TRASH

A pox of his Bedlam purity! He has spoiled half my ware.
But the best is: we lose nothing if we miss our first merchant.

LEATHERHEAD

It shall be hard for him to find, or know us, when we are
translated, Joan.

[Exeunt]

Act IV, Scene i

[Enter] TROUBLE-ALL, BRISTLE, HAGGIS, COKES, OVERDO

TROUBLE-ALL

My masters, I do make no doubt but you are officers.

BRISTLE

What then, sir?

118 *what-sha-callum* need to make water
127 *miss* avoid meeting, keep clear of
    merchant customer
128–9 *are translated* (i) have moved elsewhere (ii) have disguised
    ourselves

TROUBLE-ALL

   And the King's loving and obedient subjects.

BRISTLE

   Obedient, friend? Take heed what you speak, I advise you:
Oliver Bristle advises you. His loving subjects, we grant   5
you; but not his obedient, at this time, by your leave; we
know ourselves a little better than so; we are to command,
sir, and such as you are to be obedient. Here's one of his
obedient subjects, going to the stocks, and we'll make you
such another, if you talk.   10

TROUBLE-ALL

   You are all wise enough i' your places, I know.

BRISTLE

   If you know it, sir, why do you bring it in question?

TROUBLE-ALL

   I question nothing, pardon me. I do only hope you have
warrant for what you do, and so, quit you, and so, multiply
you.   *He goes away again*   15

HAGGIS

   What's he?—Bring him up to the stocks there. Why bring
you him not up?

                [TROUBLE-ALL] *comes again*

TROUBLE-ALL

   If you have Justice Overdo's warrant, 'tis well; you are safe;
that is the warrant of warrants. I'll not give this button for
any man's warrant else.   20

BRISTLE

   Like enough, sir. But let me tell you, an you play away your
buttons thus, you will want 'em ere night; for any store I see
about you, you might keep 'em, and save pins, I wussc.

                [TROUBLE-ALL] *goes away*

OVERDO

   [*Aside*] What should he be, that doth so esteem and advance
my warrant? He seems a sober and discreet person! It is a   25

   7 *than so* than that
  14–15 *quit you . . . you* God reward you and increase your family
  22–3 *night; . . . you,* ed. (night, . . . you: F)
  22 *store* plenty, abundant supply
  24 *should* might, can
      advance extol (OED, Advance *v.*, 12)

---

  5 *Oliver Bristle.* At III.i, 8, Haggis called him 'Davy Bristle', but Jonson
appears to have forgotten this.

comfort to a good conscience to be followed with a good
fame in his sufferings. The world will have a pretty taste by
this, how I can bear adversity; and it will beget a kind of
reverence toward me, hereafter, even from mine enemies,
when they shall see I carry my calamity nobly, and that it   30
doth neither break me nor bend me.

HAGGIS
Come, sir, here's a place for you to preach in. Will you put
in your leg?

They put him in the stocks

OVERDO
That I will, cheerfully.

BRISTLE
O' my conscience, a seminary! He kisses the stocks.   35

COKES
Well, my masters, I'll leave him with you. Now I see him
bestowed, I'll go look for my goods, and Numps.

HAGGIS
You may, sir, I warrant you. Where's the tother bawler?
Fetch him too. You shall find 'em both fast enough.

[Exit COKES*]*

OVERDO
[Aside] In the midst of this tumult, I will yet be the author   40
of mine own rest, and, not minding their fury, sit in the
stocks in that calm as shall be able to trouble a triumph.

[TROUBLE-ALL] *comes again*

TROUBLE-ALL
Do you assure me upon your words? May I undertake for
you, if I be asked the question, that you have this warrant?

HAGGIS
What's this fellow, for God's sake?   45

TROUBLE-ALL
Do but shew me 'Adam Overdo', and I am satisfied.

Goes out

BRISTLE
He is a fellow that is distracted, they say—one Trouble-all.

---

35 *seminary* recusant (cf. II. i, 33)
41 *rest* (i) tranquillity of mind (ii) arrest
42 *trouble* mar

---

33 *leg.* The stocks used here secure the victim by one leg only, not two, as
was more normal. See also the s.d. at IV.vi, 73.

He was an officer in the court of Pie-powders here last year,
and put out on his place by Justice Overdo.

OVERDO

Ha!   50

BRISTLE

Upon which he took an idle conceit, and's run mad upon't.
So that, ever since, he will do nothing but by Justice Overdo's
warrant: he will not eat a crust, nor drink a little, nor make
him in his apparel ready. His wife, sir-reverence, cannot
get him make his water, or shift his shirt, without his   55
warrant.

OVERDO

[Aside] If this be true, this is my greatest disaster! How
am I bound to satisfy this poor man, that is, of so good a
nature to me, out of his wits, where there is no room left
for dissembling!   60

[TROUBLE-ALL] comes in

TROUBLE-ALL

If you cannot shew me 'Adam Overdo', I am in doubt of
you. I am afraid you cannot answer it.   Goes again

HAGGIS

Before me, neighbour Bristle, and now I think on't better,
Justice Overdo is a very parantory person.

BRISTLE

O! are you advised of that? And a severe justicer, by your 65
leave.

OVERDO

[Aside] Do I hear ill o' that side, too?

BRISTLE

He will sit as upright o' the bench, an you mark him, as a
candle i' the socket, and give light to the whole court in
every business.   70

49 *on* of
51 *took an idle conceit* became the victim of a groundless delusion
53–4 *make him in his apparel ready* get dressed
55 *shift* change
58 *is,* Ed. (is F)
   of as a consequence of
62 *answer it* give a satisfactory answer
63 *Before me* upon my word
64 *parantory* peremptory
65 *are you advised* have you taken note

HAGGIS
But he will burn blue, and swell like a boil, God bless us,
an he be angry.

BRISTLE
Ay, and he will be angry too, when 'has list, that's more;
and when he is angry, be it right or wrong, he has the law
on's side ever. I mark that too.　　　　　　　　　　　　　　75

OVERDO
[*Aside*] I will be more tender hereafter. I see compassion
may become a Justice, though it be a weakness, I confess,
and nearer a vice than a virtue.

HAGGIS
Well, take him out o' the stocks again. We'll go a sure way
to work; we'll ha' the ace of hearts of our side, if we can.　　80
　　　　　　　　　　　　　They take the Justice out

　　　　　　　[*Enter*] POCHER, BUSY, PURECRAFT

POCHER
Come, bring him away to his fellow there. Master Busy, we
shall rule your legs, I hope, though we cannot rule your
tongue.

BUSY
No, minister of darkness, no, thou canst not rule my tongue;
my tongue it is mine own, and with it I will both knock and　　85
mock down your Bartholmew-abhominations, till you be
made a hissing to the neighbour parishes round about.

HAGGIS
Let him alone, we have devised better upon't.

PURECRAFT
And shall he not into the stocks then?

BRISTLE
No, mistress, we'll have 'em both to Justice Overdo, and let　　90
him do over 'em as is fitting. Then I, and my gossip Haggis,
and my beadle Pocher are discharged.

73 *'has list* ed. (his list F) feels so inclined
80 *of* on
87 *hissing* object of scorn and opprobrium (cf. Jeremiah, xix. 8)
92 *discharged* freed of responsibility

---

86 *Bartholmew-abhominations*. This spelling of 'abomination', very common
in the sixteenth century, arose from the mistaken view that the word
was derived from 'ab homine', meaning 'inhuman'. Jonson, who knew
better, puts this form of the word in Busy's mouth as a further indication
of the preacher's ignorance.

PURECRAFT

O, I thank you, blessed, honest men!

BRISTLE

Nay, never thank us, but thank this madman that comes
here, he put it in our heads. 95

[TROUBLE-ALL] *comes again*

PURECRAFT

Is he mad? Now heaven increase his madness, and bless it,
and thank it! Sir, your poor handmaid thanks you.

TROUBLE-ALL

Have you a warrant? An you have a warrant, shew it.

PURECRAFT

Yes, I have a warrant out of the Word, to give thanks for
removing any scorn intended to the brethren. 100

TROUBLE-ALL

It is Justice Overdo's warrant that I look for; if you have not
that, keep your word, I'll keep mine. Quit ye, and multiply
ye.

[*Exeunt all but* TROUBLE-ALL]

Act IV, Scene ii

[*Enter to him*] EDGWORTH, NIGHTINGALE

EDGWORTH

Come away, Nightingale, I pray thee.

TROUBLE-ALL

Whither go you? Where's your warrant?

EDGWORTH

Warrant for what, sir?

TROUBLE-ALL

For what you go about; you know how fit it is. An you have
no warrant, bless you, I'll pray for you, that's all I can do. 5

Goes out

EDGWORTH

What means he?

NIGHTINGALE

A madman that haunts the Fair; do you not know him? It's
marvel he has not more followers after his ragged heels.

97 *it*! Ed. (it, F)
99 *the Word* the Bible

EDGWORTH

Beshrew him, he startled me; I thought he had known of our
plot. Guilt's a terrible thing! Ha' you prepared the costard-   10
monger?

NIGHTINGALE

Yes, and agreed for his basket of pears. He is at the corner
here, ready. And your prize, he comes down, sailing, that
way, all alone, without his protector. He is rid of him, it
seems.   15

EDGWORTH

Ay, I know. I should ha' followed his protectorship for a
feat I am to do upon him; but this offered itself so i' the
way, I could not let it scape. Here he comes. Whistle. Be
this sport called 'Dorring the Dottrel'.

[Enter] COKES

NIGHTINGALE   *Whistles*
Wh, wh, wh, wh, etc.   20

[Enter] COSTARD-MONGER

COKES

By this light, I cannot find my gingerbread-wife, nor my
hobby-horse-man, in all the Fair, now, to ha' my money
again. And I do not know the way out on't, to go home for
more. Do you hear, friend, you that whistle, what tune is
that you whistle?   25

NIGHTINGALE

A new tune I am practising, sir.

COKES

Dost thou know where I dwell, I pray thee? Nay, on with
thy tune; I ha' no such haste for an answer. I'll practise
with thee.

9 *Beshrew* curse, a plague on
12 *agreed* settled on a price
13 *prize* prey (Cokes is seen as a ship to be captured)
17–18 *i' the way* invitingly, opportunely
23 *again* back

19 *Dorring the Dottrel*. Hoaxing the simpleton. 'To dor' was 'to make a fool
of', and the dottrel is a kind of plover proverbial for its foolishness
(Tilley, D364) in allowing itself to be easily caught. The fatuous Norfolk
squire in Jonson's next play, *The Devil is an Ass*, is called Fitz-Dottrell.

COSTARD-MONGER
> Buy any pears, very fine pears, pears fine.   30
>   NIGHTINGALE *sets his foot afore him, and he falls with his*
>   *basket*

COKES
> God's so! A muss, a muss, a muss, a muss!

COSTARD-MONGER
> Good gentleman, my ware, my ware! I am a poor man.
> Good sir, my ware.

NIGHTINGALE
> Let me hold your sword, sir, it troubles you.

COKES
> Do, and my cloak, an thou wilt, and my hat, too.   35
>   COKES *falls a-scrambling whilst they run away with his things*

EDGWORTH
> A delicate great boy! Methinks he out-scrambles 'em all. I
> cannot persuade myself but he goes to grammar-school yet,
> and plays the truant today.

NIGHTINGALE
> Would he had another purse to cut, Zekiel!

EDGWORTH
> Purse! A man might cut out his kidneys, I think, and he   40
> never feel 'em, he is so earnest at the sport.

NIGHTINGALE
> His soul is half-way out on's body at the game.

EDGWORTH
> Away, Nightingale, that way!
>   [*Exit* NIGHTINGALE *with sword, cloak, and hat*]

COKES
> I think I am furnished for Cather'ne pears, for one under-
> meal. Gi' me my cloak.   45

COSTARD-MONGER
> Good gentleman, give me my ware.

COKES
> Where's the fellow I ga' my cloak to? My cloak? and my hat?
> Ha! God's lid, is he gone? Thieves, thieves! Help me to cry,
> gentlemen.   *He runs out*

EDGWORTH
> Away, costermonger, come to us to Ursla's.   50
>   [*Exit* COSTARD-MONGER]

---

31 *muss* scramble
35 s.d. COKES *falls . . . things* (at l. 34 in F)
44–5 *undermeal* afternoon meal, snack

Talk of him to have a soul? 'Heart, if he have any more than
a thing given him instead of salt, only to keep him from
stinking, I'll be hanged afore my time, presently. Where
should it be, trow? In his blood? He has not so much to'ard
it in his whole body as will maintain a good flea. And if he   55
take this course, he will not ha' so much land left as to rear
a calf within this twelvemonth. Was there ever green plover
so pulled? That his little overseer had been here now, and
been but tall enough, to see him steal pears in exchange for
his beaver-hat and his cloak thus! I must go find him out   60
next, for his black box, and his patent, it seems he has, of
his place; which I think the gentleman would have a reversion of, that spoke to me for it so earnestly.   [*Exit*]

                    He [COKES] *comes again*

COKES

Would I might lose my doublet, and hose too, as I am an
honest man, and never stir, if I think there be anything but   65
thieving and coz'ning i' this whole Fair. Bartholmew Fair,
quoth he! An ever any Bartholmew had that luck in't that I
have had, I'll be martyred for him, and in Smithfield too.
I ha' paid for my pears. A rot on 'em, I'll keep 'em no longer.
                    Throws away his pears
You were choke-pears to me. I had been better ha' gone to   70
mum-chance for you, I wusse. Methinks the Fair should
not have used me thus, an 'twere but for my name's sake. I

---

58 *pulled* plucked clean
61 *patent, it seems* ed. (Patent (it seemes) F)
70 *choke-pears* (i) coarse unpalatable pears (ii) a harsh reproof
71 *mum-chance* dicing game popular among costermongers
   for instead of

51–3 *Talk . . . stinking.* An allusion to the notion that just as salt preserves
   meat so the soul prevents man from going rotten, which he does, of
   course, when the soul leaves the body. H & S aptly quote Herrick's
   epigram:
        The body's salt, the soule is; which when gon,
        The flesh soone sucks in putrifaction. (*Works*, ed. L. C. Martin,
                                Oxford, 1956, p. 332.)
61–3 *patent . . . reversion of.* Edgworth thinks the box contains a document
   confirming Wasp in his position as Cokes's tutor, and that Quarlous
   wants the document in order to make sure of taking over Wasp's position.
68 *martyred . . . Smithfield too.* A reference to the Smithfield Martyrs, the
   Protestants who were burned there during the reign of Mary Tudor.

would not ha’ used a dog o’ the name so. O, Numps will
triumph now!

TROUBLE-ALL *comes again*

Friend, do you know who I am? Or where I lie? I do not   75
myself, I’ll be sworn. Do but carry me home, and I’ll please
thee, I ha’ money enough there. I ha’ lost myself, and my
cloak and my hat, and my fine sword, and my sister, and
Numps, and Mistress Grace, a gentlewoman that I should
ha’ married, and a cut-work handkercher she ga’ me, and   80
two purses, today. And my bargain o’ hobby-horses and
gingerbread, which grieves me worst of all.

TROUBLE-ALL

By whose warrant, sir, have you done all this?

COKES

Warrant? Thou art a wise fellow indeed—as if a man need a
warrant to lose anything with.   85

TROUBLE-ALL

Yes, Justice Overdo’s warrant a man may get and lose with,
I’ll stand to’t.

COKES

Justice Overdo? Dost thou know him? I lie there, he is my
brother-in-law, he married my sister. Pray thee shew me the
way; dost thou know the house?   90

TROUBLE-ALL

Sir, shew me your warrant. I know nothing without a
warrant, pardon me.

COKES

Why, I warrant thee. Come along, thou shalt see I have
wrought pillows there, and cambric sheets, and sweet bags
too. Pray thee guide me to the house.   95

TROUBLE-ALL

Sir, I’ll tell you. Go you thither yourself first alone; tell
your worshipful brother your mind; and but bring me
three lines of his hand, or his clerk’s, with ‘Adam Overdo’

75 *lie* lodge
76 *carry* escort, take
   please satisfy, reward
80 *cut-work* embroidered
93 *thee. Come along*, ed. (thee, come along: F)
94 *wrought* embroidered
   sweet bags bags containing fragrant herbs to perfume the linen

underneath. Here I'll stay you, I'll obey you, and I'll guide
you presently.   100

COKES

[*Aside*] 'Slid, this is an ass, I ha' found him. Pox upon me,
what do I talking to such a dull fool?—Farewell. You are a
very coxcomb, do you hear?

TROUBLE-ALL

I think I am. If Justice Overdo sign to it, I am, and so we
are all. He'll quit us all, multiply us all.   105

[*Exeunt*]

Act IV, Scene iii

[*Enter*] GRACE. They (QUARLOUS, WINWIFE) *enter with their*
swords drawn

GRACE

Gentlemen, this is no way that you take. You do but breed
one another trouble and offence, and give me no contentment at all. I am no she that affects to be quarrelled for, or
have my name or fortune made the question of men's swords.

QUARLOUS

'Slood, we love you.   5

GRACE

If you both love me, as you pretend, your own reason will
tell you but one can enjoy me; and to that point there leads
a directer line than by my infamy, which must follow if you
fight. 'Tis true—I have professed it to you ingenuously—
that, rather than to be yoked with this bridegroom is ap-   10
pointed me, I would take up any husband, almost, upon any
trust; though Subtlety would say to me—I know—he is a
fool, and has an estate, and I might govern him, and enjoy a
friend beside. But these are not my aims. I must have a

99 *stay* wait for
101 *found him* discovered his true character, sized him up
 3 *affects* likes
 6 *pretend* claim
10 *is* who is
11 *take up* accept
   almost, ed. (almost F)
11–12 *upon any trust* without further investigation of his credentials
12 *he* Cokes
14 *friend* lover

husband I must love, or I cannot live with him. I shall ill   15
make one of these politic wives!

WINWIFE

Why, if you can like either of us, lady, say which is he, and
the other shall swear instantly to desist.

QUARLOUS

Content, I accord to that willingly.

GRACE

Sure you think me a woman of an extreme levity, gentlemen,   20
or a strange fancy, that, meeting you by chance in such a
place as this, both at one instant, and not yet of two hours'
acquaintance, neither of you deserving afore the other of me,
I should so forsake my modesty, though I might affect one
more particularly, as to say, 'This is he', and name him.   25

QUARLOUS

Why, wherefore should you not? What should hinder you?

GRACE

If you would not give it to my modesty, allow it yet to my
wit; give me so much of woman, and cunning, as not to
betray myself impertinently. How can I judge of you, so far
as to a choice, without knowing you more? You are both   30
equal and alike to me, yet; and so indifferently affected by
me, as each of you might be the man, if the other were
away; for you are reasonable creatures; you have understanding and discourse; and if fate send me an understanding husband, I have no fear at all but mine own   35
manners shall make him a good one.

QUARLOUS

Would I were put forth to making for you, then.

GRACE

It may be you are; you know not what's toward you. Will
you consent to a motion of mine, gentlemen?

16 *politic* scheming
28 *wit* intelligence
    cunning knowledge of the world
29 *impertinently* unbecomingly
31 *indifferently affected* impartially regarded
33 *away; for* ed. (away. For F)
34 *discourse* the ability to reason
37 *put forth to making* apprenticed to be trained
38 *toward* in store for
39 *motion* proposal, suggestion

WINWIFE

Whatever it be, we'll presume reasonableness, coming from   40
you.

QUARLOUS

And fitness, too.

GRACE

I saw one of you buy a pair of tables, e'en now.

WINWIFE

Yes, here they be, and maiden ones too, unwritten in.

GRACE

The fitter for what they may be employed in. You shall   45
write, either of you, here a word or a name, what you like
best, but of two or three syllables at most. And the next
person that comes this way—because Destiny has a high
hand in business of this nature—I'll demand which of the
two words he or she doth approve; and, according to that   50
sentence, fix my resolution, and affection, without change.

QUARLOUS

Agreed, my word is conceived already.

WINWIFE

And mine shall not be long creating after.

GRACE

But you shall promise, gentlemen, not to be curious to know
which of you it is, is taken; but give me leave to conceal that   55
till you have brought me, either home, or where I may
safely tender myself.

WINWIFE

Why, that's but equal.

QUARLOUS

We are pleased.

GRACE

Because I will bind both your endeavours to work together,   60
friendly and jointly, each to the other's fortune, and have

43 *tables* writing tablets
46 *either* each
46–7 *what you like best* whichever you prefer
55 *is, is taken* Ed. (is, taken F)
57 *tender myself* offer myself for acceptance
58 *but equal* fair enough

48–9 *because Destiny . . . nature.* Alluding to one or more proverbs:
'Marriage is destiny' (Tilley, M682); 'Marriage and magistrate be
destinies of heaven' (Tilley, M680); and the familiar 'Wedding and
hanging go by destiny' (Tilley, W232).

myself fitted with some means to make him that is forsaken
a part of amends.

QUARLOUS

These conditions are very courteous. Well, my word is out
of the *Arcadia*, then: 'Argalus'.　　　　　　　　　　　65

WINWIFE

And mine out of the play: 'Palemon'.

TROUBLE-ALL *comes again*

TROUBLE-ALL

Have you any warrant for this, gentlemen?

QUARLOUS ⎫
WINWIFE ⎭

Ha?

TROUBLE-ALL

There must be a warrant had, believe it.

WINWIFE

For what?　　　　　　　　　　　　　　　　　　　70

TROUBLE-ALL

For whatsoever it is, anything indeed, no matter what.

QUARLOUS

'Slight, here's a fine ragged prophet, dropped down i' the
nick!

TROUBLE-ALL

Heaven quit you, gentlemen.

QUARLOUS

Nay, stay a little. Good lady, put him to the question.　　75

GRACE

You are content, then?

WINWIFE ⎫
QUARLOUS ⎭

Yes, yes.

GRACE

Sir, here are two names written—

---

62 *forsaken* rejected, refused
63 *a part of* some
72-3 *i' the nick* at exactly the right moment

---

65 *Argalus*. A character in Sir Philip Sidney's *Arcadia*, whose love for
Parthenia forms one of the episodes in that work.
66 *Palemon*. Either Palamon in *The Two Noble Kinsmen* by Shakespeare
and Fletcher, first performed in 1613, or Palaemon in Samuel Daniel's
The Queen's Arcadia, played at Christ Church, Oxford, on 30 August
1605, during the course of a royal visit to the University.

TROUBLE-ALL
 Is Justice Overdo one?

GRACE
 How, sir? I pray you read 'em to yourself—it is for a wager 80
 between these gentlemen—and, with a stroke or any difference, mark which you approve best.

TROUBLE-ALL
 They may be both worshipful names for aught I know, mistress, but Adam Overdo had been worth three of 'em, I
 assure you, in this place; that's in plain English. 85

GRACE
 This man amazes me! I pray you, like one of 'em, sir.

TROUBLE-ALL
 I do like him there, that has the best warrant. Mistress, to
 save your longing, and multiply him, it may be this.
            [*He marks the book*]
 But I am aye still for Justice Overdo, that's my conscience.
 And quit you.   [*Exit*] 90

WINWIFE
 Is't done, lady?

GRACE
 Ay, and strangely as ever I saw! What fellow is this, trow?

QUARLOUS
 No matter what, a fortune-teller we ha' made him. Which
 is't, which is't?

GRACE
 Nay, did you not promise, not to enquire? 95

      [*Enter*] EDGWORTH

QUARLOUS
 'Slid, I forgot that, pray you pardon me. Look, here's our
 Mercury come; the licence arrives i' the finest time, too! 'Tis
 but scraping out Cokes his name, and 'tis done.

79 *Justice* Ed. (*Iudice* F)
80 *to yourself* silently
81–2 *difference* distinguishing mark
87 *warrant.* Ed. (warrant, F)
88 *and multiply him* Ed. (and (multiply him) F)
89 *aye* Ed. (I F)
 conscience conviction
94 *is't?* Ed. (is't. F)

97 *Mercury*. As well as being the messenger of the gods, Mercury was also
 the god of thieves.

WINWIFE
How now, lime-twig? Hast thou touched?

EDGWORTH
Not yet, sir; except you would go with me, and see't, it's   100
not worth speaking on. The act is nothing, without a witness.
Yonder he is, your man with the box, fallen into the finest
company, and so transported with vapours. They ha' got
in a northern clothier, and one Puppy, a western man, that's
come to wrestle before my Lord Mayor anon, and Captain   105
Whit, and one Val Cutting, that helps Captain Jordan to
roar, a circling boy; with whom your Numps is so taken that
you may strip him of his clothes, if you will. I'll undertake
to geld him for you; if you had but a surgeon ready, to sear
him. And Mistress Justice, there, is the goodest woman!   110
She does so law 'em all over, in terms of justice, and the
style of authority, with her hood upright, that—that I
beseech you come away, gentlemen, and see't.

QUARLOUS
'Slight, I would not lose it for the Fair. What'll you do, Ned?

 99 *lime-twig* thief, one whose fingers are 'limed' so that things stick
    to them
    touched? Ed. (touch'd. F) carried out the theft
100 *sir;* Ed. (Sir, F)
    except unless
103 *vapours. They* Ed. (vapours, they F)
110 *goodest* most important
112 *upright, that—that* ed. (vpright—that F)
113 *come away* come along

---

104 *a western man.* Cornwall was famous for its wrestlers.
105 *before my Lord Mayor.* Wrestling in the presence of the Lord Mayor was
    a regular feature of Bartholomew Fair on the afternoon of the opening
    day.
107 *a circling boy.* Since no other example of this term is known, it is
    difficult to say precisely what it means. Cutting is evidently a 'roarer';
    he makes use of a circle for quarrelling purposes (see IV.iv, 115–22);
    and he 'gives the lie in circle', i.e., circuitously, indirectly (*OED*, Circle,
    sb., †24., quoting from *The Alchemist*, III.iv, 38–9). The last of these
    activities is probably the reason for the term.
111 *law* ed. (loue F) argue with, lay down the law to. It is difficult to see how
    one can 'love . . . in terms of justice, and the style of authority'. Nor is
    it what Mistress Overdo does at IV.iv, 125–8. Nashe, in *Nashes Lenten
    Stuffe* (1599), launches a vigorous attack on lawyers' jargon, and then
    continues: 'I stand lawing heere' (Nashe, iii. 216. 16). Mistress Overdo
    also 'stands lawing'. If Jonson wrote 'lawe', as this editor believes he did,
    a compositor might easily read it as 'loue'.

WINWIFE
Why, stay here about for you; Mistress Wellborn must not   115
be seen.

QUARLOUS
Do so, and find out a priest i' the mean time; I'll bring the
licence.—Lead, which way is't?

EDGWORTH
Here, sir, you are o' the backside o' the booth already, you
may hear the noise.   120

[Exeunt]

Act IV, Scene iv

[Enter] KNOCKEM, NORTHERN, PUPPY, CUTTING, WHIT, WASP,
MISTRESS OVERDO

KNOCKEM
Whit, bid Val Cutting continue the vapours for a lift, Whit,
for a lift.

NORTHERN
I'll ne mare, I'll ne mare, the eale's too meeghty.

KNOCKEM
How now, my Galloway Nag, the staggers? Ha! Whit, gi'
him a slit i' the forehead. Cheer up, man; a needle and   5
thread to stitch his ears. I'd cure him now, an I had it, with
a little butter, and garlic, long-pepper, and grains. Where's
my horn? I'll gi' him a mash, presently, shall take away this
dizziness.

PUPPY
Why, where are you, zurs? Do you vlinch, and leave us i' the   10
zuds, now?

1 *for a lift* in preparation for a theft
4 *the staggers* disease of horses, marked by a staggering gait
7 *long-pepper* very strong kind of pepper
  grains refuse of malt
8 *horn* drenching-horn
10 *vlinch* flinch (as pronounced in the West Country), weaken in
  your drinking
10–11 *i' the zuds* (literally, in the suds) i.e., in trouble

---

3 *ne mare . . . too meeghty.* No more, the ale's too mighty. Jonson's attempt
to represent the northern dialect.
4 *Galloway Nag.* Breed of small horses from the south-west of Scotland,
noted for their hardiness and powers of endurance.
4–7 *gi' him . . . grains.* The cure recommended in Jonson's day for a horse
suffering from the staggers.

NORTHERN

I'll ne mare, I is e'en as vull as a paiper's bag, by my troth, I.

PUPPY

Do my northern cloth zhrink i' the wetting, ha?

KNOCKEM

Why, well said, old flea-bitten, thou'lt never tire, I see.

They fall to their vapours again

CUTTING

No, sir, but he may tire, if it please him.   15

WHIT

Who told dee sho? that he vuld never teer, man?

CUTTING

No matter who told him so, so long as he knows.

KNOCKEM

Nay, I know nothing, sir, pardon me there.

[*Enter*] EDGWORTH, QUARLOUS

EDGWORTH

They are at it still, sir, this they call vapours.

WHIT

He shall not pardon dee, captain, dou shalt not be pardoned.   20
Pre'de shweetheart, do not pardon him.

CUTTING

'Slight, I'll pardon him, an I list, whosoever says nay to't.

QUARLOUS

Where's Numps? I miss him.

WASP

Why, I say nay to't.

QUARLOUS

O there he is!   25

KNOCKEM

To what do you say nay, sir?

Here they continue their game of vapours, which is nonsense:
every man to oppose the last man that spoke, whether it con-
cerned him, or no

12 *paiper's* piper's
26 s.d. *Here they . . . no* (at l. 23 in F)

13 *Do my . . . wetting.* The complaint that Northern cloth shrank easily was
   a common one.
14 *flea-bitten . . . tire.* 'A flea-bitten horse never tires' was a proverb (Tilley,
   H640). 'Flea-bitten' refers to the horse's colour—dappled.

WASP
To anything, whatsoever it is, so long as I do not like it.

WHIT
Pardon me, little man, dou musht like it a little.

CUTTING
No, he must not like it at all, sir; there you are i' the wrong.

WHIT
I tink I be; he musht not like it, indeed.   30

CUTTING
Nay, then he both must and will like it, sir, for all you.

KNOCKEM
If he have reason, he may like it, sir.

WHIT
By no meansh, captain, upon reason, he may like nothing
upon reason.

WASP
I have no reason, nor I will hear of no reason, nor I will look   35
for no reason, and he is an ass that either knows any, or looks
for't from me.

CUTTING
Yes, in some sense you may have reason, sir.

WASP
Ay, in some sense, I care not if I grant you.

WHIT
Pardon me, thou ougsht to grant him nothing, in no shensh,   40
if dou do love dyshelf, angry man.

WASP
Why then, I do grant him nothing; and I have no sense.

CUTTING
'Tis true, thou hast no sense indeed.

WASP
'Slid, but I have sense, now I think on't better, and I will
grant him anything, do you see?   45

KNOCKEM
He is i' the right, and does utter a sufficient vapour.

CUTTING
Nay, it is no sufficient vapour, neither, I deny that.

KNOCKEM
Then it is a sweet vapour.

CUTTING
It may be a sweet vapour.

WASP
Nay, it is no sweet vapour, neither, sir; it stinks, and I'll   50
stand to't.

WHIT

Yes, I tink it doesh shtink, captain. All vapour doesh shtink.

WASP

Nay, then it does not stink, sir, and it shall not stink.

CUTTING

By your leave, it may, sir.

WASP

Ay, by my leave, it may stink; I know that.   55

WHIT

Pardon me, thou knowesht nothing; it cannot by thy leave,
angry man.

WASP

How can it not?

KNOCKEM

Nay, never question him, for he is i' the right.

WHIT

Yesh, I am i' de right, I confesh it; so ish de little man too.   60

WASP

I'll have nothing confessed that concerns me. I am not i' the
right, nor never was i' the right, nor never will be i' the right,
while I am in my right mind.

CUTTING

Mind? Why, here's no man minds you, sir, nor anything else.
                              They drink again

PUPPY

Vriend, will you mind this that we do?   65

QUARLOUS

Call you this vapours? This is such belching of quarrel as I
never heard. Will you mind your business, sir?

EDGWORTH

You shall see, sir.

NORTHERN

I'll ne mair, my waimb warks too mickle with this aureadly.

EDGWORTH

Will you take that, Master Wasp, that nobody should mind   70
you?

WASP

Why? What ha' you to do? Is't any matter to you?

---

67 *mind your business* get on with your job (of stealing the licence)
69 *waimb warks too mickle* stomach is too upset
72 *What ha' you to do* what business of yours is it

EDGWORTH

No, but methinks you should not be unminded, though.

WASP

Nor I wu' not be, now I think on't; do you hear, new
acquaintance, does no man mind me, say you?　　　　　75

CUTTING

Yes, sir, every man here minds you, but how?

WASP

Nay, I care as little how as you do; that was not my question.

WHIT

No, noting was ty question; tou art a learned man, and I am
a valiant man, i'faith la; tou shalt speak for me, and I vill
fight for tee.　　　　　80

KNOCKEM

Fight for him, Whit? A gross vapour; he can fight for himself.

WASP

It may be I can, but it may be I wu' not, how then?

CUTTING

Why, then you may choose.

WASP

Why, and I'll choose whether I'll choose or no.　　　　　85

KNOCKEM

I think you may, and 'tis true; and I allow it for a resolute
vapour.

WASP

Nay, then I do think you do not think, and it is no resolute
vapour.

CUTTING

Yes, in some sort he may allow you.　　　　　90

KNOCKEM

In no sort, sir, pardon me, I can allow him nothing. You mistake the vapour.

WASP

He mistakes nothing, sir, in no sort.

WHIT

Yes, I pre dee now, let him mistake.

73 *unminded* left unnoticed
90, 93 *sort* (i) sense (ii) company

WASP

A turd i' your teeth! Never pre dee me, for I will have noth-   95
ing mistaken.

KNOCKEM

Turd, ha, turd? A noisome vapour! Strike, Whit.

They fall by the ears
[EDGWORTH *steals the licence from the box, and exit*]

MISTRESS OVERDO

Why gentlemen, why gentlemen, I charge you upon my
authority, conserve the peace. In the King's name, and my
husband's, put up your weapons; I shall be driven to com-   100
mit you myself, else.

QUARLOUS

Ha, ha, ha!

WASP

Why do you laugh, sir?

QUARLOUS

Sir, you'll allow me my Christian liberty. I may laugh, I hope.

CUTTING

In some sort you may, and in some sort you may not, sir.   105

KNOCKEM

. Nay, in some sort, sir, he may neither laugh, nor hope, in
this company.

WASP

Yes, then he may both laugh and hope in any sort, an't please
him.

QUARLOUS

Faith, and I will then, for it doth please me exceedingly.   110

WASP

No exceeding neither, sir.

KNOCKEM

No, that vapour is too lofty.

QUARLOUS

Gentlemen, I do not play well at your game of vapours, I
am not very good at it, but—

97 s.d. *They fall by the ears* they fight
100–1 *commit you* send you to prison
111 *exceeding* excess, going too far

CUTTING
Do you hear, sir? I would speak with you in circle!   115
He draws a circle on the ground

QUARLOUS
In circle, sir? What would you with me in circle?

CUTTING
Can you lend me a piece, a Jacobus, in circle?

QUARLOUS
'Slid, your circle will prove more costly than your vapours,
then. Sir, no, I lend you none.

CUTTING
Your beard's not well turned up, sir.   120

QUARLOUS
How, rascal? Are you playing with my beard? I'll break
circle with you.
They draw all, and fight

PUPPY   }
NORTHERN   }
Gentlemen, gentlemen!

KNOCKEM
Gather up, Whit, gather up, Whit. Good vapours!
[*Exeunt* KNOCKEM *and* WHIT *with the cloaks*]

MISTRESS OVERDO
What mean you? Are you rebels, gentlemen? Shall I send   125
out a sergeant-at-arms, or a writ o' rebellion, against you?
I'll commit you, upon my womanhood, for a riot, upon my
justice-hood, if you persist.
[*Exeunt* QUARLOUS, CUTTING]

WASP
Upon your justice-hood? Marry, shit o' your hood! You'll
commit? Spoke like a true Justice of Peace's wife, indeed, 130
and a fine female lawyer! Turd i' your teeth for a fee, now.

MISTRESS OVERDO
Why, Numps, in Master Overdo's name, I charge you.

WASP
Good Mistress Underdo, hold your tongue.

---

117 *Jacobus* gold coin, 'sovereign', issued by James I
130 *commit* (i) send to prison (ii) fornicate

115–22 *Do you . . . with you.* The drawing of the circle is an indirect challenge,
  which Quarlous fails to understand. Cutting then asks for the loan of a
  Jacobus, knowing that it will be refused and thus provide the pretext for
  the final insult, his playing with Quarlous's beard which precipitates the
  fight.

MISTRESS OVERDO
Alas! poor Numps.

WASP
Alas! And why alas from you, I beseech you? Or why poor   135
Numps, Goody Rich? Am I come to be pitied by your
tuftaffeta now? Why, mistress, I knew Adam, the clerk, your
husband, when he was Adam Scrivener, and writ for twopence a sheet, as high as he bears his head now, or you your
hood, dame.   140

The watch comes in [*accompanied by* WHIT]

What are you, sir?

BRISTLE
We be men, and no infidels. What is the matter here, and the
noises? Can you tell?

WASP
Heart, what ha' you to do? Cannot a man quarrel in quietness, but he must be put out on't by you? What are you?   145

BRISTLE
Why, we be His Majesty's Watch, sir.

WASP
Watch? 'Sblood, you are a sweet watch, indeed. A body
would think, an you watched well o' nights, you should be
contented to sleep at this time o' day. Get you to your fleas,
and your flock-beds, you rogues, your kennels, and lie down 150
close.

BRISTLE
Down? Yes, we will down, I warrant you.—Down with him
in His Majesty's name, down, down with him, and carry him
away, to the pigeon-holes.

[WASP *is arrested*]

MISTRESS OVERDO
I thank you, honest friends, in the behalf o' the Crown, and 155

136 *Goody* Goodwife
137 *tuftaffeta* a kind of taffeta with a pile or nap arranged in tufts
  (*OED*)
145 *put out on't* debarred from doing it
148 *watched* (i) stayed awake (ii) did your duties as watchmen
154 *pigeon-holes* stocks

---

138 *Adam Scrivener*. There may be an allusion here to Chaucer's little poem
  'Chaucers Wordes unto Adam, his own Scriveyn', reproving Adam for
  his carelessness in copying.
140 s.d. *accompanied by* WHIT ed. (not in F). Whit's entry here, like his exit
  at 124, is demanded by his collusion with the Watch established in III.i.

the peace, and in Master Overdo's name, for suppressing
enormities.

WHIT

Stay, Bristle, here ish a noder brashe o' drunkards, but very
quiet, special drunkards, will pay dee five shillings very well.
Take 'em to dee, in de graish o' God: one of 'em does   160
change cloth for ale in the Fair here, te toder ish a strong
man, a mighty man, my Lord Mayor's man, and a wrestler.
He has wreshled so long with the bottle, here, that the man
with the beard hash almosht streek up hish heelsh.

BRISTLE

'Slid, the Clerk o' the Market has been to cry him all the Fair   165
over, here, for my Lord's service.

WHIT

Tere he ish, pre de taik him hensh, and make ty best on him.
            [*Exit watch with* WASP, NORTHERN, PUPPY]
How now, woman o' shilk, vat ailsh ty shweet faish? Art tou
melancholy?

MISTRESS OVERDO

A little distempered with these enormities. Shall I entreat a   170
courtesy of you, Captain?

WHIT

Entreat a hundred, velvet voman, I vill do it, shpeak out.

MISTRESS OVERDO

I cannot with modesty speak it out, but—
            [*She whispers to him*]

WHIT

I vill do it, and more, and more, for dee. What Ursla, an't be
bitch, an't be bawd, an't be!   175

            [*Enter*] URSLA

URSLA

How now, rascal? What roar you for, old pimp?

158 *brashe* Ed. (brash F) brace
164 *streek up hish heelsh* struck up his heels, i.e., overthrown him
165 *cry* summon
166 *Lord's* Lord Mayor's
170 *distempered with* upset by
176 *for, old pimp?* Ed. (for? old Pimpe. F)

163–4 *the man with the beard.* A kind of drinking-jug, pot-bellied but with a
    narrow neck decorated with a bearded face.
165 *Clerk o' the Market.* An officer appointed by the City to collect market
    dues and inspect the market.

WHIT
Here, put up de cloaks, Ursh, de purchase. Pre dee now, shweet Ursh, help dis good brave voman to a jordan, an't be.

URSLA
'Slid, call your Captain Jordan to her, can you not?

WHIT
Nay, pre dee leave dy consheits, and bring the velvet woman   180
to de—

URSLA
I bring her? Hang her! Heart, must I find a common pot for every punk i' your purlieus?

WHIT
O good voordsh, Ursh; it ish a guest o' velvet, i' fait la!

URSLA
Let her sell her hood, and buy a sponge, with a pox to her.   185
My vessel? Employed, sir. I have but one, and 'tis the bottom of an old bottle. An honest proctor and his wife are at it within. If she'll stay her time, so.

WHIT
As soon ash tou cansht, shweet Ursh. Of a valiant man I tink I am the patientsh man i' the world, or in all Smithfield.   190

[*Enter* KNOCKEM]

KNOCKEM
How now, Whit? Close vapours? stealing your leaps? covering in corners, ha?

WHIT
No fait, Captain, dough tou beesht a vishe man, dy vit is a mile hence now. I vas procuring a shmall courtesy for a woman of fashion here.   195

MISTRESS OVERDO
Yes, Captain, though I am Justice of Peace's wife, I do love men of war, and the sons of the sword, when they come before my husband.

KNOCKEM
Say'st thou so, filly? Thou shalt have a leap presently, I'll horse thee myself else.   200

---

177 *purchase.* Ed. (purchase, F) booty
183 *your purlieus* the brothel areas
185–6 *her. My vessel? Employed, sir.* ed. (her, my vessell, employed Sir. F)
192 *covering* (technical term for a stallion mating with a mare) copulating

URSLA

Come, will you bring her in now? And let her take her turn?

WHIT

Gramercy, good Ursh, I tank dee.

MISTRESS OVERDO

Master Overdo shall thank her.　　　　　　　　[*Exit*]

Act IV, Scene v

[Enter to them] LITTLEWIT, WIN

LITTLEWIT

Good Gammer Urs, Win and I are exceedingly beholden to
you, and to Captain Jordan, and Captain Whit. Win, I'll be
bold to leave you i' this good company, Win, for half an
hour or so, Win, while I go and see how my matter goes
forward, and if the puppets be perfect. And then I'll come　　5
and fetch you, Win.

WIN

Will you leave me alone with two men, John?

LITTLEWIT

Ay, they are honest gentlemen, Win, Captain Jordan and
Captain Whit, they'll use you very civilly, Win. God b'w'you,
Win.　　　　　　　　　　　　　　　　　　　[*Exit*]　　10

URSLA

What's her husband gone?

KNOCKEM

On his false gallop, Urs, away.

URSLA

An you be right Bartholmew-birds, now shew yourselves so.
We are undone for want of fowl i' the Fair here. Here will be
Zekiel Edgworth, and three or four gallants with him at　　15
night, and I ha' neither plover nor quail for 'em. Persuade
this between you two, to become a bird o' the game, while
I work the velvet woman within, as you call her.

KNOCKEM

I conceive thee, Urs! Go thy ways.　　　　[*Exit* URSLA]
Dost thou hear, Whit? Is't not pity my delicate dark chest-　　20

201　*take* Ed. (talke F)
　5　*be perfect* know their parts, are word-perfect
　12　*false gallop* Ed. (false, gallop F) canter, with a quibble on 'false'
　　　= 'unwise'
　14　*fowl* 'birds', wenches
　16　*neither plover nor quail* no wenches at all
　19　*ways.* Ed. (waies, F)

nut here—with the fine lean head, large forehead, round
eyes, even mouth, sharp ears, long neck, thin crest, close
withers, plain back, deep sides, short fillets, and full flanks;
with a round belly, a plump buttock, large thighs, knit
knees, straight legs, short pasterns, smooth hoofs, and short   25
heels—should lead a dull honest woman's life, that might
live the life of a lady?

WHIT

Yes, by my fait and trot, it is, Captain. De honesht woman's
life is a scurvy dull life, indeed, la!

WIN

How, sir? Is an honest woman's life a scurvy life?   30

WHIT

Yes, fait, shweetheart, believe him, de leef of a bondwoman!
But if dou vilt harken to me, I vill make tee a free-woman,
and a lady; dou shalt live like a lady, as te captain saish.

KNOCKEM

Ay, and be honest too, sometimes; have her wires, and her
tires, her green gowns, and velvet petticoats.   35

WHIT

Ay, and ride to Ware and Romford i' dy coash, shee de
players, be in love vit 'em; sup vit gallantsh, be drunk, and
cost de noting.

KNOCKEM

Brave vapours!

WHIT

And lie by twenty on 'em, if dou pleash, shweetheart.   40

WIN

What, and be honest still? That were fine sport.

WHIT

'Tish common, shweetheart, tou may'st do it, by my hand.

23 *plain* flat
26 *honest* (i) respectable (ii) chaste
27 *lady* (i) woman of rank (ii) 'lady of pleasure'
34 *wires* frames of wire used to stiffen ruffs and to support the hair
35 *tires* head-dresses and dresses in general
41 *still? That* Ed. (still, that F)
42 *it,* Ed. (it F)

---

35 *green gowns.* Knockem is quibbling; 'to give a wench a green gown' was
   to seduce her by rolling her over in the grass. Hence green gowns came
   to be associated with prostitutes.
36 *Ware and Romford.* Ware, famous for its 'great bed' (eleven feet square),
   and Romford were notorious as places of assignation within easy reach
   of London.

It shall be justified to ty husband's faish, now: tou shalt be
as honesht as the skin between his hornsh, la!

KNOCKEM
Yes, and wear a dressing, top and topgallant, to compare with   45
e'er a husband on 'em all, for a fore-top. It is the vapour of
spirit, in the wife, to cuckold, nowadays, as it is the vapour
of fashion, in the husband, not to suspect. Your prying cat-
eyed citizen is an abominable vapour.

WIN
Lord, what a fool have I been!   50

WHIT
Mend then, and do everyting like a lady hereafter; never
know ty husband from another man.

KNOCKEM
Nor any one man from another, but i' the dark.

WHIT
Ay, and then it ish no dishgrash to know any man.

[*Enter* URSLA]

URSLA
Help, help here!   55

KNOCKEM
How now? What vapour's there?

URSLA
O, you are a sweet ranger, and look well to your walks!
Yonder is your punk of Turnbull, Ramping Alice, has fallen
upon the poor gentlewoman within, and pulled her hood
over her ears, and her hair through it.   60

ALICE *enters, beating the Justice's wife*

MISTRESS OVERDO
Help, help, i' the King's name!

51 *Mend* reform yourself

---

44 *as honesht . . . hornsh.* 'As honest as the skin between his brows' was, and
still is, proverbial (Tilley, S506), but Whit substitutes the horns of the
cuckold for 'brows'.

45-6 *dressing . . . fore-top.* The elaborate head-dresses and 'hair-dos' of the
time are described in nautical terms, comparing the effect to that of a
ship under full sail, by Shakespeare in *The Merry Wives of Windsor*,
III.iii, 46-9, and by Nashe in his *Christs Teares Over Jerusalem*, where
he writes: 'Theyr heads, with theyr top and top gallant Lawne baby-
caps, and Snow-resembled siluer curlings, they make a playne Puppet
stage of' (Nashe, ii. 137. 31-3). Got up in this fashion, Knockem says,
Win's head will be a fit match for her husband's horns (foretop).

ALICE

A mischief on you! They are such as you are that undo us
and take our trade from us, with your tuftaffeta haunches.

KNOCKEM

How now, Alice!

ALICE

The poor common whores can ha' no traffic for the privy   65
rich ones. Your caps and hoods of velvet call away our
customers, and lick the fat from us.

URSLA

Peace, you foul ramping jade, you—

ALICE

Od's foot, you bawd in grease, are you talking?

KNOCKEM

Why, Alice, I say.   70

ALICE

Thou sow of Smithfield, thou.

URSLA

Thou tripe of Turnbull.

KNOCKEM

Catamountain vapours, ha!

URSLA

You know where you were tawed lately, both lashed and
slashed you were in Bridewell.   75

ALICE

Ay, by the same token, you rid that week, and broke out the
bottom o' the cart, night-tub.

---

62 *undo* ruin
63 *tuftaffeta haunches* artificial haunches made of silk and designed to
   improve the figure
65 *for* because of
   privy clandestine
66 *velvet* Ed. (veluet, F)
69 *in grease* fat, in prime condition for killing
73 *Catamountain* wildcat, ferocious
74 *tawed* flogged
75 *slashed* cut with the scourge
76 *rid* rode in the cart for whores
77 *night-tub* tub for excrement or night-soil

---

67 *lick the fat from us.* 'To lick the fat from one's lips' was proverbial (Tilley
   F80) for depriving one of one's best customers.
75 *Bridewell.* The London prison, where sexual offenders in particular were
   confined and punished.

KNOCKEM

Why, lion face, ha! Do you know who I am? Shall I tear ruff,
slit waistcoat, make rags of petticoat, ha? Go to, vanish, for
fear of vapours. Whit, a kick, Whit, in the parting vapour.   80
                              [*They kick* ALICE *out*]
Come, brave woman, take a good heart, thou shalt be a lady
too.

WHIT

Yes fait, dey shall all both be ladies, and write Madam. I vill
do't myself for dem. *Do* is the vord, and *D* is the middle letter
of *Madam, DD*, put 'em together and make deeds, without   85
which all words are alike, la!

KNOCKEM

'Tis true. Ursla, take 'em in, open thy wardrobe, and fit 'em
to their calling. Green gowns, crimson petticoats, green
women! My Lord Mayor's green women! guests o' the game,
true bred. I'll provide you a coach, to take the air in.   90

WIN

But do you think you can get one?

KNOCKEM

O, they are as common as wheelbarrows where there are
great dunghills. Every pettifogger's wife has 'em; for first he
buys a coach, that he may marry, and then he marries that he
may be made cuckold in't. For if their wives ride not to their   95
cuckolding, they do 'em no credit. 'Hide and be hidden, ride
and be ridden', says the vapour of experience.
                    [*Exeunt* URSLA, WIN, MISTRESS OVERDO]

Act IV, Scene vi

[*Enter to them*] TROUBLE-ALL

TROUBLE-ALL

By what warrant does it say so?

79 *petticoat, ha?* ed. (petticoat? ha! F)
83 *write* sign themselves, style themselves
93 *pettifogger* lawyer of inferior status
97 *ridden* mounted sexually by a man

---

79 *waistcoat*. When worn without a gown over it, the waistcoat was the
  mark of a prostitute, who was sometimes called a 'waistcoateer'.
88–9 *green women . . . green women*. (i) loose women, whores (ii) female
  equivalents of the 'green men', i.e., men dressed in green to represent
  wild men of the woods or woodwoses, as they were called, who were a
  common feature of the Lord Mayor's Show.

KNOCKEM

Ha! mad child o' the Pie-powders, art thou there? Fill us a
fresh can, Urs, we may drink together.

TROUBLE-ALL

I may not drink without a warrant, Captain.

KNOCKEM

'Slood, thou'll not stale without a warrant, shortly. Whit,   5
give me pen, ink and paper. I'll draw him a warrant presently.

TROUBLE-ALL

It must be Justice Overdo's!

KNOCKEM

I know, man. Fetch the drink, Whit.

WHIT

I pre dee now, be very brief, Captain; for de new ladies stay
for dee.   10

KNOCKEM

O, as brief as can be; here 'tis already. 'Adam Overdo'.

TROUBLE-ALL

Why, now I'll pledge you, Captain.

KNOCKEM

Drink it off. I'll come to thee, anon, again.

                                                         [*Exeunt*]

                    [*Enter*] QUARLOUS, EDGWORTH

QUARLOUS   *To the cutpurse*

Well, sir. You are now discharged; beware of being spied,
hereafter.   15

EDGWORTH

Sir, will it please you, enter in here at Ursla's, and take part
of a silken gown, a velvet petticoat, or a wrought smock. I am
promised such, and I can spare any gentleman a moiety.

QUARLOUS

Keep it for your companions in beastliness, I am none of 'em,
sir. If I had not already forgiven you a greater trespass, or   20
thought you yet worth my beating, I would instruct your
manners to whom you made your offers. But go your ways,
talk not to me, the hangman is only fit to discourse with you;

---

3 *we* which we
5 *stale* urinate
16 *will it* if it will
   take part partake
18 *moiety* share, portion
21-2 *I would . . . offers* I would teach you proper behaviour towards
   the man to whom you make your offers

the hand of beadle is too merciful a punishment for your
trade of life.   [*Exit* EDGWORTH]   25
I am sorry I employed this fellow, for he thinks me such:
Facinus quos inquinat, aequat. But it was for sport. And would
I make it serious, the getting of this licence is nothing to me,
without other circumstances concur. I do think how
impertinently I labour, if the word be not mine that the   30
ragged fellow marked; and what advantage I have given Ned
Winwife in this time now of working her, though it be mine.
He'll go near to form to her what a debauched rascal I am,
and fright her out of all good conceit of me. I should do so by
him, I am sure, if I had the opportunity. But my hope is in her   35
temper yet; and it must needs be next to despair, that is
grounded on any part of a woman's discretion. I would give,
by my troth, now, all I could spare, to my clothes and my
sword, to meet my tattered soothsayer again, who was my
judge i' the question, to know certainly whose word he has   40
damned or saved. For, till then, I live but under a reprieve.
I must seek him. Who be these?

Enter WASP *with the officers*

WASP
Sir, you are a Welsh cuckold, and a prating runt, and no
constable.

BRISTLE
You say very well. Come, put in his leg in the middle roundel,   45
and let him hole there.

WASP
You stink of leeks, metheglin, and cheese, you rogue.

26 *such* such a one as he is
27–8 *would I make it serious* if I wanted to take it seriously
30 *impertinently* pointlessly
32 *working* influencing
33 *form* state explicitly
34 *conceit* opinion
36 *temper* character
38 *to* down to but not including
43 *runt* ignoramus
45 *roundel* round hole (of the stocks)
47 *metheglin* Welsh mead
    cheese, you Ed. (cheese. You F)

27 *Facinus quos inquinat, aequat.* 'Crime puts those it corrupts on the same
    footing' (Lucan, *Pharsalia*, v. 290).

BRISTLE

Why, what is that to you, if you sit sweetly in the stocks in the
mean time? If you have a mind to stink too, your breeches sit
close enough to your bum. Sit you merry, sir.   50

QUARLOUS

How now, Numps?

WASP

It is no matter how; pray you look off.

QUARLOUS

Nay, I'll not offend you, Numps. I thought you had sat there
to be seen.

WASP

And to be sold, did you not? Pray you mind your business,   55
an you have any.

QUARLOUS

Cry you mercy, Numps. Does your leg lie high enough?

[Enter] HAGGIS, OVERDO, BUSY

BRISTLE

How now, neighbour Haggis, what says Justice Overdo's
worship to the other offenders?

HAGGIS

Why, he says just nothing. What should he say? Or where   60
should he say? He is not to be found, man. He ha' not been
seen i' the Fair, here, all this livelong day, never since seven
o'clock i' the morning. His clerks know not what to think on't.
There is no court of Pie-powders yet. Here they be
returned.   65

BRISTLE

What shall be done with 'em, then, in your discretion?

HAGGIS

I think we were best put 'em in the stocks, in discretion—
there they will be safe in discretion—for the valour of an
hour, or such a thing, till his worship come.

BRISTLE

It is but a hole matter if we do, neighbour Haggis. Come, sir,   70
here is company for you. Heave up the stocks.

---

66 *discretion* opinion
68 *valour* length (literally, value or quantity)

67–8 *in discretion . . . in discretion*. (i) as an act of prudence (ii) in separation.
    The proverb 'Discretion is the better part of valour' (Tilley, D354)
    seems to be in Haggis's muddled mind, since he goes on to speak of
    'valour' (= space, length).

WASP

[*Aside*] I shall put a trick upon your Welsh diligence, perhaps.

As they open the stocks, WASP *puts his shoe on his hand, and slips it in for his leg*

BRISTLE

Put in your leg, sir.

QUARLOUS

What, Rabbi Busy! Is he come?   75

They bring BUSY *and put him in*

BUSY

I do obey thee; the lion may roar, but he cannot bite. I am glad to be thus separated from the heathen of the land, and put apart in the stocks, for the holy cause.

WASP

What are you, sir?

BUSY

One that rejoiceth in his affliction, and sitteth here to   80
prophesy the destruction of Fairs and May-games, Wakes, and Whitsun-ales, and doth sigh and groan for the reformation of these abuses.

[They put OVERDO *in the stocks]*

WASP

And do you sigh and groan too, or rejoice in your affliction?

OVERDO

I do not feel it, I do not think of it, it is a thing without me.   85
Adam, thou art above these batteries, these contumelies. *In te manca ruit fortuna,* as thy friend Horace says; thou art one, *Quem neque pauperies, neque mors, neque vincula terrent.* And therefore, as another friend of thine says—I think it be thy friend Persius—*Non te quaesiveris extra.*   90

---

86 *batteries* series of heavy blows

82 *Whitsun-ales.* Parish festivals held at Whitsuntide and given over to feasting, sports, and merrymaking, Whitsun ales were opposed by the Puritans.

85 *it is a thing without me.* Overdo expresses the Stoic doctrine that no external factors can have any effect on the man who is conscious of his own virtue.

87 *In te manca ruit fortuna.* Fortune maims herself when she attacks you (Horace, *Satires,* II.vii. 88).

88 *Quem . . . terrent.* Whom neither poverty, nor death, nor shackles can affright (ibid., 84).

90 *Non . . . extra.* Look to no one outside yourself (Persius, *Satires,* i. 7).

QUARLOUS
What's here? A stoic i' the stocks? The fool is turned
philosopher.

BUSY
Friend, I will leave to communicate my spirit with you, if I
hear any more of those superstitious relics, those lists of
Latin, the very rags of Rome, and patches of Popery.   95

WASP
Nay, an you begin to quarrel, gentlemen, I'll leave you. I ha'
paid for quarrelling too lately. Look you, a device, but
shifting in a hand for a foot. God b'w'you.   *He gets out*

BUSY
Wilt thou then leave thy brethren in tribulation?

WASP
For this once, sir.   [*Exit*]   100

BUSY
Thou art a halting neutral—stay him there, stop him—that
will not endure the heat of persecution.

BRISTLE
How now, what's the matter?

BUSY
He is fled, he is fled, and dares not sit it out.

BRISTLE
What, has he made an escape? Which way? Follow, neigh-   105
bour Haggis.   [*Exit* HAGGIS]

[*Enter*] PURECRAFT

PURECRAFT
O me! In the stocks! Have the wicked prevailed?

BUSY
Peace, religious sister, it is my calling, comfort yourself, an
extraordinary calling, and done for my better standing, my
surer standing, hereafter.   110
The madman enters

TROUBLE-ALL
By whose warrant, by whose warrant, this?

93 *leave* cease
94 *lists* strips, selvages, shreds
97-8 *but shifting in a hand for a foot* merely slipping in a hand in
    place of a foot

───────────────────────────────

91 *A stoic . . . stocks.* The association of Stoics with stocks (= senseless
    things) was a fairly common witticism (cf. *The Taming of the Shrew*,
    I.i, 31).

QUARLOUS

O, here's my man dropped in, I looked for.

OVERDO

Ha!

PURECRAFT

O good sir, they have set the faithful here to be wondered at;
and provided holes for the holy of the land. 115

TROUBLE-ALL

Had they warrant for it? Shewed they Justice Overdo's hand?
If they had no warrant, they shall answer it.

[*Enter* HAGGIS]

BRISTLE

Sure you did not lock the stocks sufficiently, neighbour Toby!

HAGGIS

No? See if you can lock 'em better.

BRISTLE

They are very sufficiently locked, and truly, yet something 120
is in the matter.

TROUBLE-ALL

True, your warrant is the matter that is in question; by what
warrant?

BRISTLE

Madman, hold your peace; I will put you in his room else,
in the very same hole, do you see? 125

QUARLOUS

How? Is he a madman?

TROUBLE-ALL

Shew me Justice Overdo's warrant, I obey you.

HAGGIS

You are a mad fool, hold your tongue.

TROUBLE-ALL

In Justice Overdo's name, I drink to you, and here's my
warrant. *Shews his can* 130

[*Exeunt* HAGGIS, BRISTLE]

OVERDO

[*Aside*] Alas, poor wretch! How it earns my heart for him!

QUARLOUS

[*Aside*] If he be mad, it is in vain to question him. I'll try,

112 *man* Ed. (man! F)
 I whom I
127 *warrant,* Ed. (warrant. F)
131 *earns* grieves

though.—Friend, there was a gentlewoman shewed you two
names, some hour since, Argalus and Palemon, to mark in a
book. Which of 'em was it you marked?   135

TROUBLE-ALL
I mark no name but Adam Overdo; that is the name of
names; he only is the sufficient magistrate; and that name I
reverence. Shew it me.

QUARLOUS
[*Aside*] This fellow's mad indeed. I am further off now than
afore.   140

OVERDO
[*Aside*] I shall not breathe in peace till I have made him
some amends.

QUARLOUS
[*Aside*] Well, I will make another use of him, is come in my
head: I have a nest of beards in my trunk, one something
like his.   [*Exit*]   145

The watchmen come back again

BRISTLE
This mad fool has made me that I know not whether I have
locked the stocks or no; I think I locked 'em.

TROUBLE-ALL
Take Adam Overdo in your mind, and fear nothing.

BRISTLE
'Slid, madness itself, hold thy peace, and take that.

TROUBLE-ALL
Strikest thou without a warrant? Take thou that.   150
The madman fights with 'em, and they leave open the stocks

BUSY
We are delivered by miracle. Fellow in fetters, let us not
refuse the means; this madness was of the spirit. The malice
of the enemy hath mocked itself.

[*Exeunt* BUSY, OVERDO]

PURECRAFT
Mad do they call him! The world is mad in error, but he is
mad in truth. I love him o' the sudden—the cunning man   155
said all true—and shall love him more and more. How well it
becomes a man to be mad in truth! O, that I might be his

---

133 *though.—Friend*, Ed. (though, friend: F)
144 *nest* set, collection
     trunk trunk-hose, baggy padded breeches reaching to the knee
146 *I have* Ed. (I I haue F)
150 s.d. *The madman . . . stocks* (at l.149 in F)

yoke-fellow, and be mad with him! What a many should we
draw to madness in truth with us!   [*Exit*]
The watch, missing them, are affrighted

BRISTLE
How now? All scaped? Where's the woman? It is witchcraft!   160
Her velvet hat is a witch, o' my conscience, or my key, t'one!
The madman was a devil, and I am an ass; so bless me, my
place, and mine office!
[*Exeunt*]

Act V, Scene i

[*Enter*] LEATHERHEAD, FILCHER, SHARKWELL

LEATHERHEAD
Well, Luck and Saint Bartholmew! Out with the sign of our
invention, in the name of Wit, and do you beat the drum the
while. All the foul i' the Fair, I mean all the dirt in Smithfield
—that's one of Master Littlewit's carwhitchets now—will be
thrown at our banner today, if the matter does not please the   5
people. O the motions that I, Lantern Leatherhead, have
given light to, i' my time, since my Master Pod died!
Jerusalem was a stately thing, and so was *Nineveh*, and *The
City of Norwich*, and *Sodom and Gomorrah*, with the rising o'
the prentices, and pulling down the bawdy-houses there,   10
upon Shrove Tuesday; but *The Gunpowder Plot*, there was a

161 *t'one* the one or the other
1–2 *sign of our invention* painted cloth depicting the subject of the
puppet-shew
4 *carwhitchets* puns
6 *motions* puppet-shews
10 *prentices,* Ed. (prentises; F)

---

s.d. LEATHERHEAD Ed. (LANTHORNE. F). From this point onwards to the
end of the play Leatherhead is almost consistently LANTHORNE or
LANTERNE in stage directions and LAN. in speech prefixes. Transformed
from hobby-horse-seller into puppet-master and suitably disguised for
the new role, he has taken on another identity which prevents Cokes
from recognizing him. See his whispered request to Littlewit at V.iii, 48.
7 *my Master Pod.* F has the marginal note 'Pod *was a Master of motions
before him.*' Jonson also refers to Pod in *Every Man Out of His Humour*
(IV.v, 62) and in two of his *Epigrams*, xcvii and cxxix.
8–9 *Jerusalem . . . Gomorrah.* The destruction of Jerusalem by the
Romans, the fall of Nineveh in which Jonah and the whale figured
prominently, the building of Norwich, and the destruction of Sodom
and Gomorrah were common themes for puppet-shews.
9–11 *rising . . . Shrove Tuesday.* The apprentices of London made a
regular habit of wrecking brothels and playhouses on Shrove Tuesday.

get-penny! I have presented that to an eighteen-, or twenty-
pence audience, nine times in an afternoon. Your home-born
projects prove ever the best, they are so easy, and familiar.
They put too much learning i' their things nowadays; and   15
that, I fear, will be the spoil o' this. Littlewit? I say,
Micklewit! if not too mickle! Look to your gathering there,
Goodman Filcher.

FILCHER
I warrant you, sir.

LEATHERHEAD
An there come any gentlefolks, take twopence apiece,   20
Sharkwell.

SHARKWELL
I warrant you, sir; threepence an we can.

                                                    [*Exeunt*]

Act V, Scene ii

The Justice comes in like a porter

OVERDO
This later disguise, I have borrowed of a porter, shall carry
me out to all my great and good ends; which, however inter-
rupted, were never destroyed in me. Neither is the hour of
my severity yet come, to reveal myself, wherein, cloud-like,
I will break out in rain and hail, lightning and thunder,   5
upon the head of enormity. Two main works I have to
prosecute first: one is to invent some satisfaction for the
poor kind wretch who is out of his wits for my sake; and
yonder I see him coming. I will walk aside, and project for it.

              [*Enter*] WINWIFE, GRACE

WINWIFE
I wonder where Tom Quarlous is, that he returns not; it may   10
be he is struck in here to seek us.

12 *get-penny* draw, profitable operation
14 *projects* designs
   familiar readily understood
16 *spoil* spoiling, ruination
17 *mickle* great
   gathering collecting of entrance money (technical theatrical term)
1–2 *carry me out to* enable me to achieve
7 *prosecute first:* ed. (prosecute: first, F)
   invent find, devise
9 *project* think of some plan
11 *is struck* has turned

GRACE
  See, here's our madman again.

[*Enter*] QUARLOUS, PURECRAFT. QUARLOUS, *in the habit of the
  madman, is mistaken by* MISTRESS PURECRAFT

QUARLOUS
  [*Aside*] I have made myself as like him as his gown and cap
  will give me leave.
PURECRAFT
  Sir, I love you, and would be glad to be mad with you in   15
  truth.
WINWIFE
  [*Aside*] How? My widow in love with a madman?
PURECRAFT
  Verily, I can be as mad in spirit as you.
QUARLOUS
  By whose warrant? Leave your canting. [*To* GRACE] Gentle-
  woman, have I found you?—Save ye, quit ye, and multiply   20
  ye.—Where's your book? 'Twas a sufficient name I marked,
  let me see't, be not afraid to shew't me.
                He desires to see the book of MISTRESS GRACE
GRACE
  What would you with it, sir?
QUARLOUS
  Mark it again, and again, at your service.
GRACE
  Here it is, sir; this was it you marked.   25
QUARLOUS
  Palemon! Fare you well, fare you well.
WINWIFE
  How, Palemon!
GRACE
  Yes, faith, he has discovered it to you now, and therefore
  'twere vain to disguise it longer; I am yours, sir, by the
  benefit of your fortune.   30
WINWIFE
  And you have him, Mistress, believe it, that shall never give
  you cause to repent her benefit, but make you rather to think
  that in this choice she had both her eyes.

19 *canting* Puritan jargon
30 *benefit* favour, kindness

33 *she had both her eyes.* Winwife is referring to the proverb 'Fortune is
  blind (= blindfolded)' (Tilley, F604).

GRACE
I desire to put it to no danger of protestation.
[*Exeunt* GRACE, WINWIFE]
QUARLOUS
Palemon the word, and Winwife the man!   35
PURECRAFT
Good sir, vouchsafe a yoke-fellow in your madness; shun not
one of the sanctified sisters, that would draw with you, in
truth.
QUARLOUS
Away! You are a herd of hypocritical proud ignorants, rather
wild than mad; fitter for woods, and the society of beasts,   40
than houses, and the congregation of men. You are the
second part of the society of canters, outlaws to order and
discipline, and the only privileged church-robbers of
Christendom. Let me alone. Palemon the word, and Winwife
the man!   45
PURECRAFT
[*Aside*] I must uncover myself unto him, or I shall never enjoy
him, for all the cunning men's promises.—Good sir, hear me,
I am worth six thousand pound; my love to you is become
my rack; I'll tell you all, and the truth, since you hate the
hypocrisy of the parti-coloured brotherhood. These seven   50
years, I have been a wilful holy widow only to draw feasts
and gifts from my entangled suitors. I am also, by office, an
assisting sister of the deacons, and a devourer, instead of a
distributor, of the alms. I am a special maker of marriages for
our decayed brethren with our rich widows, for a third part of   55
their wealth, when they are married, for the relief of the poor
elect; as also our poor handsome young virgins' with our

35, 45 *man!* Ed. (man? F)
48 *you is* Ed. (you, is F)
49 *truth,* Ed. (truth: F)
50 *parti-coloured* of several colours, i.e., inconsistent
57 *virgins'* ed. (Virgins, F), i.e., virgins' marriages

34 *put . . . protestation.* An allusion to the proverb 'Too much protesting
makes the truth suspected' (Tilley, P614); cf. *Hamlet*, III.ii, 225: 'The
lady doth protest too much, methinks'.
42 *second . . . canters.* The first part of the society of canters would be
those who spoke thieves' cant, i.e., the rogues and vagabonds of the
time. Thomas Harman, in his *A Caveat or Warning for Common Cursi-
tors* (1566), provides some specimens of this cant. The pamphlet is
edited by A. V. Judges in his *The Elizabethan Underworld*, London,
1930.

wealthy bachelors or widowers, to make them steal from
their husbands, when I have confirmed them in the faith, and
got all put into their custodies. And if I ha' not my bargain,   60
they may sooner turn a scolding drab into a silent minister
than make me leave pronouncing reprobation and damnation unto them. Our elder, Zeal-of-the-land, would have
had me; but I know him to be the capital knave of the land,
making himself rich by being made feoffee in trust to   65
deceased brethren, and cozening their heirs by swearing the
absolute gift of their inheritance. And thus, having eased my
conscience, and uttered my heart with the tongue of my love
—enjoy all my deceits together, I beseech you. I should not
have revealed this to you, but that in time I think you are   70
mad; and I hope you'll think me so too, sir.

QUARLOUS
Stand aside, I'll answer you presently.
                              He considers with himself of it
Why should not I marry this six thousand pound, now I
think on't? And a good trade too, that she has beside, ha?
The tother wench, Winwife is sure of; there's no expectation   75
for me there! Here I may make myself some saver yet, if she
continue mad; there's the question. It is money that I want;
why should I not marry the money, when 'tis offered me?
I have a licence and all; it is but razing out one name and
putting in another. There's no playing with a man's fortune!   80
I am resolved! I were truly mad, an I would not!—Well,
come your ways, follow me; an you will be mad, I'll shew
you a warrant!   *He takes her along with him*

PURECRAFT
Most zealously, it is that I zealously desire.
                              The Justice calls him

OVERDO
Sir, let me speak with you.   85

61 *into* Ed. (in to F)
65 *feoffee in trust* trustee invested with a freehold estate in land (*OED*)
69 *together, I* Ed. (together. I F)
70 *in time* not too late
71 *sir.* Ed. (Sir? F)
72 s.d. *considers* Ed. (*consider* F)
75 *Winwife* Ed. (*Winwife*, F)
76 *saver* compensation for loss (gambler's term)

61 *silent minister.* One of the Puritan clergy who had been put out of their
   livings as a result of the Hampton Court conference of 1604. Cf. I.ii,
   60–1 and note.

QUARLOUS
By whose warrant?

OVERDO
The warrant that you tender and respect so: Justice Overdo's!
I am the man, friend Trouble-all, though thus disguised, as
the careful magistrate ought, for the good of the republic in
the Fair, and the weeding out of enormity. Do you want a   90
house, or meat, or drink, or clothes? Speak; whatsoever it is,
it shall be supplied you. What want you?

QUARLOUS
Nothing but your warrant.

OVERDO
My warrant? For what?

QUARLOUS
To be gone, sir.   95

OVERDO
Nay, I pray thee stay. I am serious, and have not many
words nor much time to exchange with thee; think what may
do thee good.

QUARLOUS
Your hand and seal will do me a great deal of good; nothing
else in the whole Fair, that I know.   100

OVERDO
If it were to any end, thou should'st have it willingly.

QUARLOUS
Why, it will satisfy me—that's end enough—to look on. An
you will not gi' it me, let me go.

OVERDO
Alas! thou shalt ha' it presently. I'll but step into the
scrivener's hereby, and bring it. Do not go away.   105

The JUSTICE *goes out*

QUARLOUS
Why, this madman's shape will prove a very fortunate one,
I think! Can a ragged robe produce these effects? If this be
the wise Justice, and he bring me his hand, I shall go near to
make some use on't.

The JUSTICE *returns*

87 *tender* have regard for
88–9 *as the careful magistrate ought* as befits the watchful magistrate
89 *republic* state, commonwealth
91 *Speak; whatsoever* ed. (speake whatsoeuer F)
102 *me—that's end enough—to* ed. (me, that's end enough, to F)
     on at
109 s.d. *The* JUSTICE *returns* Ed. (*and returns.* F)

He is come already!   110

OVERDO

Look thee! here is my hand and seal, 'Adam Overdo'. If there
be anything to be written above in the paper, that thou
want'st now, or at any time hereafter, think on't. It is my
deed, I deliver it so. Can your friend write?

QUARLOUS

Her hand for a witness, and all is well.   115

OVERDO

With all my heart.   *He urgeth* MISTRESS PURECRAFT

QUARLOUS

[*Aside*] Why should not I ha' the conscience to make this a
bond of a thousand pound now? Or what I would else?

OVERDO

Look you, there it is; and I deliver it as my deed again.

QUARLOUS

Let us now proceed in madness.   120

                    He takes her in with him

OVERDO

Well, my conscience is much eased; I ha' done my part.
Though it doth him no good, yet Adam hath offered
satisfaction! The sting is removed from hence. Poor man, he
is much altered with his affliction, it has brought him low!
Now for my other work: reducing the young man I have   125
followed so long in love, from the brink of his bane to the
centre of safety. Here, or in some such-like vain place, I
shall be sure to find him. I will wait the good time.

Act V, Scene iii

[*Enter*] COKES, SHARKWELL, FILCHER

COKES

How now? What's here to do? Friend, art thou the Master of
the Monuments?

117 *ha' the conscience* have the effrontery (*OED*, Conscience, 12.)
118 *pound now?* Ed. (pound? now, F)
125 *reducing* leading back
126 *bane* destruction, ruin
128 *good time* propitious moment
  1 *to do* going on

1–2 *Master of the Monuments.* Exactly what Cokes has in mind is not
clear. He obviously takes Sharkwell for an official in charge of effigies,
perhaps seeing him, as H & S suggest, as the equivalent of the guide
who took people around Westminster Abbey.

SHARKWELL

   'Tis a motion, an't please your worship.

OVERDO

   [*Aside*] My fantastical brother-in-law, Master Bartholmew
Cokes!   5

COKES

   A motion, what's that?   *He reads the bill*
'The ancient modern history of *Hero and Leander*, otherwise
called *The Touchstone of True Love*, with as true a trial of
friendship between Damon and Pythias, two faithful friends
o' the Bankside'? Pretty i'faith! What's the meaning on't? Is't   10
an interlude? or what is't?

FILCHER

   Yes, sir. Please you come near, we'll take your money within.
                 The boys o' the Fair follow him [COKES]

COKES

   Back with these children; they do so follow me up and down.

                [*Enter*] LITTLEWIT

LITTLEWIT

   By your leave, friend.

FILCHER

   You must pay, sir, an you go in.   15

LITTLEWIT

   Who, I? I perceive thou know'st not me. Call the master o'
the motion.

SHARKWELL

   What, do you not know the author, fellow Filcher? You must
take no money of him; he must come in *gratis*. Master
Littlewit is a voluntary; he is the author.   20

  4 *fantastical* fanciful, unpredictable
11 *interlude* play
20 *voluntary* volunteer, amateur, one who serves without pay

---

7–10 *The ancient . . . Bankside.* The puppet play, like the 'tedious brief
   scene of young Pyramus/And his love Thisby; very tragical mirth' in *A
   Midsummer Night's Dream*, is a burlesque of the kind of interlude
   (l. 11) that was popular in the early years of Elizabeth's reign, and, in
   particular, of Richard Edwards's *The Excellent Comedie of two the
   moste faithfullest Freendes, Damon and Pithias.* 'Newly Imprinted' in
   1571, this work is described in the Prologue to it (l. 38) as a 'tragical
   comedy'. Marlowe's *Hero and Leander*, which is brutally travestied by
   Littlewit, had first appeared in print in 1598 and had proved enorm-
   ously popular. It had also been burlesqued, in prose, by Nashe, in his
   Nashes Lenten Stuffe (1599); see Nashe, iii. 195–201.

LITTLEWIT
Peace, speak not too loud; I would not have any notice taken
that I am the author, till we see how it passes.

COKES
Master Littlewit, how dost thou?

LITTLEWIT
Master Cokes! you are exceeding well met. What, in your
doublet and hose, without a cloak or a hat?   25

COKES
I would I might never stir, as I am an honest man, and by
that fire; I have lost all i' the Fair, and all my acquaintance
too. Didst thou meet anybody that I know, Master Littlewit?
My man Numps, or my sister Overdo, or Mistress Grace?
Pray thee, Master Littlewit, lend me some money to see the   30
interlude here. I'll pay thee again, as I am a gentleman—if
thou'lt but carry me home, I have money enough there.

LITTLEWIT
O sir, you shall command it. What, will a crown serve you?

COKES
I think it will. What do we pay for coming in, fellows?

FILCHER
Twopence, sir.   35

COKES
Twopence? There's twelvepence, friend. Nay, I am a gallant,
as simple as I look now, if you see me with my man about me,
and my artillery, again.

LITTLEWIT
Your man was i' the stocks e'en now, sir.

COKES
Who, Numps?   40

LITTLEWIT
Yes, faith.

COKES
For what i'faith? I am glad o' that. Remember to tell me on't
anon; I have enough now! What manner of matter is this,

---

22 *passes* goes down, is received
27 *fire* probably refers to the fire in Ursla's booth, but could be the
   fire of hell
31 *gentleman—if* ed. (Gentleman. If F)
34 *will. What* Ed. (well, what F)
37 *as simple as* humble though
38 *artillery* full equipment
42 *i'faith?* Ed. (i'faith, F)

Master Littlewit? What kind of actors ha' you? Are they good
actors?   45

[*Enter*] LEATHERHEAD

LITTLEWIT
Pretty youths, sir, all children, both old and young, here's
the master of 'em—

LEATHERHEAD *whispers to* LITTLEWIT

LEATHERHEAD
Call me not Leatherhead, but Lantern.

LITTLEWIT
—Master Lantern, that gives light to the business.

COKES
In good time, sir! I would fain see 'em, I would be glad to   50
drink with the young company. Which is the tiring-house?

LEATHERHEAD
Troth sir, our tiring-house is somewhat little; we are but
beginners yet, pray pardon us; you cannot go upright in't.

COKES
No? Not now my hat is off? What would you have done with
me if you had had me, feather and all, as I was once today?   55
Ha' you none of your pretty impudent boys, now, to bring
stools, fill tobacco, fetch ale, and beg money, as they have at
other houses? Let me see some o' your actors.

LITTLEWIT
Shew him 'em, shew him 'em. Master Lantern, this is a
gentleman that is a favourer of the quality.   60

50 *In good time* well met
50–1 *glad to drink* Ed. (glad drinke F)
51 *tiring-house* area at the back of the stage where the actors dressed
   (attired) themselves
53 *go upright* walk without stooping
60 *quality* acting profession

46–7 *Pretty youths . . . 'em.* Probably an allusion to the Children of the
   Chapel Royal, for whom Edwards, their Master, wrote *Damon and
   Pithias*; though it could refer to the Boys' Companies which enjoyed a
   great revival in the early seventeenth century.
48 *Call me . . . Lantern.* Leatherhead does not wish to be recognized by
   Cokes, whom he has swindled.
56–8 *Ha' you . . . houses.* There is a splendid satirical account of the way
   in which the young fops who sat on the stage behaved in Thomas
   Dekker's *The Gull's Horn-Book* (1609); see *Thomas Dekker*, ed. E. D.
   Pendry, London, 1967, pp. 98–102.

OVERDO

[*Aside*] Ay, the favouring of this licentious quality is the
consumption of many a young gentleman; a pernicious
enormity.

                    He [LEATHERHEAD] *brings them out in a basket*

COKES

What, do they live in baskets?

LEATHERHEAD

They do lie in a basket, sir, they are o' the small players.   65

COKES

These be players minors, indeed. Do you call these players?

LEATHERHEAD

They are actors, sir, and as good as any, none dispraised, for
dumb shows: indeed, I am the mouth of 'em all!

COKES

Thy mouth will hold 'em all. I think one Taylor would go
near to beat all this company, with a hand bound behind him.   70

LITTLEWIT

Ay, and eat 'em all, too, an they were in cake-bread.

COKES

I thank you for that, Master Littlewit, a good jest! Which is
your Burbage now?

LEATHERHEAD

What mean you by that, sir?

COKES

Your best actor. Your Field?   75

---

62 *consumption* financial ruin
68 *mouth* interpreter, voice
71 *in cake-bread* made of cake-bread

---

69 *one Taylor*. There may be as many as three allusions here: (i) to the
   notion that tailors are cowardly, enshrined in the proverb 'Nine tailors
   make a man' (Tilley, T23); (ii) to the actor Joseph Taylor, a member of
   the company that first played *Bartholmew Fair*; (iii) to John Taylor, the
   water-poet as he was called, who had challenged William Fennor, a
   pamphleteer and hack-writer, to a combat of wit at the Hope Theatre in
   October 1614. Fennor, having accepted the challenge, failed to show up.
71 *eat 'em all*. Tailors were popularly supposed to have enormous appetites.
73 *Burbage*. Richard Burbage, who died in 1619, was the leading player of
   the King's Men, Shakespeare's company, and the most celebrated actor
   of the time.
75 *Field*. Nathan Field (1587–1619?) was the chief actor of the Lady
   Elizabeth's Servants when they put on *Bartholmew Fair*. A dramatist as
   well as a player, Field was on very good terms with Jonson.

LITTLEWIT
Good i'faith! You are even with me, sir.

LEATHERHEAD
This is he that acts young Leander, sir. He is extremely
beloved of the womenkind, they do so affect his action, the
green gamesters that come here; and this is lovely Hero; this
with the beard, Damon; and this, pretty Pythias. This is the   80
ghost of King Dionysius in the habit of a scrivener, as you
shall see anon, at large.

COKES
Well, they are a civil company, I like 'em for that. They offer
not to fleer, nor jeer, nor break jests, as the great players do.
And then there goes not so much charge to the feasting of   85
'em, or making 'em drunk, as to the other, by reason of their
littleness. Do they use to play perfect? Are they never
flustered?

LEATHERHEAD
No, sir, I thank my industry and policy for it; they are as
well-governed a company, though I say it—And here is young   90
Leander, is as proper an actor of his inches, and shakes his
head like an hostler.

COKES
But do you play it according to the printed book? I have read
that.

78 *affect his action* like his acting (with a quibble on 'action' =
   'sexual activity')
79 *green gamesters* young loose wenches
81 *the habit of a scrivener* cf. V. iv, 297.
82 *at large* in full
83 *Well*, Ed. (Well F)
84 *fleer* gibe, laugh mockingly
   great adult, full-grown
87 *perfect* word-perfect
91 *of his inches* for his size

91-2 *shakes . . . hostler.* There may be an allusion here to the actor William
   Ostler, a member of the King's Men.
93 *the printed book.* Marlowe's *Hero and Leander* (1598) and, with Chapman's continuation of it, 1598, 1600, 1606, 1609, 1613. The first four
   lines run thus:
> On Hellespont, guilty of true love's blood,
> In view and opposite two cities stood,
> Sea-borderers, disjoin'd by Neptune's might:
> The one Abydos, the other Sestos hight.

LEATHERHEAD
By no means, sir.   95
COKES
No? How then?
LEATHERHEAD
A better way, sir. That is too learned and poetical for our
audience. What do they know what Hellespont is? 'Guilty of
true love's blood'? Or what Abydos is? Or 'the other Sestos
hight'?   100
COKES
Th'art i' the right, I do not know myself.
LEATHERHEAD
No, I have entreated Master Littlewit to take a little pains to
reduce it to a more familiar strain for our people.
COKES
How, I pray thee, good Master Littlewit?
LITTLEWIT
It pleases him to make a matter of it, sir. But there is no such   105
matter, I assure you. I have only made it a little easy, and
modern for the times, sir, that's all. As, for the Hellespont,
I imagine our Thames here; and then Leander I make a
dyer's son, about Puddle Wharf; and Hero a wench o' the
Bankside, who going over one morning to Old Fish Street,   110
Leander spies her land at Trig Stairs, and falls in love with
her. Now do I introduce Cupid having metamorphosed
himself into a drawer, and he strikes Hero in love with a pint
of sherry. And other pretty passages there are o' the friendship, that will delight you, sir, and please you of judgement.   115
COKES
I'll be sworn they shall. I am in love with the actors already,
and I'll be allied to them presently.—They respect gentle-

97 *sir. That* Ed. (Sir, that F)
100 *hight* called
107 *modern* up-to-date
113 *drawer* tapster
    with by means of
114 *sherry. And* Ed. (*Sherry*, and F)
117 *be allied to them* make them members of my family

109 *Puddle Wharf*. Between Blackfriars and Paul's Stairs, it was one of the
    water-gates of London.
110 *Old Fish Street*. As the name implies, the centre of the fish trade in
    Jonson's London.
111 *Trig Stairs*. Stairs leading down to the Thames next to Puddle Wharf.

men, these fellows.—Hero shall be my fairing. But which of
my fairings? Le'me see—i'faith, my fiddle! and Leander my
fiddle-stick. Then Damon my drum, and Pythias my pipe,   120
and the ghost of Dionysius my hobby-horse. All fitted.

Act V, Scene iv

[Enter] to them WINWIFE, GRACE

WINWIFE

Look, yonder's your Cokes gotten in among his playfellows;
I thought we could not miss him at such a spectacle.

GRACE

Let him alone, he is so busy he will never spy us.

LEATHERHEAD

Nay, good sir.

COKES *is handling the puppets*

COKES

I warrant thee, I will not hurt her, fellow; what, dost think   5
me uncivil? I pray thee be not jealous; I am toward a wife.

LITTLEWIT

Well, good Master Lantern, make ready to begin, that I may
fetch my wife; and look you be perfect, you undo me else i'
my reputation.

LEATHERHEAD

I warrant you, sir. Do not you breed too great an expectation   10
of it among your friends; that's the only hurter of these
things.

LITTLEWIT

No, no, no.   *[Exit]*

COKES

I'll stay here and see; pray thee let me see.

WINWIFE

How diligent and troublesome he is!   15

GRACE

The place becomes him, methinks.

OVERDO

[Aside] My ward, Mistress Grace, in the company of a
stranger? I doubt I shall be compelled to discover myself
before my time!

120 *pipe*, Ed. (*Pipe* F)
  5 *what*, Ed. (what F)
  6 *toward* about to marry
 15 *diligent and troublesome* diligently troublesome (hendiadys)
 18 *doubt* fear

[*Enter*] KNOCKEM, WHIT, EDGWORTH, WIN, MISTRESS OVERDO
[*the ladies masked*]
The door-keepers speak

FILCHER
Twopence apiece, gentlemen, an excellent motion.   20

KNOCKEM
Shall we have fine fireworks and good vapours?

SHARKWELL
Yes, Captain, and waterworks too.

WHIT
I pree dee take a care o' dy shmall lady there, Edgworth; I
will look to dish tall lady myself.

LEATHERHEAD
Welcome, gentlemen; welcome, gentlemen.   25

WHIT
Predee, mashter o' de' monshtersh, help a very sick lady
here to a chair to shit in.

LEATHERHEAD
Presently, sir.
They bring MISTRESS OVERDO *a chair*

WHIT
Good fait now, Ursla's ale and *aqua vitae* ish to blame for't.
Shit down, shweetheart, shit down and shleep a little.   30

EDGWORTH
[*To* WIN] Madam, you are very welcome hither.

KNOCKEM
Yes, and you shall see very good vapours.

OVERDO   *By* EDGWORTH
[*Aside*] Here is my care come! I like to see him in so good
company; and yet I wonder that persons of such fashion
should resort hither!   35

EDGWORTH
This is a very private house, madam.
The cutpurse courts MISTRESS LITTLEWIT

21 *vapours?* Ed. (vapours! F)
22 *waterworks* a pageant exhibited on the water (much of the puppet-
shew is supposed to take place on the Thames)
32 s.d. *By* referring to

---

36 *private house.* Edgworth quibbles on (i) house that affords us privacy
(ii) private playhouse, i.e., one that was, unlike the public theatres such
as the Globe or the Hope, entirely roofed in. It was also more expensive
than the public theatres.

LEATHERHEAD
Will it please your ladyship sit, madam?

WIN
Yes, goodman. They do so all-to-be-madam me, I think
they think me a very lady!

EDGWORTH
What else, madam? 40

WIN
Must I put off my mask to him?

EDGWORTH
O, by no means.

WIN
How should my husband know me, then?

KNOCKEM
Husband? an idle vapour. He must not know you, nor you
him; there's the true vapour. 45

OVERDO
[Aside] Yea, I will observe more of this. [To WHIT] Is this a
lady, friend?

WHIT
Ay, and dat is anoder lady, shweetheart. If dou hasht a
mind to 'em, give me twelvepence from tee, and dou shalt
have eder-oder on 'em! 50

OVERDO
Ay? [Aside] This will prove my chiefest enormity, I will
follow this.

EDGWORTH
Is not this a finer life, lady, than to be clogged with a husband?

WIN
Yes, a great deal. When will they begin, trow, in the name o' 55
the motion?

EDGWORTH
By and by, madam, they stay but for company.

KNOCKEM
Do you hear, puppet-master, these are tedious vapours;
when begin you?

LEATHERHEAD
We stay but for Master Littlewit, the author, who is gone 60
for his wife; and we begin presently.

---

38 *all-to-be-madam me* persist in calling me madam
50 *eder-oder* one or the other
55 *trow* do you think

WIN
That's I, that's I.

EDGWORTH
That was you, lady, but now you are no such poor thing.

KNOCKEM
Hang the author's wife, a running vapour! Here be ladies
will stay for ne'er a Delia o' 'em all.   65

WHIT
But hear me now, here ish one o' de ladish ashleep. Stay till
she but vake, man.

[*Enter*] *to them* WASP

The door-keepers again

WASP
How now, friends? What's here to do?

FILCHER
Twopence apiece, sir, the best motion in the Fair.

WASP
I believe you lie. If you do, I'll have my money again, and   70
beat you.

WINWIFE
Numps is come!

WASP
Did you see a master of mine come in here, a tall young
squire of Harrow o' the Hill, Master Bartholmew Cokes?

FILCHER
I think there be such a one within.   75

WASP
Look he be, you were best; but it is very likely. I wonder I
found him not at all the rest. I ha' been at the Eagle, and the
Black Wolf, and the Bull with the five legs and two pizzles—
he was a calf at Uxbridge Fair, two years agone—and at the
Dogs that dance the morris, and the Hare o' the tabor, and   80
missed him at all these! Sure this must needs be some fine
sight that holds him so, if it have him.

---

72 s.p. WINWIFE Ed. (WIN. F)

65 *a Delia*. Delia is the name of the lady to whom Samuel Daniel addressed
his sonnet sequence *Delia*, first published in 1592. Probably an anagram
of 'ideal', the name is here synonymous with 'self-important lady'.

77–80 *the Eagle . . . tabor*. Various attractions at the Fair. The 'Bull with
five legs', first mentioned at III.vi, 7, has now acquired an extra pizzle
(penis) and has been joined by some other animals, including a hare that
plays on the tabor.

COKES
  Come, come, are you ready now?
LEATHERHEAD
  Presently, sir.
WASP
  Hoyday, he's at work in his doublet and hose. Do you hear,   85
  sir? Are you employed, that you are bare-headed and so
  busy?
COKES
  Hold your peace, Numps; you ha' been i' the stocks, I hear.
WASP
  Does he know that? Nay, then the date of my authority is
  out; I must think no longer to reign, my government is at an   90
  end. He that will correct another must want fault in himself.
WINWIFE
  Sententious Numps! I never heard so much from him before.
LEATHERHEAD
  Sure Master Littlewit will not come. Please you take your
  place, sir, we'll begin.
COKES
  I pray thee do, mine ears long to be at it, and my eyes too. O   95
  Numps, i' the stocks, Numps? Where's your sword, Numps?
WASP
  I pray you intend your game, sir, let me alone.
COKES
  Well then, we are quit for all. Come, sit down, Numps; I'll
  interpret to thee. Did you see Mistress Grace? It's no
  matter neither now I think on't, tell me anon.   100
WINWIFE
  A great deal of love and care he expresses.
GRACE
  Alas! Would you have him to express more than he has?
  That were tyranny.
COKES
  Peace, ho! now, now.
LEATHERHEAD
  Gentles, that no longer your expectations may wander,   105

89–90 *date of my authority is out* term of my authority is up
91 *want* be free from
97 *intend* pay attention to
98 *quit* even (with one another)

Behold our chief actor, amorous Leander,
With a great deal of cloth lapped about him like a scarf,
For he yet serves his father, a dyer at Puddle Wharf,
Which place we'll make bold with, to call it our Abydus,
As the Bankside is our Sestos, and let it not be denied us.   110
Now, as he is beating, to make the dye take the fuller,
Who chances to come by but fair Hero in a sculler;
And seeing Leander's naked leg and goodly calf,
Cast at him, from the boat, a sheep's eye and a half.
Now she is landed, and the sculler come back;   115
By and by you shall see what Leander doth lack.

PUPPET LEANDER
   Cole, Cole, old Cole.
LEATHERHEAD   *That is the sculler's name without control.*
PUPPET LEANDER
   Cole, Cole, I say, Cole.
LEATHERHEAD   *We do hear you.*
PUPPET LEANDER   *Old Cole.*
LEATHERHEAD
   Old coal? Is the dyer turned collier? How do you sell?
PUPPET LEANDER
   A pox o' your manners, kiss my hole here, and smell.   120
LEATHERHEAD
   Kiss your hole, and smell? There's manners indeed.
PUPPET LEANDER
   Why, Cole, I say, Cole.
LEATHERHEAD   *It's the sculler you need!*
PUPPET LEANDER
   Ay, and be hanged.
LEATHERHEAD   *Be hanged? Look you yonder;*
   Old Cole, you must go hang with Master Leander.

106 *Leander*, Ed. (Leander. F)
111 *fuller* more completely
117 *Cole* often used as the name for a pander
118 *We do hear you* Ed. (roman in F)
119 *collier* (i) seller of coal (ii) term of abuse, because coal-sellers were
    black from their trade and were notorious cheats
    How at what price

106 *amorous Leander*. The words are Marlowe's (*Hero and Leander*, i. 51).
114 *Cast . . . eye*. 'He casts a sheep's eye at her' was proverbial (Tilley,
    S323) and still is.
117 *without control*. The normal meaning of this phrase is 'freely', but here
    'beyond all contradiction' would seem more to the point.

PUPPET COLE
    Where is he?
PUPPET LEANDER   *Here, Cole. What fairest of fairs*   125
    Was that fare that thou landedst but now at Trig Stairs?
COKES
  What was that, fellow? Pray thee tell me, I scarce understand
  'em.
LEATHERHEAD
    Leander does ask, sir, what fairest of fairs
    Was the fare that he landed, but now, at Trig Stairs.   130
PUPPET COLE
    It is lovely Hero.
PUPPET LEANDER   *Nero?*
PUPPET COLE   *No, Hero.*
LEATHERHEAD   *It is lovely Hero*
    Of the Bankside, he saith, to tell you truth without erring,
    Is come over into Fish Street to eat some fresh herring.
    Leander says no more, but as fast as he can,
    Gets on all his best clothes, and will after to the Swan.   135
COKES
  Most admirable good, is't not?
LEATHERHEAD
    Stay, sculler.
PUPPET COLE   *What say you?*
LEATHERHEAD   *You must stay for Leander,*
    And carry him to the wench.
PUPPET COLE   *You rogue, I am no pander.*
COKES
  He says he is no pander. 'Tis a fine language; I understand
  it now.   140
LEATHERHEAD
    Are you no pander, Goodman Cole? Here's no man says you
      are.
    You'll grow a hot Cole, it seems, pray you stay for your fare.
PUPPET COLE
    Will he come away?
LEATHERHEAD   *What do you say?*
PUPPET COLE   *I'd ha' him come away.*
LEATHERHEAD
    Would you ha' Leander come away? Why pray, sir, stay.

126 *at* Ed. (*a* F)
130 *that he* Ed. (*thhe* F)
131 *is lovely Hero* ed. (*is* Hero. F)

You are angry, Goodman Cole. I believe the fair maid   145
Came over w' you o' trust. Tell us, sculler, are you paid?

PUPPET COLE
 Yes, Goodman Hogrubber o' Pickt-hatch.

LEATHERHEAD
 How? Hogrubber o' Pickt-hatch?

PUPPET COLE   *Ay, Hogrubber o' Pickt-hatch.*
 Take you that.   The puppet strikes him over the pate

LEATHERHEAD   *O, my head!*

PUPPET COLE   *Harm watch, harm catch.*

COKES
 'Harm watch, harm catch,' he says. Very good i'faith! The   150
 sculler had like to ha' knocked you, sirrah.

LEATHERHEAD
 Yes, but that his fare called him away.

PUPPET LEANDER
 Row apace, row apace, row, row, row, row, row.

LEATHERHEAD
 You are knavishly loaden, sculler, take heed where you go.

PUPPET COLE
 Knave i' your face, Goodman Rogue.

PUPPET LEANDER   *Row, row, row, row, row, row.*   155

COKES
 He said 'knave i' your face,' friend.

LEATHERHEAD
 Ay, sir, I heard him. But there's no talking to these watermen, they will ha' the last word.

COKES
 God's my life! I am not allied to the sculler yet. He shall be
 Dauphin my boy. But my fiddle-stick does fiddle in and out   160

146 *paid?* Ed. (*paid.* F)
149 *Harm watch, harm catch* if you do harm, you suffer harm (prov-
    erbial, Tilley, H167)
151 *had like to ha' knocked* seemed on the point of beating
157–8 *watermen, they will ha' the last word* a variant on the proverbial
    'Women will have the last word' (Tilley, W723)
160 *my fiddle-stick* i.e., Leander (cf. V. iii, 119–20)

---

147 *Hogrubber o' Pickt-hatch.* Hogrubber seems to have been a derisive
    term for a swineherd, while Pickt-hatch was a very unsavoury area of
    London, the haunt of thieves and prostitutes. It looks as though Leather-
    head is being accused of bestiality.
160 *Dauphin my boy.* Also referred to by Edgar in *King Lear* (III.iv, 99) as
    'Dolphin my boy', this snatch (from some lost ballad or song?) still
    remains unexplained.

too much. I pray thee speak to him on't; tell him I would
have him tarry in my sight more.

LEATHERHEAD

I pray you be content; you'll have enough on him, sir.
   Now gentles, I take it, here is none of you so stupid,
   But that you have heard of a little god of love, called Cupid; 165
   Who out of kindness to Leander, hearing he but saw her,
   This present day and hour, doth turn himself to a drawer.
   And because he would have their first meeting to be merry,
   He strikes Hero in love to him, with a pint of sherry.
   Which he tells her from amorous Leander is sent her, 170
   Who after him into the room of Hero doth venter.

PUPPET JONAS
   A pint of sack, score a pint of sack i' the Coney.
      Puppet Leander goes into MISTRESS HERO's room

COKES

Sack? You said but e'en now it should be sherry.

PUPPET JONAS
   Why so it is; sherry, sherry, sherry.

COKES

'Sherry, sherry, sherry.' By my troth he makes me merry. I 175
must have a name for Cupid too. Let me see. Thou
mightest help me now, an thou wouldest, Numps, at a dead
lift, but thou art dreaming o' the stocks still! Do not think
on't, I have forgot it. 'Tis but a nine days' wonder, man; let
it not trouble thee. 180

WASP

I would the stocks were about your neck, sir; condition I
hung by the heels in them, till the wonder wore off from you,
with all my heart.

COKES

Well said, resolute Numps!—But hark you, friend, where is

---

171 *venter* venture
177–8 *at a dead lift* at a pinch (proverbial, Tilley, L271)
179 *a nine days' wonder* (proverbial, Tilley, W728)
181 *condition* on condition that
184 *said,* Ed. (said F)

---

172 *the Coney.* Rooms in Elizabethan inns were named not numbered.
173 *Sack? . . . sherry.* Cokes loses no opportunity of demonstrating his
    ignorance. Sack was the name by which all white wines, including
    sherry, were called.
182 *wore* Ed. (were F). Cf. 'These few days' wonder will be quickly worn'
    (2 *Henry VI*, II.iv, 69).

the friendship, all this while, between my drum, Damon,   185
and my pipe, Pythias?

LEATHERHEAD
You shall see by and by, sir.

COKES
You think my hobby-horse is forgotten too. No, I'll see 'em
all enact before I go; I shall not know which to love best,
else.   190

KNOCKEM
This gallant has interrupting vapours, troublesome vapours,
Whit, puff with him.

WHIT
No, I pre dee, Captain, let him alone. He is a child i'faith,
la!

LEATHERHEAD
Now gentles, to the friends, who in number are two,   195
And lodged in that ale-house in which fair Hero does do.
Damon, for some kindness done him the last week,
Is come fair Hero, in Fish Street, this morning to seek.
Pythias does smell the knavery of the meeting,
And now you shall see their true friendly greeting.   200

PUPPET PYTHIAS
You whoremasterly slave, you!

COKES
'Whoremasterly slave, you?' Very friendly and familiar, that.

PUPPET DAMON   *Whoremaster i' thy face,*
Thou hast lien with her thyself, I'll prove't i' this place.

COKES
Damon says Pythias has lien with her himself, he'll prove't   205
in this place.

LEATHERHEAD
They are whoremasters both, sir, that's a plain case.

PUPPET PYTHIAS
You lie like a rogue.

LEATHERHEAD   *Do I lie like a rogue?*

PUPPET PYTHIAS
A pimp and a scab.

192 *puff with* bully, quarrel with
196 *do* work
209 *scab* scoundrel

188 *my hobby-horse is forgotten.* A much-quoted line from some lost song; cf.
Hamlet, III.ii, 130.

LEATHERHEAD   *A pimp and a scab?*
    I say between you, you have both but one drab.   210
PUPPET DAMON
    You lie again.
LEATHERHEAD   *Do I lie again?*
PUPPET DAMON
    Like a rogue again.
LEATHERHEAD   *Like a rogue again?*
PUPPET PYTHIAS
    And you are a pimp again.
COKES
    And you are a pimp again, he says.
PUPPET DAMON   *And a scab again.*   215
COKES
    And a scab again, he says.
LEATHERHEAD
    And I say again, you are both whoremasters again,
    And you have both but one drab again.
                                        They fight
PUPPET DAMON   ⎫
PUPPET PYTHIAS ⎭ *Dost thou, dost thou, dost thou?*
LEATHERHEAD
    What, both at once?
PUPPET PYTHIAS   *Down with him, Damon.*   220
PUPPET DAMON
    Pink his guts, Pythias.
LEATHERHEAD   *What, so malicious?*
    Will ye murder me, masters both, i' mine own house?
COKES
    Ho! well acted my drum, well acted my pipe, well acted
    still!
WASP
    Well acted, with all my heart!   225
LEATHERHEAD
    Hold, hold your hands.
COKES
    Ay, both your hands, for my sake! for you ha' both done
    well.
PUPPET DAMON
    Gramercy, pure Pythias.
PUPPET PYTHIAS   *Gramercy, dear Damon.*

221 *Pink* pierce, stab
226 *Hold* Ed. (*Hld* F)
227 *for* Ed. (for. F)

COKES

    Gramercy to you both, my pipe, and my drum.   230

PUPPET PYTHIAS }
PUPPET DAMON } *Come now we'll together to breakfast to Hero.*

LEATHERHEAD

    'Tis well, you can now go to breakfast to Hero,
    You have given me my breakfast, with a 'hone and 'honero.

COKES

    How is it, friend, ha' they hurt thee?

LEATHERHEAD   O no!

    Between you and I, sir, we do but make shew.   235
        Thus, gentles, you perceive, without any denial,
        'Twixt Damon and Pythias here, friendship's true trial.
        Though hourly they quarrel thus, and roar each with other,
        They fight you no more than does brother with brother.
        But friendly together, at the next man they meet   240
        They let fly their anger, as here you might see't.

COKES

    Well, we have seen't, and thou hast felt it, whatsoever thou
    sayest. What's next? What's next?

LEATHERHEAD

        This while young Leander with fair Hero is drinking,
        And Hero grown drunk, to any man's thinking!   245
        Yet was it not three pints of sherry could flaw her,
        Till Cupid, distinguished like Jonas the drawer,
        From under his apron, where his lechery lurks,
        Put love in her sack. Now mark how it works.

PUPPET HERO

        O Leander, Leander, my dear, my dear Leander,   250
        I'll for ever be thy goose, so thou'lt be my gander.

COKES

    Excellently well said, fiddle! She'll ever be his goose, so he'll
    be her gander; was't not so?

231 *to Hero* with Hero
233 *me my* Ed. (*mmy* F)
234 *is it* ed. (is't F)
243 *sayest.* Ed. (sayest, F)
246 *flaw her*, Ed. (*flaw her.* F) make her drunk (earliest example in
    OED 1673)
247 *distinguished* dressed, disguised
249 *sack* (i) sherry (ii) loose gown

233 *a 'hone and 'honero.* An Irish and Scottish exclamation of grief, from the
    Irish and Gaelic 'ochòin', meaning 'alas'.

LEATHERHEAD
Yes, sir, but mark his answer, now.

PUPPET LEANDER
And sweetest of geese, before I go to bed,   255
I'll swim o'er the Thames, my goose, thee to tread.

COKES
Brave! he will swim o'er the Thames and tread his goose
tonight, he says.

LEATHERHEAD
Ay, peace, sir, they'll be angry if they hear you eaves-
dropping, now they are setting their match.   260

PUPPET LEANDER
But lest the Thames should be dark, my goose, my dear friend,
Let thy window be provided of a candle's end.

PUPPET HERO
Fear not, my gander, I protest I should handle
My matters very ill, if I had not a whole candle.

PUPPET LEANDER
Well then, look to't, and kiss me to boot.   265

LEATHERHEAD
Now here come the friends again, Pythias and Damon,
And under their cloaks they have of bacon a gammon.
DAMON and PYTHIAS enter

PUPPET PYTHIAS
Drawer, fill some wine here.

LEATHERHEAD   *How, some wine there?*
There's company already, sir, pray forbear!

PUPPET DAMON
'Tis Hero.

LEATHERHEAD   *Yes, but she will not be taken,*   270
After sack and fresh herring, with your Dunmow-bacon.

PUPPET PYTHIAS
You lie, it's Westfabian.

LEATHERHEAD   *Westphalian, you should say.*

259 *they'll* Ed. (the'll F)
260 *setting their match* fixing a time for their (amorous) encounter
263 *not,* Ed. (*not* F)

---

271 *Dunmow-bacon.* 'To fetch a flitch of bacon from Dunmow' was synonymous with marital fidelity (Tilley, F375), since the village of Dunmow, in Essex, gives a flitch of bacon to the couple who can show that
they have not quarrelled since they were married. Leatherhead's point is
that after her meal Hero will be feeling lecherous.

272 *Westphalian.* Westphalia, in Germany, was famous for its bacon and
ham.

PUPPET DAMON
>If you hold not your peace, you are a coxcomb, I would say.

LEANDER and HERO are kissing

PUPPET [PYTHIAS]
>What's here? What's here? Kiss, kiss upon kiss.

LEATHERHEAD
>Ay, wherefore should they not? What harm is in this?   275
>'Tis Mistress Hero.

PUPPET DAMON   Mistress Hero's a whore.

LEATHERHEAD
>Is she a whore? Keep you quiet, or, sir knave, out of door.

PUPPET DAMON
>Knave out of door?

PUPPET HERO   Yes, knave, out of door.

PUPPET DAMON
>Whore out of door.

PUPPET HERO   I say, knave, out of door.

Here the PUPPETS quarrel and fall together by the ears

PUPPET DAMON
>I say, whore, out of door.

PUPPET PYTHIAS   Yea, so say I too.   280

PUPPET HERO
>Kiss the whore o' the arse.

LEATHERHEAD   Now you ha' something to do:
>You must kiss her o' the arse, she says.

PUPPET DAMON ⎫
PUPPET PYTHIAS ⎭   So we will, so we will

[They kick her]

PUPPET HERO
>O my haunches, O my haunches, hold, hold!

LEATHERHEAD   Stand'st thou still?
>Leander, where art thou? Stand'st thou still like a sot,
>And not offer'st to break both their heads with a pot?   285
>See who's at thine elbow there! Puppet Jonas and Cupid.

PUPPET JONAS
>Upon 'em, Leander, be not so stupid.

They fight

PUPPET LEANDER
>You goat-bearded slave!

PUPPET DAMON   You whoremaster knave!

PUPPET LEANDER
>Thou art a whoremaster.

PUPPET JONAS   Whoremasters all.

LEATHERHEAD
> *See, Cupid with a word has ta'en up the brawl.*   290

KNOCKEM
These be fine vapours!

COKES
By this good day they fight bravely! Do they not, Numps?

WASP
Yes, they lacked but you to be their second, all this while.

LEATHERHEAD
> *This tragical encounter, falling out thus to busy us,*
> *It raises up the ghost of their friend Dionysius,*   295
> *Not like a monarch, but the master of a school,*
> *In a scrivener's furred gown, which shews he is no fool.*
> *For therein he hath wit enough to keep himself warm.*
> *'O Damon,' he cries, 'and Pythias, what harm*
> *Hath poor Dionysius done you in his grave,*   300
> *That after his death you should fall out thus, and rave,*
> *And call amorous Leander whoremaster knave?'*

PUPPET DIONYSIUS
> *I cannot, I will not, I promise you, endure it.*

Act V, Scene v

[Enter] to them BUSY

BUSY
Down with Dagon, down with Dagon! 'Tis I, will no longer
endure your profanations.

LEATHERHEAD
What mean you, sir?

BUSY
I will remove Dagon there, I say, that idol, that heathenish
idol, that remains, as I may say, a beam, a very beam, not a   5

---

298 *wit enough . . . warm* proverbial (Tilley, K10)
  1 *will* who will, and I will

295-6 *Dionysius . . . school.* According to some accounts, Dionysius the
    younger, tyrant of Syracuse (367–343 B.C.) became a schoolmaster after
    his abdication.
  1 *Dagon.* The national god of the Philistines, represented as half man and
    half fish, was regarded as the very type of an idol. Hence comes Busy's
    ridiculous equation of the puppets, whom he sees as idols, with Dagon.
    See I Samuel, v.

beam of the sun, nor a beam of the moon, nor a beam of a
balance, neither a house-beam, nor a weaver's beam, but a
beam in the eye, in the eye of the brethren; a very great
beam, an exceeding great beam; such as are your stage-
players, rhymers, and morris-dancers, who have walked   10
hand in hand, in contempt of the brethren, and the cause;
and been borne out by instruments of no mean countenance.

LEATHERHEAD

Sir, I present nothing but what is licensed by authority.

BUSY

Thou art all licence, even licentiousness itself, Shimei!

LEATHERHEAD

I have the Master of the Revels' hand for't, sir.   15

BUSY

The Master of Rebels' hand, thou hast—Satan's! Hold thy
peace; thy scurrility shut up thy mouth; thy profession is
damnable, and in pleading for it, thou dost plead for Baal.
I have long opened my mouth wide, and gaped, I have gaped
as the oyster for the tide, after thy destruction, but cannot   20
compass it by suit, or dispute; so that I look for a bickering,
ere long, and then a battle.

KNOCKEM

Good Banbury-vapours.

6–7 *beam of a balance* transverse bar from the ends of which the
    scales of a balance are suspended
7 *weaver's beam* cylinder in a loom
7–8 *a beam in the eye* alluding to the figure of the mote and the
    beam (Matthew, vii. 3–5)
12 *borne out* supported
    instruments agents (of the devil)
    countenance position, rank
17 *thy scurrility shut up* let thy scurrility shut up
19–20 *gaped as the oyster for the tide* proverbial (Tilley, O114)
21 *bickering* skirmish

---

14 *Shimei.* Shimei, who cursed David, had, according to David himself,
    God's authority (licence) for doing it (II Samuel, xvi. 5–13).
15 *Master of the Revels.* An officer of the court who was responsible for,
    among other things, the licensing of plays.
18 *Baal.* The heathen god of the Midianites whose altar was cast down by
    Gideon (Judges, vi. 25–32). Busy sees himself as a Gideon.

COKES

Friend, you'd have an ill match on't if you bicker with him here; though he be no man o' the fist, he has friends that will go to cuffs for him. Numps, will not you take our side? 25

EDGWORTH

Sir, it shall not need; in my mind, he offers him a fairer course—to end it by disputation!—Hast thou nothing to say for thyself, in defence of thy quality?

LEATHERHEAD

Faith, sir, I am not well studied in these controversies between the hypocrites and us. But here's one of my motion, Puppet Dionysius, shall undertake him, and I'll venture the cause on't. 30

COKES

Who? My hobby-horse? Will he dispute with him?

LEATHERHEAD

Yes, sir, and make a hobby-ass of him, I hope. 35

COKES

That's excellent! Indeed he looks like the best scholar of 'em all. Come, sir, you must be as good as your word, now.

BUSY

I will not fear to make my spirit and gifts known! Assist me, zeal, fill me, fill me, that is, make me full.

WINWIFE

What a desperate, profane wretch is this! Is there any ignorance or impudence like his? To call his zeal to fill him against a puppet? 40

GRACE

I know no fitter match than a puppet to commit with an hypocrite!

25 *here;* Ed. (here, F)
26 *him.* Ed. (him, F)
27 *need;* Ed. (need, F)
29 *quality* profession
32 *undertake him* take him on
43 *commit* do battle

43 s.p. GRACE Ed. (QVA. F). As Waith points out, Quarlous is not on stage. Having made his exit at V.ii, 120, he does not return until the opening of V.vi. A misreading of 'GRA.' as 'QVA.' by the compositor is the likeliest explanation of the mistake.

BUSY
First, I say unto thee, idol, thou hast no calling.   45

PUPPET DIONYSIUS
You lie, I am called Dionysius.

LEATHERHEAD
The motion says you lie, he is called Dionysius i' the matter,
and to that calling he answers.

BUSY
I mean no vocation, idol, no present lawful calling.

PUPPET DIONYSIUS
Is yours a lawful calling?   50

LEATHERHEAD
The motion asketh if yours be a lawful calling.

BUSY
Yes, mine is of the spirit.

PUPPET DIONYSIUS
Then idol is a lawful calling.

LEATHERHEAD
He says, then idol is a lawful calling! For you called him
idol, and your calling is of the spirit.   55

COKES
Well disputed, hobby-horse!

BUSY
Take not part with the wicked, young gallant. He neigheth
and hinnyeth, all is but hinnying sophistry. I call him idol
again. Yet, I say, his calling, his profession is profane; it is
profane, idol.   60

PUPPET DIONYSIUS
It is not profane!

LEATHERHEAD
It is not profane, he says.

BUSY
It is profane.

47 *matter* puppet-play, text
57 *wicked,* Ed. (wicked F)

---

45 *no calling.* As Busy explains at l.49, he means 'no lawful occupation'.
The Puritans, and opponents of the stage in general, took the view
that acting was not a genuine occupation at all; and they had the law on
their side, for the player was liable to arrest as a rogue and a vagabond,
unless he could show that he was in the service of the court or of some
great man. It was for this reason that each acting company secured the
patronage of a member of the royal family, or of a noble, and called
themselves 'The Lord Chamberlain's Men', 'The Lady Elizabeth's
Servants', and the like.

PUPPET DIONYSIUS
It is not profane.
BUSY
It is profane.   65
PUPPET DIONYSIUS
It is not profane.
LEATHERHEAD
Well said, confute him with 'not', still. You cannot bear him
down with your base noise, sir.
BUSY
Nor he me with his treble creaking, though he creak like the
chariot wheels of Satan. I am zealous for the cause—   70
LEATHERHEAD
As a dog for a bone.
BUSY
And I say it is profane, as being the page of Pride, and the
waiting-woman of Vanity.
PUPPET DIONYSIUS
Yea? What say you to your tire-women, then?
LEATHERHEAD
Good.   75
PUPPET DIONYSIUS
Or feather-makers i' the Friars, that are o' your faction of faith?
Are not they, with their perukes, and their puffs, their fans, and
their huffs, as much pages of Pride, and waiters upon Vanity?
What say you? What say you? What say you?
BUSY
I will not answer for them.   80
PUPPET DIONYSIUS
Because you cannot, because you cannot. Is a bugle-maker a
lawful calling? Or the confect-maker's?—Such you have there.
—Or your French fashioner? You'd have all the sin within
yourselves, would you not? would you not?

69 *creaking* speaking in a strident tone
74 *tire-women* dressmakers
77 *puffs* soft protuberant mass of material on the dress
78 *huffs* paddings used to raise the shoulders of dresses
81 *bugle-maker* maker of tube-shaped glass beads
82 *confect-maker's* that of the maker of sweetmeats
83 *fashioner* tailor or dressmaker

---

76 *feather-makers i' the Friars.* The traders in feathers, who lived in the
    Blackfriars area, also happened to be Puritans. The contradiction
    between their occupation, ministering to vanity, and their religious
    leanings did not escape their opponents.

BUSY
No, Dagon. 85

PUPPET DIONYSIUS
What then, Dagonet? Is a puppet worse than these?

BUSY
Yes, and my main argument against you is that you are an
abomination; for the male among you putteth on the apparel
of the female, and the female of the male.

PUPPET DIONYSIUS
You lie, you lie, you lie abominably. 90

COKES
Good, by my troth, he has given him the lie thrice.

PUPPET DIONYSIUS
*It is your old stale argument against the players, but it will not
hold against the puppets, for we have neither male nor female
amongst us. And that thou may'st see, if thou wilt, like a
malicious purblind zeal as thou art!* 95
The PUPPET *takes up his garment*

EDGWORTH
By my faith, there he has answered you, friend, by plain
demonstration.

PUPPET DIONYSIUS
*Nay, I'll prove, against e'er a Rabbin of 'em all, that my
standing is as lawful as his; that I speak by inspiration, as well
as he; that I have as little to do with learning as he; and do* 100
scorn her helps as much as he.

BUSY
I am confuted, the cause hath failed me.

PUPPET DIONYSIUS
Then be converted, be converted.

LEATHERHEAD
Be converted, I pray you, and let the play go on!

BUSY
Let it go on. For I am changed, and will become a beholder 105
with you!

86 *Dagonet* King Arthur's fool
99 *standing* profession

88–9 *an abomination . . . male.* This 'old stale argument against the players',
used long before 1614 and long after it, is based on Deuteronomy, xxii.
5: 'The woman shall not wear that which pertaineth unto a man, neither
shall a man put on a woman's garment: for all that do so are abomination unto the Lord thy God'. The text was indeed an inviting weapon
for the enemies of a theatre in which all female roles were played by
boys.

COKES

That's brave i'faith. Thou hast carried it away, hobby-horse.
On with the play!

The JUSTICE *discovers himself*

OVERDO

Stay. Now do I forbid, I, Adam Overdo! Sit still, I charge
you.   110

COKES

What, my brother-i'-law!

GRACE

My wise guardian!

EDGWORTH

Justice Overdo!

OVERDO

It is time to take enormity by the forehead, and brand it; for
I have discovered enough.   115

Act V, Scene vi

[*Enter*] *to them*, QUARLOUS (*like the madman*), PURECRAFT

QUARLOUS

Nay, come, Mistress bride. You must do as I do now. You
must be mad with me, in truth. I have here Justice Overdo
for it.

OVERDO

Peace, good Trouble-all; come hither, and you shall trouble
none. I will take the charge of you and your friend too. (*To*   5
the cutpurse and MISTRESS LITTLEWIT) You also, young man,
shall be my care, stand there.

EDGWORTH

Now mercy upon me.

The rest are stealing away

107 *carried it away* won
  5 *too.* Ed. (too, F)
  6 *man*, Ed. (man F)

---

s.d. *Enter to them*, QUARLOUS (*like the madman*), PURECRAFT Ed. (*To them*,
QVARLOVS. (*like the Man-man*) PVRECRAFT. (*a while after*) IOHN. *to them*
TROVBLE-ALL. VRSLA. NIGHTIGALE. F). Since Quarlous is speaking to
Dame Purecraft as he enters, it is clear that the words *a while after* are
intended to apply to John Littlewit, who does not appear until l. 13.

KNOCKEM
  Would we were away, Whit! These are dangerous vapours;
  best fall off with our birds, for fear o' the cage.   10
OVERDO
  Stay, is not my name your terror?
WHIT
  Yesh faith, man, and it ish for tat we would be gone, man.

                    [*Enter*] LITTLEWIT

LITTLEWIT
  O gentlemen, did you not see a wife of mine? I ha' lost my
  little wife, as I shall be trusted, my little pretty Win. I left
  her at the great woman's house in trust yonder, the pig-   15
  woman's, with Captain Jordan and Captain Whit, very good
  men, and I cannot hear of her. Poor fool, I fear she's stepped
  aside. Mother, did you not see Win?
OVERDO
  If this grave matron be your mother, sir, stand by her, *et
  digito compesce labellum*; I may perhaps spring a wife for you   20
  anon. Brother Bartholmew, I am sadly sorry to see you so
  lightly given, and such a disciple of enormity, with your
  grave governor Humphrey. But stand you both there in the
  middle place; I will reprehend you in your course. Mistress
  Grace, let me rescue you out of the hands of the stranger.   25
WINWIFE
  Pardon me, sir, I am a kinsman of hers.
OVERDO
  Are you so? Of what name, sir?
WINWIFE
  Winwife, sir.
OVERDO
  Master Winwife? I hope you have won no wife of her, sir.
  If you have, I will examine the possibility of it at fit leisure. 30

  9 *Whit!* Ed. (*Whit*, F)
 10 *fall off* withdraw
    cage gaol
 12 *gone*, Ed. (gone F)
 17 *fool* sweet
 17–18 *stepped aside* gone astray
 20 *spring* put up (as a partridge is 'put up' from cover)
 24 *course* turn

 ───

 19–20 *et digito compesce labellum*. Adapted from Juvenal (*Satires*, i. 160):
    'and check any movement of your lips with your finger', i.e., 'don't give
    yourself away'.

Now to my enormities! Look upon me, O London! and see
me, O Smithfield! the example of Justice, and Mirror of
Magistrates; the true top of formality, and scourge of
enormity. Hearken unto my labours and but observe my
discoveries; and compare Hercules with me, if thou dar'st,   35
of old; or Columbus, Magellan, or our countryman Drake of
later times. Stand forth you weeds of enormity and spread.
(*To* BUSY) First, Rabbi Busy, thou superlunatical hypocrite.
(*To* LANTERN) Next, thou other extremity, thou profane professor of puppetry, little better than poetry. (*To the horse-*   40
courser, and cutpurse) Then thou strong debaucher, and
seducer of youth—witness this easy and honest young man.
(*Then* CAPTAIN WHIT *and* MISTRESS LITTLEWIT) Now thou
esquire of dames, madams, and twelvepenny ladies; now my
green madam herself of the price. Let me unmask your   45
ladyship.

LITTLEWIT
O my wife, my wife, my wife!

OVERDO
Is she your wife? *Redde te Harpocratem!*

Enter TROUBLE-ALL [*followed by* URSLA *and* NIGHTINGALE]

TROUBLE-ALL
By your leave, stand by, my masters, be uncovered.

URSLA
O stay him, stay him! Help to cry, Nightingale. My pan, my   50
pan!

OVERDO
What's the matter?

NIGHTINGALE
He has stolen Gammer Ursla's pan.

TROUBLE-ALL
Yes, and I fear no man but Justice Overdo.

OVERDO
Ursla? Where is she? O the sow of enormity, this! (*To* URSLA   55

33 *formality* legal procedure
37 *enormity and spread* ed. (enormity, and spread F) wide-spread
    enormity (hendiadys)
42 *easy* compliant, credulous
49 *by*, Ed. (by F)
    be uncovered take off your hats (as a sign of respect)

---

48 *Redde te Harpocratem.* Transform yourself into Harpocrates (the god of
    silence, born with his finger on his lips).

and NIGHTINGALE) Welcome. Stand you there; you, songster, there.

URSLA

An please your worship, I am in no fault. A gentleman stripped him in my booth, and borrowed his gown and his hat; and he ran away with my goods here for it.   60

OVERDO

(*To* QUARLOUS) Then this is the true madman, and you are the enormity!

QUARLOUS

You are i' the right, I am mad but from the gown outward.

OVERDO

Stand you there.

QUARLOUS

Where you please, sir.   65

          MISTRESS OVERDO *is sick, and her husband is silenced*

MISTRESS OVERDO

O lend me a basin, I am sick, I am sick. Where's Master Overdo? Bridget, call hither my Adam.

OVERDO

How?

WHIT

Dy very own wife, i'fait, worshipful Adam.

MISTRESS OVERDO

Will not my Adam come at me? Shall I see him no more then?   70

QUARLOUS

Sir, why do you not go on with the enormity? Are you oppressed with it? I'll help you. Hark you, sir, i' your ear— your 'innocent young man', you have ta'en such care of all this day, is a cutpurse, that hath got all your brother Cokes his things, and helped you to your beating and the stocks.   75
If you have a mind to hang him now, and shew him your magistrate's wit, you may; but I should think it were better

56 *you,* Ed. (you F)
58 *in no fault* not to blame
70 *at* to
72 *oppressed with* overwhelmed by

---

67 *Bridget.* The most probable explanation of the mention of this character, not heard of elsewhere in the play, is that Mistress Overdo, waking from her drunken stupor, imagines herself at home and calls a servant of this name.

recovering the goods, and to save your estimation in
pardoning him. I thank you, sir, for the gift of your ward,
Mistress Grace; look you, here is your hand and seal, by the   80
way. Master Winwife, give you joy, you are Palemon, you are
possessed o' the gentlewoman, but she must pay me value,
here's warrant for it. And honest madman, there's thy gown
and cap again; I thank thee for my wife. (*To the widow*) Nay,
I can be mad, sweetheart, when I please, still; never fear me.   85
And careful Numps, where's he? I thank him for my licence.

WASP
    How!

QUARLOUS
    'Tis true, Numps.

WASP
    I'll be hanged then.   WASP *misseth the licence*

QUARLOUS
    Look i' your box, Numps. [*To* OVERDO] Nay, sir, stand not   90
    you fixed here, like a stake in Finsbury to be shot at, or the
    whipping post i' the Fair, but get your wife out o' the air, it
    will make her worse else. And remember you are but Adam,
    flesh and blood! You have your frailty. Forget your other
    name of Overdo, and invite us all to supper. There you and   95
    I will compare our 'discoveries', and drown the memory of
    all enormity in your biggest bowl at home.

COKES
    How now, Numps, ha' you lost it? I warrant 'twas when thou
    wert i' the stocks. Why dost not speak?

WASP
    I will never speak, while I live, again, for aught I know.   100

78 *estimation* reputation
81 *Winwife*, Ed. (*Win-wife* F)
85 *fear me* fear for me, doubt it
90 *Look* Ed. (Loke F)

78–9 *in pardoning him* ed. (in im F). The Folio reading does not make
    sense. The purely conjectural insertion of 'pardoning', on the assump-
    tion that the compositor omitted it, as he omitted other words, balances
    'recovering the goods' and fits in with the conclusion of the comedy.
    'Pardon' is not an unusual word at the end of a Jonsonian comedy.
    Justice Clement tells Brainworm that he 'deserues to bee pardon'd for
    the wit o' the offence' (*Every Man in His Humour*, V.iii, 113–14), and
    Face asks for, and receives, Lovewit's pardon (*The Alchemist*, V.iii, 83).
82 *pay me value*. Because Quarlous is now Grace's guardian.
91 *a stake . . . shot at*. Finsbury Fields were a place of recreation for the
    citizens of London, and one of its attractions was archery contests.

OVERDO

Nay, Humphrey, if I be patient, you must be so too. [*To them all*] This pleasant conceited gentleman hath wrought upon my judgement, and prevailed. I pray you take care of your sick friend, Mistress Alice, and, my good friends all—

QUARLOUS

And no enormities.   105

OVERDO

I invite you home with me to my house, to supper. I will have none fear to go along, for my intents are *ad correctionem, non ad destructionem; ad aedificandum, non ad diruendum.* So lead on.

COKES

Yes, and bring the actors along, we'll ha' the rest o' the play   110
at home.

                                      [*Exeunt*]

THE END

THE EPILOGUE

Your Majesty hath seen the play, and you
    Can best allow it from your ear and view.
You know the scope of writers, and what store
    Of leave is given them, if they take not more,
And turn it into licence. You can tell   5
    If we have used that leave you gave us well;
Or whether we to rage or licence break,
    Or be profane, or make profane men speak.
This is your power to judge, great sir, and not
    The envy of a few. Which if we have got,   10
We value less what their dislike can bring,
    If it so happy be, t' have pleased the King.

101–2 s.d. *To them all* ed. (not in F)
102 *pleasant conceited* merrily disposed
  2 *allow* sanction, license
  3 *store* Ed. (*store*, F)
  8 *speak.* Ed. (*speake?* F)

107–8 *ad . . . diruendum.* To correct, not destroy; to build up, not to tear down.

The Malcontent

JOHN MARSTON

Edited by
BERNARD HARRIS

ABBREVIATIONS

Bullen	*The Works of John Marston,* ed. A.H. Bullen (1887).
Davenport	*The Poems of John Marston,* ed. Arnold Davenport (1961).
Harrier	*The Malcontent,* ed. R.C. Harrier (1963).
Harrison	*The Malcontent,* ed. G.B. Harrison (1933)
Lucas	The Complete Works of John Webster, Vol. III, ed. F.L. Lucas (1927).
Wine	The Malcontent, ed. M.L. Wine (1964).
Wood	The Works of John Marston, ed. H. A. Wood (1934).

THE

MALCONTENT.

Augmented by *Marston*.

With the Additions played by the Kings
Maiesties servants.

Written by *Ihon Webster*.

1 6 0 4.

AT LONDON
Printed by V.S. for William Aspley, and
are to be sold at his shop in Paules
Church-yard.

BENIAMINO IONSONIO

POETAE
ELEGANTISSIMO
GRAVISSIMO

AMICO   5
SVO CANDIDO ET CORDATO

IOHANNES MARSTON
MVSARVM ALVMNVS

ASPERAM HANC SVAM THALIAM

D.D.   10

1 BENIAMINO Q1, Q2 (BENIAMINI Q)
10 *D.D.* 'Dat Dedicatque'

1–10 'To Benjamin Jonson, most refined and serious poet, and his
sincere, wise friend, John Marston, disciple of the Muses, gives and
dedicates this his rough-comedy.'

To the Reader

I am an ill orator; and in truth, use to indite more honestly than eloquently, for it is my custom to speak as I think, and write as I speak.

In plainness therefore understand, that in some things I have willingly erred, as in supposing a Duke of Genoa, and in taking names different from that city's families: for which some may wittily accuse me; but my defence shall be as honest, as many reproofs unto me have been most malicious. Since (I heartily protest) it was my care to write so far from reasonable offence, that even strangers, in whose state I laid my scene, should not from thence draw any disgrace to any, dead or living. Yet in despite of my endeavours, I understand, some have been most unadvisedly over-cunning in misinterpreting me, and with subtlety (as deep as hell) have maliciously spread ill rumours, which springing from themselves, might to themselves have heavily returned. Surely I desire to satisfy every firm spirit, who, in all his actions, proposeth to himself no more ends than God and virtue do, whose intentions are always simple: to such I protest, that with my free understanding I have not glanced at disgrace of any, but of those whose unquiet studies labour innovation, contempt of holy policy, reverend, comely superiority, and established unity: for the rest of my supposed tartness, I fear not but unto every worthy mind it will be approved so general and honest as may modestly pass with the freedom of a satire. I would fain leave the paper; only one thing afflicts me, to think that scenes invented merely to be spoken should be enforcively published to be read, and that the least hurt I can receive is to do myself the wrong. But since others otherwise would do me more, the least inconvenience is to be accepted. I have myself, therefore, set forth this comedy; but so, that my enforced absence must much rely upon the printer's discretion: but I shall entreat slight errors in orthography may be as slightly overpassed; and that the unhandsome shape which this trifle in reading presents may be

5

10

15

20

25

30

35

8 *wittily* knowingly
22 *innovation* revolution
32 *but so* in such circumstances

pardoned, for the pleasure it once afforded you when it was
presented with the soul of lively action.

Sine aliqua dementia nullus Phoebus.

I. M.   40

---

39 Q, Q2 (*Me mea sequentur fata* Q1)

---

39 *Sine . . . Phoebus.* 'No poet is without some madness' (perhaps based
on *Nullum magnum ingenium sine mixtura dementiae fuit*, Seneca,
De Tranq. Animi, xvii, 10).
The replaced quotation, 'My fates follow me', may indicate Marston's
interest in the Orestes theme.

Dramatis Personae

GIOVANNI ALTOFRONTO, disguised MALEVOLE, sometime Duke of Genoa
PIETRO IACOMO, Duke of Genoa
MENDOZA, a minion to the Duchess of Pietro Iacomo   5
CELSO, a friend to Altofronto
BILIOSO, an old choleric marshal
PREPASSO, a gentleman usher
FERNEZE, a young courtier, and enamoured on the Duchess [Aurelia]   10
FERRARDO, a minion to Duke Pietro Iacomo
EQUATO ⎫
GUERRINO ⎭ two courtiers
PASSARELLO, fool to Bilioso

AURELIA, Duchess to Duke Pietro Iacomo   15
MARIA, Duchess to Duke Altofronto
EMILIA ⎫
BIANCA ⎭ two ladies attending the Duchess [Aurelia]
MAQUERELLE, an old panderess

[CAPTAIN OF THE CITADEL   20
MERCURY, PRESENTER OF THE MASQUE
GUARDS, COURTIERS, and PAGES

Scene: Genoa

Actors of the King's Men, at the Globe Theatre, who appear in the Induction: 25

| WILLIAM SLY | RICHARD BURBAGE | HENRY CONDELL |
| JOHN SINKLO | | JOHN LOWIN] |

14 *Passarello* Q (not in Q1, Q2)

The Induction

Enter W. SLY, *a* TIRE-MAN *following him with a stool*

TIRE-MAN

Sir, the gentlemen will be angry if you sit here.

SLY

Why? We may sit upon the stage at the private house. Thou dost not take me for a country gentleman, dost? Dost think I fear hissing? I'll hold my life thou took'st me for one of the players.　　　　　　　　　　　　　　　　　　　　　　　　　　　5

TIRE-MAN

No, sir.

SLY

By God's lid, if you had, I would have given you but six-pence for your stool. Let them that have stale suits sit in the galleries. Hiss at me! He that will be laughed out of a tavern or an ordinary shall seldom feed well or be drunk in good　　10 company. Where's Harry Condell, Dick Burbage and Will Sly? Let me speak with some of them.

TIRE-MAN

An't please you to go in, sir, you may.

SLY

I tell you, no. I am one that hath seen this play often, and can give them intelligence for their action. I have most of the　　15 jests here in my table-book.

Enter SINKLO

SINKLO

Save you, coz.

SLY

O cousin, come, you shall sit between my legs here.

s.d. *tire-man* dresser and property-man
　7 *lid* eye-lid (slid Q)
　10 *ordinary* eating-house
　11 *Dick* (D: Q)
　　　Will (W: Q)
　15 *intelligence* information
　16 *table-book* note-book

---

　2 *sit . . . house.* The habit which gallants had of sitting on the stage, whether at the private or public theatres, is best described in Dekker's *Gull's Horn-book* (1609).

489

SINKLO

No indeed, cousin, the audience then will take me for a viol-
da-gamba, and think that you play upon me.   20

SLY

Nay, rather that I work upon you, coz.

SINKLO

We stayed for you at supper last night at my cousin Honeymoon's the woollen-draper. After supper we drew cuts for a
score of apricocks, the longest cut still to draw an apricock.
By this light, 'twas Mistress Frank Honeymoon's fortune   25
still to have the longest cut: I did measure for the women.
What be these, coz?

Enter D. BURBAGE, H. CONDELL, J. LOWIN

SLY

The players. God save you.

BURBAGE

You are very welcome.

SLY

I pray you know this gentleman my cousin, 'tis Master   30
Doomsday's son, the usurer.

CONDELL

I beseech you, sir, be covered.

SLY

No, in good faith, for mine ease. Look you, my hat's the
handle to this fan. God's so, what a beast was I, I did not
leave my feather at home. Well, but I'll take an order with 35
you.

Puts his feather in his pocket

BURBAGE

Why do you conceal your feather, sir?

SLY

Why? Do you think I'll have jests broken upon me in the
play, to be laughed at? This play hath beaten all your

19–20 *viol-da-gamba* bass viol, held between the legs
23 *drew cuts* drew lots, using straws or sticks, and bawdy
34 *fan* i.e. feather
   God's so from 'Catso' (Ital. *cazzo*, penis)
35 *feather* ed. (father Q)

---

33 *for mine ease.* 'Possibly an echo of Osric's affected refusal to put on his
   hat in *Hamlet*, V. 2. 110', but also 'seems to have been a current polite
   expression' (Lucas).

gallants out of the feathers: Blackfriars hath almost spoiled   40
Blackfriars for feathers.

SINKLO

God's so, I thought 'twas for somewhat our gentlewomen at
home counselled me to wear my feather to the play, yet I am
loath to spoil it.

SLY

Why, coz?   45

SINKLO

Because I got it in the tilt-yard. There was a herald broke my
pate for taking it up, but I have worn it up and down the
Strand, and met him forty times since, and yet he dares not
challenge it.

SLY

Do you hear, sir, this play is a bitter play?   50

CONDELL

Why, sir, 'tis neither satire nor moral, but the mean passage
of a history. Yet there are a sort of discontented creatures
that bear a stingless envy to great ones, and these will wrest
the doings of any man to their base, malicious applyment.
But should their interpretation come to the test, like your   55
marmoset, they presently turn their teeth to their tail and
eat it.

SLY

I will not go so far with you, but I say, any man that hath
wit may censure (if he sit in the twelve-penny room), and I
say again, the play is bitter.   60

BURBAGE

Sir, you are like a patron that, presenting a poor scholar to a
benefice, enjoins him not to rail against anything that stands
within compass of his patron's folly. Why should not we
enjoy the ancient freedom of poesy? Shall we protest to the
ladies that their painting makes them angels, or to my   65

---

51 *mean passage* plain narration
54 *applyment* application   59 *censure* judge

40–1 *Blackfriars ... feathers.* The acting of the play at the Blackfriars
theatre has affected the trade of the feather-makers of the locality.
56–7 *marmoset ... it.* 'This seems a confused recollection of the beaver's
supposed habit, when hunted for its stones, of biting them off itself'
(Lucas, citing Pliny, *Naturalis Historia*, xxxii. 3).
59 *twelve-penny room.* 'A sort of large box in the lowest tier of galleries,
directly adjoining the stage' (Lucas); Dekker's *Gull's Horn-book* is
again descriptive.

young gallant that his expense in the brothel shall gain him
reputation? No sir, such vices as stand not accountable to
law should be cured as men heal tetters, by casting ink upon
them. Would you be satisfied in anything else, sir?

SLY

Ay, marry would I. I would know how you came by this play?   70

CONDELL

Faith, sir, the book was lost, and because 'twas pity so good
a play should be lost, we found it and play it.

SLY

I wonder you would play it, another company having an
interest in it?

CONDELL

Why not Malevole in folio with us, as Jeronimo in decimo-   75
sexto with them? They taught us a name for our play, we call
it *One for another*.

SLY

What are your additions?

BURBAGE

Sooth, not greatly needful, only as your sallet to your great
feast, to entertain a little more time, and to abridge the not-   80
received custom of music in our theatre. I must leave you,
sir.   *Exit* BURBAGE

SINKLO

Doth he play the Malcontent?

CONDELL

Yes, sir.

SINKLO

I durst lay four of mine ears, the play is not so well acted as   85
it hath been.

CONDELL

O no, sir, nothing *ad Parmenonis suem*.

---

68 *tetters* skin-eruptions
79 *sallet* salad
80 *entertain* pass   *abridge* cut short

---

87 *ad . . . suem*: 'compared with Parmeno's pig'. Plutarch, in *Symposiaca
problemata*, V. i, tells of one Parmeno who used to imitate the grunting
of a pig so well that his admirers declared the sound of a real pig as
nothing 'compared with Parmeno's pig'. Lucas points out that Holland's
translation of Plutarch had appeared in 1603, and that Condell here
rebukes Sinklo for being carried away by opinion about the quality
of the boys' acting before the men have been seen.

LOWIN
Have you lost your ears, sir, that you are so prodigal of laying them?

SINKLO
Why did you ask that, friend?   90

LOWIN
Marry sir, because I have heard of a fellow would offer to lay a hundred-pound wager, that was not worth five bawbees; and in this kind you might venture four of your elbows. Yet God defend your coat should have so many.

SINKLO
Nay, truly, I am no great censurer, and yet I might have been   95
one of the college of critics once. My cousin here hath an excellent memory indeed, sir.

SLY
Who, I? I'll tell you a strange thing of myself, and I can tell you for one that never studied the art of memory, 'tis very strange too.   100

CONDELL
What's that, sir?

SLY
Why, I'll lay a hundred pounds I'll walk but once down by the Goldsmiths' Row in Cheap, take notice of the signs, and tell you them with a breath instantly.

LOWIN
'Tis very strange.   105

SLY
They begin as the world did, with Adam and Eve. There's in all just five and fifty. I do use to meditate much when I come to plays too. What do you think might come into a man's head now, seeing all this company?

CONDELL
I know not, sir.   110

SLY
I have an excellent thought: if some fifty of the Grecians that were crammed in the horse belly had eaten garlic, do you not think the Trojans might have smelt out their knavery?

94 *defend* forbid

---

92 *bawbees*. Scotch coin, equivalent to halfpenny; 'possibly an allusion to James's needy Scotch followers' (Lucas).
107 *five and fifty*: 'ten fair dwelling-houses and fourteen shops' according to Stow's reckoning (Dyce).
111 *an excellent thought*: prompted by garlic fumes.

CONDELL
Very likely.
SLY
By God, I would they had, for I love Hector horribly.   115
SINKLO
O but coz, coz—
'Great Alexander, when he came to the tomb of Achilles,
Spake with a big loud voice, "O thou thrice blessed and
happy".'
SLY
Alexander was an ass to speak so well of a filthy cullion.   120
LOWIN
Good sir, will you leave the stage? I'll help you to a private
room.
SLY
Come, coz, let's take some tobacco. Have you never a pro-
logue?
LOWIN
Not any, sir.   125
SLY
Let me see, I will make one extempore. Come to them, and
fencing of a congee with arms and legs, be round with them
—'Gentlemen, I could wish for the women's sakes you had
all soft cushions: and gentlewomen, I could wish that for the
men's sakes you had all more easy standings'. What would   130
they wish more but the play now? And that they shall have
instantly.   *Exeunt*

        An imperfect ode, being but one staff,
              spoken by the Prologue
To wrest each hurtless thought to private sense
    Is the foul use of ill-bred impudence:
        Immodest censure now grows wild,   5
            All over-running.
        Let innocence be ne'er so chaste,

115 *they* ed. (he Q)   127 *fencing of a cong e* performing an elaborate bow
title *staff* stanza
_____

117–19 *Great ... happy.* Sinklo's version of John Harvey's hexameters:

    Noble *Alexander*, when he came to the tomb of *Achilles*,
    Sighing spake with a bigge voice: O thrice blessed *Achilles*':

this version of Petrarch, Sonnet CLIII, was printed in Gabriel Harvey's
Three proper, and wittie, familiar Letters to Spenser (1580).

Yet at the last
She is defiled,
With too nice-brained cunning.   10
O you of fairer soul,
Control,
With an Herculean arm,
This harm;
And once teach all old freedom of a pen,   15
Which still must write of fools, while'st writes of men.

THE MALCONTENT

Vexat censura columbas

Act I, Scene i

The vilest out-of-tune music being heard
Enter BILIOSO *and* PREPASSO

BILIOSO
Why, how now? Are ye mad, or drunk, or both, or what?
PREPASSO
Are ye building Babylon there?
BILIOSO
Here's a noise in court, you think you are in a tavern, do you
not?
PREPASSO
You think you are in a brothel-house, do you not? This   5
room is ill-scented.

Enter one with a perfume

So, perfume, perfume; some upon me, I pray thee. The duke
is upon instant entrance; so, make place there.

title *censura* Q1, Q (*censurae* Q2)

---

title *Vexat . . . columbas.* Juvenal, *Satires*, II, 63. 'The context is Laronia's
   defence of women by citing male offences: "de nobis post haec tristis
   sententia fertur? dat veniam corvis, vexat censura columbas." "After
   these things what evil judgment can be put on us women. [The criti-
   cising male] absolves the crows and passes judgment on the doves".'
   (Harrier.) This motto introduces Malevole's attack on the courtiers.

Act I, Scene ii

Enter the DUKE PIETRO, FERRARDO, COUNT EQUATO,
COUNT CELSO *before*, *and* GUERRINO

PIETRO
Where breathes that music?

BILIOSO
The discord rather than the music is heard from the malcontent Malevole's chamber.

FERRARDO
Malevole!

MALEVOLE
(*Out of his chamber*) Yaugh, God o' man, what dost thou   5
there? Duke's Ganymede, Juno's jealous of thy long stockings. Shadow of a woman, what wouldst, weasel? Thou lamb
o' court, what dost thou bleat for? Ah, you smooth-chinned
catamite!

PIETRO
Come down, thou ragged cur, and snarl here. I give thy   10
dogged sullenness free liberty; trot about and bespurtle
whom thou pleasest.

MALEVOLE
I'll come among you, you goatish-blooded toderers, as
gum into taffeta, to fret, to fret. I'll fall like a sponge into
water, to suck up, to suck up. Howl again. I'll go to church,   15
and come to you.   [*Exit*]

PIETRO
This Malevole is one of the most prodigious affections that

5 (*Out of his chamber*) probably upper-stage
6 *Ganymede* a son of Troas, ravished away for his beauty to be
cup-bearer to Zeus
7 *lamb* favourite
9 *catamite* male prostitute
10 *ragged* Q (rugged Q1, Q2)
11 *bespurtle* bespatter
14 *gum . . . fret* inferior or defective taffeta was gummed; hence
it frayed or 'fretted'
15 *church* Q, Q2 (I'll pray Q1)
17 *affections* dispositions

---

7 *Shadow of a woman.* Inverted commonplace: see Ben Jonson's song
'That women are but men's shadows'.
13 *toderers.* The word clearly indicates libertinism, though its etymology
is obscure; a 'tod' is a fox.

ever conversed with nature; a man, or rather a monster, more
discontent than Lucifer when he was thrust out of the
presence. His appetite is insatiable as the grave, as far from   20
any content as from heaven. His highest delight is to procure
others' vexation, and therein he thinks he truly serves
heaven; for 'tis his position, whosoever in this earth can be
contented is a slave and damned; therefore does he afflict all
in that to which they are most affected. The elements   25
struggle within him; his own soul is at variance within herself. His speech is halter-worthy at all hours. I like him,
faith, he gives good intelligence to my spirit, makes me
understand those weaknesses which others' flattery palliates.
Hark, they sing.   30

Act I, Scene iii

[A song]
Enter MALEVOLE *after the song*

[PIETRO]
See, he comes. Now shall you hear the extremity of a malcontent. He is as free as air; he blows over every man.—And
sir, whence come you now?

MALEVOLE
From the public place of much dissimulation, the church.

PIETRO
What didst there?   5

MALEVOLE
Talk with a usurer; take up at interest.

PIETRO
I wonder what religion thou art of?

MALEVOLE
Of a soldier's religion.

PIETRO
And what dost think makes most infidels now?

MALEVOLE
Sects, sects. I have seen seeming Piety change her robe so   10
oft that sure none,but some arch-devil can shape her a new
petticoat.

23 *position* argument
26–7 *within herself* Q (not in Q1, Q2)
4 *the church* Q (not in Q2; deleted from majority of extant copies
of Q1: see Wine, p. 18)
6 *take up* borrow
11 *new* Q1, Q2 (not in Q)

PIETRO

O, a religious policy.

MALEVOLE

But damnation on a politic religion! I am weary—would I
were one of the duke's hounds now.   15

PIETRO

But what's the common news abroad, Malevole? Thou
dogg'st rumour still.

MALEVOLE

Common news? Why, common words are, 'God save ye',
'Fare ye well'; common actions, flattery and cosenage; common things, women and cuckolds. And how does my little   20
Ferrard? Ah, ye lecherous animal, my little ferret, he goes
sucking up and down the palace into every hen's nest like
a weasel. And to what dost thou addict thy time to now,
more than to those antique painted drabs that are still
affected of young courtiers, Flattery, Pride, and Venery?   25

FERRARDO

I study languages. Who dost think to be the best linguist of
our age?

MALEVOLE

Phew! the devil. Let him possess thee, he'll teach thee to
speak all languages most readily and strangely; and great
reason, marry, he's travelled greatly i' the world, and is   30
everywhere.

FERRARDO

Save i' the court.

MALEVOLE

Ay, save i' the court. (*To* BILIOSO) And how does my old
muckhill overspread with fresh snow? Thou half a man, half
a goat, all a beast! How does thy young wife, old huddle?   35

BILIOSO

Out, you improvident rascal!

14–15 *I . . . now* Q, Q2 (not in Q1)
19 *cosenage* cheating
35 *huddle* miserly old man

28–31 *Phew! . . . everywhere.* Diabolic possession was supposed to bring
   the gift of tongues; see Jonson's *The Devil is an Ass*, V. v. (Wood).
33–4 *And . . . snow?* Cf. 'Yon's but a muckhill ouer-spred with snow',
   The Scourge of Villanie VII, 'A Cynick Satyr' 154; there are other
   self-borrowings from this satire.
34-5 *Thou . . . beast!* Cf. 'Oh villaine indiscreet, vnseasonable. Halfe a man
   halfe a goat, and all a beast' (*Il pastor fido*, II. vi, 1602, trans. Sig. G).

MALEVOLE

Do, kick, thou hugely-horned old duke's ox, good Master
Make-Pleas.

PIETRO

How dost thou live nowadays, Malevole?

MALEVOLE

Why, like the knight, Sir Patrick Penlolians, with killing o'   40
spiders for my lady's monkey.

PIETRO

How dost spend the night, I hear thou never sleep'st?

MALEVOLE

O no, but dream the most fantastical. O Heaven! O fubbery,
fubbery!

PIETRO

Dream? What dream'st?   45

MALEVOLE

Why, methinks I see that signior pawn his foot-cloth, that
metreza her plate; this madam takes physic that t'other
monsieur may minister to her; here is a pander jewelled;
there is a fellow in shift of satin this day that could not
shift a shirt t'other night; here a Paris supports that Helen,   50
there's a Lady Guinever bears up that Sir Lancelot. Dreams,
dreams, visions, fantasies, chimeras, imaginations, tricks,
conceits! (*To* PREPASSO) Sir Tristram Trimtram, come aloft,
Jackanapes, with a whim-wham; here's a knight of the land

---

38 *Make-Pleas* (Make-pleece Qq; Make-Please Wine)
43 *fubbery* deceit   46 *foot-cloth* caparizon
47 *metreza* mistress (Ital.)   49 *shift* change
53–4 *come aloft, Jackanapes* ape-ward's cry
54 *whim-wham* trifle ('reduplication with vowel-variation, like
  flim-flam, trim-tram' O.E.D.)

---

40 *Sir Patrick Penlolians.* Q, Q2 (Penlohans Q1 corrected; Penlobrans Q1
  uncorrected; Wine). Probably Marston was continuing his typified
  nomenclature; Florio offers 'Pendule labbra, bigge, downe-hanging
  blabberd-lips'; there is 'the Irish Lord, S. Patrick' in *The Dutch
  Courtesan*, II. i.
40–1 *killing . . . monkey.* Bawdy; cf. Petulant's sneer to Witwoud 'Carry
  your Mistress's Monkey a Spider', *The Way of the World*, IV. ix.
54–8 *knight . . . huge.* 'Catito' is a coinage from 'cat', or 'tipcat', a boys'
  game, which like 'trap' or 'trapball', and riding at the ring (a form of
  jousting in which the rider tried to put his lance through a suspended
  ring), offer themselves readily to Malevole's suggestiveness about the
  courtiers' immorality. 'Lancelot' and 'Lady Guinevere' had already
  become type-names for debauched chivalry.

of Catito shall play at trap with any page in Europe; do the   55
sword-dance with any morris-dancer in Christendom; ride
at the ring till the fin of his eyes look as blue as the welkin,
and run the wild-goose chase even with Pompey the huge.

PIETRO
You run—

MALEVOLE
To the devil. Now, Signior Guerrino, that thou from a most   60
pitied prisoner shouldst grow a most loathed flatterer! Alas,
poor Celso, thy star's oppressed; thou art an honest lord,
'tis pity.

EQUATO
Is't pity?

MALEVOLE
Ay, marry is't, philosophical Equato, and 'tis pity that thou,   65
being so excellent a scholar by art, shouldst be so ridiculous
a fool by nature. I have a thing to tell you, Duke; bid 'em
avaunt, bid 'em avaunt.

PIETRO
Leave us, leave us.
                          Exeunt all saving PIETRO *and* MALEVOLE
Now, sir, what is't?   70

MALEVOLE
Duke, thou art a becco, a cornuto.

PIETRO
How!

MALEVOLE
Thou art a cuckold.

PIETRO
Speak! Unshale him quick.

MALEVOLE
With most tumbler-like nimbleness.   75

PIETRO
Who? By whom? I burst with desire.

MALEVOLE
Mendoza is the man makes thee a horned beast. Duke, 'tis
Mendoza cornutes thee.

PIETRO
What conformance? Relate! short, short!

57 *fin* rim
62 *oppressed* in decline
71 *becco, cornuto* cuckold (Ital.)
74 *Unshale* unshell, disclose
79 *conformance* confirmation

MALEVOLE

As a lawyer's beard.   80

'There is an old crone in the court, her name is Maquerelle,
She is my mistress, sooth to say, and she doth ever tell me.'
Blurt o' rhyme, blurt o' rhyme! Maquerelle is a cunning
bawd, I am an honest villain, thy wife is a close drab, and
thou art a notorious cuckold. Farewell, Duke.   85

PIETRO

Stay, stay.

MALEVOLE

Dull, dull Duke, can lazy patience make lame revenge?
O God, for a woman to make a man that which God never
created, never made!

PIETRO

What did God never make?   90

MALEVOLE

A cuckold. To be made a thing that's hoodwinked with
kindness, whilst every rascal fillips his brows; to have a coxcomb with egregious horns pinned to a lord's back, every
page sporting himself with delightful laughter, whilst he
must be the last must know it—pistols and poniards, pistols 95
and poniards!

PIETRO

Death and damnation!

MALEVOLE

Lightning and thunder!

PIETRO

Vengeance and torture!

MALEVOLE

Catzo!   100

PIETRO

O, revenge!

MALEVOLE

Nay, to select among ten thousand fairs
A lady far inferior to the most,
In fair proportion both of limb and soul;
To take her from austerer check of parents,   105
To make her his by most devoutful rites,
Make her commandress of a better essence
Than is the gorgeous world even of a man;

83 *Blurt* expletive ('a fig for' *O.E.D.*)
84 *close drab* secret whore
92–3 *coxcomb* fool's-cap
100 *Catzo!* penis (Ital. *cazzo*)

To hug her with as raised an appetite
As usurers do their delved-up treasury,   110
(Thinking none tells it but his private self);
To meet her spirit in a nimble kiss,
Distilling panting ardour to her heart;
True to her sheets, nay, diets strong his blood,
To give her height of hymeneal sweets—   115

PIETRO
O God!

MALEVOLE
Whilst she lisps, and gives him some court *quelquechose*,
Made only to provoke, not satiate;
And yet, even then the thaw of her delight
Flows from lewd heat of apprehension,   120
Only from strange imagination's rankness,
That forms the adulterer's presence in her soul,
And makes her think she clips the foul knave's loins.

PIETRO
Affliction to my blood's root!

MALEVOLE
Nay think, but think what may proceed of this; adultery is   125
often the mother of incest.

PIETRO
Incest?

MALEVOLE
Yes, incest. Mark—Mendoza of his wife begets perchance a
daughter. Mendoza dies. His son marries this daughter. Say
you? Nay, 'tis frequent, not only probable, but no question   130
often acted, whilst ignorance, fearless ignorance, clasps his
own seed.

PIETRO
Hideous imagination!

MALEVOLE
Adultery? Why, next to the sin of simony 'tis the most
horrid transgression under the cope of salvation!   135

PIETRO
Next to simony?

MALEVOLE
Ay, next to simony, in which our men in next age shall not
sin.

111 *tells* counts
117 *quelquechose* dainty, unsubstantial morsel
123 *clips* embraces
135 *cope of salvation* heaven

PIETRO

Not sin? Why?

MALEVOLE

Because (thanks to some churchmen) our age will leave them 140
nothing to sin with. But adultery—O dullness!—should
show exemplary punishment, that intemperate bloods may
freeze but to think it. I would dam him and all his generation, my own hands should do it. Ha! I would not trust
heaven with my vengeance anything. 145

PIETRO

Anything, anything, Malevole! Thou shalt see instantly
what temper my spirit holds. Farewell; remember I forget
thee not; farewell. *Exit* PIETRO

MALEVOLE

Farewell.
Lean thoughtfulness, a sallow meditation,
Suck thy veins dry! Distemperance rob thy sleep! 150
The heart's disquiet is revenge most deep.
He that gets blood, the life of flesh but spills,
But he that breaks heart's peace, the dear soul kills.
Well, this disguise doth yet afford me that
Which kings do seldom hear, or great men use— 155
Free speech. And though my state's usurped,
Yet this affected strain gives me a tongue
As fetterless as is an emperor's.
I may speak foolishly, ay, knavishly,
Always carelessly, yet no one thinks it fashion 160
To poise my breath; for he that laughs and strikes
Is lightly felt, or seldom struck again.
Duke, I'll torment thee; now my just revenge
From thee than crown a richer gem shall part.
Beneath God, naught's so dear as a calm heart. 165

Act I, Scene iv

Enter CELSO

CELSO

My honoured lord—

MALEVOLE

Peace, speak low! Peace, O Celso, constant lord,

141–2 *should show* ed. (shue should Q)
143 *dam* choke
150 *Distemperance* mental or physical disturbance
161 *poise* weigh

Thou to whose faith I only rest discovered,
Thou, one of full ten millions of men,
That lovest virtue only for itself,   5
Thou, in whose hands old Ops may put her soul,
Behold forever-banished Altofront,
This Genoa's last year's duke. O truly noble,
I wanted those old instruments of state,
Dissemblance and suspect. I could not time it, Celso;   10
My throne stood like a point in midst of a circle,
To all of equal nearness; bore with none;
Reigned all alike; so slept in fearless virtue,
Suspectless, too suspectless; till the crowd,
Still lickerous of untried novelties,   15
Impatient with severer government,
Made strong with Florence, banished Altofront.

CELSO
Strong with Florence! Ay, thence your mischief rose;
For when the daughter of the Florentine
Was matched once with this Pietro, now duke,   20
No stratagem of state untried was left,
Till you of all—
MALEVOLE   Of all was quite bereft.
Alas, Maria too, close prisoned,
My true-faith'd duchess, i' the citadel.

CELSO
I'll still adhere; let's mutiny and die.   25

MALEVOLE
O no! Climb not a falling tower, Celso,
'Tis well held desperation, no zeal,
Hopeless to strive with fate. Peace! Temporise.
Hope, hope, that never forsak'st the wretched'st man,
Yet bidd'st me live, and lurk in this disguise.   30
What, play I well the free-breathed discontent?
Why, man, we are all philosophical monarchs or natural
fools. Celso, the court's afire; the duchess' sheets will smoke
for't ere it be long. Impure Mendoza, that sharp-nosed lord,
that made the cursed match linked Genoa with Florence,   35
now broad-horns the duke, which he now knows. Discord to
malcontents is very manna; when the ranks are burst, then
scuffle Altofront.

6 *Ops* goddess of plenty
9 *wanted* lacked   10 *time it* temporise
12 *bore with* favoured   15 *lickerous of* eager for
17 *Made strong* allied   20 *this* ed. (his Q)

CELSO

  Ay, but durst?

MALEVOLE

  'Tis gone; 'tis swallowed like a mineral;   40
  Some way t'will work—Phewt! I'll not shrink.
  He's resolute who can no lower sink.

     BILIOSO *entering*, MALEVOLE *shifteth his speech*

  O the father of maypoles! Did you never see a fellow whose
whole strength consisted in his breath, respect in his office,
religion in his lord, and love in himself? Why then, behold. 45

BILIOSO

  Signior.

MALEVOLE

  My right worshipful lord: your court night-cap makes you
have a passing high forehead.

BILIOSO

  I can tell you strange news, but I am sure you know them
already; the duke speaks much good of you. 50

MALEVOLE

  Go to, then; and shall you and I now enter into a strict
friendship?

BILIOSO

  Second one another?

MALEVOLE

  Yes.

BILIOSO

  Do one another good offices? 55

MALEVOLE

  Just. What though I called thee old ox, egregious wittol,
broken-bellied coward, rotten mummy? Yet, since I am in
favour—

BILIOSO

  Words of course, terms of disport. His grace presents you
by me a chain, as his grateful remembrance for—I am 60
ignorant for what. Marry, ye may impart. Yet howsoever—
come—dear friend. Dost know my son?

MALEVOLE

  Your son?

BILIOSO

  He shall eat woodcocks, dance jigs, make possets, and play

40 *mineral* medicine   45 *religion in* ed. (religion on Q)
56 *wittol* cuckold
64 *possets* hot drinks of milk curdled with liquor and spiced

at shuttlecock with any young lord about the court. He   65
has as sweet a lady, too; dost know her little bitch?

MALEVOLE
'Tis a dog, man.

BILIOSO
Believe me, a she-bitch! O 'tis a good creature; thou shalt
be her servant. I'll make thee acquainted with my young
wife too. What, I keep her not at court for nothing. 'Tis   70
grown to supper time; come to my table; that, anything I
have, stands open to thee.

MALEVOLE
(*To* CELSO) How smooth to him that is in state of grace,
How servile is the rugged'st courtier's face.
What profit, nay what nature would keep down,   75
Are heaved to them are minions to a crown.
Envious ambition never sates his thirst,
Till, sucking all, he swells and swells, and bursts.

BILIOSO
I shall now leave you with my always-best wishes, only let's
hold betwixt us a firm correspondence, a mutual-friendly-   80
reciprocal-kind of steady-unanimous-heartily-leagued—

MALEVOLE
Did your signiorship ne'er see a pigeon-house that was
smooth, round and white without, and full of holes and stink
within? Ha' ye not, old courtier?

BILIOSO
O yes, 'tis the form, the fashion of them all.   85

MALEVOLE
Adieu, my true court-friend; farewell, my dear Castilio.
                                        Exit BILIOSO

CELSO
Yonder's Mendoza.

MALEVOLE
(*Descries* MENDOZA) True, the privy key.

CELSO
I take my leave, sweet lord.   *Exit* CELSO

MALEVOLE   'Tis fit, away!

69 *servant* lover
76 *are* who are
80 *correspondence* agreement
86 *Castilio* Baldassare Castiglione
87 *privy key* bawdy allusion to intimacy

Act I, Scene v

Enter MENDOZA, *with three or four suitors*

MENDOZA
Leave your suits with me; I can and will. Attend my secre-
tary; leave me.   [*Exeunt suitors*]
MALEVOLE
Mendoza, hark ye, hark ye. You are a treacherous villain.
God b' wi' ye.
MENDOZA
Out, you base-born rascal!   5
MALEVOLE
We are all the sons of heaven, though a tripe-wife were our
mother. Ah, you whoreson, hot-reined he-marmoset! Aegis-
thus!—didst ever hear of one Aegisthus?
MENDOZA
'Gisthus?
MALEVOLE
Ay, Aegisthus; he was a filthy incontinent fleshmonger, such   10
a one as thou art.
MENDOZA
Out, grumbling rogue!
MALEVOLE
Orestes, beware Orestes!
MENDOZA
Out, beggar!
MALEVOLE
I once shall rise.   15
MENDOZA
Thou rise?
MALEVOLE
Ay, at the resurrection.
No vulgar seed but once may rise, and shall;
No king so huge, but 'fore he die may fall.   *Exit*
MENDOZA
Now, good Elysium, what a delicious heaven is it for a man   20
to be in a prince's favour! O sweet God! O pleasure! O
fortune! O all thou best of life! What should I think, what
say, what do? To be a favourite, a minion! To have a general

6 *tripe-wife* tripe-seller
7 *hot-reined* lascivious
7–8 *Aegisthus* Clytemnestra's lover, who cuckolded Agamemnon
13 *Orestes* Agamemnon's son, and his avenger

timorous respect observe a man, a stateful silence in his
presence, solitariness in his absence, a confused hum and   25
busy murmur of obsequious suitors training him; the cloth
held up, and way proclaimed before him; petitionary vassals
licking the pavement with their slavish knees, whilst some odd
palace-lamprels that engender with snakes, and are full of
eyes on both sides, with a kind of insinuated humbleness fix   30
all their delights upon his brow. O blessed state, what a
ravishing prospect doth the Olympus of favour yield! Death,
I cornute the duke! Sweet women, most sweet ladies—nay,
angels! By heaven, he is more accursed than a devil that
hates you, or is hated by you; and happier than a god that   35
loves you, or is beloved by you. You preservers of mankind,
life-blood of society, who would live—nay, who can live
without you? O paradise, how majestical is your austerer
presence! How imperiously chaste is your more modest face!
But, O, how full of ravishing attraction is your pretty,   40
petulant, languishing, lasciviously-composed countenance!
These amorous smiles, those soul-warming sparkling
glances, ardent as those flames that singed the world by
heedless Phaeton. In body how delicate, in soul how witty,
in discourse how pregnant, in life how wary, in favours how   45
judicious, in day how sociable, and in night how—O
pleasure unutterable! Indeed, it is most certain, one man
cannot deserve only to enjoy a beauteous woman. But a
duchess? In despite of Phoebus I'll write a sonnet instantly
in praise of her.   *Exit*   50

Act I, Scene vi

Enter FERNEZE *ushering* AURELIA, EMILIA *and* MAQUERELLE
bearing up her train, BIANCA *attending: all go out but* AURELIA,
MAQUERELLE, *and* FERNEZE

AURELIA
  And is't possible? Mendoza slight me, possible?

24 *observe* defer to
   stateful dignified
26 *training* following in his train
29 *lamprels* young lampreys
33 *cornute* make cuckold
44 *Phaeton* Phaeton lost control of the horses of the sun and was
   slain by Zeus with a thunderbolt
49 *Phoebus* Phoebus Apollo, god of poetry

FERNEZE

Possible? What can be strange in him that's drunk with
favour, grows insolent with grace? Speak, Maquerelle, speak.

MAQUERELLE

To speak feelingly, more, more richly in solid sense than
worthless words, give me those jewels of your ears to receive   5
my enforced duty. As for my part, (FERNEZE *privately feeds*
MAQUERELLE'S *hands with jewels during this speech*) 'tis well
known I can put up anything, can bear patiently with any
man; but when I heard he wronged your precious sweetness,
I was enforced to take deep offence. 'Tis most certain he   10
loves Emilia with high appetite; and, as she told me (as you
know, we women impart our secrets one to another) when she
repulsed his suit, in that he was possessed with your
endeared grace, Mendoza most ingratefully renounced all
faith to you.   15

FERNEZE

Nay, called you—speak, Maquerelle, speak.

MAQUERELLE

By heaven, 'witch!' 'dried biscuit!', and contested blush-
lessly he loved you but for a spurt or so.

FERNEZE

For maintenance.

MAQUERELLE

Advancement and regard.   20

AURELIA

O villain! O impudent Mendoza!

MAQUERELLE

Nay, he is the rustiest-jawed, the foulest-mouthed knave in
railing against our sex. He will rail against women—

AURELIA

How? How?

MAQUERELLE

I am ashamed to speak't, I.   25

AURELIA

I love to hate him, speak.

MAQUERELLE

Why, when Emilia scorned his base unsteadiness, the black-
throated rascal scolded, and said—

AURELIA

What?

8 *put up* Q1 (put Q, Q2); bawdy
22 *jawed* ed. (iade Q, iawde Q1, Q2)

MAQUERELLE
  Troth, 'tis too shameless.   30
AURELIA
  What said he?
MAQUERELLE
  Why, that at four women were fools, at fourteen drabs, at
  forty bawds, at fourscore witches, and at a hundred, cats.
AURELIA
  O unlimitable impudency!
FERNEZE
  But as for poor Ferneze's fixed heart,   35
  Was never shadeless meadow drier parched
  Under the scorching heat of heaven's dog
  Than is my heart with your enforcing eyes.
MAQUERELLE
  A hot simile.
FERNEZE
  Your smiles have been my heaven, your frowns my hell,   40
  O pity, then; grace should with beauty dwell.
MAQUERELLE
  Reasonable perfect, by'r lady.
AURELIA
  I will love thee, be it but in despite
  Of that Mendoza. 'Witch!' Ferneze, 'witch!'—
  Ferneze, thou art the duchess' favourite;   45
  Be faithful, private; but 'tis dangerous.
FERNEZE
  His love is lifeless, that for love fears breath;
  The worst that's due to sin, O would 'twere death.
AURELIA
  Enjoy my favour. I will be sick instantly and take physic;
  therefore, in depth of night visit—   50
MAQUERELLE
  Visit her chamber, but conditionally, you shall not offend
  her bed. By this diamond.

33 *and at a* ed. (and a Qq)
37 *heaven's dog* Sirius
38 *enforcing* compelling
51 *conditionally* on condition

47-8 *His . . . death.* Cf. *Il pastor fido*, III. iv:

    she loues too little that feares death
  Would gods death were the worst that's due to sin (Sig H3v).

FERNEZE
By this diamond.   *Gives it to* MAQUERELLE
MAQUERELLE
Nor tarry longer than you please. By this ruby.
FERNEZE
By this ruby.   *Gives again*   55
MAQUERELLE
And that the door shall not creak.
FERNEZE
And that the door shall not creak.
MAQUERELLE
Nay, but swear.
FERNEZE
By this purse.   *Gives her his purse*
MAQUERELLE
Go to; I'll keep your oaths for you: remember, visit.   60

Enter MENDOZA, *reading a sonnet*

AURELIA
'Dried biscuit!' Look where the base wretch comes.
MENDOZA
'Beauty's life, heaven's model, love's queen'—
MAQUERELLE
That's his Emilia.
MENDOZA
'Nature's triumph, best on earth'—
MAQUERELLE
Meaning Emilia.   65
MENDOZA
'Thou only wonder that the world hath seen'—
MAQUERELLE
That's Emilia.
AURELIA
Must I then hear her praised? Mendoza!
MENDOZA
Madam, your excellency is graciously encountered; I have
been writing passionate flashes in honour of— *Exit* FERNEZE   70
AURELIA
Out, villain, villain!
O judgement, where have been my eyes? What
Bewitched election made me dote on thee?

70 *flashes* outbursts
73 *election* choice

What sorcery made me love thee? But begone,
Bury thy head. O that I could do more 75
Than loathe thee! Hence, worst of ill!
No reason ask, our reason is our will.

Exit with MAQUERELLE

MENDOZA

Women? Nay, Furies! Nay, worse, for they torment only the
bad, but women good and bad. Damnation of mankind!
Breath, hast thou praised them for this? And is't you, 80
Ferneze, are wriggled into smock-grace? Sit sure. O that I
could rail against these monsters in nature, models of hell,
curse of the earth, women that dare attempt anything, and
what they attempt they care not how they accomplish;
without all premeditation or prevention, rash in asking, 85
desperate in working, impatient in suffering, extreme in
desiring, slaves unto appetite, mistresses in dissembling,
only constant in unconstancy, only perfect in counter-
feiting; their words are feigned, their eyes forged, their
sighs dissembled, their looks counterfeit, their hair false, 90
their given hopes deceitful, their very breath artificial. Their
blood is their only god. Bad clothes and old age are only the
devils they tremble at. That I could rail now!

Act I, Scene vii

Enter PIETRO, *his sword drawn*

PIETRO

A mischief fill thy throat, thou foul-jawed slave!
Say thy prayers.

MENDOZA   I ha' forgot 'em.

PIETRO   Thou shalt die.

MENDOZA

So shalt thou. I am heart-mad.

PIETRO   I am horn-mad.

MENDOZA

Extreme mad?

77 *ask* Q (else Q1, Q2)
81 *smock-grace* intimate favour
85 *prevention* anticipation
89 *forged* cosmetically enhanced
90 *sighs* ed. (sights Q)
  3 *heart-mad* distracted
    horn-mad enraged; also cuckolded

PIETRO   Monstrously mad.

MENDOZA   Why?

PIETRO

   Why? Thou, thou hast dishonoured my bed.   5

MENDOZA

   I? Come, come, sit. Here's my bare heart to thee,
   As steady as is this centre to the glorious world;
   And yet, hark, thou art a cornuto—but by me?

PIETRO

   Yes, slave, by thee.

MENDOZA

   Do not, do not, with tart and spleenful breath,   10
   Lose him can lose thee. I offend my duke?
   Bear record, O ye dumb and raw-aired nights,
   How vigilant my sleepless eyes have been
   To watch the traitor; record, thou spirit of truth,
   With what debasement I ha' thrown myself   15
   To under-offices, only to learn
   The truth, the party, time, the means, the place,
   By whom, and when, and where, thou wert disgraced!
   And am I paid with 'slave!'? Hath my intrusion
   To places private and prohibited,   20
   Only to observe the closer passages—
   Heaven knows with vows of revelation—
   Made me suspected, made me deemed a villain?
   What rogue hath wronged us?

PIETRO   Mendoza, I may err.

MENDOZA

   Err? 'Tis too mild a name. But err and err,   25
   Run giddy with suspect, 'fore through me thou know
   That which most creatures save thyself do know—
   Nay, since my service hath so loathed reject,
   'Fore I'll reveal, shalt find them clipped together.

PIETRO

   Mendoza, thou know'st I am a most plain-breasted man.   30

MENDOZA

   The fitter to make cuckold. Would your brows were most
   plain too!

PIETRO

   Tell me; indeed I heard thee rail—

---

7 *centre* earth   16 *under-offices* menial occupations
21 *closer passages* secret incidents   26 *suspect* suspicion
28 *reject* rejection

MENDOZA

   At women, true. Why, what cold phlegm could choose,
   Knowing a lord so honest, virtuous,   35
   So boundless-loving, bounteous, fair-shaped, sweet,
   To be condemned, abused, defamed, made cuckold?
   Heart! I hate all women for't: sweet sheets, wax lights,
   antique bed-posts, cambric smocks, villainous curtains,
   arras pictures, oiled hinges, and all the tongue-tied lascivi-   40
   ous witnesses of great creatures' wantonness. What salvation
   can you expect?

PIETRO

   Wilt thou tell me?

MENDOZA

   Why, you may find it yourself; observe, observe.

PIETRO

   I ha' not the patience. Wilt thou deserve me? Tell, give it.   45

MENDOZA

   Tak't. Why, Ferneze is the man, Ferneze. I'll prove't; this
   night you shall take him in your sheets. Will't serve?

PIETRO

   It will; my bosom's in some peace. Till night—

MENDOZA

   What?

PIETRO

   Farewell.   50

MENDOZA

   God! How weak a lord are you!
   Why, do you think there is no more but so?

PIETRO

   Why?

MENDOZA

   Nay, then will I presume to counsel you.
   It should be thus: you, with some guard, upon the sudden   55
   Break into the princess' chamber; I stay behind,
   Without the door through which he needs must pass;
   Ferneze flies—let him; to me he comes; he's killed
   By me—observe, by me. You follow; I rail,
   And seem to save the body. Duchess comes,   60
   On whom (respecting her advancèd birth
   And your fair nature) I know—nay, I do know—
   No violence must be used. She comes; I storm,
   I praise, excuse Ferneze, and still maintain

34 *phlegm* dullness   40 *arras* tapestry
45 *deserve* earn desert or reward from

The duchess' honour; she for this loves me;   65
I honour you, shall know her soul, you mine;
Then naught shall she contrive in vengeance
(As women are most thoughtful in revenge)
Of her Ferneze, but you shall sooner know't
Than she can think't. Thus shall his death come sure;   70
Your duchess brain-caught; so, your life secure.

PIETRO
It is too well, my bosom and my heart:
When nothing helps, cut off the rotten part.   *Exit*

MENDOZA
Who cannot feign friendship can ne'er produce the effects of
hatred. Honest fool duke, subtle lascivious duchess, silly   75
novice Ferneze—I do laugh at ye! My brain is in labour till
it produce mischief, and I feel sudden throes, proofs sensible
the issue is at hand.
As bears shape young, so I'll form my devise,
Which grown, proves horrid; vengeance makes men wise.   80
                                                    [*Exit*]

[Act I, Scene viii]

Enter MALEVOLE *and* PASSARELLO

MALEVOLE
Fool, most happily encountered; can'st sing, fool?

PASSARELLO
Yes, I can sing, fool, if you'll bear the burden; and I can play
upon instruments, scurvily, as gentlemen do. O that I had

---

71 *brain-caught* tricked   75 *silly* naive (seely Q)
77 *sensible* evident   2 *bear the burden* sing the refrain

74–5 *Who . . . hatred.* Cf. *Il pastor fido*, II. iv:

Who cannot friendship faine,
Cannot truly hate. (Sig. Fv).

79–80 *As . . . horrid.* Cf. *Il pastor fido*, III. vi:

For as the Beare is wont with licking to giue shape
To her mishapen brood, that else were helplesse borne,
Eu'n so a Louer to his bare desire,
That in the birth was shapeless, weake and fraile,
Giuing but forme and strength begetteth loue:
Which whilst t'is young and tender, then t'is sweet,
But waxing to more yeares, more cruell growes,
That in the end (Mirtillo) an inueterate affect
Is euer full of anguish and defect. (Sig. I2r).

been gelded! I should then have been a fat fool for a
chamber, a squeaking fool for a tavern, and a private fool for   5
all the ladies.

MALEVOLE
You are in good case since you came to court, fool; what,
guarded, guarded!

PASSARELLO
Yes, faith, even as footmen and bawds wear velvet, not for
an ornament of honour, but for a badge of drudgery; for now   10
the duke is discontented I am fain to fool him asleep every
night.

MALEVOLE
What are his griefs?

PASSARELLO
He hath sore eyes.

MALEVOLE
I never observed so much.   15

PASSARELLO
Horrible sore eyes; and so hath every cuckold; for the roots
of the horns spring in the eyeballs, and that's the reason the
horn of a cuckold is as tender as his eye, or as that growing
in the woman's forehead twelve years since, that could not
endure to be touched. The duke hangs down his head like a   20
columbine.

MALEVOLE
Passarello, why do great men beg fools?

PASSARELLO
As the Welshman stole rushes when there was nothing else
to filch—only to keep begging in fashion.

MALEVOLE
Pooh! Thou givest no good reason; thou speakest like a fool.   25

PASSARELLO
Faith, I utter small fragments, as your knight courts your
city widow with jingling of his gilt spurs, advancing his

7 *in good case* well-dressed
8 *guarded* wearing facing or embroidery on his fool's coat
22 *beg fools* the king could grant custody of idiots, and the profits of
their estates, to those who sued for them
27 *jingling . . . advancing* Q corrected (something of his guilt: some
aduancing Q uncorrected)

18–20 *growing . . . touched.* Probably Margaret Griffith of Montgomery-
shire, described in a pamphlet of 1588 as having a four-inch horn in
the middle of her forehead.

bush-coloured beard, and taking tobacco. This is all the mirror
of their knightly complements. Nay, I shall talk when my
tongue is a-going once; 'tis like a citizen on horseback, ever-   30
more in a false gallop.

MALEVOLE
And how doth Maquerelle fare nowadays?

PASSARELLO
Faith, I was wont to salute her as our English women are at
their first landing in Flushing—I would call her whore; but
now that antiquity leaves her as an old piece of plastic t'work   35
by, I only ask her how her rotten teeth fare every morning,
and so leave her. She was the first that ever invented perfumed smocks for the gentlewomen, and woollen shoes for
fear of creaking, for the visitant. She were an excellent lady,
but that her face peeleth like Muscovy glass.   40

MALEVOLE
And how doth thy old lord that hath wit enough to be a
flatterer, and conscience enough to be a knave?

PASSARELLO
O excellent; he keeps, beside me, fifteen jesters to instruct
him in the art of fooling, and utters their jests in private to
the duke and duchess; he'll lie like to your Switzer or lawyer;   45
he'll be of any side for most money.

MALEVOLE
I am in haste, be brief.

PASSARELLO
As your fiddler when he is paid. He'll thrive, I warrant you,
while your young courtier stands like Good Friday in Lent—
men long to see it, because more fatting days come after it;   50
else he's the leanest and pitiful'st actor in the whole pageant.
Adieu, Malevole.

MALEVOLE
O world most vile, when thy loose vanities,
Taught by this fool, do make the fool seem wise!

PASSARELLO
You'll know me again, Malevole?   55

28 *bush-* Q corrected (high Q uncorrected)
29 *complements* accomplishments (also pun on book-title)
30–31 *citizen . . . gallop* lacking riding skill
34 *Flushing* the city was in English hands for several years after
   1585 as security for a loan from Elizabeth to the Dutch
35 *plastic* wax or clay model for sculpture
40 *Muscovy glass* mica or talc
41 *lord* i.e. Bilioso

MALEVOLE

O, ay, by that velvet.

PASSARELLO

Ay, as a pettifogger by his buckram bag. I am as common
in the court as an hostess's lips in the country; knights, and
clowns, and knaves, and all share me; the court cannot
possibly be without me. Adieu, Malevole.   *Exeunt*   60

Act II, Scene i

Enter MENDOZA *with a sconce, to observe* FERNEZE'S *entrance,
who, whilst the act is playing, enter[s] unbraced, two pages before
him with lights, is met by* MAQUERELLE, *and conveyed in. The
pages are sent away*

MENDOZA

He's caught! The woodcock's head is i' the noose.
Now treads Ferneze in dangerous path of lust,
Swearing his sense is merely deified.
The fool grasps clouds, and shall beget centaurs;
And now, in strength of panting faint delight,   5
The goat bids heaven envy him; good goose,
I can afford thee nothing
But the poor comfort of calamity, pity.
Lust's like the plummets hanging on clock lines,
Will ne'er ha' done, till all is quite undone.   10
Such is the course salt sallow lust doth run,
Which thou shalt try. I'll be revenged. Duke, thy suspect;
Duchess, thy disgrace; Ferneze, thy rivalship—
Shall have swift vengeance. Nothing so holy,
No band of nature so strong,   15
No law of friendship so sacred,
But I'll profane, burst, violate,
'Fore I'll endure disgrace, contempt and poverty.
Shall I, whose very 'hum' struck all heads bare,

57 *pettifogger* inferior lawyer, conducting petty cases
s.d. *sconce* lantern
       act . . . playing the music between the acts
       unbraced in undress
 1 *woodcock* dupe; woodcock were easily taken in snares
 3 *merely* completely
 4 *fool . . . centaurs* Ixion begat the Centaurs upon a cloud
 9 *plummets* weights
11 *salt* salacious
12 *suspect* suspicion

Whose face made silence, creaking of whose shoe   20
Forced the most private passages fly ope,
Scrape like a servile dog at some latched door?
Learn now to make a leg, and cry 'Beseech ye,
Pray ye, is such a lord within?'—be awed
At some odd usher's scoffed formality?   25
First sear my brains! *Unde cadis, non quo, refert.*
My heart cries 'Perish all!' How! how! What fate
Can once avoid revenge that's desperate?
I'll to the duke; if all should ope—if? tush!
Fortune still dotes on those who cannot blush.   *Exit*   30

Act II, Scene ii

Enter MALEVOLE *at one door,* BIANCA, EMILIA, *and* MAQUERELLE
at the other door

MALEVOLE
Bless ye, cast o' ladies. Ha, Dipsas! how dost thou, old coal?
MAQUERELLE
Old coal?
MALEVOLE
Ay, old coal; methinks thou liest like a brand under billets of
green wood. He that will inflame a young wench's heart,
let him lay close to her an old coal that hath first been fired, a   5
panderess, my half-burnt lint, who, though thou canst not
flame thyself, yet art able to set a thousand virgins' tapers
afire.—And how doth Janivere thy husband, my little peri-
winkle? Is he troubled with the cough o' the lungs still?
Does he hawk o' nights still? He will not bite.   10

23 *make a leg* bow
26 *sear* Q1, Q2 (seate Q)
   Unde ... refert 'Whence you fall, not whither, matters' (based
   on Seneca, *Thyestes*, 925–6)
 1 *cast* pair
   Dipsas! Q corrected (dip-sawce Q uncorrected)
 3 *under billets* Q (under these billets Q1, Q2)   6 *lint* tinder
 8 *Janivere* January (See Chaucer's *Merchant's Tale*)

1 *Dipsas.* The name is derived from a serpent whose bite caused un-
quenchable thirst; it is also the name of a bawd in Ovid's *Amores*,
I. viii, and of the enchantress in Lyly's *Endymion*; these allusions seem
equally apt.
   old coal. 'A Maquerela, in plaine English a Bawde, Is an old char-cole,
that hath been burnt her selfe, and therefore is able to kindle a whole
greene coppice', Overbury's *Characters* (Bullen).

BIANCA

No, by my troth, I took him with his mouth empty of old
teeth.

MALEVOLE

And he took thee with thy belly full of young bones; marry,
he took his maim by the stroke of his enemy.

BIANCA

And I mine by the stroke of my friend.   15

MALEVOLE

The close stock! O mortal wench! Lady, ha' ye now no
restoratives for your decayed Jasons? Look ye, crab's guts
baked, distilled ox-pith, the pulverised hairs of a lion's
upper lip, jelly of cock-sparrows, he-monkey's marrow, or
powder of fox-stones? And whither are all you ambling now?   20

BIANCA

To bed, to bed.

MALEVOLE

Do your husbands lie with ye?

BIANCA

That were country-fashion, i' faith.

MALEVOLE

Ha' ye no foregoers about you? Come, whither in good deed,
la now?   25

MAQUERELLE

In good indeed, la now, to eat the most miraculously admirably, astonishable-composed posset with three curds, without any drink. Will ye help me with a he-fox?—Here's the
duke.   *The ladies go out*

MALEVOLE

(*To* BIANCA) Fried frogs are very good, and French-like too.   30

Act II, Scene iii

Enter DUKE PIETRO, COUNT CELSO, COUNT EQUATO, BILIOSO,
FERRARDO, *and* MENDOZA

PIETRO

The night grows deep and foul; what hour is't?

16 *stock* stoccado, fencing thrust
17 *Jasons* Jason accomplished his tasks with the help of Medea's
    magic potions
17–20 *crab's . . . fox-stones* alleged aphrodisiacs
20 *powder* Q1, Q2 (powlder Q)
    are all you Q1, Q2 (are you Q)
23 *country-fashion* bawdy, as Hamlet to Ophelia

CELSO
  Upon the stroke of twelve.
MALEVOLE
  Save ye, duke.
PIETRO
  From thee—Begone, I do not love thee! Let me see thee no
  more, we are displeased.   5
MALEVOLE
  Why, God be with thee! Heaven hear my curse—may thy
  wife and thee live long together.
PIETRO
  Begone, sirrah.
MALEVOLE
  'When Arthur first in court began'—Agamemnon, Menelaus
  —was ever any duke a cornuto?   10
PIETRO
  Begone, hence.
MALEVOLE
  What religion wilt thou be of next?
MENDOZA
  Out with him!
MALEVOLE
  With most servile patience—Time will come
  When wonder of thy error will strike dumb   15
  Thy bezzled sense.
  Slaves i' favour! Ay, marry, shall he rise?
  Good God! how subtle hell doth flatter vice,
  Mounts him aloft, and makes him seem to fly;
  As fowl the tortoise mocked, who to the sky   20
  Th'ambitious shellfish raised. Th'end of all
  Is only that from height he might dead fall.
BILIOSO
  Why, when? Out ye rogue! Begone, ye rascal!
MALEVOLE
  I shall now leave ye with all my best wishes.
BILIOSO
  Out, ye cur!   25

---

  9 'When . . . began' opening line of ballad (See 2 Henry IV, II. iv)
    Agamemnon—Menelaus cuckolded princes, like King Arthur
 16 bezzled befuddled
 17 Slaves i' favour Wine (slaues I fauour, I mary shall he, rise, Qq)
 20-1 fowl . . . raised See Aesop's fable of the tortoise and the eagle
    (Aesop, ed. Halm, No. 419)

MALEVOLE
Only let's hold together a firm correspondence.
BILIOSO
Out!
MALEVOLE
A mutual, friendly-reciprocal, perpetual kind of steady-
unanimous-heartily-leagued—
BILIOSO
Hence, ye gross-jawed peasantly—out, go!   30
MALEVOLE
Adieu, pigeon-house! Thou burr that only stickest to nappy
fortunes; the serpigo, the strangury, an eternal, uneffectual
priapism seize thee!
BILIOSO
Out, rogue!
MALEVOLE
May'st thou be a notorious wittoly pander to thine own wife,   35
and yet get no office, but live to be the utmost misery of
mankind, a beggarly cuckold.   *Exit*
PIETRO
It shall be so.
MENDOZA
It must be so, for where great states revenge
'Tis requisite the parts which piety   40
And loft respect forbears be closely dogged.
Lay one into his breast shall sleep with him,
Feed in the same dish, run in self-faction,
Who may discover any shape of danger;
For once disgraced, displayèd in offence,   45

31 *nappy* rough
32 *serpigo* creeping skin disease, ringworm
   strangury bladder disability, causing painful urination
33 *priapism* penis erection
39 *states* statesmen
40 *parts* factions
   which ed. (with Qq)
41 *loft* Q, Q2 (soft Q1)
44 *discover* Q, Q2 (dissuer Q1)
45 *displayèd* Q, Q2 (discouered Q1)

39–41 *It . . . dogged.* Mendoza's advice is obscurely phrased; the required
sense would seem to be that great men should set close watch upon
those factious subjects who withhold due loyalty and respect: Aurelia
is here the subject of the conversation, and her behaviour seems a
clue to the thinking.

It makes man blushless, and man is (all confess)
More prone to vengeance than to gratefulness.
Favours are writ in dust, but stripes we feel,
Depraved nature stamps in lasting steel.

PIETRO
You shall be leagued with the duchess!   50

EQUATO
The plot is very good.

MENDOZA
You shall both kill, and seem the corse to save.

FERRARDO
A most fine brain-trick.

CELSO
(*Tacite*) Of a most cunning knave.

PIETRO
My lords, the heavy action we intend   55
Is death and shame, two of the ugliest shapes
That can confound a soul; think, think of it.
I strike, but yet like him that 'gainst stone walls
Directs his shafts, rebounds in his own face;
My lady's shame is mine; O God, 'tis mine!   60
Therefore I do conjure all secrecy;
Let it be as very little as may be—
Pray ye, as may be.
Make frightless entrance, salute her with soft eyes,
Stain naught with blood—only Ferneze dies,   65
But not before her brows. O gentlemen,
God knows I love her! Nothing else, but this—
I am not well. If grief, that sucks veins dry,
Rivels the skin, casts ashes in men's faces,
Bedulls the eye, unstrengthens all the blood,   70
Chance to remove me to another world,
As sure I once must die, let him succeed.
I have no child; all that my youth begot
Hath been your loves, which shall inherit me;
Which as it ever shall, I do conjure it,   75
Mendoza may succeed: he's noble born,
With me of much desert.

CELSO
(*Tacite*) Much!

54 (*Tacite*) silently, aside
61 *conjure* implore
65 *Stain* Q1 (Strain Q, Q2)
69 *Rivels* wrinkles   72 *him* i.e. Mendoza

PIETRO
    Your silence answers 'Ay';
    I thank you. Come on now. O that I might die   80
    Before her shame's displayed! Would I were forced
    To burn my father's tomb, unhele his bones,
    And dash them in the dirt, rather than this!
    This both the living and the dead offends;
    Sharp surgery where naught but death amends.   85
                                 Exit with the others

Act II, Scene iv

Enter MAQUERELLE, EMILIA, *and* BIANCA, *with the posset*

MAQUERELLE
    Even here it is; three curds in three regions individually
    distinct; most methodical, according to art composed, with-
    out any drink.

BIANCA
    Without any drink?

MAQUERELLE
    Upon my honour; will you sit and eat?   5

EMILIA
    Good—the composure, the receipt, how is't?

MAQUERELLE
    'Tis a pretty pearl; by this pearl (how dost with me?) thus
    it is: seven and thirty yolks of Barbary hens' eggs, eighteen
    spoonfuls and a half of the juice of cocksparrow bones, one
    ounce, three drams, four scruples, and one quarter of the   10
    syrup of Ethiopian dates, sweetened with three-quarters of
    a pound of pure candied Indian eringoes; strewed over with
    the powder of pearl of America, amber of Cataia, and lamb-
    stones of Muscovia.

BIANCA
    Trust me, the ingredients are very cordial, and no question   15
    good, and most powerful in restoration.

---

  82 *unhele* strip off covering (vnheale Q; vnhill Q1, Q2)
    1–2 *three . . . distinct* junkets of curds and similar dishes are
      composed in layers, usually sweet and sour
    6 *composure* composition
    7 *pearl* Emilia has to buy the information
      (*how . . . me?*) 'how does it become me?' (Neilson)
    12 *eringoes* roots of sea holly
    13 *Cataia* Cathay (China)
    13–14 *lamb-stones* lamb's fry   15 *cordial* invigorating

MAQUERELLE

I know not what you mean by restoration, but this it doth:
it purifieth the blood, smootheth the skin, enliveneth the eye,
strengtheneth the veins, mundifieth the teeth, comforteth the
stomach, fortifieth the back, and quickeneth the wit; that's   20
all.

EMILIA

By my troth, I have eaten but two spoonfuls, and methinks
I could discourse most swiftly and wittily already.

MAQUERELLE

Have you the art to seem honest?

BIANCA

Ay, thank advice and practice.   25

MAQUERELLE

Why then, eat me of this posset, quicken your blood, and
preserve your beauty. Do you know Doctor Plaster-face? By
this curd, he is the most exquisite in forging of veins,
sprightening of eyes, dyeing of hair, sleeking of skins,
blushing of cheeks, surphling of breasts, blanching and   30
bleaching of teeth, that ever made an old lady gracious by
torchlight; by this curd, la.

BIANCA

We are resolved, what God has given us we'll cherish.

MAQUERELLE

Cherish anything saving your husband; keep him not too
high lest he leap the pale. But for your beauty, let it be your
saint, bequeath two hours to it every morning in your closet.
I ha' been young, and yet in my conscience I am not above
five and twenty, but believe me, preserve and use your
beauty, for youth and beauty once gone, we are like beehives
without honey, out o' fashion apparel that no man will wear;   40
therefore, use me your beauty.

EMILIA

Ay, but men say—

MAQUERELLE

Men say? Let men say what they will; life o' woman, they are

---

19 *mundifieth* cleans
29 *sprightening* making vivacious
30 *surphling* washing with sulphur water or other cosmetics
34–5 *keep . . . pale* the spirited beast will leap the fence; also bawdy
41 *use* put to use

ignorant of your wants. The more in years, the more in perfection they grow; if they lose youth and beauty, they gain   45
wisdom and discretion. But when our beauty fades, goodnight with us. There cannot be an uglier thing to see than
an old woman; from which, O pruning, pinching, and painting, deliver all sweet beauties.

BIANCA
Hark! Music.   50

MAQUERELLE
Peace, 'tis the duchess' bed-chamber. Good rest, most
prosperously-graced ladies.

EMILIA
Good night, sentinel.

BIANCA
'Night, dear Maquerelle.   *Exeunt all but* MAQUERELLE

MAQUERELLE
May my posset's operation send you my wit and honesty,   55
and me your youth and beauty: the pleasing'st rest.
                                        Exit MAQUERELLE

Act II, Scene v

A song

Whilst the song is singing, enter MENDOZA *with his sword drawn,
standing ready to murder* FERNEZE *as he flies from the duchess'
chamber*

ALL
[*Within*] Strike, strike!

AURELIA
[*Within*] Save my Ferneze! O save my Ferneze!

Enter FERNEZE *in his shirt, and is received upon* MENDOZA'S
sword

ALL
[*Within*] Follow! Pursue!

AURELIA
[*Within*] O save Ferneze!

          [MENDOZA] *thrusts his rapier in* FERNEZE

MENDOZA
Pierce, pierce! Thou shallow fool, drop there.   5

44 *your* Q (our Q1, Q2)
5 s.d. Wine (after l. 8 Q, Q2; not in Q1)

He that attempts a princess' lawless love
Must have broad hands, close heart, with Argus' eyes,
And back of Hercules; or else he dies.

Enter AURELIA, DUKE PIETRO, FERRARDO, BILIOSO, CELSO, *and*
EQUATO

ALL
Follow, follow!
MENDOZA
Stand off, forbear, ye most uncivil lords!   10
PIETRO
Strike!
MENDOZA
Do not. Tempt not a man resolved.

MENDOZA *bestrides the wounded body of* FERNEZE *and seems to
save him*

Would you, inhuman murderers, more than death?
AURELIA
O poor Ferneze!
MENDOZA
Alas, now all defence too late.
AURELIA
                                  He's dead.   15
PIETRO
I am sorry for our shame. Go to your bed.
Weep not too much, but leave some tears to shed
When I am dead.
AURELIA
What, weep for thee? My soul no tears shall find.
PIETRO
Alas, alas, that women's souls are blind.   20
MENDOZA
Betray such beauty?
Murder such youth? Contemn civility?
He loves him not that rails not at him.
PIETRO
Thou canst not move us; we have blood enough;
And please you, lady, we have quite forgot   25
All your defects; if not, why then—

7 *Argus* Argos Panoptes had eyes all over his body
8 *Hercules* See IV. v, ll. 58–9
12 *s.d.* Q1, Q2 (not in Q)

AURELIA
Not.
PIETRO
Not. The best of rest, good night.

Exit PIETRO *with other courtiers*

AURELIA
Despite go with thee!
MENDOZA
Madam, you ha' done me foul disgrace; you have wronged   30
him much loves you too much. Go to, your soul knows you
have.
AURELIA
I think I have.
MENDOZA
Do you but think so?
AURELIA
Nay, sure, I have; my eyes have witnessed thy love; thou   35
hast stood too firm for me.
MENDOZA
Why, tell me, fair-cheeked lady, who even in tears art
powerfully beauteous, what unadvised passion struck ye
into such a violent heat against me? Speak; what mischief
wronged us? What devil injured us? Speak.   40
AURELIA
That thing ne'er worthy of the name of man—Ferneze.
Ferneze swore thou lov'st Emilia,
Which, to advance, with most reproachful breath
Thou both didst blemish and denounce my love.
MENDOZA
Ignoble villain, did I for this bestride   45
Thy wounded limbs? For this, rank opposite
Even to my sovereign? O God, for this,
Sunk all my hopes, and with my hopes, my life?
Ripped bare my throat unto the hangman's axe?
Thou most dishonoured trunk! Emilia?   50
By life, I know her not—Emilia?
Did you believe him?
AURELIA   Pardon me, I did.
MENDOZA
Did you? And thereupon you graced him?
AURELIA
I did.

46 *rank* take stand
46–7 *For . . . sovereign?* Q1, Q2 (not in Q)

MENDOZA

Took him to favour, nay, even clasped with him? 55

AURELIA

Alas, I did.

MENDOZA

This night?

AURELIA

This night.

MENDOZA

And in your lustful twines the duke took you?

AURELIA

A most sad truth. 60

MENDOZA

O God! O God! how we dull honest souls,
Heavy-brained men, are swallowed in the bogs
Of a deceitful ground, whilst nimble bloods,
Light-jointed spirits, pent, cut good men's throats,
And scape. Alas, I am too honest for this age, 65
Too full of phlegm and heavy steadiness;
Stood still whilst this slave cast a noose about me:
Nay, then to stand in honour of him and her
Who had even sliced my heart!

AURELIA

Come; I did err, and am most sorry I did err. 70

MENDOZA

Why, we are both but dead; the duke hates us;
And those whom princes do once groundly hate,
Let them provide to die; as sure as fate,
Prevention is the heart of policy.

AURELIA

Shall we murder him? 75

MENDOZA

Instantly?

AURELIA

Instantly; before he casts a plot,
Or further blaze my honour's much-known blot.
Let's murder him.

MENDOZA

I would do much for you; will ye marry me? 80

64 *pent* Q1, Q2 (spent Q)
72 *groundly* thoroughly
73 *provide* make ready
74 *Prevention* anticipation
78 *blaze* proclaim

AURELIA

I'll make thee duke. We are of Medicis,
Florence our friend; in court my faction
Not meanly strengthful; the duke then dead,
We well-prepared for change; the multitude
Irresolutely reeling; we in force;   85
Our party seconded; the kingdom mazed;
No doubt of swift success all shall be graced.

MENDOZA

You do confirm me, we are resolute;
Tomorrow look for change; rest confident.
'Tis now about the immodest waist of night;   90
The mother of moist dew with pallid light
Spreads gloomy shades about the numbèd earth.
Sleep, sleep, whilst we contrive our mischief's birth.
This man I'll get inhumed. Farewell; to bed;
Ay kiss thy pillow, dream, the duke is dead. *Exit* AURELIA   95
So, so, good night. How fortune dotes on impudence! I am
in private the adopted son of yon good prince. I must be
duke. Why, if I must, I must. Most silly lord, name me? O
heaven! I see God made honest fools to maintain crafty
knaves. The duchess is wholly mine too; must kill her   100
husband to quit her shame—much! then marry her. Ay, O
I grow proud in prosperous treachery!
As wrestlers clip, so I'll embrace you all,
Not to support, but to procure your fall.

Enter MALEVOLE

MALEVOLE

God arrest thee.   105

MENDOZA

At whose suit?

MALEVOLE

At the devil's. Ah, you treacherous, damnable monster! How
dost? How dost, thou treacherous rogue? Ah ye rascal, I am
banished the court, sirrah.

MENDOZA

Prithee, let's be acquainted; I do love thee, faith.   110

MALEVOLE

At your service, by the Lord, la! Shall's go to supper? Let's

86 *mazed* confused
87 *of* by means of
94 *inhumed* buried
95 *kiss thy* Q1, Q2 (kiss the Q)   98 *silly* Q1, Q2 (seely Q)

be once drunk together, and so unite a most virtuously
strengthened friendship; shall's, Huguenot, shall's?

MENDOZA
Wilt fall upon my chamber tomorrow morn?

MALEVOLE
As a raven to a dunghill. They say there's one dead here,   115
pricked for the pride of the flesh.

MENDOZA
Ferneze. There he is; prithee, bury him.

MALEVOLE
O most willingly; I mean to turn pure Rochelle churchman, I.

MENDOZA
Thou churchman? Why? Why?

MALEVOLE
Because I'll live lazily, rail upon authority, deny kings'   120
supremacy in things indifferent, and be a pope in mine own
parish.

MENDOZA
Wherefore dost thou think churches were made?

MALEVOLE
To scour ploughshares; I ha' seen oxen plough up altars.
Et nunc seges ubi Sion fuit.   125

MENDOZA
Strange.

MALEVOLE
Nay, monstrous! I ha' seen a sumptuous steeple turned to a
stinking privy; more beastly, the sacredest place made a dog's
kennel; nay, most inhuman, the stoned coffins of long-dead
Christians burst up and made hogs' troughs. *Hic finis Priami.* 130
Shall I ha' some sack and cheese at thy chamber? Good night,
good mischievous incarnate devil, good night, Mendoza.
Ah, you inhuman villain, good night; 'night, fub.

MENDOZA
Good night; tomorrow morn.   *Exit* MENDOZA

MALEVOLE
Ay, I will come, friendly damnation, I will come. I do descry   135

113 *Huguenot* confederate (Fr. Hugues; Ger. eidgenoss)
118 *Rochelle churchman* La Rochelle was a centre of relief for
    Huguenots during periods of persecution
125 *et nunc . . . fuit* 'And now corn grows where Sion was' (based on
    'Jam seges est ubi Troja fuit', Ovid, *Heroides*, l. 53)
130 *Hic finis Priami* 'Here was Priam's end' (based on 'Haec finis
    Priami fatorum', Virgil, *Aeneid* II, l. 554)
133 *fub* cheat

cross-points; honesty and courtship straddle as far asunder
as a true Frenchman's legs.

FERNEZE

O!

MALEVOLE

Proclamations, more proclamations!

FERNEZE

O, a surgeon!   140

MALEVOLE

Hark! Lust cries for a surgeon; what news from limbo? How
does the grand cuckold, Lucifer?

FERNEZE

O help, help! Conceal and save me.

FERNEZE *stirs, and* MALEVOLE *helps him up, and conveys him*
away

MALEVOLE

Thy shame more than thy wounds do grieve me far;
Thy wounds but leave upon thy flesh some scar;   145
But fame ne'er heals, still rankles worse and worse;
Such is of uncontrollèd lust the curse.
Think what it is in lawless sheets to lie;
But, O, Ferneze, what in lust to die.
Then thou that shame respects, O, fly converse   150
With women's eyes and lisping wantonness.
Stick candles 'gainst a virgin wall's white back,
If they not burn, yet at the least they'll black.
Come, I'll convey thee to a private port,
Where thou shalt live (O happy man) from court.   155
The beauty of the day begins to rise,
From whose bright form night's heavy shadow flies.
Now 'gins close plots to work, the scene grows full,
And craves his eyes who hath a solid skull.   *Exeunt*

Act III, Scene i

Enter DUKE PIETRO, MENDOZA, COUNT EQUATO *and* BILIOSO

PIETRO

'Tis grown to youth of day; how shall we waste this light?
My heart's more heavy than a tyrant's crown. Shall we go
hunt? Prepare for field.   *Exit* EQUATO

136 *cross-points* tricks (pun on dancing term)
142 *does* Q1, Q2 (doth Q)   146 *fame* ill report
154 *port* place of refuge   155 *from* away from

MENDOZA
Would ye could be merry.
PIETRO
Would God I could! Mendoza, bid 'em haste. *Exit* MENDOZA   5
I would fain shift place. O vain relief!
Sad souls may well change place, but not change grief;
As deer, being struck, fly thorough many soils,
Yet still the shaft sticks fast, so—
BILIOSO
A good old simile, my honest lord.   10
PIETRO
I am not much unlike to some sick man
That long desired hurtful drink; at last
Swills in and drinks his last, ending at once
Both life and thirst. O would I ne'er had known
My own dishonour! Good God, that men should desire   15
To search out that, which being found, kills all
Their joy of life! To taste the tree of knowledge,
And then be driven from out paradise.
Canst give me some comfort?
BILIOSO
My lord, I have some books which have been dedicated to   20
my honour, and I ne'er read 'em, and yet they had very fine
names: *Physic for Fortune, Lozenges of Sanctified Sincerity*,
very pretty works of curates, scriveners, and schoolmasters.
Marry, I remember one Seneca, Lucius Annaeus Seneca—
PIETRO
Out upon him! He writ of temperance and fortitude, yet   25
lived like a voluptuous epicure, and died like an effeminate
coward. Haste thee to Florence.
Here, take our letters, see 'em sealed; away.
Report in private to the honoured duke
His daughter's forced disgrace; tell him at length   30
We know too much; due compliments advance.
There's naught that's safe and sweet but ignorance.
                                                   Exit DUKE
                    Enter BIANCA
BILIOSO
Madam, I am going ambassador for Florence; 'twill be great
charges to me.

8 *soils* stretches of water in which hunted animals try to lose scent
34 *charges* expense

---

22 *Physic for Fortune.* Petrarch's *De Remediis Utriusque Fortunae* (1386)
was translated by Thomas Twyne as *Physicke against Fortune* (1579).

BIANCA

No matter, my lord, you have the lease of two manors come   35
out next Christmas; you may lay your tenants on the greater
rack for it; and when you come home again, I'll teach you
how you shall get two hundred pounds a year by your teeth.

BILIOSO

How, madam?

BIANCA

Cut off so much from housekeeping; that which is saved by   40
the teeth, you know, is got by the teeth.

BILIOSO

'Fore God, and so I may; I am in wondrous credit, lady.

BIANCA

See the use of flattery; I did ever counsel you to flatter
greatness, and you have profited well. Any man that will do
so shall be sure to be like your Scotch barnacle—now a   45
block, instantly a worm, and presently a great goose. This it
is to rot and putrefy in the bosom of greatness.

BILIOSO

Thou art ever my politician. O, how happy is that old lord
that hath a politician to his young lady! I'll have fifty gentlemen shall attend upon me; marry, the most of them shall be   50
farmers' sons, because they shall bear their own charges;
and they shall go apparelled thus, in sea-water-green suits,
ash-colour cloaks, watchet stockings, and popinjay-green
feathers—will not the colours do excellent?

BIANCA

Out upon't! They'll look like citizens riding to their friends   55
at Whitsuntide, their apparel just so many several parishes.

BILIOSO

I'll have it so; and Passarello, my fool, shall go along with
me; marry, he shall be in velvet.

BIANCA

A fool in velvet?

BILIOSO

Ay, 'tis common for your fool to wear satin; I'll have mine   60
in velvet.

BIANCA

What will you wear then, my lord?

35–6 *come out* expire
42 *credit* reputation   53 *watchet* light blue

45 *Scotch barnacle.* An account 'Of the Goose tree, Barnacle tree, or the
tree bearing Geese' is in Gerard's *Herball* (1597), Chap. 188.

BILIOSO

Velvet too; marry, it shall be embroidered, because I'll differ
from the fool somewhat. I am horribly troubled with the
gout; nothing grieves me but that my doctor hath forbidden   65
me wine, and you know your ambassador must drink. Didst
thou ask thy doctor what was good for the gout?

BIANCA

Yes; he said ease, wine and women were good for it.

BILIOSO

Nay, thou hast such a wit. What was good to cure it, said he?

BIANCA

Why, the rack; all your empirics could never do the like cure   70
upon the gout the rack did in England, or your Scotch boot.
The French harlequin will instruct you.

BILIOSO

Surely, I do wonder how thou, having for the most part of
thy lifetime been a country body, shouldst have so good a
wit.   75

BIANCA

Who, I? Why, I have been a courtier thrice two months.

BILIOSO

So have I this twenty year, and yet there was a gentleman-
usher called me coxcomb t'other day, and to my face too.
Was't not a backbiting rascal? I would I were better travelled,
that I might have been better acquainted with the fashions of   80
several countrymen; but my secretary, I think he hath sufficiently instructed me.

BIANCA

How, my lord?

BILIOSO

'Marry, my good lord', quoth he, 'your lordship shall ever
find amongst a hundred Frenchmen, forty hot-shots;   85
amongst a hundred Spaniards, threescore braggarts; amongst
a hundred Dutchmen, fourscore drunkards; amongst a
hundred Englishmen, fourscore and ten madmen; and
amongst a hundred Welshmen—'

BIANCA

What, my lord?   90

70 *empirics* sect of empirical physicians
71 *Scotch boot* instrument of torture by which legs were crushed
72 *harlequin* (Herlakeene Q) referred to probably because the Scotch
    boot was used in Scotland and France
81 *several countrymen* of several countries

BILIOSO

'Fourscore and nineteen gentlemen.'

BIANCA

But since you go about a sad embassy, I would have you go
in black, my lord.

BILIOSO

Why, dost think I cannot mourn unless I wear my hat in
cypress like an alderman's heir? That's vile, very old, in   95
faith.

BIANCA

I'll learn of you shortly. O we should have a fine gallant of
you, should not I instruct you. How will you bear yourself
when you come into the Duke of Florence' court?

BILIOSO

Proud enough, and 'twill do well enough. As I walk up and   100
down the chamber I'll spit frowns about me, have a strong
perfume in my jerkin, let my beard grow to make me look
terrible, salute no man beneath the fourth button, and 'twill
do excellent.

BIANCA

But there is a very beautiful lady there; how will you enter- 105
tain her?

BILIOSO

I'll tell you that when the lady hath entertained me. But to
satisfy thee, here comes the fool.

Enter PASSARELLO

Fool, thou shalt stand for the fair lady.

PASSARELLO

Your fool will stand for your lady most willingly and most   110
uprightly.

BILIOSO

I'll salute her in Latin.

PASSARELLO

O, your fool can understand no Latin.

BILIOSO

Ay, but your lady can.

PASSARELLO

Why then, if your lady take down your fool, your fool will   115
stand no longer for your lady.

91 *gentlemen* Welshmen were proverbially proud of their pedigrees
95 *cypress* light, transparent material of silk and linen, used for
veiling
103 *salute . . . button* make no low bows

BILIOSO

A pestilent fool! 'Fore God, I think the world be turned
upside down too.

PASSARELLO

O no, sir; for then your lady, and all the ladies in the palace,
should go with their heels upward, and that were a strange   120
sight you know.

BILIOSO

There be many will repine at my preferment.

PASSARELLO

O ay, like the envy of an elder sister that hath her younger
made a lady before her.

BILIOSO

The duke is wondrous discontented.   125

PASSARELLO

Ay, and more melancholic than a usurer having all his money
out at the death of a prince.

BILIOSO

Didst thou see Madam Floria today?

PASSARELLO

Yes, I found her repairing her face today; the red upon the
white showed as if her cheeks should have been served in for   130
two dishes of barberries in stewed broth, and the flesh to
them a woodcock.

BILIOSO

A bitter fool! Come, madam, this night thou shalt enjoy me
freely, and tomorrow for Florence.

                              [*Walks* BIANCA *aside: exit* BIANCA]

PASSARELLO

What a natural fool is he that would be a pair of bodies to a   135
woman's petticoat, to be trussed and pointed to-them. Well,
I'll dog my lord, and the word is proper; for when I fawn
upon him he feeds me; when I snap him by the fingers, he
spits in my mouth. If a dog's death were not strangling, I
had rather be one than a serving-man; for the corruption of   140
coin is either the generation of a usurer, or a lousy beggar.

                                                        [*Exit*]

122 *preferment* advancement
131 *barberries* Barbary hens
133 *fool* punning on fowl, carried on through 'trussed and pointed'
     below
135 *bodies* punning on bodice
136 *trussed and pointed* tied with points (laces)

Act III, Scene ii

Enter MALEVOLE *in some frieze gown, whilst* BILIOSO *reads his
patent*

MALEVOLE

   I cannot sleep; my eyes' ill-neighbouring lids
   Will hold no fellowship. O thou pale sober night,
   Thou that in sluggish fumes all sense doth steep,
   Thou that gives all the world full leave to play,
   Unbend'st the feebled veins of sweaty labour.   5
   The galley-slave, that all the toilsome day
   Tugs at his oar against the stubborn wave,
   Straining his rugged veins, snores fast;
   The stooping scythe-man that doth barb the field
   Thou mak'st wink sure. In night all creatures sleep;   10
   Only the malcontent, that 'gainst his fate
   Repines and quarrels—alas, he's goodman tell-clock;
   His sallow jaw-bones sink with wasting moan;
   Whilst others' beds are down, his pillow's stone.

BILIOSO

   Malevole.   15

MALEVOLE

   Elder of Israel, thou honest defect of wicked nature and
   obstinate ignorance, when did thy wife let thee lie with her?

BILIOSO

   I am going ambassador to Florence.

MALEVOLE

   Ambassador? Now, for thy country's honour, prithee do
   not put up mutton and porridge in thy cloak-bag. Thy young   20
   lady wife goes to Florence with thee too, does she not?

BILIOSO

   No, I leave her at the palace.

MALEVOLE

   At the palace? Now discretion shield man! For God's love,

s.d. *frieze* woollen cloth with heavy nap
     patent commission as ambassador
  9 *barb* mow
  12 *tell-clock* calling the hours of night watches
  16 *Elder of Israel* wicked old judge (Harrier cites Thomas Nashe,
     Pierce Penilesse: Works ed. McKerrow and Wilson, I, p. 188)

---

16 *thou . . . nature.* Cf. *Il pastor fido*, II. vi:
       'Dryed *Carogne*, defect of wicked nature' (Sig. G)
   (*Carogne* = carrion).

let's ha' no more cuckolds. Hymen begins to put off his
saffron robe. Keep thy wife i' the state of grace. Heart   25
o' truth, I would sooner leave my lady singled in a bordello
than in the Genoa palace.
Sin there appearing in her sluttish shape,
Would soon grow loathsome, even to blushes' sense;
Surfeit would choke intemperate appetite,   30
Make the soul scent the rotten breath of lust.
When in an Italian lascivious palace,
A lady guardianless,
Left to the push of all allurement,
The strongest incitements to immodesty,   35
To have her bound, incensed with wanton sweets,
Her veins filled high with heating delicates,
Soft rest, sweet music, amorous masquerers,
Lascivious banquets, sin itself gilt o'er,
Strong fantasy tricking up strange delights,   40
Presenting it dressed pleasingly to sense,
Sense leading it unto the soul, confirmed
With potent example, impudent custom,
Enticed by that great bawd, Opportunity;
Thus being prepared, clap to her easy ear   45
Youth in good clothes, well-shaped, rich,
Fair-spoken, promising-noble, ardent, blood-full,
Witty, flattering—Ulysses absent,
O Ithaca, can chastest Penelope hold out?

BILIOSO
Mass, I'll think on't; farewell.   *Exit* BILIOSO   50
MALEVOLE
Farewell; take thy wife with thee; farewell.
To Florence, um? It may prove good, it may;
And we may once unmask our brows.

24–5 *Hymen . . . robe* god of marriage, usually dressed in saffron robe
     in dramatic representations; Bilioso imperils his marriage by
     going abroad without his wife
26 *singled* alone
   bordello brothel
28 *there* in the bordello
30 *choke* ed. (cloke Q)   37 *delicates* delicacies
44 *Opportunity* often so described (See *The Rape of Lucrece*, l. 886)
49 *Ithaca, can chastest* Q1, Q2 (Ithacan, chastest Q.)

──

40–4 *Strong . . . Opportunity.* For Marston's use of these terms, and their
     indebtedness to Epictetus, see Davenport, pp. 346–7; the vocabulary
     is used again at III. iii, 72–5.

Act III, Scene iii

Enter COUNT CELSO

CELSO
    My honoured lord.

MALEVOLE
    Celso, peace! How is't? Speak low, pale fears
    Suspect that hedges, walls and trees have ears.
    Speak, how runs all?

CELSO
    I' faith, my lord, that beast with many heads,   5
    The staggering multitude, recoils apace;
    Though thorough great men's envy, most men's malice,
    Their much intemperate heat hath banished you,
    Yet now they find envy and malice ne'er
    Produce faint reformation.   10
    The duke, the too soft duke, lies as a block,
    For which two tugging factions seem to saw,
    But still the iron through the ribs they draw.

MALEVOLE
    I tell thee, Celso, I have ever found
    Thy breast most far from shifting cowardice   15
    And fearful baseness: therefore, I'll tell thee, Celso,
    I find the wind begins to come about;
    I'll shift my suit of fortune.
    I know the Florentine—whose only force,
    By marrying his proud daughter to this prince,   20
    Both banished me, and made this weak lord duke—
    Will now forsake them all, be sure he will.
    I'll lie in ambush for conveniency,
    Upon their severance to confirm myself.

CELSO
    Is Ferneze interred?   25

MALEVOLE
    Of that at leisure; he lives.

CELSO
    But how stands Mendoza? How is't with him?

MALEVOLE
    Faith, like a pair of snuffers; snibs filth in other men and
    retains it in himself.

19 *only force* power alone
24 *confirm* strengthen
28 *snibs* snubs, reproves   29 *himself* Q1, Q2 (itself Q)

CELSO

He does fly from public notice, methinks, as a hare does   30
from hounds; the feet whereon he flies betrays him.

MALEVOLE

I can track him, Celso.
O, my disguise fools him most powerfully;
For that I seem a desperate malcontent
He fain would clasp with me; he is the true slave   35
That will put on the most affected grace
For some vile second cause.

Enter MENDOZA

CELSO   He's here.
MALEVOLE   Give place.
                                                Exit CELSO

Illo, ho, ho, ho! Art there, old truepenny? Where hast thou
spent thyself this morning? I see flattery in thine eyes and
damnation in thy soul. Ha, thou huge rascal!   40

MENDOZA

Thou art very merry.

MALEVOLE

As a scholar *futuens gratis.* How doth the devil go with thee
now?

MENDOZA

Malevole, thou art an arrant knave.

MALEVOLE

Who I? I have been a sergeant, man.   45

MENDOZA

Thou art very poor.

MALEVOLE

As Job, an alchemist, or a poet.

MENDOZA

The duke hates thee.

MALEVOLE

As Irishmen do bum-cracks.

MENDOZA

Thou hast lost his amity.   50

MALEVOLE

As pleasing as maids lose their virginity.

42 *futuens gratis* 'fornicating free' (Harrier cites Seneca, *Epistle*
   XLIV, quoting Plato)
45 *sergeant* sheriff's officer
49 *As . . . cracks* Irish objections to wind-breaking seem proverbial
   (Harrier cites Nashe, *ed. cit.* same page)

MENDOZA

Would thou wert of a lusty spirit; would thou wert noble.

MALEVOLE

Why, sure my blood gives me I am noble; sure I am of noble
kind, for I find myself possessed with all their qualities;
love dogs, dice and drabs, scorn wit in stuff-clothes, have   55
beat my shoemaker, knocked my seamstress, cuckold[ed]
my pothecary, and undone my tailor. Noble? Why not?
Since the Stoic said, *Neminem servum non ex regibus, neminem
regem non ex servis esse oriundum*—only busy Fortune touses,
and the provident Chances blends them together. I'll give   60
you a simile; did you e'er see a well with two buckets?
Whilst one comes up full to be emptied, another goes down
empty to be filled; such is the state of all humanity. Why,
look you, I may be the son of some duke; for, believe me,
intemperate lascivious bastardy makes nobility doubtful. I   65
have a lusty daring heart, Mendoza.

MENDOZA

Let's grasp! I do like thee infinitely. Wilt enact one thing
for me?

MALEVOLE

Shall I get by it? ([MENDOZA] *gives him his purse*) Command
me; I am thy slave beyond death and hell.   70

MENDOZA

Murder the duke.

MALEVOLE

My heart's wish, my soul's desire, my fantasy's dream, my
blood's longing, the only height of my hopes! How, O God,
how? O how my united spirits throng together, so strengthen
my resolve!   75

MENDOZA

The duke is now a-hunting.

MALEVOLE

Excellent, admirable, as the devil would have it! Lend me,
lend me rapier, pistol, cross-bow; so, so, I'll do it.

MENDOZA

Then we agree?

53 *gives* shows
55 *drabs* whores   *stuff-clothes* coarse cloth garments
58-9 *Neminem . . . oriundum* 'There is no slave not born of kings,
    no king not born of slaves' (Seneca, *Epistle* XLIV, again quoting
    Plato)
59 *only* alone   *touses* puts in disorder
67 *grasp* embrace   69 *get* gain

MALEVOLE

As Lent and fishmongers. Come, *a-cap-a-pe*, how? Inform.   80

MENDOZA

Know that this weak-brain'd duke, who only stands on
Florence' stilts, hath out of witless zeal made me his heir, and
secretly confirmed the wreath to me after his life's full point.

MALEVOLE

Upon what merit?

MENDOZA

Merit! By heaven, I horn him; only Ferneze's death gave me   85
state's life.

Tut, we are politic, he must not live now.

MALEVOLE

No reason, marry. But how must he die now?

MENDOZA

My utmost project is to murder the duke, that I might have
his estate, because he makes me his heir; to banish the
duchess, that I might be rid of a cunning Lacedaemonian,   90
because I know Florence will forsake her; and then to marry
Maria, the banished Duke Altofront's wife, that her friends
might strengthen me and my faction; this is all, la.

MALEVOLE

Do you love Maria?

MENDOZA

Faith, no great affection, but as wise men do love great   95
women, to ennoble their blood and augment their revenue.
To accomplish this now, thus now. The duke is in the forest
next the sea; single him, kill him, hurl him in the main, and
proclaim thou sawest wolves eat him.

MALEVOLE

Um; not so good. Methinks when he is slain, to get some   100
hypocrite, some dangerous wretch that's muffled o'er with
feigned holiness, to swear he heard the duke on some steep
cliff lament his wife's dishonour, and in an agony of his
heart's torture, hurled his groaning sides into the swollen
sea.—This circumstance well made sounds probable, and   105
hereupon the duchess—

MENDOZA

May well be banished. O unpeerable invention! Rare! Thou
god of policy! It honeys me.

80 *a-cap-a-pe* from head to foot   83 *point* end
90 *Lacedaemonian* slang for 'whore' (Spartan women had unaccus-
    tomed equality with men)
107 *unpeerable* peerless

MALEVOLE
Then fear not for the wife of Altofront; I'll close to her.

MENDOZA
Thou shalt, thou shalt. Our excellency is pleased. Why wert   110
not thou an emperor? When we are duke I'll make thee some
great man sure.

MALEVOLE
Nay, make me some rich knave, and I'll make myself some
great man.

MENDOZA
In thee be all my spirit.   115
Retain ten souls, unite thy virtual powers;
Resolve; ha, remember greatness. Heart, farewell.

Enter CELSO

The fate of all my hopes in thee doth dwell. [*Exit* MENDOZA]

MALEVOLE
Celso, didst hear? O heaven, didst hear
Such devilish mischief? Sufferest thou the world   120
Carouse damnation even with greedy swallow,
And still dost wink, still does thy vengeance slumber?
If now thy brows are clear, when will they thunder?
[*Exeunt*]

Act III, Scene iv

Enter PIETRO, FERRARDO, PREPASSO, *and three* PAGES

FERRARDO
The dogs are at a fault.   *Cornets like horns*

PIETRO
Would God nothing but the dogs were at it! Let the deer
pursue safely, the dogs follow the game, and do you follow
the dogs. As for me, 'tis unfit one beast should hunt another.
I ha' one chaseth me. An't please you, I would be rid of ye a   5
little.

FERRARDO
Would your grief would as soon leave you as we to quietness.

PIETRO
I thank you.   *Exeunt* FERRARDO *and* PREPASSO
Boy, what dost thou dream of now?

109 *close to* come to terms with
116 *virtual* effective

PAGE

Of a dry summer, my lord, for here's a hot world towards.   10
But, my lord, I had a strange dream last night.

PIETRO

What strange dream?

PAGE

Why, methought I pleased you with singing, and then I
dreamed you gave me that short sword.

PIETRO

Prettily begged. Hold thee, I'll prove thy dream true; take't.   15

PAGE

My duty; but still I dreamed on, my lord, and methought,
and't shall please your excellency, you would needs out of
your royal bounty give me that jewel in your hat.

PIETRO

O, thou didst but dream, boy; do not believe it; dreams
prove not always true. They may hold in a short sword, but   20
not in a jewel. But now, sir, you dreamed you had pleased
me with singing; make that true as I have made the other.

PAGE

Faith, my lord, I did but dream; and dreams, you say,
prove not always true. They may hold in a good sword, but
not in a good song. The truth is, I ha' lost my voice.   25

PIETRO

Lost thy voice, how?

PAGE

With dreaming, faith. But here's a couple of sirenical rascals
shall enchant ye. What shall they sing, my good lord?

PIETRO

Sing of the nature of women, and then the song shall be
surely full of variety, old crotchets and most sweet closes;   30
it shall be humorous, grave, fantastic, amorous, melancholy,
sprightly, one in all, and all in one.

PAGE

All in one?

PIETRO

By'r lady, too many. Sing; my speech grows culpable of
unthrifty idleness; sing.   35

Song

10 *dry summer* to dream of a dry summer is proverbial
27 *sirenical* siren-like, alluring
30 *crotchets* quarter-notes; pun on whimsical fancies
   closes cadences; also bawdy   33 *All in one?* bawdy

Act III, Scene v

Enter MALEVOLE, *with cross-bow and pistol*

PIETRO
Ah, so, so; sing. I am heavy; walk off; I shall talk in my
sleep; walk off.   *Exeunt* PAGES
MALEVOLE
Brief, brief; who? The duke? Good heaven, that fools should
stumble upon greatness! Do not sleep, duke—give ye good
morrow. You must be brief, duke. I am fee'd to murder thee   5
—start not. Mendoza, Mendoza hired me; here's his gold,
his pistol, cross-bow and sword; 'tis all as firm as earth. O
fool, fool, choked with the common maze of easy idiots,
credulity! Make him thine heir? What, thy sworn murderer?
PIETRO
O, can it be?   10
MALEVOLE
Can?
PIETRO
Discovered he not Ferneze?
MALEVOLE
Yes, but why? but why? For love to thee?—Much, much!—
To be revenged upon his rival, who had thrust his jaws awry,
who being slain, supposed by thine own hands, defended by   15
his sword, made thee most loathsome, him most gracious
with thy loose princess; thou, closely yielding egress and
regress to her, madest him heir, whose hot unquiet lust
straight toused thy sheets, and now would seize thy state.
Politician! Wise man! Death, to be led to the stake like a bull   20
by the horns, to make even kindness cut a gentle throat!
Life, why art thou numbed? Thou foggy dullness, speak!
Lives not more faith in a home-thrusting tongue than in
these fencing tip-tap courtiers?

Enter CELSO *with a hermit's gown and beard*

PIETRO
Lord Malevole, if this be true—   25
MALEVOLE
If? Come, shade thee with this disguise. If? Thou shalt

17 *closely* secretly
19 *toused* rumpled
25 *Pietro* ed. (Celso Qq)

handle it; he shall thank thee for killing thyself. Come,
follow my directions, and thou shalt see strange sleights.

PIETRO
World, whither wilt thou?

MALEVOLE
Why, to the devil. Come, the morn grows late;   30
A steady quickness is the soul of state.   *Exeunt*

Act IV, Scene i

Enter MAQUERELLE *knocking at the ladies' door*

MAQUERELLE
Medam, medam, are you stirring medam? If you be stirring,
medam—if I thought I should disturb ye—

[*Enter* PAGE]

PAGE
My lady is up, forsooth.

MAQUERELLE
A pretty boy; faith, how old art thou?

PAGE
I think fourteen.   5

MAQUERELLE
Nay, and ye be in the 'teens—are ye a gentleman born? Do
you know me? My name is Medam Maquerelle; I lie in the
old Cunnycourt—

[PAGE]
See, here the ladies.

Enter BIANCA *and* EMILIA

BIANCA
A fair day to ye, Maquerelle.   10

EMILIA
Is the duchess up yet, sentinel?

MAQUERELLE
O ladies, the most abominable mischance! O dear ladies, the
most piteous disaster! Ferneze was taken last night in the
duchess' chamber. Alas! the duke catched him and killed
him.   15

---

31 *state* statecraft
 8 *Cunnycourt* rabbit-warren (Lat. cuniculus) bawdy

BIANCA
> Was he found in bed?

MAQUERELLE
> O no, but the villainous certainty is, the door was not bolted,
> the tongue-tied hatch held his peace; so the naked truth is,
> he was found in his shirt, whilst I, like an arrant beast, lay
> in the outward chamber, heard nothing; and yet they came   20
> by me in the dark, and yet I felt them not, like a senseless
> creature as I was. O beauties, look to your busk-points—if
> not chastely, yet charily. Be sure the door be bolted. Is your
> lord gone to Florence?

BIANCA
> Yes, Maquerelle.   25

MAQUERELLE
> I hope you'll find the discretion to purchase a fresh gown
> for his return. Now, by my troth, beauties, I would ha' ye
> once wise: he loves you, pish! he is witty, bubble! fair-
> proportioned, mew! nobly born, wind! Let this be still your
> fixed position: esteem me every man according to his good   30
> gifts, and so ye shall ever remain most dear, and most
> worthy to be most dear ladies.

EMILIA
> Is the duke returned from hunting yet?

MAQUERELLE
> They say not yet.

BIANCA
> 'Tis now in midst of day.   35

EMILIA
> How bears the duchess with this blemish now?

MAQUERELLE
> Faith, boldly; strongly defies defame, as one that hath a duke
> to her father. And there's a note to you: be sure of a stout
> friend in a corner, that may always awe your husband. Mark
> the 'haviour of the duchess now: she dares defame, cries   40
> 'Duke, do what thou canst, I'll quit mine honour'; nay, as
> one confirmed in her own virtue against ten thousand
> mouths that mutter her disgrace, she's presently for dances.

18 *hatch* half-door
22 *busk-points* the whalebone busk of stays was fastened to the
    front by lace points
29–32 *Let ... ladies* See the Dedication to Sir Philip Sidney's
    Arcadia (1590); 'most deare, and most worthy to be most deare
    Lady'
41 *quit* requite, clear   43 *presently* immediately

Enter FERRARDO

BIANCA
  For dances?
MAQUERELLE
  Most true.   45
EMILIA
  Most strange. See, here's my servant, young Ferrardo. How
  many servants thinkest thou I have, Maquerelle?
MAQUERELLE
  The more, the merrier: 'twas well said, use your servants as
  you do your smocks, have many, use one, and change often,
  for that's most sweet and courtlike.   50
FERRARDO
  Save ye, fair ladies, is the duke returned?
BIANCA
  Sweet sir, no voice of him as yet in court.
FERRARDO
  'Tis very strange.
BIANCA
  And how like you my servant, Maquerelle?
MAQUERELLE
  I think he could hardly draw Ulysses' bow; but, by my   55
  fidelity, were his nose narrower, his eyes broader, his hands
  thinner, his lips thicker, his legs bigger, his feet lesser, his
  hair blacker, and his teeth whiter, he were a tolerable sweet
  youth, i' faith. And he will come to my chamber, I will read
  him the fortune of his beard.   60

Cornets sound

FERRARDO
  Not yet returned I fear; but the duchess approacheth.

Act IV, Scene ii

Enter MENDOZA *supporting* [AURELIA]: GUERRINO. *The ladies that
are on the stage rise.* FERRARDO *ushers in* AURELIA, *and then takes
a lady to tread a measure*

AURELIA
  We will dance—music!—we will dance.

46 *servant* lover
54–60 *And how . . . beard* they are speaking about the page
s.d. *measure* dance

GUERRINO
'Les quanto', lady, 'Pensez bien', 'Passa regis', or 'Bianca's
brawl'?

AURELIA
We have forgot the brawl.

FERRARDO
So soon? 'Tis wonder.   5

GUERRINO
Why, 'tis but two singles on the left, two on the right, three
doubles forward, a traverse of six round; do this twice; three
singles side, galliard trick of twenty, coranto-pace; a figure
of eight, three singles broken down, come up, meet, two
doubles, fall back, and then honour.   10

AURELIA
O Daedalus, thy maze! I have quite forgot it.

MAQUERELLE
Trust me, so have I, saving the falling back, and then
honour.

                    Enter PREPASSO

AURELIA
Music, music!

PREPASSO
Who saw the duke? The duke?   15

                    Enter EQUATO

AURELIA
Music!

11 *Daedalus* Daedalus constructed the maze, or Cretan labyrinth,
   for Minos
15 *Equato* ed. (*Pre*: Q)

2–3 *'Les quanto'* . . . *brawl*. 'Les quanto' may be 'a courtlie daunce called
   Les Guanto', cited by Bullen from A. Mundy, *Banquet of Daintie
   Conceits* (1588); 'Passa regis' is possibly a 'King's Jig' (Wood); and
   'Bianca's brawl' is probably a provocative jest. The brawl (Fr. *branle*)
   was sometimes danced in a ring, sometimes 'at length'. Guerrino here
   begins a 'branle double'. A galliard was usually in triple time, its steps
   consisting of five movements of the feet ('cinquepace') and a characteristic leap, hence 'trick of twenty' may be an emphatic description of
   the 'sault'; 'coranto-pace' indicates a lively dance (Fr. *courante*);
   'broken down' means 'singly'. Guerrino clearly leads the company
   into a disorganised climax. For an account of a great variety of French
   dances see Jehan Tabouret, anagrammatised into Thoinot Arbeau,
   Orchésographie, 1588–9; for the music hear 'Court Dances of Medieval
   France', from Arbeau's *Orchésographie*, Telemann Society recording,
   Mono TV 4008.

EQUATO
  The duke? Is the duke returned?
AURELIA
  Music!

Enter CELSO

CELSO
  The duke is either invisible, or else is not.
AURELIA
  We are not pleased with your intrusion upon our private   20
  retirement. We are not pleased; you have forgot yourselves.

Enter a PAGE

CELSO
  Boy, thy master? Where's the duke?
PAGE
  Alas, I left him burying the earth with his spread joyless
  limbs. He told me he was heavy, would sleep; bid me walk
  off, for that the strength of fantasy oft made him talk in his   25
  dreams. I straight obeyed, nor ever saw him since; but,
  whereso'er he is, he's sad.
AURELIA
  Music, sound high, as is our heart! Sound high!

Act IV, Scene iii

Enter MALEVOLE, *and* PIETRO *disguised like an hermit*

MALEVOLE
  The duke—peace!—the duke is dead.
AURELIA
  Music!
MALEVOLE
  Is't music?
MENDOZA
  Give proof.
FERRARDO
  How?   5
CELSO
  Where?
PREPASSO
  When?
MALEVOLE
  Rest in peace, as the duke does; quietly sit. For my own part,
  I beheld him but dead, that's all. Marry, here's one can give
  you a more particular account of him.   10

MENDOZA
    Speak, holy father, nor let any brow within this presence
    fright thee from the truth. Speak confidently and freely.

AURELIA
    We attend.

PIETRO
    Now had the mounting sun's all-ripening wings
    Swept the cold sweat of night from earth's dank breast,   15
    When I (whom men call Hermit of the Rock)
    Forsook my cell, and clambered up a cliff,
    Against whose base the heady Neptune dashed
    His high-curled brows; there 'twas I eased my limbs,
    When, lo! my entrails melted with the moan   20
    Someone, who far 'bove me was climbed, did make—
    I shall offend.

MENDOZA
    Not.

AURELIA
    On.

PIETRO
    Methinks I hear him yet—'O female faith!   25
    Go sow the ingrateful sand, and love a woman.
    And do I live to be the scoff of men,
    To be the wittol-cuckold, even to hug
    My poison! Thou knowest, O truth!
    Sooner hard steel will melt with southern wind,   30
    A seaman's whistle calm the ocean,
    A town on fire be extinct with tears,
    Than women, vowed to blushless impudence,
    With sweet behaviour and soft minioning,
    Will turn from that where appetite is fixed.   35
    O powerful blood, how thou dost slave their soul!
    I wash'd an Ethiop, who, for recompense
    Sullied my name. And must I then be forced
    To walk, to live thus black? Must? Must? Fie!
    He that can bear with "must", he cannot die'.   40
    With that he sighed so passionately deep
    That the dull air even groaned. At last, he cries,
    'Sink shame in seas, sink deep enough!', so dies.
    For then I viewed his body fall and souse
    Into the foamy main. O then I saw   45

41 *so* Q1 (too Q, Q2)
44 *souse* plunge heavily

That which methinks I see; it was the duke,
Whom straight the nicer-stomached sea belched up.
But then—

MALEVOLE
Then came I in; but 'las, all was too late,
For even straight he sunk.

PIETRO   Such was the duke's sad fate.   50

CELSO
A better fortune to our Duke Mendoza!

OMNES
Mendoza!

Cornets flourish

MENDOZA
A guard, a guard!

Enter a GUARD

We, full of hearty tears
For our good father's loss—
For so we well may call him   55
Who did beseech your loves for our succession—
Cannot so lightly over-jump his death
As leave his woes revengeless. (*To* AURELIA) Woman of
                                                        shame,
We banish thee for ever to the place
From whence this good man comes; nor permit,   60
On death, unto the body any ornament;
But base as was thy life, depart away.

AURELIA
Ungrateful—

MENDOZA
Away!

AURELIA
Villain, hear me.   65

PREPASSO *and* GUERRINO *lead away* [AURELIA]

MENDOZA
Begone! My lords,
Address to public council; 'tis most fit,
The train of Fortune is borne up by wit.
Away! Our presence shall be sudden; haste.

All depart saving MENDOZA, MALEVOLE *and* PIETRO

MALEVOLE
Now, you egregious devil; ha, ye murdering politician, how   70
dost, duke? How dost look now? Brave duke, i' faith!

67 *address to* prepare for

MENDOZA
How did you kill him?

MALEVOLE
Slatted his brains out, then soused him in the briny sea.

MENDOZA
Brained him and drowned him too?

MALEVOLE
O 'twas best, sure work. For, he that strikes a great man, let   75
him strike home, or else 'ware, he'll prove no man. Shoulder
not a huge fellow, unless you may be sure to lay him in the
kennel.

MENDOZA
A most sound brain-pan! I'll make you both emperors.

MALEVOLE
Make us Christians, make us Christians!   80

MENDOZA
I'll hoist ye, ye shall mount.

MALEVOLE
To the gallows, say ye? Come: *Praemium incertum petit
certum scelus.* How stands the progress?

MENDOZA
Here, take my ring unto the citadel;
Have entrance to Maria, the grave duchess   85
Of banished Altofront. Tell her we love her.
Omit no circumstance to grace our person. Do't.

MALEVOLE
I'll make an excellent pander. Duke, farewell; 'dieu, adieu,
duke.

MENDOZA
Take Maquerelle with thee, for 'tis found   90
None cuts a diamond but a diamond.   *Exit* MALEVOLE
Hermit, thou art a man for me, my confessor;
O thou selected spirit, born for my good,
Sure thou wouldst make an excellent elder
In a deformed church—   95
Come, we must be inward; thou and I all one.

73 *Slatted* knocked
78 *kennel* gutter
82–3 *Praemium . . . scelus* 'He seeks uncertain reward, certain guilt'
    (based on 'praemium incertum petis Certum scelus', Seneca,
    Phoenissae, ll. 632–3)
88–9 *'dieu . . . duke* grotesque Marstonian word-play
95 *deformed church* irregular, i.e. Puritan (Wine)
96 *inward* intimate

PIETRO

I am glad·I was ordained for ye.

MENDOZA

Go to, then; thou must know that Malevole is a strange
villain; dangerous, very dangerous; you see how broad 'a
speaks, a gross-jawed rogue. I would have thee poison him.   100
He's like a corn upon my great toe, I cannot go for him, he
must be cored out; he must. Wilt do't, ha?

PIETRO

Anything, anything.

MENDOZA

Heart of my life! Thus, then. To the citadel;
Thou shalt consort with this Malevole;   105
There being at supper, poison him. It shall be laid
Upon Maria, who yields love or dies.
Scud quick like lightning!

PIETRO

Good deeds crawl, but mischief flies.   *Exit* PIETRO

Enter MALEVOLE

MALEVOLE

Your devilship's ring has no virtue. The buff-captain, the   110
sallow Westphalian gammon-faced zaza cries, 'Stand out!';
must have a stiffer warrant, or no pass into the castle of
comfort.

MENDOZA

Command our sudden letter. Not enter, sha't? What place is
there in Genoa but thou shalt? Into my heart, into my very   115
heart. Come, let's love—we must love, we two, soul and
body.

MALEVOLE

How didst like the hermit? A strange hermit, sirrah.

MENDOZA

A dangerous fellow, very perilous. He must die.

MALEVOLE

Ay, he must die.   120

---

99 *broad* freely
110 *virtue* effect, referring to l. 84
    buff-captain leather-jerkined captain of the citadel
111 *Westphalian gammon-faced* pig-faced ('That Westphalian gamon
    Cloue-stuck face', *Scourge of Villanie*, VII, l. 115: Westphalian
    pigs produced good bacon)
    zaza possibly from 'huszar' (Hung.), military freebooter
114 *sha't?* shalt not?

MENDOZA
Thou'st kill him. We are wise; we must be wise.
MALEVOLE
And provident.
MENDOZA
Yea, provident. Beware an hypocrite;
A churchman once corrupted, O avoid!—
A fellow that makes religion his stalking-horse,   125
Shoots under his belly, he breeds a plague.
Thou shalt poison him.
MALEVOLE
Ho, 'tis wondrous necessary. How?
MENDOZA
You both go jointly to the citadel;
There sup, there poison him. And Maria,   130
Because she is our opposite, shall bear
The sad suspect, on which she dies, or loves us.
MALEVOLE
I run.   *Exit* MALEVOLE
MENDOZA
We that are great, our sole self-good still moves us.
They shall die both, for their deserts crave more   135
Than we can recompense; their presence still
Imbraids our fortunes with beholdingness,
Which we abhor; like deed, not doer. Then conclude,
They live not to cry out ingratitude.
One stick burns t'other, steel cuts steel alone: 140
'Tis good trust few; but O, 'tis best trust none.
                                              Exit MENDOZA

121 *Thou'st* Thou must
126 *Shoots . . . belly* marginal in Q, Q2 (not in Q1)
131 *opposite* opponent
132 *sad suspect* heavy suspicion
137 *Imbraids* upbraids
     beholdingness indebtedness

125–6 *A fellow . . . plague.* Wood suggests that 'Shoots under his belly' is
not a marginal addition but a stage direction, and that Mendoza 'goes
through the motion of shooting under the belly of his horse'. The
actor's direction seems unprofessionally vague; does he shoot under
his own belly or Malevole's? The force of 'shoots' seems required to
bring the mental context of 'breeds a plague' into adequate intelligibility.
I have accommodated the words in the text where Marston seems most
probably to have been intending they should be placed.

Act IV, Scene iv

Enter MALEVOLE *and* PIETRO, *still disguised, at several doors*

MALEVOLE

How do you? How dost, duke?

PIETRO

O, let the last day fall; drop, drop on our cursed heads! Let
heaven unclasp itself, vomit forth flames!

MALEVOLE

O, do not rant, do not turn player—there's more of them
than can well live one by another already. What, art an infidel   5
still?

PIETRO

I am amazed, struck in a swoon with wonder! I am commanded to poison thee.

MALEVOLE

I am commanded to poison thee, at supper.

PIETRO

At supper?   10

MALEVOLE

In the citadel.

PIETRO

In the citadel?

MALEVOLE

Cross-capers! Tricks! Truth o' heaven, he would discharge
us as boys do eldern guns, one pellet to strike out another.
Of what faith art now?   15

PIETRO

All is damnation, wickedness extreme; there is no faith in
man.

MALEVOLE

In none but usurers and brokers, they deceive no man; men
take 'em for bloodsuckers, and so they are. Now God
deliver me from my friends!   20

PIETRO

Thy friends?

MALEVOLE

Yes, from my friends; for from mine enemies I'll deliver
myself. O, cut-throat friendship is the rankest villainy!
Mark this Mendoza, mark him for a villain; but heaven will
send a plague upon him for a rogue.   25

4 *rant* ed. (rand Q2, Q; raue Q1)
14 *eldern guns* popguns of elder wood

PIETRO

O world!

MALEVOLE

World! 'Tis the only region of death, the greatest shop of
the devil, the cruelest prison of men, out of the which none
pass without paying their dearest breath for a fee. There's
nothing perfect in it but extreme, extreme calamity, such as   30
comes yonder.

Act IV, Scene v

Enter AURELIA, *two halberts before, and two after, supported by*
CELSO *and* FERRARDO; AURELIA *in base mourning attire*

AURELIA

To banishment! Led on to banishment!

PIETRO

Lady, the blessedness of repentance to you.

AURELIA

Why? Why? I can desire nothing but death,
Nor deserve anything but hell.
If heaven should give sufficiency of grace   5
To clear my soul, it would make heaven graceless;
My sins would make the stock of mercy poor,
O, they would tire heaven's goodness to reclaim them.
Judgement is just, yet from that vast villain;
But sure, he shall not miss sad punishment   10
'Fore he shall rule. On to my cell of shame!

PIETRO

My cell 'tis, lady; where, instead of masques,
Music, tilts, tourneys, and such courtlike shows,
The hollow murmur of the checkless winds
Shall groan again, whilst the unquiet sea   15
Shakes the whole rock with foamy battery.
There, usherless, the air comes in and out;
The rheumy vault will force your eyes to weep,
Whilst you behold true desolation;

30 *perfect* completed
s.d. *halberts* guards bearing halberds (combination of spear and
        battle-axe)
  8 *tire* Q, Q2 (try Q1)
  9 *yet* even though
 10 *sad* heavy
 17 *usherless* unannounced, without warning

A rocky barrenness shall pierce your eyes,   20
Where all at once one reaches where he stands,
With brows the roof, both walls with both his hands.

AURELIA

It is too good. Blessed spirit of my lord,
O, in what orb so'er thy soul is throned
Behold me worthily most miserable!   25
O, let the anguish of my contrite spirit
Entreat some reconciliation.
If not, O joy, triumph in my just grief!
Death is the end of woes, and tears' relief.

PIETRO

Belike your lord not loved you, was unkind.   30

AURELIA

O heaven!
As the soul loved the body, so loved he;
'Twas death to him to part my presence,
Heaven to see me pleased.
Yet I, like to a wretch given o'er to hell,   35
Brake all the sacred rites of marriage,
To clip a base, ungentle, faithless villain;
O God, a very pagan reprobate!—
What should I say? Ungrateful, throws me out,
For whom I lost soul, body, fame, and honour.   40
But 'tis most fit. Why should a better fate
Attend on any who forsake chaste sheets,
Fly the embrace of a devoted heart,
Joined by a solemn vow 'fore God and man,
To taste the brackish blood of beastly lust   45
In an adulterous touch? O ravenous immodesty,
Insatiate impudence of appetite!
Look, here's your end; for mark what sap in dust,
What sin in good, even so much love in lust.
Joy to thy ghost, sweet lord, pardon to me.   50

CELSO

'Tis the duke's pleasure this night you rest in court.

AURELIA

Soul, lurk in shades; run shame from brightsome skies,
In night the blind man misseth not his eyes.

                    Exit [with CELSO, FERRARDO *and halberts]*

45 *brackish* salty, licentious
46 *immodesty* excess
47 *impudence* shamelessness

MALEVOLE
Do not weep, kind cuckold; take comfort, man; thy betters
have been beccos: Agamemnon, emperor of all the merry   55
Greeks, that tickled all the true Trojans, was a cornuto;
Prince Arthur, that cut off twelve kings' beards, was a
cornuto; Hercules, whose back bore up heaven, and got
forty wenches with child in one night—
PIETRO
Nay, 'twas fifty.   60
MALEVOLE
Faith, forty's enow, a' conscience—yet was a cornuto.
Patience; mischief grows proud; be wise.
PIETRO
Thou pinchest too deep, art too keen upon me.
MALEVOLE
Tut, a pitiful surgeon makes a dangerous sore; I'll tent thee
to the ground. Thinkest I'll sustain myself by flattering thee,   65
because thou art a prince? I had rather follow a drunkard,
and live by licking up his vomit, than by servile flattery.
PIETRO
Yet great men ha' done it.
MALEVOLE
Great slaves fear better than love, born naturally for a coal-
basket, though the common usher of princes' presence,   70
Fortune, hath blindly given them better place. I am vowed
to be thy affliction.
PIETRO
Prithee be; I love much misery, and be thou son to me.
MALEVOLE
Because you are an usurping duke—

Enter BILIOSO

(*To* BILIOSO) Your lordship's well returned from Florence.   75

64 *pitiful* full of pity
   tent clean out a lanced wound to prevent festering
69-70 *born . . . basket* for servile tasks

64-5 *Tut . . . ground.* Cf. *Il pastor fido*, III. v:

> How much I grieue for thee: and if I haue
> Piers't with my wordes thy soule, like a Phisicion I
> Haue done, who searcheth first the wound
> Where it suspected is: be quiet then
> Good Nimph, and do not contradict that which
> Is writ in heau'n aboue of thee. (Sig. L4v.)

BILIOSO
Well returned, I praise my horse.

MALEVOLE
What news from the Florentines?

BILIOSO
I will conceal the great duke's pleasure; only this was his
charge: his pleasure is, that his daughter die; Duke Pietro
be banished, for banishing his blood's dishonour; and that   80
Duke Altofront be re-accepted. This is all; but I hear Duke
Pietro is dead.

MALEVOLE
Ay, and Mendoza is duke; what will you do?

BILIOSO
Is Mendoza strongest?

MALEVOLE
Yet he is.   85

BILIOSO
Then yet I'll hold with him.

MALEVOLE
But if that Altofront should turn straight again?

BILIOSO
Why, then I would turn straight again.
'Tis good run still with him that hath most might;
I had rather stand with wrong, than fall with right.   90

MALEVOLE
What religion will you be of now?

BILIOSO
Of the duke's religion, when I know what it is.

MALEVOLE
O Hercules!

BILIOSO
Hercules? Hercules was the son of Jupiter and Alcmena.

MALEVOLE
Your lordship is a very witt-all.   95

BILIOSO
Wittol?

MALEVOLE
Ay, all-wit.

BILIOSO
Amphitryo was a cuckold.

MALEVOLE
Your lordship sweats; your young lady will get you a cloth

80 *banishing* proclaiming, a pun on 'ban'
98 *Amphitryo* Amphytryon was Alcmena's husband

for your old worship's brows.   *Exit* BILIOSO   100

Here's a fellow to be damned; this is his inviolable maxim,
'Flatter the greatest, and oppress the least'—a whoreson
flesh-fly, that still gnaws upon the lean, galled backs.

PIETRO

Why dost then salute him?

MALEVOLE

Faith, as bawds go to church, for fashion sake. Come, be   105
not confounded; thou art but in danger to lose a dukedom.
Think this:—this earth is the only grave and Golgotha
wherein all things that live must rot; 'tis but the draught
wherein the heavenly bodies discharge their corruption, the
very muckhill on which the sublunary orbs cast their excre-   110
ments. Man is the slime of this dung-pit, and princes are the
governors of these men; for, for our souls, they are as free as
emperors, all of one piece; there goes but a pair of shears
betwixt an emperor and the son of a bagpiper—only the
dyeing, dressing, pressing, glossing makes the difference.   115
Now, what art thou like to lose?
A jailor's office to keep men in bonds,
Whilst toil and treason all life's good confounds.

PIETRO

I here renounce for ever regency.
O Altofront, I wrong thee to supplant thy right,   120
To trip thy heels up with a devilish sleight,
For which I now from throne am thrown; world tricks
                                                     abjure,
For vengeance, though't comes slow, yet it comes sure.
O I am changed; for here, 'fore the dread power,
In true contrition I do dedicate   125
My breath to solitary holiness,
My lips to prayer; and my breast's care shall be
Restoring Altofront to regency.

MALEVOLE

Thy vows are heard, and we accept thy faith.

                                 Undisguiseth himself

                  Enter FERNEZE *and* CELSO

108 *draught* privy
110 *sublunary* lying between the orbit of moon and earth
113–14 *there . . . bagpiper* they are cut out of the same cloth ('There
        went but a pair of shears between them', proverbial phrase)
115 *glossing* finishing
118 *confounds* destroys

Banish amazement. Come, we four must stand full shock of   130
Fortune; be not so wonder-stricken.

PIETRO

Doth Ferneze live?

FERNEZE

For your pardon.

PIETRO

Pardon and love. Give leave to recollect
My thoughts, dispersed in wild astonishment.   135
My vows stand fixed in heaven, and from hence
I crave all love and pardon.

MALEVOLE

Who doubts of providence
That sees this change? A hearty faith to all!
He needs must rise, who can no lower fall,   140
For still impetuous vicissitude
Touseth the world; then let no maze intrude
Upon your spirits. Wonder not I rise,
For who can sink, that close can temporise?
The time grows ripe for action; I'll detect   145
My privat'st plot, lest ignorance fear suspect.
Let's close to counsel, leave the rest to fate;
Mature discretion is the life of state.   *Exeunt*

Act V, Scene i

Enter BILIOSO *and* PASSARELLO

BILIOSO

Fool, how dost thou like my calf in a long stocking?

PASSARELLO

An excellent calf, my lord.

BILIOSO

This calf hath been a reveller this twenty year. When
Monsieur Gundi lay here ambassador, I could have carried
a lady up and down at arm's end in a platter; and I can tell   5
you, there were those at that time who, to try the strength
of a man's back and his arm, would be coistered. I have

140 *who* Q1, Q2 (not in Q)
142 *Touseth* Q, Q2 (Looseth Q1)
      maze amazement
145 *detect* reveal
147 *close* meet
  7 *coistered* curled up (probably nonce word, and bawdy)

measured calves with most of the palace, and they come
nothing near me; besides, I think there be not many armours
in the arsenal will fit me, especially for the headpiece. I'll tell   10
thee—

PASSARELLO
What, my lord?

BILIOSO
I can eat stewed broth as it comes seething off the fire; or a
custard as it comes reeking out of the oven; and I think there
are not many lords can do it. A good pomander—a little   15
decayed in the scent, but six grains of musk ground with
rose-water, and tempered with a little civet, shall fetch her
again presently.

PASSARELLO
O ay, as a bawd with aqua-vitae.

BILIOSO
And, what, dost thou rail upon the ladies as thou wert wont?   20

PASSARELLO
I were better roast a live cat, and might do it with more
safety. I am as secret to thieves as their painting. There's
Maquerelle, oldest bawd, and a perpetual beggar. Did you
never hear of her trick to be known in the city?

BILIOSO
Never.   25

PASSARELLO
Why, she gets all the picture-makers to draw her picture;
when they have done, she most courtly finds fault with them
one after another, and never fetcheth them. They, in revenge
of this, execute her in pictures as they do in Germany, and
hang her in their shops. By this means is she better known   30
to the stinkards than if she had been five times carted.

BILIOSO
'Fore God, an excellent policy.

PASSARELLO
Are there any revels tonight, my lord?

BILIOSO
Yes.

PASSARELLO
Good my lord, give me leave to break a fellow's pate that   35
hath abused me.

15 *pomander* perfume ball, carried or worn
17 *fetch* restore
31 *stinkards* mob
    carted convicted bawds were carted to Bridewell for whipping

BILIOSO
  Whose pate?
PASSARELLO
  Young Ferrardo, my lord.
BILIOSO
  Take heed, he's very valiant; I have known him fight eight
  quarrels in five days, believe it.   40
PASSARELLO
  O, is he so great a quarreller? Why then, he's an arrant
  coward.
BILIOSO
  How prove you that?
PASSARELLO
  Why thus. He that quarrels seeks to fight; and he that seeks
  to fight, seeks to die; and he that seeks to die, seeks never to   45
  fight more; and he that will quarrel and seeks means never
  to answer a man more, I think he's a coward.
BILIOSO
  Thou canst prove anything.
PASSARELLO
  Anything but a rich knave, for I can flatter no man.
BILIOSO
  Well, be not drunk, good fool; I shall see you anon in the   50
  presence.   [Exeunt]

  Enter MALEVOLE *and* MAQUERELLE, *at several doors opposite,*
                              singing

MALEVOLE
  'The Dutchman for a drunkard,'
MAQUERELLE
  'The Dane for golden locks,'
MALEVOLE
  'The Irishman for usquebaugh,'
MAQUERELLE
  'The Frenchman for the (   ).'   55
MALEVOLE
  O, thou art a blessed creature! Had I a modest woman to
  conceal, I would put her to thy custody; for no reasonable
  creature would ever suspect her to be in thy company. Ha,
  thou art a melodious Maquerelle, thou picture of a woman
  and substance of a beast!   60

  54 *usquebaugh* whiskey (or any spirits; 'aqua vitae', Ir. 'uisge
     bheatha')
  55 ( ) obviously 'pox', but not necessarily either said or printed

Enter PASSARELLO

MAQUERELLE

O, fool, will ye be ready anon to go with me to the revels? The hall will be so pestered anon.

PASSARELLO

Ay, as the country is with attorneys.

MALEVOLE

What hast thou there, fool?

PASSARELLO

Wine. I have learned to drink since I went with my lord   65
ambassador; I'll drink to the health of Madam Maquerelle.

MALEVOLE

Why, thou wast wont to rail upon her.

PASSARELLO

Ay, but since I borrowed money of her, I'll drink to her health now, as gentlemen visit brokers, or as knights send venison to the city, either to take up more money, or to pro-   70
cure longer forbearance.

MALEVOLE

Give me the bowl. I drink a health to Altofront, our deposed duke.

PASSARELLO

I'll take it; so. Now I'll begin a health to Madam Maquerelle.

MALEVOLE

Pugh! I will not pledge her.   75

PASSARELLO

Why, I pledged your lord.

MALEVOLE

I care not.

PASSARELLO

Not pledge Madam Maquerelle? Why, then will I spew up your lord again with this fool's finger.

MÁLEVOLE

Hold; I'll take it.   80

MAQUERELLE

Now thou hast drunk my health, fool, I am friends with thee.

PASSARELLO

Art? Art?
     'When Griffon saw the reconciled quean,
       Offering about his neck her arms to cast,

---

62 *pestered* crowded
70 *take up* borrow
71 *forbearance* credit
83 *Griffon* a hero in Ariosto's *Orlando Furioso*

He threw off sword and heart's malignant stream,   85
And lovely her below the loins embrac'd.'
Adieu, Madam Maquerelle.   *Exit* PASSARELLO

MALEVOLE

And how dost thou think o' this transformation of state now?

MAQUERELLE

Verily, very well; for we women always note, the falling of
the one is the rising of the other; some must be fat, some   90
must be lean; some must be fools, and some must be lords;
some must be knaves, and some must be officers; some must
be beggars, some must be knights; some must be cuckolds,
and some must be citizens. As for example, I have two
court dogs, the most fawning curs, the one called Watch,   95
th'other Catch; now I, like Lady Fortune, sometimes love
this dog, sometimes raise that dog, sometimes favour Watch,
most commonly fancy Catch. Now, that dog which I favour,
I feed; and he's so ravenous that what I give he never chaws
it, gulps it down whole, without any relish of what he has,   100
but with a greedy expectation of what he shall have. The
other dog now—

MALEVOLE

No more dog, sweet Maquerelle, no more dog. And what
hope hast thou of the Duchess Maria? Will she stoop to the
duke's lure; will she come, thinkest?   105

MAQUERELLE

Let me see; where's the sign now? Ha' ye e'er a calendar?
Where's the sign, trow you?

MALEVOLE

Sign! Why, is there any moment in that?

MAQUERELLE

O, believe me, a most secret power. Look ye, a Chaldean or
an Assyrian (I am sure 'twas a most sweet Jew) told me,   110
court any woman in the right sign, you shall not miss. But
you must take her in the right vein then; as, when the sign
is in Pisces, a fishmonger's wife is very sociable; in Cancer,
a precisian's wife is very flexible; in Capricorn, a merchant's

---

89–90 *the falling . . . other* Maquerelle, for bawdy purposes, reverses
      the proverbial phrasing 'The rising of one man is the falling of
      another' (Erasmus, *Adagia* II, 1055 C: *Bona nemini hora est, quin
      alcui sit mala*)
104 *stoop* swoop, descend
105 *lure* falconer's device for recalling hawks
      come Q1, Q2 (cowe Q)
106 *sign* astrological sign of the zodiac   114 *precisian's* puritan's

wife hardly holds out; in Libra, a lawyer's wife is very tract-   115
able, especially if her husband be at the term; only in
Scorpio 'tis very dangerous meddling. Has the duke sent any
jewel, any rich stones?

Enter CAPTAIN

MALEVOLE
Ay, I think those are the best signs to take a lady in—
By your favour, signior, I must discourse with the Lady   120
Maria, Altofront's duchess. I must enter for the duke.

CAPTAIN
She here shall give you interview. I received the guardian-
ship of this citadel from the good Altofront, and for his use
I'll keep it, till I am of no use.

MALEVOLE
Wilt thou? O heavens, that a Christian should be found in a   125
buff-jerkin! Captain Conscience, I love thee, Captain. We
attend.   *Exit* CAPTAIN
And what hope hast thou of this duchess' easiness?

MAQUERELLE
'Twill go hard. She was a cold creature ever; she hated
monkeys, fools, jesters, and gentlemen-ushers extremely.   130
She had the vile trick on't, not only to be truly modestly
honourable in her own conscience, but she would avoid the
least wanton carriage that might incur suspect; as God bless
me, she had almost brought bed-pressing out of fashion; I
could scarce get a fine for the lease of a lady's favour once in   135
a fortnight.

MALEVOLE
Now, in the name of immodesty, how many maidenheads
hast thou brought to the block?

MAQUERELLE
Let me see. Heaven forgive us our misdeeds!—Here's the
duchess.   140

Act V, Scene ii

Enter MARIA *and* CAPTAIN

MALEVOLE
God bless thee, lady.

MARIA
Out of thy company.

116 *term* law-court session
133 *carriage* behaviour
135 *fine* fee

MALEVOLE
We have brought thee tender of a husband.

MARIA
I hope I have one already.

MAQUERELLE
Nay, by mine honour, madam, as good ha' ne'er a husband   5
as a banished husband; he's in another world now. I'll tell
ye, lady, I have heard of a sect that maintained, when the
husband was asleep, the wife might lawfully entertain
another man, for then her husband was as dead; much more
when he is banished.   10

MARIA
Unhonest creature!

MAQUERELLE
Pish! Honesty is but an art to seem so. Pray ye, what's
honesty, what's constancy, but fables feigned, odd old fools'
chat, devised by jealous fools to wrong our liberty?

MALEVOLE
Molly, he that loves thee is a duke, Mendoza; he will main-   15
tain thee royally, love thee ardently, defend thee powerfully,
marry thee sumptuously, and keep thee in despite of
Rosicleer or Donzel del Phoebo. There's jewels; if thou wilt,
so; if not, so.

MARIA
Captain, for God's sake, save poor wretchedness   20
From tyranny of lustful insolence!
Enforce me in the deepest dungeon dwell
Rather than here; here round about is hell.
O my dear'st Altofront, where'er thou breathe,
Let my soul sink into the shades beneath,   25
Before I stain thine honour; this thou hast:
And long as I can die, I will live chaste.

MALEVOLE
'Gainst him that can enforce, how vain is strife!

MARIA
She that can be enforced has ne'er a knife.
She that through force her limbs with lust enrolls,   30

3 *tender* offer, on Mendoza's behalf
15 *Molly* (Mully Qq) familiar form of Maria, Mary: 'Molly' was
possibly already a term for a prostitute
18 *Rosicleer Donzel del Phoebo* heroes in *The Mirror of Knighthood*,
Spanish popular romance trans. 1583–1601
20 *sake* Q (loue Q1, Q2)
29 *She . . . knife* Lucrece afterwards stabbed herself

Wants Cleopatra's asps and Portia's coals.
God amend you.   *Exit with* CAPTAIN

MALEVOLE
　　Now, the fear of the devil for ever go with thee! Maquerelle,
　　I tell thee, I have found an honest woman. Faith, I perceive,
　　when all is done, there is of women, as of all other things,   35
　　some good, most bad; some saints, some sinners. For as
　　nowadays no courtier but has his mistress, no captain but
　　has his cockatrice, no cuckold but has his horns, and no fool
　　but has his feather, even so, no woman but has her weakness
　　and feather too, no sex but has his—I can hunt the letter   40
　　no farther. [*Aside*] O God, how loathsome this toying is to
　　me! That a duke should be forced to fool it! Well, *Stultorum
　　plena sunt omnia*; better play the fool lord than be the fool
　　lord.—Now, where's your sleights, Madam Maquerelle?

MAQUERELLE
　　Why, are ye ignorant that 'tis said a squeamish, affected   45
　　niceness is natural to women, and that the excuse of their
　　yielding is only (forsooth) the difficult obtaining? You must
　　put her to't; women are flax, and will fire in a moment.

MALEVOLE
　　Why, was the flax put into thy mouth, and yet thou—Thou
　　set fire? Thou inflame her?   50

MAQUERELLE
　　Marry, but I'll tell ye now, you were too hot.

MALEVOLE
　　The fitter to have inflamed the flaxwoman.

MAQUERELLE
　　You were too boisterous, spleeny; for indeed—

MALEVOLE
　　Go to, thou art a weak pandress; now I see,
　　Sooner earth's fire heaven itself shall waste,   55
　　Than all with heat can melt a mind that's chaste.
　　Go thou, the duke's lime-twig! I'll make the duke turn thee
　　out of thine office. What, not get one touch of hope, and had
　　her at such an advantage!

MAQUERELLE
　　Now, o' my conscience, now I think in my discretion, we   60

31 *Wants . . . coals* Cleopatra died of snake bites; Portia, wife of
　　Brutus, swallowed fire
38 *cockatrice* whore
42-3 *Stultorum . . . omnia* 'All places are full of fools' (Cicero,
　　Epistolae ad Familiares, ix. 22)
57 *lime-twig* twig smeared with bird-lime; snare for Maria

did not take her in the right sign; the blood was not in the
true vein, sure.   *Exit*

Enter BILIOSO

BILIOSO
Make way there! The duke returns for the enthronement.
Malevole—

MALEVOLE
Out, rogue!   65

BILIOSO
Malevole!

MALEVOLE
'Hence, ye gross-jawed peasantly—out, go!'

BILIOSO
Nay, sweet Malevole, since my return I hear you are become
the thing I always prophesied would be, an advanced virtue,
a worthily employed faithfulness, a man o' grace, dear   70
friend. Come; what? *Si quoties peccant homines.*—If as often
as courtiers play the knaves honest men should be angry—
why, look ye, we must collogue sometimes, forswear sometimes.

MALEVOLE
Be damned sometimes.   75

BILIOSO
Right. *Nemo omnibus horis sapit*; no man can be honest at all
hours. Necessity often depraves virtue.

MALEVOLE
I will commend thee to the duke.

BILIOSO
Do; let us be friends, man.

MALEVOLE
And knaves, man.   80

BILIOSO
Right; let us prosper and purchase; our lordships shall live
and our knavery be forgotten.

MALEVOLE
He that by any ways gets riches, his means never shames
him.

67 *'Hence . . . go!'* refers to II. iii, 30
71 *Si . . . homines* 'If as often as men sin' (Ovid, *Tristia* II, 33–4,
'si, quotiens peccant homines, sua fulmina mittat/Iuppiter, exiguo
tempore inermis erit'); Malevole completes the thought in his
own terms   73 *collogue* pretend
76 *Nemo . . . sapit* Pliny, *Naturalis Historia*, Bk. VII, xli. 2
81 *purchase* acquire wealth

BILIOSO
True.   85
MALEVOLE
For impudency and faithlessness are the main stays to
greatness.
BILIOSO
By the Lord, thou art a profound lad.
MALEVOLE
By the Lord, thou art a perfect knave. Out, ye ancient
damnation!   90
BILIOSO
Peace, peace! And thou wilt not be a friend to me as I am a
knave, be not a knave to me as I am thy friend and disclose
me. Peace! Cornets!

Act V, Scene iii

Enter PREPASSO *and* FERRARDO, *two* PAGES *with lights,* CELSO
and EQUATO, MENDOZA *in duke's robes, and* GUERRINO

MENDOZA
On, on; leave us, leave us.
                                   Exeunt all saving MALEVOLE
Stay, where is the hermit?
MALEVOLE
With Duke Pietro, with Duke Pietro.
MENDOZA
Is he dead? Is he poisoned?
MALEVOLE
Dead, as the duke is.   5
MENDOZA
Good, excellent. He will not blab; secureness lives in secrecy.
Come hither, come hither.

1–17 *On . . . man.* After these opening lines Q has a repetitious scene
   entrance:
                        Enter MALEVOLE *and* MENDOZA
 MENDOZA
  Hast been with Maria?
 MALEVOLE
  As your scrivener to your usurer, I have dealt about taking of
  this commodity; but she's cold-frosty.

If, as editors suggest, Marston intended to cancel the first eighteen
lines and recommence the scene with only Malevole and Mendoza, he
may have been prompted by stage economy; but he would soon realise
that Mendoza's decision to kill Maria would not find a place.

MALEVOLE

Thou hast a certain strong villainous scent about thee my
nature cannot endure.

MENDOZA

Scent, man? What returns Maria? What answer to our suit?   10

MALEVOLE

Cold, frosty; she is obstinate.

MENDOZA

Then she's but dead; 'tis resolute, she dies.
Black deed only through black deed safely flies.

MALEVOLE

Pugh! *Per scelera semper sceleribus tutum est iter.*

MENDOZA

What, art a scholar? Art a politician? Sure, thou art an arrant   15
knave.

MALEVOLE

Who, I? I ha' been twice an under-sheriff, man. Well, I will
go rail upon some great man, that I may purchase the
bastinado, or else go marry some rich Genoan lady, and
instantly go travel.   20

MENDOZA

Travel, when thou art married?

MALEVOLE

Ay, 'tis your young lord's fashion to do so, though he was so
lazy, being a bachelor, that he would never travel so far as
the university; yet when he married her, tails off, and Catso!
for England.   25

MENDOZA

And why for England?

MALEVOLE

Because there is no brothel-houses there.

MENDOZA

Nor courtesans?

MALEVOLE

Neither; your whore went down with the stews, and your
punk came up with your puritan.   30

MENDOZA

Canst thou empoison? Canst thou empoison?

---

14 *Per . . . iter* 'The safest way through crimes is always by crimes'
   (Seneca, *Agamemnon* I, 115)
19 *bastinado* beating
24 *tails off* turns tail
30 *punk* whore; a common charge of hypocrisy

MALEVOLE
Excellently; no Jew, 'pothecary, or politician better. Look ye,
here's a box; whom wouldst thou empoison? Here's a box
[*Gives it*] which, opened and the fume taken up in conduits
thorough which the brain purges itself, doth instantly for   35
twelve hours' space bind up all show of life in a deep senseless sleep. Here's another [*Gives it*] which, being opened
under the sleeper's nose, chokes all the power of life, kills
him suddenly.

MENDOZA
I'll try experiments; 'tis good not to be deceived—so, so;   40
Catso!

Seems to poison MALEVOLE

Who would fear that may destroy?
Death hath no teeth or tongue;
And he that's great, to him are slaves
Shame, murder, fame, and wrong—   45
Celso!

Enter CELSO

CELSO
My honoured lord?

MENDOZA
The good Malevole, that plain-tongued man,
Alas, is dead on sudden, wondrous strangely.
He held in our esteem good place. Celso,   50
See him buried, see him buried.

CELSO
I shall observe ye.

MENDOZA
And Celso, prithee let it be thy care tonight
To have some pretty show, to solemnise
Our high instalment; some music, masquery.   55
We'll give fair entertain unto Maria,
The duchess to the banished Altofront.
Thou shalt conduct her from the citadel
Unto the palace; think on some masquery.

CELSO
Of what shape, sweet lord?   60

MENDOZA
What shape? Why, any quick-done fiction—
As some brave spirits of the Genoan dukes

34 *conduits* Q corrected (*comodities* Q uncorrected)
61 *What* ed. (*Why* Qq)

To come out of Elysium, forsooth,
Led in by Mercury, to gratulate
Our happy fortune—some such anything,   65
Some far-fet trick, good for ladies, some stale toy
Or other, no matter so't be of our devising.
Do thou prepar't, 'tis but for a fashion sake;
Fear not, it shall be graced man, it shall take.

CELSO
All service.   70

MENDOZA
All thanks; our hand shall not be close to thee. Farewell.
(*Aside*) Now is my treachery secure, nor can we fall;
Mischief that prospers men do virtue call.
I'll trust no man; he that by tricks gets wreaths,
Keeps them with steel; no man securely breathes   75
Out of deserved ranks; the crowd will mutter, 'fool';
Who cannot bear with spite, he cannot rule.
The chiefest secret for a man of state
Is, to live senseless of a strengthless hate.   *Exit* MENDOZA

MALEVOLE
(*Starts up and speaks*) Death of the damned thief! I'll make   80
one i' the masque; thou shalt ha' some brave spirits of the
antique dukes.

CELSO
My lord, what strange delusion?

MALEVOLE
Most happy, dear Celso; poisoned with an empty box! I'll
give thee all, anon. My lady comes to court; there is a whirl   85
of fate comes tumbling on; the castle's captain stands for me,
the people pray for me, and the great leader of the just
stands for me. Then courage, Celso—
For no disastrous chance can ever move him
That leaveth nothing but a God above him.   [*Exeunt*]   90

Enter PREPASSO *and* BILIOSO, *two* PAGES *before them*;
MAQUERELLE, BIANCA *and* EMILIA

BILIOSO
Make room there, room for the ladies! Why, gentlemen,

---

64 *gratulate* greet
66 *far-fet trick* clever device; also bawdy, 'far fet and dear bought
   is good for ladies'
71 *close* niggardly
74 *wreaths* crowns (Harrison)
79 *senseless* indifferent

will not ye suffer the ladies to be entered in the great
chamber? Why, gallants! And you, sir, to drop your torch
where the beauties must sit too!

PREPASSO

And there's a great fellow plays the knave; why dost not   95
strike him?

BILIOSO

Let him play the knave, o' God's name; think'st thou I have
no more wit than to strike a great fellow? The music! More
lights! Revelling-scaffolds! Do you hear? Let there be oaths
enow ready at the door; swear out the devil himself. Let's   100
leave the ladies, and go see if the lords be ready for them.

All save the ladies depart

MAQUERELLE

And by my troth, beauties, why do you not put you into the
fashion? This is a stale cut, you must come in fashion. Look
ye, you must be all felt, felt and feather, a felt upon your bare
hair. Look ye, these tiring things are justly out of request now.   105
And—do you hear?—you must wear falling-bands, you must
come into the falling fashion; there is such a deal o' pinning
these ruffs, when the fine clean fall is worth all. And again, if you
should chance to take a nap in the afternoon, your falling-
bands requires no poting-stick to recover his form; believe   110
me, no fashion to the falling, I say.

BIANCA

And is not Signior Sir Andrew a gallant fellow now?

MAQUERELLE

By my maidenhead, la, honour and he agree as well together
as a satin suit and woollen stockings.

EMILIA

But is not Marshall Make-room, my servant in reversion, a   115
proper gentleman?

MAQUERELLE

Yes, in reversion, as he had his office; as in truth he hath all
things in reversion. He has his mistress in reversion, his
clothes in reversion, his wit in reversion, and indeed is a

104 *felt* hat
105 *tiring things* head-dresses
106 *falling-bands* collars, falling flat from the neck, and replacing
       ruffs in fashion
110 *poting-stick* poking-stick, for setting pleats
112 *Sir Andrew* ed. St. Andrew Q, Q2 (S. Andrew Iaques Q1; possibly
       a deleted joke on James I's Scottish courtiers)
115 *reversion* succession

suitor to me for my dog in reversion. But, in good verity, la,   120
he is as proper a gentleman in reversion as—and indeed, as
fine a man as may be, having a red beard and a pair of warped
legs.

BIANCA

But, i' faith, I am most monstrously in love with Count
Quidlibet-in-Quodlibet; is he not a pretty, dapper, unidle   125
gallant?

MAQUERELLE

He is even one of the most busy-fingered lords; he will put
the beauties to the squeak most hideously.

[*Enter* BILIOSO]

BILIOSO

Room! Make a lane there! The duke is entering. Stand
handsomely for beauties' sake. Take up the ladies there. So;   130
cornets, cornets!

Act V, Scene iv

Enter PREPASSO, *joins to* BILIOSO; *two* PAGES *and lights,* FERRARDO,
MENDOZA; *at the other door two* PAGES *with lights, and the*
CAPTAIN *leading in* MARIA; *the* DUKE *meets* MARIA *and closeth*
with her. The rest fall back

MENDOZA

Madam, with gentle ear receive my suit;
A kingdom's safety should o'er-peise slight rites,
Marriage is merely nature's policy.
Then, since unless our royal beds be joined,
Danger and civil tumult frights the state,   5
Be wise as you are fair, give way to fate.

MARIA

What wouldst thou, thou affliction to our house?
Thou ever-devil, 'twas thou that banished'st
My truly noble lord.

MENDOZA

I?   10

122–3 *red . . . legs* possibly referring to Jonson's description of
     Marston in *Poetaster*
122 *warped* (warpt Q1, Q2; wrapt Q)
125 *Quidlibet-in-Quodlibet* 'Who you will of What you will' (Cf.
     Justice Quodlibet in *The Dutch Courtesan*)
s.d. *DUKE* i.e. Mendoza
   2 *o'er-peise* outweigh

MARIA

Ay, by thy plots, by thy black stratagems.
Twelve moons have suffered change since I beheld
The lovèd presence of my dearest lord.
O thou far worse than death! He parts but soul
From a weak body; but thou, soul from soul   15
Dissever'st, that which God's own hand did knit.
Thou scant of honour, full of devilish wit!

MENDOZA

We'll check your too-intemperate lavishness; I can and will.

MARIA

What canst?

MENDOZA

Go to; in banishment thy husband dies.   20

MARIA

He ever is at home that's ever wise.

MENDOZA

You'st ne'er meet more; reason should love control.

MARIA

Not meet?
She that dear loves, her love's still in her soul.

MENDOZA

You are but a woman, lady; you must yield.   25

MARIA

O, save me, thou innated bashfulness;
Thou only ornament of woman's modesty!

MENDOZA

Modesty? Death, I'll torment thee!

MARIA

Do; urge all torments; all afflictions try;
I'll die, my lords, as long as I can die.   30

MENDOZA

Thou obstinate, thou shalt die! Captain,
That lady's life is forfeited to justice;
We have examined her, and we do find
She hath empoisonèd the reverend hermit.
Therefore, we command severest custody.   35
Nay, if you'll do's no good,
You'st do's no harm; a tyrant's peace is blood.

MARIA

O thou art merciful! O gracious devil,

22 *You'st* You must
26 *innated* innate
32 *forfeited* Q1, Q2 (fortified Q)

Rather by much let me condemnèd be
For seeming murder than be damned for thee!   40
I'll mourn no more; come, girt my brows with flowers;
Revel and dance, soul, now thy wish thou hast;
Die like a bride, poor heart; thou shalt die chaste.

Enter AURELIA *in mourning habit*

AURELIA
'Life is a frost of cold felicity,
And death the thaw of all our vanity'—   45
Was't not an honest priest that wrote so?
MENDOZA
Who let her in?
BILIOSO
                    Forbear.
PREPASSO
                    Forbear.
AURELIA
Alas, calamity is everywhere;
Sad misery, despite your double doors,
Will enter even in court.   50
BILIOSO
Peace!
AURELIA
I ha' done. One word—take heed! I ha' done.

Enter MERCURY *with loud music*

MERCURY
Cyllenian Mercury, the god of ghosts,
From gloomy shades that spread the lower coasts,
Calls four high-famed Genoan dukes to come   55
And make this presence their Elysium;
To pass away this high triumphal night
With song and dances, court's more soft delight.
AURELIA
Are you god of ghosts? I have a suit depending in hell
betwixt me and my conscience; I would fain have thee help   60
me to an advocate.

44–5 '*Life . . . vanity*' Thomas Bastard, *Chrestoleros*, iv, 32 (1598);
    Bastard was vicar of Bere Regis
53 *Cyllenian Mercury* Mercury's birthplace was Mount Cyllene
54 *coasts* regions
59 *depending* pending

BILIOSO
Mercury shall be your lawyer, lady.

AURELIA
Nay faith, Mercury has too good a face to be a right lawyer.

PREPASSO
Peace, forbear! Mercury presents the masque.

*Cornets: the song to the cornets; which playing, the masque
enters:* MALEVOLE, PIETRO, FERNEZE, *and* CELSO *in white robes,
with dukes' crowns upon laurel-wreaths, pistolets and short
swords under their robes*

MENDOZA
Celso, Celso, court Maria for our love. Lady, be gracious, yet   65
grace—

MARIA
With me, sir?

MALEVOLE *takes his wife to dance*

MALEVOLE   Yes, more loved than our breath,
With you I'll dance.

MARIA   Why, then you dance with death.
But come sir, I was ne'er more apt to mirth.
Death gives eternity a glorious breath;   70
O, to die honoured, who would fear to die!

MALEVOLE
They die in fear who live in villainy.

MENDOZA
Yes, believe him, lady, and be ruled by him.

PIETRO
Madam, with me?

PIETRO *takes his wife* AURELIA *to dance*

AURELIA
                    Wouldst then be miserable?

PIETRO
I need not wish.   75

AURELIA
O, yet forbear my hand; away, fly, fly!
O seek not her that only seeks to die!

PIETRO
Poor loved soul!

62 *Mercury . . . lady* Mercury is patron of lawyers
65 *Celso* Mendoza mistakes the disguised Malevole
   court Q1, Q2 (count Q)

AURELIA
                  What, wouldst court misery?
PIETRO
    Yes.
AURELIA
            She'll come too soon. O my grieved heart!
PIETRO
    Lady, ha' done, ha' done.   80
    Come, let's dance; be once from sorrow free.
AURELIA
    Art a sad man?
PIETRO   Yes, sweet.
AURELIA   Then we'll agree.

    FERNEZE *takes* MAQUERELLE; *and* CELSO, BIANCA: *then the
        cornets sound the measure; one change and rest*

FERNEZE
    (*To* BIANCA) Believe it, lady; shall I swear?
    Let me enjoy you in private and I'll marry you, by my soul.
BIANCA
    I had rather you would swear by your body; I think that   85
    would prove the more regarded oath with you.
FERNEZE
    I'll swear by them both to please you.
BIANCA
    O, damn them not both to please me, for God's sake.
FERNEZE
    Faith, sweet creature, let me enjoy you tonight, and I'll
    marry you tomorrow-fortnight, by my troth, la.   90
MAQUERELLE
    On his troth, la! Believe him not; that kind of cony-
    catching is as stale as Sir Oliver Anchovy's perfumed jerkin.
    Promise of matrimony by a young gallant to bring a virgin
    lady into a fool's paradise, make her a great woman, and then
    cast her off—'tis as common, as natural to a courtier, as   95
    jealousy to a citizen, gluttony to a puritan, wisdom to an
    alderman, pride to a tailor, or an empty handbasket to one
    of those sixpenny damnations. Of his troth, la! Believe him
    not; traps to catch polecats!

91–2 *cony-catching* deceiving (card-sharping term)
92 *perfumed* jerkins were sometimes rubbed with oil
98 *sixpenny damnations* cheap whores
99 *polecats* whores

MALEVOLE
   (*To* MARIA) Keep your face constant; let no sudden passion   100
   Speak in your eyes.
MARIA
   O my Altofront!
PIETRO
                    [*To* AURELIA] A tyrant's jealousies
 . Are very nimble; you receive it all.
AURELIA
   My heart, though not my knees, doth humbly fall
   Low as the earth to thee.   105
PIETRO
   Peace. Next change. [*To* MARIA] No words.
MARIA
   Speech to such? Ay, O what will affords!

      Cornets sound the measure over again: which danced,
                         they unmask

MENDOZA
   Malevole!

      They environ MENDOZA, *bending their pistols on him*

MALEVOLE
   No.
MENDOZA
   Altofront! Duke Pietro! Ferneze! Ha!   110
ALL
   Duke Altofront! Duke Altofront!

                    Cornets, a flourish

MENDOZA
   Are we surpris'd? What strange delusions mock
   Our senses? Do I dream? Or have I dreamt
   This two days' space? Where am I?

                    They seize upon MENDOZA

MALEVOLE
   Where an arch-villain is.   115
MENDOZA
   O lend me breath till I am fit to die;
   For peace with heaven, for your own souls' sake,
   Vouchsafe me life.

103 *receive* suffer, and understand
116 *breath till* Q, Q2 (breath to liue till Q1)

PIETRO

Ignoble villain, whom neither heaven nor hell,
Goodness of God or man, could once make good.   120

MALEVOLE

Base, treacherous wretch, what grace canst thou expect,
That hast grown impudent in gracelessness?

MENDOZA

O life!

MALEVOLE

Slave, take thy life.
Wert thou defenced, through blood and wounds,   125
The sternest horror of a civil fight;
Would I achieve thee; but prostrate at my feet,
I scorn to hurt thee. 'Tis the heart of slaves
That deigns to triumph over peasants' graves;
For such thou art, since birth doth ne'er enroll   130
A man 'mong monarchs, but a glorious soul.
O, I have seen strange accidents of state!—
The flatterer like the ivy clip the oak,
And waste it to the heart; lust so confirmed
That the black act of sin itself not shamed   135
To be termed courtship.
O they that are as great as be their sins,
Let them remember that th'inconstant people
Love many princes merely for their faces
And outward shows; and they do covet more   140
To have a sight of these than of their virtues.
Yet thus much let the great ones still conceive,
When they observe not heaven's imposed conditions,
They are no kings, but forfeit their commissions.

MAQUERELLE

O good my lord, I have lived in the court this twenty year;   145
they that have been old courtiers and come to live in the
city, they are spited at and thrust to the wall like apricocks,
good my lord.

BILIOSO

My lord, I did know your lordship in this disguise; you
heard me ever say if Altofront did return I would stand for   150

127 *achieve* make an end of
139 *princes* Wine (princes Q uncorrected; men Q corrected)
142 *conceive* ed. (conceale Q)
144 *kings* Wine (kings Q uncorrected; men Q corrected)

133–4 *The flatterer . . . heart.* A commonplace from Plutarch.

him; besides, 'twas your lordship's pleasure to call me wittol
and cuckold; you must not think, but that I knew you, I
would have put it up so patiently.

MALEVOLE

(*To* PIETRO *and* AURELIA) You o'er-joyed spirits, wipe your
        long wet eyes;
Hence with this man (*Kicks out* MENDOZA); an eagle takes not
          flies. 155
(*To* PIETRO *and* AURELIA) You to your vows; and thou unto
       the suburbs. (*To* MAQUERELLE)
(*To* BILIOSO) You to my worst friend I would hardly give;
Thou art a perfect old knave. (*To* CELSO *and the* CAPTAIN)
         All-pleased, live
You two unto my breast; (*To* MARIA) thou to my heart.
The rest of idle actors idly part.   160
And as for me, I here assume my right,
To which I hope all's pleased: to all, goodnight.

     Cornets, a flourish.

           Exeunt omnes

    F I N I S

Epilogus

Your modest silence, full of heedy stillness,
Makes me thus speak: a voluntary illness
Is merely senseless; but unwilling error,
Such as proceeds from too rash youthful fervour,
May well be called a fault, but not a sin;   5
Rivers take names from founts where they begin.
Then let not too severe an eye peruse
The slighter brakes of our reformed Muse,
Who could herself her self of faults detect,
But that she knows 'tis easy to correct,   10

153 *put it up* put up with it
154 *o'er-joyed* Q, Q2 (are ioyd Q1)
155 *an . . . flies* (Erasmus, *Adagia* II, 761 E, *Aquila non captat muscas*:
  Pettie-Young, *Civile Conversation*, I 200, 'the Eagle catcheth
  not flies')
156 *suburbs* brothels were situated in the suburbs
160 *The . . . part.* Q, Q2 (not in Q1)
 2 *illness* fault
 3 *merely* wholly
 8 *brakes* errors

Though some men's labour; troth, to err is fit,
As long as wisdom's not professed, but wit.
Then till another's happier Muse appears,
Till his Thalia feast your learned ears
To whose desertful lamps pleased Fates impart   15
Art above Nature, Judgment above Art,
   Receive this piece, which hope nor fear yet daunteth;
   He that knows most, knows most how much he wanteth.

FINIS

14 *Thalia* the Muse of Comedy

A Trick to Catch the Old One

———— ⌇⌇⌇⌇⌇⌇⌇/◎/⌇⌇⌇⌇⌇⌇ ————

THOMAS MIDDLETON

Edited by
G. J. WATSON

ABBREVIATIONS

1. Texts of *A Trick*:

Q1 = The first edition, 1608.
Q2 = The second edition, 1616.
Dyce = A. Dyce, ed., *The Works of Thomas Middleton*, 5 vols., ii, 1840.
Bullen = A. H. Bullen, ed., *The Works of Thomas Middleton*, 8 vols., ii, 1885.
Ellis = H. Ellis, ed., *Thomas Middleton*, The Mermaid Series, 2 vols., i, 1887.
Sampson = M. W. Sampson, ed., *Thomas Middleton*, New York, 1915.
Spencer = H. Spencer, ed., *Elizabethan Plays*, Boston, 1933.
Baskervill = C. R. Baskervill *et al.*, edd., *Elizabethan and Stuart Plays*, New York, 1934.

2. Other works:

Bowers = F. Bowers, ed., *The Dramatic Works of Thomas Dekker*, 4 vols., 1953–61.
Chambers = E. K. Chambers, *The Elizabethan Stage*, 4 vols., 1923.
Greg = W. W. Greg, *A Bibliography of the English Printed Drama to the Restoration*, 4 vols., 1939–59.
Grosart = A. B. Grosart, ed., *The Life and Complete Works in Prose and Verse of Robert Greene*, 15 vols., 1881–6.
Herford and Simpson = C. H. Herford and P. and E. Simpson, edd., *Ben Jonson*, 11 vols., 1925–52.

A
Tricke to Catch the
Old-one.

As it hath beene often in Action, both
at Paules, and the Black-
Fryers.

*Prefented before his Maieftie on
New-yeares night laft.*

Compofde by T.M.

AT LONDON
Printed by G: E. and are to be fold by *Henry Rockytt*,
at the long ſhop in the Poultrie vnder
the Dyall. 1608.

[DRAMATIS PERSONAE

THEODORUS WITGOOD
PECUNIUS LUCRE, *his uncle*
WALKADINE HOARD
ONESIPHORUS HOARD, *his brother*
LIMBER ⎫
KIX   ⎪
LAMPREY ⎬ *friends to* HOARD
SPITCHCOCK ⎭
HARRY DAMPIT ⎫ *usurers*
GULF   ⎭
SAM FREEDOM, *son to* LUCRE'S WIFE
MONEYLOVE
HOST
SIR LANCELOT

GEORGE, *servant to* LUCRE
ARTHUR, *servant to* HOARD

CREDITORS, GENTLEMEN, DRAWER,
  VINTNER,   BOY,   SCRIVENER,
  SERVANTS, SERGEANTS, *etc.*

COURTESAN
WIFE *to* LUCRE
NIECE *to* HOARD
LADY FOXSTONE
AUDREY, *servant to* DAMPIT

Scene: *A Leicestershire town* (I. i and I. ii),
then London]

590

[Act I, Scene i]

Enter WITGOOD, *a Gentleman, solus*

WITGOOD

All's gone! still thou'rt a gentleman, that's all; but a poor
one, that's nothing. What milk brings thy meadows forth
now? Where are thy goodly uplands and thy downlands? All
sunk into that little pit, lechery. Why should a gallant pay
but two shillings for his ordinary that nourishes him, and   5
twenty times two for his brothel that consumes him?
But where's Long-acre? in my uncle's conscience, which is
three years' voyage about; he that sets out upon his
conscience never finds the way home again—he is either
swallowed in the quicksands of law-quillets, or splits upon   10
the piles of a *praemunire*; yet these old fox-brained and
ox-browed uncles have still defences for their avarice, and
apologies for their practices, and will thus greet our follies:

He that doth his youth expose
To brothel, drink, and danger,   15
Let him that is his nearest kin
Cheat him before a stranger.

And that's his uncle, 'tis a principle in usury. I dare not visit
the city: there I should be too soon visited by that horrible
plague, my debts, and by that means I lose a virgin's love,   20

5 *ordinary* meal in an eating-house or tavern
7 *Long-acre* term applied generally to any estate
7 *conscience* regard for the dictates of conscience
10 *law-quillets* legal subtleties or quibbles
11 *praemunire* a sheriff's writ
12 *ox-browed* cuckolded (or stupid—cf. V. ii, 193)
12 *still* always

4 *little . . . lechery.* Cf. Coverdale's Bible (1535), *Prov.* xxii. 14, 'The
   mouth of an harlot is a depe pytt.'
4–6 *Why . . . him?* Cf. Dekker and Webster's *Westward Ho!*, 1604:
   'Your Farmers that would spend but three pence on his [*sic*] ordinarie,
   would lauish halfe a Crowne on his Leachery' (Bowers, ii, III. iii,
   15–16). Witgood's expensive ordinary would be in keeping with his
   status as a gallant.
7–11 Lucre's lack of compunction is compared to the ocean in its bound-
   lessness; to be dependent on his finer feelings is like making a long and
   dangerous voyage which must end in shipwreck. See III. i, 183, where
   the same metaphor is used.

591

her portion and her virtues. Well, how should a man live now,
that has no living; hum? Why, are there not a million of men
in the world, that only sojourn upon their brain, and make
their wits their mercers; and am I but one amongst that
million and cannot thrive upon't? Any trick, out of the   25
compass of law, now would come happily to me.

Enter COURTESAN

COURTESAN
My love.
WITGOOD
My loathing! hast thou been the secret consumption of my
purse? and now com'st to undo my last means, my wits? wilt
leave no virtue in me, and yet thou never the better?   30
Hence, courtesan, round-webbed tarantula,
That dryest the roses in the cheeks of youth!
COURTESAN
I have been true unto your pleasure, and all your lands
thrice racked, was never worth the jewel which I prodigally
gave you, my virginity;   35
Lands mortgaged may return and more esteemed,
But honesty, once pawned, is ne'er redeemed.
WITGOOD
Forgive: I do thee wrong
To make thee sin and then to chide thee for't.
COURTESAN
I know I am your loathing now: farewell.   40
WITGOOD
Stay, best invention, stay.
COURTESAN
I that have been the secret consumption of your purse, shall I
stay now to undo your last means, your wits? Hence
courtesan, away!

23–4 *make . . . mercers* rely on their wits to keep up appearances
25–6 *out . . . law* not punishable by law
31 ed. prose in Qq
31 *round-webbed* 'referring to the hooped farthingale?' (Sampson)
34 *racked* rented at excessively high rates
37 *honesty* chastity
41 *invention* device (referring to her as the instrument for his scheme)

31 *tarantula*. The spider traditionally 'turns all into Excrement and
Venom' (Swift, *The Battle of the Books*). Cf. Donne's 'The spider love,
which transubstantiates all' ('Twicknam Garden'), and IV. v, 26.

WITGOOD

    I prithee, make me not mad at my own weapon, stay (a thing   45
few women can do, I know that, and therefore they had need
wear stays); be not contrary. Dost love me? Fate has so cast
it that all my means I must derive from thee.

COURTESAN

    From me! Be happy then;
What lies within the power of my performance   50
Shall be commanded of thee.

WITGOOD   Spoke like
An honest drab i'faith; it may prove something.
What trick is not an embryon at first,
Until a perfect shape come over it?

COURTESAN

    Come, I must help you, whereabouts left you?   55
I'll proceed.
Though you beget, 'tis I must help to breed.
Speak, what is't? I'd fain conceive it.

WITGOOD

    So, so, so; thou shall presently take the name and form upon
thee of a rich country widow, four hundred a year valiant, in   60
woods, in bullocks, in barns and in rye-stacks; we'll to
London, and to my covetous uncle.

COURTESAN

    I begin to applaud thee; our states being both desperate,
they're soon resolute. But how for horses?

WITGOOD

    Mass, that's true; the jest will be of some continuance. Let   65
me see; horses now, a bots on 'em! Stay, I have acquaintance
with a mad host, never yet bawd to thee; I have rinsed the
whoreson's gums in mull-sack many a time and often; put

45 *a thing* i.e., to be staid or steadfast
47–8 *Fate . . . thee* run on ed. as new par. Qq
47 *cast* planned
51–4 ed. prose in Qq
60 *valiant* worth
64 *resolute* decided
66 *bots* a common disease of worms, affecting the gums of horses
67 *mad* merry
68 *mull-sack* sack heated, sweetened and spiced

---

64 *they're.* Q1 they'are. The only instance in this play of the 'Jonsonian'
    apostrophe to indicate elision, which other modern editors overlook.
67 *bawd.* As Spencer notes, innkeepers were apt to be procurers. See
    I. ii, 17–18.

but a good tale into his ear now, so it come off cleanly, and
there's horse and man for us, I dare warrant thee.   70

COURTESAN

Arm your wits then
Speedily; there shall want nothing in me,
Either in behaviour, discourse or fashion,
That shall discredit your intended purpose.
I will so artfully disguise my wants,   75
And set so good a courage on my state,
That I will be believed.

WITGOOD

Why, then, all's furnished; I shall go nigh to catch that old
fox, mine uncle. Though he make but some amends for my
undoing, yet there's some comfort in't—he cannot otherwise   80
choose (though it be but in hope to cozen me again) but
supply any hasty want that I bring to town with me. The
device well and cunningly carried, the name of a rich widow,
and four hundred a year in good earth, will so conjure up a
kind of usurer's love in him to me, that he will not only desire   85
my presence—which at first shall scarce be granted him,
I'll keep off a' purpose—but I shall find him so officious to
deserve, so ready to supply! I know the state of an old man's
affection so well; if his nephew be poor indeed, why, he lets
God alone with him; but if he be once rich, then he'll be the   90
first man that helps him.

COURTESAN

'Tis right the world; for in these days an old man's love to
his kindred is like his kindness to his wife, 'tis always done
before he comes at it.

WITGOOD

I owe thee for that jest. Begone, here's all my wealth;   95
prepare thyself, away! I'll to mine host with all possible
haste, and with the best art, and most profitable form, pour

69 *cleanly* cleverly, adroitly
71–4 ed. prose in Qq
76 *set . . . state* assume such confidence (or boldness) in the value of
   my estate
79–80 *for my undoing* for ruining me
81 *cozen* cheat
87–8 *officious to deserve* eager to become entitled to reward
89–90 *lets . . . him* leaves it to God to look after him
92 *right . . . world* precisely the way of the world
93 *kindness* love (here in a specifically sexual sense)
95 *owe* am indebted to

the sweet circumstance into his ear, which shall have the gift
to turn all the wax to honey.   [*Exit* COURTESAN]
How now? oh, the right worshipful seniors of our country!   100

[*Enter* ONESIPHORUS HOARD, LIMBER, *and* KIX]

ONESIPHORUS
Who's that?
LIMBER
Oh, the common rioter, take no note of him.
WITGOOD
[*Aside*] You will not see me now; the comfort is,
Ere it be long you will scarce see yourselves.   [*Exit*]
ONESIPHORUS
I wonder how he breathes; h'as consumed all   105
Upon that courtesan!
LIMBER   We have heard so much.
ONESIPHORUS
You have heard all truth. His uncle and my brother
Have been these three years mortal adversaries.
Two old tough spirits, they seldom meet but fight,
Or quarrel when 'tis calmest;   110
I think their anger be the very fire
That keeps their age alive.
LIMBER
What was the quarrel, sir?

98 *gift* power
100 *now* ed. no Qq
102 *common rioter* notorious profligate
103–10 ed. prose in Qq

100ff. *Onesiphorus, Limber, Kix.* Proper names can be substituted for the
    numerals of Qq's speech headings on the evidence of the following
    lines and of V. ii, 46ff. Onesiphorus, a Puritan name actually in use,
    means 'profit-bearing', with an obvious irony; Kix is a dried up stalk,
    and Limber's name refers ironically to his age. For a full discussion of
    Middleton's nomenclature, see W. Power, 'Middleton's Way with
    Names', *NQ*, New Series VII (1960), 26–29 and ff.
106 *that courtesan.* This easy, familiar reference is of some importance to our
    appreciation of the dénouement. F. S. Boas, *An Introduction to Stuart
    Drama*, 1946, p. 223 writes: 'the disclosure of the widow's real identity
    in the short final act is too forced and abrupt as it comes from . . .
    Onesiphorus . . . Limber and Kix . . . who have merely caught sight
    of the courtesan for a moment in the opening scene'. But, as Middleton
    deftly indicates here, she was evidently a figure of some notoriety in
    the town: the recognition and horror in V. ii is very adequately pre-
    pared for.

ONESIPHORUS

Faith, about a purchase, fetching over a young heir; Master
Hoard, my brother, having wasted much time in beating   115
the bargain, what did me old Lucre, but as his conscience
moved him, knowing the poor gentleman, stepped in
between 'em and cozened him himself.

LIMBER

And was this all, sir?

ONESIPHORUS

This was e'en it, sir; yet for all this I know no reason but the   120
match might go forward betwixt his wife's son and my niece;
what though there be a dissension between the two old men,
I see no reason it should put a difference between the two
younger; 'tis as natural for old folks to fall out, as for young
to fall in! A scholar comes a-wooing to my niece: well, he's   125
wise, but he's poor; her son comes a-wooing to my niece: well,
he's a fool, but he's rich—

LIMBER

Ay, marry, sir?

ONESIPHORUS

Pray, now, is not a rich fool better than a poor philosopher?

LIMBER

One would think so, i'faith!   130

ONESIPHORUS

She now remains at London with my brother, her second
uncle, to learn fashions, practise music; the voice between
her lips, and the viol between her legs; she'll be fit for a
consort very speedily. A thousand good pound is her
portion; if she marry, we'll ride up and be merry.   135

KIX

A match, if it be a match!   *Exeunt*

114 *purchase* profit (from a shady deal)
114 *fetching over* cheating
115–16 *beating . . . bargain* haggling
125 *fall in* make up after a quarrel
125 *A scholar* Moneylove (see I. iii)
134 *consort* pun on (i) concert (ii) husband
136 *A match* agreed

---

114 *purchase.* The word was closely associated with the world of coney-
catching. Robert Greene, in *A Notable Discovery of Cozenage*, 1591,
glosses some of the sharpers' most common expressions: 'The partie
that taketh vp the Connie, the Setter . . . The monie that is won,
Purchase' (Grosart, x, 38). The fetching over of a young heir—or any
rich young fool—is the most common motif of coney-catching literature.

[Act I, Scene ii]

Enter at one door, WITGOOD, *at the other*, HOST

WITGOOD
Mine host!

HOST
Young Master Witgood.

WITGOOD
I have been laying all the town for thee.

HOST
Why, what's the news, bully Hadland?

WITGOOD
What geldings are in the house, of thine own? Answer me to   5
that first.

HOST
Why, man, why?

WITGOOD
Mark me what I say: I'll tell thee such a tale in thine ear,
that thou shalt trust me spite of thy teeth, furnish me with
some money, willy-nilly, and ride up with me thyself *contra*   10
voluntatem et professionem.

HOST
How? Let me see this trick, and I'll say thou hast more art
than a conjuror.

WITGOOD
Dost thou joy in my advancement?

HOST
Do I love sack and ginger?   15

WITGOOD
Comes my prosperity desiredly to thee?

HOST
Come forfeitures to a usurer, fees to an officer, punks to an
host, and pigs to a parson desiredly? why, then, la.

3 *laying* searching   4 *bully* a familiar term of address
4 *Hadland* a humorous title for one who formerly owned land and
has lost it. Cf. 'Lackland'
9 *spite . . . teeth* despite yourself
10–11 *contra . . . professionem* against your will and profession
12 *How* What? (exclamation of surprise)
17 *punks* prostitutes. Cf. I. i, 67
18 *pigs . . . parson* proverbial reference to the time when the parson
collected his tithe in kind
18 *la* exclamation, meaningless in itself, usually accompanying an
emphatic statement

WITGOOD
> Will the report of a widow of four hundred a year, boy, make
> thee leap, and sing, and dance, and come to thy place again?   20

HOST
> Wilt thou command me now? I am thy spirit; conjure me
> into any shape.

WITGOOD
> I ha' brought her from her friends, turned back the horses
> by a sleight; not so much as one amongst her six men, goodly
> large yeomanly fellows, will she trust with this her purpose: 25
> by this light, all unmanned, regardless of her state, neglectful
> of vainglorious ceremony, all for my love; oh, 'tis a fine little
> voluble tongue, mine host, that wins a widow.

HOST
> No, 'tis a tongue with a great T, my boy, that wins a widow.

WITGOOD
> Now sir, the case stands thus: good mine host, if thou lov'st   30
> my happiness, assist me.

HOST
> Command all my beasts i'th' house.

WITGOOD
> Nay, that's not all neither; prithee take truce with thy joy,
> and listen to me. Thou know'st I have a wealthy uncle i'th'
> city, somewhat the wealthier by my follies; the report of this   35
> fortune, well and cunningly carried, might be a means to
> draw some goodness from the usuring rascal; for I have put
> her in hope already of some estate that I have either in land
> or money: now, if I be found true in neither, what may I
> expect but a sudden breach of our love, utter dissolution of   40
> the match, and confusion of my fortunes for ever?

HOST
> Wilt thou but trust the managing of thy business with me?

WITGOOD
> With thee? Why, will I desire to thrive in my purpose? Will I
> hug four hundred a year, I that know the misery of nothing?
> Will that man wish a rich widow, that has never a hole to   45
> put his head in? With thee, mine host? Why, believe it, sooner
> with thee than with a covey of counsellors!

HOST
> Thank you for your good report, i'faith, sir, and if I stand
> you not in stead, why then let an host come off *hic et haec*

29 *great* capital
49–50 *hic . . . hostis* 'a pun on the meaning *host* and *enemy* is intended'
    (Baskervill), though the phrase does not have any literal import

hostis, a deadly enemy to dice, drink, and venery. Come,   50
where's this widow?

WITGOOD

Hard at Park End.

HOST

I'll be her serving-man for once.

WITGOOD

Why, there we let off together, keep full time; my thoughts
were striking then just the same number.   55

HOST

I knew't; shall we then see our merry days again?

WITGOOD

Our merry nights—which never shall be more seen.   *Exeunt*

[Act I, Scene iii]

Enter at several doors, old LUCRE, *and old* HOARD,
Gentlemen [i.e. LAMPREY, SPITCHCOCK, SAM FREEDOM
and MONEYLOVE] *coming between them, to pacify 'em*

LAMPREY

Nay, good Master Lucre, and you, Master Hoard, anger is
the wind which you're both too much troubled withal.

HOARD

Shall my adversary thus daily affront me, ripping up the
old wound of our malice, which three summers could not
close up? into which wound the very sight of him drops   5
scalding lead instead of balsamum.

LUCRE

Why, Hoard, Hoard, Hoard, Hoard, Hoard; may I not pass
in the state of quietness to mine own house? Answer me to
that, before witness, and why? I'll refer the cause to honest,
even-minded gentlemen, or require the mere indifferences   10
of the law to decide this matter. I got the purchase, true;
was't not any man's case? Yes. Will a wise man stand as a

50 *venery* lechery
52 *Hard* near-by
52 *Park End* probably no particular locality is intended
s.d. *several* different
10 *indifferences* impartiality. The plural form is historically correct
12–13 *as . . . bawd* as a third party

s.d. *Lamprey, Spitchcock.* A lamprey was an eel-like fish, and a spitchcock a
fried eel (see V. ii, 20–22).

bawd, whilst another wipes his nose of the bargain? No, I
answer no in that case.

LAMPREY
Nay, sweet Master Lucre.   15

HOARD
Was it the part of a friend? no, rather of a Jew—mark what I
say—when I had beaten the bush to the last bird, or, as I may
term it, the price to a pound, then like a cunning usurer to
come in the evening of the bargain, and glean all my hopes
in a minute? to enter, as it were, at the back door of the   20
purchase? for thou never cam'st the right way by it.

LUCRE
Hast thou the conscience to tell me so, without any impeach-
ment to thyself?

HOARD
Thou that canst defeat thy own nephew, Lucre, lap his lands
into bonds, and take the extremity of thy kindred's forfei-   25
tures, because he's a rioter, a wastethrift, a brothel-master,
and so forth—what may a stranger expect from thee, but
vulnera dilacerata, as the poet says, dilacerate dealing?

LUCRE
Upbraid'st thou me with nephew? Is all imputation laid upon
me? What acquaintance have I with his follies? If he riot,   30
'tis he must want it; if he surfeit, 'tis he must feel it; if he
drab it, 'tis he must lie by't; what's this to me?

HOARD
What's all to thee? Nothing, nothing; such is the gulf of thy

13 *wipes his nose* cheats him
16 *Jew* the type of heartlessness on the Elizabethan stage
19 *evening . . . bargain* at the eleventh hour in the chaffering
24 *defeat* dispossess
26 *wastethrift, brothel-master* according to the *OED*, first used by
   Middleton   32 *drab* whore
33 *gulf* instability (literally, voracious belly, a conventional attribute
   of the usurer)

---

17 *beaten . . . bird.* 'One beats the bush and another catches the bird' is
   proverbial, but it is possible that Middleton was here thinking of
   Greene's *Black Book's Messenger*, 1592, where a catalogue of the terms
   of city roguery runs: 'He that drawes the fish to the bait, *the Beater*.
   The Tauerne where they goe, *the Bush*. The foole that is caught, *the
   Bird . . .* The fetching in a Conny, *beating the Bush*' (Grosart, xi, 7).
28 *vulnera dilacerata.* Lacerated wounds. Untraced, and possibly non-
   existent. The comic point is in the inflated language, the pomposity, of
   Hoard's anger.

desire, and the wolf of thy conscience; but be assured, old
Pecunius Lucre, if ever fortune so bless me, that I may be at   35
leisure to vex thee, or any means so favour me, that I may
have opportunity to mad thee, I will pursue it with that
flame of hate, that spirit of malice, unrepressed wrath, that I
will blast thy comforts.

LUCRE
Ha, ha, ha!   40

LAMPREY
Nay, Master Hoard, you're a wise gentleman.

HOARD
I will so cross thee.

LUCRE
And I thee.

HOARD
So without mercy fret thee.

LUCRE
So monstrously oppose thee!   45

HOARD
Dost scoff at my just anger? Oh, that I had as much power
as usury has over thee!

LUCRE
Then thou wouldst have as much power as the devil has over
thee.

HOARD
Toad!   50

LUCRE
Aspic!

HOARD
Serpent!

LUCRE
Viper!

SPITCHCOCK
Nay gentlemen, then we must divide you perforce.

LAMPREY
When the fire grows too unreasonable hot, there's no better   55
way than to take off the wood.

> *Exeunt. Manent* SAM *and* MONEYLOVE

42 *cross* thwart, oppose
51 *Aspic* asp   56 s.d. *Manent* ed. *Manet* Qq

---

34 *wolf*. Usurers were often likened to wolves: see Sir Thomas Wilson,
A Discourse upon Usury, 1572, where they are described as 'greedie
cormoraunte wolfes in deede, that rauyn vp both beaste and man.'

SAM

A word, good signior.

MONEYLOVE

How now, what's the news?

SAM

'Tis given me to understand, that you are a rival of mine in
the love of Mistress Joyce, Master Hoard's niece: say me ay,   60
say me no.

MONEYLOVE

Yes, 'tis so.

SAM

Then look to yourself: you cannot live long. I'm practising
every morning; a month hence I'll challenge you.

MONEYLOVE

Give me your hand upon't; there's my pledge I'll meet you!   65
        Strikes him.   *Exit*

SAM

Oh, oh!—What reason had you for that, sir, to strike before
the month? You knew I was not ready for you, and that made
you so crank. I am not such a coward to strike again, I
warrant you. My ear has the law of her side for it burns
horribly. I will teach him to strike a naked face, the longest   70
day of his life; 'slid, it shall cost me some money, but I'll
bring this box into the Chancery.   *Exit*

[Act I, Scene iv]

Enter WITGOOD *and the* HOST

HOST

Fear you nothing, sir; I have lodged her in a house of credit,
I warrant you.

WITGOOD

Hast thou the writings?

HOST

Firm, sir.

---

67 *month* ed. mouth Q1
68 *crank* aggressively cocky
68 *again* back
70 *naked* defenceless, unprotected
72 *box* possibly a pun on *box* meaning (i) blow (ii) case
72 *Chancery* the Lord Chancellor's court, the highest court of
        judicature next to the House of Lords
3 *writings* the spurious documents presented to Lucre at II. i, 35

[*Enter* DAMPIT *and* GULF, *who talk apart*]

WITGOOD

Prithee, stay, and behold two the most prodigious rascals   5
that ever slipped into the shape of men: Dampit, sirrah, and
young Gulf, his fellow caterpillar.

HOST

Dampit? Sure I have heard of that Dampit.

WITGOOD

Heard of him? Why, man, he that has lost both his ears may
hear of him: a famous infamous trampler of time; his   10
own phrase. Note him well: that Dampit, sirrah, he in the
uneven beard, and the serge cloak, is the most notorious,
usuring, blasphemous, atheistical, brothel-vomiting rascal,
that we have in these latter times now extant, whose first
beginning was the stealing of a masty dog from a farmer's   15
house.

HOST

He looked as if he would obey the commandments well,
when he began first with stealing.

WITGOOD

True. The next town he came at, he set the dogs together
by th' ears.   20

  7 *caterpillar* extortioner
 10 *trampler* attorney, petty solicitor
 15 *masty* mastiff
 17 *commandments* ed. commandment Qq
 19-20 *set . . . ears* set men at variance (proverbial)

---

  4 s.d. Other editors place the entry of Dampit and Gulf at l. 30. Apart
    from what seems the physical proof that they enter now, in Witgood's
    description of Dampit, surely the scene gains added comic point by
    the presence of the two usurers, 'conversing apart' during Witgood's
    unflattering comments. This kind of situation is repeated in the play,
    in III. i, 121–236, IV. i, 37–95, and IV. iv, 165–75. Dampit's name is
    self-explanatory, as the song in IV. v makes quite clear; for Gulf, see
    gloss at I. iii, 33.
  9 *lost . . . ears.* A legal punishment; hence the implication may be: 'Any
    criminal would know of Dampit.'
 10 *trampler.* With Dampit's later account of his frenetic activity and his
    'trashing' and 'trotting' about his business, the accurate descriptiveness
    of the cant word (apparently first used by Middleton) becomes clear.
 12 *uneven . . . cloak.* This has led some commentators on the play to think
    that Dampit is a caricature of a real person, but the unkempt beard and
    serge cloak were typical of the poor (see M. C. Linthicum, *Costume in
    the Drama of Shakespeare and his Contemporaries*, 1936, p. 89), or, as
    here, of those who pretended to poverty.

HOST

A sign he should follow the law, by my faith.

WITGOOD

So it followed, indeed; and being destitute of all fortunes,
staked his masty against a noble, and by great fortune his dog
had the day. How he made it up ten shillings I know not, but
his own boast is that he came to town but with ten shillings in   25
his purse, and now is credibly worth ten thousand pound!

HOST

How the devil came he by it?

WITGOOD

How the devil came he not by it? if you put in the devil once,
riches come with a vengeance. H'as been a trampler of the
law, sir, and the devil has a care of his footmen. The rogue   30
has spied me now: he nibbled me finely once too; a pox
search you—oh, Master Dampit!—the very loins of thee!—
cry you mercy, Master Gulf, you walk so low I promise you
I saw you not, sir!

GULF

He that walks low walks safe, the poets tell us.   35

WITGOOD

[*Aside*] And nigher hell by a foot and a half than the rest of
his fellows.—But, my old Harry!

DAMPIT

My sweet Theodorus!

WITGOOD

'Twas a merry world when thou cam'st to town with ten
shillings in thy purse.   40

DAMPIT

And now worth ten thousand pound, my boy; report it,

23 *noble* a gold coin worth 6s. 8d.
33 *cry . . . mercy* beg your pardon

---

30 *footmen.* Continuing the 'trampling' imagery associated with Dampit's
    job.
35 *low.* Witgood had meant that Gulf was of such a low stature (see IV. v,
    126, 159) that he had overlooked him. Gulf, however, takes the word as
    meaning 'humble', and his penchant for the classics (see IV. v, 149)
    causes him to refer obliquely to the idea of the ancient 'poets' that one
    avoided the wrath of the gods by living humbly (cf. 3 *Henry VI*, IV. vi,
    19–20). Witgood's swift *sotto voce* riposte neatly deflates this piece of
    philosophising.
38 *Theodorus* = gift of God. W. Power, 'Middleton's Way with Names',
    p. 60, suggests that Witgood's two names, taken together, might be
    interpreted as meaning: 'cleverness is God's gift to man'.

Harry Dampit, a trampler of time, say, he would be up in
a morning, and be here with his serge gown, dashed up to
the hams in a cause; have his feet stink about Westminster
Hall, and come home again; see the galleons, the galleasses,   45
the great armadas of the law; then there be hoys and petty
vessels, oars and scullers of the time; there be picklocks of the
time too. Then would I be here, I would trample up and
down like a mule; now to the judges, 'May it please your
reverend-honourable fatherhoods'; then to my counsellor,   50
'May it please your worshipful patience'; then to the
examiner's office, 'May it please your mastership's gentleness'; then to one of the clerks, 'May it please your worshipful lousiness', for I find him scrubbing in his codpiece; then
to the Hall again, then to the chamber again—   55

WITGOOD
And when to the cellar again?

DAMPIT
E'en when thou wilt again! Tramplers of time, motions of
Fleet Street, and visions of Holborn; here I have fees of one,
there I have fees of another; my clients come about me, the

44 *have . . . stink* Cf. III. iv, 68
44–5 *Westminster Hall* where the law courts were held until 1882
45 *galleasses* heavy galleys
46 *hoys* small coasting vessels
47 *oars* rowing boats. Similarly, *scullers* means sculling boats
47 *picklocks* Dampit turns from the officers of the law to its trans-
   gressors, probably his clients
50 *counsellor* the legal advocate
52 *examiner's* function was to take the depositions of witnesses
54 *scrubbing* scratching (because of lice)
54 *codpiece* a bagged appendage to the front of the breeches
57 *motions* puppets or puppet-shows

43 *dashed.* Bespattered with mud. Dekker in *News from Hell* (1606) describes lawyers' clerks as being 'durtied vp to the hammes with trudging
   vp and downe to get pelfe, and with fishing for gudgeons' (A. B. Grosart,
   ed., *The Non-Dramatic Works of Thomas Dekker*, 5 vols., 1884–86, ii,
   94).
57–8 *motions . . . Holborn.* The precise meaning here is obscure. Perhaps
   we need take it only as another example of Dampit's energetic inco-
   herence. Spencer glosses: 'We tramplers of time move along Fleet
   Street, on our business errands, with the mechanical regularity of
   puppets. You may see us . . . also in Holborn . . . Hence, we are
   visions of Holborn.' These two streets, favourite haunts of sharpers (see
   Greene's *Notable Discovery of Cozenage*, Grosart, x, 15), are mentioned
   in the song which begins IV. v.

fooliaminy and coxcombry of the country; I still trashed and   60
trotted for other men's causes. Thus was poor Harry
Dampit made rich by others' laziness, who, though they
would not follow their own suits, I made 'em follow me with
their purses.

WITGOOD

Didst thou so, old Harry?   65

DAMPIT

Ay, and I soused 'em with bills of charges, i'faith; twenty
pound a year have I brought in for boat-hire, and I never
stepped into boat in my life.

WITGOOD

Tramplers of time!

DAMPIT

Ay, tramplers of time, rascals of time, bull-beggars!   70

WITGOOD

Ah, thou'rt a mad old Harry! Kind Master Gulf, I am bold to
renew my acquaintance.

GULF

I embrace it, sir.   *Music.*   *Exeunt*

[Act II, Scene i]

Enter LUCRE

LUCRE

My adversary evermore twits me with my nephew, forsooth,
my nephew; why may not a virtuous uncle have a dissolute
nephew? What though he be a brotheller, a wastethrift, a common surfeiter, and, to conclude, a beggar; must sin in him
call up shame in me? Since we have no part in their follies,   5
why should we have part in their infamies? For my strict
hand toward his mortgage, that I deny not, I confess I had an

60 *fooliaminy* fools (with *coxcombry*, the first of the many coinages
   Middleton is to put into Dampit's mouth. See also III. iv, 45–6
   and IV. v, 25, 48–9)
60 *trashed* walked or ran through mud and mire
66 *soused* ed. (souc'st Q1 = sauced?) swindled. Cf. modern *soaked*
70 *bull-beggars* hob-goblins, scare-crows
s.d. ed. *Incipit ACT.* 2. Qq
 1 *twits* censures, upbraids

73 s.d. *Music.* Particularly popular in the theatres of the boy actors, which
   derived originally from 16th-century choir schools.

uncle's pen'worth: let me see, half in half, true. I saw neither
hope of his reclaiming, nor comfort in his being, and was it
not then better bestowed upon his uncle, than upon one of   10
his aunts?—I need not say bawd, for everyone knows what
'aunt' stands for in the last translation.

[*Enter* SERVANT]

Now, sir?

SERVANT

There's a country serving-man, sir, attends to speak with your
worship.   15

LUCRE

I'm at best leisure now; send him in to me. [*Exit* SERVANT]

Enter HOST *like a serving-man*

HOST

Bless your venerable worship.

LUCRE

Welcome, good fellow.

HOST

[*Aside*] He calls me thief at first sight, yet he little thinks
I am an host!   20

LUCRE

What's thy business with me?

HOST

Faith, sir, I am sent from my mistress to any sufficient
gentleman indeed, to ask advice upon a doubtful point; 'tis
indifferent, sir, to whom I come, for I know none, nor did my
mistress direct me to any particular man, for she's as mere a   25
stranger here as myself; only I found your worship within,
and 'tis a thing I ever loved, sir, to be dispatched as soon
as I can.

LUCRE

[*Aside*] A good blunt honesty, I like him well.—What is thy
mistress?   30

HOST

Faith, a country gentlewoman and a widow, sir. Yesterday

14 SERVANT ed. *Ser.* 2 Qq
18 *good fellow* cant name for a thief
22 *sufficient* well-to-do
31–2 *Yesterday . . . us* we originally intended to leave (London)
    yesterday

---

8 *uncle's pen'worth.* To 'uncle' was to cheat or swindle.

was the first flight of us, but now she intends to stay till a
little term business be ended.

LUCRE
Her name, I prithee?

HOST
It runs there in the writings, sir, among her lands: Widow   35
Medler.

LUCRE
Medler? Mass, have I never heard of that widow?

HOST
Yes, I warrant you, have you, sir; not the rich widow in
Staffordshire?

LUCRE
Cuds me, there 'tis indeed; thou hast put me into memory;   40
there's a widow indeed, ah, that I were a bachelor again!

HOST
No doubt your worship might do much then, but she's
fairly promised to a bachelor already.

LUCRE
Ah, what is he, I prithee?

HOST
A country gentleman too, one whom your worship knows   45
not, I'm sure; h'as spent some few follies in his youth, but
marriage, by my faith, begins to call him home, my mistress
loves him, sir, and love covers faults, you know: one Master
Witgood, if ever you have heard of the gentleman?

LUCRE
Ha? Witgood, say'st thou?   50

HOST
That's his name indeed, sir; my mistress is like to bring him
to a goodly seat yonder—four hundred a year, by my faith.

LUCRE
But, I pray, take me with you.

HOST
Ay, sir?

LUCRE
What countryman might this young Witgood be?   55

HOST
A Leicestershire gentleman, sir.

---

33 *term business* legal matters, transacted during the court terms.
    See III. i, 96 and note
40 *Cuds* a corruption of *God's*
53 *take . . . you* tell me your meaning

LUCRE

[*Aside*] My nephew, by th' mass, my nephew! I'll fetch out
more of this, i'faith; a simple country fellow, I'll work't out
of him.—And is that gentleman, say'st thou, presently to
marry her?   60

HOST

Faith, he brought her up to town, sir; h'as the best card in
all the bunch for't, her heart; and I know my mistress will
be married ere she go down; nay, I'll swear that, for she's
none of those widows that will go down first, and be married
after; she hates that, I can tell you, sir.   65

LUCRE

By my faith, sir, she is like to have a proper gentleman and a
comely; I'll give her that gift!

HOST

Why, does your worship know him, sir?

LUCRE

I know him! Does not all the world know him? Can a man of
such exquisite qualities be hid under a bushel?   70

HOST

Then your worship may save me a labour, for I had charge
given me to enquire after him.

LUCRE

Enquire of him? If I might counsel thee, thou shouldst never
trouble thyself furder; enquire of him of no more but of me;
I'll fit thee! I grant he has been youthful, but is he not now   75
reclaimed? Mark you that, sir; has not your mistress, think
you, been wanton in her youth? If men be wags, are there not
women wagtails?

HOST

No doubt, sir.

LUCRE

Does not he return wisest, that comes home whipped with his   80
own follies?

HOST

Why, very true, sir.

LUCRE

The worst report you can hear of him, I can tell you, is that
he has been a kind gentleman, a liberal, and a worthy; who
but lusty Witgood, thrice noble Witgood!   85

63 *go down* to the country; with an obvious *double entendre*
66 *proper* handsome
70 *bushel* the reference is to *Matt.* v. 15
74 *furder* further   78 *wagtails* wantons

HOST

Since your worship has so much knowledge in him, can you
resolve me, sir, what his living might be? My duty binds me,
sir, to have a care of my mistress's estate; she has been ever a
good mistress to me, though I say it.. Many wealthy suitors
has she non-suited for his sake; yet, though her love be so   90
fixed, a man cannot tell whether his non-performance may
help to remove it, sir; he makes us believe he has lands and
living.

LUCRE

Who, young Master Witgood? Why, believe it, he has as
goodly a fine living out yonder—what do you call the place?   95

HOST

Nay, I know not, i'faith.

LUCRE

Hum—see, like a beast, if I have not forgot the name—puh!
And out yonder again, goodly grown woods and fair meadows;
pax on't; I can never hit of that place neither.—He? Why,
he's Witgood of Witgood Hall, he an unknown thing!   100

HOST

Is he so, sir? To see how rumour will alter! Trust me, sir,
we heard once he had no lands, but all lay mortgaged to
an uncle he has in town here.

LUCRE

Push! 'tis a tale, 'tis a tale.

HOST

I can assure you, sir, 'twas credibly reported to my mistress.   105

LUCRE

Why, do you think, i'faith, he was ever so simple to mortgage
his lands to his uncle, or his uncle so unnatural to take the
extremity of such a mortgage?

HOST

That was my saying still, sir.

LUCRE

Puh, never think it.   110

---

90 *non-suited* this pun on the legal and matrimonial meanings of the
    word is used again at III. i, 95
91 *non-performance* failure to fulfil promises
97 *puh* pooh   99 *pax* pox
104 *Push* Pish. The use of this exclamation is one of Middleton's
    trademarks (see also II. i, 227, III. i, 202)
107–8 *take . . . of* exact the full amount on
109 *That . . . still* That was the story I was always told

HOST

Yet that report goes current.

LUCRE

Nay, then you urge me: cannot I tell that best that am his uncle?

HOST

How, sir? What have I done!

LUCRE

Why, how now! In a swoon, man?   115

HOST

Is your worship his uncle, sir?

LUCRE

Can that be any harm to you, sir?

HOST

I do beseech you, sir, do me the favour to conceal it. What a beast was I to utter so much! Pray, sir, do me the kindness to keep it in; I shall have my coat pulled o'er my ears, an't   120 should be known; for the truth is, an't please your worship, to prevent much rumour and many suitors, they intend to be married very suddenly and privately.

LUCRE

And dost thou think it stands with my judgement to do them injury? Must I needs say the knowledge of this marriage   125 comes from thee? Am I a fool at fifty-four? Do I lack subtlety now, that have got all my wealth by it? There's a leash of angels for thee: come, let me woo thee; speak, where lie they?

HOST

So I might have no anger, sir—

LUCRE

Passion of me, not a jot; prithee, come.   130

HOST

I would not have it known it came by my means.

LUCRE

Why, am I a man of wisdom?

HOST

I dare trust your worship, sir, but I'm a stranger to your

111 *goes current* is in general circulation
112–3 lineation ed. Cannot . . . Vncle Qq as separate line
115 *swoon* ed. Sowne Qq (= swoon, See *OED*, 'sound', v^4.)
118 *you* ed. your Q1
120 *I . . . ears* I will be stripped of my livery (see l. 147 below), i.e., I will lose my job   *120 an* if   127 *leash* a set of three
128 *angels* gold coins worth ten shillings each, having on one side the figure of St Michael overcoming the dragon
131 HOST ed. *Hostis* Q1

house; and to avoid all intelligencers, I desire your worship's
ear.   135

LUCRE

[*Aside*] This fellow's worth a matter of trust.—Come, sir.
[HOST *whispers to him*] Why, now, thou'rt an honest lad.—
Ah, sirrah nephew!

HOST

Please you, sir, now I have begun with your worship, when
shall I attend for your advice upon that doubtful point? I   140
must come warily now.

LUCRE

Tut, fear thou nothing; tomorrow's evening shall resolve
the doubt.

HOST

The time shall cause my attendance.   *Exit*

LUCRE

Fare thee well.—There's more true honesty in such a country 145
servingman than in a hundred of our cloak companions: I
may well call 'em companions, for since blue coats have been
turned into cloaks, we can scarce know the man from the
master.—George!

                    [*Enter* GEORGE]

GEORGE

Anon, sir.   150

LUCRE

List hither: [*whispers*]—keep the place secret. Commend
me to my nephew; I know no cause, tell him, but he might
see his uncle.

GEORGE

I will, sir.

LUCRE

And, do you hear, sir, take heed you use him with respect and 155
duty.

GEORGE

[*Aside*] Here's a strange alteration: one day he must be
turned out like a beggar, and now he must be called in like
a knight!   *Exit*

134 *intelligencers* spies
140 *that . . . point* i.e., the nature of Witgood's living
146 *companions* a term of familiarity or contempt

147–8 *blue . . . cloaks*. The blue coat, the traditional livery of the serving man,
    seems to have been discarded at some time in the very early 17th
    century.

LUCRE

Ah, sirrah, that rich widow! four hundred a year! beside, I 160
hear she lays claim to a title of a hundred more. This falls
unhappily that he should bear a grudge to me now, being
likely to prove so rich. What is't, trow, that he makes me a
stranger for? Hum—I hope he has not so much wit to apprehend that I cozened him: he deceives me then. Good heaven, 165
who would have thought it would ever have come to this
pass! yet he's a proper gentleman, i'faith, give him his due—
marry, that's his mortgage; but that I never mean to give him.
I'll make him rich enough in words, if that be good; and if it
come to a piece of money I will not greatly stick for't: there 170
may be hope of some of the widow's lands, too, may one day
fall upon me if things be carried wisely.

[*Enter* GEORGE]

Now, sir, where is he?

GEORGE

He desires your worship to hold him excused; he has such
weighty business it commands him wholly from all men. 175

LUCRE

Were those my nephew's words?

GEORGE

Yes, indeed, sir.

LUCRE

[*Aside*] When men grow rich, they grow proud too, I perceive that. He would not have sent me such an answer once
within this twelvemonth; see what 'tis when a man's come 180
to his lands!—Return to him again, sir; tell him his uncle
desires his company for an hour; I'll trouble him but an hour,
say; 'tis for his own good, tell him; and, do you hear, sir, put
'worship' upon him. Go to, do as I bid you; he's like to be a
gentleman of worship very shortly. 185

GEORGE

[*Aside*] This is good sport, i'faith. *Exit*

LUCRE

Troth, he uses his uncle discourteously now. Can he tell what
I may do for him? Goodness may come from me in a minute,
that comes not in seven year again. He knows my humour;
I am not so usually good; 'tis no small thing that draws 190

161 *title* deed of property   163 *trow* do you suppose
165 *cozened* cheated
165 *he . . . then* he is not the fool I took him for
170 *stick for* grudge   189 *humour* disposition

kindness from me, he may know that an he will. The chief
cause that invites me to do him most good is the sudden
astonishing of old Hoard, my adversary. How pale his
malice will look at my nephew's advancement! With what a
dejected spirit he will behold his fortunes, whom but last day   195
he proclaimed rioter, penurious makeshift, despised
brothel-master! Ha, ha! 'twill do me more secret joy than my
last purchase, more precious comfort than all these widow's
revenues.

[*Enter* GEORGE]

Now, sir.   200

GEORGE

With much entreaty he's at length come, sir.   [*Exit*]

Enter WITGOOD

LUCRE

Oh, nephew, let me salute you, sir! You're welcome,
nephew.

WITGOOD

Uncle, I thank you.

LUCRE

Y'ave a fault, nephew; you're a stranger here. Well, heaven   205
give you joy!

WITGOOD

Of what, sir?

LUCRE

Hah, we can hear!
You might have known your uncle's house, i'faith,
You and your widow; go to, you were too blame,   210
If I may tell you so without offence.

WITGOOD

How could you hear of that, sir?

LUCRE   Oh, pardon me,
It was your will to have it kept from me,
I perceive now.

WITGOOD

Not for any defect of love, I protest, uncle.   215

198 *purchase* see I. i, 114
201 s.d. *Enter* WITGOOD after l. 200 in Qq
209–11 ed. prose in Qq   213–14 ed. prose in Qq
213 *it kept* so Q1. Most later editions follow Q2's kept it

---

210 *too blame*. 'In the 16–17th c. the *to* was misunderstood as *too*, and *blame*
was taken as adj. = *blameworthy, culpable*' (*OED*, 'blame', *v*., 6). See
also l. 260 below.

LUCRE

Oh, 'twas unkindness, nephew! fie, fie, fie.

WITGOOD

I am sorry you take it in that sense, sir.

LUCRE

Puh, you cannot colour it, i'faith, nephew.

WITGOOD

Will you but hear what I can say in my just excuse, sir?

LUCRE

Yes, faith, will I, and welcome.   220

WITGOOD

You that know my danger i'th' city, sir, so well, how great
my debts are, and how extreme my creditors, could not out
of your pure judgement, sir, have wished us hither.

LUCRE

Mass, a firm reason indeed.

WITGOOD

Else, my uncle's house, why 't'ad been the only make-match. 225

LUCRE

Nay, and thy credit.

WITGOOD

My credit? Nay, my countenance. Push, nay, I know, uncle,
you would have wrought it so by your wit you would have
made her believe in time the whole house had been mine.

LUCRE

Ay, and most of the goods too.   230

WITGOOD

La, you there; well, let 'em all prate what they will, there's
nothing like the bringing of a widow to one's uncle's house.

LUCRE

Nay, let nephews be ruled as they list, they shall find their
uncle's house the most natural place when all's done.

WITGOOD

There they may be bold.   235

LUCRE

Life, they may do anything there, man, and fear neither

---

216 *unkindness* ingratitude. Baskervill glosses 'unnaturalness, forgetfulness of the relationship due a relative'
227 *countenance* support of my façade (of wealth)
231 *La* see I. ii, 18

---

232 *uncle's house.* Sampson suggests that this may have been a slang term for
the residence of an 'aunt', i.e. bawd.

beadle nor summoner. An uncle's house! a very Cole Harbour!
Sirrah, I'll touch thee near now: hast thou so much interest
in thy widow that by a token thou couldst presently send for
her?   240

WITGOOD
Troth, I think I can, uncle.

LUCRE
Go to, let me see that!

WITGOOD
Pray command one of your men hither, uncle.

LUCRE
George!

[Enter GEORGE]

GEORGE
Here, sir.   245

LUCRE
Attend my nephew! [WITGOOD *whispers to* GEORGE, *who then
goes out*] [*Aside*] I love a' life to prattle with a rich widow;
'tis pretty, methinks, when our tongues go together; and
then to promise much and perform little—I love that sport
a' life i'faith. Yet I am in the mood now to do my nephew   250
some good, if he take me handsomely.—What, have you
dispatched?

WITGOOD
I ha' sent, sir.

LUCRE
Yet I must condemn you of unkindness, nephew.

WITGOOD
Heaven forbid, uncle!   255

LUCRE
Yes, faith, must I; say your debts be many, your creditors
importunate, yet the kindness of a thing is all, nephew; you
might have sent me close word on't, without the least danger
or prejudice to your fortunes.

237 *summoner* a petty officer whose function was to warn people to
     appear in court
238–9 *interest in* claim on   258 *close* secret

237 *Cole Harbour.* A warren of tenements by the Thames above London
    Bridge. 'It was regarded as a sanctuary where debtors and malefactors
    were safe from the law' (Spencer), and where, as may be inferred from
    III. i, 227–8, marriages could be hastily solemnised. (*Cole* = cheat,
    sharper).

WITGOOD

Troth, I confess it, uncle, I was too blame there; but, indeed,   260
my intent was to have clapped it up suddenly, and so have
broke forth like a joy to my friends, and a wonder to the
world. Beside, there's a trifle of a forty pound matter toward
the setting of me forth; my friends should never have
known on't; I meant to make shift for that myself.   265

LUCRE

How, nephew? let me not hear such a word again, I beseech
you—shall I be beholding to you?

WITGOOD

To me? Alas, what do you mean, uncle?

LUCRE

I charge you upon my love: you trouble nobody but myself.

WITGOOD

Y'ave no reason for that, uncle.   270

LUCRE

Troth, I'll never be friends with you while you live, an you
do.

WITGOOD

Nay, an you say so, uncle, here's my hand, I will not do't.

LUCRE

Why, well said! there's some hope in thee when thou wilt be
ruled; I'll make it up fifty, faith, because I see thee so   275
reclaimed. Peace, here comes my wife with Sam, her
tother husband's son.

[*Enter* WIFE *and* SAM]

WITGOOD

Good aunt—

SAM

Cousin Witgood! I rejoice in my salute: you're most
welcome to this noble city governed with the sword in the   280
scabbard.

WITGOOD

[*Aside*] And the wit in the pommel—good Master Sam
Freedom, I return the salute.

264 *setting . . . forth* equipping me, fitting me out
267 *beholding* common in early 17th century for *beholden* (see II. i, 313,
    III. i, 71, IV. iv, 54)
277 *tother* a common form of *other*
282 *wit . . . pommel* the amount of wit in the knob on the hilt of a
    sword

LUCRE
By the mass, she's coming; wife, let me see now how thou
wilt entertain her.   285

WIFE
I hope I am not to learn, sir, to entertain a widow; 'tis not so
long ago since I was one myself.

[Enter COURTESAN]

WITGOOD
Uncle—

LUCRE
She's come indeed!

WITGOOD
My uncle was desirous to see you, widow, and I presumed   290
to invite you.

COURTESAN
The presumption was nothing, Master Witgood: is this your
uncle, sir?

LUCRE
Marry am I, sweet widow, and his good uncle he shall find
me; ay, by this smack that I give thee, thou'rt welcome.—   295
Wife, bid the widow welcome the same way again.

SAM
[Aside] I am a gentleman now too, by my father's occupation,
and I see no reason but I may kiss a widow by my father's
copy; truly, I think the charter is not against it; surely these
are the words: 'The son, once a gentleman, may revel it,   300
though his father were a dauber;' 'tis about the fifteenth
page—I'll to her—
[Offers to kiss the COURTESAN, *who repulses him]*

LUCRE
Y'are not very busy now; a word with thee, sweet widow—

SAM
[Aside] Coad's nigs! I was never so disgraced, since the hour
my mother whipped me.   305

LUCRE
Beside, I have no child of mine own to care for; she's my

285 *entertain* receive
292 *your* ed. yours Q1
295 *smack* kiss
299 *copy* example
299 *charter* i.e., of one of the trade guilds
301 *dauber* plasterer
304 *Coad's nigs* God's nigs, a meaningless oath

second wife, old, past bearing; clap sure to him, widow; he's
like to be my heir, I can tell you.

COURTESAN

Is he so, sir?

LUCRE

He knows it already, and the knave's proud on't; jolly rich   310
widows have been offered him here i'th' city, great merchants'
wives, and do you think he would once look upon 'em?
Forsooth, he'll none. You are beholding to him i'th' country,
then, ere we could be; nay, I'll hold a wager, widow, if he
were once known to be in town, he would be presently sought   315
after; nay, and happy were they that could catch him first.

COURTESAN

I think so.

LUCRE

Oh, there would be such running to and fro, widow, he
should not pass the streets for 'em; he'd be took up in one
great house or other presently. Fah! they know he has it, and   320
must have it. You see this house here, widow; this house
and all comes to him, goodly rooms, ready furnished, ceiled
with plaster of Paris, and all hung above with cloth of arras.—
Nephew!

WITGOOD

Sir.   325

LUCRE

Show the widow your house; carry her into all the rooms and
bid her welcome.—You shall see, widow. [*Aside to* WITGOOD]
Nephew, strike all sure above an thou beest a good boy—ah!

WITGOOD

Alas, sir, I know not how she would take it.

LUCRE

The right way, I warrant t'ee. A pox, art an ass? Would I   330
were in thy stead! Get you up; I am ashamed of you.—
[*Exeunt* WITGOOD *and* COURTESAN] So, let 'em agree as they
will now; many a match has been struck up in my house a'
this fashion: let 'em try all manner of ways, still there's

---

315 *presently* immediately
323 *cloth of arras* rich tapestries, in which figures and scenes (often
    Biblical) were woven in colour

---

323 *above.* All modern editors, with the exception of Spencer, follow Q2's
    about, but it seems more probable that Lucre is referring to the upstairs
    rooms.

nothing like an uncle's house to strike the stroke in. I'll hold   335
my wife in talk a little.—Now, Jinny, your son there goes a-
wooing to a poor gentlewoman but of a thousand portion;
see my nephew, a lad of less hope, strikes at four hundred a
year in good rubbish.

WIFE

Well, we must do as we may, sir.   340

LUCRE

I'll have his money ready told for him again he come down.
Let me see, too;—by th' mass, I must present the widow
with some jewel, a good piece a' plate, or such a device; 'twill
hearten her on well. I have a very fair standing cup, and a
good high standing cup will please a widow above all other   345
pieces.   *Exit*

WIFE

Do you mock us with your nephew?—I have a plot in my
head, son; i'faith, husband, to cross you.

SAM

Is it a tragedy plot, or a comedy plot, good mother?

WIFE

'Tis a plot shall vex him. I charge you, of my blessing, son   350
Sam, that you presently withdraw the action of your love
from Master Hoard's niece.

SAM

How, mother!

WIFE

Nay, I have a plot in my head, i'faith. Here, take this chain of
gold, and this fair diamond; dog me the widow home to her   355
lodging, and at thy best opportunity fasten 'em both upon
her—nay, I have a reach; I can tell you thou art known what
thou art, son, among the right worshipful, all the twelve
companies.

339 *rubbish* land   341 *again* against, i.e. before
344 *standing* ed. stranding Q1 i.e., on a stem or base (but probably
        with a *double entendre*)
353 *How* see I. ii, 12   357 *reach* scheme

---

335 *to strike the stroke.* Cf. l. 328 above. This may have sexual connotations (cf.
    Titus Andronicus, II. i, 117–18 and 129–31, and Eric Partridge, *Shake-
    speare's Bawdy*, 1947, p. 196). McKerrow's *Nashe*, iii, 122 indicates that a
    striker was a wencher; but the context in which the phrase recurs at
    III. i, 250 suggests that perhaps this is simply a vigorous way of saying
    'to seal up a bargain'.
358–9 *twelve companies.* The twelve merchants' guilds—or unions—in the
    city of London. See V. ii, 22.

SAM

Truly, I thank 'em for it.   360

WIFE

He? he's a scab to thee; and so certify her thou hast two
hundred a year of thyself, beside thy good parts—a proper
person and a lovely. If I were a widow, I could find it in my
heart to have thee myself, son; ay, from 'em all.

SAM

Thank you for your good will, mother, but indeed I had   365
rather have a stranger; and if I woo her not in that violent
fashion that I will make her be glad to take these gifts ere I
leave her, let me never be called the heir of your body.

WIFE

Nay, I know there's enough in you, son, if you once come
to put it forth.   370

SAM

I'll quickly make a bolt or a shaft on't.   *Exeunt*

[Act II, Scene ii]

Enter HOARD *and* MONEYLOVE

MONEYLOVE

Faith, Master Hoard, I have bestowed many months in the
suit of your niece, such was the dear love I ever bore to her
virtues; but since she hath so extremely denied me, I am to
lay out for my fortunes elsewhere.

HOARD

Heaven forbid but you should, sir. I ever told you my niece   5
stood otherwise affected.

MONEYLOVE

I must confess you did, sir; yet, in regard of my great loss of
time, and the zeal with which I sought your niece, shall I
desire one favour of your worship?

HOARD

In regard of those two, 'tis hard but you shall, sir.   10

MONEYLOVE

I shall rest grateful. 'Tis not full three hours, sir, since the
happy rumour of a rich country widow came to my hearing.

361 *scab . . . thee* scoundrel compared to thee
371 *make . . . . on't* do it one way or another (proverbial—literally, use
       a thick arrow or a slender one)
  6 *affected* disposed

HOARD
How? a rich country widow?

MONEYLOVE
Four hundred a year landed.

HOARD
Yea?   15

MONEYLOVE
Most firm, sir, and I have learned her lodging; here my suit
begins, sir: if I might but entreat your worship to be a
countenance for me, and speak a good word—for your words
will pass—I nothing doubt but I might set fair for the
widow; nor shall your labour, sir, end altogether in thanks,   20
two hundred angels—

HOARD
So, so, what suitors has she?

MONEYLOVE
There lies the comfort, sir, the report of her is yet but a
whisper, and only solicited by young riotous Witgood,
nephew to your mortal adversary.   25

HOARD
Ha! art certain he's her suitor?

MONEYLOVE
Most certain, sir, and his uncle very industrious to beguile
the widow, and make up the match!

HOARD
So! very good!

MONEYLOVE
Now, sir, you know this young Witgood is a spendthrift,   30
dissolute fellow.

HOARD
A very rascal.

MONEYLOVE
A midnight surfeiter.

HOARD
The spume of a brothel-house.

MONEYLOVE
True, sir! Which being well told in your worship's phrase,   35
may both heave him out of her mind, and drive a fair way for
me to the widow's affections.

HOARD
Attend me about five.

17–18 *be . . . countenance* seem favourable to
35 *phrase* manner of expression (*OED, s.v.*, 1. Cf. 1. 47 below)

MONEYLOVE

    With my best care, sir.   *Exit*

HOARD

    Fool, thou hast left thy treasure with a thief,   40
    To trust a widower with a suit in love!
    Happy revenge, I hug thee! I have not only the means laid
    before me, extremely to cross my adversary, and confound
    the last hopes of his nephew, but thereby to enrich my state,
    augment my revenues, and build mine own fortunes greater;   45
    ha, ha!
    I'll mar your phrase, o'erturn your flatteries,
    Undo your windings, policies, and plots,
    Fall like a secret and dispatchful plague
    On your secured comforts. Why, I am able   50
    To buy three of Lucre, thrice outbid him,
    Let my out-monies be reckoned and all.

Enter three CREDITORS

1 CREDITOR

    I am glad of this news.

2 CREDITOR

    So are we, by my faith.

3 CREDITOR

    Young Witgood will be a gallant again now.   55

HOARD

    [*Listening*] Peace!

1 CREDITOR

    I promise you, Master Cockpit, she's a mighty rich widow.

2 CREDITOR

    Why, have you ever heard of her?

1 CREDITOR

    Who? Widow Medler? she lies open to much rumour.

40–1 ed. prose in Qq
47 *phrase* gush of words in praise or flattery (*OED, s.v.*, 4)
49–52 ed. prose in Qq
49 *dispatchful* deadly
49 *plague* ed. plauge Q1
52 *out-monies* money lent out or invested and not immediately
    liquid

---

59 *open*. Another name for medlar, the fruit, was 'openarse'. See IV. v,
    142. The name is also appropriate for a prostitute because the fruit is
    not ready to eat until it is almost rotten (cf. *As You Like It*, III. ii,
    124–9).

3 CREDITOR
Four hundred a year, they say, in very good land.   60

1 CREDITOR
Nay, take't of my word, if you believe that, you believe the
least.

2 CREDITOR
And to see how close he keeps it!

1 CREDITOR
Oh, sir, there's policy in that, to prevent better suitors.

3 CREDITOR
He owes me a hundred pound, and I protest I never looked   65
for a penny.

1 CREDITOR
He little dreams of our coming; he'll wonder to see his
creditors upon him.   *Exeunt*

HOARD
Good, his creditors; I'll follow. This makes for me:
All know the widow's wealth; and 'tis well known   70
I can estate her fairly, ay, and will.
In this one chance shines a twice happy fate:
I both deject my foe, and raise my state.   *Music*   *Exit*

[Act III, Scene i]

[Enter] WITGOOD *with his* CREDITORS

WITGOOD
Why, alas, my creditors, could you find no other time to
undo me but now? Rather your malice appears in this than
the justness of the debt.

1 CREDITOR
Master Witgood, I have forborne my money long.

WITGOOD
I pray, speak low, sir; what do you mean?   5

2 CREDITOR
We hear you are to be married suddenly to a rich country
widow.

WITGOOD
What can be kept so close but you creditors hear on't? Well,
'tis a lamentable state, that our chiefest afflicters should

63 *close* secret
69–71 ed. prose in Qq
69 *makes . . . me* works in my favour
73 *state* estate
s.d. ed. *Incipit ACT. 3.* Qq

first hear of our fortunes. Why, this is no good course, i'faith,   10
sirs; if ever you have hope to be satisfied, why do you seek
to confound the means that should work it? There's neither
piety, no, nor policy in that. Shine favourably now, why, I
may rise and spread again, to your great comforts.

1 CREDITOR
He says true, i'faith.   15

WITGOOD
Remove me now, and I consume for ever.

2 CREDITOR
Sweet gentleman!

WITGOOD
How can it thrive which from the sun you sever?

3 CREDITOR
It cannot, indeed!

WITGOOD
Oh, then, show patience! I shall have enough   20
To satisfy you all.

1 CREDITOR   Ay, if we could
Be content, a shame take us.

WITGOOD   For, look you,
I am but newly sure yet to the widow,
And what a rend might this discredit make!
Within these three days will I bind you lands   25
For your securities.

1 CREDITOR   No, good Master Witgood,
Would 'twere as much as we dare trust you with!

WITGOOD
I know you have been kind; however, now,
Either by wrong report, or false incitement,
Your gentleness is injured. In such   30
A state as this a man cannot want foes.
If on the sudden he begin to rise,
No man that lives can count his enemies.
You had some intelligence, I warrant ye,
From an ill-willer.   35

2 CREDITOR
Faith, we heard you brought up a rich widow, sir, and were
suddenly to marry her.

13 *piety* early form of *pity*
20–6 ed. prose in Qq
23 *sure* betrothed
28–31 ed. prose in Qq
34–5 ed. prose in Qq

WITGOOD

Ay, why there it was, I knew 'twas so: but since you are so
well resolved of my faith toward you, let me be so much
favoured of you, I beseech you all—   40

ALL

Oh, it shall not need, i'faith, sir—

WITGOOD

As to lie still awhile, and bury my debts in silence, till I be
fully possessed of the widow; for the truth is—I may tell you
as my friends—

ALL

Oh, oh, oh—   45

WITGOOD

I am to raise a little money in the city, toward the setting
forth of myself, for mine own credit, and your comfort. Now,
if my former debts should be divulged, all hope of my
proceedings were quite extinguished!

1 CREDITOR

[*Aside to* WITGOOD] Do you hear, sir? I may deserve your   50
custom hereafter; pray let my money be accepted before a
stranger's. Here's forty pound I received as I came to you;
if that may stand you in any stead, make use on't—nay, pray
sir, 'tis at your service.

WITGOOD

[*Aside*] You do so ravish me with kindness that   55
I'm constrained to play the maid, and take it!

1 CREDITOR

[*Aside*] Let none of them see it, I beseech you.

WITGOOD

[*Aside*] Fah!

1 CREDITOR

[*Aside*] I hope I shall be first in your remembrance
After the marriage rites.

WITGOOD   [*Aside*] Believe it firmly.   60

1 CREDITOR

So.—What, do you walk, sirs?

2 CREDITOR

I go.—[*Aside to* WITGOOD] Take no care, sir, for money to
furnish you; within this hour I'll send you sufficient.—
Come, Master Cockpit, we both stay for you.

39 *resolved* convinced
55–6 ed. prose in Qq
56 *play . . . it* say no—and acquiesce (proverbial)
59–60 ed. prose in Qq

3 CREDITOR

I ha' lost a ring i'faith, I'll follow you presently [*Exeunt* 1   65
and 2 CREDITORS]—but you shall find it, sir; I know your
youth and expenses have disfurnished you of all jewels;
there's a ruby of twenty pound price, sir; bestow it upon
your widow.—What, man, 'twill call up her blood to you;
beside, if I might so much work with you, I would not have   70
you beholding to those blood-suckers for any money.

WITGOOD

Not I, believe it.

3 CREDITOR

They're a brace of cut-throats!

WITGOOD

I know 'em.

3 CREDITOR

Send a note of all your wants to my shop, and I'll supply you   75
instantly.

WITGOOD

Say you so? Why, here's my hand then, no man living shall
do't but thyself.

3 CREDITOR

Shall I carry it away from 'em both then?

WITGOOD

I'faith, shalt thou!   80

3 CREDITOR

Troth, then I thank you, sir.

WITGOOD

Welcome good Master Cockpit!   *Exit* [3 CREDITOR]
Ha, ha, ha! why, is not this better now, than lying a-bed? I
perceive there's nothing conjures up wit sooner than poverty,
and nothing lays it down sooner than wealth and lechery!   85
This has some savour, yet oh! that I had the mortgage from
mine uncle as sure in possession as these trifles! I would
forswear brothel at noon day, and muscadine and eggs at
midnight.

Enter COURTESAN

COURTESAN

Master Witgood? where are you?   90

WITGOOD

Holla!

69 *blood* sexual appetite
79 *carry . . . away* win the day
88 *muscadine* a rich wine, taken with eggs as an aphrodisiac

COURTESAN
Rich news!

WITGOOD
Would 'twere all in plate.

COURTESAN
There's some in chains and jewels. I am so haunted with
suitors, Master Witgood, I know not which to dispatch first.   95

WITGOOD
You have the better term, by my faith.

COURTESAN
Among the number,
One Master Hoard, an ancient gentleman.

WITGOOD
Upon my life, my uncle's adversary.

COURTESAN
It may well hold so, for he rails on you,   100
Speaks shamefully of him.

WITGOOD   As I could wish it.

COURTESAN
I first denied him, but so cunningly,
It rather promised him assured hopes,
Than any loss of labour.

WITGOOD   ·   Excellent.

COURTESAN
I expect him every hour, with gentlemen,   105
With whom he labours to make good his words,
To approve you riotous, your state consumed,
Your uncle—

WITGOOD
Wench, make up thy own fortunes now, do thyself a good
turn once in thy days. He's rich in money, moveables, and   110
lands; marry him, he's an old doting fool, and that's worth
all; marry him, 'twould be a great comfort to me to see thee
do well, i'faith; marry him, 'twould ease my conscience
well to see thee well bestowed; I have a care of thee, i'faith.

97–8 ed. prose in Qq   107–8 ed. prose in Qq
107 *approve* prove
110 *moveables* personal property

96 *term.* Witgood is playing with the two senses of *suitor*. During the
court sessions, when London was full of litigants, not only the lawyers
but also the prostitutes did very well for themselves. Cf. Dekker's and
Webster's *Westward Ho!*, 1604, III. iii, 13–14: 'there were many
Punkes in the Towne (as you know our Tearme is their Tearme)'.

COURTESAN

Thanks, sweet Master Witgood.   115

WITGOOD

I reach at farder happiness: first, I am sure it can be no harm
to thee, and there may happen goodness to me by it. Prosecute it well: let's send up for our wits, now we require their
best and most pregnant assistance!

COURTESAN

Step in, I think I hear 'em.   *Exit* [*with* WITGOOD]   120

Enter HOARD *and* GENTLEMEN *with the* HOST
[*as*] *serving-man*

HOARD

Art thou the widow's man? By my faith, sh'as a company of
proper men then.

HOST

I am the worst of six, sir; good enough for blue-coats.

HOARD

Hark hither: I hear say thou art in most credit with her.

HOST

Not so, sir.   125

HOARD

Come, come, thou'rt modest. There's a brace of royals;
prithee, help me to th' speech of her.

HOST

I'll do what I may, sir, always saving myself harmless.

HOARD

Go to, do't, I say; thou shalt hear better from me.

HOST

[*Aside*] Is not this a better place than five mark a year   130
standing wages? Say a man had but three such clients in a

116 *farder* farther
118 *our* ed. out Q1
123 *blue-coats* see II. i, 147
126 *royals* gold pieces worth about fifteen shillings
130 *mark* Middleton is using a term familiar to his audience as
    equivalent in England to 13s. 4d., though there was no actual coin
    of this amount
131 *standing* fixed

---

120 s.d. GENTLEMEN. Dyce suggests that these are Lamprey and Spitchcock,
but see IV. i, where they are distinguished from numbered 'Gentlemen'.
However, Middleton was careless about naming and counting his lesser
characters (see III. iii, first s.d.), and the practical, theatrical point of
view would support Dyce's suggestion.

day, methinks he might make a poor living on't; beside, I was
never brought up with so little honesty to refuse any man's
money; never. What gulls there are a' this side the world!
Now know I the widow's mind, none but my young master   135
comes in her clutches. Ha, ha, ha!   *Exit*

HOARD

Now, my dear gentlemen, stand firmly to me;
You know his follies, and my worth.

1 GENTLEMAN   We do, sir.

2 GENTLEMAN

But, Master Hoard, are you sure he is not i'th' house now?

HOARD

Upon my honesty I chose this time   140
A' purpose, fit; the spendthrift is abroad.
Assist me; here she comes.

[Enter COURTESAN]

Now, my sweet widow.

COURTESAN

Y'are welcome, Master Hoard.

HOARD

Dispatch, sweet gentlemen, dispatch.—
I am come, widow, to prove those my words   145
Neither of envy sprung nor of false tongues,
But such as their deserts and actions
Do merit and bring forth, all which these gentlemen,
Well known and better reputed, will confess.

COURTESAN

I cannot tell   150
How my affections may dispose of me,
But surely if they find him so desertless,
They'll have that reason to withdraw themselves.
And therefore, gentlemen, I do entreat you,
As you are fair in reputation,   155
And in appearing form, so shine in truth.
I am a widow, and, alas, you know,
Soon overthrown; 'tis a very small thing
That we withstand, our weakness is so great.

134 *gulls* dupes
137–8 ed. prose in Qq
146 *envy* malice
147 *their* i.e., Witgood's and Lucre's
148–9 ed. prose in Qq

Be partial unto neither, but deliver,   160
  Without affection, your opinion.

HOARD

  And that will drive it home.

COURTESAN

  Nay, I beseech your silence, Master Hoard;
  You are a party.

HOARD   Widow, not a word!

1 GENTLEMAN

  The better first to work you to belief,   165
  Know neither of us owe him flattery,
  Nor t'other malice, but unbribed censure,
  So help us our best fortunes.

COURTESAN   It suffices.

1 GENTLEMAN

  That Witgood is a riotous, undone man,
  Imperfect both in fame and in estate,   170
  His debts wealthier than he, and executions
  In wait for his due body, we'll maintain
  With our best credit and our dearest blood.

COURTESAN

  Nor land nor living, say you? Pray, take heed
  You do not wrong the gentleman!

1 GENTLEMAN   What we speak   175
  Our lives and means are ready to make good.

COURTESAN

  Alas, how soon are we poor souls beguiled!

2 GENTLEMAN

  And for his uncle—

HOARD   Let that come to me.
  His uncle, a severe extortioner;
  A tyrant at a forfeiture; greedy of others'   180
  Miseries; one that would undo his brother,
  Nay, swallow up his father, if he can,
  Within the fathoms of his conscience.

161 *affection* prejudice
167 *t'other* i.e., Witgood (the *him* of the previous line refers to Hoard)
167 *censure* judgement
171 *executions* seizure of the goods or person of a debtor in default of
    payment
174–5 ed. prose in Qq
180–2 lineation ed.

_____

183 *fathoms.* See I. i, 7–11 and note.

1 GENTLEMAN
Nay, believe it, widow,
You had not only matched yourself to wants,   185
But in an evil and unnatural stock.

HOARD
[*Aside*] Follow hard, gentlemen, follow hard!

COURTESAN
Is my love so deceived? Before you all
I do renounce him; on my knees I vow
He ne'er shall marry me.   190

WITGOOD
[*Looking in*] Heaven knows he never meant it!

HOARD
[*Aside to* GENTLEMEN] There, take her at the bound.

1 GENTLEMAN
Then with a new and pure affection,
Behold yon gentleman, grave, kind, and rich,
A match worthy yourself; esteeming him,   195
You do regard your state.

HOARD
[*Aside to* GENTLEMEN] I'll make her a jointure, say.

1 GENTLEMAN
He can join land to land, and will possess you
Of what you can desire.

2 GENTLEMAN   Come, widow, come.

COURTESAN
The world is so deceitful!

1 GENTLEMAN   There 'tis deceitful,   200
Where flattery, want, and imperfection lies;
But none of these in him; push!

COURTESAN   Pray, sir—

1 GENTLEMAN
Come, you widows are ever most backward when you should
do yourselves most good; but were it to marry a chin not
worth a hair now, then you would be forward enough! Come,   205
clap hands, a match.

HOARD
With all my heart, widow.—Thanks, gentlemen.
I will deserve your labour, and thy love.

COURTESAN
Alas, you love not widows but for wealth!
I promise you I ha' nothing, sir.

192 *at the bound* at the first opportunity   198–9 ed. prose in Qq
204–5 *chin . . . hair* an impecunious youngster

HOARD   Well said, widow,   210
  Well said; thy love is all I seek, before
  These gentlemen.
COURTESAN   Now I must hope the best.
HOARD
  My joys are such they want to be expressed.
COURTESAN
  But, Master Hoard, one thing I must remember you of,
  before these gentlemen, your friends: how shall I suddenly   215
  avoid the loathed soliciting of that perjured Witgood, and his
  tedious, dissembling uncle, who this very day hath appointed
  a meeting for the same purpose too, where, had not truth
  come forth, I had been undone, utterly undone.
HOARD
  What think you of that, gentlemen?   220
1 GENTLEMAN
  'Twas well devised.
HOARD
  Hark thee, widow: train out young Witgood single; hasten
  him thither with thee, somewhat before the hour, where, at
  the place appointed, these gentlemen and myself will wait
  the opportunity, when, by some sleight removing him from   225
  thee, we'll suddenly enter and surprise thee, carry thee
  away by boat to Cole Harbour, have a priest ready, and
  there clap it up instantly. How lik'st it, widow?
COURTESAN
  In that it pleaseth you, it likes me well.
HOARD
  I'll kiss thee for those words.—Come, gentlemen;   230
  Still must I live a suitor to your favours,
  Still to your aid beholding.
1 GENTLEMAN   We're engaged, sir;
  'Tis for our credits now to see't well ended.
HOARD
  'Tis for your honours, gentlemen; nay, look to't;
  Not only in joy, but I in wealth excel.—   235
  No more sweet widow, but sweet wife, farewell.
COURTESAN
  Farewell, sir.   *Exeunt* [HOARD *and* GENTLEMEN]

210–12 ed. prose in Qq
215 *suddenly* shortly
217 *very* ed. very uery Q1
222 *train out* entice, decoy
229 *likes* is pleasing to

Enter WITGOOD

WITGOOD
Oh, for more scope! I could laugh eternally! Give you joy,
Mistress Hoard; I promise your fortune was good, forsooth;
y'ave fell upon wealth enough, and there's young gentlemen   240
enow can help you to the rest. Now it requires our wits; carry
thyself but heedfully now, and we are both—

[*Enter* HOST]

HOST
Master Witgood, your uncle.

WITGOOD
[*Aside to* COURTESAN] Cuds me! remove thyself a while; I'll
serve for him.   [*Exeunt* COURTESAN *and* HOST]   245

Enter LUCRE

LUCRE
Nephew, good morrow, nephew.

WITGOOD
The same to you, kind uncle.

LUCRE
How fares the widow? Does the meeting hold?

WITGOOD
Oh, no question of that, sir.

LUCRE
I'll strike the stroke, then, for thee; no more days.   250

WITGOOD
The sooner the better, uncle. Oh, she's mightily followed!

LUCRE
And yet so little rumoured!

WITGOOD
Mightily! Here comes one old gentleman, and he'll make her
a jointure of three hundred a year, forsooth; another wealthy
suitor will estate his son in his lifetime, and make him weigh   255
down the widow; here a merchant's son will possess her with
no less than three goodly lordships at once, which were all
pawns to his father.

LUCRE
Peace, nephew, let me hear no more of 'em; it mads me. Thou
shalt prevent 'em all. No words to the widow of my coming   260

---

245 *Entre* LUCRE ed. after l. 243 Qq
250 *days* postponements, days of grace (usurers' language. See IV. v,
77)
257 *lordships* estates   260 *prevent* get ahead of, anticipate

hither. Let me see—'tis now upon nine; before twelve,
nephew, we will have the bargain struck, we will, i'faith, boy.

WITGOOD

Oh, my precious uncle!   *Exit* [*with* LUCRE]

[Act III, Scene ii]

[*Enter*] HOARD *and his* NIECE

HOARD

Niece, sweet niece, prithee, have a care to my house; I leave
all to thy discretion. Be content to dream awhile; I'll have a
husband for thee shortly; put that care upon me, wench, for
in choosing wives and husbands I am only fortunate; I have
that gift given me.   *Exit*   5

NIECE

But 'tis not likely you should choose for me,
Since nephew to your chiefest enemy
Is he whom I affect; but, oh, forgetful!
Why dost thou flatter thy affections so,
With name of him that for a widow's bed   10
Neglects thy purer love? Can it be so,
Or does report dissemble?

[*Enter* GEORGE]

How now, sir?

GEORGE

A letter, with which came a private charge.

NIECE

Therein I thank your care. [*Exit* GEORGE] I know this hand:
Reads 'Dearer than sight, what the world reports of me,   15
yet believe not; rumour will alter shortly. Be thou constant;
I am still the same that I was in love, and I hope to be the
same in fortunes.
                    Theodorus Witgood.'
I am resolved; no more shall fear or doubt   20
Raise their pale powers to keep affection out.   *Exit*

8 *affect* love   11 *it* ed. in Q1
20 *resolved* convinced

---

262 *i'faith*. Other editors print *faith*, probably because the initial *i* of Q1's
    ifaith is badly damaged.

[Act III, Scene iii]

Enter, with a DRAWER, HOARD *and two* GENTLEMEN

DRAWER
You're very welcome, gentlemen.—Dick, show those
gentlemen the Pomegranate, there.
HOARD
Hist!
DRAWER
Up those stairs, gentlemen.
HOARD
Pist! drawer—   5
DRAWER
Anon, sir.
HOARD
Prithee, ask at the bar if a gentlewoman came not in lately.
DRAWER
William, at the bar, did you see any gentlewoman come in
lately? Speak you ay, speak you no?
[WILLIAM] *Within*
No, none came in yet but Mistress Florence.   10
DRAWER
He says none came in yet, sir, but one Mistress Florence.
HOARD
What is that Florence? a widow?
DRAWER
Yes, a Dutch widow.
HOARD
How?
DRAWER
That's an English drab, sir; give your worship good   15
morrow.   [*Exit*]

2 *Pomegranate* tavern rooms were named thus instead of numbered

---

s.d. *two* GENTLEMEN. Note Q1's assignment of speech, l. 30. Spencer's theory
that this *two* 'indicates reduction of personnel in the interest of economy'
is untenable, since it suggests a playhouse provenance for the MS of Q1,
to which all the evidence runs counter. In light of the fact that the first
gentleman seems to 'join their hands' at III. i, 206, it is best to explain
the anomaly as being due to authorial carelessness about minor characters. See III. i, 120, IV. v, 5, and V. ii, 19 and 41. As at III. i, 120 the
'two Gentlemen' are probably Lamprey and Spitchcock.
1 *Dick*. Off-stage, like William at l. 10.

HOARD

   A merry knave, i'faith! I shall remember a Dutch widow the
longest day of my life.

1 GENTLEMAN

   Did not I use most art to win the widow?

2 GENTLEMAN

   You shall pardon me for that, sir; Master Hoard knows I took   20
her at best vantage.

HOARD

   What's that, sweet gentlemen, what's that?

2 GENTLEMAN

   He will needs bear me down that his art only wrought with
the widow most.

HOARD

   Oh, you did both well, gentlemen, you did both well, I   25
thank you.

1 GENTLEMAN

   I was the first that moved her.

HOARD   You were, i'faith.

2 GENTLEMAN

   But it was I that took her at the bound.

HOARD

   Ay, that was you; faith, gentlemen, 'tis right.

1 GENTLEMAN

   I boasted least, but 'twas I joined their hands.   30

HOARD

   By th' mass, I think he did. You did all well,
Gentlemen, you did all well; contend no more.

1 GENTLEMAN

   Come, yon room's fittest.

HOARD   True, 'tis next the door.

                       Exit [*with* GENTLEMEN]

      Enter WITGOOD, COURTESAN, [DRAWER] *and* HOST

DRAWER

   You're very welcome; please you to walk up stairs, cloth's
laid, sir.   35

COURTESAN

   Upstairs? troth, I am weary, Master Witgood.

WITGOOD

   Rest yourself here awhile, widow; we'll have a cup of muscadine in this little room.

30 1 GENTLEMAN ed. 3. Qq
31–2 ed. prose in Qq   37 *muscadine* see III. i, 88

DRAWER

A cup of muscadine? You shall have the best, sir.

WITGOOD

But, do you hear, sirrah?   40

DRAWER

Do you call? Anon, sir.

WITGOOD

What is there provided for dinner?

DRAWER

I cannot readily tell you, sir; if you please, you may go into
the kitchen and see yourself, sir; many gentlemen of worship
do use to do it, I assure you, sir.   [*Exit*]   45

HOST

A pretty familiar prigging rascal, he has his part without
book!

WITGOOD

Against you are ready to drink to me, widow, I'll be present
to pledge you.

COURTESAN

Nay, I commend your care, 'tis done well of you.   50

                                          [*Exit* WITGOOD]

'Las, what have I forgot!

HOST

What, Mistress?

COURTESAN

I slipped my wedding ring off when I washed, and left it at my
lodging; prithee run, I shall be sad without it.   [*Exit* HOST]
So, he's gone!—Boy!   55

                        [*Enter* BOY]

BOY

Anon, forsooth.

COURTESAN

Come hither, sirrah: learn secretly if one Master Hoard, an
ancient gentleman, be about house.

BOY

I heard such a one named.

COURTESAN

Commend me to him.   60

                Enter HOARD *with* GENTLEMEN

46 *prigging* haggling or suave. The cant word need not be taken in
   any strictly literal sense
46–7 *without book* off by heart   48 *Against* before
51 *'Las* ed. asse Qq. A letter has obviously dropped out in Q1

HOARD
I'll do thy commendations!
COURTESAN
Oh, you come well: away, to boat, begone.
HOARD
Thus wise men are revenged, give two for one.   *Exeunt*

Enter WITGOOD *and* VINTNER

WITGOOD
I must request
You, sir, to show extraordinary care;   65
My uncle comes with gentlemen, his friends,
And 'tis upon a making.
VINTNER   Is it so?
I'll give a special charge, good Master Witgood.
May I be bold to see her?
WITGOOD   Who, the widow?
With all my heart, i'faith, I'll bring you to her!   70
VINTNER
If she be a Staffordshire gentlewoman, 'tis much if I know
her not.
WITGOOD
How now? boy, drawer!
VINTNER
Hie!

[*Enter* BOY]

BOY
Do you call, sir?   75
WITGOOD
Went the gentlewoman up that was here?
BOY
Up, sir? she went out, sir.
WITGOOD
Out, sir?
BOY
Out, sir: one Master Hoard with a guard of gentlemen carried
her out at back door, a pretty while since, sir.   80
WITGOOD
Hoard? death and darkness, Hoard?

64–7 ed. prose in Qq
67 *upon a making* concerning a matchmaking
68–9 ed. prose in Qq   69 *the* ed. he Qq

---

61 *I'll.* Eleven of the extant copies of Q1 read 'I bee' (which modern
editors emend to 'Ay, boy'); only three have the correct 'Ile'.

Enter HOST

HOST
  The devil of ring I can find!
WITGOOD
  How now, what news? where's the widow?
HOST
  My mistress? is she not here, sir?
WITGOOD
  More madness yet.
HOST   She sent me for a ring.   85
WITGOOD
  A plot, a plot! To boat! she's stole away!
HOST
  What?

Enter LUCRE *with* GENTLEMEN

WITGOOD
  Follow, enquire old Hoard, my uncle's adversary—
                                        [*Exit* HOST]
LUCRE
  Nephew, what's that?
WITGOOD   Thrice miserable wretch!
LUCRE
  Why, what's the matter?
VINTNER   The widow's borne away, sir.   90
LUCRE
  Ha? passion of me!—A heavy welcome, gentlemen.
1 GENTLEMAN
  The widow gone?
LUCRE   Who durst attempt it?
WITGOOD
  Who but old Hoard, my uncle's adversary?
LUCRE
  How!
WITGOOD
  With his confederates.   95
LUCRE
  Hoard, my deadly enemy! Gentlemen, stand to me,
  I will not bear it, 'tis in hate of me;
  That villain seeks my shame, nay thirsts my blood;
  He owes me mortal malice.
  I'll spend my wealth on this despiteful plot,   100
  Ere he shall cross me and my nephew thus.

98-9 ed. prose in Qq
98 *thirsts* ed. thrifts Qq

WITGOOD
  So maliciously.

Enter HOST

LUCRE
  How now, you treacherous rascal?
HOST
  That's none of my name, sir.
WITGOOD
  Poor soul, he knew not on't.   105
LUCRE
  I'm sorry. I see then 'twas a mere plot.
HOST
  I traced 'em nearly—
LUCRE   Well?
HOST   And hear for certain
  They have took Cole Harbour.
LUCRE   The devil's sanctuary!
  They shall not rest, I'll pluck her from his arms.
  Kind and dear gentlemen,   110
  If ever I had seat within your breasts—
1 GENTLEMAN
  No more, good sir, it is a wrong to us,
  To see you injured; in a cause so just
  We'll spend our lives, but we will right our friends.
LUCRE
  Honest and kind! come, we have delayed too long: 115
  Nephew, take comfort; a just cause is strong.
WITGOOD
  That's all my comfort, uncle.
        Exeunt [LUCRE, GENTLEMEN, VINTNER *and* BOY]
             Ha, ha, ha!
  Now may events fall luckily, and well:
  He that ne'er strives, says wit, shall ne'er excel.   *Exit*

107 *nearly* closely
107–8 lineation ed.
110–11 lineation ed.   117 s.d. ed. after l. 116 Qq
119 *wit*, ed. wit Qq (Wit is personified again at IV. iii, 52)

---

108 *Cole Harbour*. See II. i, 237, and the ironic contrast in Lucre's view of
  the place.

[Act III, Scene iv]

Enter DAMPIT, *the Usurer, drunk*

DAMPIT

When did I say my prayers? In anno '88, when the great
armada was coming; and in anno '99, when the great
thundering and lightning was, I prayed heartily then, i'faith,
to overthrow Poovies' new buildings; I kneeled by my
great iron chest, I remember.   5

[*Enter* AUDREY]

AUDREY

Master Dampit, one may hear you, before they see you; you
keep sweet hours, Master Dampit; we were all abed three
hours ago.

DAMPIT

Audrey?

AUDREY

Oh, y'are a fine gentleman.   10

DAMPIT

So I am, i'faith, and a fine scholar. Do you use to go to bed so
early, Audrey?

AUDREY

Call you this early, Master Dampit?

DAMPIT

Why, is't not one of clock i'th' morning? Is not that early
enough? Fetch me a glass of fresh beer.   15

3 *lightning* ed. Lighting Q1   11 *bed* ed. bed Bed Q1

---

s.d. *Usurer*. Presumably Dampit turned to usury after his 'trampling' days
   were done. He continues to be spoken of as both petty lawyer and
   usurer throughout the play (see especially IV. v, 12, 54, 151).

2 '99. Most modern editors emend either to '*89* or to '*98*, when John
   Stow's *Survey of London*, 1603, records tremendous storms (none such
   is recorded for '99). Emendation is unnecessary: as Spencer says, 'the
   point is the long lapse of time' between Dampit's praying fits, and there
   is no reason to suppose that Middleton aspired to meteorological accuracy.

4 *Poovies*'. Sampson notes tentatively that a certain Povey erected a
   timber building in Paul's Churchyard, after James I, in 1605 and 1607,
   had ordered no more houses in the city to be built of wood. It had to be
   pulled down. This identification is not conclusive, however. E. H.
   Sugden, *A Topographical Dictionary to the Works of Shakespeare and
   His Fellow Dramatists*, 1925, p. 418, says that possibly Powis House, at
   one corner of Lincoln's Inn Fields, is meant, but Spencer may be right
   when he suggests that the name 'may be taken at random and intended
   merely to illustrate Dampit's malevolence'.

AUDREY
Here, I have warmed your nightcap for you, Master Dampit.

DAMPIT
Draw it on then.—I am very weak, truly; I have not eaten
so much as the bulk of an egg these three days.

AUDREY
You have drunk the more, Master Dampit.

DAMPIT
What's that?   20

AUDREY
You mought, an you would, Master Dampit.

DAMPIT
I answer you I cannot. Hold your prating; you prate too
much and understand too little. Are you answered? Give
me a glass of beer.

AUDREY
May I ask you how you do, Master Dampit?   25

DAMPIT
How do I? I'faith, naught.

AUDREY
I never knew you do otherwise.

DAMPIT
I eat not one penn'ort' of bread these two years. Give me a
glass of fresh beer—I am not sick, nor I am not well.

AUDREY
Take this warm napkin about your neck, sir, whilst I help to   30
make you unready.

DAMPIT
How now, Audrey-prater, with your scurvy devices, what
say you now?

AUDREY
What say I, Master Dampit? I say nothing but that you are
very weak.   35

DAMPIT
Faith, thou hast more coney-catching devices than all
London!

---

21 *mought* obsolete form of *might*
31 *make . . . unready* undress you
36 *coney-catching devices* cheating stratagems

---

28 *not one penn'ort' of bread.* Dampit has some of Falstaff's characteristics:
cf. Falstaff's 'one halfpennyworth of bread to this intolerable deal of
sack.' (1 *Henry IV*, II. iv, 598–9).

AUDREY
Why, Master Dampit, I never deceived you in all my life!

DAMPIT
Why was that? Because I never did trust thee.

AUDREY
I care not what you say, Master Dampit!   40

DAMPIT
Hold thy prating. I answer thee, thou art a beggar, a quean,
and a bawd; are you answered?

AUDREY
Fie, Master Dampit! a gentleman, and have such words?

DAMPIT
Why, thou base drudge of infortunity, thou kitchen-stuff
drab of beggary, roguery and coxcombry, thou cavernesed   45
quean of foolery, knavery and bawdreaminy, I'll tell thee
what, I will not give a louse for thy fortunes.

AUDREY
No, Master Dampit? And there's a gentleman comes a-
wooing to me, and he doubts nothing but that you will get me
from him.   50

DAMPIT
I? If I would either have thee or lie with thee for two
thousand pound, would I might be damned! Why, thou base,
impudent quean of foolery, flattery and coxcombry, are you
answered?

AUDREY
Come, will you rise and go to bed, sir?   55

DAMPIT
Rise, and go to bed too, Audrey? How does Mistress Proserpine?

AUDREY
Fooh—

41 *quean* strumpet
44 *infortunity* misfortune
44 *kitchen-stuff* refuse, slops
45 *cavernesed* cavernous? (i.e., she is like a cavern full of foolery)
46 *bawdreaminy* bawdry
49 *doubts* fears
56 *Mistress* ed. Misters Q1

56–7 *Mistress Proserpine.* Probably Dampit's surrealistically drunken
name for a bawd or prostitute 'in the liberties'. He could mean Audrey
herself, implying that she is a witch (Proserpine was sometimes identified with Hecate). Middleton intended Dampit to be incoherent.

DAMPIT

She's as fine a philosopher of a stinkard's wife as any within
the liberties—fah, fah, Audrey!   60

AUDREY

How now, Master Dampit?

DAMPIT

Fie upon't, what a choice of stinks is here! What hast thou
done, Audrey? Fie upon't, here's a choice of stinks indeed!
Give me a glass of fresh beer, and then I will to bed.

AUDREY

It waits for you above, sir.   65

DAMPIT

Foh! I think they burn horns in Barnard's Inn; if ever I
smelt such an abominable stink, usury forsake me.   [*Exit*]

AUDREY

They be the stinking nails of his trampling feet, and he
talks of burning of horns.   *Exit*

[Act IV, Scene i]

Enter at Cole Harbour, HOARD, *the* WIDOW, [LAMPREY, SPITCH-
COCK] *and* GENTLEMEN, *he married now*

1 GENTLEMAN

Join hearts, join hands,
In wedlock's bands,
Never to part
Till death cleave your heart;
You shall forsake all other women;   5
You lords, knights, gentlemen and yeomen.
What my tongue slips,
Make up with your lips.

60 *liberties* suburbs, in which the brothels flourished
62 *is here* ed. here is Qq
66 *horns* either ink-wells (made of horn) or the translucent horn used
   to protect leaves of paper in reading
68 *stinking . . . feet* see I. iv, 44
s.d.ed. *Incipit ACT.* 4.Qq
   1–4 lineation ed.
   7 *slips* neglects, overlooks
   7–8 lineation ed.

---

66 *Barnard's Inn.* An Inn of Chancery, on the south side of Holborn. The
reference to the burning of horns is probably best understood as a wild
flight of the drunkard's 'fantastical' imagination.

HOARD
> Give you joy, Mistress Hoard; let the kiss come about.
> > [*Knocking*]
> Who knocks? Convey my little pig-eater out.   10

LUCRE [*within*]
> Hoard!

HOARD
> Upon my life, my adversary, gentlemen.

LUCRE [*within*]
> Hoard, open the door, or we will force it ope:
> Give us the widow.

HOARD   Gentlemen, keep 'em out.

LAMPREY
> He comes upon his death that enters here.   15

LUCRE [*within*]
> My friends assist me.

HOARD   He has assistants, gentlemen.

LAMPREY
> Tut, nor him, nor them, we in this action fear.

LUCRE [*within*]
> Shall I, in peace, speak one word with the widow?

COURTESAN
> Husband and gentlemen, hear me but a word.

HOARD
> Freely, sweet wife.

COURTESAN   Let him in peaceably;   20
> You know we're sure from any act of his.

HOARD
> Most true.

COURTESAN
> You may stand by and smile at his old weakness;
> Let me alone to answer him.

HOARD   Content,
> 'Twill be good mirth, i'faith; how think you gentlemen?   25

LAMPREY
> Good gullery!

HOARD   Upon calm conditions let him in.

9 *come about* circulate
10 *pig-eater* a term of endearment
20–1 ed. prose in Qq
23–4 ed. prose in Qq
23 COURTESAN ed *Lu.* Qq
24 *let . . . alone* leave it to me
26 *gullery* trickery

LUCRE [*within*]
   All spite and malice—
LAMPREY   Hear me, Master Lucre:
   So you will vow a peaceful entrance
   With those your friends, and only exercise
   Calm conference with the widow, without fury,   30
   The passage shall receive you.
LUCRE [*within*]   I do vow it.
LAMPREY
   Then enter and talk freely, here she stands.

            Enter LUCRE, [GENTLEMEN, *and* HOST]

LUCRE
   Oh, Master Hoard, your spite has watched the hour;
   You're excellent at vengeance, Master Hoard.
HOARD
   Ha, ha, ha!
LUCRE   I am the fool you laugh at: 35
   You are wise, sir, and know the seasons well.
   Come hither, widow: why is it thus?
   Oh, you have done me infinite disgrace,
   And your own credit no small injury!
   Suffer mine enemy so despitefully   40
   To bear you from my nephew! oh, I had
   Rather half my substance had been forfeit,
   And begged by some starved rascal!
COURTESAN
   Why, what would you wish me do, sir?
   I must not overthrow my state for love: 45
   We have too many precedents for that;
   From thousands of our wealthy undone widows
   One may derive some wit. I do confess,
   I loved your nephew, nay, I did affect him,
   Against the mind and liking of my friends;   50
   Believed his promises, lay here in hope
   Of flattered living, and the boast of lands:
   Coming to touch his wealth and state indeed,

27–9 ed. prose in Qq
28 *entrance* trisyllabic
32 s.d. ed. after *receive you*, l. 31, in Qq
33–7 ed. prose in Qq
41–3 lineation ed.
49 *affect* love
50 *friends* ed. friend Q1
52 *flattered* too favourably represented

It appears dross; I find him not the man,
Imperfect, mean, scarce furnished of his needs;   55
In words, fair lordships, in performance, hovels:
Can any woman love the thing that is not?

LUCRE
Broke you for this?

COURTESAN   Was it not cause too much?
Send to enquire his state: most part of it
Lay two years mortgaged in his uncle's hands.   60

LUCRE
Why, say it did, you might have known my mind;
I could have soon restored it.

COURTESAN
Ay, had I but seen any such thing performed,
Why, 'twould have tied my affection, and contained
Me in my first desires: do you think, i'faith,   65
That I could twine such a dry oak as this,
Had promise in your nephew took effect?

LUCRE
Why, and there's no time past; and rather than
My adversary should thus thwart my hopes,
I would—   70

COURTESAN
Tut, y'ave been ever full of golden speech.
If words were lands, your nephew would be rich.

LUCRE
Widow, believe it, I vow by my best bliss,
Before these gentlemen, I will give in
The mortgage to my nephew instantly,   75
Before I sleep or eat.

1 GENTLEMAN   We'll pawn our credits,
Widow, what he speaks shall be performed
In fulness.

LUCRE   Nay, more: I will estate him
In farder blessings; he shall be my heir.
I have no son;   80
I'll bind myself to that condition.

COURTESAN
When I shall hear this done, I shall soon yield
To reasonable terms.

LUCRE   In the mean season,

56 *performance* fulfilment of promises
61–70 ed. prose in Qq
76–8 ed. prose in Qq   82–3 ed. prose in Qq

Will you protest, before these gentlemen,
To keep yourself as you are now at this present?   85
COURTESAN
I do protest before these gentlemen,
I will be as clear then, as I am now.
LUCRE
I do believe you. Here's your own honest servant,
I'll take him along with me.
COURTESAN   Ay, with all my heart.
LUCRE
He shall see all performed and bring you word.   90
COURTESAN
That's all I wait for.
HOARD
What, have you finished, Master Lucre? Ha, ha, ha, ha!
LUCRE
So laugh, Hoard, laugh at your poor enemy, do;
The wind may turn, you may be laughed at too.
Yes, marry, may you, sir.—Ha, ha, ha!   95
HOARD   *Exeunt* [LUCRE, GENTLEMEN *and* HOST]
Ha, ha, ha! If every man that swells in malice
Could be revenged as happily as I,
He would choose hate and forswear amity.
What did he say, wife, prithee?
COURTESAN
Faith, spoke to ease his mind.
HOARD   Oh—oh—oh!   100
COURTESAN
You know now little to any purpose.
HOARD
True, true, true.
COURTESAN   He would do mountains now.
HOARD
Ay, ay, ay, ay.
LAMPREY   Y'ave struck him dead, Master Hoard.
SPITCHCOCK
And his nephew desperate.
HOARD   I know't, sirs, I.
Never did man so crush his enemy!   *Exeunt* 105

87 *clear* pure   93–5 ed. prose in Qq
102 *do mountains* give the world (to regain the 'widow')
104 *And* ed. I and Q1

---

85 Lucre does not know that Hoard's marriage has already taken place.

[Act IV, Scene ii]

Enter LUCRE *with* GENTLEMEN [*and* HOST], *meeting* SAM FREEDOM

LUCRE
My son-in-law, Sam Freedom! Where's my nephew?

SAM
O man in lamentation, father!

LUCRE
How?

SAM
He thumps his breast like a gallant dicer that has lost his
doublet, and stands in's shirt to do penance.   5

LUCRE
Alas, poor gentleman.

SAM
I warrant you may hear him sigh in a still evening to your
house at Highgate.

LUCRE
I prithee, send him in.

SAM
Were it to do a greater matter, I will not stick with you, sir,   10
in regard you married my mother.   [*Exit*]

LUCRE
Sweet gentlemen, cheer him up; I will but fetch the mortgage, and return to you instantly.   *Exit*

1 GENTLEMAN
We'll do our best, sir.—See where he comes,
E'en joyless and regardless of all form.   15

[*Enter* WITGOOD]

2 GENTLEMAN
Why, how now, Master Witgood? Fie, you a firm scholar,
and an understanding gentleman, and give your best parts
to passion?

1 GENTLEMAN
Come, fie!

1 *son-in-law* stepson
1 ed. as two lines in Qq (my . . . lawe/*Sam* . . . Nephew?)
10 *stick . . . you* begrudge you
16 *how now* ed. how Q1   18 *passion* sorrow

---

2 *O man in lamentation.* There was an old tune 'O man in desperation',
mentioned in Nashe's *Summer's Last Will and Testament*, 1600, and
Peele's *The Old Wives' Tale*, 1590.

WITGOOD
  Oh, gentlemen—   20
1 GENTLEMAN
  Sorrow of me, what a sigh was there, sir!
  Nine such widows are not worth it.
WITGOOD
  To be borne from me by that lecher, Hoard!
1 GENTLEMAN
  That vengeance is your uncle's, being done
  More in despite to him, than wrong to you.   25
  But we bring comfort now.
WITGOOD   I beseech you, gentlemen—
2 GENTLEMAN
  Cheer thyself, man, there's hope of her, i'faith!
WITGOOD
  Too gladsome to be true.

Enter LUCRE

LUCRE   Nephew, what cheer?
  Alas, poor gentleman, how art thou changed!
  Call thy fresh blood into thy cheeks again: 30
  She comes—
WITGOOD   Nothing afflicts me so much
  But that it is your adversary, uncle,
  And merely plotted in despite of you.
LUCRE
  Ay, that's it mads me, spites me! I'll spend my wealth ere
  he shall carry her so, because I know 'tis only to spite me.   35
  Ay, this is it.—Here, nephew [*giving a paper*], before these
  kind gentlemen I deliver in your mortgage, my promise to
  the widow; see, 'tis done. Be wise, you're once more master
  of your own; the widow shall perceive now, you are not alto-
  gether such a beggar as the world reputes you: you can make   40
  shift to bring her to three hundred a year, sir.
1 GENTLEMAN
  Berlady, and that's no toy, sir.
LUCRE
  A word, nephew.
1 GENTLEMAN [*to* HOST]
  Now you may certify the widow.

28–31 ed. prose in Qq
33 *merely* simply, absolutely
35 *carry* win
42 *Berlady* By our Lady

LUCRE

You must conceive it aright, nephew, now; 45
To do you good I am content to do this.

WITGOOD

I know it, sir.

LUCRE

But your own conscience can tell I had it
Dearly enough of you.

WITGOOD   Ay, that's most certain.

LUCRE

Much money laid out, beside many a journey 50
To fetch the rent; I hope you'll think on't, nephew.

WITGOOD

I were worse than a beast else, i'faith.

LUCRE

Although to blind the widow and the world
I out of policy do't, yet there's a conscience, nephew.

WITGOOD

Heaven forbid else!

LUCRE   When you are full possessed, 55
'Tis nothing to return it.

WITGOOD

Alas, a thing quickly done, uncle.

LUCRE

Well said! you know I give it you but in trust.

WITGOOD

Pray let me understand you rightly, uncle:
You give it me but in trust? 60

LUCRE

No.

WITGOOD

That is, you trust me with it.

LUCRE

True, true.

WITGOOD

[Aside] But if ever I trust you with it again, would I might
be trussed up for my labour! 65

LUCRE

You can all witness, gentlemen, and you, sir yeoman?

HOST

My life for yours, sir, now I know my mistress's mind so

45–54 ed. prose in Qq
65 *trussed up* hanged
67 *so* ed. to Q1 too Q2

    well toward your nephew; let things be in preparation and
I'll train her hither in most excellent fashion.   *Exit*

LUCRE

    A good old boy—wife, Jinny!   70

Enter WIFE

WIFE

    What's the news, sir?

LUCRE

    The wedding day's at hand: prithee, sweet wife, express thy
housewifery; thou'rt a fine cook, I know't; thy first husband
married thee out of an alderman's kitchen; go to, he raised
thee for raising of paste. What! here's none but friends;   75
most of our beginnings must be winked at.—Gentlemen, I
invite you all to my nephew's wedding against Thursday
morning.

1 GENTLEMAN

    With all our hearts, and we shall joy to see
    Your enemy so mocked.

LUCRE   He laughed at me,   80
    Gentlemen; ha, ha, ha!   *Exeunt [all but* WITGOOD]

WITGOOD   He has no conscience, faith,
    Would laugh at them; they laugh at one another!
    Who then can be so cruel? Troth, not I;
    I rather pity now, than aught envy.
    I do conceive such joy in mine own happiness,   85
    I have no leisure yet to laugh at their follies.
    [*To the mortgage*] Thou soul of my estate I kiss thee,
    I miss life's comfort when I miss thee.
    Oh, never will we part again,
    Until I leave the sight of men.   90
    We'll ne'er trust conscience of our kin,
    Since cozenage brings that title in.   [*Exit*]

69 *train* entice
70 *Jinny* ed. Girnne Qq
79–82 ed. prose in Qq
84 *envy* bear malice
85–6 ed. prose in Qq
92 *Since . . . in* since cozenage (or cousinship) introduces that name
    (i.e., of *kin*). Another variant of the cousin-cozen pun

[Act IV, Scene iii]

Enter three CREDITORS

1 CREDITOR
I'll wait these seven hours but I'll see him caught.

2 CREDITOR
Faith, so will I.

3 CREDITOR
Hang him, prodigal, he's stripped of the widow.

1 CREDITOR
A' my troth, she's the wiser; she has made the happier choice;
and I wonder of what stuff those widows' hearts are made of,   5
that will marry unfledged boys before comely thrum-chinned
gentlemen.

Enter a BOY

BOY
News, news, news!

1 CREDITOR
What, boy?

BOY
The rioter is caught.   10

1 CREDITOR
So, so, so, so! It warms me at the heart; I love a' life to see
dogs upon men. Oh, here he comes.

Enter WITGOOD *with* SERGEANTS

WITGOOD
My last joy was so great it took away the sense of all future
afflictions. What a day is here o'ercast! How soon a black
tempest rises!   15

1 CREDITOR
Oh, we may speak with you now, sir! What's become of
your rich widow? I think you may cast your cap at the
widow, may you not, sir?

2 CREDITOR
He a rich widow? Who, a prodigal, a daily rioter, and a
nightly vomiter? He a widow of account? He a hole i'th'   20
Counter!

WITGOOD
You do well, my masters, to tyrannize over misery, to afflict

6   *thrum-chinned* bearded. The *thrum* was the waste end of the warp
20 *hole* one of the worst cells
21 *Counter* a city prison for debtors

the afflicted; 'tis a custom you have here amongst you; I
would wish you never leave it, and I hope you'll do as I bid
you.   25

1 CREDITOR
Come, come, sir, what say you extempore now to your bill
of a hundred pound? A sweet debt, for frotting your doublets.

2 CREDITOR
Here's mine of forty.

3 CREDITOR
Here's mine of fifty.   30

WITGOOD
Pray, sirs—you'll give me breath?

1 CREDITOR
No sir, we'll keep you out of breath still; then we shall be sure
you will not run away from us.

WITGOOD
Will you but hear me speak?

2 CREDITOR
You shall pardon us for that, sir; we know you have too fair a   35
tongue of your own: you overcame us too lately, a shame take
you! We are like to lose all that for want of witnesses; we
dealt in policy then: always when we strive to be most politic
we prove most coxcombs; *non plus ultra*. I perceive by us
we're not ordained to thrive by wisdom, and therefore we   40
must be content to be tradesmen.

WITGOOD
Give me but reasonable time, and I protest I'll make you
ample satisfaction.

1 CREDITOR
Do you talk of reasonable time to us?

WITGOOD
'Tis true, beasts know no reasonable time.   45

2 CREDITOR
We must have either money or carcass.

WITGOOD
Alas, what good will my carcass do you?

---

27 *frotting* rubbing with perfume. Cf. Jonson's *Cynthia's Revels*,
   V. iv, 312

---

39 *non plus ultra*. No farther. A reference to the *ne plus ultra* said to have
   been inscribed on the Pillars of Hercules (Gibraltar and Mt. Abyla),
   the traditional limit to navigation.

3 CREDITOR

Oh 'tis a secret delight we have amongst us! We that are used
to keep birds in cages, have the heart to keep men in prison,
I warrant you.   50

WITGOOD

[*Aside*] I perceive I must crave a little more aid from my
wits: do but make shift for me this once, and I'll forswear
ever to trouble you in the like fashion hereafter; I'll have
better employment for you, an I live.—You'll give me leave,
my masters, to make trial of my friends, and raise all means   55
I can?

1 CREDITOR

That's our desires, sir.

Enter HOST

HOST

Master Witgood.

WITGOOD

Oh, art thou come?

HOST

May I speak one word with you in private, sir?   60

WITGOOD

No, by my faith, canst thou; I am in hell here, and the devils
will not let me come to thee.

CREDITORS

Do you call us devils? You shall find us Puritans.—Bear him
away; let 'em talk as they go; we'll not stand to hear 'em.—
Ah, sir, am I a devil? I shall think the better of myself as   65
long as I live: a devil, i'faith!   *Exeunt*

Act IV, Scene iv

Enter HOARD

HOARD

What a sweet blessing hast thou, Master Hoard, above a
multitude! Wilt thou never be thankful? How dost thou think
to be blest another time? Or dost thou count this the full
measure of thy happiness? By my troth, I think thou dost:
not only a wife large in possessions, but spacious in content: 5
she's rich, she's young, she's fair, she's wise; when I wake, I
think of her lands—that revives me; when I go to bed, I dream

63 CREDITORS ed. *Cit.* (i.e., Citizens) Qq (mod. eds. erroneously
    emend to 1 CRED.)
6 *wise* ed. wife Q1

of her beauty—and that's enough for me; she's worth four
hundred a year in her very smock, if a man knew how to use it.
But the journey will be all, in troth, into the country; to ride to   10
her lands in state and order following my brother and other
worshipful gentlemen, whose companies I ha' sent down for
already, to ride along with us in their goodly decorum beards,
their broad velvet cassocks, and chains of gold twice or thrice
double; against which time I'll entertain some ten men of   15
mine own into liveries, all of occupations or qualities: I will
not keep an idle man about me; the sight of which will so
vex my adversary Lucre—for we'll pass by his door of
purpose, make a little stand for the nonce, and have our
horses curvet before the window—certainly he will never   20
endure it, but run up and hang himself presently!

[Enter SERVANT]

How now, sirrah, what news? Any that offer their service to
me yet?

SERVANT

Yes, sir, there are some i'th' hall that wait for your worship's
liking, and desire to be entertained.   25

HOARD

Are they of occupation?

SERVANT

They are men fit for your worship, sir.

HOARD

Say'st so? send 'em all in! *[Exit* SERVANT] To see ten men ride
after me in watchet liveries, with orange-tawny capes, 'twill
cut his comb, i'faith.   30

Enter ALL [*i.e.,* TAILOR, BARBER, PERFUMER, FALCONER,
and HUNTSMAN]

13 *decorum* noun used in its original adjectival function
14 *cassocks* long loose coats, often worn by usurers
15–16 *entertain . . . into liveries* employ as servants
19 *the* ed. omitted Qq
29 *watchet* sky blue
30 s.d. after l. 32 in Qq

---

21 *hang himself.* The traditional end for a usurer when overtaken by
despair. See C. T. Wright, 'Some Conventions Regarding the Usurer
in Elizabethan Literature', *SP*, XXXI (1934), 192–6.
29 *orange-tawny.* Cf. Bacon's *Of Usury: 'Vsurers* should have Orange-
tawney Bonnets, because they doe *Judaize*' (E. Arber, ed., *A Harmony
of the Essays . . . of Francis Bacon*, 1895, p. 541).

How now? Of what occupation are you, sir?

TAILOR

A tailor, an't please your worship.

HOARD

A tailor? Oh, very good: you shall serve to make all the liveries.—What are you, sir?

BARBER

A barber, sir.   35

HOARD

A barber? very needful: you shall shave all the house, and, if need require, stand for a reaper i'th' summer time.—You, sir?

PERFUMER

A perfumer.

HOARD

I smelt you before. Perfumers, of all men, had need carry   40
themselves uprightly, for if they were once knaves they would be smelt out quickly.—To you, sir?

FALCONER

A falconer, an't please your worship.

HOARD

Sa ho, sa ho, sa ho!—And you, sir?

HUNTSMAN

A huntsman, sir.   45

HOARD

There, boy, there, boy, there, boy! I am not so old but I have pleasant days to come. I promise you, my masters, I take such a good liking to you, that I entertain you all; I put you already into my countenance, and you shall be shortly in my livery; but especially you two, my jolly falconer and my   50
bonny huntsman, we shall have most need of you at my wife's manor houses i'th' country; there's goodly parks and champion grounds for you; we shall have all our sports within ourselves; all the gentlemen o'th' country shall be beholding to us and our pastimes.   55

FALCONER

And we'll make your worship admire, sir.

39 *perfumer* one who fumigates or perfumes rooms
44 *Sa ho* a hawking cry
46 *There, boy* a hunting cry
49 *countenance* favour
53 *champion* champaign
56 *your* ed. you Q1
56 *admire* wonder

HOARD

Say'st thou so? do but make me admire, and thou shalt want
for nothing.—My tailor!

TAILOR

Anon, sir.

HOARD

Go presently in hand with the liveries.   60

TAILOR

I will, sir.

HOARD

My barber.

BARBER

Here, sir.

HOARD

Make 'em all trim fellows, louse 'em well—especially my
huntsman—and cut all their beards of the Polonian fashion.   65
—My perfumer.

PERFUMER

Under your nose, sir.

HOARD

Cast a better savour upon the knaves, to take away the scent
of my tailor's feet, and my barber's lotium-water.

PERFUMER

It shall be carefully performed, sir.   70

HOARD

But you, my falconer and huntsman, the welcom'st men
alive, i'faith!

HUNTSMAN

And we'll show you that, sir, shall deserve your worship's
favour.

HOARD

I prithee, show me that. Go, you knaves all, and wash your   75
lungs i'th' buttery, go. [*Exeunt* TAILOR, BARBER, PERFUMER,
FALCONER, *and* HUNTSMAN] By th' mass, and well remembered, I'll ask my wife that question. Wife, Mistress Jane
Hoard!

Enter COURTESAN, *altered in apparel*

69 *lotium-water* stale urine, used as a hair-wash

---

65 *Polonian fashion.* Sampson quotes Fynes Moryson's *Itinerary*, 1617:
'The Polonians [Poles] shave all their heads close, excepting the haire
of the forehead, which they nourish very long and cast back to the hinder
part of the head.' Hoard is probably punning on 'pole', the traditional
symbol of the barber's profession.

COURTESAN
Sir, would you with me?   80

HOARD
I would but know, sweet wife, which might stand best to thy
liking, to have the wedding dinner kept here or i'th' country?

COURTESAN
Hum!—faith, sir, 'twould like me better here; here you were
married, here let all rites be ended.

HOARD
Could a marquess give a better answer? Hoard, bear thy head   85
aloft, thou'st a wife will advance it.

[Enter HOST *with a letter]*

What haste comes here now? Yea, a letter? Some dreg of my
adversary's malice. Come hither; what's the news?

HOST
A thing that concerns my mistress, sir. [*Gives letter to*
COURTESAN]

HOARD
Why then it concerns me, knave!   90

HOST
Ay, and you, knave, too (cry your worship mercy): you are
both like to come into trouble, I promise you, sir: a precontract.

HOARD
How? a precontract, say'st thou?

HOST
I fear they have too much proof on't, sir. Old Lucre, he runs   95
mad up and down, and will to law as fast as he can; young
Witgood laid hold on by his creditors, he exclaims upon you
a't'other side, says you have wrought his undoing by the
injurious detaining of his contract.

HOARD
Body a' me!   100

HOST
He will have utmost satisfaction;
The law shall give him recompense, he says.

COURTESAN
[*Aside*] Alas, his creditors so merciless! my state being yet
uncertain, I deem it not unconscionable to furder him.

85 *marquess* marchioness
85-6 *bear . . . it* 'An unconscious allusion to the horns of the cuckold'
    (Spencer)   87 *Yea* ed. yee Qq
92 *precontract* legally binding betrothal agreement

HOST

  True, sir,—   105

HOARD

  Wife, what says that letter? Let me construe it.

COURTESAN

  Curst be my rash and unadvised words! [*Tears letter and stamps on it*]

  I'll set my foot upon my tongue,

  And tread my inconsiderate grant to dust.

HOARD

  Wife—   110

HOST

  [*Aside*] A pretty shift, i'faith! I commend a woman when she can make away a letter from her husband handsomely, and this was cleanly done, by my troth.

COURTESAN

  I did, sir!

  Some foolish words I must confess did pass,   115

  Which now litigiously he fastens on me.

HOARD

  Of what force? Let me examine 'em.

COURTESAN

  Too strong, I fear: would I were well freed of him!

HOARD

  Shall I compound?

COURTESAN

  No, sir, I'd have it done some nobler way   120

  Of your side; I'd have you come off with honour;

  Let baseness keep with them. Why, have you not

  The means, sir? The occasion's offered you.

HOARD

  Where? How, dear wife?

COURTESAN

  He is now caught by his creditors; the slave's needy, his   125
debts petty; he'll rather bind himself to all inconveniences than rot in prison; by this only means you may get a release from him. 'Tis not yet come to his uncle's hearing; send speedily for the creditors; by this time he's desperate, he'll set his hand to anything: take order for his debts, or dis-   130
charge 'em quite: a pax on him, let's be rid of a rascal!

113 *cleanly* adroitly
119 *compound* make a financial concession (in light of what follows, a
    long-standing arrangement is meant)
122–3 ed. prose in Qq

HOARD
  Excellent!
  Thou dost astonish me.—Go, run, make haste;
  Bring both the creditors and Witgood hither.
HOST
  [*Aside*] This will be some revenge yet.   [*Exit*]   135
HOARD
  In the mean space I'll have a release drawn.—Within there!

[*Enter* SERVANT]

SERVANT
  Sir?
HOARD
  Sirrah, come take directions; go to my scrivener.
COURTESAN
  [*Aside*] I'm yet like those whose riches lie in dreams;
  If I be waked, they're false; such is my fate,   140
  Who ventures deeper than the desperate state.
  Though I have sinned, yet could I become new,
  For, where I once vow, I am ever true.
HOARD
  Away, dispatch; on my displeasure, quickly. [*Exit* SERVANT]
  Happy occasion! Pray heaven he be in the right vein now to   145
  set his hand to't, that nothing alter him; grant that all his
  follies may meet in him at once, to besot him enough! I
  pray for him i'faith, and here he comes.

[*Enter* WITGOOD *and* CREDITORS]

WITGOOD
  What would you with me now, my uncle's spiteful adversary?
HOARD
  Nay, I am friends.
WITGOOD   Ay, when your mischief's spent.   150
HOARD
  I heard you were arrested.

132–4 ed. prose in Qq
137 SERVANT ed. l. Qq
147–8 lineation ed. I . . . comes Qq as separate line
151–2 lineation ed.

---

138 *scrivener.* Not merely a penman, but a notary, and one who, like the
  lawyer and the usurer, lives on the misfortunes of others. 'An usurer is
  one that puts his money to the unnatural act of generation, and the
  scrivener is his bawd' (Tilley, U28). This general characterisation
  persisted—cf. Pope's *Epistle to Cobham*, l. 106: 'Will sneaks a Scriv'ner,
  an exceeding knave'.

WITGOOD   Well, what then?
You will pay none of my debts, I am sure.
HOARD
A wise man cannot tell;
There may be those conditions 'greed upon
May move me to do much.
WITGOOD   Ay, when?—   155
'Tis thou, perjured woman! (Oh, no name
Is vild enough to match thy treachery!)
That art the cause of my confusion.
COURTESAN
Out, you penurious slave!
HOARD
Nay, wife, you are too froward;   160
Let him alone; give losers leave to talk.
WITGOOD
Shall I remember thee of another promise
Far stronger than the first?
COURTESAN   I'd fain know that.
WITGOOD
'Twould call shame to thy cheeks.
COURTESAN   Shame!
WITGOOD   Hark in your ear.
—[*Draws* COURTESAN *aside*] Will he come off, think'st thou,   165
and pay my debts roundly?
COURTESAN
Doubt nothing; there's a release a-drawing and all, to which
you must set your hand.
WITGOOD
Excellent!
COURTESAN
But methinks, i'faith, you might have made some shift to dis-   170
charge this yourself, having in the mortgage, and never have
burdened my conscience with it.
WITGOOD
A' my troth, I could not, for my creditors' cruelties extend
to the present.
COURTESAN
No more.—   175
Why, do your worst for that, I defy you.

155–6 lineation ed.
155 *when* exclamation of impatience   157 *vild* vile
161 *give . . . talk* proverbial   162–3 ed. prose in Qq
164–6 lineation ed.   175–6 lineation ed.

WITGOOD

Y'are impudent: I'll call up witnesses.

COURTESAN

Call up thy wits, for thou hast been devoted
To follies a long time.

HOARD   Wife, y'are too bitter.—

Master Witgood, and you, my masters, you shall hear a mild   180
speech come from me now, and this it is: 't 'as been my
fortune, gentlemen, to have an extraordinary blessing
poured upon me a'late, and here she stands; I have wedded
her and bedded her, and yet she is little the worse. Some
foolish words she hath passed to you in the country, and   185
some peevish debts you owe here in the city; set the hare's
head to the goose-giblet: release you her of her words, and
I'll release you of your debts, sir.

WITGOOD

Would you so? I thank you for that, sir; I cannot blame you,
i'faith.   190

HOARD

Why, are not debts better than words, sir?

WITGOOD

Are not words promises, and are not promises debts, sir?

HOARD

He plays at back-racket with me.

1 CREDITOR

Come hither, Master Witgood, come hither; be ruled by fools
once.   [CREDITORS *draw* WITGOOD *aside*]   195

2 CREDITOR

We are citizens, and know what belong to't.

1 CREDITOR

Take hold of his offer; pax on her, let her go. If your debts
were once discharged, I would help you to a widow myself
worth ten of her.

3 CREDITOR

Mass, partner, and now you remember me on't, there's   200
Master Mulligrub's sister newly fallen a widow.

178–9 ed. prose in Qq   186 *peevish* silly
186–7 *set . . . giblet* give tit for tat (proverbial)
193 *back-racket* the return of the ball in tennis, hence fig. a counter-
       charge, a *tu quoque*

201 *Mulligrub's.* Another example of Middleton's penchant for grotesque
    names. The mulligrubs was 'a fit of megrims or spleen' (*OED*). There
    is a Master Mulligrub in Marston's *The Dutch Courtesan*, 1605.

1 CREDITOR

Cuds me, as pat as can be! There's a widow left for you, ten
thousand in money, beside plate, jewels, *et cetera*; I warrant
it a match; we can do all in all with her. Prithee dispatch;
we'll carry thee to her presently.   205

WITGOOD

My uncle will never endure me, when he shall hear I set my
hand to a release.

2 CREDITOR

Hark, I'll tell thee a trick for that. I have spent five hundred
pound in suits in my time; I should be wise. Thou'rt now a
prisoner; make a release; take't of my word, whatsoever a   210
man makes as long as he is in durance, 'tis nothing in law,
not thus much.   [*Snaps his fingers*]

WITGOOD

Say you so, sir?

3 CREDITOR

I have paid for't, I know't.

WITGOOD

Proceed then, I consent.   215

3 CREDITOR

Why, well said.

HOARD

How now, my masters; what, have you done with him?

1 CREDITOR

With much ado, sir, we have got him to consent.

HOARD

Ah-a-a! and what came his debts to now?

1 CREDITOR

Some eight score odd pounds, sir.   220

HOARD

Naw, naw, naw, naw, naw! Tell me the second time; give me
a lighter sum. They are but desperate debts, you know,
never called in but upon such an accident; a poor, needy
knave, he would starve and rot in prison. Come, come, you
shall have ten shillings in the pound, and the sum down   225
roundly.

1 CREDITOR

You must make it a mark, sir.

HOARD

Go to, then; tell your money in the mean time; you shall find

202 *Cuds* see II. i, 40
222 *desperate* 'bad', i.e. irretrievable
227 *mark* see III. i, 130

little less there.—Come, Master Witgood, you are so
unwilling to do yourself good now.   230

[*Enter* SCRIVENER]

Welcome, honest scrivener.—Now you shall hear the release
read.

SCRIVENER
[*Reads*] Be it known to all men by these presents, that I,
Theodorus Witgood, gentleman, sole nephew to Pecunius
Lucre, having unjustly made title and claim to one Jane   235
Medler, late widow of Anthony Medler, and now wife to
Walkadine Hoard, in consideration of a competent sum of
money to discharge my debts, do forever hereafter disclaim
any title, right, estate, or interest in or to the said widow,
late in the occupation of the said Anthony Medler, and now 240
in the occupation of Walkadine Hoard; as also neither to lay
claim by virtue of any former contract, grant, promise, or
demise, to any of her manors, manor houses, parks, groves,
meadow-grounds, arable lands, barns, stacks, stables, dove-
holes, and coney-burrows; together with all her cattle,   245
money, plate, jewels, borders, chains, bracelets, furnitures,
hangings, moveables, or immoveables. In witness whereof I,
the said Theodorus Witgood, have interchangeably set to
my hand and seal before these presents, the day and date
above written.   250

WITGOOD
What a precious fortune hast thou slipped here, like a beast
as thou art!

HOARD
Come, unwilling heart, come.

WITGOOD
Well, Master Hoard, give me the pen; I see
'Tis vain to quarrel with our destiny. [*Signs*]   255

HOARD
Oh, as vain a thing as can be; you cannot commit a greater
absurdity, sir. So, so; give me that hand now: before all
these presents, I am friends forever with thee.

233 *presents* the present document (*OED*, 'present', *sb.*[1] 2. b.)
243 *demise* conveyance or transfer of an estate by will or lease
243 *manors* ed. Mannor Qq   244 *dove-holes* dove-houses
245 *coney-burrows* rabbit warrens
245 *cattle* chattels (*OED*, 'cattle', *sb.*, 3)
247 *immoveables* ed. immouerables Q1
249 *presents* witnesses (*OED* 'present', *sb.*[1], 2)
251 *slipped* let slip

WITGOOD

Troth, and it were pity of my heart now, if I should bear you
any grudge, i'faith.   260

HOARD

Content. I'll send for thy uncle against the wedding dinner;
we will be friends once again.

WITGOOD

I hope to bring it to pass myself, sir.

HOARD

How now? is't right, my masters?

1 CREDITOR

'Tis something wanting, sir; yet it shall be sufficient.   265

HOARD

Why, well said; a good conscience makes a fine show
nowadays. Come, my masters, you shall all taste of my wine
ere you depart.

ALL

We follow you, sir.

                [*Exeunt* HOARD, COURTESAN *and* SCRIVENER]

WITGOOD

[*Aside*] I'll try these fellows now.—A word, sir; what, will   270
you carry me to that rich widow now?

1 CREDITOR

Why, do you think we were in earnest, i'faith? Carry you to a
rich widow? We should get much credit by that: a noted
rioter! a contemptible prodigal! 'Twas a trick we have
amongst us to get in our money. Fare you well, sir.   275

                                        Exeunt [CREDITORS]

WITGOOD

Farewell, and be hanged, you short pig-haired, ram-headed
rascals! He that believes in you shall never be saved, I warrant
him. By this new league I shall have some access unto my love.

                        She is above

NIECE

Master Witgood!

WITGOOD

My life!   280

NIECE

Meet me presently; that note directs you [*throwing it down*];
I would not be suspected. Our happiness attends us. Farewell!

WITGOOD

A word's enough.   *Exeunt*

276 *pig-haired* the citizens wore their hair short
276 *ram-headed* cuckolded   283 s.d. after l. 282 in Qq

[Act IV, Scene v]

DAMPIT, *the usurer, in his bed;* AUDREY *spinning by;* [BOY]
Song [*by* AUDREY]

Let the usurer cram him, in interest that excel,
There's pits enow to damn him, before he comes to hell;
In Holborn some, in Fleet Street some,
Where'er he come, there's some, there's some.

DAMPIT
Trahe, traheto, draw the curtain, give me a sip of sack more.   5

Enter GENTLEMEN [*i.e.,* LAMPREY *and* SPITCHCOCK]

LAMPREY
Look you, did not I tell you he lay like the devil in chains,
when he was bound for a thousand year?

SPITCHCOCK
But I think the devil had no steel bedstaffs; he goes beyond
him for that.

LAMPREY
Nay, do but mark the conceit of his drinking; one must wipe   10
his mouth for him with a muckinder, do you see, sir?

2 *pits* brothels and taverns
3 *Holborn . . . Fleet Street* where Dampit conducted his business.
  Cf. I. iv, 57–8
8 *bedstaffs* stout staves laid loose across the old wooden bedsteads,
  to support the bedding
10 *conceit* peculiarity   11 *muckinder* handkerchief or bib

---

s.d. He would have been 'discovered' on the inner stage when the curtain
  he refers to was drawn back.
1–4 The song is by Thomas Ravenscroft, a chorister at Paul's, and is
  reprinted in 'Melismata' (1611), a collection of his lyrics. In Q1, it lacks
  the first two lines, probably as a result of a compositor's blunder. They
  run:
      My master is so wise, so wise, that he's proceeded wittol,
      My mistress is a fool, a fool, and yet 'tis the most get-all.
  See A. J. Sabol, 'Ravenscroft's "Melismata" and the Children of
  Paul's', *RN*, XII (1959), 3–9.
6–7 See *Revelation*, xx, 2. Sampson suggests that Dampit is chained to the
  'great iron chest' (III. iv, 5), but it is unlikely that the Biblical reference
  need be taken so literally, especially in the light of the s.d. which opens
  this scene. Further, 'hanging in chains' seems to have been a traditional
  end for the usurer: see Dekker's *Work for Armourers* (*The Non-Dramatic
  Works*, ed. Grosart, iv, 164) and his *If This Be Not a Good Play, the
  Devil Is In It*, V. iv, 253–4.

SPITCHCOCK

Is this the sick trampler? Why, he is only bed-rid with
drinking.

LAMPREY

True, sir. He spies us.

DAMPIT

What, sir Tristram? You come and see a weak man here, a   15
very weak man.

LAMPREY

If you be weak in body, you should be strong in prayer, sir.

DAMPIT

Oh, I have prayed too much, poor man.

LAMPREY

There's a taste of his soul for you.

SPITCHCOCK

Fah, loathsome!   20

LAMPREY

I come to borrow a hundred pound of you, sir.

DAMPIT

Alas, you come at an ill time; I cannot spare it, i'faith; I ha'
but two thousand i'th' house.

AUDREY

Ha, ha, ha!

DAMPIT

Out, you gernative quean, the mullipood of villainy, the   25
spinner of concupiscency!

Enter other GENTLEMAN [*i.e.,* SIR LANCELOT]

LANCELOT

Yea, gentlemen, are you here before us? How is he now?

LAMPREY

Faith, the same man still: the tavern bitch has bit him i'th'
head.

12 *trampler* See I. iv, 10
25 *gernative* addicted to 'girning', or grumbling
25 *mullipood* dirty toad (?). See *OED, s.v. mull* and *pode*
27 *Yea* ed. Yee Qq   28–9 *tavern . . . head* he is drunk (proverbial)

---

15 *Tristram.* In the various revivals of the Tristram story which began in
the late 15th century, the famous lover had become a mere gallant, and
his name was loosely applied to any libertine. Lamprey does not display
a licentious bent in the play: Dampit is simply playing on his name,
lampreys supposedly being strongly aphrodisiac.
26 *spinner.* Audrey is literally spinning, but *spinner* probably = *spider*
here. See I. i, 31.

LANCELOT

We shall have the better sport with him; peace!—And how   30
cheers Master Dampit now?

DAMPIT

Oh, my bosom Sir Lancelot, how cheer I! Thy presence is
restorative.

LANCELOT

But I hear a great complaint of you, Master Dampit, among
gallants.   35

DAMPIT

I am glad of that, i'faith; prithee, what?

LANCELOT

They say you are waxed proud a' late, and if a friend visit you
in the afternoon, you'll scarce know him.

DAMPIT

Fie, fie! Proud? I cannot remember any such thing; sure I
was drunk then.   40

LANCELOT

Think you so, sir?

DAMPIT

There 'twas, i'faith, nothing but the pride of the sack, and so
certify 'em.—Fetch sack, sirrah!

BOY

A vengeance sack you once!

[Exit, and returns presently with sack]

AUDREY

Why, Master Dampit, if you hold on as you begin, and lie a   45
little longer, you need not take care how to dispose your
wealth; you'll make the vintner your heir.

DAMPIT

Out, you babliaminy, you unfeathered, cremitoried quean,
you cullisance of scabiosity!

AUDREY

Good words, Master Dampit, to speak before a maid and a   50
virgin.

DAMPIT

Hang thy virginity upon the pole of carnality!

---

48 *babliaminy* babbler
48 *cremitoried* 'burnt, syphilitic. *Unfeathered* implies that she has lost
  her hair from the pox' (Spencer)
49 *cullisance* a corruption of *cognizance* = heraldic badge
49 *scabiosity* syphilis

AUDREY

Sweet terms! My mistress shall know 'em.

LAMPREY

Note but the misery of this usuring slave: here he lies, like a
noisome dunghill, full of the poison of his drunken blas-   55
phemies, and they to whom he bequeaths all grudge him the
very meat that feeds him, the very pillow that eases him.
Here may a usurer behold his end. What profits it to be a
slave in this world, and a devil i'th' next?

DAMPIT

Sir Lancelot, let me buss thee, Sir Lancelot; thou art the only   60
friend that I honour and respect.

LANCELOT

I thank you for that, Master Dampit.

DAMPIT

Farewell, my bosom Sir Lancelot.

LANCELOT

Gentlemen, an you love me, let me step behind you, and one
of you fall a-talking of me to him.   65

LAMPREY

Content.—Master Dampit.

DAMPIT

So, sir.

LAMPREY

Here came Sir Lancelot to see you e'en now.

DAMPIT

Hang him, rascal!

LAMPREY

Who, Sir Lancelot?   70

DAMPIT

Pythagorical rascal!

LAMPREY

Pythagorical?

DAMPIT

Ay, he changes his cloak when he meets a sergeant.

60 *buss* kiss

---

53 *My mistress*. This is the only time that we hear of Dampit's wife. It may
be an authorial slip, an example of episodic intensification. But see note
on IV. v, 1–4 above.
71–3 A debasement of the Pythagorean doctrine of the transmigration of
souls. Cf. Jonson's *Cynthia's Revels*, 1601, IV. iii, 146; and Middleton's
Your Five Gallants, 1605, V. i, 108–9: 'That Pythagorical rascal! in a
gentleman's suit today, in a knight's tomorrow.'

LANCELOT
What a rogue's this!

LAMPREY
I wonder you can rail at him, sir; he comes in love to see you.   75

DAMPIT
A louse for his love! His father was a comb-maker; I have no
need of his crawling love. He comes to have longer day, the
superlative rascal!

LANCELOT
'Sfoot, I can no longer endure the rogue!—Master Dampit,
I come to take my leave once again, sir.   80

DAMPIT
Who? my dear and kind Sir Lancelot, the only gentleman of
England? Let me hug thee; farewell, and a thousand.

LAMPREY
Composed of wrongs and slavish flatteries!

LANCELOT
Nay, gentlemen, he shall show you more tricks yet; I'll give
you another taste of him.   85

LAMPREY
Is't possible?

LANCELOT
His memory is upon departing.

DAMPIT
Another cup of sack!

LANCELOT
Mass, then 'twill be quite gone! Before he drink that, tell him
there's a country client come up, and here attends for his   90
learned advice.

LAMPREY
Enough.

DAMPIT
One cup more, and then let the bell toll; I hope I shall be
weak enough by that time.

LAMPREY
Master Dampit.   95

DAMPIT
Is the sack spouting?

LAMPREY
'Tis coming forward, sir. Here's a countryman, a client of
yours, waits for your deep and profound advice, sir.

77 *crawling* continuing the *louse* image
77 *longer day* more time to pay off his debts
82 *farewell . . . thousand* a thousand times farewell

DAMPIT

A coxcombry? Where is he? Let him approach; set me up a
peg higher.　　　　　　　　　　　　　　　　　　100

LAMPREY

You must draw near, sir.

DAMPIT

Now, good man fooliaminy, what say you to me now?

LANCELOT

Please your good worship, I am a poor man, sir—

DAMPIT

What make you in my chamber then?

LANCELOT

I would entreat your worship's device in a just and honest　　105
cause, sir.

DAMPIT

I meddle with no such matters; I refer 'em to Master No-
man's office.

LANCELOT

I had but one house left me in all the world, sir, which was
my father's, my grandfather's, my great-grandfather's; and　　110
now a villain has unjustly wrung me out, and took possession
on't.

DAMPIT

Has he such feats? Thy best course is to bring thy *ejectione
firmae*, and in seven year thou may'st shove him out by the
law.　　　　　　　　　　　　　　　　　　　　115

LANCELOT

Alas, an't please your worship, I have small friends and less
money.

DAMPIT

Hoyday! this gear will fadge well. Hast no money? Why,
then, my advice is thou must set fire o'th' house and so get
him out.　　　　　　　　　　　　　　　　　　120

LAMPREY

That will break strife, indeed.

---

104 *make* do
105 *device* an intentional malapropism
113–14 *ejectione firmae* writ of ejectment whereby a person ousted
　　from an estate for years may recover possession of it
114 *firmae* ed. *firme* Qq
118 *gear* business
118 *fadge* succeed
121 *break* broach, breech

LANCELOT
I thank your worship for your hot counsel, sir.—Altering but
my voice a little, you see he knew me not; you may observe
by this that a drunkard's memory holds longer in the voice
than in the person. But, gentlemen, shall I show you a sight?   125
Behold the little dive-dapper of damnation, Gulf the
usurer, for his time worse than t'other.

Enter HOARD *with* GULF

LAMPREY
What's he comes with him?
LANCELOT
Why, Hoard, that married lately the Widow Medler.
LAMPREY
Oh, I cry you mercy, sir.   130
HOARD
Now, gentlemen visitants, how does Master Dampit?
LANCELOT
Faith, here he lies e'en drawing in, sir, good canary as fast as
he can, sir; a very weak creature, truly, he is almost past
memory.
HOARD
Fie, Master Dampit! you lie lazing abed here, and I come to   135
invite you to my wedding dinner; up, up, up!
DAMPIT
Who's this? Master Hoard? Who hast thou married, in the
name of foolery?
HOARD
A rich widow.
DAMPIT
A Dutch widow?   140
HOARD
A rich widow; one Widow Medler.
DAMPIT
Medler? She keeps open house.
HOARD
She did, I can tell you, in her tother husband's days; open
house for all comers; horse and man was welcome, and room
enough for 'em all.   145

126 *dive-dapper* dabchick, a small diving waterfowl
127 *for his time* considering the duration of his activities
132 *canary* a light, sweet wine from the Canary Islands
142 *open house* see II. ii, 59

DAMPIT

There's too much for thee, then; thou may'st let out some to
thy neighbours.

GULF

What, hung alive in chains? O spectacle! bed-staffs of steel?
O monstrum horrendum, informe, ingens, cui lumen ademptum!
O Dampit, Dampit, here's a just judgement shown upon   150
usury, extortion, and trampling villainy!

LANCELOT

This is excellent, thief rails upon the thief!

GULF

Is this the end of cut-throat usury, brothel, and blasphemy?
Now may'st thou see what race a usurer runs.

DAMPIT

Why, thou rogue of universality, do not I know thee? Thy   155
sound is like the cuckoo, the Welsh ambassador; thou
cowardly slave, that offers to fight with a sick man when his
weapon's down! Rail upon me in my naked bed? Why, thou
great Lucifer's little vicar, I am not so weak but I know a
knave at first sight. Thou inconscionable rascal! thou that   160
goest upon Middlesex juries, and will make haste to give up
thy verdict, because thou wilt not lose thy dinner, are you
answered?

GULF

An't were not for shame—   *draws his dagger*

---

149 *O . . . ademptum* O fearful monster, misshapen, huge, deprived of
    sight (*Aeneid*, III. 658)
152 *This is excellent* ed. This exlent Qq
153–4 lineation ed. Is . . . Vsury Qq as separate line
158 *upon . . . bed* upon me undressed in bed

---

156 *cuckoo . . . ambassador.* Welsh raiding bands used to descend on the
    English border to fight and plunder 'about Cuckoe tymes', according to
    an anonymous play *The Welsh Ambassador*, 1623. See Gwyn Williams,
    'The Cuckoo, the Welsh Ambassador', *MLR*, LI (1956), 223–5.
158 *naked bed.* An allusion to Hieronimo's much-ridiculed line in Kyd's
    The Spanish Tragedy, 1587, II. v, i: 'What outcries pluck me from my
    naked bed . . . ?'
161 *Middlesex juries.* Frequently a subject for complaints. Cf. Ben Jonson's
    Every Man in His Humour, 1616, I. ii, 88–9, and Herford and Simpson's
    note (ix, 350), in which they quote the reputed saying of a Tudor bishop:
    'A London jury would find Abel guilty of the murder of Cain'. And see
    Tilley, J104: 'A London (Kentish, Middlesex) jury hang half and save
    half.'

DAMPIT
>Thou wouldst be hanged then.   165

LAMPREY
>Nay, you must exercise patience, Master Gulf, always, in a
>sick man's chamber.

LANCELOT
>He'll quarrel with none, I warrant you, but those that are
>bed-rid.

DAMPIT
>Let him come, gentlemen, I am armed; reach my close-stool   170
>hither.

LANCELOT
>Here will be a sweet fray anon; I'll leave you, gentlemen.

LAMPREY
>Nay, we'll along with you.—Master Gulf—

GULF
>Hang him, usuring rascal!

LANCELOT
>Push, set your strength to his, your wit to his.   175

AUDREY
>Pray, gentlemen, depart; his hour's come upon him.—Sleep
>in my bosom, sleep.

LANCELOT
>Nay, we have enough of him, i'faith; keep him for the house.
>Now make your best.
>For thrice his wealth I would not have his breast.   180

GULF
>A little thing would make me beat him, now he's asleep.

LANCELOT
>Mass, then 'twill be a pitiful day when he wakes. I would be
>loath to see that day come.

GULF
>You overrule me, gentlemen, i'faith.   *Exeunt*

[Act V, Scene i]

Enter LUCRE *and* WITGOOD

WITGOOD
>Nay, uncle, let me prevail with you so much;
>I'faith, go, now he has invited you.

172 *sweet* with reference to its odoriferous possibilities
176 *his . . . him* he is on the point of death
184 GULF ed. L*ul*: Q1   s.d. ed. *ACTVS.* Qq

LUCRE

I shall have great joy there when he has borne away the
widow.

WITGOOD

Why, la, I thought where I should find you presently; uncle,   5
a' my troth, 'tis nothing so.

LUCRE

What's nothing so, sir? Is not he married to the widow?

WITGOOD

No, by my troth, is he not, uncle.

LUCRE

How?

WITGOOD

Will you have the truth on't? He is married to a whore,   10
i'faith.

LUCRE

I should laugh at that.

WITGOOD

Uncle, let me perish in your favour if you find it not so, and
that 'tis I that have married the honest woman.

LUCRE

Ha! I'd walk ten mile a' foot to see that, i'faith.   15

WITGOOD

And see't you shall, or I'll never see you again.

LUCRE

A quean, i'faith? Ha, ha, ha!   *Exeunt*

[Act V, Scene ii]

Enter HOARD, *tasting wine, the* HOST *following in a livery cloak*

HOARD

Pup, pup, pup, pup! I like not this wine. Is there never a
better tierce in the house?

HOST

Yes, sir, there are as good tierce in the house as any are in
England.

HOARD

Desire your mistress, you knave, to taste 'em all over; she has   5
better skill.

---

2 *tierce* cask. The host puns in the following lines on other meanings
  of the word: a band or company (of soldiers), or a thrust in
  fencing

HOST

[*Aside*] Has she so? The better for her, and the worse for you.

Exit

HOARD

Arthur!

[*Enter* ARTHUR]

Is the cupboard of plate set out?

ARTHUR

All's in order, sir.   [*Exit*]   10

HOARD

I am in love with my liveries every time I think on 'em; they
make a gallant show, by my troth.—Niece!

[*Enter* NIECE]

NIECE

Do you call, sir?

HOARD

Prithee, show a little diligence, and overlook the knaves a
little; they'll filch and steal today, and send whole pasties   15
home to their wives; an thou beest a good niece, do not see
me purloined.

NIECE

Fear it not, sir.—[*Aside*] I have cause: though the feast be
prepared for you, yet it serves fit for my wedding dinner too.

[*Exit*]

Enter two Gentlemen [*i.e.*, LAMPREY *and* SPITCHCOCK]

HOARD

Master Lamprey and Master Spitchcock, two the most   20
welcome gentlemen alive! Your fathers and mine were all
free o'th'fishmongers.

LAMPREY

They were indeed, sir. You see bold guests, sir, soon
entreated.

HOARD

And that's best, sir.—   25

[*Enter* SERVANT]

How now, sirrah?

9 *cupboard of plate* a side-board for the display of plate, or the
service of plate itself
22 *free o'th' fishmongers* members of that one of the great city companies (with an obvious allusion to the 'fishiness' of the names—
see I. iii, first s.d. and note)

SERVANT
  There's a coach come to th'door, sir.   [*Exit*]
HOARD
  My Lady Foxstone, a' my life!—Mistress Jane Hoard, wife!
  —Mass, 'tis her Ladyship indeed!

                   [*Enter* LADY FOXSTONE]

  Madam, you are welcome to an unfurnished house, dearth of   30
  cheer, scarcity of attendance.
LADY FOXSTONE
  You are pleased to make the worst, sir.
HOARD
  Wife!

                   [*Enter* COURTESAN]

LADY FOXSTONE
  Is this your bride?
HOARD
  Yes, madam.—Salute my Lady Foxstone.   35
COURTESAN
  Please you, madam, a while to taste the air in the garden?
LADY FOXSTONE
  'Twill please us well. *Exeunt* [LADY FOXSTONE *and* COURTESAN]
HOARD
  Who would not wed? The most delicious life!
  No joys are like the comforts of a wife.
LAMPREY
  So we bachelors think, that are not troubled with them.   40

                   [*Enter* SERVANT]

SERVANT
  Your worship's brother with another ancient gentleman are
  newly alighted, sir.   [*Exit*]
HOARD
  Master Onesiphorus Hoard? Why, now our company begins
  to come in.

          [*Enter* ONESIPHORUS HOARD, LIMBER *and* KIX]

  My dear and kind brother, welcome, i'faith.   45

35 *Foxstone* ed. *Foxtone* Qq

---

41 *another ancient gentleman.* The servant may have only noticed one old
   man with Onesiphorus, but all the evidence is that Middleton was
   careless about the introduction and numbering of his minor characters.
   See III. iii, first s.d.

ONESIPHORUS
You see we are men at an hour, brother.

HOARD
Ay, I'll say that for you, brother; you keep as good an hour
to come to a feast as any gentleman in the shire.—What, old
Master Limber and Master Kix! Do we meet, i'faith, jolly
gentlemen?   50

LIMBER
We hope you lack guests, sir?

HOARD
Oh, welcome, welcome! we lack still such guests as your
worships.

ONESIPHORUS
Ah, sirrah brother, have you catched up Widow Medler?

HOARD
From 'em all, brother; and I may tell you, I had mighty   55
enemies, those that stuck sore; old Lucre is a sore fox, I can
tell you, brother.

ONESIPHORUS
Where is she? I'll go seek her out; I long to have a smack at
her lips.

HOARD
And most wishfully, brother, see where she comes.   60

[*Enter* COURTESAN *and* LADY FOXSTONE]

Give her a smack now we may hear it all the house over.

Both [*i.e.,* COURTESAN *and* ONESIPHORUS HOARD] *turn back*

COURTESAN
Oh, heaven, I am betrayed! I know that face.

HOARD
Ha, ha, ha! Why, how now? Are you both ashamed?—Come,
gentlemen, we'll look another way.

ONESIPHORUS
Nay, brother, hark you: come, y'are disposed to be merry?   65

HOARD
Why do we meet else, man?

ONESIPHORUS
That's another matter; I was never so 'fraid in my life but
that you had been in earnest.

HOARD
How mean you, brother?

61 *smack* ed. smerck Qq

ONESIPHORUS
> You said she was your wife?   70

HOARD
> Did I so? By my troth, and so she is.

ONESIPHORUS
> By your troth, brother?

HOARD
> What reason have I to dissemble with my friends, brother?
> If marriage can make her mine, she is mine! Why?

ONESIPHORUS
> Troth, I am not well of a sudden. I must crave pardon,   75
> brother; I came to see you but I cannot stay dinner, i'faith.

HOARD
> I hope you will not serve me so, brother.

LIMBER
> By your leave, Master Hoard—

HOARD
> What now? what now? Pray, gentlemen, you were wont to
> show yourselves wise men.   80

LIMBER
> But you have shown your folly too much here.

HOARD
> How?

KIX
> Fie, fie! A man of your repute and name!
> You'll feast your friends, but cloy 'em first with shame.

HOARD
> This grows too deep; pray, let us reach the sense.   85

LIMBER
> In your old age dote on a courtesan—

HOARD
> Ha?

KIX
> Marry a strumpet!

HOARD
> Gentlemen!

ONESIPHORUS
> And Witgood's quean!   90

HOARD
> Oh! nor lands, nor living?

ONESIPHORUS
> Living!

HOARD
> [to COURTESAN] Speak!

COURTESAN
  Alas, you know at first, sir,
  I told you I had nothing.   95
HOARD
  Out, out! I am cheated; infinitely cozened!
LIMBER
  Nay, Master Hoard—

Enter WITGOOD *and* LUCRE

HOARD
  A Dutch widow, a Dutch widow, a Dutch widow!
LUCRE
  Why, nephew, shall I trace thee still a liar?
  Wilt make me mad? Is not yon thing the widow?   100
WITGOOD
  Why, la, you are so hard a' belief, uncle!
  By my troth, she's a whore.
LUCRE   Then thou'rt a knave.
WITGOOD
  Negatur argumentum, uncle.
LUCRE
  Probo tibi, nephew: he that knows a woman to be a quean
  must needs be a knave; thou say'st thou know'st her to be   105
  one; *ergo*, if she be a quean, thou'rt a knave.
WITGOOD
  Negatur sequela majoris, uncle, he that knows a woman to be
  a quean must needs be a knave; I deny that.
HOARD
  Lucre and Witgood, y'are both villains; get you out of my
  house!   110
LUCRE
  Why, didst not invite me to thy wedding dinner?
WITGOOD
  And are not you and I sworn perpetual friends before witness,
  sir, and were both drunk upon't?
HOARD
  Daintily abused! Y'ave put a junt upon me!

  99–102 ed. prose in Qq
  103 *Negatur argumentum* Proof is denied
  104 *Probo tibi* I'll prove it to you (*Probo* . . . Nephew Qq as separate
      line)
  107 *Negatur sequela majoris* The conclusion of your major premise is
      denied
  114 *junt* trick

LUCRE
   Ha, ha, ha!
HOARD   A common strumpet!
WITGOOD   Nay, now   115
   You wrong her, sir; if I were she, I'd have
   The law on you for that; I durst depose for her
   She ne'er had common use, nor common thought.
COURTESAN
   Despise me, publish me: I am your wife;
   What shame can I have now but you'll have part?   120
   If in disgrace you share, I sought not you;
   You pursued me, nay, forced me;
   Had I friends would follow it,
   Less than your action has been proved a rape.
ONESIPHORUS
   Brother!   125
COURTESAN
   Nor did I ever boast of lands unto you,
   Money, or goods; I took a plainer course
   And told you true I'd nothing.
   If error were committed, 'twas by you;
   Thank your own folly. Nor has my sin been   130
   So odious but worse has been forgiven;
   Nor am I so deformed but I may challenge
   The utmost power of any old man's love.—
   She that tastes not sin before, twenty to one but she'll taste
   it after; most of you old men are content to marry young   135
   virgins, and take that which follows; where, marrying one
   of us, you both save a sinner, and are quit from a cuckold for
   ever.
   And more, in brief, let this your best thoughts win,
   She that knows sin, knows best how to hate sin.   140
HOARD
   Cursed be all malice! Black are the fruits of spite,

115–18 ed. prose in Qq
119 *publish* denounce, 'show up'
130–3 ed. prose in Qq
136 *where* whereas
137 *quit from* saved from the danger of becoming

139–40 Q1 has inverted commas before these lines to emphasise their
sententious character. This was a fashionable practice in certain printing
houses of the time; but the commas might well have been in Middleton's
MS, if, as seems likely, he wanted to emphasise the artificiality of the
speeches of 'repentance'.

And poison first their owners. Oh, my friends,
I must embrace shame, to be rid of shame!
. Concealed disgrace prevents a public name.
Ah, Witgood! ah, Theodorus.   145

WITGOOD
Alas, sir, I was pricked in conscience to see her well
bestowed, and where could I bestow her better than upon
your pitiful worship? Excepting but myself, I dare swear
she's a virgin; and now, by marrying your niece, I have
banished myself for ever from her. She's mine aunt now, by   150
my faith, and there's no meddling with mine aunt, you know
—a sin against my nuncle.

COURTESAN
[kneeling] Lo, gentlemen, before you all
In true reclaiméd form I fall.
Henceforth for ever I defy   155
The glances of a sinful eye,
Waving of fans (which some suppose
Tricks of fancy), treading of toes,
Wringing of fingers, biting the lip
The wanton gait, th'alluring trip,   160
All secret friends and private meetings,
Close-borne letters and bawds' greetings,
Feigning excuse to women's labours
When we are sent for to th'next neighbours,
Taking false physic, and ne'er start   165

150 *aunt* pun on *aunt* = *mistress*
152 *nuncle* a common corruption of *uncle*
155 *defy* renounce
158 *fancy* love
159 *wringing* clasping
161 *friends* lovers
162 *Close* secretly

156–7 Cf. the Palinode to Jonson's *Cynthia's Revels:* 'From wauing **of**
     fannes, coy glaunces, glickes, cringes, and all such simpring humours
     . . . Good MERCVRY defend vs.'
158–9 Cf. Dekker's and Webster's *Northward Ho!,* II. ii, 11ff.: 'what
     treads of the toe, salutations by winckes, discourse by bitings of the
     lip, amorous glances, sweete stolne kisses when your husbands backs
     turn'd, would passe betweene them.' See also III. ii, 109: 'Marke how
     she wrings him by the fingers.'
163–4 Another frequently mentioned wifely deceit—see Nashe's *Christ's
     Tears over Jerusalem,* 1593, (McKerrow, ii, 151), and Middleton's own
     Black Book, 1604, (Bullen, viii, 35).

To be let blood, though sign be at heart,
Removing chambers, shifting beds,
To welcome friends in husbands' steads,
Them to enjoy, and you to marry,
They first served, while you must tarry,   170
They to spend, and you to gather,
They to get, and you to father—
These and thousand thousand more,
New reclaimed, I now abhor.

LUCRE

Ah, here's a lesson, rioter, for you.   175

WITGOOD

[*kneeling*] I must confess my follies; I'll down too.
And here for ever I disclaim
The cause of youth's undoing, game,
Chiefly dice, those true outlanders,
That shake out beggars, thieves, and panders,   180
Soul-wasting surfeits, sinful riots,
Queans' evils, doctors' diets,
'Pothecaries' drugs, surgeons' glisters,
Stabbing of arms for a common mistress,
Riband favours, ribald speeches,   185
Dear perfumed jackets, penniless breeches,
Dutch flapdragons, healths in urine,

179 *outlanders* foreigners
182 *Queans' evils* syphilis. 'A quibbling antithesis to king's evil'
    (Sampson). Cf. *Macbeth*, IV. iii, 146
186 *perfumed jackets* see IV. iii, 27
187 *flapdragons* raisins, or similar objects, set on fire and drunk in wine
    as they flamed. Dutchmen were supposed to be experts in the art
187 *healths . . . urine* another extravagance of the gallants; it was
    drunk mixed with wine

---

166 *Hence* dangerous. 'According to the directions for bleeding in old
    almanacs, blood was to be taken from particular parts under particular
    planets' (Dyce). Cf. *Northward Ho!*, III. i, 129–32: 'how many seuerall
    loues of Plaiers, of Vaulters, of Lieutenants haue I entertain'd . . . and
    now to let bloud when the signe is at the heart?'
183 *glisters*. Suppositories, enemas. Greene in *A Quip for an Upstart
    Courtier* sneers at the taking of clysters as being an affectation of the
    would be gallant (see Grosart, xi, 248).
184 *Stabbing of arms.* Drinking the blood mixed with wine in a health to
    one's mistress was a common practice. Cf. the palinode to *Cynthia's
    Revels*: 'From stabbing of armes, flap-dragons, healths, whiffes, and all
    such swaggering humours . . . Good MERCVRY defend vs', and Marston's
    The Dutch Courtesan, 1605, IV. i.

Drabs that keep a man too sure in—
I do defy you all.
Lend me each honest hand, for here I rise 190
A reclaimed man, loathing the general vice.

HOARD
So, so, all friends! The wedding dinner cools.
Who seem most crafty prove oft times most fools. [*Exeunt*]

FINIS

New Mermaids

New Mermaid drama books

Paperback drama texts from Ernest Benn

New Mermaids present modern-spelling, fully annotated
editions of classic English plays, including works by Marlowe,
Jonson, Webster, Congreve, Sheridan, and Wilde. Each volume
includes a biography of the writer, a critical introduction to
the play, discussions of dates and sources, and a bibliography.

Arden of Faversham

edited by Martin White,
University of Bristol

160 pages
0 510-33508-X £3.25

Three Late Medieval Morality Plays

(Everyman, Mankind, Mundus et Infans)

edited by Geoffrey Lester,
University of Sheffield

204 pages
0 510-33505-5 £3.50

Francis Beaumont

The Knight of the Burning Pestle

edited by Michael Hattaway,
University of Kent

144 pages
0 510-33202-1 £3.25

George Chapman

Bussy D'Ambois

edited by Maurice Evans

160 pages
0 510-33202-1 £3.25

Chapman, Jonson and Marston

Eastward Ho!

edited by C. G. Petter

192 pages
0 510-33311-7 £3.25

William Congreve

The Double Dealer

edited by John Ross, Massey
University

168 pages
0 510-33504-7 £3.25

Love for Love

edited by Malcolm Kelsall,
University College, Cardiff

158 pages
0 510-33662-0 £3.25

The Way of the World

edited by Brian Gibbons,
University of Zurich

152 pages
0 510-33672-8 £3.25

Thomas Dekker

The Shoemakers' Holiday

edited by David Palmer,
University of Manchester

128 pages
0 510-33721-X £3.25

John Dryden

All for Love

edited by N. J. Andrew

144 pages
0 510-33711-2 £3.25

Sir George Etherege

The Man of Mode

edited by John Barnard,
University of Leeds

200 pages
0 510-33500-4 £3.25

George Farquhar

The Beaux' Stratagem

edited by Michael Cordner,
University of York

160 pages
0 510-33781-3 £3.25

The Recruiting Officer

edited by John Ross, Massey
University

184 pages
0 510-33731-7 £3.25

John Ford

'Tis Pity She's a Whore

edited by Brian Morris,
University College, Lampeter

128 pages
0 510-34145-4 £3.25

Oliver Goldsmith

She Stoops to Conquer

edited by Tom Davis,
University of Birmingham

132 pages
0 510-34142-X £3.25

Jasper Heywood/Seneca

Thyestes

edited by Joost Daalder,
Flinders University

144 pages
0 510-39010-2 £3.95

Ben Jonson

The Alchemist
edited by Douglas Brown

176 pages
0 510-33606-X £3.25

Bartholmew Fair
edited by G. R. Hibbard,
University of Waterloo,
Ontario

216 pages
0 510-33710-4 £3.25

Epicoene
edited by R. V. Holdsworth,
University of Manchester

224 pages
0 510-34154-3 £3.25

Every Man in his Humour
edited by Martin Seymour-
Smith

160 pages
0 510-33636-1 £3.25

Volpone
edited by Philip Brockbank,
Shakespeare Institute,
University of Birmingham

208 pages
0 510-34157-8 £3.25

Thomas Kyd

The Spanish Tragedy
edited by J. R. Mulryne,
University of Warwick

176 pages
0 510-33707-4 £3.25

Christopher Marlowe

Doctor Faustus
edited by Roma Gill,
University of Sheffield

128 pages
0 510-33821-6 £3.25

Edward the Second
edited by W. Moelwyn
Merchant, University of Exeter

144 pages
0 510-33806-2 £3.25

The Jew of Malta
edited by T. W. Craik,
University of Durham

128 pages
0 510-33836-4 £3.25

Tamburlaine Parts I & II
edited by J. W. Harper,
University of York

208 pages
0 510-33851-8 £3.25

John Marston

The Malcontent

edited by Bernard Harris,
University of York

144 pages
0 510-33906-9 £3.25

Philip Massinger

The City Madam

edited by T. W. Craik,
University of Durham

128 pages
0 510-34006-7 £3.25

A New Way to Pay Old Debts

edited by T. W. Craik,
University of Durham

128 pages
0 510-34021-0 £3.25

Thomas Middleton

A Chaste Maid in Cheapside

edited by Alan Brissenden,
University of Adelaide

136 pages
0 510-34121-7 £3.25

A Game at Chess

edited by J. W. Harper,
University of York

128 pages
0 510-34136-5 £3.25

A Trick to Catch the Old One

edited by G. J. Watson,
University of Aberdeen

144 pages
0 510-34141-9 £3.25

Women Beware Women

edited by Roma Gill,
University of Sheffield

144 pages
0 510-34166-7 £3.25

Thomas Middleton and Thomas Dekker

The Roaring Girl

edited by Andor Gomme,
University of Keele

192 pages
0 510-34138-1 £3.25

Thomas Middleton and William Rowley

The Changeling

edited by Patricia Thomson, University of Sussex

128 pages
0 510-34106-3 £3.25

A Fair Quarrel

edited by R. V. Holdsworth, University of Manchester

176 pages
0 510-34108-X £3.25

George Peele, Nicholas Udall, etc.

Three Sixteenth Century Comedies

(The Old Wife's Tale, Gammer Gurton's Needle, Roister Doister)

edited by Charles Whitworth, University of Birmingham

240 pages
0 510-33509-8 £4.95

Richard Brinsley Sheridan

The Rivals

edited by Elizabeth Duthie, University College, Cardiff

160 pages
0 510-34141-1 £3.25

OD   O level Eng Lit 1983-4-5-6
SU   A level Eng Lit 1983

The School for Scandal

edited by F. W. Bateson

200 pages
0 510-34364-3 £3.25

J. M. Synge

The Playboy of the Western World

edited by Malcolm Kelsall, University College, Cardiff

128 pages
0 510-33771-6 £3.25

Cyril Tourneur

The Atheist's Tragedy

edited by Brian Morris, St Davids University College, & Roma Gill, University of Sheffield

144 pages
0 510-33751-1 £3.25

The Revenger's Tragedy

edited by Brian Gibbons, University of Zurich

144 pages
0 510-34206-X £3.25

Sir John Vanbrugh

The Provoked Wife

edited by James L. Smith, University of Southampton

160 pages
0 510-34252-3 £3.25

The Relapse

edited by Bernard Harris, University of York

160 pages
0 510-34262-0 £3.25

John Webster

The Devil's Law-Case

edited by Elizabeth M. Brennan, University of London

192 pages
0 510-34296-5 £3.25

The Duchess of Malfi

edited by Elizabeth M. Brennan, University of London

160 pages
0 510-34306-6 £3.25

The White Devil

edited by Elizabeth M. Brennan, University of London

208 pages
0 510-34321-X £3.25

Oscar Wilde

The Importance of Being Earnest

edited by Russell Jackson, The Shakespeare Institute, University of Birmingham

192 pages
0 510-34143-8 £3.25

Lady Windermere's Fan

edited by Ian Small, University of Birmingham

176 pages
0 510-34153-5 £3.25

Two Society Comedies

(An Ideal Husband, A Woman of No Importance)

edited by Russell Jackson, Shakespeare Institute, University of Birmingham & Ian Small, University of Birmingham

336 pages
0 510-33511-X £4.95

William Wycherley

The Country Wife

edited by John Dixon Hunt, University of London

160 pages
0 510-343521-X £3.25

The Plain Dealer

edited by James L. Smith, University of Southampton

216 pages
0 510-33503-9 £3.25